Shale Trek

Jeff Scott

Methanol Press

Dedicated to Edwin, Rhian, Medi & Gethin Jones
and
i.m of Stephanie Macleod 1965-1996

"the past falls open anywhere"
Michael Donaghy (1954-2004)
Collected Poems (Picador 2009)

First published in Great Britain by
Methanol Press
2 Tidy Street
Brighton
East Sussex BN1 4EL

For a complete catalogue of current and forthcoming publications please write to the address above, or visit our website at www.methanolpress.com

ISBN 978-0-9553103-9-3
A catalogue for this book is available from the British Library

Editor in absentia: Michael Payne
Word Wrangler: Graham Russel
Stenographer: Vy Shepherd
Book & Cover Design: Vicky Holtham
Cover Photograph: Jeff Scott

Printed in the UK by Lightning Source

INTRODUCTION

Each year I vow not to write another but the road to hell is paved with good intentions. The book you have in your hand continues my examination of the question 'what is speedway?' that I embarked on when I travelled to every track in the country in 2005, 2006, 2007 and 2008. This odyssey resulted in the publication of the books *Showered in Shale, Shifting Shale, Concrete for Breakfast* and *Quantum of Shale*. This is really more of the same but also something different. It's not a club history nor the (auto) biography of a rider but a snapshot and my personal journey round every stadium that staged the sport in Britain – this time during 2009. Again, it was a pleasure to be able to have a reason to visit every track in the country. Though I could only write about what I encountered, I've again tried to capture some of the characters that make up some parts of the speedway world as well as vaguely attempt to delve beneath the surface of what I've seen. Many people went out of their way to be kind, tell me their thoughts on speedway or comment on my books. What notionally started out as a philosophical quest has continued to take a somewhat anthropological and sociological turn.

When writing this book I have tried to adhere to the lessons I was given previously by my editor and writing coach Michael Payne as well as building upon encouragement from the late Michael Donaghy who suggested I write about what I know or love. Anyone familiar with my blog or my previous books will know that I'm not adverse to some pointless navel-gazing, pretentiousness and facetiousness. Nonetheless, I hope that you can forgive these faults and mostly enjoy the chance to travel to the tracks again in my company as much as I relished the visits.

Lastly, without the riders prepared to risk their lives on high-powered bikes without brakes on various tracks – for our entertainment and to make their living – there would be no sport to watch in this country. In our everyday lives, we often take our own mortality for granted and, equally, we make light of speedway injuries as part and parcel of the sport, often forgetting that every rider is someone's brother, son, partner, husband or father. Hopefully we can all remember this every time a critical comment nearly passes our lips.

There you have it. I hope that you enjoy your journey.

Brighton

May 24th 2010

CONTENTS

CHAPTER 1

Newport
"It just looks like there's been a lick of paint but, behind the scenes, so much has gone on!"

15th March

The 2009 British Speedway season opens on a Sunday at 1 p.m. in the Hayley Stadium, Newport, South Wales where a field of 18 riders (including the two reserves) compete to land the first silverware of the season, the Prince of Wales Trophy. More importantly, this afternoon's event is also the Tim Stone Memorial Meeting. It was the late Tim Stone's hard work, vision and determination that saw speedway reintroduced to South Wales when Newport returned to speedway in 1997. As the club owner and promoter, Tim ran Newport Speedway in his own inimitable way until his tragic premature death aged 55 on April 26th 2008 on his way to visit his mum in hospital. Further tragedy struck the family when she died shortly afterwards and they were buried together in a joint funeral on May 8th. Matters off the track threw the club into crisis and forced their sudden dramatic withdrawal from British Speedway. Since the last home meeting on Sunday April 20th 2008 (which Newport lost to Redcar by 47-46), uncertainty eventually gave way to optimism and the club has been saved from extinction by the father and son combination of Steve and Nicky Mallett, previous long-term sponsors of the club through Mallett Transport. In fact, the club will have a Newport-born Welsh management team in the form of Promoters Steve and Nicky Mallett, Programme Editor and Commercial Manager Gareth Rogers and his brother Laurence Rogers who will jointly manage the Wasps team along with the legendary Neil Street. A glance down the list of club officials in the programme reveals that a huge number of the personnel who previously occupied positions of authority at the club still remain in situ under the new regime. Steve Mallett intended to get Tim Stone's stepdad Ken Wood to open the meeting but, sadly, he too passed away before this Tim Stone Memorial Meeting could be staged. In his place Newport star of yesteryear, Phil Crump, will do the honours before the formal re-launch of speedway in Wales. Phil rode for the club when it was based at Somerton Park and, interestingly, Tim Stone was a member of Phil's support team in the 1970s. The re-launch of the club is founded on the hard work and determination of many people. Steve Mallett goes out of his way to thank, "The Manager of the Lloyds TSB Bank, who supported my business proposal for the acquisition without whom none of this would have been possible. In a difficult economic climate a positive decision was made and since then we have enjoyed such good will and input from those with the sport at heart locally." Sensibly not listing all the people who have helped in case he accidentally misses any of them out, Steve also expresses, "Heartfelt gratitude for all those who've helped us upgrade various areas of the stadium both on and off the track."

Three or so hours before the scheduled start time it's already a scorching hot day. Steve Mallett takes the time to welcome me to the club when I arrive. Despite the large number of last-minute activities still to be completed and the stream of people who require his authorisation or insight, Steve also kindly provides a table for my book display in a prime position just inside the turnstiles located next to the programme stall and SWARM (South Wales Aid to Riders and Machinery) club table they use to sell raffle tickets to raise money for the riders' equipment fund. Steve wears a precisely ironed coloured shirt with tie and sports his box-fresh BSPA jacket with pride. He's friendly and apparently oblivious to the hubbub of activity by the large open metal gates close to the entrance turnstiles as people flit in and out of the stadium with boxes on their way to the first-bend refreshment kiosk. I'm soon left to my own devices. Changes in the stadium are immediately obvious, most notably a bright yellow portacabin plonked right next to the home-straight grandstand. It's festooned in the new eye-catching Wasps club logo designed by Steve Mallett's younger son, Thomas. The new design is definitely distinctive and showcased to great effect on the portacabin. The new promoters at the club have appointed experienced practitioners to most positions of responsibility and authority within the club. The trackshop is no exception since it's run by the ex-Poole and Somerset promoter Mike Golding and his partner Anita Lewis along with her daughter, Katie. Though not so brightly coloured, another highly visible addition to the stadium furniture is an inflatable air-fence positioned in front of the wooden boards that used to suffice as the club safety furniture. Though this element of safety equipment has yet to become mandatory across the Premier League, the arrival of Mike Golding at the club has seen this inflatable safety equipment move with him from Somerset to Newport (it's almost as well travelled as a speedway rider since it was previously at Peterborough). There have in fact been numerous other changes to the stadium infrastructure since the demise of the Tim Stone regime that aren't easily spotted but are, nonetheless, significant. The track has been dug up, completely re-laid and now uses a material with a much higher clay content. You'd be forgiven for not noticing this change though you can't fail to see that it has been recently watered since it glistens moistly in the bright morning sunshine. The centre green looks much as it always did but, in the interim, has also seen the drainage improved. The dressing rooms have been refurbished, there's a new medical room under the grandstand (replacing the caravan that used to serve this purpose for the last 10 years), and the new bar area has been remodelled and completed. And, though they won't be in evidence this afternoon, every Newport rider has been issued with a team suit for the first time ever. There are also plans to install floodlights when the economic situation improves and the Mallett business plan is, apparently, robust enough to support such an investment. The initial team speedway meeting at Hayley Stadium will take place next weekend. Somewhat synchronistically, the day before that the Wasps travel to Rye House (for a Premier Trophy meeting) where the last Newport meeting was staged under the Tim Stone promotion on Saturday April 26th 2008.

New era air fence

Red Nose day team photo

One of the familiar faces back at the club is Dave. He runs the programme stall and busily opens the first box of programme of the new season in preparation for the anticipated rush of fans through the turnstiles at 11 a.m. Like so many volunteers at the club, he's pleased that speedway has returned to Newport. The warm sunshine has made his thoughts turn to Tim Stone. "It was always nice for Tim. Many a morning it was raining but, at 1 p.m., it would clear so Tim could get his speedway on!" The unseasonably warm temperature has caught Dave out, "It took me 45 minutes to walk here and I'm soaked. I was going to wear my shorts but I didn't want to upset anyone." Promoter Steve Mallett arrives with a youngster in tow to check that everything is as it should be at the programme stall. Informed of a last-minute minor oversight, Steve immediately issues instructions to the youngster, "Go and see Mam and tell her we forgot to do a float for the programme seller!"

Back straight crowd

Steve's very much a hands-on promoter who's unafraid to get his hands dirty though, dressed in his smart BSPA jacket, today they'll only get metaphorically messy. He proceeds to instruct the car parking detail attired in bright yellow high-visibility jackets about how exactly he'd like to see them control and supervise the rough-hewn car park – with its surface made from clinker taken from the demolished adjacent steelworks – outside Hayley Stadium. Away by the main grandstand and luminous trackshop, familiar faces chat amiably together as the loudspeakers test *Dancing Queen* loudly over the public address system. The always cheerful club Incident Recorder, Gavin Morrison, approves of the arrival of the new safety fence but doesn't believe it will eliminate drama and incident from the Tim Stone Memorial Meeting. "No matter what, we always see an incident here!" Neither of us mentions the dip on the inside of the third bend that historically causes difficulty for riders. Club Presenter and Public Relations Officer, Gareth Rogers looks very managerial in a box-fresh anorak replete with a slogan on the back that says "FEEL THE BUZZ". I gather this is the new club mission statement-cum-slogan. Today, it definitely describes anticipation levels inside and outside the stadium. Away from his duties at Hayley Stadium, Gareth has his fingers in a variety of sporting metaphorical pies. He's also what I suppose could be described as the editor of Len Silver's forthcoming autobiography which, if I were the blurb writer for the book keen to identify some newsworthy hyperbole, I would probably trumpet as a "fascinating story of triumph over adversity". In his capacity as Rye House Speedway owner and promoter, Len Silver notoriously pays fastidious attention to all aspects of his club. It would be a big surprise if this attention to presentational detail didn't also apply to his autobiography. Unusually in an age of ghost writers, Len has penned his own life story. Meanwhile, Gareth has collated 45,000 words of anecdotes, something he characterises as "A Who's Who of Speedway Talking About Len! We're just waiting on Allen Trump to get it printed – I'll get Len to chase him!" Nearby, Craig Wright has also returned to the club as start marshal. At one point he was the youngest start marshal in British Speedway (and might still be), "Nick was pestering me. It's great to be back! No mechanicking [for Karl Mason] this year for me, except if the Wasps or Hornets need me. I doubt they will today. Though we could do with an electrician 'cause the speakers on the centre green have blown up! We need them there so they don't deafen the fans in the grandstand."

Club photographer, Hywel Lloyd rushes up to promoter Steve Mallett, "Tell Laurence I want all the Newport riders out at 12 on the dot – no messing!" The team photograph might not happen then, "That could be a problem as we have a team meeting then!" On my way to the pits area I bump into Laurence Rogers who suggests with pride, "You should see the new changing rooms!" Also walking purposefully round the stadium is SCB consultant track inspector and in-demand track builder/curator Colin Meredith who, dressed dapperly in black overalls with a yellow De Walt logo, greets me warmly, "I'm here this year!" When I arrive in the still almost completely deserted pits area, David Dean – the man listed in the programme as the track curator – has a quizzical expression on his face. "A new broom sweeps clean. I was hoping for the job as trackman but that's gone to Colin. I was promised it in December but, a week ago, I heard I didn't have the job! It's a bit of a kick in the balls! Still, we'll see, the old man is around here somewhere too – though he's retired nowadays."[1] Talk of the track prompts Peter Brookes to expand on recent changes. "There's a lot more clay in the track, it will take a while to settle down. It just looks like there's been a lick of paint but, behind the scenes, so much has gone on! It all looked good on the surface [when Tim was here] but we had to redo the electrics and put in ceilings in the loos. So much! There's a high water table and, now the drains have been done, it should make a real difference! Streetie always says how hard it is to prepare a track in the afternoon. We could do with a bit of cloud cover really to stop it drying out. There will be a blue groove later and, probably, some dust – but there won't be any holes!" We're then joined by another man also keen to remember Tim Stone. "You always knew where you stood with Tim. Peter and Dave have been here since the start and, they will tell you, Tim always started things but didn't always finish them! The bar has been crying out to be developed ever since but, now, it is!" David Dean insists I have a tour of the Home and Away dressing rooms. He missed his vocation as an estate agent though, even the most hyper-professional of these, would struggle to generate the level of enthusiasm and pride he takes in the facilities, let alone the tile work. The Away dressing room is a particular favourite, "Look at how much better this is! We had to knock a wall down. It's night and day isn't it?" Outside the shower area there's a large instruction notice, PLEASE DO NOT CLEAN KEVLARS OR BOOTS IN THE SHOWER. Back out in the bright sunshine of the pits, close to the Away riders' section there's another bright yellow portacabin that David waves at airily, "The junior riders' changing room will be finished shortly". Proudly thorough, he also highlights the medical facilities "have been updated".

Back by the entrance turnstiles Steve Girdwood from ReRun Productions has arrived just 10 minutes before the gates open to set up his stall of DVDs adjacent to the trackshop He then immediately rushes off to the pits area to film some rider interviews prior to the start of the races to determine the winner of the Prince of Wales Trophy. "We've got three meetings today! I'd like to have been at Eastbourne [for the Dean Barker farewell meeting] but this is the start of a new era! I'm going to Swindon later for the 60th Anniversary meeting." By the time I return to my book

[1] Cost control measures would see Colin Meredith leave the club in June to be replaced by David.

display table, Janet's got her raffle tickets at the ready behind the SWARM table, "It's looking like a proper track, isn't it? A proper track! It must be Sunday as my eyes and nose is running." In anticipation of a rush of eager fans, on the adjacent table Dave fiddles with the programmes, "We have 1400 programmes. I have to account for all of them!" Janet chips in, "We've got to pay for them now!" Dave shrugs, "Everyone has to! When we cleared out Tim's office we found a filing cabinet full of old programmes." Presentation and promotion play a key part in the smooth running of any speedway meeting and this applies to events off the track just as much as the action on it. Janet tells me conspiratorially, "If you have two books [of raffle tickets] you sell more than if you've got one 'cause they buy one of each!"

Earlier in the trackshop, I'd admired the range of new Wasps and Hornets merchandise, the frequent use of the new club logo and the 'Feel the Buzz' slogan. Initially my eyes had been drawn to mugs adorned with the slogan "Born to Watch Speedway Forced to Work!" These are available to purchase at a cost of £5.50 but, by the cash register, is arguably the speedway photograph of the season taken at the Club Press and Practice day. Namely all the riders posing partially clothed or nearly naked – apart from their green mankinis! Judged from the red noses they all wear, this must've been a Red Nose Day sponsored dare. It's safe to say that some riders are happier to pose in the buff than others! Their speedway boots provide a further air of incongruity to an already surreal photograph. Nicky Mallett really stands out as the only person who's refused to remove his shirt though, as a concession to nudity, he has loosened his tie! It's definitely a photograph that will provoke strong reactions! On the SWARM stall, Janet studies the Red Nose mankinis' photo carefully, "Some of them were braver than others!" Steve from ReRun expresses delight, "Fantastic isn't it! I was there and filmed it for the crashes and cock-ups DVD." There's quite a range of expertise on hand inside Hayley Stadium to consult about this photograph. Later when I spot off-duty SCB Referee Christina Turnbull, she laughs, "What was it they say at the end of *Crimewatch*? Don't have nightmares!" We're joined by Mark Lemon's wife Emma whose opinion I canvass, "I live with that! At least he took his boxers off and went for it!" I also gain the expert opinion of Reading Racers club historian Arnie Gibbons. He initially refuses to be drawn on his opinions on the quality of the photograph or the mankini models. "My word, I think Mark Lemon was quite cold!"

Though he didn't exactly throw himself heart and soul into the Red Nose Day photograph, Newport co-promoter Nicky Mallett enjoys meeting and greeting the speedway public as they stream through the turnstiles. He has a manner that wouldn't be out of place in the reception area of an expensive American resort hotel (or B&Q) since he greets the customers with a broad smile and phrases like: "thanks for coming!" "great to see you!" and "good to be back!" Notoriously, the publicly issued speedway new season rules and regulations quickly undergo massive changes once the action starts and individual promoters coax, wheedle and test them to destruction. Various rules and regulations are soon (often contradictorily) amended. Sadly these subsequent amendments often aren't made available to the public, so we have to content ourselves with a version of the rules flash frozen in time that no longer really apply to the sport that we then watch throughout the season. Apart from these ongoing amendments, a number of unknown written rules also exist. Apparently, one of these is that whoever the youngest promoter is in the country, they must wear industrial quantities of high strength hair gel as well as indulge a creative penchant for vivid hair colouring. That's definitely the case if judged by the tonsorial styles most recently sported by Jonathan Chapman and, now, by Nicky Mallett. Nicky is 22. He rode both speedway and Grasstrack with enthusiasm before he inherited the mantle of the 'Youngest Speedway Promoter in the Country' from Jonathan. We should collectively be delighted that some authority figures within our sport are – in age terms – nowadays much more closely related to the riders than the average fan. Along with his promotional acumen, Jonathan is well known for his distinctive, often challenging but frequently changing hairstyle. Though Nicky hasn't quite gone the full hog and availed himself of any red hues, he certainly hasn't stinted on the hair gel or failed to perfect that 'just got out of bed look'. It's all elegantly set off by his comparatively subtle use of hair colour. Nicky's smart attire also grabs attention and, like his father, he sports his British Speedway promoter's jacket with pride. This amazes one fan who rushes up to exclaim, "Eh, Nicky Mallett in a suit! Good luck to you, mate!" Said fan ostentatiously shakes Nicky's hand and nods to the throng of people who mill about by the entrance turnstiles, programme stall, refreshment kiosk and trackshop, "They're all coming out of the woodwork again!"

Amongst the early arrivals are Somerset fans Tiny Tim and Johnny Sometimes. Since the death of their friend Speedway Dave, Johnny Sometimes is beset with both real and imagined medical concerns for which Tiny Tim has little tolerance. Younger by some distance, he holds a more optimistic outlook on health matters and life in general. "I've been out of work for eight months. I've applied to be the DVD commentator at Somerset this season. I applied to Pete [Ballinger] from Clean Cut. I hope I get it as I've followed the Rebels since the start and I'm passionate about my speedway but, for DVDs, you have to be neutral." [2] Johnny Sometimes butts in, "Unlike the bloke at Newcastle [Andrew Dalby] who still brings up three years ago. [3] It's on the DVD; George English brings it up too! I won't ever go back there."

[Tim] "I can see 20 Somerset fans in yellow and black. It's the best thing to happen to speedway all winter – Newport coming back! They got an air-fence too!"

[Johnny] "They need it here!"

The demise of Newport robbed Somerset of their closest speedway rivals for nearly 11 months. The reopening of Hayley Stadium will see friendly hostilities resume again next weekend.

The ubiquitous Arnie Gibbons still mourns the closure of Smallmead Stadium – this ensures his beloved Reading Racers won't be a member of the Premier League this season. "The meeting's starting early today so that Mads [Korneliussen] and Neils-Kristen Iversen can ride at Swindon. But I've just heard that Neils-Kristen Iversen is replaced by Jason Doyle! Without Reading, the closest track to me is Rye House which is 75 minutes away and Swindon which is 85 minutes away. Journey times home make life tough to see speedway this year! Fundamentally though, from 1989 to 1999, I survived without seeing Reading at Smallmead – 'cause of work – but saw them away. I saw my speedway elsewhere. I have been back to Smallmead to take some photographs. It's awful! Have you seen the one someone took through the broken window of the back stand? It'll be flattened in the next six months and be match-day parking for the Madejski [Stadium]. I have no inside knowledge but I am economically literate so I have no grounds for optimism that the club is going to open again in the near future! The club nearly went out of existence before we dropped back down to the Premier League and, on the crowds we used to get, it's not a surprise. I guess that it might have been a financial struggle. Mark Legg has disappeared. I heard that some riders weren't paid for the last few weeks – no wonder they weren't enthusiastic about the End-of-an-Era meeting! It will be interesting to see what will happen at Berwick this season. Peter Waite, when he was there, instilled a real sense of community and it would be good if that could be carried on. Peter always built his teams to a budget and I think he has to be respected for that." We're briefly interrupted by the arrival of Mercedes-driving trackshop entrepreneur Dave 'The Rat' Rattenberry resplendent in a baseball cap with Ghana written in large letters. Innocently Arnie enquires, "Have you got the speedway concession here too?" Dave brusquely informs him that this concession is held by Mike Golding. Arnie continues "I expect I'll see most of my speedway this season at Rye House. It gets an unfairly hard time. It surprises you how often it's good! Sometimes it can be less than exciting but that's much less often than people make out. Len Silver is very professional and puts on a very good show. He goes out of his way to give credit to the opposition – if he thinks they've put up a good show! The flip side is that Len will criticise them, if he thinks they haven't tried. Last season, Edinburgh and King's Lynn were a couple of the best meetings I saw anywhere. Some teams just fold before they get there. Sometimes someone like Newcastle or Glasgow give it a go. I love Conference League racing so that appeals too! Joe Haines and Linus Sundstrom are good riders who will be improving. I don't think that the Elite League will be as bad as people make out it's going to be either. Once you take Leigh Adams out – the big name everyone wants to knock down – the range is very even. It could be very exciting! If you look at it geographically: in the Elite League, only Belle Vue is in the North, whereas the Premier League is so northern biased. If you could split the country into North and South, [in the Premier League] Stoke is in the south!"

Our conversation about speedway borders is interrupted by the arrival of 76-year-old Eastbourne fan Sid Greatley who, rather surprisingly, isn't elsewhere at Arlington for the Dean Barker farewell meeting. "I won't go down there 'cause he's already had a testimonial! He pissed it all away!" Arnie is quick to defend Deano, "To be fair to Mr Barker, his testimonial was a proper testimonial by modern standards. He gave good service to Eastbourne for the correct amount of time. It's not his fault that his career has been happening long enough to have an End-of-Career Benefit. That's perfectly acceptable! Nobody is suggesting that Billy Hamill shouldn't have one when his career is just about

[2] Tiny Tim gets the job but struggles to maintain his desire for neutrality on all occasions

[3] There were incidents on and off the track in a high-spirited Newcastle v. Somerset Premier League meeting staged in 2005.

the same length as Dean Barker's." The expression on Sid's face indicates that perhaps he's not in full agreement with Arnie. Instead he moves off to buy a wodge of programmes before he hunts for exciting souvenirs from the trackshop. Easily swayed by the media hype that surrounds him, I confess to Arnie that I'd be excited to see Emil Sayfutdinov race in the Elite League. Arnie tells me I'm likely to be disappointed, "I don't think he's coming. He can't get a visa! You know – with all my travel – I still haven't seen him, which bugs me! He's supposedly in the process of applying for a Polish passport – that's from the British Speedway Forum so you'd be advised to check and treat that suggestion with a pinch of salt. It would be a shame if he joined Rune Holta in the Polish team. Aside from the fact it undermines the credibility of the sport – not that it needs much help! – the Russians have a lot of promising young riders." Arnie then proceeds to confidently pronounce a series of exotically named but mysterious young Russian riders. "There's Artem Laguta (younger brother of Grigory), Danil Ivanov who won the 2007 Russian Under-21 championship (Sayfutdinov was second) and Artem Vodyakov. In a few years Russia could have a strong national team. For the first time since the 1970s, Russia will have a stronger team than the USA!"

With admission prices around the industry norm – £15 (adults), £11.50 (concessions), £4 (children) – the unexpected sunshine allied to the excitement at the reintroduction of speedway to Newport plus the first chance to see some action on the shale, there's a good-sized crowd inside Hayley Stadium. Off-duty referee, Chris Durno, is impressed, "It's a good crowd. It's the most crowded I've seen it here in years!" I'm surprised to see Wolves promoter Chris Van Straaten at the stadium, "Yes, it's a good crowd – we start tomorrow". I'm later told that he has a supervisory function at Newport Speedway and will be there to mentor and help guide them through the trials and travails of their first season. Chris Van Straaten is a well-travelled promoter who oversaw the successful reintroduction of speedway to Redcar and, prior to his successful incumbency at Wolverhampton, he was, of course, at Cradley. Though he's a man with a dry wit, he's also a man of few words who keeps his own counsel when he interacts with the speedway public. Chris moves away to stand on the first bend and is soon deep in conversation with Dave Rattenberry whose Wolverhampton trackshop franchise is a vital and lucrative outpost of his merchandising empire. I quiz John Rich why he isn't standing with Rat, "Have you seen who he's standing with? You get filled in there too!"

Prior to the meeting there's an immaculately observed minute's silence for the late Tim Stone. Once this courtesy has been observed and Tim wistfully remembered, the riders get pushed off by assorted mechanics and helpers to conduct a few quick practice laps while, over the public address system, Gareth Rogers gleefully exclaims, "The bikes are roaring which means the new era starts!" A glance at the racecard inside the programme reveals a high calibre line-up for the first heat of the new era under the Mallett management at Hayley Stadium. Mark Lemon, Chris Kerr, Kevin Doolan and Ben Barker race before the Wasps number 1 wins comfortably followed home by a competitive Kevin Doolan. Throughout, a man close to me screams, "Come on, Ben!" Although above the roar of the engines it would be impossible for Ben to be motivated by these imprecations, he nonetheless nearly snatches second place on the finish line from Doolan who, this season, will ply his trade for the Workington Comets.

Now that the crowd is settled within the stadium, I snatch a few words with Grandma Mallett. "The pressure has been up to here [gestures above her head]. There's been so much work behind the scenes! We just need to get this one out of the way and hope we can get the fans back like it was." The second race of the afternoon is won easily by David Howe from the gate. Jason Doyle's hopes of the Tim Stone Memorial Trophy end before he can even leave the start line when he gets completely snagged on the tapes and is disqualified for his troubles by referee Dan Holt. It's a disaster for the rider but definitely doesn't alter Arnie's earlier opinion about the absence of Neils-Kristian Iversen ("We can live without him"). Once the race finally gets underway, it's won by another Wasp, Craig Watson in a time of 61.37, nearly three seconds outside his own track record of 58.38 set on 3rd August 2003. Second-place Nicolai Klindt races determinedly and prompts Arnie to observe, "I should think Klindt will get into the Danish team but, to say he'll be world champion, is pushing it. It's even worse here! The problem is we're so short of British candidates that anyone who shows promise gets saddled with that label. A couple of years ago it was Josh Auty and he's made his way up to Sheffield reserve!" Though the racing has barely begun a noticeable blue groove has already appeared on the track. Dust also already starts to billow over some sections of the crowd. I'm stood by a man who's clearly used to dust inhalation at Hayley Stadium. He notes philosophically, "They used to say to the crowd: 'Can you throw the shale back!'" The next race features yet another easy win – this time for Mads Korneliussen though there's some brief excitement when Ty Proctor aggressively passes Emil Kramer at the start of the second lap. Arnie Gibbons wears the vexed expression of a man in the midst of a mental struggle with the likely complexities the Mallett family may face in their first speedway season, though he's sympathetic to their impending plight. "The problem is often the unrealistic cost structures that new promoters can get caught up with! The most expensive thing to do is flying foreign riders in and out but, even if you don't do that, there's the signing-on fees and the points money. It's best not to pay guarantees as often it can hit the riders' form, like it did with Mark Lemon last season!"

This afternoon additional on-track entertainment is provided by reserve races and races-cum-displays from the Men in Black. These are leavened throughout the main event every four heats. The first reserve race of the afternoon immediately showcases the huge gulf in standard that presently exists between the Premier League and National League levels of the sport in Britain. Karl Mason wins by the proverbial country mile ahead of a game but badly off-the-pace Jay Pickard. The sixth race of the afternoon features an exciting blast round the outside down the home straight by Mads Korneliussen who hammers past Nicolai Klindt before the race is stopped for the first test of the inflatable safety equipment by Jordan Frampton. Jordan hits the bend-four air-fence with such velocity that he punctures one of the panels. Gareth Rogers exclaims, "Let's hope he's okay and the fence is as well!" We're 35 minutes into the meeting and we have our first unscheduled relatively lengthy delay of the afternoon. It's pleasantly warm in the sunshine but cool in the shade. Some of the crowd savour the first proper sunshine of the spring but, by 2 p.m. on a mid-March afternoon, the power of the sun quickly declines. The enjoyment of impromptu centre-green and pits interviews conducted by an ebullient Gareth Rogers is almost as intermittent as the warmth of the sunshine because of problems with the public address system. On the back-straight speakers, there's an in-depth but audibly indistinct interview with Mark Lemon to enjoy. Bizarrely, the music is amplified well enough to be heard clearly. For those of the crowd who can hear announcements, Gareth apologies for the problems with the public address system. "It's rather obvious that we've now become aware of that and will certainly be working on it! It's mainly the speakers on the far side. We're sorting some of the inconsistencies that have been pointed out in the PA system. That's a technical matter and we can sort it out but, if you can strain your ears, at least the action on the track has been great!"

With the air-fence repairs completed, heat 6 is rerun. Chris Kerr gets as far as the first bend before he runs into the back of Nicolai Klindt and is thrown from his bike. Clearly the master of his own destiny and close encounter with the shale surface of the track, Kerr remounts only to find that the referee has stopped the race and ordered all three riders back to the start line. The fan next to me is mystified by the decision, "He was up and going, dunno why he's done that?" In true speedway fashion, the re-rerun sees Nicolai Klindt out gate the red-helmeted Mads Korneliussen who'd led by some distance in the first rerun. The lady in the trackshop tells me that the Red Nose Day photographs have sold well before she comments favourably upon the hardiness of the riders, "It was freezing when they took it as well!" Heat 8 sees Craig Watson win his second race of the afternoon after a close contest with Ben Barker from the last bend to the finish line. Judged by Ben's celebrations, he feels he's definitely snatched it on the line but, the referee ignores speedway's equivalent of the gamesmanship seen during throw-in appeals and, instead, adjudges Craig Watson the victor. Two comfortable wins for Watson along with a win and a second place for Lemon appears to confirm the pundits' pre-season predictions that the new promotional team at Newport have compiled an experienced squad capable of a strong 2009 challenge for Premier League honours. The pundits at the *Speedway Star* certainly thought so, since they predicted an almost unprecedented seventh place. When interviewed by the magazine, Wasps fan Andrew Horder felt confident enough to forecast a top-four finish! Along with the all-action Jordan Frampton also in the Wasps team – assuming he avoids too many encounters with the air-fence – a positive season looks in prospect. Recent Premier League campaigns have seen Newport finish bottom (2005 and 2007), hardly start their fixtures (2008) or achieve the heady heights of 13th (out of 14 in 2006).

Over the tannoy Gareth Rogers continues to luxuriate in the quality of the spectacle served up by Craig Watson and Ben Barker during heat 8. "Well, the race of the meeting so far, not just a great race but a contrast in riding styles!" After the Men in Black treat us to another of their demonstration races, the curatorial track staff spend considerable time engaged in an orgy of track grading and watering. This enforced break in proceedings allows Gareth to inform those members of the crowd (who can hear him) of some housekeeping matters, "Two announcements from the speedway management. If you are standing up watching the speedway, please don't do so in front of the windows [of the home-straight grandstand] – rather obvious I'd have thought that!" I completely fail to hear the remainder of his announcement since gremlins again crackle noisily through the PA system. The interval is long enough for Mads

Korneliussen to contemplate the meaning of life. Whatever conclusions he reaches remain unknown though he does decide to withdraw from the meeting ("with mechanical difficulties"). Gareth attempts to boost our collective anticipation levels for the final race of the meeting, "That 21st heat will carry some serious money – £1000 for first, £750 for second and £500 for third!" These are the kind of figures to concentrate riders' minds early season.

If Chris Kerr is going to remain in contention for a place in the final, then he's going to have to try to remain on his bike more often than he's managed earlier. The first attempt to run heat 10 sees him, once again, suddenly depart from his machine on the first bend. Depart puts it a bit strongly. To be exact, he manages to get stuck under the air-fence with his equipment. Once extricated, he's able to take his place in the rerun since the referee Daniel Holt adjudges he'd become trapped there as a result of first-bend bunching. Gareth Rogers talks up the clash between the previously undefeated Craig Watson and David Howe. The excitement he generates in the crowd about this notional duel for mastery ends almost as soon as the tapes rise since Craig Watson shoots from the gate to record yet another supremely untroubled race win. David Howe does manage to enter the first corner in second place but is then passed at speed on the exit from the second bend by Chris Kerr. Three wins from three rides. Craig Watson's closest challenger – Kevin Doolan – immediately imitates Watson to gate and storm to victory from the tapes. The next reserve race of the afternoon splits heat 12 from heat 13. Once more Karl Mason emerges victorious, albeit after the race is awarded following the disqualification of Richard Andrews. Nicky Mallett continues to enthusiastically work the crowd as he slowly wends his way towards the Speedway Office. Like so many others this afternoon, I congratulate him on the return of the club and, more significantly, a "good crowd". He smiles, "it looks so but, I'm just about to count up, so we'll know then!"

After the interval, heat 13 proves incredibly unlucky for both Craig Watson and also for the 2009 Premier League ambitions of the Newport Wasps since he crashes badly on the back straight. Craig is fortunate not to be collected by Nick Simmons who, somehow, manages to avoid his stricken rival with a display of sharp reactions. Unluckily the crash happens a few metres past the newly installed air-fence. The almost imperceptible dividing line between good and ill fortune that affects life as well as speedway is double underlined by Watson's accident. Rumours of a damaged back sweep the stadium as the medical staff attend to the stricken rider and the ambulance remains parked close by. Whatever the exact nature of his injuries, it's clear that he will require a trip to Royal Gwent hospital. There's some measure of relief amongst concerned members of the crowd when subsequent rumour sweeps the stadium that Craig has suffered a knee injury. This relief proves premature since, when full details of the accident emerge, we learn the Aussie has suffered what the *Speedway Star* later call a "splintering and twisting to a bone above his left knee". When a bone in your body disintegrates like a crushed digestive biscuit from an injury sustained at work, thoughts inevitably turn to the future quality of life that will be enjoyed by that individual, let alone the more narrow concerns of whether they will resume their speedway career. After an inordinate delay, the racing resumes. The result of the rerun is somewhat academic but, nonetheless, won by Mark Lemon in the second-slowest time of the afternoon. Like London buses, one accident follows another. Though injuries are part and parcel of a dangerous sport, heat 14 sees an even more dramatic crash that involves Jason Doyle and Ty Proctor. They would have sustained much more serious injuries had they not encountered the comparative soft landing of the first-bend air-fence. The referee adjudges Jason Doyle at fault for the stoppage and disqualifies him from the rerun but, since shortly afterwards, he would also depart to the Royal Gwent hospital, such considerations are rendered moot by the injury to his weakened shoulder. Ty Proctor is unable to race in the rerun and takes no further part in the meeting. When International Film School Wales visit Hayley Stadium to make a film on speedway, Mark Lemon confirms to them the ever-present danger faced daily by riders. He stresses for the cameras that he's seen friends "being fatally killed". [4]

As a consequence of these dramatic incidents – along with the delays caused by on-track treatment and subsequent ambulance journeys – it's decided to cut short the meeting programme. In practical terms, this means that heats 17-20 are scrubbed from the racecard with the qualifiers for the final determined by their respective points position at the end of four races (rather than five). Among the crowd, the sense of an anticlimax is palpable but much less so for the four riders still in contention for the prize money. Kevin Doolan emerges victorious with the trophy and a cheque for £1000. He's joined on the podium by three-times winner of the Prince of Wales Trophy, David Howe. Third place

[4] This evocative film can be seen at http://www.vimeo.com/4549589

is taken by Ben Barker ahead of the (for once) slow-starting Mark Lemon. Kevin Doolan becomes the eighth rider to win the Prince of Wales Trophy since 1969. An august list of previous trophy winners includes Barry Briggs, Jim Airey, Ole Olsen, Anders Michanek, Phil Crump and Reidar Eide. Until this afternoon, David Howe regularly emerges victorious and, with triumphs in 2003, 2005 and 2007, in sequential terms initially looked favourite to do so again. Those fans keen to go to Blunsdon to see the Swindon 60th Anniversary meeting have to leave the stadium pronto, thereby missing the post-meeting auction in the bar scheduled to feature diverse lots such as the day's race jackets and the rider mankinis! Mads Korneliussen's earlier withdrawal from the meeting means that he's probably already in the pits at Swindon before many of us even leave the Hayley Stadium car park.

15th March Prince of Wales Trophy Winner: Kevin Doolan

CHAPTER 2

Swindon

"I know I sound a bit of an anorak but I've got my own virtual Platinum Helmet competition."

15th March

The drive from Newport to Swindon is enlivened with the Top 20 chart from 12th March 1969 that features Glen Campbell singing *Wichita Lineman*. For reasons I can't quite put my finger on, it sounds somehow evocative of a time when speedway was in its (second) heyday. Given the notorious unfaltering loyalty of the dedicated dyed-in-the-wool speedway fan, "And I need you more than want you, and I want you for all time" seems oddly apposite. Traffic reports and national news interrupt my oral trip down memory lane. Think-tank proposals to add 50p per unit on to alcohol in order to stamp out binge drinking is derided by Minister James Purnell, who muddledly comments, "The irresponsible majority are being punished for the irresponsible minority!"

Swindon's Speedway's 60th Anniversary Celebration meeting opens the season at the Abbey Stadium in Lady Lane, Blunsdon. Maybe the 2009 term will be the one when the Robins finally end 42 years of notional 'hurt' and add to their 1967 triumph in the British League. Given how thin on the ground trophies have been since then, they don't exactly need a large cabinet to fit in the Premier League Knock-Out Cup (2000), the Premier League Four-Team Championship trophy (2003) and whatever gets presented as a result of their recent consecutive wins in the Elite League Pairs Championship (2004 and 2005). Swindon also enjoyed some success prior to the recent era. Whether or not they have any trophies for this period remains unknown, but records show they were National League Division 2 Champions (1956), National League Champions (1957), Midland Cup winners in (1967, 1968 and 1994) and also British League Division 2 Pairs Champions in 1994. Tonight's meeting has been extensively trailed in the local media and also nationally, with frequent adverts in the *Speedway Star* that feature an attractive montage of great Swindon riders of yesteryear (from 1949 to the present). Swindon co-promoters Terry Russell and Gary Patchett have assembled a strong field to whet the appetite of speedway fans starved of track action throughout the close season winter months. Regrettably, though advertised as appearing, both Jaroslaw Hampel and Emil Sayfutdinov have cried off from the 60th Anniversary Celebration. This is something of a disappointment for those keen to see the exciting young Russian Sayfutdinov in action round the fast Blunsdon circuit. The only chance that British speedway fans will now have to see him on home shale is at Cardiff. Another man nowadays rarely sighted on British shale – but no stranger to these shores since he lives in Stevenage – is Nicki Pedersen, who'll blow away his speedway cobwebs tonight in Wiltshire.

When I arrive inside the hallowed portals of the Abbey Stadium, Paul Oughton, commercial admin supremo for the Swindon Robins, looks extremely tired. "I've had a very busy week. We've had go-karting, the press and practice, the season launch and a signing at George White Motorcycles. They're the largest independent motorcycle retailer in the UK. They're a Robins team partner. They're named after a Swindon rider who started the business, but they've got a young owner called Steve Gallicott, who started there as an apprentice and built it up all the way through and eventually bought it." We're interrupted when the Swindon team manager, Alun Rossiter, arrives with sunglasses perched on top of his head like a supermodel, even though it's close to dusk and the air already has a noticeable chill. He's rather managerially stopped by to check the running order sheet with Paul Oughton and, satisfied that he has confirmed his role in the itinerary, departs smartish. The ongoing corporatisation of British speedway sees Alun dressed in a smart black Robins top and, like shop workers the world over nowadays, he has his name on the breast pocket. Also smartly dressed is a nearby member of the track-staff, who sports box-fresh blue overalls with AC Nurden emblazoned in large letters across it. Rhetorically he wonders, "What other sport would people volunteer and turn up every week and through the winter? My wife says I'm mad when I come down over the winter but, then, lots of us do!" Although the turnstiles have yet to open, the public address system blares into life. Below cloudy skies, Steve Harley and Cockney Rebel open proceedings with the misleading meteorological news, "Here Comes the Sun". A casual glance along the queue of fans who patiently wait to enter the stadium confirms that Rosco is the only person in sunglasses. The lyric "seems years since it's been here" has a certain resonance for speedway fans deprived of track action since the end of October 2008.

Dress and anticipation levels run high throughout the stadium. At the entrance turnstiles the staff member looks forlorn and, in a slightly panicked voice, tells another man "The programmes haven't arrived yet!" Swindon speedway uber-fan, speedway historian and the most prodigious living speedway author, Robert Bamford sports a slightly perplexed look. "I felt okay until I walked through the gates and Terry Russell said to me 'Make a list of all the legends and when they rode here'. He must think I still work here! " Even before the deleterious economic climate arrived, speedway promoters regularly look for opportunities to beat costs from their supply chain wherever possible. Though Gutenberg and Caxton probably had their own issues, the recent decision by the Swindon Speedway promotion to invest in hi-tech printing equipment – an all-singing, all-dancing photocopier in old money – with which to print their own programmes sounds a good idea in theory when the salesman is in the room or on the 'phone but, in practice, massively underestimates the difficulty and complexity involved to produce a professional-looking document. To the casual or untutored eye, programmes probably pretty well write themselves but, invariably, this massively underestimates the time and effort that goes into producing the copy, let alone the administration required to collate all the photographs, adverts and advertisers' PDFs. Once you have the base materials collated, you usually require a good working relationship with a professional printer to ensure that the latest iteration of your programme is produced to a tight deadline (and your agreed budget). While some or all these factors might well have been factored in, it's a brave man who tries to beat costs out of the supply chain just before the first major meeting of your season. However, the Swindon promotion are these iconoclastic brave men, so they've chosen the official souvenir programme to be the guinea pig for their new printing equipment. In the manner of Frazer from *Dad's Army*, Robert Bamford provides an update on progress. "Have you heard about the programme fiasco? Chris [Seaward] was here until midnight last night printing them but, 'cause one machine broke down, he only did 157 copies, so they had to get a Bristol firm to do an emergency run at a substantial cost!" Though the season is only a few hours old, in addition to photocopier equipment issues, misfortune has also struck riders on the track. Unaware I'd been at Newport, Rob asks, "Did you hear Watson has gone to hospital?" I mention that Jason Doyle has also visited said establishment. Briefly concerned, Rob then moves on to an analysis of the high-quality field assembled for this evening's meeting, "They've had three withdrawals here, including the Russian!" "Emil was the one I wanted to see, apart from Nicki." He nods, "So did lots of people!"

The turnstiles open and a part delivery of the emergency print run of Swindon 60th Anniversary programmes are seized upon with the enthusiasm pigeons reserve for breadcrumbs at Trafalgar Square. Oblivious to the popularity of this document, Swindon co-promoter Gary Patchett is deep in conversation with Chris Louis by the refreshment stall. Over by the track shop, a speedway fan wears an incredible selection of speedway badges to create a chain-mail effect as if he's about to use them as body armour in the recreation of the Battle of Blunsdon. In the absence of such a battle, he turns out to be Paul Collins from Bristol who's gone to speedway since 1977. "My dad took me to the old Bristol stadium. I used to go to different tracks and buy all the badges. I used to get the new ones from every track each season as well – but it got too much." [Waves proudly at badges], "I've still got a big bag of them at home." Apparently able to pardon his own non-attendance, an Eastbourne speedway fan rushes up to my display table and demands to know, "Why aren't you at Dean Barker's testimonial?" Unable to answer the question himself, he changes tack, "It's like old times with Bob [Dugard] back in charge at Eastbourne. But you have to wonder how many new fans will come along. When I chat to people in Hailsham, they don't know there's speedway at Arlington!"

Inside the downstairs "conservatory bar" of the home-straight grandstand, Darcia Gingell and her boyfriend staff the Robins Pits Crew stand. Though they're a relatively new supporters organisation, Darcia tells me proudly, "We're nearly at a milestone now. At the end of last year we were £5 short of donating £5,000. 2009 is our fourth year and all monies raised go to the Riders' Equipment Fund. We've had 28 join this year so far. It's £5 for adults and £3 for kids. You get a programme board as a welcome gift, you get a signed birthday card in the post and junior members get a pack with a teddy bear, badges, pens and regular newsletter. You get invited to a pits party at the stadium where you can meet Leigh Adams on 24th March. It's the first time we've been offered the stadium to use." Darcia waves the specially commissioned "Supporting the Swindon Robins" programme board (used by the Robins Pit Crew members on tour), along with a pen and a newsletter. It's all too hard to resist and I join to become member number 29. News that I can have a birthday card "signed by anyone" at the Swindon Speedway club is the part of the offer that tips the scales for me. I'm tempted to ask for my birthday card to be signed by Terry Russell but, in the end, decide to settle for the collectors' item that's a birthday card signed by Rosco. This duly arrives on my birthday and has the added bonus that it features Rosco's smiling photo on the front.

Crowds gather

By 5.20 p.m., interest levels at my bookstall have remained catatonic, though a number of fans come up to complain that the official souvenir programme (priced at £4) has already sold out. "There's not many people in here to have run out of programmes already!" Over the public address system a member of the Robins match-day presentational team (that usually comprises Richard Crowley and Clive Fisher) tells those fans already within the stadium, "We've got a very special guest here tonight – Jeff Scott – I'm not quite sure what he's got, but I expect it's his books!" Unable to leave South Wales as early as Mads Korneliussen, Reading uber-fan and official club historian Arnie Gibbons nonetheless hotfoots it from Gwent to Wiltshire. "The new promotion have clearly changed some things, but also retained some of its old features. One local wag said to me, 'They say it's the finest training ground in the country [pause] for the St John Ambulance.' Kevin Doolan won apparently. There was a half-hour delay after Doyle, like Watson, fell when leading easily. I left as they were explaining what I said they should do anyway – which was scrap heats 17-20!" Dave Rattenberry has also been to Newport. He passes summary judgement on the meeting and track, "Bloody terrible!" In my mind's eye, I can picture a bullion van with hi-tech security parked outside in the Abbey Stadium car park. I ask Rat, "Are you Chris Van Straaten's driver?" "No! I thought the track was the same as usual – bloody terrible! What can you do when riders get injured, though?"

Paul Collins

Our conversation is interrupted by the arrival of an extremely territorial group of old age pensioner Swindon fans who greatly resent my table whenever it appears in the general proximity of their favoured vantage point. They harrumph and ostentatiously move one of the bins; though, since they're all dressed as smartly as if they've come direct to the stadium from a church service, this doesn't seem sensible behaviour. Over the public address system fans are encouraged to visit the "Pit crew stand in the conservatory bar in front of the main grandstand". Though the meeting at Newport also featured exhibition rides from the Men in Black, weirdly they're also on show at Swindon's 60th Anniversary Celebration. A quick glance at them and their equipment reveals that they're a completely different Men in Black team. Either they're imposters and impersonators or, maybe, they've been cloned. In fact, to avoid a high-speed dash down the M4 motorway, it turns out that there are a sufficient number of enthusiasts and vintage machines to ensure that various troupes of 'Men in Black' can simultaneously perform at different venues in the country on the same day. Dave Rattenberry roves on the lookout for famous riders of yesteryear. He's already spotted and tracked down ex-Swindon hero Martin Ashby, "I followed him into the toilets – he was in the toilet having a pee before me."

Sunset over Blunsdon

Though Rat still relives the thrill of this encounter it must have been a few minutes beforehand since, out on the track, Martin is with the group of "Legends" as they circle slowly past on a trailer waving to the crowd as they enjoy a stately celebratory circuit of Blunsdon. The Legends don't quite seem to have dressed for the weather. This is unfortunate since they get to stand on the truck on the centre green slowly getting colder while only a selection of them are each interviewed in turn. Clive Fisher soon warms to his task but, before he does so, makes an important announcement. "In 60 years of speedway, obviously, some of these riders are no longer with us and the latest of those we'd like to remember is Robert Stanley Kilby. We don't think a minute's silence is appropriate so please put your hands together for a minute's celebration!" I much prefer the formality of a minute's silence. However, the fans in the stadium clap with such gusto for this commemorative minute that their loud applause clearly signals the warm esteem and respect in which Bob Kilby is held locally. Along with the Legends, Rosco is also on the centre green to talk about the meeting and the season ahead. Before he launches into some well-rehearsed *bons mots*, Rosco offers a few emollient words about the lack of availability of the official souvenir programmes. "I'm led to believe by Terry Russell that, if you haven't got a programme, you'll be able to get one by ordering online from our website. We had a few technical problems beyond our means!" As a stop-gap measure to satisfy disgruntled fans, photocopies of the race-card are given out to the punters. Speedway invariably attracts avid, obsessive collectors of statistics and memorabilia, particularly programmes. The idea that such an event could take place without the chance to get your hands on the key document of the day has quite a few dentures tightly clenched. The announcer tries to assuage the mood before it turns from peeved to really miffed. "We understand that there are more supplies on the way – we will inform you when they arrive!" While Rosco spoke about his expectations for the season ahead, Dave Rat notes *sotto voce*, "Peter Adams at the Wolves forum said, deadpan, 'One thing against Swindon … they've got Alun Rossiter!'".

When the action gets underway, the difference in perceived level of speed between Hayley Stadium and Abbey Stadium is so phenomenal that it can't be solely attributed to track size (or quantity of shale). The first race is won at breakneck speed by Chris Harris. The second race appears even faster, though it's won in a slightly slower time by home favourite Leigh Adams, who takes until the start of the first bend of lap three to pass the often fast-starting Chris Holder. The third race of the afternoon is led until the fourth bend by jet-propelled American Robin Ryan Fisher. Ryan appears to struggle with his own speed and takes off on a wild trajectory that loses his lead. He then immediately follows that up with a virtuoso rear of his bike on the entry to the next lap (to relegate himself to third), before a wide line into the penultimate corner of the race guarantees his last position. One thing is for sure, things are never dull on the track when Flyin' Ryan features in a race! Eastbourne fan Sid Greatley has made a rocket-propelled trip across from South Wales in his Vauxhall Nova – despite the poor visibility of its sticker-strewn windows – dressed in his trademark brightly coloured 2005 vintage Eastbourne Eagles anorak. Sid furrows his brow in the manner of a concerned ward orderly as he recalls the injuries that afflicted this afternoon's Prince of Wales Trophy. "Craig Watson has broken his pelvis and Jason Doyle has broken his arm. That's all I can tell yer! Craig Watson has retired – his missus has said it's not worth getting injured!" Heat 4 features a ring rusty start from Nicki Pedersen. He completely fails to make the gate but his trademark confidence, competitive spirit allied to sheer strength of mind somehow takes him into second place. Though not quite on the gas, Nicki showcases his traditional busy use of the handlebars with the thousand micro adjustments it apparently invariably requires to get maximum speed out of his steed. The surprise race leader is a rejuvenated Antonio Lindback who rides with great acceleration but, nonetheless, still finds himself racing neck-and-neck with the current World Champion. The decisive moment to the race sees Antonio get slightly out of shape (on the second bend of the second lap) but, rather than seize the moment, Nicki decides discretion is the better part of valour and, unusually, throttles back to settle for an untroubled second place. Behind them we're treated to a ding-dong battle between 2009 Robin Simon Stead and 2008 Blunsdon favourite Mads Korneliusson.

There's a brief break for some track care during which fans are implored, "Please, please don't use flash photography – it's dangerous and illegal!" The calibre of the field along with the chance to shake off the speedway watching cobwebs has attracted a large number of Polish people to Wiltshire. They congregate under a large Polish flag enhanced with the word Leszno spelt out in large letters. They enthusiastically smoke and drink in noisy but amiable fashion. Rather than fail to make the gate, Nicki Pedersen makes a slow but majestic start to heat 5, apparently in some slow-motion race for the second bend with Charlie Gjedde. Nicki soon abandons the pretence of close competition to pull away and win with considerable ease. He looks remarkably fast when picked out against the darkness by the bright glare of the Blunsdon floodlights along the back straight. The seventh race of the 60th Anniversary meeting is sufficiently varied to hold our collective attention throughout. An engine failure robs Ryan Fisher of any opportunity to career wildly across the shale surface. Last year's Robins hero, Jurica Pavlic, appears completely out of touch and definitely would fail to score but for the mechanical difficulties that has robbed Fisher of power. Up front and spotlit under the lights, Antonio Lindback looks even speedier than Nicki Pedersen as he zooms away from Blunsdon track expert Leigh Adams. Stood at the border of the yellow hash marks that demarcate the safety zone at the bottom of the home-straight grandstand stairs, speedway fan Mike Butler marvels at this race defeat for Adams, rather than the race win for Lindback. "It was nice to see Adams beaten twice on his own track! Fisher can gate but he just can't hold it". Speedway writer and one time member of the Lindback speedway team, Brian Burford passes. I ask him, "Is Antonio's success down to you?" Brian reveals that Tony Rickardsson has come from Sweden to Swindon to help out his prodigy in the pits, "Nah, he has another bloke helping him who knows a bit about speedway! Not that everyone knows him funnily enough. There was a media bloke in the pits trying to interview Gordon Day [Poole press officer] and, he pointed out Tony and said 'You should interview that bloke over there – he knows quite a bit'. None the wiser the media bloke says, 'Who is he?' Gordon smiles, only to be asked again, 'No, who is he?' Amazingly Gordon has to tell him, 'He's six-times World Champion, Tony Rickardsson!'"

To test the mettle of the incredibly proactive security man in charge of the hashed safety area at the base of the stairs, the melting-pot-of-nations feel to the meeting continues when another group of Poles gather there to drink, smoke and enjoy the action. Rather unbelievably (to my mind), this group of Poles are from Basingstoke! Emil Kazmierski and Lukasz Kokot both work at RAF Odiham. Yet more astonishingly for me since I grew up there, though, the other two Poles Jarek Jakuszkowiak and Krzysztof Dlugaszek live in the bright lights of Basingstoke, they work for Ashby Signs on the Youngs Industrial Estate in Tadley (though the Post Office in their wisdom describe it as Aldermaston – the village a few miles away). In speedway terms, Tadley is famous for its resident Paul Hunsdon. Without any invitation, Jarek makes it abundantly clear that the days can drag in Tadley and he believes entertainment levels remain minimal. However, Jarek is enthusiastically keen to spread the word about the delights of his home speedway track, "You should go to Leszno [smacks lips] it's excellent!" When I knowledgeably point to the huddle of fans a few yards away and say, "The man over there with the big flag is from Leszno". Jarek earnestly replies, "Yes he is! But we don't know him, we're from Basingstoke!"

Given the lack of big tracks in British speedway, I don't wish to colour the opinion of these enthusiastic Polish speedway fans by pre-warning them that all British speedway tracks aren't quite the same size as Swindon. Emil is keen to experience the local speedway culture "We're going to go to Reading – it's only a small way from Basingstoke!" Mike Butler breaks the sad news that it's shut. A pained look briefly crosses Emil's face, "Really! No!" The Poles chatter among themselves and continue their informal chain-smoking contest. Alert to stranger danger, Mike felt visitors swelled this afternoon's crowd in South Wales, "I'd say 30 to 40 per cent of the people there today were not local. He's [Steve Mallett] got to build up the local support. I went to Newport versus Birmingham [before] and there was 300 fans. It was like a morgue!"

The frenetic pace with which one race follows another could make you think that the riders have to shoot off to another speedway meeting elsewhere afterwards. Heat 9 continues the chequered evening experienced by Ryan Fisher when he falls on the third bend of the first lap to earn a disqualification. Interestingly, before the red lights come on, Charlie Gjedde lays his bike down on the fourth bend but is allowed back into the rerun. In heat 10, Antonio Lindback's third quick start of the evening ensures his third comfortable win. Henfield-based Mike Butler forecasts a stampede for Antonio's signature, "The promoters are going to be all over him! Newport need a new No. 1!" The pre-meeting formbook dictates that Chris Holder should come under pressure from Kenneth Bjerre or Jurica Pavlic but, instead, Simon Stead wins the race. Heat 12 should presage a classic battle between Leigh Adams and Nicki Pedersen – particularly after Chris Harris suffers an engine failure on the start line – but it's a routine, another day at the office, win for the Australian. Leigh Adams is arguably this afternoon's most popular rider, if judged by the vociferous reception his every moment on the track attracts from the contingent of chain-smoking Poles based around the Leszno flag. Victory sends them into a level of celebration and ecstasy that ensures the less boisterous crowd members who surround them stand out like Mormons in a brothel. "LEE AD-DAMS! LEE LEE ODD-HAMS!" they burble in unison extremely loudly.

It turns out Mike Butler is a man of many obsessions. "I've been to 989 Step 7 and above football grounds. I hope to do 11 more this season". The concept of Step 7 makes watching football sound like listening to parents discuss the class and year their child is in. I gather that Conference League football is Step 1 but I'm not exactly sure. Football is definitely something that Mike feels passionately about. "But the *Times* misquoted me! They got out of me I was recently divorced and they said I got divorced because I was such a sad ground-hopper, which wasn't the case – the divorce not the ground-hopping! I'm a Brentford season ticket holder, but I'm nothing like as serious as some of the ground-hoppers. Some people don't count the ground unless they stop the ball. Others don't count nil-nils. Some went twice to Stenhousemuir for nil-nils. Some don't count a ground if they haven't seen all 90 minutes so, if the coach gets there 5 minutes late, they don't get out of the coach if they can't see the full 90 minutes. Others have to have a programme for it to count as a visit. This can be a bit of a problem when they visit clubs that don't produce a programme! To get round it: they write their own programme and get it printed up – then, they send 20 programmes to the club and buy one!" This is truly obsessive behaviour! But, before I can explore whether he has their name and number (so that I can put him in contact with the Swindon promotion to ensure that their programme printing goes more smoothly in the future), Mike reveals that he knows award-winning, highly regarded *Northern Echo* veteran sports reporter, Mike Amos. "He arranged the first ground hop, in the early 90s, where we saw nine matches in three days! There were 500 hoppers on the first one."

It's not all football with Mike [Butler], he's also obsessive about his speedway and, as befits his IT background and statistical inclination, he's kept comprehensive electronic records of his speedway exploits. Nowadays they're electronic records but, obviously, they started out held in traditional paper format. Mike is proprietarily proud of these tabulations since he's invented his own somewhat complicated taxonomy (after he saw his first speedway meeting in 1976). "I have completed 1977 and 1978 'One Man's Speedway Seasons' and I'm now on to 1979. Unfortunately, having to work full-time it's taken me approximately six months to complete each season including checking and verification. But, when I retire, I hope to improve upon this. In the slight hope that, one day, I'll get up to date while I'm still active enough to go to meetings! It's great bedtime reading but the target audience is about three". Mike later shares with me some of these spreadsheets (the 1976 version also features some fantasy teams and a fantasy four-team tournament). Mike starts with his 'Riders seen in consecutive seasons' spreadsheet that also lists his best and worst meetings of the season. Whenever his record keeping takes a bizarre but detailed journey down an interesting speedway side street, incredibly complicated spreadsheets invariably follow. One spreadsheet features rider-by-rider analysis of all those Mike saw ride in 1976. I can't quite comprehend all the information that appears. However, if I look at the example of Peter Collins, Mike saw him ride at Waterden Road on 24 September 1976 and also two nights later at Arlington. Cumulative away scores by track are provided along with a calculated match average. There are winning times and these rider-based spreadsheets also record any second-half appearances. Based on what Mike saw, Peter Collins's top opponents in 1976 were Paul Gachet, Trevor Geer and Gordon Kennett. This snapshot of speedway as experienced by Mike is certainly a unique optic through which to view the sport. Ultimately, it's arguably the most honest representation that there can be since, really, we all experience our speedway riders and meetings through the events we really saw them ride at (rather than those we read about or, in the modern way, see on television or via the Internet)!

Even more innovatively, Mike's invented his own speedway competition. "I know I sound a bit of an anorak but I've got my own virtual Platinum Helmet competition. Only me and my cousin, Paul Baston, live in my virtual world! I went to my first meeting on 8 August 1976 and that started a purely theoretical title [competition] based on actual results from then. Whoever wins my first race of my season – and only the other three – can take it. To try and explain: Jason Doyle was the winter holder in 2008 since he won it in a challenge at the end of the season. He automatically held the Platinum Helmet over the winter. This afternoon at the Welsh Open, Doyle was excluded from heat 3 and Craig Watson thereby became the Platinum Helmet holder when he won the race. He defended it successfully by winning the eighth race and again rode a good race in heat 10 to retain the helmet. When he crashed in heat 13, he lost the helmet and Mark Lemon then gained it by winning the race. He held it until the Final where he finished last and, because the heat was won by Kevin Doolan, Doolan now holds it! It tends to stay years in the Elite League and then switches to the Premier League." Later Mike sends me his spreadsheet for his Platinum Helmet theoretical competition. It reads like a Who's Who of Speedway populated with illustrious winners, though it's equally possible for less exalted riders to hold the crown. It's not without controversy. In 1983 Kenny Carter was "stripped of the title" because "there were no challengers" during this season. For the same reason, Dennis Sigalos is stripped of the title in 1985, Marvyn Cox in 1993, Gary Havelock in 1996, Steve Johnston in 1998, Dave Mullett in 2003 and, finally, Craig Watson in 2005. Clearly these riders have been stripped of their titles either because they no longer ride or because Mike fails to see them during that particular season. It's a clever variation on the *Speedway Star*'s Fantasy League that some claim increases speedway fan interest in the on-track action and its associated results.

Back out on the Blunsdon track, heat 13 ends in another victory for Leigh Adams. Clive Fisher tries to compete with the voluble Poles when he exclaims, "It's SLEE Adams." If the Platinum Helmet is only ever retained by winners then, even though the imaginary Platinum Helmet is already held under lock and key in the back of Kevin Doolan's van, the men who'd be most likely to succeed at Blunsdon tonight are Nicki Pedersen, Leigh Adams and a massively rejuvenated Antonio Lindback, who races to a supremely untroubled and massively impressive five-ride maximum. However, speedway like life often isn't fair and the 60th Anniversary meeting has become infected with the *faux* 'excitement' bacillus that necessitates we fans are routinely subjected to a further couple of semi-finals and a final to, thereby, 'determine' the actual 'winner' of the meeting. My slightly old-fashioned view of the speedway world would dictate that, since Antonio emerged victorious from all his races, he should be presented with the trophy. However, the endlessly unsatisfied lusts prompted by our on-the-go consumerist culture, apparently conditions even speedway fans to require frequent peaks of additional stimulation rather than endure the comparative boredom of a cumulative triumph. While sudden death penalties (in football) appeal, the Speedway Grand Prix emphasises its banality at every meeting they stage with its glorified 20-heat qualification process prior to semi-finals and final. Sadly, from my point of view, the Swindon promotion have also decided to ape that iniquitous structure. The consequence for Antonio Lindback is that he suffers his first defeat in semi-final number one but still, somehow, qualifies for the Grand Final where he finishes fourth. The innate futile iniquity of said qualification process rears its head when – with only one win from five rides – Krzysztof Kasprzak scrapes into semi-final number two and, from there, progresses to the final after he finishes second behind Leigh Adams. Leigh's victory is greeted by tumultuous applause. While the elimination stage of the meeting inexorably progresses towards some briefly felt euphoria in the Lady Lane area of Swindon for those of the Leigh Adams persuasion, Mike Butler reveals that he's yet more interests away from football and speedway. "Until last month I was Sussex individual bridge champion, though not in the same league as my father who could automatically count and memorise any cards played in any card game". My boast that I play cribbage prompts derision, "That's not really cards!" The vague coincidence that half of the splinter group of Polish speedway supporters stood by my table work in Tadley is nothing compared to the vortex of coincidence that affects other aspects of Mike's life but, sadly, news of the Grand Final line up interrupts us. However, news of Mike's birth in March 1958 ("Gary Numan was born the day after me") would definitely over-excite Swindon Speedway historian Robert Bamford who – based on the 52 times he's seen him in concert – maintains, "Gazza is a simply sensational live act!"

Just prior to the Grand Final, Wayne Russell emerges from the Speedway Office still resiliently affable after an ongoing succession of visits from disgruntled speedway programme collectors. With the crowd distracted, it's now safe for him to emerge chrysalis-like into the stadium proper and linger by the track-shop to chat with Nick Barber (who's also suffered a deluge of programme availability enquiries). Nick takes the opportunity to try to quiz Wayne about the situation. "Don't talk to me about the programmes! We bought two machines that can print, collate and staple our programmes. But yesterday one broke down and, after 11 hours on the other one, we got 160 copies. This morning we PDF'd it to an outside printer. We haven't got all the copies we want and we understand people are unhappy. We're unhappy! Many other promotions wouldn't have bothered but our fans and the 60th Anniversary are important to us!" [1]

[1] After the meeting, the club issue a statement of apology that also contains good news about programme availability. "Prior to yesterday's 60th Anniversary Celebration meeting problems were encountered with the printing of the souvenir programme. During Saturday evening every effort was made to find an alternative producer and eventually we were able to prevail, at the last minute, upon the services of Cove Digital, Bristol. To say that they 'pulled a rabbit out of the hat' would be an understatement as the alternative was a very real possibility that we would have been left without programmes at all for last night's event. Because of the tight deadline Cove were working to we were only able to receive limited quantities of the programme, probably about half of the anticipated demand. We sincerely apologise for any inconvenience that was caused, especially to those supporters that patiently waited for us to print a complimentary race-card. We trust that this did not detract from what was a superb night's racing. However, the programme will be available for anyone to purchase, either by application online, by post or at the race office from this coming Thursday when we entertain Swedish Champions, Lejonen Lions in an International Challenge match."

Keen to change the subject, Wayne quizzes Nick about events at Arlington where another member of the Barber family, Johnny, has been on track-shop duty with the perpetually cheerful Martin Dadswell.
[Wayne] "You know how it was [the crowd] at Dean Barker's?
[Nick] "Okay – but not brilliant!"
[Wayne] "I rang him to wish him well. Originally, I think, he'd organised the 8th [March] that's why we went for the 15th before it was clear that the season wouldn't start until the 15th!"

Whatever the rights, wrongs or benefits of the protracted process by which tonight's winner is found, the crowd funnel away through the stadium gates in cheerful mood after the presentations give Leigh Adams the opportunity to offer a few platitudinous words. These centre upon his delight to have marked the start of the 2009 season in, what he hopes, will eventually be a propitious manner for all Swindon fans.

15th March Swindon Speedway 60th Anniversary Celebration Winner: Leigh Adams

Swindon: *"I know I sound a bit of an anorak but I've got my own virtual Platinum Helmet competition."*

CHAPTER 3

London:

"All the best-looking girls used to go and, if you wanted to see them on a Friday night, you had to go too!"

18th March

A glance in your e-mail junk folder isn't usually the most uplifting activity though there's often a wealth of notionally useful medical information contained there. However, it's lucky I do occasionally check otherwise I would have missed the news from David H. Willis, Chairman of the National Sporting Club that my book *Concrete for Breakfast* is shortlisted in the Best Biography category (person, place, sport or event) for the 2009 British Sports Book Awards. This Award along with many others would be presented after a celebratory but expensive lunch in March 2009 at the Sheraton Park Lane Hotel in London. The British Book Awards are in their seventh year and the slightly less famous cousin of the widely reported and, arguably, more prestigious William Hill Sports Book of the Year. Obviously, I was hugely delighted to receive news of my unexpected nomination and I suspect I was the only self-published author to attend. This is quite something in itself. It was even more of an honour to tacitly represent and showcase British Speedway at such a high profile sports media occasion. Whether this will lead the members of the press to give speedway more thought and coverage in the future remains open to doubt. Given that this is a prize that you can't enter I can only assume that the lovely review of my book by Ian McMillan in the *Times* prompted my consideration. I have no connection to Ian (though I did once see him give a poetry reading at the University of Brighton). He's a man of many talents. Not only is he Poet in Residence at Barnsley Football Club and an occasional witty guest on *Have I Got News For You* but he's also the regular editor and presenter of the highly regarded BBC Radio 3 programme on poetry and language, *The Verb.* [1]

A glance down the list of the other contenders for the Best Biography prize reveals that my speedway book will be up against other titles that cover sports as diverse as boxing, golf, cycling, formula 1 and the Olympics. All these books are published by major publishers and, even more worryingly and without any conscious research, I'm already aware of three of them! The brilliantly titled *Sex, Lies and Handlebar Tape* was serialised in the sadly now defunct *Observer Sports Monthly* (it's about the French Tour de France cyclist Jacques Anquetil), *The Austerity Olympics* by Jane Hampton reviewed favourably in quite a few newspapers, while Kasia Boddy's book *Boxing: A Cultural History* won praise in the *Daily Telegraph* – described by their reviewer David Flusfeder as, "compendious and thoroughly fascinating". Even worse, author Boddy had researched widely to draw a broad canvas looking at boxing "as it has been represented in literature, art and film". David Flusfeder is a successful novelist, sometime television critic and also a journalist who writes engagingly about poker and the books he reviews. Like his fiction, this review draws you in from the first sentence, "On the day of his mother's funeral, the poet Byron occupied himself in sparring rather than escort the coffin into the family vault". [2] Overall, the shortlist of nominated books is some cause for trepidation. However, the truism of all prize draws and, of course, the lottery is that you have to be in it to win it! Hopefully the judges of the Best Biography category Jon Waldman, Mihir Bose and Ian Payne will look favourably upon my book.

[1] Always enjoyable *Guardian* television critic Nancy Banks-Smith recently mentioned Ian. "Ian McMillan who wrote a poem to Barnsley's German goalkeeper, 'Lars Leese, Tall as the Trees'. Lars ungratefully complained that 'Leese wasn't pronounced like that at all'." Ignoring that Ian does have quite a strong but mellifluous Yorkshire accent, in this country we have a well-deserved reputation for pronouncing foreigners' names whatever way we like. For example, in speedway Charlie Gjedde continues to tongue-tie speedway presenters at many tracks around the country. According to the rider (and you'd like to think he'd know) the official pronunciation of Gjedde is Gu-yay-da.

[2] One section of David's review does give slight grounds for guarded hope. "Some of her remarks can be tendentious: is James Joyce's *Ulysses*, really, albeit only "some of the time", a boxing novel? But, apart from some clunky excursions at the end into the work of Norman Mailer, Bob Dylan and Sylvester Stallone, which read like professional attempts to impose meaning and consistency where there is none, it is an excellent, well-written and beautifully illustrated book." Worryingly, David isn't a man to lash round praise unnecessarily or, at least he didn't, when I knew him at university.

One slight but further cause for concern about possible future glory is that the National Sporting Club appears to have rechristened me Jim Scott in their shortlist for this award.

In an ideal world I would like to have taken everybody who's helped at any stage with any of my speedway books along to the champagne reception prior to the lunch held at the Sheraton Park Hotel in Piccadilly ahead of the Awards ceremony itself. The event is sponsored by an array of forward-thinking companies: Sky Sports, The *Times*, Llanllyr Source, Ladbrokes and Littlehampton Book Services. Collectively, these companies sound quite something when you see them name checked on the ticket for the event, "Be a part of the atmosphere to witness some of Britain's finest sporting writers battle it out to take home the winning trophies." I'm genuinely quite excited and almost apprehensive to be invited. Prior to the big day itself, my mum and I differ slightly about my dress code. I'm in favour of a slightly toned down version of speedway casual, albeit without the brightly coloured anorak, whereas she's more of the school of thought that you probably only get invited to these events once in a lifetime and, therefore, should dress your smartest. Like so many times previously her advice is spot on since the ticket for the event when it arrives states "Dress is Lounge Suit". Middle age and my expanded waistline mean I have to get my suit altered so that it doesn't cut me in two at the event. On the day my mum dresses glamorously with a mint green top while my dad wears his "special suit". He's a man who likes to keep numerous mementoes from the past. The treasure trove of receipts and papers Dad finds in his suit pockets indicate that his suit is a minimum of 41 years old, based on the 1968 receipt from the Durley Hall Hotel in Bournemouth where we spent our summer holidays that year. There's also an invite to the Queen's visit and garden party at the Atomic Weapons Research Establishment in Aldermaston on June 29th 1979 (held after the Queen had opened a new building). The final receipt is dated 1983 (probably the last time my dad wore the suit – though it still fits him perfectly) from a now defunct French pseudo-rustic Brighton restaurant (Le Grandgousier) that back then verged on the swanky. We visited to celebrate my graduation from Sussex University with my then girlfriend, the diminutive dark-haired Kate Buchan. Unlike modern students, a visit to a restaurant was a rare event and this was certainly exotic enough to have served us raw vegetables (crudités) and peculiar strong-tasting cold meat (rather fatty-looking salami).

On a bright sunny March day, I arrive early at the Sheraton Park Lane Hotel. It's a large building on Piccadilly opposite Green Park. You enter through an impressive set of rotating doors, noticeable for the brass shined within an inch of its life and its shockingly clean glass (despite its proximity to a busy main road crowded with slow-moving traffic). Inside the hotel entrance, the noise of the street is immediately lost as you instantly find yourself cast back in time by its olde-worlde ostentation, so beloved of American visitors. It's such a posh hotel that it's impossible to find the reception area though there is a plush large tearoom decorated in the style of the 1940s albeit with a menu priced for Russian oligarchs. I relax on one of the many massive sofas to wait for my parents who will, continuing a Scott tradition for all events or when catching public transport, inevitably arrive massively early. From the vantage point of my sofa, I can see signs for the "Ladies and Gentlemen's Hairdressing Saloon" though it takes me much longer to spot that the Sheraton staff have kindly displayed a discreet sign that advises similarly misplaced attendees like myself, "Your event is in the Ballroom – please take a right around the corner". This separate section of the hotel is so large that it has its own equally impressive entrance area. While I wait in one part of the building concerned my parents are late, they stand in another part of the building with exactly the same assumption. Already at home in the bar area, my father sips complimentary champagne cocktails, while my mother and I both stick to orange juice. This conference and reception area of the hotel is clearly fit for purpose with a large, long bar and numerous small but tall tables you can stand by to nibble the deluxe but slightly stale crisps. Though I'd mislaid my parents, I'm still one of the first arrivals. A quick check of the seating plan finds us on Table 21 some distance back from the stage. In terms of proximity to the stage, it's the locational equivalent of Siberia, albeit mercifully close to the exits in the event of fire. The view below from the balcony area of the bar reveals a ballroom already laid out with 25 circular tables each with 12 seats. Last-minute sound checks are the order of the day on the stage, photographers fuss about nearby checking their camera positions while staff make adjustments to the cutlery, glasses and napkins. Back in the bar, waiters circle with drink-laden trays but don't have enough guests so can chat amongst themselves ("Look out for Gabby Logan!"). Suddenly as if they'd all arrived as part of a giant coach party, the bar area transforms within minutes from the plush hush of a church confessional box – albeit one lit like a brothel with a myriad of shiny surfaces – to a roar and babble so raucous that you'd half think that many people are speed drinking on an empty stomach the Italian Prosecco that doubles as the champagne for this reception. Stood slightly to our side is the aforementioned

Gabby Logan, glamorously dressed, high heeled and studiously deep in conversation on her mobile phone.

On my return from the grand gentlemen's toilets replete with shoe shines (black or brown), impressive sinks and unguents, I discover that my parents have, true to the outgoing northerners that they are, chatted with Gabby. My mum confirms what all the men in the room have already noticed "She's got very high heels on". My mum confides in Gabby that, in her opinion, she'd been unfairly knocked out of the dancing (or '*Strictly*' as those in the know call it). My dad quizzed her about her lost Welsh accent. "I come from Wales but I'm more from middle England now. I lived in Wales 'til I was four and came back when I was 19". My dad thinks that Gabby said she lives or lived in Neath but can't quite remember. Mum's distracted by a man who repeatedly stares over since he arrived half an hour ago ("He keeps looking over"). Just my luck to be ignored by Gabby and visually stalked by some besuited bloke. The man in question turns out to be Jonathan Sim the Sky Sports Press Officer. Jonathan enjoys a varied and demanding brief, particularly given the vast array of sports that Sky so skilfully present on their satellite channel. Football is obviously the jewel in the crown of their sporting presentations but speedway is also an important franchise for the company. Jonathan tells me that he's here because Sky sponsor the British Sports Book Awards. He's noticed my book on the shortlist of the Best Biography section but my half-playful suggestion, "I hope you put in a good word for me with the judges", gets short shrift, "It was nothing to do with me!" I gather if they'd asked Jonathan, he wouldn't have put in a good word. Apart from Gabby and Jonathan, another face it's a surprise to recognise in the crowd is that of David Grant. He's here for the piss up with Littlehampton Book Services but away from the Awards is co-founder of the business publishing company Infinite Ideas (one divided by zero gives you infinity) and is the author of the highly praised novel Elephant published by Beautiful Books. [3]

Walk this way

Proud parents

Last minute preparations

The chance for further discussion is cut short when we're summoned to take our places at our nominated tables inside the ballroom. Prior to the meal, the Chairman of the National Sporting Club, David Willis sets the scene for the afternoon's events in avuncular and theatrical fashion with a few words from the podium. He thanks all the sponsors, assembled guests and is clearly a capable public speaker since he soon has the audience laughing, "The late John Smith sadly made a wonderful speech and dropped down dead two hours later, I hope that doesn't happen to me!" Though it subsequently turns out to be a bit of a Bermuda Triangle, there are a number of other nominees sat at Table 21. Opposite me and sat quite close to my dad is Simon Briggs whose book, *Don't Mention the Score: A Masochist's History of the England Football Team* is nominated for the Best Football book section. He's come along to the event with his editor from publishers Quercus. When not wittily bathing in the misery that is the usual lot of an England football supporter, Simon also writes for the *Telegraph*. He cuts a slightly reticent and reserved

[3] Beautiful Books is a great name for a publishing company and their publisher, Simon Petherick, cuts a distinctive figure at book fairs throughout the world. His pride in his own appearance would quickly lead anyone to the impression that the company has been named after him. Simon is definitely no stranger to the mirror, men's styling products or the fashionable shops of Central London but, just like you shouldn't judge a book by its cover, the mid-life crisis first novel that he commissioned from David Grant, with its wit and storytelling, illustrates his publishing acumen.

figure and mostly converses with his publisher throughout the meal. Possibly he'd expected more prestigious company at his table. Sensibly his editor's brought along a copy of his book and, as you'd expect from a highly regarded publishing company, the material's presented extremely well. This is a book much more after my dad's heart. He soon quizzes Simon, "Have you got any of the old players in it?" He should really have added the qualifier 'from the North East' to his question. My dad would chat to anyone about footballers like Len Shackleton, Jackie Millburn, Willie Watson or Wilf Mannion. My dad's clear enthusiasm for North Eastern football of yesteryear is partially shared by Simon Briggs who reacts (possibly diplomatically) to my Dad's question "Have you got a favourite player?" with "Out of this? Probably Mannion."

Sat to my left are a charming and affable couple, Peter Burns and his pregnant wife Annabel. They're from the Edinburgh-based publishing company Birlinn who have a wide range of imprints. They're at this Award event with their author David Barnes whose book *The Accies: Cradle of Scottish Rugby* is nominated in the Best Rugby Book award section. David Barnes used to live close to Powderhall and, so, knew about speedway! He explains his memories to his publisher, "It used to get big crowds. Sounds silly but it used to appear glamorous! All the best-looking girls used to go and, if you wanted to see them on a Friday night, you had to go too!" Peter and his wife flew down from Edinburgh especially for the ceremony leaving behind their 2-year-old. Peter modestly talks down any expectation of victory for David but, despite their management of my and their expectations, they're clearly extremely proud that the quality and content of their book has been recognised. It's lavishly illustrated with colour and black-and-white photos throughout. The book runs to 464 pages and is available in a trade hardback edition priced at £25 as well as in a limited edition print run of 150 individually numbered books case bound in real cloth with a protective slipcase (signed by David Sole and Michael Blair) at £100 each. Originally commissioned to celebrate The Accies sesquicentennial year (150th anniversary to you and me), "I don't know if you have heard of The Accies but they're very important to the formation of rugby in the UK! The book only came out in mid-November due to the late delivery of the manuscript but we're very happy with how it's gone and the coverage. To be invited here last December was a surprise but one we're extremely proud of!" A man who sits to their left has an initially impenetrable accent joins in our conversation. I ask Peter, "The chappie next to you, is he foreign?" "Scottish!", he sounds more foreign than that. In fact the strangely spoken man is David Barnes, author of said acclaimed rugby book. He's also incredibly unassuming and modest. Our talk ranges widely and it soon becomes clear that while speedway fans bemoan their lack of national print and broadcast media coverage, we do so unfairly since the situation is far far worse for Scottish rugby teams! "We wish we were on Sky every week. Actually we are – Sky Alba – in bloody Gaelic! The best we can hope for is that our teams play Welsh clubs so that we can get it on their channels!" After nearly two decades' experience of Publishing Conference Dinners I'm surprised at the high quality of the food they serve at the Sheraton Park Lane Hotel. My mum's got a few questions about the mystery ingredients on her starter plate ("What are they?" "Peppers and courgettes"), with main meal ("What are they?" "No idea at all") though she pronounces the dessert too sweet!. Since her heart operation, my mum's developed a taste for savoury food and completely lost her sweet tooth as well as her previously minimal taste for alcohol. Since her recovery from this operation, her energy levels have massively increased and she looks wonderful having dropped two dress sizes. Her joy and our delight at these physical changes are subsequently tempered by the sad discovery that not all of them are due to her heart operation.

With the appetiser of our lunchtime dining at an end, the main course of the Award presentations gets underway in earnest when David Willis, Chairman of the National Book Awards, takes to the stage in typically flamboyant manner. He speaks with the assurance of someone confident enough to be the centre of attention or judged by the warmth and wit of his own performance. David deservedly garners the full attention of the packed ballroom. "There are a number of people we'd like to welcome, silver medallist Cox of the Men's Eight in the Beijing 2008 Olympics, Acer Nethercott, the great grand Frank Maloney, former England cricketer Ed Smith, racing's Brough Scott, Irish rugby player and British Lyons' Stewart McKinney as well as all our sponsors to whom we're all extremely grateful!" There are a number of housekeeping announcements. Basically, awards will be announced in turn. Images of the shortlisted books will be projected onto the giant screen that's the backdrop of the stage. On stage during each award there'll be the sponsor, the judge, a special guest and, of course, shortly afterwards – the lucky winner! All will then pose for a celebratory photograph before we move swiftly on to the next award. David Willis issues a few further pointers, "The winner's acceptance speech should be limited to 40 minutes! As we all know, Awards functions of this kind are quite dreadful! In all, there are 37 authors shortlisted to receive these various awards and 30 of these authors are going to go away disappointed! I'm wondering, was it worth buying that new tie? To put this crushing disappointment into context – even to get here with the huge number of sports books that there are published nowadays is an achievement! I invite you to all sit back and enjoy this stratosphere of pleasure and ambrosia!"

The first Award for the Best Illustrated Title is sponsored by Llanllyr Source who've won the Queen's Award for Enterprise and International Trade 2008. In July/August 2007 *Imbibe Magazine* Tasting Panel judged them to have the "best water". On stage with Mark, from the sponsors, is Mick Fitzgerald who's introduced as "One of our favourite National Hunt jockeys. Like so many who race horses for a living, he has faced extreme danger and has the injuries to prove it! [He broke his neck in four places]". David Willis jokes with Mick, "I know I told you it was a non-speaking part but I lied!" David then immediately encourages Mick to announce the name of the winner until he's corrected about the order of ceremony he'd just himself announced by this very much on-the-ball National Hunt jockey. David handles this unforced error with elegant chagrin. "No, No, I got that wrong! We've got to see the nominations first! If you come often enough you get it right!" After we've seen the five books that comprise this category, Ed Whitaker's announced as the winner for his book, *In The Frame, Great Racing Photographs* (published by *Racing Post*).

The next category is for Best New Writer sponsored by Ladbrokes for whom Chris Palmer does the honours. He's joined on stage by judge Jim Cockin and from Somerset, cricketer Marcus Trescothick. Judge Jim is positively evangelical about his work, "I think this is the most exciting category to judge. We had to choose between two outstanding books. Runner-up is George Kimball with his book on boxing Four Kings. After much deliberation, the judges chose *When Friday Comes* by James Montague, "We found our fresh voice – in a world where people are still hell bent on misunderstanding each other!" Sadly the victorious author isn't able to come up on stage because he's in Beirut (where he's editor of *Time Out*, Beirut). From Mainstream Publishing, Bill Campbell deputises and barely sets foot on stage before he states, "This is a truly incredible book ... anyone in love with football or the world should read it!"

The next Award – for Best Rugby Book – is sponsored by Getty Images. Mere talk of this award provokes a small flurry of anticipation on our table, not just amongst the Birlinn gang. Rick from Getty Images is joined by judge Alan Pearey and former Welsh Captain, Michael Owen from Saracens. Helpfully for any of us in the audience unable to identify the rugby player on stage, David Willis offers guidance, "Michael's the big one!" Keen to get an insider's opinion David seizes the moment to enquire about the Six Nations, "Do the Irish have a chance at the weekend?" Michael bites back with a "No chance!" Having briefly imposed himself, David withdraws, "I'm sorry, let's look at the shortlist again, I'm sorry about that". Judge Alan observes, "We thought the bar was raised a little bit on this category. A riveting and near the knuckle account of Welsh rugby written by Alun Carter and Nick Bishop called *Seeing Red: Twelve Tumultuous Years in Welsh Rugby* caught our attention as did Paul Rees's *The Resurrection Men: Wales Grand Slam 2008* which was a superb book and, from Scotland, we had an unbelievably thorough history of the Edinburgh Accies club from David Barnes. We had some great books to choose from and we ended up choosing Alun Carter's *Seeing Red*." On our table David Barnes takes his near miss with great humility, "That was the book I'd most like to read out of all of them!" Winning author Alun Carter bounds onto the stage to tell us, "The inspiration for the book probably came from being sacked! A lot of people have had that experience in Welsh rugby!" Alun proceeds to give thanks to the many people who've helped him, offers gratitude for his experiences in Welsh rugby at Pontypool and then strikes an optimistic note, "I'm not bitter – I'm thankful for my involvement in Welsh rugby and we're coming good again!" The author gleefully poses for his celebratory photograph while, on the microphone, David Willis makes a point to inform us that a digitally enhanced picture of Alun will shortly be whizzed down to the *Swansea Post* as well as to Pontypridd.

Next up is the Best Cricket Book category sponsored by Littlehampton Book Services. I believe the judge is called Stephen but I'm slightly distracted by the news that David Willis has a brother, "I'm delighted to introduce my brother Bob Willis – the most successful England Captain of the 1980s who currently holds the record for the most 'Not Out' innings in all of Test cricket! It just shows the effect he had on others. He's also known for going out to bat having forgotten his bat and got 40 yards before he remembered! I do hope that he's not going to give us any tips because the last time he was here in 2005 my brother said 'put your savings and house on Australia to win the Ashes'. He assured us that it was the best bet and the most solid bet! There were quite a lot of homeless publishers and journalists after that! He may well have started the whole credit crunch thing personally". Once Bob Dylan fan Bob Willis arrives on stage, the family resemblance to his brother is unmistakable. Though it's only a short distance from his table to the stage, we can all see hint of the lope in his gait that made him so distinctive on the cricket pitch. That said, his hair is less frizzy than it was in his pomp and prime. Bob eases gently into some repartee about his brother's comments, "I would just like to correct David on behalf of Courtney Walsh – he now has the most 'Not Outs' in Test cricket!" Discussions about the chosen books then continue apace and we're given a glimpse into the mechanics of selection, "We discussed thirty books before we arrived at a long list of nine and a shortlist of five. We liked *What Sport Tells us About Life* by Ed Smith. It was the usual Ed Smith product: enthralling and well written. However, the two best books out of the five we have chosen were Bob Woolmer's *Art and Science of Cricket*. This was remarkable and covered everything from forward defensive strokes to Sex and the Test Cricketer. So there was something for everyone! After a tense run-off we've chosen Stephen Chalke's *The Way it Was* which is a neatly written social and cricketing history." Quite what it is about this Sports Awards ceremony I don't know but Stephen is another modest author. "Oh, I'm going to say something; it's a bit embarrassing [to be selected]". Stephen confesses the genesis of this project started when he wrote a, "monthly column for Wisden [*Cricketer* magazine] nine years ago. It's a wonderful game cricket! There's no game like it to play or to write about! Currently cricket is at the crossroads with lots of money coming into it: some of it honest, some of it real. I just hope that the people who are looking after it remember how it was, when they plan how it could be!"

Ladbrokes also sponsor the Best Football Book category. On stage, Kieran O'Brien from Ladbrokes is joined by Scots football writer and journalist Patrick Barclay of *The Times* (most recently ex-*Sunday Telegraph* but, like a well travelled footballer, is also ex-*Guardian*, ex-*Independent* and ex-*Observer*) who was a late stand-in, "for the former very celebrated Premiership referee Graham Poll". From the mini-competition within a competition point of view of our table, Patrick quickly name-checks Simon Briggs's book *Don't Mention The Score*, "It's a book about England that, as a Scot, I enjoyed! It's a lovely book that captures the essence of new England supporters forgetting their bad memories of the past. Still I think I can speak for the whole panel when I say judging this award has been the easiest piece of work since one book stood out from all the others. Jonathan Wilson's *Inverting the Pyramid* which is magnificent, absolutely riveting and will do for football tactics what Simon Inglis did for football grounds. It will make everyone think afresh about everything in the game! And it should also help football illustrators – hopefully, they do now know where the sweeper goes!"

Though I've missed it from my account of the Awards ceremony until the category of Best Biography every judge and commentator on the Award had the good grace to name check all the books within each category. It's a basic courtesy that easily and simply acknowledges the achievement of every book/author to make it this far, even if they don't emerge victorious in the final analysis. Sadly this approach isn't taken by voluble judge Ian Payne (who switched from BBC Radio 5 to Sky Sports but remains for many a poor man's Jeff Stelling). I'd always assumed 'Payney' was a nickname until Ian narcissistically shares with us his version of the afternoon so far. "First of all I'd just like to say that I think we should have a separate category for revealing comments made by the Sports Book industry in a recession." Delighting in the sound of his own voice and apparently convinced we've all come along to this dinner specifically to hear him pontificate, Ian self-importantly shares his 'celebrity' bar banter to reveal his "friend" Graham Poll "said definitively that Gallas was off-side". Maybe in a room of sports journalists with a ready availability of alcohol, it's always highly likely they'd talk shop. However, a few minutes of insider talk from Ian Payne on the already widely reported Premiership Top Four symbolically captures the difficulty that any sport – even football outside the Premiership bubble (let alone a minority one like speedway) – faces in its quest for attention from the major sports media (whether print, broadcast or online). Deprived of the oxygen of attention, minority sports decline in the shadow of the corporatised fame of the all-consuming Premiership sporting juggernaut. Without any acknowledgement of the also-ran titles in this category, after some more navel gazing we learn that the judges "came to an almost unanimous decision. It was difficult to separate the two books – *Sex, Lies and Handlebar Tape* by Paul Howard on Jacques Anquetil and Christopher Hilton's book about Clay Regazzoni, Regga who lost the use of his legs after a horrendous accident in America". I'm not sure where the other nominated writers for this category sit within the room but table 21 is definitely the Bermuda Triangle of the event with its trio of modest, also-ran authors thrown together. In sharp contrast to this judge, author Christopher Hilton is charming and diffidently underplays his skill as a writer when accepts his award. "I've been doing the words for 45 years now. I'm delighted to receive this award but, if my book persuades a youngster in a wheelchair to look at their life differently, then it will be worth more than anything!"

Without further ado, David Willis highlights that we've now come to the main event of the afternoon – namely news of the winner of the Best Autobiography award. Mark Pougatch and Frank Maloney join Jonathan Sim from sponsors Sky Sports on stage. One of the contenders Mick Fitzgerald has written an autobiography entitled *Better Than Sex* ("each to his own, Mick!") Marcus Trescothick's *Coming Back to Me* and James Whitham's *What A Good Do* all get mentions as does Sir Bobby Charlton's *My England Years.* Given that Sir Bobby isn't at the event it's probably safe to assume that he's not the winner! We're then told about the "stand-out two books", *In Pursuit of Glory* by Bradley Wiggins and *Black and Blue* by Paul Canoville. There's a brief pause for dramatic effect before a surprised and sheepish Paul Canoville makes his way up to the podium to deliver a sincere, heartfelt and moving speech. "I dunno what to say! I wanted to mention my two kids. I'm so honoured. It's a stepping stone. This book has opened doors for me, I'm truly blessed! I want to thank my mum. She'll be surprised [affects West Indian accent] 'What you get it for?' Oh, my gosh! What am I supposed to tell the kids at school?" Whenever you see clips of emotional acceptance speeches at the Oscars or similar showbiz events, an understandable reaction is to question the sincerity of the wishes expressed. However, in this instance, Paul Canoville seems genuinely overwhelmed and touched by the idea that his book could genuinely merit selection as a deserving prize winner at the British Sports Book of the Year Awards 2009 ceremony. The majority of the audience laugh along with Paul and, like many others of those present, I'm swept along in the pride and joy he feels at this achievement. My mum's delighted on Paul's behalf but, nonetheless, leans over to tell me, "We've done so many things with you that we would never have done if you weren't our son. Whoever would have thought you'd be a writer and we would ever get to come to a ceremony like this – in a place like this? He's the winner and his mum will be very proud of him but I'm just as proud of you! Not everyone can win but it's good that you were one of the last six!"

18th March British Sports Book Awards 2009 Winner: National Sporting Club (for staging this event).

CHAPTER 4

Isle of Wight

"I don't apologise that I'm patriotic. We need to help British youngsters reach a world stage at a lot earlier age and we have to do it as a nation!"

7th April

The 2009 British Speedway season sees the third tier of the racing structure operate under a brand new moniker, the National League. Actually while everyone gets used to the demise of the old moniker – the Conference League – there is a small element of confusion as to whether we should call this the National Development League or the National League. The Speedway Rulebook is often consulted by fans and speedway officials alike in the manner that lawyers and theologists refer to their key canonical texts. The SCB Rulebook doesn't clarify the exact designation either since it manages to refer to both to the NDL and the NL! Rather like many people continue to refer to Lakeside as Arena, it will take some time before people cease to call this the Conference League. Whatever it's called, the inaugural meeting of the newly founded National League tier will take place on the Isle of Wight when the Islanders meet their new local regional rivals the Bournemouth Buccaneers in a Challenge meeting. It's also the debut British Speedway appearance for the Buccaneers since they've only just come into existence, albeit that they'll race as the junior club of that Rolls-Royce of clubs – the Poole Pirates.

Though only the first week of April, it's a gloriously sunny spring afternoon when I arrive in the reception area of the Wightlink Island Ferry office. I fully expect to find Dave Pavitt coordinating ferry tickets, riders and last-minute phone calls about travel arrangements. But, with a new dawn about to rise in British Speedway, he has made a prompt start and sailed across on an earlier ferry to Ryde. In his place another familiar face/figure, Roy Collins, is sat on the metal chairs of the Wightlink ticket office waiting area. Roy is a man who wears many hats, "If they gave out figures for what I do, I'd have a long list after me name. I'm sort of the Commercial Director. I do all sorts – sell advertising, sorting stuff out, sorting printers out. I do lots but I'm working for nothing!"

While Roy tries to recall and accurately list his various responsibilities, a continuous stream of riders, their mechanics and/or parents interrupt our conversation. Islanders number 8, Scott Meakins arrives to collect his ferry tickets. This prompts Roy to try to get some of the vital start of season paperwork completed. "How many of you are there? [hands over form] Can you make sure you put your registration down [speaks to young gentleman with him] and you're Berwick – you're the short one!" In the Islanders number 7 race tabard tonight is their reserve: tall Dan Berwick. Apart from his involvement with speedway on the Isle of Wight, Roy also has responsibilities for motorcycling generally in this part of the world. "I'm Southern Centre ACU Chairman. This covers Sussex, this end of Dorset, up to the M4 and Wiltshire and includes the Isle of Wight and the Channel Islands. I used to visit but Head Office has decided they want to go on the jollies nowadays. I'm a Trustee of the ACU Benevolent Fund." His friend John Bramall, editor of the monthly magazine, *The Sporting Motorcyclist*, accompanies Roy this afternoon. "It's entirely voluntary. We produce 64 pages monthly. We have 2,500 subscribers." I've never heard of the magazine and ask what exactly is meant by the term "Sporting Motorcyclist". John furrows his brow, "Motorcycles means different things to different people. I like grasstrack and speedway but then there are also enduros and road bikes which, if you compared them to speedway, never the twain shall meet." Shortly afterwards he digs in the boot of his red Lada to find some recent back issues. "It includes ACU entry forms and regulations but we try and make it readable as well so the public read it! We have started to have general articles. Things have been a bit interrupted recently as I've just moved down to Fareham from Woking. I've come down to baby sit. My daughter had a baby last summer; it's our first grandchild,

Kieran. With the move, things have been a bit upside down. It's a good magazine!" [1] While we've talked magazines, Roy has continued to administer arrivals keen to go on the 4 o'clock ferry sailing.

[Roy] "You are?"

[Man] "Gavin Sedgmen."

[Roy] "At last! How many in the van?"

[Gavin] "How long's a piece of string?"

[Roy] "I ask the silly questions."

[Gavin] "Four."

Hearing I'm without transport from Ryde – where the ferry docks – to Ashey Road, John Bramall kindly volunteers to give me a lift in his red Skoda. Another passenger in the car will be a diffident young man who's stood with our group and turns out to be a reporter from the *Speedway Star*, "I'm Paul Burbidge". Anyone who reads the *Speedway Star* on a regular basis will have seen the Paul Burbidge by-line. It's increasingly appeared on a diverse range of articles about speedway personalities, clubs and major events. Paul belongs to the new generation of young reporters who bring youthful verve, insight and élan to their writing on the sport. Though he only lives 70 miles from the Isle of Wight, Paul hasn't previously been to a speedway meeting there. His trip this afternoon and evening to the Challenge Meeting against Bournemouth will form the basis for a subsequent two-page article in the *Speedway Star* about a trip to what he describes as "British Speedway's unique outpost". [2]

When I suggest to Paul that he's the only one in our group not working for nothing he replies, "Well, sort of ..." Paul tries to establish with Roy what attractions he can look forward to on the Island but doesn't thrill to news there's a brand new Tesco on the Island. "I'm doing a feature on the logistics of running the Club on the Island. It looks like a massive logistical exercise getting everyone across the Solent to the Stadium. I haven't been to the Island since I was 10, I think". Paul covers football as well as speedway but it sounds like speedway is his first love. Apart from his work with the *Speedway Star*, he also produces reports and articles for the *Bournemouth Echo*, the *Dorset Echo* and the Press Association. "I do a bit of football at Portsmouth for them. I get more work if they stay in the Premiership! The Internet has changed a lot of the week's news. It's very different nowadays to what it was. We've got to move with the times!" Roy's keen to let us know that he too has embraced new technology, "I use the Internet to sell the advertising boards. I sent two invoices by post and 34 by email." With an assortment of speedway riders' vans and various other vehicles just about to be given the signal they can drive onto the ferry, we make our way out to John Bramall's red Skoda with Roy on his mobile phone still orchestrating yet more administration. Paul has a brief panic about his ticket, ("Did you give me mine?") Roy remains phlegmatic ("I thought I did"). While we wait for permission to drive on board, Paul gives a brief run through his speedway reporting career. "I've been doing it since 2003 really, since the Pirates did the treble!" In recent years Poole have been used to considerable success on the track, large crowds and, of course, from a press point of view, there's the addition benefit that if you get to deal with the best Press Officer in British Speedway, Gordie Day. Paul treats it a privilege to cover Poole and to work with Mr Day, "He does talk in riddles sometimes but, if you listen long enough, it all falls into place!" Discussion of other local clubs prompts further proud talk from Roy about the Isle of Wight speedway club. "I think the marvellous thing with our speedway programmes over here is that we print them at half-twelve on the day of the meeting and then have them at the track. If it's raining, we don't print them and save that way! More tracks should do that – they'd save money and be more accurate. If we get an injury on the Monday night, then we can make sure it's correct in the programme the next day. Sheffield do something similar." Paul's keen to visit a number of the speedway clubs he hasn't been to before and report on them for the *Speedway Star*, "I'd like to go to Workington!" News that I'm a Sunderland fan prompts Paul to confess, "I want Newcastle to stay in the Premiership – they're a big club – it's the bloke at the top who's the

[1] *The Sporting Motorcyclist* issues I saw are packed with a wide variety of information. Readers are advised to subscribe ["if you're a competitor you'll need this"] and each issue contains, "entry forms and regulations, information, previews and reports on meetings and social events, news from the ACU and over 160 clubs in the Southern, South Eastern and South Midland centres, fixtures, championship tables and photos." A one year subscription costs £22 (first-class post or £20 second class post) all cheques should be made payable to *The Sporting Motorcyclist* and sent to Andy Wood, 30 Westways, Edenbridge, Kent TN8 6AA

[2] His report starts, "For those who have always fancied watching an overseas meeting, there is no need to find a hotel in Sweden or Poland. You don't even have to book the cheap flight which drops you a thousand miles from the track. In fact, the perfect overseas trip starts in Portsmouth....There was no way I could miss this night. As well as the Islanders making their National League bow, the visiting Bournemouth Buccaneers were making their debut appearance in British Speedway".

problem!" Roy interrupts, "I used to follow Reading [speedway] when I worked in Camberley for a while."
[Paul] "What did you make of their Elite League experiment?"
[Roy harrumphs] "Not much. That silly idiot [John Postlethwaite] upset all the regulars by changing the name. They're the Racers really. Always have been always will be! I used to watch them at Tilehurst. I can still name the team. Mick Bell, Bernie Leigh, Richard May, Dag Lovaas, Geoff Curtis and Anders Michanek." Though we only have to drive from the car park to the deck of the ferry, Roy could regale us with many stories of speedway past and present. The sight of a giant vehicle about to be driven onto the ferry prompts Roy to recall his recent brush with big vehicles on the Island. "They brought a 10-ton blade over last summer. It took 45 minutes to drive to the track and four changes of the traffic lights to turn the corner. The police waved us on but a vehicle like that can only go very slowly, even in high gear. When it tried to go up a hill, it couldn't make it! You have to go into neutral to change the gears. I was two cars behind it when the brakes failed and it started rolling back. Ten tons! He turned it into a hedge. It didn't damage it [the hedge] much, strange to say. We did have a two-mile queue though!"

By now we've parked up the Skoda, made our way up the internal stairs of the ferry to the plush seating area that surrounds the café bar and, with a report to compile and later write, Paul seizes his chance to disappear and/or work. "I'm just going to mingle!" Though regular ferry passengers have become inured to its appeal, the journey from Portsmouth to the Island across the Solent on a sunny afternoon is an absolute pleasure to experience from the outside deck of the ferry. As we leave the port, we're assailed with numerous safety announcements. These could fill a more nervous passenger with thoughts of their imminent demise when the ferry sinks. After I've taken careful note of the instructions to do with evacuation procedures, lifeboats and inflatable life vests we're also reminded, "For safety reasons, do not throw lighted cigarettes over the side of the boat." I assume the issue isn't so much that there isn't enough water to extinguish the embers but more that the red-hot cinders might blind fellow passengers in the breeze that the ferry inevitably creates on its journey over to the Island. The sight of Portsmouth in the sunshine as it recedes into the distance never fails to appeal. However, this afternoon we're also treated to the impressive sight in the near distance of the world's biggest warship, the super Carrier *USS Theodore Roosevelt*. Home to a crew of 5,500, made up of American pilots, engineers and sailors. The 103,000 tonne vessel has a giant 1,150 foot flight deck. Even though it's anchored some distance away, it still looks huge on the horizon. Hardly surprising, given the sheer scale of this nuclear-powered warship. She stands 252 foot tall with 20 decks, a fleet of 90 aircraft and is as long as the Empire State Building is high.

Already comfortable on board our vessel, and sat at a table with their refreshments, are the Islanders Programme Editor and Announcer, Bryn Williams, and Maxwell Richards owner of Southampton-based Pegasus Speed Needs who operates the spares van franchise at three British speedway tracks: Swindon, Poole and the Isle of Wight ("I used to do Oxford, Reading and Eastbourne as well!"). Maxwell is a smartly dressed man dressed in his trademark smart overalls and sports a hairstyle with echoes of a teddy-boy quiff that must have been much more luxuriant in his youth. Maxwell has the look of a man unafraid of hard work and, afterwards on the journey home, I discover that he has a wealth of fascinating stories – many from the 10 years he spent in Saudi Arabia as a diver. Though Pegasus boast an impressive array of speedway, grasstrack and longtrack supplies, the business is ultimately is only a hobby for Maxwell. Nonetheless, it's a fun occupation that also enables him to participate in the casual freemasonry that characterises the inner circle of the speedway community. After his time in Saudi during its glory growth years of the 70s, Maxwell strongly believes modern Britain has gone badly downhill. Equally used to socialising with Saudi princes and assorted members of the Saudi Royal family, Maxwell is just at home in conversation with the riders, mechanics and Bryn Williams. Though the season has barely started, Bryn confesses, "I'm tired. I'm pleased I didn't go last night [to Belle Vue]; it was a farce and only run 'cause Sky were there! I've got enough to do anyway. I'm on the Island tonight, King's Lynn tomorrow, Arena on Friday, Rye on Saturday, Rye on Sunday and then Tuesday back here at the Isle of Wight." When I arrive Maxwell has just posed the question, "Guess how much the ESO fuel tank went for on eBay?" I'm so naive that I didn't even know that there would be a burgeoning market for the fuel tanks of yesteryear so I've absolutely no idea whether £267 represents a bargain or financial foolishness! Maxwell would still have many more speedway bikes, parts and equipment to sell on eBay but for the fire that ripped through his property last summer. "They evacuated 250 people and closed the road off. It took 10 fire engines to put it out. It was on the news! Afterwards I had the insurance Gestapo crawl all over my warehouse since it caught fire last August. One thing I'd say to everyone is photograph every single item in your house. You need it to make an insurance claim. If you can't

Isle of Wight: *"I don't apologise that I'm patriotic. We need to help British youngsters reach a world stage at a lot earlier age and we have to do it as a nation!"*

see it [after the fire] you can't claim it! There was nothing left. Everything melted. It was amazing – bikes, engines, scaffolding poles!"

Talk of excessive heat has Bryn come over all wistful for warmer climes since he returned from his winter away in Australia, "I've had the central heating on 24 hours a day". Maxwell warms to his theme of the iniquities of the insurance Gestapo, "Fighting the insurance is a nightmare!" Isle of Wight Islanders Incident Recorder, Chris Golding looks sympathetic, "What was the cause? Did you find out?" "Yeah, bloody squirrels! I leave nuts for the birds and the squirrels. They reckon they were the ones who started it." Quite what the squirrels did exactly we don't learn since Gavin Sedgmen comes over to renew his acquaintances with Bryn. His son Ryan rides tonight in the number 3 race tabard for the Wight Link Islanders. Gavin also has another son in the country, Justin, who'll ride in the Premier League for Somerset this season. Compared to the distances in Australia, it must appear that all British speedway tracks are remarkably handy, no matter whereabouts you're based. Gavin's already put in the miles. "We went to Somerset and had a spin round there. He went pretty quick actually." The smooth quality of the track surface in Somerset gains some praise and stands out in even sharper relief to the Sedgmen family after their trip to Stoke.
[Bryn] "Stoke is never the smoothest."
[Gavin] "The track itself was alright, it's just a tired old stadium – she's done a mile or two. They haven't used the dog track for years. The tarps are all perished; grass is growing up through the tyres. It don't look that attractive! [For Justin] It's pretty cutthroat. You go to a track you haven't seen or can't visualise and you're out in heat 1. [At Somerset] it's a good track and they've got good facilities and a big fence to cut the breeze off the fans. They're the ones you have to look after! It was freezing bloody cold at Stoke but, tell you what, it's the only track in England we haven't been offered a cup of tea!" Later outside on deck as we look back towards Portsmouth, I ask, "Will Ryan be here the whole season?" "I have two sons over here – at Somerset and the Isle of Wight. I'm just staying till the end of the month to help them settle in. They live in Swindon, which is very central. One son who's 17 will do his driving test – you have to be 18 to do it in Oz. You know, this must be one of the most beautiful journeys to a speedway track anywhere in the world!" Because of the tide, this afternoon it's a longer journey than usual and, stood in the spring sunshine, we savour the view and the breeze until the announcement we must all return to our vehicles.

Back in John Bramall's Skoda, Roy Collins reveals that age has its complications, "I need one pair of glasses to drive and another pair to read the map. The first time I went to Czechoslovakia, I had to find a track in a field in the rain – it was a nightmare!"
[John Bramall] "Pardubice – probably wouldn't pass health and safety in this country."
[Roy] "I dunno. What about King's Lynn? If you move that bit of wood aside there's a concrete wall and Armco barrier."

Since this is Paul Burbidge's first trip to the Island, Roy is keen to provide information on what will greet him after a short drive from the ferry terminal. "These people who ride small tracks well, when they come to our one, they're 20 mph faster on the first corner. We change things when we can. A year or so

Chris Johnson warms up

Practice starts

The NL is born

ago we had a delivery of 365 tons of chalk on the last bend. We crushed it and banked it up with 500 tons of bricked rubble. I spent hours doing that banking. We have a 50-year lease, with 48 years to go, planning permission for 35 meetings a year and we mustn't start the engines until 7. If we have an accident, we can run from 9:30 until 10. I'm biased but I think it's the best-looking speedway track in the whole of the British Isles!"
[Paul] "This is a huge night for Bournemouth! The test will be the size of the crowd when they race at home. There's a slight problem that Poole are away at Ipswich that night. I don't think many will go and watch the Pirates. They'll stay and watch the Buccaneers meeting!" On arrival we all go our separate ways. Paul heads off towards the pits in search of rider interviews and I go to the Speedway Office in search of the Islanders experienced Promoter Dave Pavitt. [3]

Inside the Speedway Office door located at the top of the stairs of the stadium clubhouse, Dave Pavitt's behind his desk multi-tasking. There's an impressive number of piles of paper scattered throughout the room and on top of his desk. Something of a surprise to see is a computer connected to the Internet. Not exactly the greatest lover of posters on speedway forums, Pav clearly has some occasional use for the information superhighway that is the World Wide Web. Though I've only popped in for a quick chat, Pav is under the impression I've specifically come to interview him about the formation of the National League and the decision of the club to become one of its inaugural members. Pav definitely wears his promotional hat with pride this afternoon. Whatever the reason, Pav is keen to tell any gentleman of the press in his general vicinity (or on the phone) about the benefits of the National League or, alternatively, the thinking behind why the Isle of Wight have dropped down from the Premier League to the National League. With little or no preamble Dave launches into a succinct summary of the situation with the speed of delivery that wouldn't disgrace Peter O'Sullivan at the end of an exciting horse race commentary. "I only have about 10 minutes. For two or three years, we've been thinking about the National League. It's all my baby! It was quite obvious that we needed to do something. The Premier League, in my opinion, gets stronger and stronger every year. Like a rose you should prune it. If it's never pruned, it's not strong enough. The Premier League is a successful business. Some teams are stronger than others. You can't cut the points to help the weaker teams and [for the Islanders] the writing has been on the wall for a while. It was a struggle to track a competitive team but I was loath to join the Conference League 'cause I believe the Isle of Wight needs to be in a professional league. What infuriated me was you could never name a settled team [in the Conference League] and, when you did develop young riders, Premier League teams would come and steal from you and you wouldn't get paid because there wasn't a system in place to reward you for your efforts! I knew one day we'd have to go down this road. For the last two previous AGMs, I've been trying to get things off the ground with very slow success. Because I was on the Management Committee in 2008 – my third term – I was fortunate that the then members of the Management Committee saw that the time was right for a third professional league to start. In November 2008, we had an inaugural meeting of all the existing Conference League chairmen along with Peter Morrish – now National League coordinator – to thrash out what we were all aiming to do. I took that back to the Management Committee. They knew I had a vested interest, but wanted to listen! We had various other meetings and tabled a motion in Spain at the AGM and it went through by acclaim. The only objection was from Matt Ford who has now become a founder member of the League. He thought it was such a good idea that everyone would want to join it! But, the points he objected to were valid. We had to make a few rules with regards to riders and averages but also we must bear in mind we must be protective of clubs who have teams in higher leagues already: like King's Lynn, Scunthorpe, Rye House and, now, Bournemouth. Tonight we have our first ever National League meeting against ourselves and the Bournemouth Buccaneers. This will be a bedding-in year where we'll be making sure that the rules and regulations become adapted to suit realities. Already we've come across some teething problems with the averages and the percentages given but we've adapted them. In 2010, we'll all re-declare, possibly with one or two other clubs. I do believe this will be a great help to bring on British

[3] Paul describes his journey to and arrival at the stadium. "On route to Smallbrook I had no idea what to expect on my arrival. Roy assured me that I was visiting the best looking speedway venue in the British Isles. I could certainly see what he meant when we pulled into the car park. While there are a number of stadiums around the country which are badly in need of renovation or at least a lick of paint, Smallbrook is certainly one of the tidiest I have visited. The track was surrounded by grass; and there was a well maintained grandstand with proper seating on the home straight, and a fantastic clubhouse complete with gymnasium and a viewing balcony. Roy led me inside to meet Dave Pavitt. I'd spoken to him many times over the phone during the winter, but it was great to meet one of the sport's promoting giants in person for the first time. Giant is definitely the word to describe the tall and imposing Pavitt, who warmly shook my hand and welcomed me to the club he's promoted for over 11 years.

Isle of Wight: *"I don't apologise that I'm patriotic. We need to help British youngsters reach a world stage at a lot earlier age and we have to do it as a nation!"*

speedway riders which we desperately need!" [4]

"In the National Development League, they'll be able to race more sincerely and more competitively as it's a professional league. Their abilities will shine through in the National League more than in the Conference League! For example, Brendan Johnson will be racing in Hungary in the World Under-19s and, I think, he'll do better because of the National League. What I mean is, had it still been the Conference League, I don't think he'd have been ready to do that! I don't apologise that I'm patriotic. We need to help British youngsters reach a world stage at a lot earlier age and we have to do it as a nation! If I get the same crowd level in the National Development League, we'll make money. We lost tons of money in 2008. [5] Maybe, in hindsight, we were going a bit stale in the Premier. Only in hindsight, mind you. The £10 [admission fee] will be attractive – especially for the holidaymaker. I've sold nearly the same number of season tickets for this year as last year, albeit at the lower rate. I believe at £10, this can only help us increase our crowds. We're a unique club here, we're a tourist attraction – we survive 'cause of the tourists in the summer and, but for them and Wightlink, there definitely would be no speedway here! I only came here for a year in 1998 on a one-year contract and I'm still here! [6] But it's okay for us! We don't run another team!" Our conversation is interrupted and ends abruptly when a man arrives with a mock-up of a poster. Pav is delighted with what he's shown, "You're a star! It looks lovely!" Pleased at his reception, the man confirms, "You've got a new colour photocopier haven't you? I can do it on disk so you can print it yourself!"

Over by the pits I bump into the other Dave I view to be synonymous with the speedway club on the Isle of Wight – Dave Croucher. He's in the company of Paul Burbidge and, after we've exchanged pleasantries, I make an error when I describe the third tier of speedway as the National Development League. Though Pav has also used this term, Crouch immediately puts me right, "It's the National League not the National Development League!" Paul Burbidge agrees with Crouch's version of the nomenclature, "The National Development League devalues the product!" Given that he now has responsibilities at Somerset, I'm surprised that Crouch has come over to the Island. "I'm here tonight 'cause I have an interest in five riders – two for Bournemouth and three for the Isle of Wight. Also, it's partly social and it's the first meeting for this League!"

The stadium infrastructure looks pretty much as I remember it from last season though I hadn't previously noticed the disabled viewing platform area on bend number one. On the nearby road, a horse-drawn carriage goes by. They say that a trip to the Isle of Wight is like going back in time though I always understood this to be the 1950s not the 1850s. The lady in the refreshment kiosk readies her equipment in preparation for the first-night rush through the turnstiles. I make the mistake of praising the double belly burger that's actually sold in the bar, "No, we don't do that! We do the triple with three slices of bacon and cheese!" In and around the pits area the Buccaneers management team are out in full force. Joint team manager Neil Vatcher is with Poole co-promoter and Bournemouth Chairman Giles Hartwell, fellow team manager Garry May and press officer Gordie Day. Garry offers no real predictions on either the meeting or the season ahead. "Well, it's a challenge. We've put on a strong side but we'll lose some of them when they ride for their Premier League sides!" He doesn't specify which riders but a glance at the line-up indicates that he definitely could sometimes find himself without Jay Herne and Jerran Hart. I'm not quite sure of the arrangements that apply to riders like Luke Priest, Mark Baseby and Kyle Newman. One member of the Bournemouth team well used to life on the Island is Gordie Day. "I used to work here for David. In fact, for three years I was pits marshal here for David. I remember the first ever meeting here. What a lovely family to be part of – speedway! We're all gypsies really! It can drive you up the wall – as you know – but, at the end of the day, everyone knows everyone

[4] During the close season Buxton co-promoter Richard Moss would comment: "The new league set-up has been more professional rules-wise but has also come with added expense which has been tough in the current economic climate. Both points money and travel costs have significantly increased over the last year and it has been a tough year financially for the club." Buxton speedway club have, of course, been widely praised for how they embody what many see as the true ethos of the old Conference League. It is an approach that, traditionally, has seen them nurture riders rather than compete for silverware at all costs.

[5] The unique ownership structure of the Isle of Wight Speedway Club means there's an Annual General Meeting where all shareholders can inspect the Club accounts. From a financial point of view, apparently this didn't make the best ever reading. It was widely reported that the average crowd size in 2008 for the Islanders was 343

[6] When Pav met Paul Burbidge, he explains something similar, "The Isle of Wight put in an application to join the Premier League and they needed an experienced promoter to guide them in the first year, just as I'm doing at Somerset this year. The Directors of the company employed me for a season. It was only a 1-year contract and that was made quite plain, but 11 years later I'm still enjoying it. When I went there I was just running the speedway, but now I run the whole stadium. It's still a lovely little place. The way we manage to run speedway in the quiet months with so few supporters compared to other clubs is incredible."

else!" Gordie definitely has an extensive speedway network. He meets and greets pretty well everyone who passes us. We're briefly interrupted by Crouch who has some last-minute instructions for the Bournemouth team, "Gordon, I'm sure you remember – at quarter past seven we need them all lined up in numerical order for the parade." Gordie does indeed remember.

Since I understand Gordie is Krzysztof Kasprzak's speedway agent, I tell him how amazingly quick Krzysztof looked at Arlington on Saturday night when he visited with Belle Vue. His speed round the track really caught the eye. "You saw on Saturday night, what I saw in Krzysztof Kasprzak in 2002. Zenon does his engines – they're always 10% too strong and you spend the whole meeting trying to knock them off and Zenon won't let you! My job is to make sure Krzysztof has the sponsors and that they're happy and he's happy. I try to make sure that everything he wants is where he wants it! You get to know and understand different riders when you work with them and Krzysztof is very easy to work with. He has many sponsors and one of them is Mrs Day, well, Angry Dodo Productions – it's an anagram of my name. It's a music production company. I heard Krzysztof say to Nicki Pedersen once when he pointed to his Angry Dodo logo, "This is the sponsor you want!" If there are any clouds on the metaphorical speedway horizon, Gordie believes they are economic. "We only had 800 for the meeting against Swindon!" While I clutch at the straw that this perhaps could be expected since the meeting was being shown live on Sky, Gordie dismisses my attempt to find some consolation, "Yes – but it's Poole we're talking about!"

Gordie's keen interest in and love of music isn't something I previously knew about. "Bournemouth has been a real breeding ground for musicians in this country. I remember when Tony Blackburn was a singer in a band called Tony Blackburn and the Rovers. They were just a Bournemouth band. Shows his sense of humour hasn't changed at all. I saw Zoot Money and the Big Roll Band with Andy Summers playing lead guitar for them – he'd later go on to gain world fame with The Police. I saw all my heroes at the Winter Gardens. So many people played there or got their big breaks there. Some perfected their skills outside – Ralph McTell and Al Stewart were both buskers in and around Bournemouth during the early 60s. I played for a band called the Stoolpigeons from 1963 to 1965 (they split up in 1966) before leaving to work in London. I played for a number of bands in and around the London until coming back to the Poole area in 1973. The last gig I played was 1989 in Seattle in Washington State. We played quite a few times in America. Phil Katz from Seattle started me and my wife going to America. I played with him. He's a Professor of Mathematics and his son is a humongous guitarist and works for Disney. I love America. The people are so friendly and there are those beautiful lakes in Seattle. I went there in 1979 and 80 and learnt about Japanese, Vietnamese and Chinese food for the first time. We had a seven-week holiday and it took me months to get used to England again and not being able to go out at 9 o'clock to eat and to eat anything we liked! The music community is just as close as the speedway community."

The chance for further reminiscence is interrupted by the roar of the bikes in the pits as the preparations for the first ever National League meeting start to get properly underway. Out on the track a gorilla on a quad bike provides some motorised entertainment as it circuits the Smallbrook Stadium track. Bryn Williams wonders aloud over the tannoy, "I don't know if that's Dave Pavitt on the bike?" He proceeds to welcome "the visitors from Dorset who used to be in Hampshire when I did my O levels". Close to the pits fence but positioned slightly further along so that they can also overlook activity in the pits, the fourth bend of the track and still enjoy a panoramic view of the stadium, are Albert and Eileen Shepherd. They're dedicated Islanders fans wrapped up warmly against the elements. They eagerly await the first race of the season. Tonight they're also proud parents since their son, Kevin, will this season be joint Islanders team manager (along with former rider Chris Hunt). Albert regales me with some harrowing tales from his childhood that nowadays would be seen as just cause to leave you with lifelong trauma and a very jaundiced view of humanity. Instead, Albert takes great pride in his family, his 28 years in the Navy and his speedway club. Though he's 77 tomorrow, he has a youthful outlook belied by his chronological age. Before the meeting starts a popular stalwart of the Islanders pits crew on race night, Buzz Terry, who passed away during the close season is fondly remembered.

As a result of their arrival in the National League, the Isle of Wight will enjoy the rivalry with a number of new local competitors from Dorset: namely Weymouth's Wildcats and tonight's comparatively geographically closer neighbours, the Bournemouth Buccaneers. The first ever National League race is won by Tom Brown who, although he's third at the end of the second lap, by the exit of the second bend on the third lap he finds the lead. Tom then doesn't

Isle of Wight: *"I don't apologise that I'm patriotic. We need to help British youngsters reach a world stage at a lot earlier age and we have to do it as a nation!"*

relinquish his advantage, despite strong pressure from Jay Herne. It's a spectacle that impresses Bryn Williams, "What a cracking race to start the season! If it's that quality all year – well!" Though the Islanders open the meeting in positive fashion, the highly regarded Buccaneers record a maximum heat advantage in heat 2 to go into a lead they fail to relinquish for the remainder of the meeting. Islanders' reserve Andy Braithwaite enjoys a torrid opening lap when he strikes the safety fence with great force as he exits the fourth bend of the first lap. Placed in third at the time, though he tries to rejoin the race, Andy sensibly retires before he makes it to the next bend. Medical news from the pits soon reveals a dislocated finger. In fact, Andy could have sustained further injuries but his badly swollen hand prevents exact diagnosis. Albert Shepherd believes that the quality of the racing served up in the National League should be equivalent to that of the Premier League but, if he has one anxiety, it's the inexperience of the riders. "It's great to be back but I wonder about the accidents in the National League." The third heat showcases Ryan Sedgmen's first race of the night, but he ends up in last place during a race where the riders are strung out like a line of washing. The cloudless sky remains and the disappearance of the sunshine causes temperatures to drop dramatically. Dave Pavitt is clearly keenly aware of local climatic conditions judged by the greatcoat and cap that he wears. It's an outfit that gives him the appearance of an extra from a Moscow street scene in a John le Carré episode on the telly. The fourth race of the meeting sees Nick Simmons and Jerran Hart via for supremacy on the first and second bends of the second lap before the Islanders' captain becomes the second home rider to triumph tonight. The race action hasn't quite caught Bryn's eye as much as some of the stadium furniture, "You can probably see a few electronic signs on the home straight – they look a bit flash! Our thanks go to Elite Signs in Poole." Jay Herne wins the fifth race with some ease. Indeed, his first race defeat at the hands of Tom Brown turns out to be the only time he's headed by any rival during this particular meeting. In the number 3 race tabard, Ryan Sedgmen records his first ever National League points when he finishes third. It's a hard-won point since Andrew Aldridge spends all four laps in hot pursuit, apparently somehow attached to Ryan's back wheel but unable to quite find the speed required to get past. Bryn Williams provides a low key medical update on Andy Braithwaite ("He has hurt his hand") before he praises the Buccaneers, "With the kind agreement of the Bournemouth managers [and the referee], as it's a challenge, Scott Meakins [Islanders number 8] is allowed to take his [Braithwaite's] ride."

Heat 7 features a flier from the start line for Luke Priest. He powers ahead until Nick Simmons calls upon his Smallbrook Stadium expertise to sweep past the Buccaneer with considerable ease round the outside of banked third and fourth bends. Ben Hopwood is fortunate to finish second in heat 8 after Andrew Aldridge nearly sneaks past him during the run-in from the last bend (his charge halts when he suffers untimely engine problems signalled by a dramatic puff of smoke close to the finish line). The ninth race sees Ryan Sedgmen continue his race-by-race improvement to finish second behind Jerran Hart. Ryan's followed home so closely by teammate Brendan Johnson that you half expect to find his tyre is stuck to the exhaust. Tom Brown wins the last race before the interval. The interval break is taken with the scores relatively poised at 27-33. Prior to the race I'd heard Dave Pavitt issue instructions to the track staff, "We'll grade and blade after the next one and bring some of that dirt back from the outside!" Dressed against the cold of a Russian winter, Pav expresses some satisfaction that his dream of a professional National League is finally underway, "I'm happy! It's a big crowd. I prefer to be 6 ahead than 6 behind, of course!" Albert Shepherd is equally delighted the season is underway, albeit his satisfaction is tempered by some disappointment at the first three races of Ben Hopwood's National League season. Keen to support his club and its riders, Albert had bought a rolling chassis for Ben Hopwood to help with his mechanical preparations, "I expected more of Ben I must admit. Still it's the first meeting of the season and everyone's a bit rusty! It's bloody wonderful to see a big crowd particularly after the club's heavy £50,000 loss last season."

During the interval, Bryn reiterates his earlier appeal on behalf of Brendan Johnson, "On May 1st and 2nd, Brendan will be going to the Under-19 championship in Hungary. It's a marvellous achievement for the rider and, just to remind you, he's looking for sponsors!" [7] Any satisfaction taken by either the Islanders management or their fans take in their 6-point deficit behind the highly fancied Bournemouth Buccaneers, quickly evaporates when things go progressively downhill after the interval. Heat 11 is both a collector's item and a curate's egg of a race. Nick Simmons suffers an engine failure at the start line, while his teammate Andy Braithwaite – who'd bravely defied medical advice to try and get back out on his bike again – fails to complete a full lap of the circuit and, once again, on the fourth bend he clatters

[7] Brendan rode in the U19 semi-final at Debrecen and finished 11th with 6 points.

into roughly the same section of the safety fence he'd struck previously. Given the high speeds achieved around Smallbrook, a swollen hand is always a handicap and sensibly, after his disqualification, Andy finally agrees to go to the hospital to get some X-rays. In the commentary-cum-referee's box that he shares with SCB official Christina Turnbull, Bryn struggles to get used to the newfangled phraseology of the 2009 Rulebook, "I can't say excluded, I have to say disqualified otherwise I'll get a fine, I'm told!" With only Buccaneers riders in the rerun – unless they do something silly like fall off or fail to race – the inevitably 5-0 race result effectively puts the meeting beyond doubt.

One rerun quickly follows another. Heat 12 stops before it's hardly got going. Ryan Sedgmen rides his bike round to the pit gate where he proceeds to have an animated discussion with his dad. Albert shrugs phlegmatically, "Ryan's at that sort of age that he'll be a nightmare to manage!" There would appear to be some wisdom in these words when, at the start of the second lap of the rerun, Ryan suddenly idles to a snail's pace and tootles round the inside of the circuit to stop on the grass of the fourth bend directly opposite the pits gate. Though the race proceeds around him, Ryan gets off his bike and gesticulates angrily towards his father Gavin who, when the race ends, studiously ignores his teenage son while he purposefully walks to collect the bike. Unluckily, shortly afterwards Ryan is the victim of team changes at the club and this dictates that he'll only ride three times for the Islanders. With the score far from poised at 28-43, the Islanders joint team managers of Kevin Shepherd and Chris Hunt decide to give Tom Brown the black-and-white helmet colour only to see the Welshman relegated to third by the time the riders reach the first bend. With Brown eventually fourth, when the black-and-white helmet colour returns to the pits it's handed onto Brendan Johnson who's then knocked off on the first bend by his own teammate, Scott Meakins. Fortunately for the Islanders, referee Christina Turnbull orders a rerun with all four riders back. Second time out Brendan flies off into the lead but is skilfully passed by a Kyle Newman blast round the outside of the fourth bend. The last race of the night sees Jerran Hart studiously adopt a head-down-and-go approach. So much so that it takes until he's half way down the back straight for Jerran to spot the red lights that Christina Turnbull illuminates immediately after the start of the race. Next time out Nick Simmons falls on the second bend of the first lap but is saved from any further pain (other than his disqualification) by the quick reactions of Tom Brown, who lays down his bike in the blink of an eye. At the third time of asking the race runs to completion and enables the Buccaneers to record yet another maximum heat advantage. Despite the use of both tactical rides, falls, engine failures and exclusions somehow contrive to ensure the Islanders only gain 7 points after the interval from the last five races (while the Buccaneers gain 24). The ease of their victory signals that the *Speedway Star* expert's prediction of fourth place for the Buccaneers could prove to be an under-estimate if the Bournemouth side continue to show such strength in depth on their travels throughout the rest of the 2009 season.

7th April Isle of Wight v. Bournemouth (National League) 34-57

CHAPTER 5

Poole

"Often after a meeting, Charles would have the officials and everyone for tea and Penguin biscuits."

11th June

Though the season is less than three months old, local rivals the Poole Pirates and the Eastbourne Eagles meet for the fifth time of the 2009 season. The Elite League 'B' fixture at Wimborne Road is the Poole Pirates 15th Elite League meeting of a campaign that's seen them massively stutter compared to the exalted standards they've previously set themselves over the last decade or so in the top tier of British speedway. A quick glance at the league table reveals that they've won three meetings, drawn one and lost ten! However, if football is a game of two halves then the same promises to be true for Poole. To aid their possible recovery, the Pirates have made team changes in the light of a new regulation that appeared in the Rulebook over the winter. This allows Elite League teams to strengthen up to a 42-point limit after they complete 12 league meetings. Good news for the Pirates faithful is that Hans Andersen is back at the club to race for the rest of the season in the Pirates number 1 race tabard. However, less welcome for the club are rumbles of discontent about the alleged 'manipulation' of rider averages. These started as whispers some weeks ago and have now built up to thunderclap levels following recent team strengthening changes at both Coventry and Poole.

Trade exhibition poster

Tensions sometimes run high between speedway promoters and, with the lure of the televised Elite League play-offs increasingly financially significant, (unsubstantiated) allegations have been thrown around like confetti during recent days. Two Poole meetings in particular have received comprehensive (usually hearsay) analysis – the away league meetings at Swindon (May 7th) and Peterborough (May 14th). The basic fact is that the ongoing poor Pirates start to the 2009 Elite League season continued. It saw them slip to a 56-39 defeat at Blunsdon and a 55-38 defeat at the East of England Showground. After the Peterborough meeting, Panthers co-promoter Mick Bratley contacted the BSPA with his suspicions that the Dorset visitors had tried to manipulate their rider averages and, as evidence, he cited one race in particular (heat 14). Publicly, Poole co-promoter Matt Ford expressed "bafflement" and sensibly highlighted that a number of other Elite League teams struggled similarly at both Abbey Stadium and the East of England Showground. Rumour of sharp practice and Spanish customs is part of the lingua franca of the contemporary vocabulary of British speedway. However, what lit the blue touchpaper isn't so much the custom and practice of rider average manipulation – often rumoured as a hardy perennial of both early- and late-season racing – but the fact that these alleged but unproven actions enable some Elite League teams to strengthen up and thereby (via the expanded six-team Elite League play-off system) seize the coveted financial prize of lucrative end-of-season Play-off meetings that arrive with the potential glory of finishing as league champions. Lakeside co-promoters Stuart Douglas and Jon Cook chose not to attend the BSPA Annual Conference held during winter 2008 (and were fined £750 for not doing so) where these changes to the EL play offs were agreed. Nonetheless, on the 27th May, they did post a potentially explosive statement on the Lakeside Hammers club website. [1]

Given the propensity of the speedway family to sweep things under the carpet and/or keep them in-house, then the mere fact that the Lakeside promotion took this action (irrespective of the content or validity of their complaint) definitively highlights that all is not well within the Elite League tier of the sport. Some people were quick to query whether this attack of conscience was entirely altruistic since other potentially heinous allegations don't attract such public opprobrium from the club. Had Morpheus suddenly found himself in Thurrock and inadvertently mistaken Jon Cook for Neo? Judged by his statement and subsequent interview with the *Speedway Star*, offered the choice of the red pill (learn the truth) or the blue pill (to return to the world as he knows it), then Jon has clearly chosen the route of speaking truth to power. Interviewed in the *Speedway Star* shortly after the Hammers website statement, Jon called for BSPA Chairman Peter Toogood to "Step aside to allow changes in the governance of the sport. The current system is open to abuse and we don't want to spend our time looking for loopholes and taking advantage of them. This sport is grey – it's as grey as the hairs on my head – and it needs to be black and white. The reason it's grey is because there is too much self- governing, people trying to do the right thing, or their perception of the right thing, to help us through. If the regulators were a bit tougher in the first place, we would get a better result for speedway."

The immutable law of gossip, innuendo and conjectural comment dictates that when enough mud is thrown, it inevitably sticks. If someone shouts stinking fish loud enough, then people take notice. If these unsubstantiated allegations and comments had been made on Internet speedway forums, then they would have (as usual) been dismissed as the wild ill-informed fantasies of a pernicious minority with axes to grind. However, since these allegations were made by key people within the sport, it provoked *Speedway Star* Managing Editor Philip Rising enough to pen a prominent comment piece. [2]

Neil 'Middlo' Middleditch was apoplectic that he had to comment upon such accusations after a lifetime for him and his family in the sport. Things were so serious that even the Bible came readily to hand in the Middleditch household, when Middlo revealed he would "Swear on my children's lives that nothing untoward went on at Peterborough". Even then some fans weren't happy with his statement highlighting that Middlo didn't make a similar offer about the disputed Swindon meeting. Mechanical failure and injury are part and parcel of the sport. Their impact can strike randomly at any time and it's unfortunate that the six retirements on the same night that the Pirates endured have sparked unwarranted speculation. Matt Ford would have preferred to open his programme notes for the Eastbourne

[1] Lakeside Speedway promoters Stuart Douglas and Jon Cook have called for a complete overhaul in the way speedway is run plus an independent inquiry into the controversy surrounding allegations of race fixing during Poole's visit to Swindon earlier this month. The pair have issued a joint statement in an attempt to save the sport from all the infighting that is in danger of undoing much of the stability winter changes have brought to the Elite League. Their statement reads as follows:

"Over the last three years we have put considerable effort into re establishing our Speedway for the enjoyment of our fans and to become a solid member of both the Elite League and the British Speedway Promoters Association (BSPA). It has become obvious during that time that the continued move towards total self governance by the BSPA through the continued weakening of the Speedway Control Bureau (SCB) is not in the best interests of the sport and presents an opportunity for individual promoters to stretch the rule book to the extreme to gain advantage.

The time has come to return back to the old values of being overseen by an independent body and for rule making to be taken out of the hands of the promoters, who will naturally vote for what they want, as opposed to what is often best for the sport.

We share the concerns of many supporters with what is alleged to have gone on at Swindon when Poole visited and a public wall of silence from the SCB and BSPA does nothing but fan the flames. For that reason we have contacted the SCB and requested an independent inquiry in to the match, so the matter can be put to rest, such is the unprecedented furore surrounding it.

Whether Poole are exonerated of blame, averages on both sides are disallowed or other action taken, an inquiry has to address this matter with urgency. We make public our actions with a heavy heart but to stay silent would suggest we do not care about the situation and the fans of Speedway. Both our own supporters, and those in opposition, deserve clarity as without them we have no Sport and Speedway cannot retain its integrity until the stigma of allegations of race fixing are addressed."

[2] "It is also high time that the BSPA carried out a root and branch review of overly complex regulations that now govern the compilation of teams in this country. The rules are a minefield and open to abuse. The *Speedway Star* would like to see a simple process that ultimately would negate the temptation to bend the rules. First and foremost, NO team should be forced to release riders at the end of any season. Those that wish to continue with the same side must be allowed to do just that. ... the current system clearly does not work."

Poole: *"Often after a meeting, Charles would have the officials and everyone for tea and Penguin biscuits."*

meeting with the joyous news of Hans Andersen's return (it's so long ago that he was known as Hans N. Andersen when he last rode for the Pirates) but, instead, makes heartfelt comment about the unfair allegations that swirl round the club as well as his perception that jealousy at the Poole Pirates success plays some part in the current furore. [3]

Fans gather by the pits

The wheels of justice at the Speedway Control Bureau usually grind slowly but, after a slow start from the tapes, they're now proceeding at breakneck speed with an investigation under the auspices of the SCB consultant administrator Graham Reeve. Tonight he'll start a series of in-depth interviews with all potential witnesses to establish the veracity these allegations. Clearly there are potentially many people to be interviewed, though suspicions remain high that additional carpets will be bought for the BSPA office or, more likely, the SCB will require a burden of proof beyond that usually required at murder trials. Peter Toogood immediately brushes aside concerns about his initial tardy response to these allegations when they originally surfaced and, instead, provides an early indicator of the potential outcome of these investigations when he pointedly reminds promoters that not only should they shut up but that the rules and regulations that they collectively supposedly adhere

4th bend fans

[3] "Among the riders, mechanics, sponsors, management and supporters, we are delighted to welcome Speedway Control Board Bureau official Graham Reeve to Wimborne Road this evening.
Graham is here to talk with the Poole Castle Cover Pirates riders about the wild allegations being chucked at the club from several rival Elite League clubs that we have been deliberately losing races to reduce our averages and strengthen the team.
Mr Reeve can be assured of our full cooperation in any matter pertaining to this. The riders will be delighted to answer any questions Graham may have.
My only hope is that tonight proves a cracking meeting against Eastbourne, so that Graham can have some sort of reason for taking time out [of] his schedule to be here this evening.
I firmly believe this entire charade by rival promotions is a smokescreen on the part of one management and pure envy on behalf of the others who should be ashamed of themselves.
I find it incredibly strange that the two meetings in particular where we are being "cited" are at Swindon and Peterborough.
Let me remind you we scored 39 points at Swindon on May 7th, which is nowhere near the sort of score I want any Poole team to score away from home. But it was exactly the same points Coventry scored at Blunsdon this season and three more than Lakeside and top of the table Wolverhampton. So if that is the case ... is every Elite League team underperforming?
We are getting accused of supposed skulduggery in heat 14 at Peterborough after Daniel Davidsson was put off 15 metres for touching the tapes.
But why would we then score a 4-2 heat advantage in the last heat from Chris Holder and Bjarne Pedersen if we were making concerted efforts to "underperform".
There is absolutely no pattern to any of these scandalous accusations and they are, in my opinion, born purely out of total envy for everything we have achieved here in 10 years.
What is remarkable about this whole episode is that one of the clubs who started this bullying game against Poole Speedway are currently in the spotlight for having a side who contravened rules and ignored the Association's management committee in a meeting recently.
And they've the gall to write that we've got questions to answer about a meeting at Swindon when they weren't even there! As top newspaper columnist Richard Littlejohn would say ... You couldn't make it up.
It's been a difficult season for us. We've won only three meetings in 16 and we're not prepared to sit around at the bottom of the table and be the whipping boys for every other Elite League side without trying to do something about it.
We are delighted to welcome Hans Andersen on board this evening, but let me make it abundantly clear it's no different to Scott Nicholls and Matej Zagar rejoining the Elite League in the last fortnight.
I have had many friends privately suggest that I should walk away from speedway after this sorry episode.
But I feel quite the opposite. By doing that it would be suggesting I have something to answer on behalf of the club. Let me assure these bullies and gangs prodding and poking Poole Speedway they will have to go a long way for me to quit. They will not win.
I have written many times about my love of this place. I am a proud Poole boy and to drive around recently and see *Daily Echo* back page headlines of "FORD IN CHEAT SENSATION" is extremely damaging against this business and my name.
But, I refer to the answer I gave earlier: Official Mr Reeve will be given my full cooperation and we'll see where the matter takes us after tonight."

specifically prevent their public comment. [4]

If ever there was a local derby meeting for Eastbourne fans to make that they went to Poole to see, then tonight's 2009 Elite League 'B' fixture is that meeting. Over recent years the greater strength of the Pirates has caused the Eagles to struggle to win at Arlington, let alone to emerge victorious on their visits to Dorset. However, the comparative weakness of the opposition rather than the strength of the Eastbourne line-up has already seen home and away triumphs for the Eagles in the early season Elite Shield. These heart-warming victories were followed up shortly afterwards with a Good Friday draw in a curtailed meeting at Wimborne Road and immediately followed by a comfortable home victory in the Elite League 'A' fixtures. Away on a caravan holiday in St Leonards, Alan Bowman (whom I recognise as a member of the Eastbourne pits track staff) and his wife Barbara have come along to savour another possible Eagles away win. Before we can discuss possible scenarios, we're joined in our car park discussions by Mike Addison who's passing but immediately stops to renew his acquaintance with fellow initiates from the glory Wimbledon years at Plough Lane. Understandably proud of his involvement in British Speedway, Mike Addison now gets his speedway kicks as a fan who attends meetings at Rye House and Poole. Though modest about his previous involvement, I quickly gather that Mike spent 20 years working for the BSPA, many of those in charge of finding sponsorship for the sport during its glory years. Mike persuaded household names like Gulf Oil, Strongbow, WD & Ho Wills and Skol to sponsor British Speedway and then managed to retain their interest. These major brands sharply contrast with the comparatively Mickey Mouse crop of brands and companies that, for example, nowadays associate themselves with the prestigious and notionally international Speedway Grand Prix. [5]

Mike recalls characters from speedway's past with fond enthusiasm. He ranges widely and assumes I have the same familiarity with the great and the good of British Speedway history that he does. "I started with Ronnie Greene at 11, worked with Charles Ochiltree on special projects and then spent 20 years at the BSPA. Another one I was closely involved with was Reg Fearman at Reading. Reg was a rider, and promoter – everything! He was a hundred percent speedway – I think he had a hairdressing business once, like Matt Ford." Mike takes justifiable pride and satisfaction in the quality of the sponsors he persuaded to involve themselves with British Speedway during his watch, "I brought them all in but I walked out over the Durex sponsorship and warned them: if you take them, everyone else will cancel! They got in others after me on big money but they brought in nothing – like I knew they would! They requested me to come back. They realised then what I'd done for them but it was too late!"

Mike's heyday was a promotional era full of strong personalities and, often, similarly sized egos. Within the inner sanctum of the sport Mike had his own personal repertoire of heroes and villains. He wasn't a fan of John Berry but proceeds to speak highly of many other people. "I loved Mike Parker – who started Hackney and Crayford – lots of people were jealous 'cause he opened all those tracks. They could have, but he had the get up and go to do it and they didn't! I went to most of their funerals: Ronnie Greene, Charles Ochiltree. I didn't know Parker was even ill to my shame. He was a man who would stand by you no matter what. He would always be there! We've had a laugh. You could speak as you found. Greene and Ochiltree didn't like him but I did. I said to Ronnie 'I like him' and he said 'You can like who you like'. You could always sort things out. Often after a meeting, Charles would have the officials and everyone for tea and Penguin biscuits. We'd stay until 2 a.m. discussing things and having a laugh. That's how it was. No one sued each other! Sure, there were disagreements and jealousies but it was what it was. I would often speak on the phone late at night with Charles. I brought them all in [Skol, Stongbow]. When they voted by one vote to accept the Durex sponsorship I packed up my folder and said 'Right I'm off!' They said, 'You can't do that' and I said 'I just have!' The next day it was [national newspaper] headlines: 'Speedway boss walks out over Durex'. I knew it would be the beginning of the end! Speedway is a family sport and I always chose the sponsors carefully. There were many great promoters then – now there's not! The one here is good. Matt Ford! He puts on a show – a good

[4] Peter Toogood confirmed to the *Speedway Star*, "I think all the items that are now out in the public domain are not actually doing our sport any good. Obviously, when situations like this occur, it's actually better to try and resolve the thing in-house, without airing our dirty washing." Quizzed about the specifics BSPA's position on the matter Peter added gnomically, "It has been handed over to the Speedway Control Bureau, so it's now up to them to take the investigation forward. There won't be anything official from the BSPA on the basis that there is now an investigation underway. We wouldn't want to make a comment on any of the items that might be investigated."

[5] In his fascinating chapter on 1976 from the forthcoming *History of British Speedway*, Wolverhampton club historian Mark Sawbridge writes, "One very positive aspect of the sport in 1976 was the level of sponsorship. With marketing 'guru' Michael Addison at the helm, many household names seemed to be queuing up to back the sport. The *Daily Mirror* sponsored the Grand Prix, Skol Lager supported the World Team Cup final, Leyland Cars backed the British League Riders' Championship, Gauloises cigarettes sponsored the NNL alternative, and so on."

spectacle! All the new promoters [of yesteryear] I used to take them to Plough Lane for a meal and a sit down to watch the speedway so they could see what it should be like. If I did it now, I'd bring them here 'cause the grandstand, the service and the spectacle impresses. Matt puts on a good show and it is a show! Some promoters just open the gates and you have heat 1 without a parade. The best promoter now would equal the worst promoter then showmanship wise! The cleverest and the shrewdest thing Matt Ford has done was starting the National League team. When it was free last week they said in the papers they had a substatial crowd – usually they get 800 – but, in three years, all of speedway will be at that level. Elite League speedway is on its last legs! It can't carry on and that's why Matt has been so clever. Everyone will see Bournemouth as their team, they'll win and people will love them. The [Elite League] crowds have dropped here but he had to do what he did with Hans Andersen and, as soon as they start to win again, the crowds will be back. I come as often as I can here as much as I can afford. It costs me 60 or 70 quid a meeting. I live in South London and come down on the train from Waterloo. I eat upstairs and get the second-last train back and my girlfriend picks me up. Have you heard of the group Boney M? Well, she used to be in it! I miss the last few races but they do a good show here. I go to Rye House too but I know Len and he's a showman to the tips of his toes! There's really not many like him. There's the one here and, oh, I don't know." Mike has also had some insight into the late 20th century Conference League incarnation of Wimbledon Speedway at Plough Lane. He's saddened by their demise. "It was always going to be hard and I understand that Ian felt he really had to fight for what he saw as the best interests of Wimbledon Speedway. You've only got to look at the history to see they were always going to shut down all the London tracks and develop them. Ronnie Greene used to say that and he was right. I said to him, 'What even here?' [Plough Lane] and he paused and said, 'Yeah, even here!'"

Inside the impressive glass-fronted back-straight grandstand, the programme lady has set up her stall adjacent to the toilets just inside the double doors that lead in one direction to the bar area and in the other to the third bend. Bournemouth Buccaneers joint team manager Garry May passes, so receives some feedback that although the official race-day magazine contains the racecard for next Thursday's (11th June) National League home meeting against the Scunthorpe Saints – none of their riders are actually listed! Understandably, with the meeting still eight days away, Garry explains, "I rang Malcolm [Vasey] up for his team but he couldn't give them 'cause there'll be changes!" The programme lady also takes the opportunity to put across popular opinion, "Lots of people don't like Bournemouth being in the Poole programme – they want their own!" Garry shrugs, "I don't do the programme! I just run the team and make sure they've all turned up!" Though the *Speedway Star* isn't officially published until the Thursday of each week because they're a Wednesday night track, Poole Pirates fans regularly have the chance to purchase the magazine a night early. Given the controversy that swirls across the Internet forums and message boards, this week's edition has even more currency than usual since it features interviews with Matt Ford, Neil Middleditch, Jon Cook, Allen Trump, Peter Toogood and Mick Bratley among others. Scandal sells. When *Speedway Star* vendor, Mike 'Starman', takes up his pitch close to the programme stall he, like the programmes, does a roaring trade. British Speedway Forum posters have been quick to ascribe blame to both the Poole and Coventry managements. Some of the criticisms of the Pirates have been done with anonymous vitriol, others with humour. Whatever their attitude, Starman has no time for such irrelevant gossip or the piffle of ill-informed opinion. "We've done something wrong [pause] allegedly. I can name you 30 riders who've been dropping rides to reduce their averages. In a recession, we don't need controversy. With Hans Andersen here it will make it more exciting! Shame that Chris Holder is out." Starman's diatribe is interrupted by a passing fan who exclaims, "Chris Holder is out?!" Starman nods, "Yeah, he's done his collarbone in on his scrambler. A rider of his calibre should be swimming or in the gym or running not out on the scrambler. If it happens to a reserve that doesn't matter but a rider like him! Someone should tell him! He probably wouldn't listen though. Everyone goes on about Hans Andersen but no one's taking so much about Scott Nicholls at Coventry? What's going on there?" I suggest that we should wait till we read the truth about the situation in the magazine Mike sells. For reasons I can't quite put my finger on, he laughs. A man who proudly clutches what looks like a copycat substandard version of a BlackBerry comes up with the latest unsubstantiated tittle tattle he's just surfed across on the Internet, "Nichols has been dropped by Coventry – huh, huh, huh!" Starman has a bee in his bonnet about ill-informed comment, like others in this part of Dorset I suspect that he'd prefer that comment is substantiated by oaths taken on the Bible, "That's just speculation! We don't know that!"

With much of the country in the grip of a sharp economic recession and Elite League crowds on the decline at Poole this season, the issue of club and meeting sponsorship assumes even greater importance in the present famine than

Poole: *"Often after a meeting, Charles would have the officials and everyone for tea and Penguin biscuits.*

it does in times of comparative feast. Poole Speedway have a proven track record of commercial acumen. To illustrate this fact, this evening the spacious area inside the posh grandstand that often serves as the post-meeting disco area is filled with a variety of corporate sponsorship display stands rather than the empty dance floor the strobe lights of the disco would usually light up later. Exhibitors rather than speedway fans form a crowd in the display area. It's full of men in dark clothing – mostly suits – who look uncomfortable in collared shirts set off by their too brightly coloured ties. They've clearly been here some time stood by their display stands or those of their rivals. Many hold beers and have smoky breath. To my untutored eye, these booths showcase the latest designs in central heating knobs, obscure but sleekly swish gas heaters, boilers and the assorted accoutrements you'd expect to see in the usually hidden world of heating, ventilation and air conditioning. Garish but obscure adverts flash up on video screens. A few speedway fans who've accidentally ventured into the exhibition area out of curiosity mingle with the trade customers but don't look quite sure what exactly they've discovered or, even, if they're allowed to be there. Stallholders exchange commercial gossip, network and catch up. Some exhibitors have called it a day, start to dismantle their stands and begin to pack them back into their sleek transport cases. After my stroll throughout the cluttered display area, I come across a poster that proclaims "You are invited to our Trade Speedway evening. Free entry to the stadium during the Trade Show before 6 p.m.". The advert promises that a wealth of suppliers and manufacturers will attend the event from 4 p.m. onwards. Some household names leap out (Ariston, Bosch and Invensys), while many others haven't previously intruded upon my consciousness (Baxi Heating UK, Polypipe or Uponor). Whether they're known widely or not, a swathe of garish company logos illustrate a poster united in their desire to persuade trade show visitors to "Place an order or open an account on the day for free drink vouchers". Buffet food is also available. However, the real message for speedway fans to remember is that members of the Plumbing Trade Supplies Association (at least those based in the South East of England) believe in the benefit of their association with the heroes of the shale and, in particular, the Poole Pirates!

Speedway nights at Wimborne Road often have additional entertainment off the track to captivate the fans. Nearly 60 years after they first teamed up as members of the all-conquering Pirates side of the early 1950s – when they became Third Division Champions (1951) and Second Division Champions (1952) – Brian Crutcher, Alan Kidd, Norman Strachan and Bill Holden attend tonight and later will be reintroduced to the Pirates faithful. Between them they have 1,142 official appearances for the club. Quartet member Alan Kidd emigrated to the Toronto area in the late 1950s but has specially made the journey back over from Canada. Apart from his illustrious career with the Pirates another claim to fame for Alan is that he was the first speedway rider ever to feature in a UK TV commercial (he advertised Players Weights cigarettes). Though apparently the illustrious quartet are all already in the stadium, a slightly harassed Gordie Day searches the grandstand and trade display area. "I'm looking for a lost 50s speedway rider. I've got four of the stars from the 50s and I need to find the one I'm missing for the photo!" Press officer for the club, Gordie is the gold standard by which speedway press officers everywhere should be judged. In all sincerity I also made this claim in my last book *Concrete for Breakfast* but Gordie is modest enough to want to immediately correct this misapprehension, "I am not the best press officer in British Speedway!" Keen to find out who is, I ask, "Who is then?" Gordie is rarely lost for words, "Eh, I dunno, but I'm not!" It's a denial that carries little weight given the photo opportunity he's keen to get taken, let alone that we're stood by a trade exhibition taking place inside a speedway stadium. "Plumbing Trade Supplies – they've had their trade fair here today and they're sponsoring tonight's meeting." We head off to the pits to continue Gordie's search where, instead, we bump into a member of the behind-the-scenes staff from the Isle of Wight – the rather tanned Malcolm Terry. He justifies his tan ("I go out on my land and work – I'll have time to lie down when I'm dead!") and his limp to us ("I did my knee in six weeks ago"). When untroubled by injury, during some weeks of the speedway season Malcolm rides in the Smallbrook second halves on old speedway equipment. "With my knee I won't be doing it but I've rode the second halves on my old JAPs. We often get a bigger crowd [at the Isle of Wight] for that than they do for the meeting!" Gordie enquires solicitously about present attendance levels.
[Malcolm] "It's running is all I'll say! It was always going to be hard. There's three or four weeks in the summer and they need that to go well otherwise well, you know?!" Talk turns to promising young riders, "Vaclav [Verner] who was over last summer and he said Simon [Gustafsson] was going to be better than his father [Henka]."
[Gordie] "He had his year ironing out his rough edges and now he's got the confidence to go with the skill and kicked

on! He's not here tonight – they've got James Holder at 7."

[Malcolm] "The step up between any League is so big. It's asking a lot to step up from the Premier League."

[Gordie] "It is but, sometimes, I wonder what they're thinking? The National League riders were complaining about the track [at Wimborne Road] and I said 'It was just the same for the Elite League riders – the only difference is that they were doing it six seconds a race quicker'."

Rumours of plummeting crowds at Wimborne Road aren't borne out by a casual glance around the stadium tonight. Already sat in his wheelchair on the pathway that overlooks the home side of the pits and the second bend of the track is Eastbourne programme editor, Mick Corby. He takes a phlegmatic view of the recent Pirates team changes, "We always seem to ride against teams the first meeting after they've re-declared, like tonight with Hans Andersen!" The riders have made their way out onto the track and the Eastbourne Eagles team get introduced to the crowd. First up is Eastbourne number 7, James Holder, someone who the announcer informs us, "is stepping in at the last minute". Mick nods, "It was the best we could do at the last minute." Cameron Woodward is presented as "knocking on the door as heat leader" while mention of Lewis Bridger immediately prompts some low-key catcalls from the Pirates faithful sat in the old-fashioned home-straight grandstand. Poole fans then show the loyalty you'd expect when they theatrically cheer the announcement of each Pirate in the line-up as they're introduced in turn. Chris Holder is absent tonight. Bizarrely programmed to ride in the number 2 race tabard, all Chris's rides are covered by rider replacement this evening ("Chris was injured in a motocross accident and we apologise for that"). The crowd greet the announcer's talk of "returning prodigal son – Hans Andersen" with a loud cacophony of air horns and cheers. Debate about Andersen's return to Dorset has been done to death on the terraces, in the press and on the forums. Elsewhere, Peterborough Panthers club owner Rick Frost cast yet another but different light on the situation in his Top Talk column in the Peterborough programme. [6]

After their warm-up laps the riders return to the pits and, shortly after, for the first race of the night go back out round to the start line where the Poole start-line girls are conspicuous by their absence. If the declining fan numbers and reduced gate receipts require cost-cutting steps at Poole, then surely cut-backs on the start-line girls' appearances takes such measures way too far! Particularly so given the iconoclasm and flair shown over recent years by Poole in their start-line girl uniform designs. After all the hullaballoo about the return of Hans Andersen, it's a surprise to see Travis McGowan (guest replacement for David Norris) win the first race of the meeting! The combination of Hans Andersen and Chris Holder will be formidable but, until the Australian recovers from injury, the Pirates are deprived of this powerhouse pairing. Ricky Kling is another Eastbourne winner in the next race though, again, the heat remains drawn. The second bend of the first lap of the third race sees the evergreen Joe Screen blast round the Eagles impetuous Lewis Bridger to put the Pirates in command and on their way to their first heat advantage of the evening helped in no small measure by a fall for Cameron Woodward whose demise is enthusiastically cheered by the crowd. Before a dramatic first lap of heat 4, the announcer issues a *mea culpa* on behalf of the club, "I'm afraid to say the Castle Cover Poole Pirates are languishing at the bottom of the Elite League!" Apology over, he then strikes a more positive note, "The re-declaration to include Hans Andersen is a shot in the arm but the news that Chris Holder had broken his collarbone was a body blow to the Pirates." Mild mannered off the track but occasionally ferocious on it,

[6] On July 2nd, Rick wrote, "I know many of you have wondered what is the truth regarding Hans Anderson [*sic*] and his 'loan' to Poole and the reasons why he left last season for Coventry before I took over the club. Briefly, Hans was owed around £60,000. This was made up of £15,000 sponsorship in 2007 from a company owned by Colin Horton that was wound up by him and as a result Hans was never paid. The remainder was for unpaid wages and for bike covers he had paid for on behalf of the club, a total of around £45,000. When I bought the club from Colin Horton one of the things I did as part of the deal was to deduct from the sale price all monies/wages owing to all riders, including Hans, and as a result Hans was paid all wages outstanding and also the money for the bike covers, leaving only the old Colin Horton debt of £15,000."

"Hans decided this year to not ride in England and to concentrate his time on the GP Series. He later changed his mind in late April, early May and decided he did want to ride in England. Since he is an asset of Peterborough he was always likely to be considered for a return to the club. However, we made the decision to stay with the team we had. Hans was told of our decision and given permission to speak to other clubs including Coventry and Poole. He agreed terms with Poole and that would normally have been the end of the matter but Poole never made any contact with Peterborough to agree the terms and conditions of the loan agreement and sign the necessary paperwork. Clearly this is contrary to the rules of the BSPA but nevertheless the BSPA accepted his inclusion in the Poole 1 to 7 declaration and to this day no signed agreement is in place yet he is still riding for Poole."

"Our take on this situation is fairly simple. We have no wish to stop Hans earning his living but we may possibly need to use him ourselves this year, in the event of injury for example, and for that reason would only have given permission for a minimum loan period of 28 days which could have been renewed or extended if we didn't need him. I have no animosity towards Hans regarding this as he is only 'the meat in the sandwich' so to speak and earning a living the only way he knows how but clearly the actions of Poole are far from transparent and are in fact dishonest, contrary to the BSPA rules and indeed civil law in that they are using our club asset without our consent and without payment. Watch this space for the next instalment!"

Bjarne Pedersen rides Ricky Kling close to the third- and fourth-bend safety fence and, in the gap he creates, powers hard underneath the youngster before he pulls away to win. Battered by the experience, Kling drops to third but, despite a mistake on the last corner, still coasts comfortably to the line ahead of an out-of-sorts Karol Baran.

While we wait between races at our vantage position that overlooks the frantic activity of the Poole section of the pits, Mick Corby reveals that during the close season he met Ian Perkin at a Wetherspoons in Redhill along with the hard-working Mr Sittingbourne Speedway, Graham Arnold. "Although we've heard all sorts of things about him and, speak as you find, I thought he was very professional! We quoted a figure for him to run at Sittingbourne and he went away and thought about it and sensibly said, 'No thanks'. It was the correct decision 'cause who would want to run in the National League this season?" While the announcer whips up the crowd with news of "A very special welcome for four people: stars of the 1950s!" – I move to watch the speedway from elsewhere in the stadium. On the first bend of heat 5 Daniel Davidsson gets thrown from his machine, "contact there with the track and the air-fence for Daniel Davidsson, he got caught in traffic". It prompts SCB match referee Phil Griffin to order a rerun with all four riders. Viewed from the fourth bend, Davey – or Dave as the programme incorrectly calls him – Watt definitely appears to have knocked off Davidsson at the very moment when (ahead of them) Joe Screen passed Travis McGowan. Though Daniel quickly dusts himself down, the air-fence sustains a puncture. Men in overalls and high visibility jackets set about repairs with great industry, "The air-fence is being repaired – well done track staff! We don't often get the chance to congratulate the track staff who make sure things run here, whatever the weather. Let's put our hands together!" It's an instruction that the assembled crowd greets with sustained silence. To pass the time, we're advised about the availability (at the photo stall on bend 3) of the Poole speedway fanzine *Pep Talk*. Founded in 1990 and available for free, albeit with the important proviso, "There's a minimum donation of 30 pence! All monies raised go to the riders." When I arrive at the stall keen to make a donation of a pound, I'm told that there are no copies available.

Joe Screen obviously likes the puncture repair handiwork of the track staff because, on the first bend of the rerun of the rerun, he kindly takes Davey Watt on a detour so close to the inflatable equipment it would be churlish not to have a close inspection of the facilities. Watt determinedly remains on his machine, proceeds to pressure Screen during the second lap before he then lags some distance behind his rival and ex teammate. Ignoring his 2009 epidemic of equipment failures, Davey Watt frequently feigns disinterest to gain psychological advantage. His tardiness here is tactical. On the third bend of the last lap, Davey winds up his response, dives hard under Screen and appears to triumph in their dash to finish line for second place ("I'll let the ref sort that one out!"). Though the race concluded excitingly, it fails to distract the young couple stood by the DVD stall who aggressively snog and rub their bodies together apparently oblivious to the on-track action. Every so often, the bloke (in a replica Pirates top) briefly draws away to quickly fill in his programme. Inspirational, on-fire guest Travis McGowan wins the race to give the Eagles a 1-5 race win and a 2-point overall lead. Nearby, though I can't imagine they're ever needed, policemen queue in the third-bend bar-cum-kiosk for refreshments.

Normal service resumes in the next race when, after initial early success for Cameron Woodward, the Pirates reply with a 5-1 from their experienced partnership of Joe Screen and Hans Andersen. First time out in heat 7, "Be-yar-nar" as the announcer likes to call him, shows great aggression when finds himself neck and neck with daredevil racer Lewis Bridger. Unafraid to hold his throttle open, Lewis refuses to be intimidated and takes a third bend lead he doesn't relinquish. There's drama during the first running of heat 8 when Karol Baran rears massively on a bike that behaves like a bucking bronco before it charges off dangerously in riderless fashion. With measured understatement, Baran's disqualification is confirmed and also we receive an explanation about his wildly exaggerated manoeuvres, "He looped the loop before his bike narrowly missed Ricky Kling." The ninth race of the night peters out after a first bend battle between Davey Watt and Joe Screen to subside into a processional follow-my-leader encounter. The comparative lack of action draws attention to a noticeable blue groove (coloured brown this evening) that serves as the racing line for every rider to unthinkingly follow. Between races, there's birthday news about the Johnson family, "Brendan Johnson will be 17 tomorrow (4th June) and it's also a 50th for Dave Johnson who receives this message with love from Sue and best wishes from Alan. It'll be an expensive week in the Johnson household!" Heat 10 sponsors

Sea View Coaches get a brief name check before we're told, "Bjarne Pedersen takes the rider replacement ride in heat 10 to make a formidable line-up with Hans Andersen – this is going to be one to watch!" It's definitely the fastest race of the night (58.97) and treats us to the magnificent sight of Bjarne in full flight. He completely blows away the fast-riding Lewis Bridger who in turn comfortably defeats a slightly out-of-sorts Hans Andersen. Bjarne is out again in the next race and narrowly avoids becoming the second Poole rider to fall for the Davey Watt sucker punch after three and a half laps of sustained listlessness. When this torpor suddenly transmogrifies into brutal determination during the race for the finish line, Bjarne effortlessly repels the attempted sneak underneath him by the cunning Australian. Under the roof of the home-straight grandstand, the Pirates fans briefly rouse themselves to chant "Bjarne! Bjarne!"

The relatively lengthy interval features discussions with the Pirates of yesteryear: Brian Crutcher, Alan Kidd, Norman Strachan and Bill Holden. The eddies of dust that the recent races raised develop into clouds after an interval that saw centre green staff use the hose to clean the air-fence adverts on the grass rather than water the track. Something must have gone on in the section of the pits occupied by Lewis Bridger since he gates with alacrity and fires away to win heat 12 with some ease ahead of Joe Screen. Exploring all race options with great tactical acumen, Eagles team manager Trevor Geer sends Lewis back out in the next race. Clearly confident and in control, Lewis brushes aside Hans Andersen at high speed on the third bend of the first lap. It's a further sign of his ongoing development as a rider that he refuses to let Hans boss him in a brutal bend that sees the youngster imperiously elbow aside his GP-experienced rival. After he wins the race, Lewis shakes hands with Hans then immediately punches the air twice with a weird anti-clockwise circular motion before he wheelies flamboyantly past the home-straight grandstand to generous congratulation from the assembled Pirates fans. Daniel Davidsson flies off on the third bend of the penultimate race when badly marooned at the back. This prompts an exasperated small bloke in an England shirt to shout, "Bloody stay there you useless prat! Go back to [trails off]". Exactly where Davidsson should go back to remains a mystery after this agitated patriot completely loses the thread of his anger. With a stricken rider in need of attention, we're treated to the weird sight of medical staff in fluorescent clothing galloping at great speed from the flagpole in the centre green past track staff still industriously cleaning air-fence banners on the grass. Ignoring the fact that Daniel Davidsson fell on his own under no pressure, the announcer confuses Poole speedway with the Bronx, "It was tough out there!" After some treatment and David's inevitable disqualification, the race is rerun with Pirates hopes pinned upon the unlikely shoulders of doubling up rider Ben Wilson in the number 6 skull-and-crossbones race tabard. Both times this race is run, Wilson gates exceptionally quickly only to lift on the second bend exit and allow Cameron Woodward through. Ben retains second place and, thereby, keeps the Pirates statistically in the meeting. At least until the third bend of the second lap when a brave outside pass by Ricky Kling ensures the Eagles 5-1 that wins them the meeting. Clearly if Chris Holder had ridden then the result would have been very different but this is no consolation to the Poole fan in the England shirt who fulminates, "They bloody need someint, bloody shit." Comment that Wilson "looked great from the gate" provides little consolation to this disgruntled Poole fan who asks rhetorically, "I wonder what [Steve] Shovlar will have to say about this one [on the British Speedway Forum afterwards]!" The announcer clutches at a non-existent straw with the claim, "The Pirates need a heat win to claim a point tonight!" While, tonight's Pirates power partnership of Hans Andersen and Bjarne Pedersen do the honours, their 5-1 only serves to massage the scoreline to 44-46. Despite this defeat, once Chris Holder returns to the track then, although they've started badly, you'd be silly to write-off the Pirates or the possibility they could still claim sixth place and thereby qualify for the Elite League Play-offs. [7]

3rd June Poole v. Eastbourne (Elite League) 44-46

Poole: *"Often after a meeting, Charles would have the officials and everyone for tea and Penguin biscuits.*

[7] Shortly afterwards, in one of the most egregious rulings made by the BSPA in recent years, the rules agreed before the start of the season for the Elite League – namely that the top six teams would be involved in the end of season play-offs – were peremptorily changed mid season and altered to ensure that only the top four teams would take part in the play-offs. Widely seen as a rather cack-handed measure to ensure that the newly strengthened Pirates definitely couldn't progress to the lucrative play-off stages, in the heat of the moment Matt Ford commented on the Club website prior to the home Elite League meeting against Lakeside on June 17th. "This meeting could possibly be our last live Sky TV meeting as an Elite League club. It is only right to see out this season first and then make our decision, and I've already alerted our team of major sponsors, especially Castle Cover, of the dilemma we find ourselves in at the current time. I think my duty as Promoter of Poole Speedway is to protect riders, sponsors and every supporter from allowing outsiders to dictate our business in future. I don't make idle threats. This has nothing to do with me throwing dummies out of the pram because we're not winning. This has everything to do with a rule that was unanimously voted on at the AGM last winter that the Elite League play-offs at the end of this season would consist of the top six clubs. Why continue in a league where we have absolutely no confidence? You cannot simply change the rules when it suits. What's going to happen next week? My fellow promoters don't like the new League points structure, so that will change too? They have opened up a can of worms which now says any rule can be changed at any time if the majority of promoters don't like it. As far as I'm concerned the play-off rule was voted on and passed and that was that until next winter's AGM. … But then my fellow Elite League promoters decided last week to move the goalposts and have a re-vote on the amount of clubs taking part in the play-offs in the middle of the season. And this time it was thrown out and reverted to four. They claim this decision is to do with Sky Sports not having the time to cover more play-offs on their schedules. That's a lame excuse. Sky Sports didn't cover the relegation play-off battles at the end of last season at Wolves, Peterborough and Edinburgh and no one batted an eyelid. … My venom is particularly targeted at – promoters – who have none of their money invested in the clubs they are representing, yet are quite happy to vote and tarnish my name and reputation. Perhaps voting should be purely for promoters whose money is invested in their respective club. That would kill off a few stinking rotten eggs in British Speedway. Poole Speedway have been accused of underhand tactics by figures in responsible positions within the sport who have yet to substantiate any proof and are happy to go public telling all in sundry what they thought went on. Have we been found guilty of any dubious tactics? The answer, of course, is no! I just hope these "employees" of rival clubs who have verbally attacked us can quantify the sort of damage they have caused to my business and our reputation as a club. They should hang their heads in shame, the lot of them. … One of my esteemed colleagues was quoted in the local paper last week saying this was the "right decision at the wrong time and that the whole idea of a team coming from sixth place to win the title would have been the death-knell of the play-off system". What planet is he on? He voted in favour of it seven months ago! And it was unanimously carried… A word for my learned colleague: This was the wrong decision at the wrong time. The only death-knell, my old friend, was changing the rules mid season."

CHAPTER 6

Eastbourne

"I think they honestly deserve to win the league because they have bought and paid for it!"

6th June

The side window of the Eastbourne trackshop proclaims "Congratulations Councillor Barber". *Argus* newspaper vendors, Lucy Cross and her fiancé Kenny Penfold, have specially prepared this large poster. Though brothers Johnny and Nick Barber are both in attendance, it's not initially clear who (or what) exactly is being congratulated. From a brochure he hands me, it turns out Nick Barber stood for election for the Conservatives in the Felixstowe Coastal Division ward during Thursday's Suffolk County Council elections. Anyone who encounters Nick at the various outposts of his speedway trackshop empire already knows him to be an unassuming knowledgeable man. Few would have suspected his political ambitions. Given some of the Spanish customs that can exist within speedway, it's refreshing to know that there are men of integrity like Nick Barber or Reading Racers Historian and Liberal Democrat Arnie Gibbons (Nick Clegg's agent when he was first elected to public office, in the 1999 Euro elections) have sufficient transparency in their lives to be able to seek public office or support those who do. It's Nick Barber's first step into politics and he's swept into office with an impressive 3,001 votes to finish nearly 200 ahead of his fellow Conservative partner in crime Councillor Graham Newman also standing in this ward. Smiling wryly, the full impact of his decision to seek office hasn't quite sunk in. It soon would on Monday when Nick attends his first council meeting and learns which committees he'll now serve on. Rather than birching for young offenders or the reintroduction of National Service, in the Felixstowe Coastal Division ward Nick ran a campaign that sought office with a slogan of "A record of action a promise of more". Judged by the election leaflet copy, in Nick's part of Suffolk, the Lib Dems and Labour not only can't organise a trip to the pub, but their collective lack of local nous now requires the firm leadership and steadying hand of those with a conservative outlook on political life. The leaflet also promised, "Your priorities are our priorities". [1] The pages of the *Daily Mail* could lead you to think that the ideology of any Conservative candidate has always to include talk of a withdrawal from Europe, tighter immigration, concern about wheelie bins as well as the restoration of hanging and flogging. However, all of these issues are noticeable by their absence from Nick's pledges.

In an ideal world, the brute reality of political life should require that all our elected representatives be judged at the ballot box on what they do rather than what they say (or, indeed, what they say they've done). Obviously, in political high office, words invariably speak louder than actions. Nick's a sincere enough man – and new enough councillor – to want to work hard to keep his promises as well as also to operate in a collegiate manner. His promise to keep Council Tax increases below 18.5% is probably manageable but control of the weather could prove even beyond his capabilities. Electors will always want to know more about the Councillor they're about to elect. His leaflet gives some insight into Nick's background and includes mention of speedway. [2]

[1] Nick outlines his priorities in six key points:

1. Protect the most vulnerable whether they be children or adults.
2. Continue to keep Council Tax rises as low as possible, particularly to benefit older people and others on limited and fixed incomes.
3. Drive down the costs of the County Council – building on the £60m already saved – so that services can meet growth in demand.
4. Do whatever we can to ensure government demands for new housing are tailored to local needs and the availability of jobs, and that every brownfield site is exploited before there is any question of building on green fields.
5. Continue to press for infrastructure improvements to match the growth of traffic at the Port, and for more permanent solutions to deal with high winds and other weather problems.
6. Asking for your support and vote to ensure we never return to the days of 18.5% Council Tax increases.

[2] "Nick Barber, born and bred in Felixstowe, attended Deben school and still lives near the town centre. After a 17-year career in the transport industry, he started up his own business in the production and design of speedway and sporting merchandise. Married, he has three daughters at home: one studying for her A levels and two at local primaries. His hobbies are, unsurprisingly, sport, speedway and his family!"

Lingering by the attractive display of speedway merchandise laid out on tables in front of the trackshop is Coventry team manager Peter Oakes along with his tanned daughter Sarah and her son Josh. Invariably unable to suppress his reporting instincts, Peter conducts an *ad hoc* interview with Nick about his nascent political career and his future ambitions. A brief article appears in the *Speedway Star* that notes Nick studious silence about his political ambitions within speedway circles prior to the election. "I didn't want to say too much because I was a little bit superstitious about it. I was really pleased to get as many votes as I did, the other successful candidate had been a candidate for the last four years." Later Nick modestly tells me that he believes he's elected because he's a local man who's "not tainted" by service in previous administrations at the County Council.

This season's arrival of journeyman speedway rider Lukas Dryml at the Eastbourne Eagles has seen the scrupulously observed politeness of the Eagles faithful in the home-straight roofed grandstand replaced by loud exuberance. Each or any mention of Lukas's name, let alone his race wins on the track gets greeted with ecstatic adulation by this section of the Arlington crowd. In recent years, some other Elite League clubs have riders who've achieved bête noir status at Arlington (or had it thrust upon them) and, as a result they get boos, catcalls or jeers. Somehow the Coventry Bees manage to assemble three such candidates for this collective opprobrium. Rather unfairly in my opinion, Adam Shields's move from Eastbourne to Lakeside with Jon Cook still ensures that he's reminded of this transfer every time he sets his tyres on the Arlington shale. Booked by the Bees as a guest tonight in place of Rory Schlein (who's at the GP qualifier in Lonigo), announcer Kevin Coombes's name check during the rider parade attracts the predictable response. Adam professes that Arlington remains his favourite racetrack and he regularly continues to perform on the track with some distinction. This evening also sees Edward Kennett return to the East Sussex area to ride a speedway meeting following his fissiparous often acrimonious full transfer to the Coventry Bees during the close season. Ostensibly, the person with the most public animus towards Edward appears to be club owner and promoter Bob Dugard. [3]

Edward enjoys a close relationship with various people at the club and, ironically, Martin Dugard often spanners for Edward or is present in his pits corner. However, tonight Martin is notable by his absence from mechanical duties, though he would subsequently continue to be regularly seen alongside Edward (and is scheduled to be in his corner at the forthcoming Cardiff Grand Prix).

[3] The first public news of Edward Kennett's intention to ride elsewhere in 2009 appears in the *Speedway Star* on 6th December. Apparently Edward requests "A one-year loan for a bigger Elite League circuit". What you get and what you want are often two different things. Ace *Argus* reporter, Brian Owen, notes that this suggestion "Was quickly developing into a fully blown transfer request after Dugard told him [Kennett] it was a permanent move or nothing. There was even talk of an £80,000 price tag as Dugard had a look at other rumoured transfer fees." The rider insists he doesn't want to leave Eastbourne on a permanent basis – he's been involved with the club since age 16 – but does want to develop as a speedway rider. "I felt it was time to move on and that I would benefit from a year at a bigger track. I ride big tracks quite well and I can improve and I always struggle when I go abroad to be big tracks. When I went to Poole for a year in 2007, I came back a better rider. I feel I can do that and come back to Eastbourne as an improved rider but Bob wasn't happy with that. He said if I go, I'm not welcome back." Bob Dugard confirms, "I would rather sell him than loan him out. Edward has always been a somewhat reluctant member of the team and we want people who are proud to put on an Eastbourne race jacket and represent us." By the next week's reports in the *Speedway Star* attitudes harden. Brian Owen reports initial talk of an £80,000 fee disappears as Bob Dugard "has since revised his asking price to £45,000." It's also reported, "Peterborough had met his revised asking price of £45,000 but the Hailsham-based rider was not willing to sign." The size of the initial suggested fee still bothers Kennett, "I think that's a bit over the top – I know I'm not worth £80,000 but that's what Bob said and it's ridiculous. That's what he wants to do and I'll just let him get on with it but it's not good at all."
Fans aren't privy to the exact ins and outs of the high-level negotiations but, by the next week, Bob fulminates after Coventry offer less than half of his revised asking price of £45,000. "They offered £20,000. That's an absolute joke." Casting doubt on the possibility that a loan may even be issued, Bob went on to comment, "It's not guaranteed that the loan would be to Coventry. He will go to whoever makes the best offer." The Eagles supremo envisions a range of alternative options, Brian Owen reports, "Ideally [he] wants Kennett to leave on a permanent deal in return for cash and/or a rider hence an attempt to swap him for Rory Schlein turned down by Coventry." Back at Brandon Stadium, Coventry Promoter Colin Pratt keeps his cards close to his chest about their move for the Eagles want-away Edward Kennett. Publicly he commented, "There's not too much to report at this stage other than the fact Edward has formally requested to leave Eastbourne and we have spoken to them about it." By January, Bob's keen to leave the previously closed door open should Edward change his mind. "Ed went on the microphone at our end of season 'do' and said he wanted to be back next season if I would have him. We talked that night. Then I got the bombshell from him that he wanted to move. No one rider, good as he may be, dictates to me. This club is far more important than one rider. I said 'If you go, you go for good'. He has only ever had one full season for us and, as you can see, he improved himself in that season more than he ever did on loan at Poole. He will get a worse deal there [Coventry] than he would have had here, I can assure him of that. I would still have him back on the simple condition that he wants to be here. If he doesn't, he goes for good. I would only let him go on loan if I really had to but I would rather go to arbitration than sell him for good. I believe he would be good value at £30,000. Don't underestimate my opinion of Edward as a rider. He has got great potential and we would have brought it out of him better than anybody. I would have seen him really pushing for our number one spot next season. I don't totally blame Ed. I think he has been badly advised in this."
Back at Brandon Stadium Colin Pratt continues to operate a 'steady as she goes' approach to press announcements about negotiations for Edward Kennett. "There's not really any change to that situation at the moment because Bob isn't accepting the deal that we're offering for Edward. If that remains the case then we'll have to go to arbitration over it."

On the microphone, Kevin Coombes – well aware of potential emotional flashpoints – informs us "We have our cheer leaders" but also sensibly notes, "this meeting needs no building up between these two experienced sides". As expected Edward receives a loud chorus of boos, something that Kevin greets in jovial fashion "That's not bad!" Former home favourite Scott Nicholls also returns tonight. After they'd completed the required 12 meetings, the Suffolk-based rider has been drafted into the re-declared Bees team as mid-season replacement for their broken leg victim Olly Allen. Under the 2009 speedway regulations, Elite League teams initially construct their team to a points limit of 40.95 but, after they race 12 league meetings, they've then the option to re-declare to a revised average of 42 points. It wouldn't be speedway if there weren't some dispute over the rules and, with the benefit of hindsight, it's plain to see that the rule-makers failed to take account of all the ramifications. Consequently, any team that quickly rode 12 meetings could change their team and, subsequently, race against other teams who hadn't had the equivalent opportunity because they (for reasons of fixture list planning and postponements) hadn't yet raced the required number of meetings to make similar changes. Objections that this alteration to the Bees line-up might not have been completely kosher were initially given credence when the use of Scott Nicholls is complicatedly ruled illegal by the sport's Management Committee a few days after his debut in the Coventry versus Ipswich meeting. Any explanation of this requires a deep breath and a clear head but, essentially, Jordan Frampton's doubling up average was deemed to be a new figure of 4.73 rather than his starting average of 3.17 – despite him having only ridden 11 league meetings and not having missed a single meeting he might have been available for. Though tonight I've come along with newcomers who have little familiarity with the rules and regulations of speedway, this dispute is something to quickly

By mid January the situation is more clearly defined. Pratt comments, "Obviously at the moment we have a disagreement with Eastbourne over Edward. We made our final offer to Eastbourne for Edward at the BSPA last Tuesday and this was refused. Edward has said he wants to move to Coventry, and Bob cannot sell him to another club without Edward's agreement. What Bob must remember is he's not dealing with cattle in a cattle market; he is dealing with human beings and sportsmen. The move will go to arbitration after 28 days have elapsed from Edward's [formal written] transfer request and we will take it from there. We have gone to arbitration when we have bought both Scott Nicholls and Lee Richardson during my time here, and that is what will happen again."

By this stage, Bob resigns himself to arbitration on April 7th, "Coventry reduced their offer to £15,000 which I see as a bargaining tactic by them before going to arbitration. They are experts in these matters whereas I have never been to arbitration over a rider but I'll go in there to give it my best."

Before the arbitration meeting, Bob changes tack and tries to offer Edward on loan to Coventry rather than lose his asset for what the *Speedway Star* called "a knockdown price". Although Bob initially ruled out such an option, the more conciliatory Eagles supremo said, "Ed can go on loan to Coventry for this year. I've already spoken to Coventry saying I'm not in favour of going to arbitration."

With the new season nearly underway, Edward Kennett again comments on close season events. "When I spoke to Bob, he said if you go, you have to go for good. I put the transfer request into the BSPA and did what he told me. Now he's turning back on his word. I'm not going to change my mind and I'm not going back down on my decision. We'll just have to wait until April for the arbitration. He hasn't phoned me or anything over the last couple of months. So I'm just going to let things happen and Coventry will be my new club."

Bob also looks at the long-term and wider ramifications of this transfer. "Coventry made a derisory offer of £20,000 and then reduced that to £15,000. People need to be very aware that this year could be very difficult financially. That will mean banks are looking seriously at any tracks that get in a deficit position. If you are going to halve the value of riders, it could put tracks in serious jeopardy. Riders are often the only assets speedway clubs have. They operate at rented stadiums, a lot of them don't even own their own tractors. Their assets are almost totally made up of riders. If you are going to devalue your own assets, the banks will look at that if you go into an overdraft situation. I'm going to arbitration for the first time in nearly 40 years in the sport. Coventry have done this more times than anybody so they will have the advantage. But they are not being clever if they get Edward at half price because it could cause more problems for tracks in the longer term."

When the day of the arbitration arrives, the meeting is postponed to enable an Elite League Promoters meeting to take place. However, bitterness still remains between the two clubs and on the pages of the *Speedway Star*, Colin Pratt refutes claims that the Coventry Bees were trying to "steal" Edward Kennett for a knockdown price and also derides suggestions from Bob Dugard that he might close down the Arlington training track if the verdict went against him. "I would remind everyone that in the first place Edward only ever wanted to go on loan, but Bob Dugard said no, and wanted an £80,000 transfer fee. It's a good job I didn't say something similar last winter when Eastbourne needed a number 1. Would they have paid £80,000 and more for Scott Nicholls? I remind him of the AGM in 2007 when Eastbourne was one of the clubs who voted for a new points limit to help strengthen them up for the following year, and it meant us losing top men. Obviously that was the whole idea behind them voting for the low limit, and it meant they gained on loan a rider we had paid a fair [and arbitrated] value for. I suppose talking about closing his junior track is his ploy to try and pump up the transfer fee, but we might all threaten to close things down if we don't get our way. What Bob must remember is that the economic climate is very different to how it was five years ago, or even one year ago." The arbitration meeting adjudication requires the Coventry Bees pay £29,000 to the Eastbourne Eagles for Edward Kennett. Afterwards Pratt comments, "I've got mixed feelings over the arbitration but that's what it's there for and we will, of course, abide by it. I do feel that in the last two arbitrations that we've been to, this one and Scott Nicholls, the valuations been over the top, but of course it's now different people involved compared to when I first started. It does mean that if any of our riders ever do want to leave, we would be seeking a fee for them like Eastbourne have, in order for us to spend elsewhere."

When Scott Nicholls moved from Ipswich to Coventry in 2005, arbitration set the fee at £36,000 and in this context, along with the initial dramatic difference in valuations, Bob Dugard professes delight at the outcome of the hearing. "The meeting was at 10.30 a.m. in the morning and when I got back to my desk at 4 p.m. there was an email waiting which said they had fixed a fee of £29,000 plus VAT. We asked for £40,000 and they offered £15,000 so the transfer fee favours us and is in our balance. We feel totally vindicated in asking for our fee and I'm delighted. It's not like football so we're not talking those sort of numbers but it's probably the biggest fee in the sport for a while. The matter is totally settled now and I just want my money. I've already sent off an invoice. A fee should have been paid before the start of the season but that was delayed by the arbitration. I am hoping they will now pay up quickly."

draw a veil over rather than even attempt to explain. As indicated by the Management Committee's subsequent decision to rescind their judgement that this team line-up was illegal, Coventry had in fact operated completely within the rules but had fallen foul of an unwritten interpretation of the regulations that had previous precedent! Namely, that fictional averages could be given to riders in teams that had re-declared even if the rider, individually, had not yet ridden the 12 meetings required to result in an actual change to their average. [4]

After Kevin Coombes completes the rider introductions, riders from both teams conduct a couple of warm-up laps and return to the pits. Bob Dugard then unexpectedly takes to the microphone to deliver some frank but clearly deeply held opinions to the assembled crowd prior to heat 1. Normally a man who shuns the limelight in preference for track maintenance duties on race day, Bob temporarily abandons his tractor to deliver an address that temporarily hushes the crowd. "You can rest assured that Coventry will pull every stroke in the book. They are renowned for that. They came in and stole Edward Kennett from us when he had agreed to ride for us and they tried to do the same with Simon Gustafsson two years ago!" Clearly alluding to Coventry Bees team that this evening includes four riders that many consider to be heat leaders (Scott Nicholls, Edward Kennett, Adam Shields and Chris Harris) Bob continues to lambast the alleged lack of a collegiate approach displayed by the visitors. "The repercussions of what they have done here today will go through the whole of the sport. They have done so much damage and they don't even realise it. Next season will show how much damage they have done!" Bob recalls discussions at the Promoters AGM in November 2008, "We all sat down there as a group of people to look at the economic situation and we agreed we were all in it together. What Coventry have done here today – they have been and ruined the sport! They can pay for the fines and all the other things. If anyone wants to compete against Coventry, they have got to find another £50,000 or £70,000 to strengthen their team. Clubs can't afford to do that and Coventry can. I think they honestly deserve to win the league because they have bought and paid for it! One thing I will say, I don't have any anger towards the Coventry riders but I do towards the management! I think what they have done is purely against the sport and they're not even bright enough to realise it!" [5]

I like to introduce as many new people to the joys of live speedway as possible. This evening Glen Campbell and his 9-year-old son, Jack, travel across from Bolnore Village near Haywards Heath to Arlington. A passionate Sunderland fan who retains his broad accent, Glen's lived in the South for well over a decade working as an aerials and satellites contractor throughout London and the South East. He's recently set up his own company Wear Communications (www.theweargroup.co.uk) and, in true speedway fashion, is a man with skilful hands useful in many trades. In recent years, the SGP and Elite League meetings shown live on Sky Sports reignited his interest in speedway. Keen to inculcate his son into the ways of the speedway world, they take full advantage of a visit to the Eastbourne pits to savour the

[4] Afterwards Peter Oakes comments on their successful appeal against the Management Committee ruling, "We simply quoted the Rulebook, which states that if a rider has not completed 12 matches, then he will remain on the average that he started on. We were told that there were Minutes which said that an average could come in after eight matches – we've studied the Minutes and indeed, there were Minutes saying there was a discussion about it. But one promoter, Matt Ford of Poole, is quoted in the Minutes as saying they should go back to the starting average (if they have not completed 12). Another promoter [Chris Van Straaten] is quoted as saying it should be after eight. There was no vote taken according to the Minutes, and no further discussion. It's not in the SCB Regulations nor the 2009 Rulebook, which is what we all go by, and they state categorically that averages don't come in until a rider has done 12 matches. I appreciate the BSPA have already enforced this imaginary rule on two other clubs [Joe Screen at Poole and Tomasz Piszcz for Birmingham] but three wrongs don't make a right." Coventry owner Avtar Sandhu also outlines concern at this situation. "There seem to be plenty of people calling for the book to be thrown at us, but what none of them can do is find a rule that we did not abide by when we re-declared our team. Our team was rejected on the afternoon of Friday May 22nd on the application of a principle suggested by the Chris Van Straaten at last November's AGM. We stress again that Mr Van Straaten's suggestion was minuted as exactly that – a suggestion. At no stage did it become an issue which was voted on and carried into the 2009 SCB Regulations, nor did it even become a supplementary regulation. The most sensible course of action the BSPA can take is to correct their error in respect of ourselves and the other clubs to which this nonexistent 'Rule' has been applied, and then continue their investigation into other serious Elite League matters at present. Moreover, we call for a decision to be made as it is in nobody's interest for this situation to be allowed to drag on, and if necessary we will prove to higher authorities that we have made our changes within the Rulebook." Though Neil Middleditch is quick to grasp his household Bible if integrity questions get raised, it's widely suspected that the higher authorities Mr Sandhu refers to aren't religious but juridical.

[5] Afterwards Coventry co-team manager Colin Pratt comments in the pages of the *Speedway Star*. "It seemed like it was a pre-planned statement, but I thought to slag off Mr Sandhu and Coventry Speedway in public like that was absolutely disgusting. He said that Coventry pull every stoke in the book, but I would suggest that he checks his own history on that. I thought when you steal something, it's when you don't have permission to have it, and you don't pay for it. Bob said Edward was for sale, and we paid. With Simon Gustafsson that's not true. If I was a Coventry supporter many of whom turned up in the pouring rain at Brandon to get a coach down to Eastbourne, I'd be wondering why I bothered to go down there again to hear a slagging off match before the meeting. But I don't know where this talk of damage to the sport comes from. He said if anyone wants to compete against Coventry they had to find £50,000 to £70,000, but we haven't had to find that – we've just used one of our own assets whilst we have injuries. What's wrong with that?"

atmosphere as well as get to see the riders, mechanics and their bikes close up. It's difficult to decide who's more impressed by this level of access as they mingle with fans, sponsors, mechanics, fellow riders and officials alike. Glen's particularly impressed to see Chris Harris diminutive as life in the flesh. From 1979 to 1985, aged between 6 and 12 Glen did motocross. "I rode for many teams throughout the region. I rode for York and District, Cleveland and Cumbria. I won the Northumbria championship in 1982 and every week me bike used to end up at John Robson's. He's the father of speedway riders Stuart and Scott Robson. He used to tune me bike and everything. He used to do all sorts of bikes, not just motocross. There were always speedway bikes around and grass track. He was very good!" Though many regular Eagles fans are absorbed by Bob's comments over the public address system, as a newcomer Glen's mystified by Bob's announcement, let alone he's no interest in the ins and outs of the politics of the situation (and his son, Jack, has even less).

Kevin Coombes records for ReRun

Though tonight's crowd is definitely a healthy one, in the pages of the local press and the *Speedway Star*, Bob's made it clear that he's dissatisfied with attendance levels and that they presently remain below the levels the club budgeted. That said, in recent weeks a slightly larger number of speedway fans than usual now congregate by the start-line area. Though speedway prides itself on its family sport credentials and the wide age range of its fans (from young children to OAPs) recent meeting have seen Eastbourne buck the trend with their choice of start-line girls drawn from the Indigo Redd Lap Dancing Club in Seaside Road, Eastbourne ("opposite the Hippodrome Theatre next to the Cash Converters"). It's fair to say that these young ladies have no self-consciousness about tight skimpy clothing or the display of their bodies. Prior to the recent Sky Sports televised meeting, it's rumoured that the behind the scenes editorial and production staff deemed the girls' shorts so tight and revealing as to be unacceptable for them to appear on their live "family" broadcast. Based on the evidence of recent meetings, though they're somewhat prone to exaggerate the entertainment on offer, it's clear that the Sky Sports team were accurate on the said tightness of the girls' under-garments. When in the pits prior to the Elite League meeting versus Peterborough at the end of May, one of these girls come over and give me a free VIP entry certificate for the Indigo Redd Lap Dancing Club. This establishment features "free topless stage show" and "2-4-1 dances". Though entry was "at management's discretion", it's over-21s only but would only be free if I arrived before 10 p.m. ("or £5 after"). I'm initially mystified why this girl singles me out as a possible user of this certificate until, 30 seconds later, she gives one to an ogle-eyed but baffled male old age pensioner stood a yard or so away from me.

Martin Dadswell in his lair

Perhaps I'm naive but I'd expect lap dancers would, at least, theoretically be able to indulge the dance aspect of their employment as well as the lap element. However, judged by their pre-race displays, it would appear that the girls put a much greater emphasis upon the gymnastic requirement of forward bends than they do upon coordinated team choreography. Some girls clearly had greater rhythm than others but collectively they coordinated their actions visually rather than intuitively. This gives their movements a jerky quality as if they were holograms beamed back to Arlington by a satellite from the far side of the moon. However, judged by the race-night crowds around the start-gate and the intense level of male interest (and amateur photography), many male

Pom Pom Girl in action

members of the Arlington faithful are able to put aside dance and moral outrage concerns to give this pre-race spectacle their full and undivided attention. As the riders came round to line-up for the first heat Jack enquired excitedly, "Is there going to be lots of crashes?" while Glen, with more than a hint of reproach in his voice, enquired "I thought you said they had lap dancers as start-girls here?" [6]

One man definitely not disappointed by the demise of the lap dancing start-girls is long-time Eagles start marshal Alan Rolfe. "They weren't interested in speedway! They didn't perform in unison! It's better on my own. I'm more comfortable now I'm back on my own!" Tonight it appears that the lap dancing girls are replaced around the stadium by a dance troupe managed by Eagles club physiotherapist, Jane Wooller. These young girls dance enthusiastically at different points throughout the meeting: stood on the centre green as well as on the stockcar track in front of the home and back-straight grandstands. Pompoms have replaced the décolletage and tight fitting clothing. The age range of these girls declines to the extent that our entertainment is now provided by schoolgirls as yet untroubled by the need to study for their GCSEs.

When the riders line up for the start of the first race, Robert Ksiezak is very noticeably the only participant not to sport Eastbourne Eagles kevlars. Davey Watt and Lukas Dryml (taking a rider replacement ride for David Norris) wear the 2009 Dugard version of kevlars while Scott Nicholls also sports the distinctive blue-and-gold Eagles colouring, albeit from a different earlier era. The choice of Lukas Dryml by Eagles team manager Trevor Geer highlights how keen the Eagles are to get some early points on the board. However, the first attempt to run the race gets no further than the first bend when, with Scott Nicholls already in the lead, the riders behind him engineer a complete tangle that sees Watt and Ksiezak thrown from their bikes. Jack Campbell can't quite believe his eyes when the first corner of his first ever live speedway meeting produces what he views to be a serious crash. Referee Dan Holt takes the view that this is first-bend bunching and so orders a rerun with all four riders back. This initial dramatic first-corner incident creates unrealistic expectations for young Jack about the number of crashes he'll see during this evening. Nonetheless, the rerun showcases some authentic speedway thrills in the form of a fast-starting, hard-fought high-speed contest between all four riders that ends in a 5-1 for the Eagles. Eastbourne extend their early lead in the second race, won easily by Simon Gustafsson ahead of Robert Ksiezak to give a surprise 9-3 scoreline. If Bob's comments over the tannoy were designed to gee-up the Eastbourne team, they've also been similarly motivated the Coventry riders with Eastbourne connections (despite, subsequent press claims that these comments were unheard by the riders since they were delivered at a "hectic time in the pits" for those actually required to race speedway). Before the tapes rise on heat 3, Kevin Coombes highlights that the Bridger/Woodward combination up against the Kennett/Shields Coventry pairing encapsulates "Eastbourne present and past all in one!" Judged by their progress to the first bend, the home riders must have left their gating gloves in the pits. Lewis completely fails to anticipate the rise of the tapes and, though he looks much faster than his teammate, Cameron Woodward only occupies third place. Up front for the next four laps, the Coventry Bees streak away while Lewis struggles even to pass Cameron. Desperate to win the chip-shop money, Lewis attempts a last-ditch inside dive under his Aussie race partner on the second bend of the last lap. Instead of positional advantage, Lewis immediately loses traction and is thrown from his machine. Lewis's fall results in his disqualification and a race awarded 5-1 to the visitors. Well tutored by Sky Sports commentary team, Glen Campbell notes, "Lewis Bridger just tried too hard there."

[6] Before I could take advantage of my VIP entry certificate – though it would require a mad dash from the speedway in order to gain entry before 10 p.m. – the *Eastbourne Herald* dated May 29th features a report headlined "Lap Dancing Club shut by Bailiffs". The report continues: "A lap dancing club in Eastbourne has been shut down. Bailiffs entered Indigo Redd in Seaside Road early on Tuesday [May 26th] with police officers and a man was arrested but later released without charge. The premises were boarded up and a notice of forfeiture plastered on the entrances warning people that landlord Hurst Springs Holdings Limited had taken possession of the building. The notice addressed to Paul David Jones and Liza-Jane Jones informed them that their lease dated June 10, 2008 was forfeited. Hours after the closure, Eastbourne Borough Council's licensing sub-committee reconvened to hear the second stage of a hearing of an application by Indigo Redd to open 24 hours a day seven days a week. The sub-committee members heard evidence from the council's noise team, the planning department and Sussex Police as well as residents regarding the issues of crime, disorder, noise and nuisance. A council spokesman said, "In reaching its decision to refuse the application, the sub-committee did not consider that the applicant had provided sufficiently compelling evidence to rebut the presumption against the granting of the application arising from the council's cumulative impact policy relating to the area in which the premises is situated. The application was refused on the grounds that an extension of hours would undermine the licensing objectives relating to crime and disorder and the prevention of nuisance. The sub-committee refused the application, having heard insufficient evidence to depart from its cumulative impact policy. It also recognised the challenges faced by Sussex Police, businesses and residents in the vicinity of Seaside Road in relation to crime, disorder, noise and nuisance and sought to balance the different needs of the leisure industry and the need to protect local businesses, residents and visitors to the town."

Heat 4 sees another win for Simon Gustafsson ahead of his partner Lukas Dryml and, more surprisingly from Glen's point of view, an out of sorts Chris Harris trails in third. Before the next race I spot that Lewis Bridger's granddad Tony is watching the action from amongst the fans rather than from pit lane. "He's trying a new engine tonight. He's really nervous that's why I'm here to keep out of the way in case I call him a wanker or someint. He's really nervous and I don't think he's that happy with it." The race doesn't go well for the Eagles power pairing of Lewis Bridger and Cameron Woodward since they're easily vanquished by Coventry Bees number 1 Scott Nicholls. Though Lewis completes all four laps, he finishes some distance behind Scott and treats us to frequent glances down at his equipment during his last two laps.

Before the tapes rise for heat 6, we learn that it's Eastbourne reserve Ricky Kling's 22nd birthday. To make the celebration of this happy event something special, Davey Watt (off gate one) and Chris Harris (gate two) decide to line up as speedway's version of Siamese twins conjoined at the elbow. However, their close relationship lasts until Harris resists a hard challenge underneath him on bend three and takes this as the signal to power away to a comfortable victory. The seventh race of the evening features a comfortable tapes-to-flag win for Adam Shields. In the pits Kevin Coombes grabs the injured David Norris for a brief update on his recovery. David estimates it will be two weeks before he recovers "but I'm not sure about the muscle!" The Hailsham-based racer needs no second invitation to savour the recent Eagles win at Wimborne Road, "They done fantastic at Poole but it just goes to show that cheating don't always win!" Kevin also grabs returning ex Eagle Adam Shields for a brief pit-lane interview. Often a reluctant interviewee, Adam invariably gives a taciturn interview and weighs his answers as if charged by the word. Nonetheless, he's happy to nail his colours to the mast about Bob Dugard's track handiwork, "It's one of my favourite tracks – if not my favourite track!"

A couple of drawn heats pass before arguably the race of the night so far arrives in heat 10. Lewis Bridger gates and fires into the corner ahead of Adam Shields while, for the first two laps, Davey Watt and Edward Kennett indulge in their own classic battle for third place. Race positions are exchanged almost corner by corner until Davey Watt eventually masters Arlington track expert Kennett after they exit of the second bend on lap three. The race advantage gives the Eagles a 4-point cushion to take into a hard-fought heat 11. Dryml and Nicholls enter the first corner side by side whereupon the Czech rider gives Scott a massive shove that forces him so wide that Ricky Kling nearly gets a birthday ride on the air-fence (until he shuts off). With so many bêtes noires to catcall, a small section of Eastbourne faithful exempt Adam Shields from his usual treatment and, instead, focus their collective ire upon returnee and previously loyal Eastbourne servant Edward Kennett. Any race that pits Lewis Bridger against Edward Kennett is always hard-fought and, heat 12 of this Elite League meeting, is no exception. Lewis flies from the inside gate but decides to ride very, very close to the air-fence in order to block the anticipated charge from gate four by Edward Kennett. Unfortunately while this does block off Kennett's charge for the front, it makes Gustafsson the meat in the sandwich until he hits the bend-two air-fence. Simon stays prostrate on the track for some time while Kevin Coombes relays news "Simon's told the paramedic he's okay". With only one Eagles in the rerun, Lewis is keen to disprove the maxim that lightning doesn't strike twice. He really revs up his bike to fire off the start line at an angle the laws of trigonometry dictate should theoretically block the outside run. Unfortunately Edward obeys the laws of speedway savvy rather than trigonometry so, instead, confidently cuts back to the inside and powers away to win the by some considerable distance. Judged by the velocity and frequency of his celebratory air punches from the last bend to the finish line, Edward takes great delight in this victory. Lewis shakes his hand while the Eastbourne fans continue to loudly revisit their collective displeasure at his close season departure.

With the Eagles advantage again back down to a slender 2-point cushion, Lukas Dryml storms away from the start to comfortably beat both Chris Harris and Scott Nicholls with Davey Watt trailed off at the back apparently mounted upon lead equipment. Cameron Woodward and Adam Shields battle shoulder to shoulder into the first bend of the second lap of the penultimate race. In the dim and distant past, this would have been the signal for Cameron to slightly back off but, with greater experience (and under the tutelage of his mechanic Ashley Wooller), recent seasons have seen Cameron add some steel to his naturally fluent racing style. Consequently, Cameron holds firm and, in a dust storm, Adam Shields suddenly finds himself fractionally behind. He decides to go down in theatrical style in the hope that referee Dan Holt will reward his performance with a disqualification for his rival. Unfortunately for Adam, though still fresh-faced Dan Holt isn't swayed by speedway's equivalent of a professional foul but, instead, decides to call the incident based on his initial snap judgement rather than how it appears a split second afterwards. With Shields disqualified from the rerun, Simon Gustafsson records his third race win of the night and with Cameron second, this Eagles 5-1 takes the score to 45-39 and ensures Eastbourne emerge victorious. Though the result is beyond doubt, the new race points system adopted for 2009 ensures that Coventry keenly contest the last race because of the possibility of the race point still on offer to them. The Eagles team manager, Trevor Geer, rewards Cameron Woodward's combative team riding performance (four bonus points in five rides) with a last-heat nomination. His faith in the young Australian is fully justified as Shields, Harris and Woodward fight hard for fractional advantage behind race winner Lukas Dryml. Though the latter heats had seen the unusual sight of a blue groove appear on the Arlington track surface, first-time young speedway visitor Jack Campbell is enthralled throughout. He's enjoyed the glamour of the battle and the fine film of dust it produces. Jack pronounces the evening "Amazing – yeah, it's been one of the best nights ever!"

When he eventually leaves the stadium, Bob Dugard will take pleasure in the 49-41 win on the track but also, off it, a crowd of around 1,500 fans that ensures that the evening is a financial success off it. Though speedway finances are usually shrouded in more mystery than the exact mechanics of the process used to select a new Pope, the 2009 season has heard Bob frequently talk to the media about the precarious economics that afflict speedway in general and Eastbourne in particular. Using Bob's own figures that the Eagles earn an average of £13.20 per spectator, this evening's crowd generates just shy of £20,000 in gate receipts.

6th June Eastbourne v. Coventry (Elite League) 49-41

CHAPTER 7

Somerset

"The little tractor from the farm they use wouldn't pull your plonker but it's better than nothing."

26th June

The traditional curtain raiser the night before the Cardiff SGP always used to be the Newport v. Glasgow Premier League meeting staged at Newport's Hayley Stadium. Though tonight they will stage a Conference League meeting against Scunthorpe, in recent seasons the Oak Tree Arena in Highbridge, Somerset, stages one of the key Super7even events, namely the Premier League Pairs Championship. In the speedway press, Somerset's general manager Dave Croucher advises any fans making the trip to set off early. "If the experiences of the last two seasons here are anything to go by, then we are going to be in for a bumper crowd, I would strongly urge fans to get to the Oak Tree Arena early to avoid any last-minute queues at the turnstiles." Over the last few seasons this meeting has also been plagued by traffic chaos in the local area. So it's hardly a surprise to hear that an accident on a motorway bridge near Bristol has resulted in the closure of the M5 in both directions (for eight hours). Fortunately for speedway fans (unless they'd set off super-early), the accident happens mid-morning giving most of those going to Highbridge time to find alternative routes. You can't ignore the M5 motorway when you visit the Oak Tree Arena. The stadium is close to one of its junctions and the back straight affords a panoramic view of said motorway. Upon arrival, I report horror news of this traffic jam to club press officer and programme editor, the avuncular Ian Belcher. Ian takes news of the southbound tailback from junctions 18 to 22 (and similar northbound traffic queues) phlegmatically. In fact he's positively nonchalant about traffic volumes. Naively I ask whether the start of Glastonbury has increased traffic volumes on the cross-country routes around Highbridge. "There's nothing on in Glastonbury. They all came on Wednesday and anyway it's nine miles away in Pilton. But Pilton Farm doesn't sound so good as Glastonbury, does it?"

Over the last 24 hours, the weather hasn't been kind to anyone in a tent at Pilton Farm nor has it been ideal that the Oak Tree Arena endured this torrential rain. The lack of early summer sunshine has left the centre green and the grass banking at the stadium looking incredibly lush. Nonetheless, the forecast for later is good and the meeting will definitely proceed. This year is the 30th staging of the Premier League Pairs Championship. Though the competition was launched in 1975 it wasn't staged from 1991 to 1993 or in 1995 and 1996. In all, 46 different riders have found themselves on the winners' rostrum. The all-time most successful Premier League Pairs rider is Carl Stonehewer and, though he still plies his trade with Redcar, tonight Gary Havelock and Ty Proctor represent the Bears. Though reputedly a fair track, the Somerset Rebels partnership of Steve Johnston and Emil Kramer start as clear favourites. With ceremonial fanfare, the voluble but friendly Australian rider Steve Johnston has signed to stay at Highbridge until 2011 after the club purchased his contract from the BSPA. At a press conference specially called to commemorate this unusually lengthy commitment (within speedway), Johnston wryly commented, "I'd like it to be a football deal; Rio Madrid paid £80m for Ronaldo so if Somerset gave me £8m, I'd be happy. They could even knock a zero off and I'd still be happy – that's the sort of guy I am!" Though press conferences rarely get beyond the platitudinous, Johno proceeds to identify some incontrovertible facts about Somerset speedway. "I've ridden for some very good clubs but this track is built on the Hancock's land and they live right next door – literally 200 metres away. It's really unusual and the great thing is they put their heart and soul into the place. The centre green here is like a football pitch and you see the stadium improve weekly." The words speedway club, speedway rider and commitment rarely appear in the same sentence nowadays. This is a state of affairs dictated by rider averages, the self-employed nature of their contractual relationship and the seemingly endless pursuit of success (within a tight financial budget) pursued by pretty well all British speedway clubs at all levels within the sport. Somerset appear to have bucked the trend and Johno looks approvingly to a shared future, "I think it will be a partnership that will be good for both of us." [1]

Inside the clubhouse a small crowd of people gather for a pre-work coffee and chat. Close by to them is a notice that proclaims that on July 18th they'll be an event called "Di's PR on the Pier". Keen Somerset Rebels fan and indefatigable Zorro admirer, Di Phillip's explains, "It's for Shrek!" The Shrek in question actually turns out to be SREF [Somerset Riders' Equipment Fund]. "It's going to be on the pier at Weston-super-Mare, I mean Burnham-on-Sea, Weston has burnt down!" Club trackshop manager Andy Griggs interrupts gleefully, "She was gonna go to the wrong pier!" Di ignores this comment to continue with her explanation, "It's the first year we've done it on the pier. Every year we've raised money. Last year the riders all had £300 each. This year so far we've given two of the young riders – Brendan Johnson and Justin Sedgmen – £374 each! And also we've got a defibrillator for here after what happened to Garry Stead. He stopped breathing a couple of times. If we could save the life of a fan or a rider that would be fantastic!"

Since this is a Super7even event, on behalf of the BSPA Nigel Pearson produces the programme. For one week only, this spares Ian Belcher his usual programme editorial duties. However, since it's such a major event for the club, Ian's press officer responsibilities are still fulfilled very seriously. Somerset co-promoter (whose first ever job at Somerset speedway was in the car park nearly 10 years previously) Debbie Hancock arrives in the clubhouse and confirms Ian's success with the press function, "He's a nightmare when he's around! There's TV, radio and newspapers all wanting to know about what we're doing here at the Oak Tree Arena. It's my second year of PR misery. I came home [to the area] from working at a local furniture company for 19 years where I did the financials. Since I was ten, we lived to the left of Brent Knoll. Mum's [Frances] a Highbridger and dad's [Bill] from Brent Knoll. I have 96 words a minute in shorthand dictation. Dad had the idea to do a little clubhouse and I helped with that. It got a bigger and bigger. Now we have conferences and all sorts from local schools to the Environment Agency. We've got five wedding receptions at the end of August, two skittles nights, dancing and, of course, speedway every Friday! I've been 10 years watching now – 12 years ago, I didn't know anything about it. Someone knocked at the door, dad went to the exhibition – he didn't like motorbikes – and it all went from there. From day one in the Conference League to say I was addicted is an understatement! To secure its future here, I went on as a co-promoter last winter." Debbie is personable, matter of fact and doesn't look her age (41). The staff roster in the programme lists Debbie as one of three co-promoters at the club along with Mr D. Pavitt and Mr P. J. Toogood. The general manager is David Croucher and, as if they already didn't have enough experienced staff on the roster, this list identifies the team manager as Ronnie Russell. Shortly afterwards Ronnie's tenure would be brought to a premature close when he decides to concentrate on his track preparation duties on behalf of his brother, Terry, at Swindon Speedway. Though she's keen to make Somerset speedway a success on behalf of her family, the fans and the local area, Debbie also looks beyond Somerset. "What would I like? I'd like to see a big, big sponsor come along so we can get further afield – someone like Coke or Vodafone. This is far more thrilling than many other sports! Though we need to get more people through the turnstiles here and in speedway generally. If we got 1,000 people a week that would be doing a good job as an individual speedway club. Imagine someone like Asda giving away freebie tickets for Sky TV meetings or the Grand Prix? People don't realise it's a professional sport. They think it's a Mickey Mouse thing." Throughout our conversation Debbie multitasks. She fusses behind the bar and tells a member of staff, "I'm gonna take the phone." It's lucky she does because it rings all the time with questions about the weather. "Most people ring up and ask 'Is the speedway on tonight?' They say things like 'I'm in Cardiff and it's raining here'. I'm polite but you think, second question?!" We move to the far side of the clubhouse where Debbie sets out the cutlery (and answers the phone) on a number of tablecloth-covered sponsors' tables. "We have the BSPA managers and promoters, Speedy Hire, Sharp Retail – our main sponsor – Spearpoint Racing, Mike Manning and, of course, Crouch and Pav. They're here to make sure I don't sink. Come to think of it, Crouch could sink even without all the jewellery." Debbie's phone rings continuously and it's clear that her many race night duties have to interrupt our conversation. She puts her hand over the mouthpiece

[1] Steve Johnston would be one of the first signings announced for 2010 by the Birmingham Brummies! He would afterwards become a Brummies "asset" in April 2010 when the club bought his contract from Somerset. Johno commented, "Birmingham is a good club and I'm only too pleased to be riding for them. It's very nice to be working with Graham and Denise Drury again and I've been very impressed with Gary Patchett so far. Everything about the place is professional, the stadium is excellent and after the disappointment over the Somerset thing it's turned into a positive for me."

Somerset: *"The little tractor from the farm they use wouldn't pull your plonker but it's better than nothing."*

of the phone, "You'd like one of my business cards? Sorry Sharpie I was just giving another interview!"

On the subject of interviews, Ian Belcher informs me that Johno is a star on local radio. "Johno is on BBC Radio Somerset at 20 to 9 when Adam Thomas does the Breakfast Show. They get on really well and Johno, as you know, is always a laugh! This week before he was on they gave a weather forecast and he said 'I just want to thank you for your description of the weather. For me it's just coloured bits, squiggly lines and pretty pictures – that's the language I can understand.' He's got a great turn of phrase, after our Rye House defeat he said 'They served us up like a dinner.'" Johno interviews are everywhere including a Q&A in the glossy Super7even programme. Asked about his first ever speedway pay packet, Johno recalls, "My debut was away at Berwick for Sheffield and I think I got 1 or 2, and these were the days when there were no guarantees or anything like that. The pay packet wasn't even enough to cover the cost of getting up there! It cost me to ride!" Worryingly for anyone who shares any journey in Johno's van we also learn, "Someone bought me a Rock Classic CD at Christmas with all the Aussie rock anthems and it's absolutely brilliant. Make sure it's clear it's rock songs not classical music! I'm not into violins and all that stuff!" Leaving aside the question of whether "classic Aussie rock anthems" is a contradiction in terms, Johno returns home every winter (November to March) to enjoy the sunshine and "make sure I get my accent back before I start to sound like a pommy!" Though known for his confident sociability, Johno reveals that he does suffer from occasional self-doubt, "That would have been on Sunday night at the pub. I'd already sunk 10 pints and had to do 5 more to keep up with everyone. I doubted whether I could do it but I rose to the challenge and got them down me!"

I launched my first speedway book *Showered in Shale* at Somerset (in 2006) and tonight I'll launch my latest speedway book *Quantum of Shale* here. I'm privileged to be able to do this at a BSPA shared event and can only do so since I've been invited by Andy Griggs, the trackshop concessionaire at Somerset. Consequently I'm by my display table when the Sheffield Speedway Massive wanders through the turnstiles. Their posse comprises ex club promoter Malcolm Wright, Scunthorpe and Sheffield presenter Shaun Leigh along with club co-promoter Dave Hoggart. They arrive just in time to see the fire engine that serves as the bowser here back onto the centre green. Dave notes, "That's the bravest decision I've seen – thinking about watering a waterlogged track!" The shock news of the death of Michael Jackson has dominated the airwaves on their journey down from South Yorkshire to Somerset. Shaun Leigh doesn't have much time for the wave of *faux* grief that dominates the airwaves and, instead, sympathises with the late Farah Fawcett Majors. "Someone rang me to say someone they know had paid £3,000 for a pair of Michael Jackson tickets for the O2. He won't get his money back! Poor old Farah Fawcett has been pushed off the front pages. She was many a teenager's fantasy!" Distinctive vehicles are suddenly the order of the day. A long white car (manufactured in the US) parks up close by the entrance turnstiles. Emblazoned with a Confederate flag, this car wouldn't be out of place in the *Dukes of Hazzard*. The Sheffield posse watch this sight wordlessly until Dave Hoggart breaks silence, "It's the Blues Brothers! It's the southern mafia!" In fact, it's the arrival of Dave Pavitt and Dave Croucher. Away from the shale Dave Hoggart works in the motor industry and the lot of any speedway

Rob Peasley collects for SRBF

Bill Hancock & Johnny Sometimes

Raffle tickets from Judith Rourke & Di Phillips

official, promoter, manager or rider is to experience many hours of joy on the British road transport system (there are 245,366.5 miles of motorable road in Britain). Giant white US cars always get a reaction, "People slow down for them on the motorway." Recent months have seen the Speedway Press [and programmes] littered with acrimonious comments and disputes among promoters. The BSPA have tried to assert their authority and have issued fines like confetti. One of those deemed to have committed a disciplinary infraction is Bob Dugard, "He's already been fined £1,000 [with £500 suspended]. Unlike some, he can afford to keep paying the fines. He has always tried to intimidate and upset the visitors [to Arlington]. It's been 30 years since I've been there but they always used to metaphorically piss in your side of the pits. The track staff wouldn't push you off and the machine examiner would harass you. It was all designed to get you angry and put you off. Is it like that nowadays?" Malcolm Wright stares off into the distance, "Everyone always says they've got the best track with the best racing here. They used to say that at Odsal [yawns theatrically]."

Inside his trackshop, Andy Griggs makes last-minute adjustments to the merchandise. On my smooth-flowing cross-country journey to the stadium, BBC Radio 4 had discussed the rise of manufacturing in China and raised an important question of product quality in the modern disposable era they elegantly summarised with the term "quality fade". I'm unclear about the exact provenience of the stock in Andy's shop but, to my untutored eye, it all looks robustly durable. There are none of the orange-tinted rider photographs that you see on souvenir mugs at some trackshops in the country. Andy is busy but instructs me, "Make sure you put in your book 'One of the best trackshops in the country, run by the entrepreneurial Andy Griggs who, by the way, isn't a councillor!' Further thoughts on local government or other matters are interrupted by Andy's ringing mobile ("For frick's sake it's not raining!"). With nearly four hours to go before the scheduled start time of 7.30 p.m., phones all over the stadium ring with astonishing regularity. In the clubhouse, Ian Belcher's rings and he takes a slightly more conciliatory stance towards predictable meteorological questions, "Yeah, yeah, it's sunny here now. They're thinking about watering the track. No, no, it's up north!" Di Phillips hovers by the display table she's set up inside the clubhouse. "Everyone knows that without the top riders things have got cheaper [for the promoters]. They should have reduced the admission prices!" Newport track photographer Hywel Lloyd interjects, "Newport were made to put up their Premier League admission fees by the BSPA!" Di continues, "And try to attract more people! Every Premier League team this season has riders who aren't really good enough!"

Shortly afterwards the usually perma-friendly Dave Pavitt walks up to my stall with a seriously pained expression that leads me to think he's been stung by a stray wasp. "Excuse me, who's given you permission to have a stall here!?" When I mistakenly laugh, Dave repeats his question firmly. "Andy Griggs" "In the trackshop?" "Yeah." Although Pav says, "That's OK," his face belies these words and he ambles off towards the pits area where he immediately corroborates my story with Andy. Shortly after I find Pav inside one of the entrance gate admissions booths fussing with the till. I ask if I should randomly ring up some big amounts for him? "Naw don't do that, Crouch'll go mental! We don't want to lose our reputation! I'm sorry if I'm a bit grumpy today but I'm running two tracks and the threat of the weather means I'm feeling under pressure! On the Island, it's been slowly picking up but we depend on the summer crowds. It was okay at half term – we could do with more of them!"

Club owner Bill Hancock stops at my stall for a few words. "If you'd said 10 years ago we'd be here now I wouldn't have believed you! We've been lucky. We had Peter Toogood and I'll always say, until I'm in my box, that he's a completely honest man to deal with! He must be the most honest man in speedway. Not like [pauses theatrically, then changes tack] ... speedway is the sport of the people. It's a family thing! You get the whole lot – grandparents in their 80s and their great-grandchildren. You've got to get on with everyone. What we have here is for speedway on a speedway night and we have all those events in the clubhouse but, really, it's for the community. Sure it costs a lot of money but, if you want to do something, you've got to do it properly! I was strimming the grass borders here last night and it was fork lightning, torrential rain right through the night until 10 this morning. Many tracks wouldn't be getting the meeting on. We're lucky to own everything here, unlike a lot of tracks where they're council owned. Speedway isn't really welcome at a lot of places! They prefer greyhounds and that. But here, we can get it on as we like it. It's a family business. My daughter gave up her job of nearly 20 years and my wife works hard, like all the family. We just live over the back."

Somerset: *"The little tractor from the farm they use wouldn't pull your plonker but it's better than nothing."*

Many people stop by my stall to admire *Quantum of Shale*. Most don't buy a copy but do share their thoughts. One old age pensioner called Roy mistakes me for someone whose opinions might have some authority in the sport if judged by the tirade of abuse he launches into about the people "from the Isle of Wight – they're a mafia who've moved to the West Country." If the new management team aren't up to his expectations, then there are also some grumbles about the stadium infrastructure, "I've just had a moan at the turnstiles about the lights over there [back straight] but, apparently, it's Bill Hancock's job and if he don't fix it I ain't gonna pay to come in anymore!" One of the country's politest young speedway riders (and martial arts black belt), Brendan Johnson arrives with his father Dave. This season Brendan plies his trade in both the Premier League (at Somerset) and National League (at the Isle of Wight). A thoughtful young man, Brendan Johnson is hardworking and analytical about his chosen vocation, "Since I've been riding here and on the continent I've come on leaps and bounds! I've ridden in Hungary, Germany and Slovenia. I scored my first ever maximum at Scunthorpe, where I broke my wrist." Brendan's dad has an even gentler manner. Dave wholeheartedly backs his son's speedway career and ambitions. He also provides financial, emotional and practical support. In addition he acts as chauffeur, "The hardest trip we've done was Germany. I drove all the way there, Brendan rode and then I drove straight back after the meeting. When we got back to the UK, I was so exhausted I couldn't drive any further!"

Stood close by to my stall is Oxford speedway fan and Speedway Riders' Benevolent Fund volunteer, Robert Peasley who rattles his collection bucket at fans as they enter through the stadium gates. Even if he didn't catch your attention with a rattle of the change in his bucket, Rob's yellow fleece top is so brightly coloured that, if it had fluorescent properties, it would double as a high-visibility jacket. Rob twirls peculiarly on the spot as he rattles the change. "I'm suddenly collecting bees that are attracted by my yellow top! We're not allowed to collect for the Speedway Riders' Benevolent Fund at Cardiff 'cause it's an international event and our fund is only for British riders! We did collect at Bradford and raised £2,000 but then they stopped it! We had a very successful Ben Fund meeting at Sheffield and raised £35,000 and Lakeside was good at the British U21 final. At Poole it wasn't 'cause they put the admission charges up to £20! £5 more than usual and they had a free National League meeting the next night so no wonder, the crowd was so poor! If you were a local, which meeting would you go to?" At present, Rob's beloved Oxford no longer race in British speedway. "The GRA [Greyhound Racing Association] do want speedway back at Oxford I've heard but they weren't happy when they weren't getting paid [by Colin Horton]!" It's become a truism (unfounded in fact) among certain speedway fans that the GRA have a hatred of speedway clubs. Such self-serving statements fly in the face of the evidence at Manchester and Birmingham where the GRA works hand in glove with the Belle Vue Aces and the Birmingham Brummies. Prior to its closure, the stadium landlords (GRA) endured a quick succession of speedway lessees of their Oxford Blackbird Leys property (Steve and Vanessa Purchase, Nigel Wagstaff, Aaron Lanney, Mick Horton and Allen Trump) so, understandably, could have reservations about the long-term viability of such relationships. Coupled with a drop in attendance levels – that preceded the current deteriorating economic climate – plus the self-imposed demotion of the club from the Elite League to the Conference League, further depressed bar and catering revenues at the stadium. Whatever the politics or income statements, Rob is an optimistic man who hopes/believes in a bright future, "If we come back, then that would leave Wimbledon as the only club to have fallen out with the GRA!"

The great and the good of speedway funnel through the turnstiles. The always smartly dressed referee Jim Lawrence (who will be meeting steward tonight) arrives with his mobile phone prominently on display strapped into a special holder on his belt. One of the Rebels tallest fans, Tiny Tim arrives. I congratulate him on his newfound fame as a speedway commentator. He has other matters on his mind – most of them money. "I can't buy your book. It's the recession; I've never been so skint! I lost me job on the first night six weeks ago when I'd dislocated my thumb. I was going to be a night manager at the McDonald's near us. I wouldn't be able to come here every week if I didn't get in free! I've tried to be like a fan when I commentate – the view is excellent [on top of the referee's box] – but sometimes when I get too excited it goes a bit and the pikey in me comes out. I don't do tonight 'cause it's a Super7even event. They asked me to do some interviews but I won't 'cause I like to drink, which I can't do on race night now!" Over the tannoy club presenter Nigel Thomas suggests that we might like to "Get a Somerset pork roll – you won't get swine flu!" After an extensive run through the various outlets available to fans tonight, Nigel continues, "Speedway author Jeff Scott is here tonight. I hear he is. Where are you, Jeff? Wave to us. He's here somewhere." On the subject of speedway personalities Mike Bennett strides past but doesn't stop to say hello ("he's his own biggest fan!"). Tim continues, "It's still a good track but not the track it was. They put down no shale and there's not so much passing. Last week we only had four passes in the whole meeting! The little tractor from the farm they use wouldn't pull your plonker but it's better than nothing. Until a few weeks ago, they didn't have a tractor that worked." They do have a bowser that works and the promotion are clearly confident that the forecast of fine weather for this evening holds true. Just before 6 o'clock, they douse the track with copious quantities of water. Unafraid to broach every controversial subject, Tiny Tim comments, "Bill [Hancock] is a nice bloke but then so is Mike Golding and who knows what went on there? I know a little bit but would like to know more!"

On the terrace outside the clubhouse Shaun Leigh and Malcolm Wright with drinks in hand savour the atmosphere. Mike Bennett pops up everywhere in the stadium ("I can't get on with that man") but again doesn't stop to chat or say hello. Shaun likes to research his chosen career, "I'm interested in sports announcing and music. There was a PhD with a three-year survey done on the impact of announcements on football and sporting crowds and they found that 93.5% or some similar really exact percentage switched off after they went on for more than 30 seconds! After 28 seconds you've got them but, after that, you've lost them! [Waves in general direction of the track] I dunno why people complain about the shale here? When the fire truck went across the track it didn't even leave a mark and think how much rain they've had here!" Programme sellers for the night John Rich and Bill Gimbeth end their duties early after the meeting programmes sell out 25 minutes before the scheduled start time. It's hard to judge whether this news indicates a failure or a success? Shaun notes, "They print them in Sheffield." The riders take to the track for the parade with quite a fanfare escorted by the local chapter of Hells Angels. Shaun isn't impressed, "Everyone does parades with a local chapter! It would be much more interesting if they had Sinclair C5s!" Personally, I think lawnmowers would be much more appealing. Shaun works at Wolverhampton, Sheffield and Scunthorpe speedway clubs (and is main announcer at Sheffield Wednesday FC). "I said to Rob Godfrey signing David Howe was a big risk. I watched him ride for years at Wolves and I always said he'd do a really good job in the Premier League but, it turns out, he's inconsistent still! He was awful when he started the season at Scunny and then, a few weeks ago, he got a maximum and a track record and then all he got was 6 points in the next meeting. I think he'll be inconsistent wherever he rides." Like many in the sport, Shaun is impressed with one young rider who's already had a dramatic impact during the opening months of the 2009 season. "Emil Sayfutdinov is young, confident and he hasn't had a big fall! So he doesn't care about reputations or who it is! It's not 'Oh, look there's Nicki' or Jason or Greg but 'there's a rider ahead of me who I have to pass to beat'. There's all that about him having an oversized engine but you'd have to be mad to do that in the GPs or anywhere really! They might do the odd little thing but a 600 [cc engine] would be madness! You can never tell just by looking anyway. Simon Lambert was a reserve last night at Sheffield [against Scunthorpe] and, in two races he was winding it on and really going for it but was at the back. Whereas, he won three others seemingly just sitting there effortlessly!"

Our conversation ends when, over the stadium speakers, we're collectively treated to lengthy introductions of each rider who'll compete tonight. Because it's their home track, the Somerset Rebels pair of Steve Johnston and Emil Kramer start out as clear pre-meeting favourites, albeit only fractionally ahead of the highly regarded King's Lynn Stars partnership of Tomas Topinka and Darcy Ward. Not only are they in the same group but, the speedway equivalent of Sod's Law dictates they've been drawn to race each other in the first race. In front of a large crowd, there's almost a hush of expectation as the riders tootle round to the tapes since it could well be a dress rehearsal for the grand final, if the pundits' predictions prove correct. Shaun laughs, "It's probably a bit early to say things – but this could be the defining heat of the meeting!" If it is to be the key race of the night, then the important lesson we immediately learn is that it looks unlikely that Somerset will triumph this evening. Topinka and Ward ride so well together that, if you didn't know better, you'd think that they rode this track every week rather than their easily vanquished rivals, for whom Steve Johnston finishes third.

The format of the meeting dictates that there are five teams in each group. Races from group A and group B alternate. Consequently, the second heat of the night features the Glasgow pair of James Grieves and Shane Parker up against another well-fancied combination from Workington, Kevin Doolan and Adrian Rymel. Sadly the race gets no further than the first bend. Out of gate 3, Shane Parker leans on Adrian Rymel (on his outside) just before things go completely wrong. Shane accelerates into the fence and appears to be clattered by Rymel's bike. Ahead of them Kevin Doolan has a delayed reaction fall when he arrives in the apex of the first corner. Confirming the evidence of our own eyes, over the public address system we're told, "Shane's in quite a bit of pain on the track there." There's a substantial delay while the paramedics from the St John Ambulance team attend to the popular stricken Glasgow Tiger. To pass the time the raffle draw is made and amazingly Tiny Tim wins £150 with "143 on the blue". When he passes my stall en route to collect his winnings from the referee's box, he's understandably gleeful. "I'll be splitting it with Johnny [Sometimes]. What did I say if I won the 50-50 draw? I'd buy a book."

Minutes earlier, I'd been up to the referee's box and accidentally witnessed Chris Durno make the 50-50 draw. He did so distractedly while on the phone to the pits, "Well, what's he doing in the pits? Only mechanics are allowed in the pits! So either he's a mechanic or he's not allowed in there! Just take the helmet off him until after the meeting and just politely ask him to leave!" [2] News that Tiny has Chris Durno to thank for his winnings prompts him to make a promise many would pay to witness, "Good man, I'll give him a kiss!" Tiny Tim straightaway fulfils his promise and gives what Chris Durno describes as "a big lager-laced wet kiss on my cheek".

Out on the track Shane continues to receive the expert ministrations of the medical team. Somerset presenter Nigel Thomas provides us with regular insights, "Just to update you, Shane Parker would get up but the paramedics won't let him because he's taken a wheel in the back from the bike." Shortly afterwards we learn, "He will be going to the hospital. This is standard procedure after a whack in the back after he's been boarded off." Obviously this refers to the medical backboard rather than the water variety they love to use at Guantanamo Bay. Clearly procedures have to be followed and, given the propensity of apparently innocuous speedway back injuries to develop and have subsequently devastating consequences for riders (let alone the Garry Stead incident at this track), it's clearly important to take great care and avoid any presumption. Once Shane is gingerly loaded into the ambulance, they transport him back into the pits but the meeting still can't proceed because the paramedic remains with Shane in the ambulance rather than on supervisory duty as the speedway regulations and insurance policies require. This gives us all the chance to really study the Super7even programme they print in Sheffield. In his introductory column for this event, BSPA chairman Peter Toogood waxes lyrical about pretty everything but the grass in the car park. His delight ranges widely and includes: the Oak Tree Arena, Super7even Series, the Premier League Pairs and his barely contained exultant pride about the British speedway representatives who will tomorrow grace the SGP in Cardiff. "I know plenty about Somerset from my time in charge of the club here, and my wife Angela and I still have many good friends at the club. Personally I was very honoured to open the Oak Tree clubhouse facility here."

In the interim, Somerset presenter Nigel updates the crowd with the news "meeting reserve Tom Brown will replace Shane Parker for the rest of the meeting and will, effectively, be a Glasgow rider tonight." Combative though he is at National League level and despite the fact that he rides for Somerset in the Premier League, Tom definitely won't be an adequate replacement for Shane. The Tigers ongoing quest for silverware will be further handicapped by the knowledge that the Oak Tree Arena isn't exactly one of James Grieves's favourite circuits. Though we're kept constantly informed, not everything Nigel says is completely audible throughout the stadium since his microphone frequently sounds like it's attacked by a manic sandpaperer or has, somehow, been linked to a badly tuned-in portable radio. The impression that he broadcasts to us from the dark side of the moon rather than the centre green is hard to avoid. During the delay, Coventry team manager Peter Oakes bustles enthusiastically around the stadium with a camera slung round his neck. He's taking photos for the next edition of his Speedway Year Book. "It's surprisingly hard to get a good action photo. It looks easy but that's deceptive! You have to admire the skill they have to make it look so easy."

Thirty minutes after the conclusion of the first race Workington comfortably win the rerun of the second heat and, as if to double underline his dislike of the circuit, James Grieves trails in last behind his National League teammate Tom Brown. The 7 points the Workington Comets pair of Doolan and Rymel plunder from this race showcases their speed round the track and sets the tone for their qualification rounds during which they only drop a solitary point (in heat 6 when Birmingham's Jason Lyons heads Kevin Doolan in the race for second place behind Adrian Rymel). Scunthorpe's chance to lift the trophy suffers a setback in their first race of the night [heat 5]. Though Magnus Karlsson leads the Somerset Rebels pair into the first bend after a display of fast reflexes, Emil Kramer quickly passes him on the back straight of the first lap and by the third corner, Johno also gets past. This maximum heat advantage steadies the Rebels campaign and

[2] The next afternoon before the Cardiff GP, Chris sheds some light on this conversation. "Glasgow machine examiner was in the pits with Jim McGregor. They had all the passes on 'cause they do it here [at Cardiff] but they were going round telling everyone what to do and the local machine examiner felt he had his toes stood on"

takes their cumulative points total to 9 points (since the pairs championship awards 4 points for first place, 3 points for second place and 2 points for third). Further cause for delight amongst the Oak Tree faithful arrives in heat 11 when Johno stalks Berwick's Josef 'Pepe' Franc for three laps until he blasts past his rival on the exit from the second bend. Briefly stood next to my table during this heat, Dave Pavitt shouts gleefully at the moment of this manoeuvre, "Ha! Ha!" Keen to show a modicum of insight I say, "He's good!" only for Pav to issue qualified praise, "Round here he is!"

If qualification for the King's Lynn Stars and the Somerset Rebels from group A is hardly ever in doubt then the same could equally be said for the Workington Comets qualification from group B. With Glasgow consigned to the metaphorical hard shoulder by Shane Parker's injury, a three-way battle for the final qualification place ensues between the Edinburgh Monarchs, Birmingham Brummies and Redcar Bears. If you worked for an Asian betting syndicate, until the riders came out for heat 12, the combination of ex-world champion Gary Havelock along with the new improved Ty Proctor looked both potent and certain to ensure the Bears qualification. However, in their race against the Workington Comets, Proctor fails to score and Gary Havelock is comprehensively third. That said, a good performance in heat 16 against the (until then) lacklustre Brummies would still guarantee their qualification. However, this completely fails to materialise and, instead, we're treated to a maximum heat advantage from Jason Lyons and Tomasz Piszcz that catapults the Brummies from also-ran fodder stuck on 5 points (after two races) to contenders with 12 points after three. Should Edinburgh now ride well in Heat 18 against the Workington Comets power combination of Doolan and Rymel they will progress to the final. However, another maximum advantage from the Brummies against the injury-hit Glasgow Tigers in heat 20, sees them sneak through to the first semi-final to pit themselves against Darcy Ward and Tomas Topinka from King's Lynn.

Any dedicated student of speedway would assume the Brummies interest in the competition would now probably end after the next race. Someone, somewhere hasn't read the script or reckons without the wily, tactical savvy of Jason Lyons who passes his fellow countryman Darcy Ward on the back straight to occupy the all-important third place behind teammate Tomasz Piszcz. After a season in which one triumphant race win had quickly followed another, it was something of novelty to see Darcy Ward flounder in fourth place during a Premier League race. Keen to immediately right this wrong – while showing great acceleration down the home straight – Ward blasts under Lyons in dramatic fashion, unseats him and, thereby, earn his disqualification from the rerun. This rash moment ensures that the Brummies will now definitely qualify for the final (barring mechanical failure). The second semi-final between Somerset and Workington also has to be rerun after a first-bend bunching incident sees Steve Johnston thrown from his machine. Based on their form up to this point, it would have been a shock if Doolan and Rymel didn't ease their way into the final. But, unpredictability is often the order of the day within speedway circles – consequently, the Rebels win easily to keep alive hopes of the wild party in the clubhouse pre-promised by Rebels management, volunteers and fans!

Because of the 10 o'clock curfew it's announced that the third-place run-off would not take place. It's a decision that the *Speedway Star* reports afterwards left King's Lynn duo of Tomas Topinka and Darcy Ward "dejected". It also doesn't please some sections of the crowd who fail to understand why the curfew regulations specified under the stadium's planning permission consent have to be adhered to so rigorously. The final as a contest is over by the first corner after Lyons and Piszcz gate with alacrity. While Johnston is able to fight his way past Tomasz Piszcz, he's unable to make any impression upon the runaway leader Jason Lyons. The Brummies victory is greeted with some delight but not the wild celebrations promised for a Rebels triumph. Though subject to some (enforced) delay, the highest compliment that you could pay match referee Chris Durno is that you wouldn't notice he's in charge of the meeting. This is in sharp contrast to the 2008 meeting held here when a nonsensical refereeing decision by Graham Flint robbed Reading of their place in the final. Though I stand to be corrected, victory for the Birmingham Brummies – under the management team of Graham and Denise Drury on behalf of club promoter Tony Mole – requires that the Perry Barr Stadium speedway office now actually gets equipped with a trophy cabinet to display their first silverware since their re-emergence as a Premier League team in 2007. Sadly Graham and Denise aren't present, so Tony Mole proudly accepts the trophy on behalf of the club. Apart from his great achievement in reintroducing the sport back into England's second city, Tony delights in this silverware and, subsequently, rarely misses the opportunity to remind Graham and Denise that they weren't there when all their hard work with the Brummies finally bore fruit.

26th June Premier League Pairs Championship Winners: Birmingham

CHAPTER 8

Cardiff

"Cardiff has an amazing atmosphere but poor racing! It's very different from all the other speedway meetings I've been to in this country."

27th June

The Cardiff Grand Prix Speedway Fayre organised by Nick Barber of Enjay Designs takes place as usual in the rugby club next door to the Millennium Stadium. For reasons that haven't yet been believably explained by the SGP organisers, the scheduled start time for the meeting has been brought forward by two hours to 5 p.m. Anyone who's been to Cardiff previously will know that the racing is unlikely to start until at least 30 minutes after that because of the tedious approach taken with the rider parades and introductions. The pre-meeting "entertainment" will also start earlier and as a result, it's widely expected that visitor numbers to the Collectors' Fayre will fall. All the stallholders you'd expect to see at such an event are in attendance and, since they didn't go to the PL Pairs at Somerset, many of them laid out attractive displays of their merchandise last night. The remainder of the stallholders (like myself) spend time humping our materials up the rugby club bar rear staircase from the nearby adjacent car park.

John Davidson, who runs the Devon Shirts stall (they manufacture race tabards for speedway in the UK), will break with his own tradition and not go to Newport tomorrow to display his merchandise at the Welsh Open. "I make 50% of what I make at Cardiff". Though he's not going to Newport tomorrow he continues to help them, "I sorted out the Men in Black with Nick [Mallett] just like I did for the first meeting they held. There'll be a Douglas, a Rudge and a JAP racing. People often see them on display but to see them in action is something else, as you know! I've always done Newport – I was Tim's friend, his only friend! Steve [Mallett] didn't know anything about it! So I'm not going! I have a young family and I'd rather see them!" Our talk turns to the 2009 Grand Prix Series and, like many people, John believes that Jason Crump will end the season as world champion. Given the prize money leaves something to be desired, fortunately Jason Crump has a significant sponsorship advantage over his rivals because of his relationship with Red Bull (whose Sydney-based global agency Kastner & Partner also has an Aussie connection). It's highly unusual (if not almost unheard of) that proper recognised worldwide brand names associate themselves with the Speedway Grand Prix series, let alone individual speedway riders. "Jason Crump has a 34-page contract with Red Bull! When did you ever hear about that in speedway? It's all come through Mark Webber [Australian Formula 1 racing driver and motorcycle enthusiast]. Jason went to watch the racing over the last 18 months and now he's sponsored by them. I thought they'd do lots of new stuff [merchandise]. Jason said Red Bull said 'No!' He wears their cap but none of his pits crew has anything with Red Bull on it! Clever really! When you think about the Red Bull brand you only think of champions! Jason gets various bonuses if he wins GPs and a really big one if he becomes world champion!"

GRT Media have the stall next to mine. Their range of well-produced DVDs, from a number of Northern speedway clubs (Newcastle, Redcar, Scunthorpe, Sheffield, Workington and Berwick) attracts good interest. GRT owner, cameraman, film editor and marketer, Bob Tasker, attends along with his wife Suzi. Unlike her husband she likes the Grand Prix series, "Bob wouldn't cross the road to watch the Elite League or the Grands Prix!" Though he watches Premier League racing on a regular basis, Bob wasn't that impressed with the staging of the PL Pairs last night at Somerset. "So, 24 races in two and a half hours and they only have one paramedic! At Newcastle, we have two, which saves what happens with Shane [in heat 2] where we waited for the paramedic to treat him on the track and then waited again for him to see him in the pits. Luckily they could run the meeting quickly by not grading the track hardly at all. It wasn't the Super7 more like the Shitty7!"

My new book attracts some interest but like many stallholders at the 2009 Cardiff Grand Prix Fayre my sales volume is down on previous years. However, the fun of Cardiff is the social occasion and the chance to catch up with likeminded people as they sociably wile away the hours before the start of the meeting. Someone with little time because of his responsibilities as Danish team manager (and also as informal advisor to his fellow countrymen who ride in the SGP) is Jan Staechmann. He wanders past with his glamorous wife Claudia. In addition to his moral support and advice, Jan looks after his riders' interests at each Grand Prix. Consequently, this photogenic couple are part of the Grand Prix circus as it moves from city to city during the speedway season. The highlight of the *Speedway Star's* extensive and usually relentlessly breathless coverage of every Grand Prix meeting is the "Harkins Report" written by the eponymous Bert Harkins. It provides the sort of first-hand behind-the-scenes nuggets of information that makes it stand out as consistently readable. Indeed, the SGP soap opera that is the focus of his column regularly features the Staechmanns. Last season we learnt where Jan proposed to Claudia and, this season, prior to the Czech Grand Prix in the Marketa Stadium in Prague, sight of Claudia's official pass prompted Bert to reflect on the possible rise of speedway WAGs ("Talking of Jan, I wonder if speedway is going the same way as football?") The track pass which Jan's English wife Claudia famously wore round her neck in Prague included her photograph and the description 'wife and girlfriend'". Rather like Tony Mole can only ever be discussed as a Kidderminster-based businessman then, for Bert, Claudia can only ever be described as 'Jan's English wife'. Jan believes Bert's column "is something different". Claudia holds its author in some affection, "Bert's such a lovely man and he knows so many people!"

The Brown family from Sheffield also stop by my table. I quickly gather that Mrs Brown is not a fan of John Postlethwaite. So much so that, on occasion in the past when she's had the chance to tell him face to face of his shortcomings, she has done so. "To be fair to him, he listened to what I had to say. I don't think he was that happy with it and passed the buck [to Paul Bellamy]". Our conversation ranges widely including some discussion of whether the new track that Reading Speedway Club have been promised will ever be built. ("Racino is a great name!"). The wonderful review that Ian McMillan gave my book *Concrete for Breakfast* in *The Times* last year doesn't impress Paul, Mr Brown senior. Or at least its author doesn't: "He started on BBC Radio Sheffield as a poet from BAARNS-LEE and he's branched out from there. He's a professional Yorkshireman!" The male side of the Brown family are fans of the Grand Prix. Paul Brown is that rarity among speedway fans, someone with a good word to say for Grand Prix Race Director Ole Olsen. "I agree with Ole Olsen – I'm one of the few people who likes slick tracks! In the Grands Prix where the [indoor] tracks are good it's often processional. Cardiff is always more exciting with its ruts – it adds drama and excitement – and, since it's the best atmosphere in speedway, it makes things even more dramatic." Given my scepticism about some aspects of the management and administration of the SGP series as well as my concern at the disbenefits it creates for British speedway, Phillip (Mr Brown junior) wonders why I'm even here, "Isn't it a bit hypocritical to go to the Cardiff Grand Prix?"

The information about my book that the BSPA kindly put on their website attracts some comment from a Swindon fan. "You must have written that [blurb] on the BSPA website. In future, you have to make sure us lesser mortals can understand it!" Edinburgh Monarchs' speedway director Mike Hunter mooches round the Memorabilia and Collectors' Fayre. Last season he easily won the prize for the most tenuous reason not to purchase my book and, even though it's only the second day it's been on sale, he quickly establishes himself as a front-runner in the 2009 version of the best excuse not to purchase contest. "I would get one but it's a bit heavy to carry round all day!" Self-evidently lighter than *Concrete for Breakfast*, Mike then allows me to persuade him to purchase a copy. After nearly a decade of releasing statements about how wonderful the Cardiff Grand Prix is and how much he'd love to be there, I'm told by a King's Lynn fan that their gifted presenter Mike Bennett has finally given up on his dream of working at this event. "Mike Bennett has said he's so disgusted with how the GPs have gone that he wouldn't do them now if he was asked on principle!" [1]

Kenneth Brown whom I originally encountered at Sheffield speedway with a battered copy of *The Mycenaeans* by

[1] Rumours of the recent flaccidity of his Cardiff ambition proves unfounded when, at the start of 2010, a Facebook campaign group about his presentation skills is started by Mike Bennett himself! I'm not on Facebook so can't establish whether Mike or his 'friends' advocate that he must be chosen to present the 2010 Cardiff GP! Mike Bennett certainly often has the smug, self-satisfied look that suggests he thinks he's the Sting of speedway so, perhaps, as a compromise, he could be booked by the organisers as the pre-meeting or interval entertainment? Not known for the sparkle of his humour or the ability to laugh at himself, Mike, subsequently, tries to pass off the existence of the Mike Bennett Speedway Presentation Legend Facebook group as a 'joke'.

Cardiff: *"Cardiff has an amazing atmosphere but poor racing! It's very different from all the other speedway meetings I've been to in this country."*

Lord William Taylour as reading material for his journey there and back, contemplates buying Robert Bamford's *2008 Speedway Yearbook* at a bargain price of £5. He eventually changes his mind, "I don't need a book of stats 'cause I've kept my own from 1946 to the present day". Scunthorpe official photographer Steve Dixon stops by with a woman who looks remarkably like his partner Debbie but isn't. The mystery lady turns out to be Deb's elder sister Barbara, "I'm here to celebrate my youngest sister's birthday!" Bob Tasker's dry wit is guaranteed to enliven any day. Close to our stalls is a speedway fan with a beer gut so large that he looks heavily pregnant. "Replica shirts seem like a good idea but looking like Joe Screen is taking things a bit far! Still, look at him this year. As Joe said on Sky last week – 'not bad for a fat bloke!'"

Crowded Fayre

Paul Cooper's photo keeps falling on the floor. Bob Tasker notes wryly, "As it's GP day, in an imitation of real life, Paul Cooper keeps falling down all the time!" Elsewhere in the Fayre Johnny Barber has glanced inside *Quantum of Shale* and immediately is concerned, "Oh no, page 35, schoolboy error! You've said John Rich when it's Bill Gimbeth – I don't know if he'll forgive you!"

Hello sailor!

Fresh from his SRBF collection duties at Somerset last night, Rob Peasley as usual provides perceptive insight. "I was just saying to Nick [Barber] that the decisive race of the meeting was when track reserve [Tom Brown] kept Tully at the back and, therefore, stopped Edinburgh getting through to the semi-final. If they had beaten Brown then Birmingham wouldn't have got through and won! I expect the Glasgow fans might remind the Monarchs fans that this happened!" Also on duty at Somerset speedway referee Chris Durno is in Cardiff with his son Tom (who forecasts a win for Bomber). Each season Chris visits every track in the country, so his eye had been immediately caught by something missing from the Somerset stadium infrastructure. "I had to do a double take when I got there and saw there was no air-fence! Then I remembered that Mike Golding took it to Newport where he runs the trackshop. You have to ask whether Shane Parker would have got injured like that if there had been one? Many refs wouldn't have got the meeting run that quickly [after the Parker crash]. Then, before the semi-final, there was a 20-minute delay while the riders put on new tyres and then, for the final, I had to wait while the riders switched their tyres round to get a new edge. They'd only had one race on it! We did the last race at 22.02 and, if Somerset gets in trouble with the curfew, they have to look to these things and how long the parade took!" Glasgow speedway fan and ex "Miss Green" start-line girl, Heather McNeilly is shocked to find herself mentioned in *Quantum of Shale*. "I can't believe you've put that in your book! Dad! Dad! Look what's in here!" Her father, Hugh, keeps a dispassionate look on his face as he stands at the tapes as assistant start marshal for the Glasgow Tigers and he adopts this well-practised expression now.

Above the start line

The earlier start time gives the atmosphere around the Millennium Stadium a strange feel since there's less time for pre-meeting drinking let alone that the heat of the afternoon is that much higher. Ostensibly the revised start time was introduced to enable fans to travel to and from Cardiff without the need to book a hotel room. Due to the scarcity and price of rooms in the Cardiff area, regular fans book their accommodation the year beforehand so, when this announcement was made, many of them would be unable to cancel without loss or penalty. Though Paul Bellamy top dog at BSI/IMG would claim live on

Cardiff: *"Cardiff has an amazing atmosphere but poor racing! It's very different from all the other speedway meetings I've been to in this country."*

television a few nights later that the aim of his organisation was to "give the fans value for money", such comments look laughably platitudinous given the historic disregard shown by BSI about unnecessary expense for SGP fans caused by their actions. The Gelsenkirchen experience still remains a sore point with all of those fans unfortunate enough to have travelled to Germany to watch an indoor meeting that ultimately didn't take place because of the weather! A full investigation was promised by BSI and apparently undertaken but, if fault has been accurately apportioned and meaningful conclusions drawn, then these results have yet to be made public. In order to "compensate" the fans for the losses they incurred in travel, food and accommodation, BSI made great play of 'generously' offering them a free ticket to a 2009 SGP of their choice (provided they only wished to have a free ticket for Copenhagen, Gothenburg or Cardiff). It typified the BSI approach to cost control that they had failed to invest sufficiently enough to ensure that they had dry shale to put inside the Veltins Arena. It's interesting that the free ticket offer reveals that, in fact, BSI don't really stage the majority of Grand Prix events but, instead, franchise these out to local promoters ambitious enough to want the reflected glory that the arrival of the SGP circus in their area notionally creates. Gelsenkirchen would have made four SGP events that BSI actually stage themselves but, sadly, this proved beyond their organisational competence. It's a cliché of advertising and sales that there's one born every day so, when potential future promoters at new venues tender to stage a forthcoming SGP round, then they will find BSI demand standards of facilities and performance that they were unable to achieve themselves! [2]

Though they proved unable to run a trip to the pub in Gelsenkirchen, nonetheless the staging of the Cardiff Grand Prix is, despite the calibre of the racing, justifiably the highlight of the SGP calendar. In the teeth of a recession, attendances were widely predicted to fall dramatically and, while the FIM don't provide independently audited attendance figures for the individual rounds of the Grand Prix Series, it's claimed attendances held up well. Historically quite how these attendances were calculated remains open to question in the absence of independent verification. Given the Millennium Stadium has a capacity way in excess of the record Cardiff speedway crowd, there are always a large number of empty seats on display at this event. To my untutored eye, these gaps look bigger than usual but, given the scale of the stadium, this would be impossible to say with any degree of certainty. Though there has been talk by BSI about "value for money" for fans it's clear that there's been cost-cutting compared to 2008. For example, huge swathes of the crowd this season haven't been provided with a free Union flag to wave enthusiastically during the event to provide valuable patriotic footage for the Sky television cameras. On the subject of television, though neither Sky nor BSI release viewing figures, a subsequent thread on the British Speedway Forum uses the official BARB figures to show that viewer numbers fell dramatically by 38% (from 268,000 in 2008 to 164,000 in 2009). Compared to the viewing figures generated by other marginal sports, these figures apparently still remain viewed as robust and cause for some satisfaction at Sky Sports. It also has to be remembered that BSI generates the most significant proportion of its income not through gate revenues but through the worldwide sale of television rights (for the live event itself, pre-recorded shown as live or various edited highlight summary packages). Speedway is an attractive television commodity to broadcast during the summer (non-footballing) months since it can fill three hours air time, is amenable to frequent commercial breaks and isn't premium priced.

Speedway enthusiast Charles McKay has kindly given me the complementary ticket he received as a result of the

[2] Each year the BSI Press Office appear to manage to ensure that the Cardiff round of the SGP – the jewel in the series crown – is invariably greeted by the print and broadcast media with a stunning lack of coverage. The sharp contrast to the lack of publicity generated about Cardiff in the print media does have the side benefit that it ensures that the small number of outlets that do cover the sport do not reveal details that BSI might not wish to appear in the public domain. Fortunately, because of the immense popularity of speedway in Poland more important facts do get into the public domain and give us some insight into the *modus operandi* of BSI. When Gorzow in Poland obtained the rights to stage a Speedway World Cup event, the local newspaper *Gazeta Lubuska* revealed that Gorzow's Town Hall (City Council) had to comply with 41 contractual conditions specified by BSI. The most important condition is that Gorzow will pay £300,000 for the rights to stage the event. In addition they have to, obviously, bear all costs of staging the event along with the purchase of advertising boards and the hire of security. They also had to provide and pay for several rooms and one apartment (in "the best hotel in town") for the BSI delegation for the duration of the event as well as pay for their air tickets, three cars and translators. Contractually BSI will also receive 250 free tickets for the best seats in the main stand and also have an option to purchase a further 50 tickets, if required, at half price. At no cost to BSI, Gorzow's Town Hall also has to "ensure availability of four girls to be present at the starting gate" and also, somewhat weirdly, these girls "must be accepted in advance" of the event by BSI. The 15-page document did identify some BSI responsibilities: notably, the provision of an air-fence, a decoration box, an advertising board to be used as background during TV interviews and clothes for the track staff (if deemed necessary). Smug executives come as standard. They also promise to supply six blank advertising banners that Gorzow Town Hall can sell the advertising space for to interested companies – on condition that these sponsoring companies meet BSI approval! Finally there are conditions of confidentiality that request Gorzow Town Hall don't undertake any activity (or voice opinion) which might be seen as harmful to the reputation, renown and image of BSI. It goes without saying that BSI can't be held responsible for any party prepared to agree to such terms and conditions.

Cardiff: *"Cardiff has an amazing atmosphere but poor racing! It's very different from all the other speedway meetings I've been to in this country."*

Gelsenkirchen fiasco. I had expected that I would find myself in a crowded grandstand area filled with fans disgruntled at their treatment by BSI. However, the organisers have sensibly looked after these potentially irked fans. Indeed, they've given us a prime location that overlooks the start line, bend 1 and the open pit area adjacent to the first bend. This section, like so many others in the stadium, is sparsely populated. No international speedway event is complete without exuberant Polish fans waving giant flags or screaming nationalistically in (beer-fuelled) ecstatic delight after every race win by a Polish national (Rune Holta included). Despite the presence of many Poles, the overall atmosphere in my section remains muted even when at 5.20 p.m. presenter Kevin Coombes exalts over the impressively loud stadium public address system, "Ladies and Gentlemen, boys and girls – let's go racing!" With his championship ambitions already arguably in tatters, the blue-helmeted Nicki Pedersen (off gate 2) makes sure that he blocks the new golden boy of the SGP Emil Sayfutdinov's run to the first bend in heat 1. This manoeuvre initially enables Kenneth Bjerre and Rune Holta to escape. By the last corner of the second lap, Emil and Rune only battle for third place until Sayfutdinov gets out of shape to prompt the Norwegian-born Pole Holta to lay down his bike with alacrity only to be disqualified by the referee for his trouble. The rerun sees Nicki Pedersen again gate but, over four laps, he can't prevent his smaller and lighter fellow countryman Kenneth Bjerre winning. Sat where I am, the flames that theatrically flare at the moment the winning rider crosses the finish line obscures the exact detail of any neck-and-neck finish. Though we're sat on the top tier of the Millennium Stadium, I can still feel the heat of these flames.

There is a case to be made that the format and frequency with which they stage the SGP rounds has led to a feeling amongst the riders, fans and television viewers, that the competition has gone stale. Though the arrival on the scene of Emil Sayfutdinov has already given the 2009 Series a much-needed shot in the arm, even this has not quite had the impact it should have given Emil's poor English and lack of photogenic appeal. Though clearly the top riders are able to benefit financially from sponsorship through their participation in the SGP series, some of the lesser lights not only have to work hard to go nowhere but they also have to bear significant infrastructure costs in order to try to effectively compete. Though set by the FIM (rather than the BSI) prize money remains frozen, paid in dollars and completely derisory. Painfully aware of how Hans Andersen was discriminated against a few years ago when he had the temerity to voice an honest opinion about his thoughts on the SGP series, nowadays no rider who takes part or wishes to take part in the series is likely to venture critical opinion. The exception to that rule (though he still has ambitions to compete in the Series in future) is Poole captain Bjarne Pedersen who believes that many riders commonly felt dissatisfaction but were reluctant to express it. "They don't want to say to the press that, 'I don't want to be in the Grand Prix'. Everybody says they want to be in it. I'm sure there are a few riders who are, or have been in the Grands Prix, that don't want to be in it, but won't say it to the press." One rider who most assuredly does want to take part is Coventry's Edward Kennett, who qualified for this event via the British final. Heat 3 is his first race of the night and, after a duel with Sebastian Ulamek, initially he's comfortably second while Andreas Jonsson and Tomasz Gollob battle behind him for third place. Edward bustles competitively but has to use all his speedway experience and skill since, compared to his rivals, he appears underpowered. This perception proves to be the case when Andreas Jonsson makes up significant ground to somehow snatch second place on the finish line. At least that's what we can see on the cameras afterwards since the flames again obscure the exact nuances.

The fourth race of the night sees an easy win for Jason Crump and it's noticeable that the 2009 Cardiff Grand Prix doesn't suffer from the variable track that's characterised previous years. In fact, the track is so road-like in its constitution that there's a complete absence of the ruts and bumps of yesteryear. Variable Cardiff track conditions have historically placed the riders in some potential danger though tonight – in the spirit of instant nostalgia – some fans in the crowd miss the excitement and drama that the unpredictability of such track conditions provides. The cock-up in shale and storage in Gelsenkirchen could be attributed to either penny pinching or poor management. During the 2009 close season in an interview with the *Speedway Star*, Speedway Control Bureau consultant track inspector Colin Meredith reveals that, since its inception, BSI took a policy decision to use inferior (but cheaper) materials to create the Cardiff track surface. "We've run at Cardiff for eight years on really bad material and it always cut up. It produced exciting racing, but it was bordering on dangerous." Though quality materials clearly cost more than lower quality alternatives, this year BSI finally invested. "They had 3,000 tons of Breedon material [from Ennstone Johnston Ltd in Breedon, Derbyshire] and transported it down to Cardiff two months previously. That is first-class material, exactly what every track should be using, but it's so expensive to transport." With safety to the fore instead of profit, Cardiff track curator Colin Meredith acknowledged "Some people have said that the track this year at Cardiff

Cardiff: *"Cardiff has an amazing atmosphere but poor racing! It's very different from all the other speedway meetings I've been to in this country."*

was boring because it lacked a bit of excitement, the track was too good – so you can't win!"

If there isn't excitement and entertainment on the track again this year, then there's certainly argy-bargy off it at the end of heat 5 when Scott Nicholls and Emil Sayfutdinov clash. According to press sources in the pits, as Scott Nicholls went out to take part in the fifth race of the night he was jostled by Emil's engine tuner Ashley Holloway, son of 'Mad Wellie' Malcolm. Whether this happened as reported, happened at all or took place after – its contribution to the post-race incident is open to debate. The ostensible on-track cause of this contretemps is clear for all to see. As they transition from the third bend to the fourth on the final lap of heat 5, Emil Sayfutdinov tries to barge his way past Scott Nicholls only to find his rival is made of sterner stuff than anticipated. Scott gives absolutely no quarter and emerges triumphant from their mini battle for third place. If there's going to be any post-race exchange of opinion between riders, then the warm-down lap or upon the return to the pits are the usual locations for said discussion. Though, subsequently, the organisers would publicly clasp their hands together in mock piety, after a decade of dull meetings the Speedway Grand Prix finally caught national and international media attention. Sadly for those who enjoy the sport, it was the action after the race (albeit on the track) that causes the interest. Though more handbags than a prizefight, the end of the warm-down lap fires the collective interest of those inside the stadium. White helmeted Scott Nicholls is on his way back to the pits when Emil Sayfutdinov zooms alongside to lean shoulder to shoulder with Scott as they near the pits gate entrance. Surprised to be butting shoulders rather than shaking hands, Scott continues to demonstrate the tenacity he exhibited on track and returns the favour. Both riders concentrate their attentions upon each other and so fail to stop their collision with the open air-fence panel rather than smoothly continue their egress into the pits. Scott casts his bike to the floor and pushes Emil's shoulder while the Russian rider initially remains on his bike. The contretemps apparently over, Scott goes to pick up his bike but instinctively (and sensibly) realises that Emil Sayfutdinov has dismounted his machine. At this point, Scott kicks over Emil's bike to create further room to repel the Russian's likely assault. Though not a surprise, Scott's immediately knocked down and, if this were a boxing match, would then receive a count to 10 from the referee. Since the Queensbury Rules don't apply, Emil Sayfutdinov lashes out with a misplaced kick while Scott springs up with speed that wouldn't disgrace a wrestler to scrabble for the chin guard on Sayfutdinov's helmet. Just as the confrontation appears to be about to enter its next stage, the smothering effect of track staff and mechanics finally starts to properly intervene. Rather than continue with the scratch-his-eyes-out strategy, Scott finally manages to punch Sayfutdinov, albeit only when the Russian is held by others in an attempt to establish calm. Apparently more of a street fighter than his English rival, Sayfutdinov fires off a punch in reply but this flails harmlessly away as he's being dragged back at that very moment by assorted helpers. Though he serves no purpose, the first speedway rider on the scene is the diminutive Tai Woffinden. The dramatic footage from the event immediately finds its way onto YouTube and a key still from the fight gets comprehensive coverage in British national newspapers including the *Sun, Telegraph, Mirror, Mail* and *Times*. Swindon track staff volunteer and author of *Blunsdon blog* – the excellent website that goes behind the scenes of curatorial life in Wiltshire – Graham Cooke is also captured (mouth open in surprise) for posterity right in the thick of the action. Family relatives have previously taken at face value Graham's reassurance that his voluntary track work involves modest almost rustic agricultural activities such as riding on tractors, shifting shale and maintaining fences. To their great surprise, it now transpires that Graham's work involves ringside action in fights between motorcyclists! Fully aware that discretion is the better part of valour Graham would afterwards comment, "Hard helmets, heavy gloves and steel shoes meant I wasn't going to get too involved until they were separated!" Speedway is obviously an adrenalin-driven sport so occasionally feelings will run high in the heat of the moment. Another possible contributory factor to the helmet-to-helmet posturing that eventually led to brief violence between Nicholls and Sayfutdinov is that his first two races in the Cardiff Grand Prix had already effectively ended any pretentions that the Russian teenager may have to be crowned World Champion in 2009. There's no doubt that Emil has already created a buzz in the speedway world with his performances in previous Grands Prix (albeit without any coverage from any recognised sports media) but, with a meagre 1 point from two races, his Cardiff performance signalled that his dream of glory might be a future goal but wasn't going to be realised during 2009.

Though it's more circus and theatre than a speedway meeting, many fans, commentators and BSI employees still make expansive claims about the Cardiff event each and every season. Prior to the meeting, when informally applying for an extension to his contract, Sky Sports speedway pundit Kelvin Tatum ramps up the hyperbole to incredible levels with the claim, "You haven't lived until you've been to a Cardiff Grand Prix!" Apparently driven to the verge

Cardiff: *"Cardiff has an amazing atmosphere but poor racing! It's very different from all the other speedway meetings I've been to in this country."*

of ecstasy by the sight of riders racing on an inferior track surface that reduces the skill element to a lottery, Kelvin summarises his many years of delight at Cardiff ("makes my hair stand on end"). If this spectacle provides such an orgasmic highlight for him, it's probably best to avoid any trips to the recycling centre or a cashpoint in Kelvin's company for fear of his reaction to such thrills. Something the lickspittle boosters invariably highlight are the deluxe Millennium Stadium facilities the attending speedway fans pay through the nose to enjoy. Few bother to mention that in a stadium of this size, many of the cheaper seats find fans seated in what Americans would call "the nose bleeds". As a consequence, we have to rely on the giant video screens to replay the drama and fine detail that we miss. Peculiarly, the most significant SGP event since the Boyce/Gollob confrontation at Hackney in 1996 doesn't appear to be worthy of any replay for the crowd inside the Millennium Stadium. After the incident the giant stadium video screens go blank until they flash up some offer that involves the endorsement of Tiger Woods and Madonna (apparently one of the few women Tiger hasn't slept with in recent years) before the screens then return to blackness for the next two minutes. When the camera feed is eventually 'safe' to be restored, a cameraman bravely ventures to the Emil Sayfutdinov corner of the pits a mechanic brusquely gestures them away. After further considerable delay, we're treated to a visual treat of a replay of the race winner (Sebastian Ulamek) as he races to the line and his post-race clenched-fist celebrations. Paid to be enthusiastic, informative and voluble throughout Cardiff, presenter Kevin Coombes takes a temporary vow of silence in the long delay before heat 6 finally gets underway.

In the absence of an execrable track that causes riders to fight for control against the ruts, the Cardiff GP becomes the speedway equivalent of a recipe for catatonia. Apart from the Nicholls/Sayfutdinov contretemps, any neutral fan at Cardiff for their first ever speedway meeting would be unlikely to return. Whether or not they do, the organisers will continue to gouge the 40,000 or so fans prepared to regularly attend. Understandably, they'll continue to bank substantial revenues they deserve for their entrepreneurial acumen, irrespective of the action on the track or "spectacle" off it. The chance to build enthusiasm or mystery about the series hasn't been helped by their choice of dull race format where, effectively, each SGP event is a lengthy qualification process for the sharp end of the evening – namely, the semi-finals and final. Even here, in recent years the cut and thrust has severely diminished. Excellence and determination are no longer absolute necessities since the riders know there will usually be further opportunities to make amends in future weeks. It's a situation that hasn't been helped in recent years by the dominance of one rider. In 2008 it was clear that Nicki Pedersen was always going to emerge triumphant as world champion and, although the 2009 series has only reached the half-way point, it's already almost a foregone conclusion that Jason Crump will (injury aside) emerge triumphant at the end of the season. Indeed, Jason wins heat 7 with great ease and when, three races later, he faces his closest ostensible rival, he imperiously sweeps Nicki Pedersen to the bend 1 air-fence before he proceeds to race away for another comfortable victory. Injury, bad luck, falls and a number of questionable refereeing decisions have blighted Nicki's 2009 world championship campaign. Speedway rumours, like gossip everywhere, whether true or false travel like wildfire. Talk before the meeting is that Nicki Pedersen has platinum engine barrels and piston heads (titanium products are banned by the FIM and the SCB – though platinum isn't listed as a banned product). This sounds unbelievable as well as unsubstantiated even more so when people say there's only been 12 made and Nicki has got them all at a price of £10,000 each! Given his performances this season so far, such talk sounds wide of the mark.

Even The Last Night of the Proms atmosphere that was previously a notable feature at Cardiff is noticeably absent without the jingoistic free Union flags. Even the volume of the music sounds to have been brought down a notch or two. Nonetheless, there are many enthusiastic Poles within the stadium keen to celebrate and you have to wonder if flag waving is a national pastime or a patriotic skill learnt at birth. The Poles aren't the only people with flags. When Hans Andersen wins heat 8, without apparent irony given his very recent arrival in Dorset, a large impressively beer-bellied Poole fan enthusiastically waves a skull and cross bones flag during his celebration lap. In the absence of any team silverware heading to Dorset this year, then this will probably be one of the rare occasions this flag gets waved in celebration.

For the past eight years, riders often haven't got as far at the first bend before they struggle to control their bike due to track conditions. However, we have to wait until Grzegorz Walasek enters the third bend on the second lap of heat 11 for the first sign of a minor loss of bike control due to the variability of the track! This is simultaneously amazing but also a sign that entertainment is conspicuous by its absence from the 2009 event. This would be a concern

Cardiff: *"Cardiff has an amazing atmosphere but poor racing! It's very different from all the other speedway meetings I've been to in this country."*

for BSI if they were frank with themselves (or cared). Even the interval entertainment – where the organisers traditionally hire the faded stars of yesteryear – appears to have suffered from dramatic cost control. Some musicians do appear but they're anonymous in terms of their presentation and insufficiently interesting for me to try to solve the mystery of their identity. As usual, Nicki Pedersen enjoys mixed fortunes with speedway officials and remains the pantomime villain for the Cardiff crowd. He does have some justification for his increasingly hair-trigger ire at the end of heat 14 when Hans Andersen cuts back inside him to snatch third place on the line. To my untutored eye, it looks like this cut back up the inside on the last bend requires Hans to ride with both wheels inside the white line. If a last place for Nicki Pedersen is a rarity then a first place for Scott Nicholls is even more of a collector's item. However, his celebration lap confrontation with Emil Sayfutdinov must have stirred his blood and temporarily rejuvenated his competitive edge. Heat 15 sees him exchange the lead for a couple of laps with Andreas Jonsson before he aggressively stamps his authority on the race. This evening it takes a special rider to find any bump on the too-smooth track surface. Rune Holta proves equal to the task in heat 16, when he finds one on the second bend and is thrown from his bike. The referee disqualifies him. Predictably enough, Jason Crump is comfortably in the lead at the point Rune discovered the bump. Jason then proceeds to win the rerun very easily.

If the BSI/IMG Press Department display ineptitude in their task of garnering widespread media coverage then their colleagues in the Commercial Department also struggle to master their job responsibilities, if judged by the adverts on display inside the Millennium Stadium. Sponsor adverts appear on the air-fences, on the centre-green A boards and also, most dramatically, on wooden posters laid on the surface of the centre green. The main sponsor of this Grand Prix must be Tobet who display the almost giant-sized bright red poster on the apex of the first corner. At the start line (and also with two posters on bend 4 as well as one close to the finish line) are much more subtle adverts that proclaim "SPREAD YOUR WINGS LESZNO" If you think of great holiday destinations then Rio, San Francisco or Sydney immediately spring to mind. Sadly the delights of Leszno as a possible holiday destination has somehow passed me by. For some reason best known to themselves but most likely because they got this gratis, Sky Sports take a couple of centre-green A boards by the podium to advertise themselves to the Sky Sports subscribers already watching at home or, possibly, to recommend their services to fans within the stadium who are presently some distance from their television sets. Actually, since we're told so often about the incredible success of the SGP being televised to 100 countries round the world, perhaps this is a stealth campaign by Sky to break into new markets? The Daily Express also have a couple of A boards in the vicinity of the podium. Some company called *Fakt* also advertise their services by the podium. Quite what these services are I'm fakt if I know? [3] In fact, when I say podium that's not correct. Relentless cost control probably dictates that at one of the few Grands Prix they actually stage, BSI no longer even supply a traditional podium but instead use numbers superimposed on a chequered floor covering to denote the position of each of the triumphant top three finishers. The lack of a step up isn't such good news for any height challenged riders.

Since I know that she loves National (Conference) League racing to the exclusion of all others, I'm shocked to get a text from Julie Martin, Weymouth Press Officer and Track Photographer from inside the Millennium Stadium. Though we've already reached Heat 19 she's not impressed with the calibre of the action or entertainment, "It's like watching paint dry!" Jules has come away on a two-night boys' speedway camping weekend – separate tents – in Penarth with Tim Webster, Luke Priest, Spud and Skippy (aka Nick Matthews, Tim Webster's mechanic). Last night, they'd enjoyed some race action at Newport speedway. Jules isn't enthralled with the early evening entertainment served up in Cardiff by the SGP inside the plush but expensive Millennium Stadium. "It's been more fun watching Craig start marshal than the racing. They have different start marshals who take it in turns. Craig is so lovely. He used to mechanic for Karl Mason." Patriotic fervour temporarily invigorates the crowd as Chris Harris lines up at the tapes for the second semi-final. His victory on a ludicrously rough track a few years back is arguably the only ever real Cardiff Grand Prix highlight! The lack of any notable or memorable incident in nearly a decade is so marked that this evening's Nicholls/Sayfutdinov's brief display of handbags already runs it close as a key historic event. BSI/IMG along with Sky Sports would probably wet themselves with delight if Chris Harris (or any British rider, please!) would again win the

[3] Later Internet research, well Wikipedia, reveals that *Fakt* is a "tabloid-style daily newspaper" that sells 500,000 per day and has an "estimated readership of 7 million". Launched in October 2003 by Axel Springer (the publishers of the German tabloid *Bild*), it employs a tried and tested approach to journalism: namely, downmarket, sensationalist and populist.

Cardiff: *"Cardiff has an amazing atmosphere but poor racing! It's very different from all the other speedway meetings I've been to in this country."*

Cardiff Grand Prix since this would boost viewing figures, provide the news media with an actual story worthy of coverage and also attract more punters through the turnstiles. Sadly, it's been a while since Chris qualified on ability as a permanent member of the SGP. Instead the afterglow of that triumph still resonates with the organisers. On the track, it's a different story illustrated again tonight by his exclusion after he's run into Hans Andersen. With patriotic dreams at an end, on the giant screens we're treated to lingering coverage of a studiously unemotional Chris Harris on a lengthy walk back from the track to his bay in the pits. In the rerun, Hans Andersen comes back out onto the track and the man sat next to Julie Martin observes, "He's come out on Emil Sayfutdinov's bike!" Even with the possible help of the giant screens I'm amazed at how this gentleman could identify such a fact. "You can see he's got a different dirt deflector, a different wheel disk and also has number 15 written on the side!" Though he makes this sound easy to spot, this gentleman clearly must have some speedway equipment expertise. Judged by the soft burr of his accent he doesn't come from either Dorset or Wales. It turns out he's Erwin Tree a New Zealander from Invercargill, "I'm on an exchange with the British and New Zealand Navy for four months in total. I'm in logistics – I'm a stores attendant. This speedway is awesome! I'm Grant Tregoning's mechanic. I've also mechanicked for Jason Bunyan and Glen Phillips. I'm so pleased I came. Cardiff has an amazing atmosphere but poor racing! It's very different from all the other speedway meetings I've been to in this country. Tonight's a night off but tomorrow I'll be with Greg at Newport – he's the only National League rider in the Welsh Open! People criticise Newport [track] but it's not as bad as Rye House with their camber where it goes up and down!" The rerun of semi-final two finds Hans Andersen slightly ahead with Nicki Pedersen on his outside. Skilled enough to go for speedway's equivalent of a professional foul, Nicki plays the percentages and falls theatrically in order to try to tempt the referee into a rerun or the disqualification of Hans Andersen. Unfortunately for Nicki, the referee's adjudication is that he's at fault for the incident and, so, disqualifies him from the rerun. Erwin's in no doubt about the situation, "He could have held it!"
[Jules] "If they didn't have the air-fence they wouldn't do that."
[Erwin] "They should do what they do at home and have concrete fences!"
The person in charge of the music isn't sympathetic to Nicki's plight either since, over the public address system, we're treated to the loud strains of *Que sera sera.*

The third rerun of the semi-final is a match race between Greg Hancock and Hans Andersen. American Greg is a rider well liked by fans and rivals alike. Nonetheless, he's not adverse to a bit of gamesmanship himself. People have pointed out before that Greg has quite a habit of moving after the start marshal lines up the riders. Though he's certain to qualify, after they have been start marshalled at the tapes Greg rolls back and rolls forward. Jules comments, "I've heard about it but not seen it!"

With six wins from six rides prior to the grand final, Jason Crump completes another successful night with the formality of his seventh straight race win tonight to treble underline his superiority in the 2009 version of the SGP. We can all admire the ability, skill and determination that enable Jason to complete his maximum. His studious professionalism, however, doesn't provide the type of barnstorming performance required to bring the crowd alive or, more importantly, sell television rights to even more broadcasters round the world in search of extensive but cheap scheduling. The Cardiff GP remains true to its theatrical roots and sadly, without the variable track surface, the quality of the 'entertainment' on offer has – even though it didn't seem possible – declined yet further! Nonetheless, neither Cardiff nor the SGP Series are going to go away any time soon so any fans bored by a dull, protracted "World Championship" format that fails to include all the best riders in the world or have a properly legitimate qualification process, will continue to have to find their so-called 'authentic' speedway kicks elsewhere.

27th June Cardiff Grand Prix Winner: Jason Crump

CHAPTER 9

Newport

"I'm sure they'd let him park his caravan here if he wanted!"

28th June

Since a brief 11-month hiatus brought on by the premature death of owner/promoter Tim Stone, the reincarnation of Newport Speedway under the father and son promotional management of Steve and Nicky Mallett is three and a half months into the 2009 season, though they've yet to financially prosper. The car park outside the stadium entrance gates is already dusty, bathed in warm sunshine and sparsely occupied with a few cars that belong to staff already at work inside the stadium. I'm immediately greeted by a smartly dressed Steve Mallett. "You're Jeff Scott, aren't you? You came here last time [for the Prince of Wales Trophy meeting] so make sure you sort Mike Golding out afterwards as he's hurting as much as the rest of us! I don't mind you being here like but Mike owns the trackshop franchise." Due to start at 1 p.m. the South Wales Argus Welsh Open Championship features a strong field of Premier League level riders many fans would pay good money to see race. They include the recent winner of the Prince of Wales Trophy Kevin Doolan along with contemporary luminaries of the Premier League racing scene like Ricky Ashworth, Ty Proctor, Ryan Fisher, David Howe, Mark Lemon and, Newport track record holder, Jordan Frampton. The profile of Jordan in the programme contains some frankly unbelievable information including the claim that his favourite film is *The Sound of Music*, It also reveals that he likes to drink Coke and eat Chinese food yet, rather than relax to the dulcet tones of Julie Andrews, he prefers Led Zeppelin, Jimi Hendrix and the Rolling Stones. Under the new management team there have been many improvements to the infrastructure. Most visibly the track now has an air-fence (courtesy of Mike Golding) and there is now a disabled viewing area on the second bend. Though new to the promotional game, Steve and Nicky have ambitiously chosen to run Newport sides in both the Premier League and the National League. Since the start of the season, the Newport Hornets have won more meetings in the National League than they've lost, while the Premier League Newport Wasps have endured a torrid start to the season with six wins (including an April Fool's Day victory at Perry Barr Stadium), one draw and thirteen losses (four of these on home shale).

It would be fair to say that frequent metaphorical sight of the Premier League wooden spoon in the Newport Trophy cabinet has educated fans to temper their wilder expectations of glory. In the bumper issue of the *Speedway Star* Keith McGhie made his own unique pre-season National League prediction that Newport would win the league and Bournemouth would finish bottom. Sadly, things didn't start as anticipated though, admirably, Steve and Nicky Mallett initially tracked an attractive side in keeping with their aspirations for silverware. However, unlike the *Field of Dreams* ("build it and they will come") the club continues to struggle to attract significant numbers of fans through the turnstiles. Any cursory due diligence undertaken by any prospective owner of the club would quickly establish that (in recent years) attendances for speedway meetings at Hayley Stadium mostly remain peopled by a loyal hardcore of fans willing to be regularly seduced by the aroma of methanol. When I wrote my first book *Showered in Shale*, Tim Stone quickly identified possible textual changes for my draft Newport chapter ("Do you have to say 'meagre crowd'? Couldn't you just say 'small crowd'? In fact, do you have to mention the crowd size at all?"). Even before the impact of the recession seeped into all three speedway leagues, it was hardly a secret that attendance levels frequently fell short of individual promoters' expectations, let alone their financial break-even point.

Based upon his frequent comments in the past few months in the pages of the *Speedway Star*, the idea that the arrival back on the scene of Newport Speedway mightn't banish the torpor and inertia of erstwhile floating speedway fans in the city and its surrounding catchment area, has come as quite a shock to Nicky Mallett. After only months in charge, British speedway's youngest promoter sounds a plaintive tone, "We're quite happy with the response to the sport returning to the city but would be lying if we said we were entirely satisfied ... we do need more fans coming through the gates thick and fast." Highlighting the competitive team they have put together, Nicky also rehearses the tried and tested favoured narrative, "Speedway was almost dead in the city until we came and saved it." If Premier League and National League attendances disappoint, then the four team tournament held at the start of May really fails to live up to expectations, "We didn't expect the best crowd in the world, but we were disappointed with the crowd." The "international" flavour of said four-team tournament excites Nicky but, given the present lack of British riding talent, pretty well every Elite and Premier League speedway meeting features an international field. By the end of May, Nicky (now 22) found a new but unusual *bête noire* namely, the Sky Sports speedway editorial team who he deemed to "Have been insulting the people of Newport." Not only did Sky Sports studiously ignore Hayley Stadium as a possible venue for a live Premier League meeting, they'd forced the club to make fixture changes and pig-headedly ignored Newport's Cinzano credentials ("prepared to race any time at any place"). Setting aside his anger for long enough to find some humour in their rejection, Nicky notes, "We certainly feel as if we've been shot out of the sky with the way we've been treated by the company ... we are attempting to bring Newport back from the doldrums ages only to be told that we are not good enough to be on TV."

Any casual reader of the *Speedway Star* or local newspaper, let alone the local radio would be in no doubt that Nicky's been "sending out a clear message – come on down and see what Newport's speedway is all about." Though found less often in print, Nicky's father Steve also reveals some exasperation. "I know there are still lots of speedway fans all round the area who haven't yet returned to watching the Wasps since we took over the club. So I'm urging them not only to come back to give us their backing through the turnstiles but also help roar the club to a successful Premier League season." Understandably the hard-core of Newport fans remain relentlessly excited but the stay-away silent majority probably don't read the *Speedway Star*, otherwise they'd have been painfully aware of the June 13th Premier League news section headline ("Wasps worry"); let alone Nicky Mallett's forecast of possible future scenarios should the stay-away fans continue to remain absent. "Fans really have to be aware that unless things pick up at the turnstiles, then we can't operate Newport Speedway at the levels we currently do. It's been hugely disappointing to see the low attendances we've seen so far and I have to say we simply can't keep throwing money at it. We've done a lot here in a short space of time but the response through the turnstiles has been way down." Even if we ignore the historic average level of attendances at the club, performances could also be a factor. Indeed the theme that the "fans deserve better" is something Nicky himself notes about the season's results so far, "The fans deserve better than what is happening at the moment ... Our family have put our heart and soul into the club and we couldn't be more disappointed than how things have gone so far. We know the fans are out there and will come back with a winning team, and that's what we intend to do." Ominously for the riders that comprise the current team line-up Nicky continues, "We will not tolerate these home defeats and we can assure our fans that this will not be continuing for much longer. I must stress that we don't want to sign any old guy just to show we will go and sign someone. We want to make sure we sign the right riders." On the assumption that the riders might occasionally glance through the pages of the *Speedway Star* (or chat to their contemporaries), they'd be under no illusion that sunk investment costs combined with poor crowd levels had already had a deleterious impact upon the financial robustness of the Newport Speedway balance sheet. Though perhaps some ambitious riders could overlook this factor, most self-employed people would naturally incline towards clients who enjoy greater financial success or, even if they don't, might prefer to sign up for those that don't advertise this fact.

By the next week's *Speedway Star*, financial news that had been comparatively buried in the team news section of the magazine suddenly splashes all over page 2 under the headline "Desperate times for Wasps". Using an inappropriately smiling photo of Nicky Mallett, the article left some observers with the feeling that Mel Brooks's *Blazing Saddles* provides the role model for his public comments. [1] As only 300 people had come along to see the Wasps triumph 50-40 in the Premier League over the equally hapless Glasgow Tigers, Nicky's downcast at the ongoing poor return from an investment rumoured to be in the region of £200,000. "The destiny of Newport Speedway is in the hand of the supporters now. If they can't come back, we're going to seriously going to have review ourselves in eight weeks time as to whether we continue or not ... We're not going to continue putting

[1] In the famous scene from *Blazing Saddles* when the Johnsons load their guns and point them at Bart, he immediately points his own pistol at his head and exclaims in a low voice, "Hold it! Next man makes a move, the [person of colour] gets it!"

money into the club, only to find that when the fans become disillusioned, we haven't got any left." Though the National League racing attracts 500 people and is 'profitable' on its lower cost base, it fails to alter the brute reality of a situation where the club is "losing money in the Premier and can't just survive on making money on one and not the other. It's not off-setting our losses enough and the reality is that unless we have more fans, the club will go. I'll have to review what I'm going to do in eight weeks time and if the fans want speedway in Newport, they must come and support it."

Outside the brightly painted yellow terrapin hut blazoned with both Newport Wasps and Newport Hornets logos that serves as the club trackshop, Mike Golding and his partner Anita Lewis erect some green garden furniture. Away from a speedway track this would be described as a gazebo. It's hot work putting up this structure in bright Welsh sunshine, let alone setting out the merchandise, but later the roof will, at least, provide some welcome shade. Basic economics dictates that if crowd numbers fall then business at the trackshop will suffer similarly, if not more so. "The last five weeks, it's been terrible here! The Hornets have had good crowds. There were 600 or so on Friday and that's good 'cause costs are lower in the National League but announcements in the *Star* by Nick that the club might close if things don't pick up isn't the way to go or good for trackshop business! Anita invested in 15 grands' worth of stock but, after replenishment, she's still got 10 grands' worth left. People aren't going to buy a £40 or £50 jacket if they think we're going to close! You're here but [fellow stallholders] Pawel Ruszkiewicz and John [Devon Shirts] haven't turned up yet. Nick and Steve don't talk to each other so who know if they'll come?"

There are still plenty of familiar faces at the track albeit, since the turnstiles are closed, they're mainly the track staff. According to the programme, Peter Brookes is in charge of race-day maintenance but he's keener to enthuse about the quality of the track prepared for the Cardiff Speedway Grand Prix yesterday. "It was a great track, wasn't it? Ole brought five of his staff and the road blade! They had to do something as this is the ninth year and they've had eight years rough tracks – so it couldn't go on!" Smiling club incident recorder Gavin Morrison nods his agreement, "Neil Street was saying that Philip Rising said it was only 500 down on last year which is amazing in a recession! They had the top shale from Denmark [and Derbyshire] and that did the trick!" When the turnstiles open, Scunthorpe track photographer Steve Dixon also has strong opinions on the event. "Andersen should have been excluded! He knew he wasn't anywhere near and felt Bomber behind him and fell off. Still the ref had a shocking meeting! Were you there for the start? One of the 10-year-olds who'd come all the way to the Millennium got excluded when he touched the tapes! What's that about? How ridiculous! They stopped any further racing when another 10-year-old broke his face." [2]

Diehard Newport fan Mark Poulton is also one of the early arrivals, "We walked into the Millennium after the meeting and thought we'd see how far we could get and got right to the track. It was rock hard!" Mark's keen to praise Newport's National League New Zealand star Grant Tregoning. "He's got a wonderful style – very smooth! He's also a very clever rider. He looks for the right line to pass. If someone's riding a bit wild, he bides his time and weighs things up before he passes! He reminds me of Leigh Adams. He's good enough to ride in the Premier League but, because of his permit/visa, he can only ride in the National League and at open meetings, like today. On Friday we saw a new Swede – Jonas Andersson – who did about 20 laps with Steve Mallett watching from the centre green. He looked excellent and they say we might sign him to pick things up or maybe Krzysztof Stojanowski who, they say, just needs to be settled. I'm sure they'd let him park his caravan here if he wanted!" Stood on the home straight savouring the atmosphere of the Newport version of the traditional rider parade is Mariusz Dubielewicz originally from Bydgoszcz (but now living in Germany for the past 10 years) who's presently on a tour that will see him take in 19 or 20 British speedway tracks in almost as many days. "It's my old dream for 20 years! For the last three years very real

[2] Steve Casey writing in his "Anoraknaphobia"' column in *Vue* – the official raceday magazine of the Belle Vue Aces – summarises his reaction to the pre-meeting entertainment. "The terrific innovation introduced to the event is allowing eight young (or very young) riders to have a ride in a couple of races before the main event. I will set the scene for you, imagine you are a young kid who has been granted the honour of having ONE ride in the biggest event on the speedway calendar. You are a touch nervous, but you are holding it together, it is early, an hour and a half before the main event. The crowd is ONLY about 20,000 people. You line up for your race ... the referee holds the tapes a fraction too long ... and BANG ... you move at the start and you just brush the tapes. If it's your call, what would YOU do? If I was the referee I would order a re-start with all four riders. After all, it is an "exhibition" race, if I was feeling particularly mean-spirited; I may have even given everyone a warning about keeping still at the tapes. If I am FIM referee Frank Ziegler, a man totally opposed to the concept of "all four back", I disqualify the "offender" and order a re-start with THREE RIDERS ONLY. After all, a rider with so much experience should know better, especially as he is all of TEN years old and that is what the compassionate Mr Ziegler did."

and, two years ago, I changed my money for pounds at not so good exchange value. I went to Plymouth two years ago and there I see Tai Woffinden for the first time and also Josh Auty who, I thought, would be just as good. But not so. Now at Sheffield, he better. I think Eastbourne's short and sharp corners. I like not so big tracks. More technical, drive not full power like Poland!" Speedway obsessive Steve Miles is also in the stadium after his trip to the Millennium last night. When Hans Andersen came out on Emil Sayfutdinov 's bike – with little on-track excitement to speak of – the Sky commentary team apparently made a mountain out of that particular molehill. "I got a text last night to say they were saying on Sky that we were ganging up on the Brits again! I don't think so. They don't need it! It was good last night but I'd love it if it went back to a one-off final! In a proper stadium, not Norden or Pocking but somewhere where they could get 40 or 50,000. Everyone would go! Imagine the atmosphere? It would have to be a proper track as temporary ones are no good really." Steve's partner Sarah shares programme duties with Steve at Peterborough although this news isn't widely known. "I'm the co-editor of the Peterborough programme but I'll let you off not knowing that as they often forget that at Peterborough too!"

Mariusz Dubielewicz

Never short of insight, Bob Tasker doesn't disappoint, "I'm pleased Jason Crump won. He was head and shoulders above the rest. It would have been a travesty if he hadn't – it was man against boys! And before Andrew Dolby tells you, I didn't make a 9-year-old girl cry, though I did shout 'Hit him, Emil'. We saw it again later on the telly back at the hotel and it was a lot funnier! Scott seemed to be upset about the way Emil rode. I couldn't see anything wrong with it myself. Scott fights like a girl and kept battering away while Emil has got a bit about him and looked like he'd done that before, judged by the couple of punches he threw before he was dragged off. If you punch up and under the helmet, you can get the chin and he certainly knew that. That upset Scott, he should try it with Michal Makovsky buzzing on his tail, he wouldn't be looking for a fight – he'd be looking for the keys for his van!" For one night each season Cardiff is a speedway Mecca. Sadly, awareness levels about the sport in the principality isn't quite what it should be, "When I checked into the Hilton on Friday night the woman behind the desk said 'Are you here for the speedway? We have some leaflets for Newport but many people don't know 'cause it ain't in the local paper enough'."

Under orders

Rumour has it that this is the 21st staging of the Welsh Open and over the public address system we're told that the exotically named Shelby Rutherford will replace Paul Fry. Unusually for a speedway meeting, this is the only change to the racecard inside the centre of the programme. Newport team manager, Laurence Rogers, is disappointed that the fans won't enjoy sight of this seasoned rider. "Paul Fry has reported in ill – that's a shame because he's a previous winner". Mike Golding takes a wry view of this illness. There's a good-sized crowd in the stadium to see this afternoon's meeting filled with "international riders". This could lead you to the conclusion that local fans prefer individual events to four team tournaments and might even be a reasonable analysis, except that crowds here on the Sunday after Cardiff traditionally are traditionally swollen by attendees from elsewhere who've been drawn to South Wales for the weekend. The meeting doesn't get underway at the scheduled start time. We're advised that there will be "a slight meeting delay for Mark Lemon's return from France." This could be a big delay!

Race action

Luckily they're definitely not still en route since Mark's wife Emma is already sat in the home-straight grandstand alongside Debbie Hancock from Somerset. Emma is keen to emphasise, "It makes it sound like he's been on holiday when he's been working!" Anticipation levels build up yet further when the two-minute warning is unofficially extended to allow Shelby Rutherford extra time to get to the line. Unfortunately when he gets there, the other riders immediately leave him behind (soon by some considerable distance). Mark Lemon wins though a rather stylish-looking Jonas Andersson follows him home. The Swede looks comfortable on a bike and is sufficiently modish to draw approving glances. Personally I'm rather taken with the epaulettes on his kevlars that simply state "Mamma & Pappa". No sooner has the first race finished than there's a brief break for the track to be watered!

During this delay in the race action, I nip to the back of the home-straight grandstand and open the door of the referee-cum-announcer's box without knocking. My presumption is quickly highlighted when the announcer barks out in Aussie strine, "Did you knock? Oh! Well go out and try that again please!" It's difficult to establish whether this is supposedly humorous or, as I suspect, some sort of schoolteacherish power trip. Either way, I go back out and knock theatrically on the door to wait for permission to enter the hallowed portals. "Come in! That was better, wasn't it!? [laughs] Have you written a book before?" I reassure him that I have and referee Stuart Wilson kindly interjects, "They're a damn good read!"

Back at my stall I check with Mike and Anita at the trackshop who on earth this person is? Anita identifies him as Shane Child ("used to be Craig Watson's mechanic") while Mike provides further detail. "'Motormouth' Shane, you mean – he's the one on last year's [Sky Sports] GP adverts shouting and everything!" Though it would be fair to say that the television adverts for the 2008 Speedway Grand Prix were a huge improvement upon some of the previous homoerotic artistic attempts, they were misleadingly trailed in the press as featuring the "honest" opinions of genuine speedway lovers selected as a result of their collective enthusiasm. Spun as representing the authentic "voice of the speedway fan", they're clearly as authentic as a Ploughman's Lunch. The star of these adverts was, indeed, an irksomely shouty, overconfident Australian who excitedly suggests we rush along to be amazed almost to orgasm at the brilliance of the on-track action. Clearly BSI liked the hysterical hyperbole of this approach so much they repeated it *ad nauseam*. Its hectoring enthusiasm was quite an irritant but, to be fair to him even though he's clearly a presenter rather than a fan, speaking as I found, all afternoon Shane's interjections added to the entertainment provided at the 2009 Welsh Open.

Shane Parker, President of the Speedway Riders' Association has wondered many times why every track in Britain doesn't have an air-fence. Newport Speedway now has the said safety furniture and throughout the meeting it gets a full and repeated test of its capabilities. On the first lap of heat 5 Sam Hurst (meeting reserve replacing Selby Rutherford – who has mechanical difficulties in the pits – replacing Paul Fry) tests the second-bend air-fence. Stood in the shade of his gazebo trackshop stall, Mike Golding looks on approvingly with proprietorial pride. "He's okay thanks to the air-fence. It tends to happen in afternoon meetings. I don't like them! It gets dusty, they take longer thinking they have all afternoon and people get bored! You should always push speedway meetings through not drag them out. It's quite an even field, there are five or six riders who could win it. Best to get an ice cream early as he tends to sell out!" One of the fancied riders in the field, Ryan Fisher, wins the rerun of Heat 5 by a street. Over the tannoy, "Motormouth" Shane lets us know about "A quick little break while we replace the air-fence on bend two". When heat 6 does eventually get underway, it soon becomes the third race to be awarded this afternoon by referee Stuart Wilson, after Ricky Ashworth hits the bend-four air-fence on his last lap when placed third. Ricky must've encountered a black cat on the way to the stadium because it was his painful-looking fall in the third heat that prompted that race to be awarded.

Another factor on a warm afternoon is the increased dust level. Moments after the riders race past us on each lap of every race – as if on a time delay – large eddies of dust billow in the direction of travel of the riders. Track staff regularly water the track but it makes no difference. [3] There's a further delay while the paramedic treats Ricky

[3] Speedway Control Board consultant track inspector Colin Meredith would comment during the close season in the *Speedway Star*. "The base is so important, if the base will absorb water then you can get a good track. If the base is rock hard, like at Newport – which is laid on a local product called slag – if you get four inches of material on the top, when it gets wet, the bike penetrates that four inches and the bikes just take it straight away... The whole problem at Newport is the base is wrong; it's like laying it on tarmac. Of course, when it's dry people say 'There are black tyre marks', but it's actually black slag that's rock hard and nothing will stick to it."

Ashworth in the pits. To pass the time "Motormouth" Shane entertains us with a programme alteration, "There's a typo in the programme for heat 10 – Leigh Lanham is number 5 not Krzysztof Stojanowski. This is now a collector's item 'cause there's an error in the programme!" if only! While we await the restart of the on-track action, off-duty speedway rider Luke Priest arrives with his friends just in time to see one of the numerous track grades of the afternoon. They're in party mood. Joining in the fun, Luke wears a brightly coloured pair of slightly oversized sunglasses with one eyeshade missing. On the subject of making a mess of my programme Krzysztof Stojanowski (whose name is so big it can only appear as "Krzysztof Stojan" for every programmed race he appears in during the meeting) falls at the start of the second lap of heat 9. Prematurely, I decide that his fall will merit his disqualification but Stuart Wilson instead excludes Sam Hurst. The rerun signals that this definitely won't be Lubos Tomicek's afternoon. Prior to heat 9, he'd only amassed 2 points but easily led the original running of the race until it stopped. A speedway's version of Sod's Law then immediately applies and, as a consequence, Lubos finishes third in the three rider rerun. The next race sees a very stylish looking Jonas Andersson win his first competitive heat at Hayley Stadium to provide the Newport fans inside the stadium with some renewed optimism about how the remainder of their Premier League season might pan out (if he decides to sign for the club). Ricky Ashworth's injuries prove too painful for him to continue and he withdraws from the rest of the meeting. The first 12 races (and track grades) of the afternoon take 105 minutes to complete and during the interval, "Motormouth" Shane makes a plaintive announcement over the public address system, "If you sponsored a heat you can come to Race Control and pay your sponsorship money!"

My stall attracts little interest though a photogenic speedway couple Barry and Alison Axtell linger long enough for us all to notice the "Made in Wales" T-shirt that just about covers her pregnant tummy. Given her North American accent, it's safe to say the T-shirt is travel memorabilia rather than a statement of fact. Other fans stop by to grumble about either the dust levels or the length of time the meeting takes to run. When the action resumes, heat 13 passes off without incident only for heat 14 to become a collector's item in terms of the sheer number of reruns required to complete it. Styled beforehand by some fans around me as the "race of death" because it features many of the leading riders (with the exception of Mark Lemon), it should be both a treat and a competitive contest. So it proves first time out when a three-rider sandwich of Fisher, Frampton and Doolan arrive en masse into the first bend to ensure carnage ensues. Jordan Frampton lays down, Kevin Doolan rides over him and Ryan Fisher glides into the mêlée as he too tries to lay his bike down. Ruled an unsatisfactory start by referee Stuart Wilson, "Motormouth" Shane wistfully ponders, "If only referee Stuart Wilson was on the button last night. Ha! Ha!" Before the race can be rerun there's a slight delay that Shane explains for us, "Jordan lost his steel shoe in that incident so the riders will have to get redressed and clean out their bikes!" When the rerun gets underway, it only lasts until the yellow-helmeted Kevin Doolan lays down his machine and this time the closely following red-helmeted Jonas Andersson runs over him. To the amazement of pretty well everyone within the stadium (and to loud objections from the home-straight grandstand) Stuart Wilson decides to disqualify Jonas Andersson. Back in the pits mystification levels are similar to that on the terraces. Afterwards Paul Burbidge would recall, "I think that was the worst decision I've seen this season and I see a lot of speedway! Laurence Rogers rang up – and he didn't have to – and said 'Are you sure about that?' There were lots of puzzled looks in the pits". Grant Tregoning's mechanic Erwin Tree also comments later, "They say Kevin Doolan said he T-boned him but how could Jonas do that from the outside?" The next instalment-cum-rerun of the race ends when Jordan Frampton finds himself in the first-bend air-fence and, once again, all three riders get called back for the next rerun. Further indication that the gods are keen to see Kevin Doolan's name etched on the trophy arrives when he falls on the second bend and, in a less than subliminal suggestion to the referee, proceeds to stand around with his hands on his hips until the decision to again invite all three riders back for a rerun is taken. Margaret Vardy's partner Steve Davies expresses surprise, "God! All three!" Bob Tasker smirks, "I think Kevin Doolan is trying to collect the shale in his kevlars to take back to Workington!" At the fifth time of asking the race starts and even manages to run to its conclusion – Ryan Fisher wins to record his fourth victory in four races. As Grant Tregoning passes with his mechanic Erwin, I enquire whether he's enjoying the step up that his participation this afternoon represents. "No, not really! I'm not making any starts. On Friday, I didn't make any starts but won all the races anyway! Today, it's totally different!"

Meeting reserve Sam Hurst takes his fourth ride of the afternoon in heat 17 and wins his first point of the afternoon with a third place finish in a race of only three riders (because of the withdrawal of Ricky Ashworth). Though he appears under-powered compared to his more illustrious rivals, until they exit the second bend Sam finds himself alongside Chris Schramm. The youngster has a distinctive riding style that apparently requires him to make repeated micro adjustments to his racing line via his handlebars in each and every corner. His baker's dozen of micro adjustments are supplemented by a peculiar bobbling movement of his head that veers towards involuntary jerks as if it's somehow connected on string to his handlebars. As he races down the straight, his excessive handlebar movement diminishes until the next bend when Sam resumes moving his handlebars nineteen to the dozen as if they're electrified and he has to hold them with wet hands. Grant Tregoning finally gates to his satisfaction and actually wins heat 18 after he holds off the close attentions of Lubos Tomicek. Afterwards he does a modest victory lap that's led out by an enthusiastically wheelying Jonas Andersson who's extremely keen to celebrate his own third place (for a final points total of 8). Heat 19 is a clash of the undefeated maximum men, Mark Lemon and Ryan Fisher. Sadly the race effectively ends as a contest when Mark fishtails to the first corner and, consequently, remains second throughout the race. The last race of the afternoon is the grand final sponsored by "Anonymous in Memory of Tim Stone". Given that it took five times to run heat 14 where Kevin Doolan found himself on the deck three times, it's hardly a surprise when he races away to win. Kevin, thereby, adds the Welsh Open Trophy to the Prince of Wales Trophy he won at the Hayley Stadium season opener on 15th March. It's a haul only a burglar could match. Maximum man Ryan Fisher finishes second while the other podium place goes to Jordan Frampton (after Mark Lemon completely fails to gate). Still, as they say, shale happens!

28th June – Welsh Open Championship Winner: Kevin Doolan

CHAPTER 10

King's Lynn

"You can have anything you like to drink so long as it comes out of the fridge!"

1st July

The highlight of my journey to King's Lynn on a gloriously hot summer's day is the sight of four police Mercedes cars as they zoom past me in quick succession on the M23 apparently involved in a high-speed chase with a vehicle I don't see. When I finally pull up next to the ski chalet-like hut that serves as the trackshop at the Norfolk Arena, my car temperature gauge tells me that it's 31 degrees centigrade with only a couple of hours to go before the meeting starts. There's a hint of a cooling breeze but, given that he's just helped unload the stock from the van with Phil Hilton, Johnny Barber is bathed in sweat, "You've arrived here on a momentous evening [theatrical pause] there's a Brit in the semi-final of Wimbledon!" Phil should be on holiday in Australia but he's had to make an emergency return after his 77-year-old father was found dead a few days ago. His words remain stoically philosophical but his expression tells a different story.

High up in the referee's box that provides a panoramic view over the track, the stadium and surrounding area (mainly fields and some industrial buildings), Nathan Hollands and his pregnant wife Cheri work together as an efficient team to ensure that the electronic scoreboard contains the correct information about tonight's meeting. Nathan reads out the rider names for each heat while Cheri enters them onto a laptop. The King's Lynn rider whose name is on everyone's lips this season is that of young gifted Australian, Darcy Ward. Nathan and Cheri visited his family when they were on honeymoon in Australia. Nathan has the devil in him, "You should ask Darcy what he can cook?"
[Cheri] "When we went to their house in Oz his dad said 'you can have anything you like to drink so long as it comes out of the fridge!' Darcy claimed he could boil a kettle but was going to fill it up with hot water! Then he said 'I can get the milk'."
[Nathan] "He can't even do toast [in the UK] mainly 'cause the toaster is different to his mum's!"
[Cheri] "I said, 'I'll teach you how to cook when you're over' and he said 'No thanks – I'll cycle round to yours to eat'."
[Nathan] "He can find McDonald's! And now he's just about to start his driving lessons, he'll be able to drive there soon."

Sadly Britain's second youngest promoter Jonathan Chapman is away at a Lenny Kravitz concert at the Brixton Academy. Johnny Barber has already taken the mickey out of Jonathan's musical taste, "He said, 'It's the only place to watch gigs' and I said 'you do know you're not black Jonathan, don't you?' He thinks he is!" Though he has now found success under his real name, Lenny originally adopted the stage name of Romeo Blue and performed with straightened hair and blue contact lenses! It was a look that the hot chick Lisa Bonet (aka Denise Huxtable from *The Cosby Show*) found attractive enough to elope with him to marry in Las Vegas in 1987. They had a daughter, Zoë Isabella in 1988, and divorced in 1993. I'd always half suspected that Jonathan was probably a boy band or heavy metal fan so it's a quite surprise to learn that he likes the comparatively retro musical style of multi-instrumentalist Lenny Kravitz. Though often multi-coloured, perhaps Jonathan's big hair is an unconscious echo of one of his musical heroes? Albeit without the pre-Raphaelite curls of Lenny's luxuriant early era hairstyle. Like Lenny Kravitz, King's Lynn speedway serve up a high quality product on a regular basis and also employ Mike Bennett as their race night presenter. Though he has an extensive list of duties, Nathan drops by the trackshop to check that everything's alright and disappoints me with the news, "Mike Bennett might not be here tonight. He picks his meetings – I reckon it'll be Kevin Moore." Everyone in the trackshop is crestfallen at this turn of events. Phil comments, "A few years ago Mike Bennett had to miss the Ashley Jones Memorial and he said 'I can't be here but if anyone has a helicopter I'd be happy to fly down from Scotland' – that's the best one I've heard!"

[Johnny] "When your first book came out Mike Bennett used to complain over the mic he wasn't in it and then, when your next one came out, he complained he was! One night Tracey [his wife] came into the shop and said, 'Is that Jeff Scott's book? Can I have a look?' I showed her the King's Lynn chapter and she read it with a slight smirk and then said with a glint in her eye, 'I dunno why he's upset, people have said far worse'!"
My latest book *Quantum of Shale* is available for purchase in the trackshop tonight but Mike Moseley isn't impressed. "I don't read crap like that!"
[Johnny] "Neither does Derek Barclay if the British Speedway Forum is to be believed!"

Continuing his tradition of initially excoriating my written work without reading it, Derek Barclay posts as his alter ego 'Parsloes 1928 nearly' and launches a one-man campaign to publicise my work. Derek appears to have more arguments with a wider range of British Speedway Forum posters than pretty well anyone else who contributes there. He bathes some riders, teams and meetings in the warm light of nostalgia, whereas others are subject to showers of leaden irony or vitriol. Never one to stint on the emoticons, Parsloes 1928 sometimes writes in the manner of someone chooching at home. His team allegiances change with dizzying speed and regularity. His more outlandish claims often get deleted when self-censorship (or complaint) dictates. Back in the real world away from the imaginary Internet world of the British Speedway Forum, there has been much talk about the increasing prevalence of topless or almost naked speedway rider photographs. The Red Nose Day Newport team photograph set the standard while at King's Lynn, not to be outdone, they have a photo of a topless Chris Schramm that has proved quite popular. Johnny is keen to highlight some key pictorial differences, "Does the Newport one have a rider holding a banana though?" Unusually for a speedway rider or, even young people generally, Chris doesn't appear to have a tattoo. Talk of tattoos inevitably takes our conversation to Amanda Buckley-Taylor's distinctive Scott Nicholls horseshoe tattoo (pictured in *Quantum of Shale*). Johnny recalls, "Amanda had a tattoo of Savalas Clouting's face done on her back and when she showed it to me I asked her 'Why have you got Severiano Ballesteros on your back?'" All this talk of tattoos and topless photographs prompts Mike Moseley to pose, with one of the over-ripe bananas he eats for medicinal purposes, in the manner of Chris Schramm. It could be a weird case of life imitating art but, thankfully, Mike doesn't expose his own untattooed torso!

Over the last three years prior to each King's Lynn meeting Johnny and Mike amuse themselves with their prediction of the scoreline ("presently it's 1-0 to Johnny").
[Mike] "I'm going for 64-28."
[Johnny] "I reckon Tommy '2-laps' Allen is the key so I'm going for 59-33."

Outside the warm confines of the trackshop, my stall is bathed in early evening sunshine. One of the early arrivals through the turnstiles is Alan Burge who wants to buy a copy of my latest book but only after, in OCD fashion, he checks the whole box for what he deems to be the perfect copy. Last year he attempted to bring a copy back for what he identified as its wrinkled paper. My stall is clearly visible from the turnstiles and I'm located like a thorn between roses with the ladies on the programme stall one side and, on the other, Julie Neal and her daughter who run a fundraising raffle for Kozza Smith. Always in search of innovation or improvement, Jonathan Chapman has pushed the envelope of programme design with his 2009 version of the King's Lynn programme. On its front cover, the moniker "Official Matchday Race-Zine" announces a document printed in four colour that's sold at a bargain price of £1. Costs are held down since it's basically an A3 sheet of glossy paper folded twice to achieve the traditional A5 speedway programme format. Nonetheless, it contains all the information that you're likely to need but, proving that you definitely can't keep all of the people happy all of the time, it has attracted complaints in some quarters as a "rip-off". I can't quite see the basis of this complaint but, like beauty, the serviceability and quality of speedway programmes remains in the eye of the beholder. When I arrived at the pits gate promoter and club owner Buster Chapman expresses some astonishment at my arrival ("What are you doing here?"). In his promoter's notes column in the Race-Zine, Buster notes, "It is great to welcome Jeff Scott here tonight who is promoting his new book *Quantum of Shale*, it has a few funny stories about our club and I would encourage you to get a copy here tonight." Johnny Barber has some sympathy, "I was speaking to Steve Miles and he said he writes the Mick Bratley bit in the programme. I was totally disillusioned; next he'll tell me Santa doesn't exist!"

This is the third week that Julie Neal has stood by the trackshop to sell raffle tickets priced at £2 each or three for £5. There are five attractive prizes. The keynote prize is a 140cc miniature pit bike, while second prize is an autographed framed painting, third prize a signed Kozza hoodie, fourth is a signed Kozza T-shirt and the fifth and final prize is a family ticket to any King's Lynn Stars home fixture. Julie is "good friends with Kozza". His devil-may-care racing style attracts plaudits but it also attracts injuries. Julie feels great sympathy for Kozza, partly because he's a long way from home but also because he's unable to ride and earn money. "He always grabs us if he needs help!" Kozza suffered an early season injury whilst riding as a doubling up rider for Ipswich but is back in the side tonight. Julie lives in Ely and, as you'd expect, is a loyal King's Lynn fan, "I've been coming 20-odd years. With us it's very social, my family come and all my friends I've made over those years." She looks too young to have such a grown-up daughter, "How my daughter loves it if I can't come. When you have an interest, then you get excited about it and want to come all the time." I ask about the riders Julie admires, "Mark Loram was always my favourite and Tony Rickardsson, of course! I used to go to World finals to see him ride. I'm pleased to see Andrew Silver back – he's riding tonight." The big question is when will the big draw take place? "I think next week Kozza's going to draw it. He can't make decisions so he could go to the end of the season!" Though more people buy raffle tickets than take an interest in my books, I still wonder if Julie should shout to attract more attention. "Nah! I just assume most people know we're here now." Visiting Rye House fans won't know about the raffle, though photographer Phil Hilton suspects that they won't travel in significant numbers. "I don't reckon many Rye fans will come as they always get stuffed by 60 odd! Then, most teams do here so that's nothing new!"

Chris Schramm & banana

Julie Neal

If it's not about speedway then the talk in the trackshop is often about medicine. Mike Moseley casually mentions, "I have to have another operation [pause] on me ears!"
[Jeff] "Pardon?"
[Mike] "I have to have another operation on me ears. When I'm working in the shop on my own I have to have a sign."
True to his word, Mike casually pulls out a torn piece of cardboard with a black felt-tipped written sign. He must be charged by the word, judged by its brevity. It also must be designed for trackshop visitors who have English as a second language: "I have hearing difficulty". Mike wonders if he might soon add back trouble to his list of ailments, "I'm not even going to start telling you about my bad back problems at this moment in time, caused no doubt by me humping boxes whilst 'The Lord' remains seated dishing out his orders!" On the drive to Norfolk, Radio 4's excellent *Thinking Allowed* programme highlights that many modern doctors are depressed by their inability to diagnose many of their patients' ailments. Most people go to the surgery expecting a magical solution when, unfortunately, they often happen to have Medically Unexplained Symptoms (MUS) – pronounced "Moose" – that their doctors are unable to explain and/or treat. The definition of action in modern medical practice is patient diagnosis since this then determines the treatment and the allocation of resources. Patients regularly present with problems the doctors can't identify and, as a result, the doctors often suffer anger, disenchantment and feelings of hopelessness. The doctors' inability to "solve" the problem often causes them to end up resenting the patients! If Mike has problems with his ears he definitely doesn't have problems with his eyesight, "Oh look who's just walked in! Ha! Ha!" As Mike Bennett strides through the turnstiles, Johnny Barber's gleeful, "Your wish has been granted!" It is indeed

Mike Moseley. Pardon?

the Great Man, the presenter some call the Sultan of Cheese. When Mike comperes Super7even events he wears a bright red jacket that gives him the look that Bela Lugosi might have if he were a Butlins' Redcoat. However, since this is merely a run-of-the-mill Premier League fixture staged on a hot evening, Mike has no need to burnish his presentational credentials, so favours his more casual jacketless rent collection officer look.

Mike quickly springs into verbal action. After he's made a few introductory comments over the loudspeaker system about the excitement he suggests we should all feel about tonight's contest, he goes walkabout and ventures over to our area. Mike enthuses stiltedly about the drinks available in the bar, the culinary delights of the Pit Stop café, the availability of Race-Zines and the weekly raffle before he lingers next to Julie Neal and her daughter. Bathed in sunshine, Mike's in priapic mood. "There's some sexy ladies down here by the trackshop so come and see the girls who'll sell you some tickets! The more tickets you buy the more you can win." Mike studiously avoids any mention of my attendance but describes at length some of the goodies on sale in the trackshop. As he walks off microphone in hand towards the centre green, it's difficult to decide if Mike is presenting or merely voicing his thoughts aloud, "sex, beer, speedway – have I forgotten something?" Though it's highly unlikely Mike really influences purchase decisions within the stadium, professionalism (and his job description) should have prompted some mention of my stall. Shortly afterwards Nathan Hollands stops to apologise for his behaviour. "I asked Mike Bennett to announce you and he said 'I'm not frickin' going too – we've had a fall out!' So I said, 'That's alright then, we won't pay you!' 'What do you mean?' he wanted to know. Don't worry I'll get someone else to mention that you're here."

Bryn Williams temporarily escapes the smoke-free confines of the referee's box to relieve his gasping lungs with a cigarette or three. Bryn tells me I'm lucky to be here and catch Mike Bennett since he's going over to Oz for three weeks, "He's going out there to establish his business. Mike will enjoy Oz 'cause they can spot bullshit a mile off!" In order to find out what obscure businesses located in the far-flung corner of the earth might require Mike Bennett's media training advice, I look up his rather magnificent Media Answers ("Managing the media – protecting your reputation") website. Based on the evidence of my ears after many visits to the Norfolk Arena, people could form the expectation that Mike's proven expertise dictates that he will train his clients to listen poorly, love the sound of their own voice, make wildly inaccurate predictions, get basic facts wrong while generally speaking with any interviewee (or to the audience) in a condescending or hectoring manner. Having set the expectations so low, it's a surprise to find that the website looks professional and appears to actually offer useful media advice. The home page of the website (www.mediaanswers.co.uk) inevitably features the main man himself as he floats above what appears to be some obscure regional airport with international pretensions, possibly Norwich or Southampton. From a sartorial point of view, with his three-button jacket, Mike looks like he's dressed for a funeral or, possibly, a second interview at an old-fashioned gentleman's outfitters. The introductory message from Mike – the exotically titled "Director of Media Answers" – is almost impossible to resist. Indeed, Mike makes a surprisingly cogent case for employing his business expertise. Albeit one slightly undermined by the lingering perception that he couches his message in way that suggests he feels his target audience might be handicapped with English as a third language (with a propensity to be slow on the uptake, dazzled by the technology involved or bamboozled by the rather straightforward concept of a media interview). Mike breathlessly talks about the complex menu of media training available for Media Answers clients as well as the various exercises that necessarily involves. Ostensibly under the impression that cameras are a relatively recent discovery, Mike informs us he's been "filming since way back in 1992!" Client training involves the emergent camera technology, doorstep interviews ("the most common type of interview") and, if you agree to hire Media Answers services, they'll kindly "recreate a media crush". Mike's accent is a little hard to understand so I'm not clear whether there's going to be a crush of people or fruit, a crash or exactly what? Possibly pitched towards repressive countries where they don't really have a sophisticated media, potential training purchasers and participants get lured in with the idea that they will get to practise a mock radio station interview ("radio is something we feel very comfortable with"). Once these trainees in far-flung corners of the world have developed in media management confidence, they'll be offered the wonderful opportunity of "sitting at the top table" being interviewed by their colleagues, involved in a "mock television" interview or, even more thrillingly, a "down the line interview". If I'd had the good fortune to have taken and graduated from his enthralling Media Answers training courses, then all Mike's schooling in the tricks and tips of the media interview trade would have been sadly wasted if I then encounter someone as petulant as Mike has been tonight. Then again, maybe this training is so comprehensive it covers how to deal with interviewers who refuse to conduct an interview or pass on basic information? Perhaps, media skill and success is really dictated by who you know rather than how Media Answers suggest you craft your approach? If that's the case, then such training isn't worth any investment since your newfound media skills and carefully crafted responses won't get revealed!

The mere suggestion of Australian sunshine or the warm glow a bottle of Bundy provides is enough to transport Bryn down memory lane. "The first time I went was in 2002 on the Lions tour organised by Graham Reeve. I'd always wanted to go so thought I might as well enjoy myself and be broke! I'd only been there three days and I agreed with the Aussie presenter that I'd wind up the crowd so I said 'You Aussie crowds don't make much noise probably 'cause you're not used to losing! You're 1-0 down so let me hear who you're rooting for!' I didn't know what that word meant out there but, from the gasp, I gathered something was up!"

On a Wednesday night during the speedway season, Johnny Barber manages the King's Lynn trackshop while his brother Nick (along with his sister Bev) run the Birmingham trackshop. The speedway press has carried news of Nick's political career and prompts a fan to speculate, "You do know that Nick Barber is a councillor? We wonder if he's going to put 100 Wulfsport jackets on his expenses!" Though the public address system can't be faulted either for its volume or clarity, Mike Bennett has surprisingly been unusually quiet but then mumbles something I don't quite catch. I turn to Mike Moseley and ask "What did he say? It's a poor track night?" Mike 'I have hearing difficulty' Moseley laughs, "NO PARADE TONIGHT! Do you want to borrow my sign?" After a prolonged bout of radio silence after his earlier sex, beer, speedway obsession, Mike effortlessly segues into his usual stream of consciousness with added bombast style of speedway presentation, "Sorry we haven't been saying anything but Rob Lyon has just been doing an interview with Sky!" Johnny Barber chortles, "It should have been Mike he means!" Gordon Brown's recent comment about David Cameron sums our collective situation up succinctly, "He has lost the art of communication but not, alas, the gift of speech!"

The Rye House 'Silver Ski' Rockets aren't the best travellers to the Norfolk Arena and their likelihood of victory is hampered still further by the absence – through injury – of Rocket number 2 Robert Mear (for whom they run rider replacement) and the highly regarded Rocket number 3 Joe Haines (for whom they have guest Carl Wilkinson). For reasons that aren't explained, the meeting gets underway 25 minutes late and, if this were tennis, Mike Bennett quickly makes his first unforced error of the evening, "Linus Sundstrum will take the rider replacement ride for Robert Mear in heat number 1 – no sorry, it will be Andrew Silver!" Actually it's Linus Sundstrum! With his wit sparkling in the early evening sunshine, Mike advises any first-time visitors in the Norfolk Arena crowd, "If you haven't been to speedway before, watch out for the red and blue helmet colours – you'll recognise them as they'll be winning all the time!" The first race of the night is the third place battle of the Linuses between the Stars Eklof and the Rockets Sundstrum. The Rockets heat leader should have taken the honours to ensure the meeting starts with a drawn heat but, unfortunately, he rears massively coming out of the second bend on the last lap and gifts Eklof the point. Up front Darcy Ward beats Chris Neath with imperious ease. Too preoccupied by the wild lands of his own internal mental landscape to listen to the race results announced by Edwin Overland, Mike Bennett continues to labour under the delusion that Andrew Silver raced in heat 1 so, as the riders idle round the track before the start of the second race, he erroneously notes, "That's very interesting, Andrew Silver looks very lively! He'll have sussed out the track by now." Stood on the centre green it probably shouldn't be beyond the wit of his observational powers to realise that the snazzy black helmet faceguard sported by Andrew Silver was surprisingly absent the first race. To the disappointment of the limited number of Rockets fans within the stadium and, of course, glamorous Kozza Smith fundraiser Julie Neal, Andrew Silver's reappearance at the Norfolk Arena lasts only two laps before he retires. During the latter stages of the race a paraglider noisily buzzes overhead. Mike Bennett foregoes his traditional unnecessary and irksome last lap commentary in order to free-associate, "We're being spied on!" Back in the trackshop Johnny Barber wonders if we've just seen the transport of the future for the King's Lynn presenter, "That's the ideal thing to get Mike down from Scotland!" The star of page 132 of *Quantum of Shale*, Michael Slattery gets name checked over the loudspeaker system, "We must say hello to one of speedway's biggest fans, Michael Slattery, a charming, charming young man!"

There's a slight break in proceedings that gifts Mike Bennett the opportunity to chunter down memory lane, "I was watching some old videos from the 60s and 70s – Ivan Mauger used to win everything! Happy days!" Talk of speedway nostalgia allows Mike to effortlessly segue into one of his favourite preoccupations – ruthless self-promotion of the King's Lynn DVDs that another company he owns produces for dedicated King's Lynn fans and insomniacs everywhere.

Scuttling from one task to another on race night, Cheryl Chapman offers a few brief words on the present financial state of British speedway. "We're holding our own in the Premier League crowd-wise but the National League only gets 200. It's lucky we own our own stadium! It's supposed to bring the youngsters through but we seem to have gone the other way!" The third race of the night features more rider difficulty on the second bend, this time for Chris Schramm who indulges in a second lap slow motion fall when placed second. Luckily, he's easily avoided by the not so closely following Rye House riders. Chris swiftly remounts to hide his embarrassment but still trails home last. The widely predicted thrashing of the Rye House Rockets doesn't look likely after three heats with the scores a comparatively close 11-7 before the next race reveals a complete lack of inclination to race from some of the competitors from Hertfordshire. Andrew Silver once again retires at the end of his second lap while Linus Sundstrum idles across the finish line in third place (at roughly 5 mph) well over half a lap behind second-placed King's Lynn Stars reserve, Jan Graversen. Demonstrating that there is more than one professional in the stadium with ready access to a microphone, Edwin Overland kindly announces my visit to promote my book.

After a slow start, one heat quickly follows another though the Rye House Rockets remain far from competitive. Their captain Chris Neath retires from heat 5 and their guest Carl Wilkinson also shows little inclination to race until, suddenly, he accelerates massively as he enters the last corner and falls. Already third, Carl suffers no loss of position and remounts to trundle home. With the scores suddenly uncompetitive at 21-9, Darcy Ward wins again imperiously. This race would have been shared but for the hash Tommy '2-laps' Allen makes of his exit from the second bend when placed third. Perched high above the racetrack, Bryn Williams briefly exits the referee's box to stand on the steps and enjoy another much-needed cigarette. "Don't do it, Bryn! I want to copyright John Barber underneath it. You can use that in your next book." If he were a Rye House fan, Johnny Barber jokes that, "he'd be feeling suicidal." Keen to provoke some interaction with the crowd, Mike Bennett solicits audience requests, "If you want to be mentioned over the mic just give the track staff a piece of paper with your name on it!" It's an offer I find difficult to resist. Desperate score lines call for tactical measures, so heat 7 sees Carl Wilkinson lines up on gate two in the black-and-white helmet colour. Sadly, like so many other riders this evening, Carl comes to grief on the second bend (on his second lap) when already trailed off in third place. This leaves Luke '747' Bowen to tootle around for third. Contradicting the collective evidence of our eyes, Mike Bennett bizarrely claims, "You can't fault that Carl Wilkinson for effort though." Johnny Barber, however, only has eyes for Luke Bowen, "I just sent my brother a text saying '747 won heat 8 – unfortunately he was in heat 7 at the time!'"

Mike Bennett conducts an interview with Chris Schramm that skilfully employs his trademark set of banal questions and, therefore, elicits no real insight. However, it does prompt Chris to speak bluntly and Mike can't help but revel in the "honesty" of these earthy comments, "For those who were offended by that [pause] tough!" Rockets team manager John Sampford quickly explores all his tactical options to send Chris Neath out on a rider replacement ride for Robert Mear in the black-and-white helmet colour for heat 8. It's a shrewd move as the visitors' diminutive captain wins the race. Unfortunately for the Rockets possible fightback, Andrew Silver finishes last. However, Andrew does put in a significantly improved performance since he actually finishes the race! When he eventually idles across the finish line considerable distance behind the rest of the field, loud ironic cheers from the home-straight grandstand greet him. Edwin Overland accentuates the positive, "Rye House have their first race winner of the night. That really deserves 6 points – which it is!" Earlier in the evening, Mike's dulcet tones had been interrupted by a loud rasping noise that thankfully temporarily drowns out the embryonic thoughts that flit across his consciousness and onto his lips. "There were more problems with the radio mic in the pits than there were with the Rockets". Just as the riders hit the last bend of heat 8, the deafening rasping noise returns to intrude over the loudspeakers and, impressively, drowns out the sound of the speedway bikes at full throttle (and Mike). The mystery sound is cack-handedly caused by Mike Bennett himself as he turns on his radio mic to pointlessly extemporise about the denouement of the race. The speedway gods continue to smile upon those inside the Norfolk Arena since these technical problems continue into heat 9 to temporarily stymie further last lap insight from Mike. If people purchase a DVD produced by Mike Bennett's company then, clearly, they already have an expectation that they'll enjoy his commentary upon the race action. However, in my experience it's an immutable law in speedway presentational circles that the more awful the presenter the greater chance that they will believe that speedway fans come to a speedway meeting in order to hear them shout banal descriptions over the roar of the bikes during the last lap of each and every race. These presenters are all of a similar age, ego and pomposity, unafraid to exhibit misguided self-confidence. There is a school of thought that says that the race action speaks for itself at a live event but this perspective definitely isn't entertained at some (nameless) tracks we've all visited!

The earlier evening disappointment of Mike Bennett's failure to interview Rye House captain, Chris Neath ("I was all set to have a word with Chris Neath") because of a rider autograph session held for young children in the pits area is finally assuaged. Jovially towering over a gaggle of children in the manner of the Child Catcher, Mike revels in the stimulation of their innocently uncritical company, "You don't want to wear out the riders [laughs] with their autograph writing!" Banter with the kiddies over, Mike then turns to the almost child-sized Chris Neath to ask, "Have you been giving the rest of the team some tips?" Chris Neath has, "Flat out is the only way to ride it! Unfortunately the track wasn't up to its usual standards early on. Usually it's super smooth but it was a bit patchy and some parts are a bit iffy! It's always the same here – you've got to attack and go flat out! It's a bit of a mental thing! Hopefully things will pick up – we're not doing well enough as a team at the moment."

Interview over, Mike strolls Fagan-like among the children, "It's a bit scary, some of the children are older than Darcy!" Trackshop helper Mike Moseley isn't impressed with the quality of the entertainment served up so far, "its sheer unadulterated crap!" Ex sports editor of the *Romford Recorder*, Peter Butcher is here to support the Rockets. A regular visitor at Lakeside, he's of the opinion, "This is the worst meeting I've seen in a decade!" However, the 2009 vintage of British speedway generally impresses him, "The product is so good this year, it's been really exciting wherever I've been!" Peter doesn't feel that the alleged shenanigans, rider average manipulation and subsequent controversy that engulfed the Poole Pirates is something that only they as club should be accused of. "For the Premier Trophy, Jason Lyons was riding at 20 mph for the first month and they went to all that trouble just to sign Manuel Hauzinger!" When the racing resumes, Darcy Ward is surprisingly beaten in heat 10. When I say beaten, that's not quite correct – more exactly, Darcy's headed home by a teammate (Linus Eklof) not a rival rider. This maximum heat advantage takes the Stars into a comfortable 23 point lead with one third of the meeting still to go. Though Chris Neath tried to rally his troops with confident-sounding inspirational talk of attacking the track and employing a positive psychology, the mere mention of possible difficulty is clearly the equivalent of a rub down with the negativity sponge for Chris himself. Indeed, he fails to gain a point in heat 11 or in his last race (heat 13). Though Chris double underlines the importance of the sport psychology, he still tries to indulge in some gamesmanship by anticipating the rise of the tapes. Unfortunately, his prediction is completely miscalculated and results in a few kangaroo jumps to ensure he finishes last.

Between races I stand optimistically by my stall before I rush up to the tall, substantial Norfolk Arena protective fence to watch the race action. While there Peter Butcher tells me "I said to Terry Russell, 'a speedway meeting should be 90 minutes or an hour and three-quarters at the most', and he looked sour and said, 'We plan to run for two hours at Swindon!'" Rockets guest rider Carl Wilkinson briefly flickers into life to win heat 12 and showcase the form that probably influenced Rye House to book him in the first place. Prior to heat 13, Peter Butcher updates me on a star performer of this season's Premier League, "Ty Proctor beat Darcy Ward twice round here!" Unfortunately for the Rockets, they have to take on the powerhouse Ward/Topinka partnership with Chris Neath and Linus Sundstrum. Before the tapes rise, there's positive news for the Rockets – when Stars reserve Kozza Smith replaces Darcy Ward. Peter shakes his head, "They're just taking the piss now!" Linus Sundstrum gates with alacrity to temporarily find himself alongside the King's Lynn riders until they exit the second bend. Tomas Topinka leads with such ease that he pulls wheelies down the home straight on laps two, three and four! Though Sundstrum gates with great speed, Chris Neath continues to be affected by the shale equivalent of the yips. Once again, his search for fractional advantage led to another bodged attempt to anticipate the rise of the tapes and another immediate relegation to the rear of the race. Peter applauds the fact that Tomas Topinka (though the weakness of his rivals left him with no choice) aggressively goes for the race win unlike some other riders who seek to massage their averages. "This nonsense with bonus points not counting in the averages [on the green sheets] is ridiculous. I've seen Tai Woffinden shut off about five times this season to let his partner win!" The penultimate race of the night should feature the Rockets Andrew Silver but mysteriously he fails to appear at the tapes and finds himself disqualified under the two-minute time allowance by referee Paul Carrington. Though he has rode in three races, Andrew's only completed eight laps! Nonetheless, Peter predicts a bright future, "Andrew Silver is a wealthy man and I reckon Len's getting him involved to take over from him!" Tommy Allen replaces Andrew and takes the speedway equivalent of the bronze when he finishes third. Luke '747' Bowen falls heavily on the last corner. It's a sight that prompts Mike Bennett to confirm what we've all just seen, "That was a very awkward fall!"

Since Mike Bennett started his meeting with an unforced error, it's only right and proper that he provides some much-needed symmetry when he concludes with (yet) another. After Mike confidently advises us that Kozza Smith will race in the nominated Heat 15, vastly experienced announcer Edwin Overland quickly interjects, "I wouldn't write in Kozza Smith just yet as he's not able to ride 'cause he's not in the top three scorers from the programmed rides!" With our programmes now covered in scrawl based on his information, Mike chortles, "If it's any consolation, my programme is stuffed as well!" Personally I don't find it any consolation. Given that four of the last five heats have produced maximum heat advantages for the homesters, Peter Butcher predicts similar medicine for the last race of the night before it's even been run, "This should be a thriller, I've already written it down as 66-27." Though it looks as one-sided as all his previous outings, Stars captain Tomas Topinka errs on the side of caution and, therefore, only wheelies down both straight during laps three and four! The ninth 5-1 of the night produces a result of 66-27 that, arguably, flatters Rye House! It has been Nigel 'Noddy' Fordham's 4,805th ever speedway meeting and has taken his grand total of speedway miles to 956,000. [1] The crowd disperses to the car park or the bar. King's Lynn promoter Buster Chapman professes himself exhausted but satisfied. "I'm tired! We've had a lot of work here with the stockcars and the speedway. I finished at midnight last night and was back at 5 a.m. It was boiling hot at 9 a.m. and it's always difficult when it's like that. We've got a busy weekend ahead and there's always lots to clear up after the stocks!"

1st July King's Lynn v. Rye House (Premier League) 66-27

[1] Since I last saw him at the Conference League Riders' Championship on the 27th September 2008 he's been to 58 more meetings and travelled a further 8,000 miles!

CHAPTER 11

Sheffield

"Most Premier League riders are only two engine blow-ups away from retiring!"

2nd July

The outer Speedway Office at Owlerton Stadium in Sheffield is already crowded when I arrive. Behind the counter, Neil Machin sits at his desk (lit cigarette in the ashtray) while, on the opposite side of the desk, Julie Reading busies herself with some paperwork. Stood in the doorway is Roger Stevens who's over from Canada to see some speedway accompanied by his Bristol-based friend Alan Sampson. Somehow the talk has turned to poetry and, from memory, Sheffield co-promoter Neil Machin recalls the some words from [Steve] Gresham's Lament.

"Come to England to seek his fame
[Something like] With his pockets stuffed with pot
He thought he could beat the lot."

Not quite satisfied with his recall of the opening lines, Neil fishes into the sheaf of papers piled on his desk and almost immediately finds a copy of the poem! Without ado or invitation, he proceeds to read this quite lengthy poem with relish.

Gresham's Lament

Crasher Gresham, was his name,
Came to Bristol, to seek his fame,
With his pockets stuffed with pot,
He thought that he could beat the lot.

He rode the tracks, night and day,
God help anyone, in his way,
His one thought was to win the race,
To hell with the rest, who couldn't keep pace.

His reputation spread far and wide,
Even his team mates tried to hide,
When asked to race along with him,
They'd turn away with a sickly grin.

He needs a partner, Teaspoon cried,
Come on one of you, you must ride,
The riders talked in vain, but it was deadlock.
Alright said Teaspoon, I'll choose Boocock.

They all cheered Booey from the heart,
He'd be alright, if he was smart,
I'll have that bugger, Booey said, just you wait and see,
I'll hit him with my helmet, if he dares to come near me.

He and Gresham made the bend,
Look out! Booey, he's no friend,
It'll be five-one to us, for sure,
But Gresham wants first place, more.

The race is fast, and all are tense,
As Gresham sends Booey into the fence,
Booey's excluded, says the Ref,
The crowd go mad, he must be blind and deaf.

Booey's protest can't be heard,
As Palmer won't believe a word,
To help him make his point more clear,
Booey belts him round the ear.

Now slowly back to the pit,
His back is hurt, his leathers split,
Sock him Dad" came a heartfelt cry,
From Little Darren, the light of his Father's eye.

With his helmet in his hand,
And both feet firmly on the sand,
I'll finish him, don't worry son,
As Booey shouts to Gresham – COME!

In just thirty seconds flat,
Gresham's lying on his back,
His teeth are out, he cannot laugh,
He'll not make the second half.

As soon as he was out of bed,
Back to the U.S.A. he fled,
Now Booey's cheered from East to West,
Everyone knows that he's the best.

Neil reads with some passion ("Look out! Booey, he's no friend"). It's quite a performance and the only break in his oration is provided by a pregnant pause and a deep sigh before he repeats the line "From Little Darren, the light of his Father's eye". Poetry and speedway aren't obvious bedfellows but clearly sufficiently addictive for Neil to have various poems mixed amongst the important BSPA and SCB documents piled high upon his desk. Quickly sifting through the pile, Neil swiftly finds another poem, this one written by Steve Casey. We're not treated to another poetic oration but, instead, Neil hands out copies. [1]

[1] *Green Light and Go*

What do you see when you go to the races?
You see crowds, you see cars, you see expectant faces,
Hot food if you're hungry, no need for the shakes,
And of course, the four madmen, on the bikes with no brakes.

You see programmes and turnstiles where you must pay to enter,
Paramedics for safety, they all stand in the centre,
The track all prepared, even graded with rakes,
Should be perfect for the madmen, on the bikes with no brakes.

[Alan] "I think that must be "78 'cause Nigel Boocock rode for Bristol that year."
[Roger] "How are your crowds, Neil?"
[Neil] "Pretty up and down really – petty sort of average. Like many other clubs I suspect we could all do with more in this bad economic climate. We've all got to work a bit harder, bolt the hatches down and survive! When I heard you were coming, I'd expected you'd be bringing a big cheque?"
[Roger] "Nah! I thought you'd have retired to Australia by now."

Their conversation is interrupted by a call from Rob Woffinden on Neil's mobile. Roger and Alan are touring the tracks and, last night, they were at Poole. Alan recalls, "Bjarne and Tai came together and there was an altercation." Neil's conversation ends and Roger wonders why with such a small speedway scene Australia ("what is it about Oz?") can produce so many world-class riders.
[Neil] "Parents invest in the kids 'cause it's a proper career for them. I think one of our big problems in this country is that we make it too difficult to make the jump up from other disciplines into speedway. Of course, historically, we got them from grasstrack and motocross."
[Alan] "So it's a lack of kids coming through?"
[Neil] "Yeah. I don't know why? But the demographics have changed across the country and it's worrying. People don't want to emulate sportsmen unless they're footballers! We've got quite a young team, the youngest is 18 and the oldest is 26. They're all pretty cool dudes but there aren't a lot of young riders."
[Roger] "Do you think if we all had standard bikes it would encourage more people?"
[Neil] "Mate, our big problem is we've always ignored the proprietary brands – engines specifically! A GM engine costs four grand and it's not worth it!"

Neil fishes back into the pile of papers, pulls out a glossy colour motorcycle catalogue and opens it to display a couple of new bikes, "This is what you get for four grand when you look for a bike. It looks like a bike and when you compare it to what you get if you spend four grand on a GM engine without anything else. It's bollocks, mate! Speedway bikes, without lights and electrics, can't cost six grand! What has also escalated the cost of speedway in the last 12 months is the value of the euro which puts costs up across the board. None of us have the crowd levels to bear these costs! It's getting like road racing three years ago. Nowadays you need a rich dad or sponsorship just to be able to ride speedway. It doesn't stop at the bike: there's the van, the bed, the sat nav, the toolboxes, the works! We haven't been open-minded about standardisation or working with the big manufacturers. There was a Honda prototype – it was the wrong engine – but we ignored the Honda model at

You hear music and air horns, all part of the fun,
You see mechanics and pushers to make the bikes run,
It's a serious business, there's no time for fakes,
Just four madmen, on track, on the bikes with no brakes.

There's a buzz in the air you could cut with a knife,
Changing tyres and wheels, it's a difficult life,
Split second decisions, no time for mistakes,
For the madmen on track on the bikes with no brakes.

We all hate the rain, daren't race if there's puddles,
The crowd looks concerned as they gather in huddles,
But to who can we turn? It's the risk each one takes,
It's of course, to the madmen on the bikes with no brakes.

The gospel according to Mick Gregory

Charles Birch

Jeff Dooley at trackshop

our peril. It was a second a lap slower but it sounded like a motorbike. It was bog standard. It was the wrong beast at the time. We all knew that! I think there's going to have to be change though. I think the divide has been crossed. Our riders can't afford to prop up their racing. We're not going to agree the terms that will allow them to support that level of equipment. Most Premier League riders are only two engine blow-ups away from retiring! Even if they're doing well on the track, there's too many people getting their quid out of them! Tuners and the like! It's a cottage industry! There's no volume and there's high prices so we're going to have to use a proprietary brand. It's all bullshit, mate. It would take 200 units to kit out the Premier League completely. It's probably five minutes' production for a global company. Sounds silly but riders don't think about what they really need as equipment. My pal, Rob Woffinden, who is the dad of Tai Woffinden who is the 18-year-old who's aiming for the moon and the stars, is the only person I know at that level that is using a Jawa clutch! Some dickhead said to him 'Do Jawa clutches really work?' Not if you're obsessed with the fashion industry, Desmond. Why do you think you would want to run Jawa clutches? Top riders like Leigh Adams get everything for naught so why would he bother to run Jawa clutches?"

We're interrupted by the arrival of a fresh-faced Birmingham Brummies rider, "What's happening with the pits?"
[Neil] "It's a work in progress. We're trying to get the builders to give us some more room."
[Rider] "I guess you've got the shaded bit."
[Neil] "What, to shelter out of the rain! Why don't you go off and lie in the sun and get sunburnt?" [Resumes his conversation] "I can't help thinking it's all about engines. I think that's the way forward. The dudes that talk about grippy tracks, if you give it to them, they can't ride it! These bikes are just set up for slick tracks! They should get rid of the twist grip and clutch and just have an ON/OFF switch – as that's how they ride nowadays. The characteristics of a current speedway bike create a slick surface. A spinning wheel that's spinning like mad will polish the surface and fling the shale to the side. Now it's all about wheel spin. I can't help thinking slick tracks produce processional racing 'cause everywhere you go it's all about the first corner."
[Roger] "We went to Newport, Eastbourne and Poole and it took about 40 races before we saw an over-take."
[Neil] "If you paid speedway riders on how many riders they passed that would be something but, instead, we pay them for points rather than the spectacle Joe Public wants to see! We're actually in a leisure industry and people forget that. If we get 1,000 in it's probably considered to be an acceptable crowd in Premier League speedway."
[Roger] "At Newport they had about 300."
[Neil] "They can't pay the bills on that! I can't pay mine on 700. We have to look at what we are giving people. When cricket, the most boring game on earth – it's been repackaged –and created a much more acceptable product. They realised they had to do something and it's about time we realised we had to do something."
[Roger] "At Costa Mesa, they have eight riders kneecap racing on a 180-metre track – the stands are packed, there's 24-30 races. Isn't that something to think off?"
[Neil] "They're all individuals – we're selling a team product here! We stage the PLRC here every year. If we get 3,000 it's a bloody good crowd. So the team event is definitely what we're selling! I do like the idea of a handicap 'cause you get lots of passing."
[Roger] "They did that in the 60s – Briggs and Fundin and the like."

[Neil] "All the people who used to go to speedway, the world's full of them, they'll all tell you speedway is first out of the gate! Our product has got quicker, the costs have gone up massively, it's got more competitive but, you have to ask yourself, for what? To take a fraction of a second off a track record? I'd like to see them all sealed engines and the best rider – the one with the most skill – will then win. Mate, we have to learn from other people's experience how to attract big crowds."
[Roger] "So the promoters would have to own 14 bikes."
[Neil] "Maybe that's the way to go, I don't know? The National League has become a bloody tough league with higher costs. Maybe we have to go back to the old National League as it was 20 years ago. People complain they don't get value for money. I don't hear anyone saying they don't get value for money for a football game! I don't hear anyone say they should play for longer. We're talking about different demographics. If you look at the back of the nationals [newspapers], I can tell you it's all football! Speedway never gets any coverage. People say that if we were at a fiver rather than 13 quid, we could double the crowd. I would be at a fiver but I don't believe we'd double the crowd. The reason we're at 13 quid is 'cause we can't survive on 12. It's not rocket science! We're an industry

that's always got to look to get an extra quid from a declining audience. I believe Sky TV should pay us enough money so that clubs can survive. I've thought about it for a long time but there's no obvious answer. Football and speedway aren't really to be compared. I believe we fall between two stools 'cause we don't attract the motorcycle community. When you and I were kids, teenagers were the motorcycle fraternity and nowadays there are 50-year-olds who don't want to leave their £8,000 bike in the car park. In speedway, we've also got this insular way to trying to reach out to people who fit our criteria rather than thinking how we can become trendy! I've been here 17 years and I don't know the answers. We all saw the Moto GP a few weeks ago and that was the most exciting last lap ever! It kept you on the edge of your seat. We have to give people a spectacle that does keep them on the edge of their seat and looks dangerous! Sometimes I look at speedway and it doesn't even look fast at some tracks you go to – usually 'cause you're too far away from the track! Go to Lakeside and stand in the bar – that's paint drying!"
[Roger] "What about Belle Vue?"
[Neil] "I haven't been to the new Belle Vue so I don't want to demean it. But, I went to the old Belle Vue and all they have in common with them is the team colours. Speedway that's close and dangerous and a spectacle and all the old – boosh – has gone! Processional, racing for the line is boring!"
[Roger] "What about betting?"
[Neil] "You'd have to do a forecast for the helmet colour order and that's difficult to do, I can tell you, over 15 heats. I've done the experiment and it's five max and four on average and most people think they get seven or eight. The boffins on the terraces would tell you they'd get half right but I reckon they'd be lucky to get a third and that differential is, maybe, where you'd make the money." Talk of speedway's future is interrupted by the trill of Neil's mobile ringing, "Ah, Chris Mills!" Listens and then asks Julie Reading ,"Have we booked Chris Mills's hotel?" The answer is affirmative so Neil continues, "I've spent all day chasing around – yes, you're booked in, [pause] okay mate, see ya. Just get your trapping head, your trapping head, it's needed!"
[Julie] "He's not the brightest. What did he want?"
[Neil] "A frickin' personal secretary is what he wants!"

Roger and Alan leave the Speedway Office to explore Owlerton Stadium while talk of housekeeping matters prompts Neil to inform Julie, "Charles Birch – who is 89 – is coming tonight. He came to the first meeting ever here in 1929." Neil asks me, "Where were you last night?" After news it was the Norfolk Arena, Neil continues, "I see that psychological barrier at King's Lynn – just like at Exeter – a lot of riders go to King's Lynn with the intention to go through the motions and not get damaged!" Neil's mind is clearly still on the earlier discussion of the way forward for British speedway. Unpredictably enough, Neil turns to the Gospels for guidance. "The Bible tells us 'Do not attempt to remove a splinter from your brother's eye, when you have a plank in your own eye!' I'm so frickin' angry at us damaging our credibility! Len Silver and I both wrote to the BSPA saying we shouldn't accept the revised Poole one-to-seven until three weeks later after there'd been a proper investigation! That would have sent a message but, now, public perceptions are that the sport is happy to go along with it and so every time someone sees a race they think 'Hold on! A few weeks ago there were riders going up to the line who didn't intend to race so maybe rider X wasn't racing just then!' Credibility is like virginity – once it's lost, you can't get it back!" The end of Neil's eloquent rail against present-day speedway iniquities is caught by ex-Sheffield speedway promoter Malcolm Wright who smiles beatifically while Neil rages Lear-like at speedway gods. I decide it's the ideal time to ask Neil, "Have you got wi-fi here?" Neil looks baffled, "What's that?" [Malcolm] "What's that?" My explanation doesn't excite them nor effectively suggest that it might be something Owlerton Stadium needs to embrace the future (or trendy element). Instead, Malcolm relates a chance speedway encounter. "I met a bloke who said 'you're Malcolm Wright'. He said 'I used to go to Sheffield speedway but I haven't been since 2006'. Then guess what he said? 'Do the toilets still smell?' Imagine, you haven't been for three years and the question you most want to ask is about the toilets!" Neil offers no comment but the pained expression on his face requires no words. Before I leave to set up my book display table by the turnstiles, Julie explains how she now works in the Speedway Office at Sheffield. "I've gone part-time at work and I only work here on Thursdays. I only live in Chesterfield. It came at the right time as I was going part-time anyway!" It doesn't feel like the right moment to ask where Janet and Betty are nowadays. They used to appear to be part of the Sheffield Speedway Office furniture (in a nice way). A cup of tea or coffee was never far away and they chain-smoked in unison with Neil Machin. Given Sheffield's industrial heritage has been swept away on a tide of progress and modernity, you could half suspect the level of smoke in the speedway office was a small form of tribute to its rich industrial past.

In the cool shade of the home-straight grandstand I introduce myself to new trackshop franchise holder Jeff Dooley and his wife, Ann as they unload the merchandise from their van and slowly set out the display tables. Prior to my visit Jeff impressively proactively got in touch via email to establish what my requirements might be on the night. In person, you can't miss his calm affable laidback manner. "I get on well with Mick [Gregory] but it's between Joan [Gregory] and Neil going to Oz that there's a little tension. Three years ago, when Mick had a table upstairs in the bar at the end of the season, he said 'I'm nearly 70 and I'll be retiring in a few years.' I asked Neil if he could bear me in mind when that happened and he said to me last winter 'It's time'. It was confirmed on 23rd December and Mick only heard a week later when Joan had already started to plan the badges. It was bound to cause some upset when it happened like that but it wasn't as if I was asking for it!" I leave them to their merchandising display and wander back to my stall. Neil Machin stops for a few more words, "Did you know it's a year since Darren [Boocock] died?" Thoughts of premature death are clearly on Neil's mind and, inevitably, his quickly turn to Rob Woffinden. "He's only 47! I think I'm destined to grow old with all of my mates dead. It's frickin' hard I tell you! I think Tai is just losing himself in his mad schedule. That's my opinion anyway. I'm beginning to think I'm a jinx with all my friends dying. They're all so frickin' young too!"

Postman photographer Andy Garner also stops by for a few brief words about his new website: Andy Garner Photography (www.agfoto.us). Though I've seen many websites with .com, .co.uk and .eu suffixes I've never seen one with a .us suffix! Andy smiles, "It's new out and I thought it would be different!" Andy follows many motorcycling codes not just speedway. His website advises, "I first got interested in photography in the early 70s while attending Road Race meetings with Barrie Scully – one of the top British riders of that era – and also going along to watch the Sheffield Tigers speedway at Owlerton Stadium." While we talk, a few yards away but relatively close to the turnstile entrance, Mick Gregory expertly sets up the small stall that he nowadays sells *Speedway Stars*, *Backtrack* and *Classic Speedway Magazine* from. It looks like he's got a specially designed display table with a sloped lectern-affect stand. It's ideal to display magazines and also creates the strong impression that Mick is about to deliver a sermon, except most vicars don't usually wear blue shorts and an apron (unless they happen to be Freemasons). I don't know if Mick has any religious inclinations or desire to pass himself off as a man of the cloth. Yesterday we learnt in the papers that (in St Leonards) a C of E vicar was arrested for conducting false marriages for immigration purposes for around 170 people. Doubtless he'll soon repent his sins. Mick wastes little time with small talk before he launches into a well-practised explanation about what he views as the close-season trackshop staff putsch at Owlerton Stadium. "They said I wasn't modern, that I hadn't moved with the time and was old-fashioned! They said people wanted to buy online and they couldn't buy online! That they complained! Supposedly they made the decision before the end of the season. I sat with Neil for an hour after the last meeting of the season – before he went to Australia – and he didn't say a word. First I knew was on Christmas Eve when Dave Hoggart phoned and asked 'How do you feel about next season?' which struck me as a weird question. I had to say I was worried about the crunch and he told me, 'We've decided not to renew your contract' – even though I didn't have a contract – 'cause I wasn't modern! 'Jeff [Dooley] has had an online business for eight years'. Apart from the way it was handled, it's the best thing that could have happened. I sell the mags and they used to create 35-40% of my profits. Before I turned up at 3 and got home at midnight and now I turn up at 6 and chat to everyone. It's sale or return on the magazines. I walk round the stadium selling them. I last did that in 1977!" Our talk of speedway trackshops gaining warp speed to embrace the wonderful world of technological progress is interrupted by the arrival of Malcolm Wright. The recent Cardiff Grand Prix finds Malcolm and Mick in agreement that the referee was hopeless but the racing was good.
[Malcolm] "I asked Stuart Wilson [referee] and he says that under FIM rules if the race is stopped, someone must be excluded."
[Mick] "Kelvin and Nigel [on the Sky television broadcast] said it should be all four back!"
[Malcolm] "I saw Colin Meredith in the pub afterwards and asked him about the track and he said it was 'cause they could buy their own shale – £35 a ton for a thousand tons – rather than use the crap from Newport. He said by tomorrow morning it'll be stored in a warehouse in Cardiff Docks for next year. You know what a logistical exercise it is doing the Cardiff track!"

Malcolm wanders off while, stood behind his lectern, Mick Gregory warms to the theme of his lecture. "It was the best thing that ever happened but how they did it was frickin' shocking! Have you seen their shop? It's a joke, if that's supposed to be the way forward. It's full of books and they haven't had anything new since the first week! Plus, they just stand there like cardboard cut-outs. Many people boycott the shop 'cause of what happened!" Based on my unscientific observation, many people also don't boycott the trackshop though there's definitely no longer a pile of unsold Tiger toys for sale. I can't tell whether these fans do or don't know or even care about these developments. Given that Mick is a well-known figure and circulates around the Stadium every week, it's highly probable the topic will be regularly broached. A fan briefly lingers by my table so I rush back to it in the hope of a sale. However, though we're bathed in warm early evening Yorkshire sunshine he points to the hill in the distance, adopts a serious expression and says, "They say if you can see that tree [points to a tree I can't see on the far-away hillside] it's going to rain [pause] if you can't see it, it is raining!" A crowd of 20 or so school children run through the entrance turnstiles and boisterously mill about by Mick Gregory's pulpit before they're marshalled off to the pits. Sheffield fan Bob contemplates the likely performance of tonight's visitors, the Birmingham Brummies. "They should do alright. Piszcz goes good here and so does Lyons! He rolls a bit, though. Tell you what Hugh Skidmore [the Tigers number 2 rider] is the find of the season!" Shortly afterwards a smartly dressed old age pensioner in a formal jacket set off with a smart yellow shirt arrives. It's Charles Birch who'll be 90 later in the year, "I remember the speedway when all that far side [points to back straight or distant tree] used to be packed! It was black cinders then. As you get older, it seems to get faster! I came to the first ever meeting here!" Some fans stop to bemoan recent allegations of average manipulation in the Elite League. Linguists often like to analyse the transmission of new words and key phrases across the UK population. The Oxford English Dictionary makes great play every year and always publicise their latest edition by highlighting the new words that have just entered the lexicon in this country. If speedway played a large part in the national consciousness, it's clear that – should people's names suddenly qualify for inclusion – Matt Fraud and Neil Fiddleditch would be strong contenders to be listed.

Minutes before tapes are due to rise, I relocate my display table adjacent to the trackshop in the deep shade of the home-straight grandstand. A prompt start at the scheduled start time suddenly becomes less likely when Shaun Leigh appeals over the stadium speaker system, "Can the track electrician go to the referee's box!" Shaun uses the time to make housekeeping announcements and, with tongue firmly in his cheek, announces that the "The Bard of Speedway" is at Owlerton tonight. Though I'm loath to declare the meeting over as a contest so early, heat 1 ends in a comprehensive maximum heat advantage for the Sheffield Tigers won by Ricky Ashworth closely escorted home by his promising young teammate Hugh Skidmore. Ever-professional Shaun tries to talk-up the competitive threat posed by tonight's visitors, the Birmingham Brummies. He must have seen a different race. What he describes as "a bit of early pressure in the early stages from Tomasz Piszcz" is a very generous description of the gentle pressure applied until the riders arrived at the second bend of the first lap! The position of the trackshop provides an excellent view of the Owlerton circuit and Jeff Dooley is a speedway fan with a keen appreciation of the fine detail of the nuances of the races staged here. "The first race Hugh Skidmore did in the Premier League he finished last 'cause he's never seen a track with so much shale! He'd ridden some second halves but, by then, there's no shale. The second time out he was third but then he had two heat wins! He's got an incredible ability to change racing lines at high speed! Also, he's quite physical for an 18-year-old. They tried to rough him up in the first bend but he was having none of it!"

Anxiety that Tigers versus the Brummies might be an uneven contest continues unabated as Sheffield dominate heats 2 and 3 to take the overall score to 14-4. Advised before the meeting by Neil Machin to wear his gating head, Chris Mills appears to have slightly misheard when he journeys to the line sporting what looks like a feather on the top of his helmet. Unless he's come as a Roman Centurion or, perhaps, thinking it's a Danny la Rue themed speedway meeting, Chris sports an unusual sartorial look. His peculiar head gear turns out to be a helmet cam and, worries that this might slow Chris's progress due to the increased wind resistance it provides, initially prove well founded. If you go to website www.mxcam.co.uk you can get a good idea of a speedway race as experienced from the rider's point of view. During the first attempt to run heat 4, Chris Mills is marooned at the back of the race so it would have been more exciting if Josh Auty had worn the helmet cam since he falls on the fourth bend of the second lap (just after Jason Lyons has passed him on the back straight). Adjudged by referee Peter Clarke to be the prime cause of the stoppage, Auty is disqualified from the rerun. To my untutored eye it was a perfectly fair pass by Jason Lyons, albeit one where he blasted aggressively under Josh – whose present lack of confidence and comparative inexperience dictates he'd most likely fall. Ahead when the race was stopped first time out, Brummies young reserve and star of the future Richard Sweetman repeats the medicine to win in some comfort a considerable distance ahead of Chris Mills. Unable to harry Josh Auty, Jason Lyons instead decides to rip into the safety fence round bends 3 and 4 (on the first lap) but somehow manages to stay on his machine.

This first Brummies heat advantage of the night promises to transmogrify into a more coordinated fight-back when Tomasz Piszcz gates brilliantly in the next race but, sadly for him and the limited number of Brummies fans in attendance, by the time the riders exit the fourth bend Richard Hall has imperiously brushed his challenge aside. Heat 6 features a duel between Ricky Ashworth and Jason Lyons, albeit with Hugh Skidmore in close pursuit. Heat 7 provides Josh Auty with another opportunity to channel his talent and aggression into points on the track. He patiently tracks Robert Ksiezak until the chance to seize second place presents itself as they vie for dominance around the second bend of the last lap. Ahead of them, Sheffield reserve Paul Cooper wins the race to confirm his early season mechanical difficulties are behind him. Jeff Dooley comments, "At the start of the season, Paul Cooper couldn't get his engines going at all and he was often a poor fourth! Sam Ermolenko was here and said 'take those engines out and I'll get them dynatested at Eddie Bull's.' They were hopeless and, when they were opened, there was nothing inside! They hadn't been doing what they said they'd been doing at the tuners so he now has his engines done by Eddie Bull and he's a different rider and, gradually, he's been getting them all dialled in!"

When you think that Birmingham have Jason Lyons and Tomasz Piszcz headlining their team, it says something about the high regard, confidence and esteem that Birmingham team manager Graham Drury holds for Richard Sweetman that he is the first rider chosen to take the black-and-white helmet colour in heat 8. It's a shrewd tactical decision though the bare fact of his race win doesn't do justice to the neck and neck thriller of a race that Hugh Skidmore and Richard generously serve up for the speedway faithful within Owlerton Stadium. Sweetman's three races have so far generated 11 points out of the Brummies cumulative total of 19! After a short delay, Graham Drury sensibly replaces the out-of-sorts Luke Priest with Richard Sweetman for the next race. However, his ability on the bike is such that the often combative Richard Hall decides to extremely aggressively show Sweetman the first bend fence. The ability on a bike of the youngster is such that, although he's now relegated behind Hall and Lyons, he nonetheless remains on his machine to fight another day. Joel Parsons revisits the scene of the crime on the next lap when he drives really hard underneath Sweetman to, thereby, condemn him to fourth place. Though he emerges at the end of the race pointless, it's a sign of the threat that Richard Sweetman potentially poses that the Sheffield riders have taken the trouble to broaden his racing experience with a demonstration of calculated almost savage on-track aggression. They've done this even though the cumulative scoreline of 36-21 indicates that it's highly unlikely that Birmingham will tonight pose anything like a serious challenge.

It's a treat to be at Owlerton Stadium this evening to see Richard Sweetman but, equally so, to be able to see Hugh Skidmore ride. He wins heat 10 with some aplomb, though the main action comes on the first bend where Ricky Ashworth gets a massive elbow along with a shove from Robert Ksiezak. Ricky does well to stay on his bike. He responds in true speedway rider fashion to wind it on throughout the remainder of the race on a wide outside line. His speed on the circuit is thrilling but not quite enough to catch the Brummies heat leader. Tomasz Piszcz wears the black-and-white helmet colour in the next and, with able support from Richard Sweetman in second place, they give Birmingham the heat advantage by the always incongruous score of 1-8 and narrow their deficit to 10 points.

After some rejuvenating interval cups of tea, suddenly we're treated to two sports in one: namely, speedway and a bike-based version of wrestling. The primary object of this rough, almost full-contact sport is Richard Sweetman who lines up for heat 12 for his sixth ride of the night. The rough treatment of his speedway education continues when Chris Mills shows a sudden violent streak – recorded as possible evidence by his helmet cam. At any level, speedway can be a tough business – this is definitely one (hopefully discouraging) message they're keen to pass onto Richard Sweetman. Tutor Chris Mills roughs up the youngster and aggressively blocks his path at every opportunity. The evidence of earlier races indicates Sweetman usually has greater speed than Mills but, suddenly, the Brummies reserve can find no way past. Some criticise the speedway experience at Sheffield as strictly high-speed-gate-and-go, yet tonight we've been treated to a series of thrilling battles for position as well as dramatic races for the chequered flag. If every meeting at every track were to contain this level of drama and incident, then word of mouth would surely ensure that crowd levels would rise.

The School of Hard Knocks that Richard Sweetman has been unofficially inducted into this evening continues its matriculation exercise in the penultimate heat when, on the first lap, he's practically assaulted by Paul Cooper. Rather than try to broadside around the corner, Paul Cooper arrows in a straight line and practically spears Sweetman at high speed on the third-bend fence (after they'd already endured a hard first corner together). Unless the Sheffield reserve has suddenly forgotten the basics of how to ride a speedway bike, the racing line Paul Cooper employs must indicate premeditated intimidation aforethought. Sweetman somehow manages to avoid being T-boned and, though he remains on his machine, understandably he prefers the comparative safety of the rear of the field (so much so that Luke Priest manages to collect his first point of the night). The Sheffield fan by my display table shakes his head philosophically, "He's been in the wrong place about three times tonight, ain't he?!" The Premier League meeting closes when Richard Hall completes his often imperious, frequently high-speed maximum when he elegantly rounds both Tomasz Piszcz and Jason Lyons on the second bend. It's the first drawn heat of the night and, despite the fact that the Brummies tactical rides generated maximum points, Sheffield run out comfortable winners in a meeting that has been a credit to the sport. The entertainment doesn't stop with the end of the Premier League meeting the Tigers promotion stage second-half racing accompanied by some practice for James Birkenshaw before the speedway finally draws to a good value close after two and a half hours of entertainment.

2nd July Sheffield v. Birmingham (Premier League) 55-41

CHAPTER 12

Scunthorpe

"It's all hearsay. Some rider's dad says it's happened! Where is the proof? There isn't any! It doesn't make any business sense."

3rd July

Upon arrival at the Eddie Wright Raceway in Normanby Road, Scunthorpe, the most obvious change to the general environs of the stadium is to the skyline. It's now decorated with intrusive wind turbines. Inside the perimeter fencing of the stadium, the advent of stockcar racing at the track has seen the erection of a permanent safety fence. The club have removed the more traditional fence they used to have and replaced it with one set into some substantial earth banking. Prior to my visit, I worried that the previous rightly praised panoramic views fans enjoyed here would be spoilt. However, even without a bike on the track surface, it's obvious that any appreciation of the visual speedway won't be negatively impacted. It might just be my imagination but the track also appears to be even bigger than I remember.

There are over four hours until the scheduled start time. Nonetheless, club co-promoter Rob Godfrey has already spent many hours at the stadium involved with the whole panoply of last-minute preparations. My impression is that Rob's never happier than when getting his hands dirty working on the track or, if time allows, helping with the preparation of the bikes in the pits. Currently, the reality of speedway club ownership combined with his promotional obligations dictates that many tasks you don't want or necessarily relish also fall your way on a day-to-day basis. Though Rob (along with Norman Beeney) developed the stadium from scratch, he's also now been involved behind the scenes in speedway enough to now have become both inured and irked by the politics of participation within this sport in Britain. "They can do what they like in the Elite League so long as they leave the Premier League alone! I have called them [BSPA] about Birmingham. They brought Hauzinger in on a 4-something average using eight matches and I want to know how they can do that? As it's not in the Rulebook!"
[Jeff] "Isn't that the phantom rule that has previous precedent?"
[Rob] "I don't care if they do that in the Elite League, we don't do that in the Premier League!"

The quality and entertainment value of the racing on offer is at the EWR is something close to Rob's heart. He can justifiably take pride in the feedback that Scunthorpe regularly receive for the quality of the racing and spectacle they serve up here on a regular basis. Nevertheless, Rob refuses to rest on his laurels and continues to seek to learn, hopefully, valuable lessons from other tracks he encounters on his journeys round the country with Scunthorpe. That said, Rob believes some rival facilities could perhaps take a leaf out of the Scorpions book. "It's a crime how some people prepare their tracks! I don't know why they prepare them that way? Or employ people who can't do a track? I wouldn't go and watch it! It's no fun seeing processional racing and big scores every week. Most of the meetings they have on the telly are awful. The benchmark has been set by the Sky Premier League meetings this season. It's been known for years that the racing is more exciting in the Premier League and, this season, we've all proved it! We can provide that level of excitement every week and Sky must ask themselves: what would it be best to show?"
[Jeff] "Rye House didn't entertain that much at King's Lynn the other night."
[Rob] "Well, the track they have there is so grippy. It's alright if you're used to it but not if you're not. I know Buster is thinking about letting the away team practise on it for half an hour. We were there last week and it was slick. It would be an excellent track if it was slick every week but Wilko said it was really, really grippy again this week. Jonathan [Chapman] has rung me about our shale and I've told them they should use it. They have too much clay! Even if they mixed it in, it would still be better!"

Comment and the recent outcry over allegations about Poole's alleged manipulation of the averages hold little interest for Rob. "I may be in a minority but I don't think Poole have done anything wrong! Why would Matt Ford go out of his way to ruin his own business when his crowds were already falling? People avoid failure so making sure you lose meetings over a period of time is going to be suicide! Anyway, it's all hearsay. Some rider's dad says it's happened! Where is the proof? There isn't any! It doesn't make any business sense."
[Jeff] "Maybe Poole want to get relegated to join the excitement of the Premier League?"
[Rob] "Why, they're champions! The best! The Elite League will exist next season and they'll be in it, you can be sure! No one from the Premier League would want to go up. Sure the money's more but the costs are even more so! No one would be that silly to even think of it! There's a divide at BSPA meetings nowadays – a more explicit one. They can have their businesses and we can run ours. Anyone who goes along to speedway knows where the excitement is!"

Rob briefly runs through some of the changes to the stadium infrastructure since my last visit. He points out the new grandstand area on the first bend, highlights the work required to build the stockcar wall and notes the introduction of the air-fence (something Rob considers is a vital safety development for all levels of speedway). He politely enquires about the key chapters in my new book *Quantum of Shale* and, when I say that I'm pleased with the insight the Redcar chapter provides into speedway finances, Rob reveals himself as not the biggest fan of ex-Redcar promoter Glyn Taylor. "He still walks around like he's someone, which can't be right when some riders still haven't been paid! He was good at promises but didn't always come through with them."

Though the turnstiles have still to open there's already quite a crowd inside the trackshop. When I stand in the doorway Pat asks Dave Rattenberry, "Did you see Tai [at the Cardiff Grand Prix] with a stud in his ear and a tattoo on his arm? It looked like a cotton bud. And the tattoo! Well!" Rather than discuss Tai's body art, the question I want an answer to is, 'How long have the wind turbines been next to the stadium?'
[Dave] "This season. At least it keeps the gypsies away!"
[Becky] "They've been there about two months now. One of them's broken – they were fixing it today."
[Jeff] "Aren't they noisy?"
[Anne Hollingsworth] "They don't make any noise, it's a myth!"
[Dave] "Anne is Mrs Redcar, Mrs Scunthorpe Speedway, I mean!"
[Jeff] "Is Rob [Godfrey] powering the floodlights off them?"
[Anne] "He wishes!"
Later Barry [Bazza] Preston – here tonight with his enthusiastic daughter, Chloe – definitely sounds like an expert on the legislation that surrounds wind turbines, "I think you can't have a residence within 800 metres of a wind turbine!"

Dave Rattenberry speaks highly of the atmosphere regularly found at Scunthorpe, "It's like a family here – it's excellent!" On the subject of families, trainee referee Daryl Clark arrives at the track along with his daughter Zoë and wife Diane. Daryl will be under the tutelage of Margaret Vardy for this evening's meeting. She's already here too and takes Daryl off to the referee's box to continue his education and smooth his induction into the rarefied world of speedway officialdom. Earlier I'd snatched a few words with Daryl, "I grew up with speedway [at Halifax]. I've done my reffing with rugby and that and I wanted to get back involved with speedway, so this seems ideal!" Daughter Zoë has recently completed the second year of her sport's therapy degree at the University of Teesside, "It'll be hard work next year – I'm a finalist and, of course, there's a speedway track nearby. Bradford closed when I was young." Her mum, Diane, interjects, "It wasn't the best track!" Diane and Zoë both take pride and a keen interest in Daryl's speedway referee apprenticeship. Daryl and Zoë both have to study, "It's about two years to qualify as a ref, I think." Given that they often travel as a family round the country together, I wonder how they feel when they hear referees in general or Daryl in particular get abused by supposedly 'knowledgeable' speedway fans. They say its water off a duck's back. Diane is quite definite about her favoured response, "If you can do a better job – do!" Julie Harrowven from the Scunthorpe Speedway Commercial Department catches the end of our conversation and nods sympathetically, "When they get really abusive, I'll walk away in case I say something!" Now that Julie's here the unspoken elephant in the room is the present health of Scunthorpe co-promoter and Premier League team manager, Kenny Smith. Earlier, when I was over in the pits, I'd seen Kenny sat behind the desk in the speedway office and, to my shame and embarrassment, I was lost for words. We said our hellos but, given his gaunt look, platitudinous enquiries about his health didn't seem either relevant or appropriate. Ever considerate of others, Kenny has told Julie to get on with her life and not to worry about him. Such things are easier said than done for many of Kenny's close friends. Kenny's positive attitude to life has gained him many friends and admirers within the tight knit speedway community. Matter of factly, Julie says Kenny's good friend Ginger Abigail (aka Ginge) has come down to stay with him, ferry him around the country and generally keep an eye out. It's an ongoing sign of Kenny's determination and strength of character that he wishes to carry on as 'normal' with his speedway duties rather than compromise them because of his illness. [1]

One definition of optimism could be the attempt to run any British speedway club at a profit. Despite the dark cloudy skies overhead at 5 p.m., we're treated to the track curatorial version of optimism – the Scunthorpe bowser trundles out onto the track and proceeds to douse it extremely heavily. The Hull-based mechanic (for Magnus Karlsson) with the dry wit, distinctively tall Paul Harvey wanders over to let me know that while I got his name right in the Scunthorpe chapters in my latest book *Quantum of Shale*, I somehow managed to call him Paul Henry in the Workington chapter. Margaret Vardy's partner Steve Davies is likened to Mr Yateman (from *Dad's Army*) in my book but to be likened to Benny from *Crossroads* is altogether a much more heinous crime. Paul remains phlegmatic, "You meet so many people, and you're bound to make mistakes!" Paul has the night off but he's been unable to stay away. He's come along with his son Reece. "Magnus is in Sweden 'cause his partner is having a baby. They're gonna call it Milo if it's a boy and I forget what they're gonna call it, if it's a girl." This talk of babies and children quickly get confusing. I'm unclear how many children Magnus actually has since, at one point, Paul claims "It's their third child" and, at another, says, "He's already got one!" Either way, Benny (aka Paul) believes, "It's a bit of a fiddle them [Scunthorpe] having a guest." Questions about UK paternity legislation have been raised. "Magnus is a UK taxpayer so he can have paternity leave of two weeks but the BSPA say he can only have two days – one day in the hospital and the next. Their argument is he's a UK resident but they don't listen." We stand and watch the slow progress of the bowser as it inches its way around dousing the shale of the Eddie Wright Raceway. "The track here is a strange mix of dirt and grit – actually change the 'g' for an 's'! If you don't wash the bike, the next day it's a bastard! Magnus likes it here but just not the track. There's only one way to ride it, which is flat out! It bring up the standard and makes all the poor riders look a lot better than they are 'cause you just have to go flat out! [Nods towards another man] That's Thorpy's ex-mechanic. He could tell you some stories! It's a wild world where Thorpy's concerned!" Paul falls silent as Margaret Vardy walks by and, once she's out of earshot, says to his son Reece, "She was the one that excluded Magnus last year in heat 15

[1] Kenny Smith lost his battle with throat cancer on the morning of Monday 13th July 2009. Only given days to live the previous week, Kenny fulfilled his pledge to manage the Scunthorpe Scorpions for one final time on Saturday 10th July 2009 when they rode against the Edinburgh Monarchs in the Premier Trophy semi-final. A Press Release from the club commented:

Kenneth Ian Smith 1954-2009 R.I.P.
After a near three-year battle against throat cancer, Kenny Smith, the Scorpions' Team Manager, died on Monday morning at 6.15 a.m. at his home in Yarm. Over recent weeks his condition had deteriorated but after being told he only had days to live early last week he pledged to lead his side one last time. On Saturday his courage was on show for all to see as, unable to walk any significant distance, he was taken around the track on the back of David Howe's bike for two emotional laps of honour.
Kenny's grandfather was one of the pioneer riders in the 1920's and he began his own racing career in grasstrack before taking up speedway in the late sixties at Doncaster. However, he will be best remembered for his days in team management at Newcastle and over the last five years with Scunthorpe. After being involved at Middlesbrough he switched to Newcastle when the Teesside club's Cleveland Park track closed. Newcastle Promoter and Team Manager, George English, soon made him Assistant Team Manager and Kenny took responsibility for the Newcastle Gems when they entered a side in the Conference League. During that time there were few young riders in the North who hadn't been influenced by Kenny and after the Gems withdrew from the Conference League Kenny offered his services to us at Scunthorpe.
Early links with his past saw Byron Bekker and Ashley Johnson join the club but he had an exceptional talent for managing riders. He was well-respected by his riders and that is no small feat in the adrenaline-filled cauldron that is a speedway pits when charged with the onerous task of taking away a rider's opportunity to earn a living. Ever since Kenny joined Scunthorpe Speedway it has benefitted from Kenny's unswerving passion for the sport and our club. His commitment and dedication to the club was rewarded in 2007 when he became a co-promoter and the club could have never wished for a greater ambassador.
A devastated Scunthorpe promoter Rob Godfrey commented: "Kenny has been a great friend and we knew his death was coming but that doesn't make it any easier. It was a very emotional night for all concerned on Saturday and we are all devastated at losing him. It has been an honour to have Kenny in our lives for the last five years. He was a great inspiration to me and he touched the hearts of so many people. He will forever be a part of Scunthorpe Speedway."
Sheffield promoter Neil Machin was one of the first to join the wave of tributes to Kenny. "One of the conditions of Scunthorpe moving into the Premier League was that they had a good man in charge as team manager. I recommended Kenny. He was dedicated to the sport and it was a mark of his courage that he was at Scunthorpe on Saturday."
Somerset General Manager Dave Croucher added "Kenny's passing is a great loss to the sport and I am sure there will be many hundreds of riders, officials and staff at tracks all over the UK who will miss his company and have happy memories of this lovely man."
Kenny's funeral will take place on Tuesday, July 21, starting with a service at the Eddie Wright Raceway from 10 am. The funeral itself will be held at Woodlands Crematorium, Brumby Wood Lane, Scunthorpe, from 11 a.m. No flowers but donations are welcome to be made to the Multiple Sclerosis Society."

at Sheffield and he didn't touch the tapes! She excluded him and he said he wasn't going to ride in the rerun and she said she'd fine him £250 if he walked out of the meeting – so he was reinstated but had to ride off 15 metres. What's the frickin' point of revving your engines off 15 metres at Sheffield? You can catch up at some tracks but there even Nicki Pedersen isn't gonna catch them!"

Track inspection

Away in the near distance, the turnstiles open and, among the initial rush of fans keen to reserve their ideal position within the stadium, are a large contingent of Workington fans. People often quite rightly highlight the number of Redcar fans you see at their away meetings but, it has to be noted, that the Workington Comets inspire similar loyalty but less fancy dress. The Comets programme editor, Barry Stephenson takes up the familiar theme of speedway riders, mechanics, managers, promoters and fans everywhere – journey times! "It's taken us five hours to get down here!" A large number of the Workington fans proudly display their allegiance with various items of Comet merchandise and clothing. Some jackets are impressively full of badges. The comparative weakness of the Scunthorpe Henderson Insurance Scorpions leads some Comets fans to confidently predict an away victory. "Mystic Mel's (alias Mel Pettit) forecasts 46-44."

Bob Tasker of GRT Media on trackshop roof

Another man with a dry wit and keen insight into the everyday foibles of the speedway world is Bob Tasker from GRT Media. He's in the process of humping his equipment up the stepladder that leads onto the roof of the trackshop. Bob also doesn't exchange Christmas cards with this evening's SCB official, Margaret Vardy. "We don't get on at all. Whenever I get into the pits I always ask the ref's if I can do so and promise I won't get in the way. She said, 'So long as you don't record anything I say!' I told her, 'I would overdub it with bike noise, if I did happen to record anything.' And she said 'No, you can't record anything I say because it could be used in future months and years!' I promised that wouldn't happen. After she'd gone, I couldn't figure out what the goodness she was going to say. I've been going to speedway for a while now but when I look at the Christmas tree [set of lights usually located close to the start line controlled by the referee] I never know what I'll see when she's on the buttons!" The friendly but modest Scorpions press officer, programme editor, speedway fanatic and now temporary team manager of the Scunthorpe PL team, Richard Hollingsworth, rushes by in a rather snazzy black Scunthorpe fleece en route to the referee's box. He nods to the leaden skies and enquires, "Is this fine enough for you?"

St John Ambulance staff & wind turbines

Comets trackshop manager Liz Fleming has travelled over from the North West with the Comets faithful to watch her beloved Workington. Because of her trackshop duties, the number of races she can usually watch uninterruptedly on race night at Derwent Park is very limited. She thinks the prospect of a good away performance by the six-man Comets is good. They operate rider replacement for their injured number 2 rider, Charles Wright, because of the wrist injury he sustained in a crash at Glasgow on 31st May (that ended his 2009 speedway season). A misdiagnosis of ligament damage subsequently led to arthritis in his wrist. Not really curious about what appears in my latest book, she nonetheless politely enquires, "Did you put in we have the worst positioned trackshop in Britain? I dunno where you're gonna go tomorrow 'cause the tractors go in and out of there now!"

Those inside the stadium are then treated to a peculiar and slightly ragged rider parade that features perfunctory introductions without bikes but also without any practice laps! When the riders approach the tapes for the first race of the evening, it's noticeable that there are no start girls (or any sign of the Scunthorpe equal opportunity initiative that saw them use a start boy). In the crowd the ex Miss Fina Invader, Wendy Jedrzejakski leaves no one in any doubt about who she supports after she screams, "Go on Viktor, Go on Viktor!" at Scunthorpe's Mr Bergstrom as he endeavours to catch the fast looking Comets rider with the distinctive snazzy white kevlars, Kevin Doolan. Unable to hear these words of encouragement above the roar of the bikes, Viktor gives wholehearted if unsuccessful chase. Workington's Craig Cook takes third place ahead of Scunthorpe's guest (in place of Magnus Karlsson) from Redcar, Ben Wilson. Dave Rattenberry isn't impressed with what he's seen, "They're gonna miss Magnus tonight!" Viktor stays in such close contact with Kevin Doolan that he ends the race completely clarted from head to foot in Scunthorpe shale. Pleased that he won't be involved in the post-meeting clean up, Paul Harvey highlights, "It's too wet!" Confirming Paul's characterisation of this circuit as a flat-out racing track, the first race looks exceptionally quick but we're unable to learn exactly how quick when Shaun Leigh informs us over the stadium speaker system, "Unfortunately there was a stopwatch malfunction in race control so we don't have a time for that one! I'm sorry!" With a third place already under his belt, Craig Cook surprisingly only manages to achieve the same position in the reserve's race. Arguably, Craig is one of the top discoveries of the 2009 season. With the platform of a motocross pedigree behind him, the 22-year-old has been on fire in the National League for Buxton and rides with increasing confidence in the Premier League for Workington. His discovery is credited to the perspicacity of Workington owner Keith Denham who, tonight, has taken over team management duties from Ian Thomas who remains absent through illness. Until the third bend of heat 3, it looks likely that John Branney will become the second consecutive Comets race winner until Simon Lambert imperiously cuts back inside him to shoot away for victory. Nonetheless, this drawn heat sees the Comets retain their overall advantage at 5-7.

Shaun Leigh tries to enthuse the crowd with the news, "Adam Allott makes his home debut for the Scorpions!" The expectant hush is noticeable by its absence though passions are aroused when Carl Wilkinson and Richard Lawson joust for lead position throughout the race. Fourth place first time out for Adam Allott fails to impress a Scunthorpe fan close to the start line, "Allott's a National League rider! He's Adam 'Adit not Allott!" Suddenly witty re-workings of riders' names are all the rage and Paul Harvey provides his own Spike Milligan-esque reworkings, "Glen Cuntingham, Rory Slime and Emiliano Sandshoe!" Injured speedway rider Jonathan Bethell makes his way round from the pits to the catering kiosk to buy a hotdog with extra onions. When I question his food choice ("nice healthy diet then?") Jonathan explains, "I'm not riding this season!" As the two-minute warning hooter sounds loudly, Jonathan proceeds to bamboozle me with well-practised talk of complicated knee operations and ACLs. He points to a rather dramatic looking brace on his knee. Rather than prolong our talk of knees and all things medical, I switch the subject to the Comets, ("Workington look good tonight"). Jonathan takes a big bite out of his hotdog and, between chews, expresses some scepticism, "Well, I dunno? That Adam Allott definitely isn't a number three!" Whichever way you access comparative team strengths, based on tonight's performance, these sides look closely matched. Heat 4 sees David Howe and Simon Lambert combine to surprisingly relegate Workington's ex-Sheffield rider and captain, Andre Compton to third place. This maximum heat advantage takes Scunthorpe into a brief lead that they immediately surrender in the next race when the Doolan/Cook partnership takes to the track for the second time in five races. Doolan again wins comfortably (this time ahead of Carl Wilkinson) to retain his 100% record and wonderfully pristine white kevlars. They're so unspeckled with shale that they could easily have come straight from the 'after' segment of a detergent commercial. A busy night looks in prospect for Craig Cook who, so far, finishes third in every race he starts. Dave Rattenberry's worries about Ben Wilson's inadequacy as a replacement for Magnus Karlsson look ill-founded when he comfortably wins heat 6 ahead of the ultra-busy Craig Cook who breaks his sequence of thirds to actually finish second (on his fourth outing in six races). A surprisingly lacklustre Andre Compton is sufficiently on the gas to relegate Viktor Bergstrom to last place. The self-confident version of David Howe is tonight in the Scunthorpe pits and proceeds to win heat 7 (sponsored by "Cido, Scunthorpe's Very Own Statto!") but gets no support from Scorpions reserve rider, Jerran Hart. Third placed Richard Lawson's white kevlars suffer inevitable severe discolouration when he's caught in the traffic that Kevin Doolan's sharp reflexes from the start gate, so far, avoid.

Scunthorpe fans rouse themselves from their collective torpor to hail Viktor Bergstrom and Simon Lambert after they hammer home the second Scorpions maximum heat advantage of the night to take their team into a 4-point

Scunthorpe : *"It's all hearsay. Some rider's dad says it's happened! Where is the proof? There isn't any! It doesn't make any business sense."*

lead. Crowd reaction and participation is obviously a learned behaviour since the Scunthorpe faithful react favourably to the news that Simon Lambert will start the next race in the red helmet colour (replacing Adam Allott). During the additional time allowed by referee Margaret Vardy, colour-blind Shaun Leigh entertains the crowd with the raffle draw. Shaun's colour blindness precludes a speedway officiating career but also causes weekly difficulties with the coloured tickets they use in the raffle draw. However, any problem has a practical solution with enough ingenuity, "See what they've done (we can't because he's stood some distance away on the centre green) they write down the numbers and the colours now 'cause, if they bring the tickets out to me, I haven't got a clue what the colour is!" When the race finally gets underway, there's a spectacular crash caused by Carl Wilkinson's loss of control on the entry to the fourth bend. He hammers into the nearby Andre Compton. Man and machine proceed to tumble-turn Siamese twins fashion in a jumble of bodies and chrome until they smash into the track wall at the exit of the fourth bend. Stood in the doorway of the trackshop Dave Rattenberry excitedly calls up to Bob Tasker filming on the roof of the trackshop, "Did you get all that Bob? Nasty crash weren't it!?" The crash is so dramatic that it wouldn't be a surprise if either or both riders suffer injuries. Thankfully both emerge unscathed, although Carl Wilkinson subsequently takes no further part in the remainder of the meeting (or the rerun after his disqualification by referee Margaret Vardy).

Partly relieved but also partly enthralled, presenter Shaun Leigh comments, "Tell you what, that was a scary looking crash!" While men and machinery receive much needed attention in the pits, a pick-up truck circles the track and Shaun observes, "He's a brave man that – going on the back of a Skoda!" There's quite a delay before the rerun of heat 9 gets underway. The actual cause of the additional delay is subject to conjecture. Over the public address system Shaun issues an appeal, "Once again, could the Clerk of the Course contact the referee immediately, if not quicker!" The rerun of heat 9 finds Andre Compton finally reunited with his gating gloves and allows Craig Cook to gain his fourth third place of the night (and his final points of the evening since he is to remain pointless in his next two rides). Ben Wilson gains his second race win in heat 10 to further assuage Dave Rattenberry's concerns about his suitability as a guest. David Howe comprehensively clarts Kevin Doolan's kevlars in EWR shale and also wins heat 11. Adam Allott wins his first home point in the Scorpions race tabard, albeit only a single point after a third place finish behind Simon Lambert in heat 12. Scunthorpe's apparent cruise to a comfortable win in the final third of the meeting suffers a brief blip during a competitive heat 13 that has Ben Wilson finish last for the second time this evening. However, when Scorpions rider of the night, Simon Lambert, follows home a suddenly rejuvenated Jerran Hart in heat 14 their maximum heat advantage ensures there's no way back for league leaders Workington. One maximum 5-1 invariably follows another to massage the final scoreline in a meeting that's been close throughout.

Afterwards Scunthorpe's speedway promoter Rob Godfrey characterises the meeting as "a bit nail-biting" before he heaps praise upon Simon Lambert, whose recent performances ensure that from next week he'll move up from reserve into the main body of the team. Taking the positives from this performance, Rob notes, "We certainly weren't firing on all cylinders tonight so to beat the League leaders by 12 points was fantastic." Also ebullient after this victory is a positively joyous Dave Rattenberry, "At least we've beaten the unpopular Workington team!" Scorpions parking supervisor Richard Heasman takes the trouble to find me, passes on his wife Sally's praise of my work but also keeps speedway in sensible context. "We have been hurt by illness here! Kenny isn't so well. He recovered so well but has gone downhill a bit. Pete Hubbard, the pit marshal, has learnt today that it's really bad news with his prostate cancer. He's known it wasn't good but that confirmed it. And, of course, Rob [Woffinden] is here tonight. If you see someone all the time you don't notice but he looks very different. He knew he was ill in Australia but didn't have it checked out until he got back. It's tragic! Tai is here with him. With so much illness, you wonder if you're a bit of a Jonah!"

3rd July Scunthorpe v. Workington (Premier League) 51-39

CHAPTER 13

Workington

"Twenty seconds! Go straight to the tapes but not over the grass!"

4th July

My Independence Day drive from a lorry park in Scunthorpe probably sees me approximately retrace the route the Workington Comets fans took on their journey home last night. Still beautiful under rainy leaden skies, the hills of the Lake District en route to Workington look wonderful. Derwent Park Stadium car park is practically deserted, apart from the odd track staff member's car, when I arrive at 3.30 p.m. It's dry here albeit with dark rain clouds overhead and jet black clouds in the distance in all directions. There's already a track staff member on guard duty by the entrance gates. From there you can quickly make your way to the Speedway Office, the pits gate that leads onto the track, the old fashioned home-straight covered grandstand and to the presently deserted pits area. Since I was here last, the pits area looks fully concreted and noticeably cleaner. In fact, even if you allow for the absence of bikes, mechanics, riders and assorted toolboxes, the ongoing attention to the stadium infrastructure undertaken during the reign of Keith Denham gives the whole speedway operation a much more spick and span appearance. Professional presentation is clearly one of Keith's priorities. Along the whole length of the Workington pits, crash barriers are already lined up opposite marked as the "Pits Viewing Area". In the near distance, there's sound of a tractor as it wends its way slowly round the track.

Another track staff member by the pits gate offers his welcome, "You're early! I'd heard rumours there was a writer coming. They open the turnstiles at 6. Rain is forecast for 4 p.m. [arrives at 3.45] but [nods to bowser] we keep watering it to make sure!" Not only is the bowser in action but the surface looks recently bladed and rolled. Workington presently top the table and, though they have the top-end strength of Steve Johnston (guest in place of injured Shane Parker) and James Grieves, it's highly unlikely that the Glasgow Tigers will provide substantial opposition. That's not quite how the bloke at the pits gate sees things, "Glasgow usually brings a good few fans and they always go well round here! They should be stronger tonight 'cause they have Steve Johnston for Shane Parker and Justin Sedgmen for I forget who? Ian Thomas was supposed to be at Scunthorpe last night and here tonight but he wasn't there. He's supposed to be recuperating but I reckon he might have done too much. Keith [Denham] has his name down in the programme as the team manager, anyway. The trackshop people usually get here at 5 to half-5 and Keith will arrive around half-5 towards 6. Would you like to go on the centre green?" After the luxury of a brief walk on the track and the centre green, I retreat to my car to escape torrential rain. No sooner does it stop lashing down than Steve Johnston pulls into the car park in a white Spearpoint-sponsored van. He's the first rider to arrive from either team but isn't quite dressed for the Costa del Workington with his close shaven head, black T-shirt and shorts. He immediately engages in cheery conversation with the small cluster of Comets staff that loiter by the car park. "That's why I frickin' took it! We're Friday to Friday at the moment. We had the Pairs last Friday. Glasgow's so fricking far that, if it's rained off, that's the weekend stuffed. This way I'm half way there and I've already frickin' paid for it! Let's hope your weatherman is right otherwise you'll be getting the first frickin' beers, that's for sure! And we'll be starting early!" No sooner has Johno disappeared into the pits with his bike, toolboxes and kit bags than Kevin Doolan pulls up in his van. One chivalrous member of the track staff volunteers to carry Kevin's toolbox but Kevin smilingly declines with a barely perceptible nod towards the bikes in the back of his van. "It's got wheels this thing which is heaps better than anything else!" Kevin provides a brief succinct review of recent team performances and his own individual ones for the track staff in person ("I only dropped my bike three times at Newport in heat 15"). In the programme, Kevin also reprises a busy week that includes Workington's third place in the Pairs at Somerset, his victory at Newport in the Welsh Open and last night's defeat at Scunthorpe. [1] My note-taking attracts the attention and disdain of one member of the track staff, "You're not from the Social, are you?" he asks (before he immediately stomps off into the stadium). The track staff member he's left behind says playfully, "I'm Mr Stephen Little". Given he's shown no paranoia about the possible investigative activities of the social security department, I suspect that's not his name. I'm still keen to find out the exact local weather forecast so I know how likely it is that my books will get soaked this evening. When I ask the pits gate man who'd just been deep in meteorological conversation with Steve Johnston, "What was that weather forecast you told Johno earlier?" He smiles, "Dunno! We made it up! You can tell Johno anything 'cause he's mad! And, 'cause he's mad, you have to!"

Kevin Doolan unloads

At the far side of the pits, close to another set of presently shuttered turnstiles, Liz Fleming and her partner Gary unpack the merchandise onto the tables inside the sea container that serves as the trackshop at Workington. With dark clouds massed overhead, weather questions dominate our conversation. Liz tells me, "It's lashing down in Keswick and that's the direction the wind's coming from but it'll probably get broken up by the hills before it gets here! If it comes from there [she points in the rough direction of the Isle of Man] that's where the most persistent rain comes from!" Last night, Gary enjoyed the Scunthorpe speedway experience, "It was cracking racing! Glasgow used to be my favourite track but now it's there!" Another member of the track staff, Anthony, passes and is consulted about the weather. "I rang Ian – the meteorological man – this morning and he said it was 'patchy and hard to predict'. We've put five tanker loads [of water] on so far." Shortly afterwards a bowser passes by the trackshop en route to a track about to receive its sixth tank-full of water. The Glasgow section of the pits is closest to the trackshop and, while they put inner tubes inside their tyres, fiddle with chains, unpack their tools or adjust back wheels, the Glasgow riders banter among themselves. Johno couldn't ever be mistaken for a shrinking violet. Stood in booth number five he banters with Glasgow reserve Lee Dicken (in booth number seven). Blond Mitchell Davey (booth six) listens intently to their conversation while he eats a banana – the skin of which he diligently places in a litterbin (after carefully reading the instructions on its lid beforehand). Like a desultory game of conversational ping-pong, Johno and Lee chat as they work. Lee Dicken expresses disappointment at the start of the season that Newport have endured so far in the Premier League. Johno admonishes him, "Don't feel frickin' sorry for Newport they just fired frickin' Lemo!" Johno proceeds to express some blunt opinions (that, for the avoidance of legal doubt, could best be expressed as "blah, blah"). It's a succinct analysis that Lee interrupts, "He's gone to Newcastle."
[Johno] "Who did they get rid off?"
[Lee] "Branney."

Gistening remodelled track

Though this sounds like some form of punishment or exile, it will be a shot in the arm for the remainder of Mark Lemon's Premier League season.

Sponsored promotional vehicle

[1] "With the curfew we didn't race off against King's Lynn but got third place on the count-back. I enjoyed watching at Cardiff on Saturday and kept fairly sober and then an early night ready for Newport on the Sunday... it was another good day at Newport on Sunday when I won the Welsh Open. That makes me the only rider to have won the Prince of Wales Trophy and the Welsh Open in the same season ... Last week I rode in the Ashley Jones Memorial at King's Lynn with the King's Lynn Legends who took on the Stars, giving me a look at the track ahead of our Premier Trophy semi-final matches."

Interestingly, the points he's already scored for Newport will see him remain top of the Wasps averages throughout the season. The close-knit nature of the speedway riding community ensures that the riders spend a great deal of time together in the pits throughout the country and Europe. One night they might be teammates and the next rivals but the thread that runs consistently through their relationships is their casual freemasonry. Consequently, there are very few secrets, while news and/or gossip, travels with lightning speed over the bush telegraph. Sadly, the loyalty shown to riders by speedway clubs hangs by a thread and is inevitably dependent upon a variety of factors often out of the control of an individual rider that can include such things as: fellow riders' averages as they cumulatively relate (on a monthly basis!) to the team building average, recent results, forthcoming fixtures, injuries, cost-cutting exercises and perceived interest levels to name but a few.
[Johno] "How are things at yours?"
[Lee] "Ross Brady's not coming back! How is it at Somerset?"
[Johno] "It's alright."

The strapline for the 2009 Workington programme (price £2.50) is "FUELLED BY EXCITEMENT". From Lee and Johno's conversation it sounds like Emil Kramer isn't only fuelled by excitement. "He was off his frickin' face. I saw the lights of the police car and I said 'I'm sorry but I'm off!' but Emil carried on. He told me to leave the smaller one and went for the bigger one! There was a policeman right behind him. He got out 11.30 the next morning and rode at Somerset that night! Ha! Ha!" Later a Glasgow fan proudly tells me that Lee has (allegedly) also had his own brushes with the Boys in Blue. "Lee Dicken was hammering down the motorway last season followed by a car that he didn't know was unmarked. When he pulled into a pub a couple of minutes later the two policemen said, 'What speed were you doing? Don't you know the speed limit?' and he admitted it so they put him in cuffs and put him in the back of the car. Then his mum came out and abused them so much they let him go saying, 'Keep to the speed limit in future and keep your mum away from us!'" While he relates this story, Mitchell Davey continues to eat more bananas (and place the skins in the litter bin). This shocks the Glasgow fan's son who cites another young – but absent through injury – Glasgow Tigers rider on the diet of the modern speedway rider, "Josh Grajczonek says none of the speedway riders eat before they ride – in case they have to have surgery!"

Workington programme editor, Barry Stephenson, is also full of the joys of the Scunthorpe speedway experience. "It was a brilliant meeting! A great track – well watered, with so many racing lines – all of them used and all of them usable!" Chris Butterworth from Grange-over-Sands stops by with his 5-year-old son, Glen, who's kitted out in an impressive quantity of Workington Comets memorabilia. Glen sports a Comets anorak and Comets cap festooned in badges while, in one hand, he holds a newly bought model of Hans Andersen and a bag of sweets in the other. Though a passionate Burnley Football Club fan, Chris has badly caught the speedway bug. "I saw the speedway on Sky and I've been coming for the last four years. It's great here! I've been bringing Glen – since he was 3½ – and he loves it! Really loves it! I never thought I'd take him more to the speedway than to watch Burnley. It's a 120-mile round trip – we go through the Lakes, go to McDonald's, get some sweets and enjoy some brilliant racing!"[2] Though people linger by my bookstall and look at the merchandise or stop for a chat, sales are very poor. One lady stops to buy a

[2] Afterwards Glen sent me a follow-up e-mail. "The meeting itself I think wasn't the best. The track was fabulous for the first 7–10 meetings with some amazing Speedway and lots of passing moves but the last 4–5 meetings have been pretty much a gater's paradise. I'm not sure why this should be the case but think that the hot weather might have something to do with it. There is just no moisture in the track and I think they have struggled to get enough water on it. I look forward to reading *Quantum of Shale* and hope that you might get a chance to visit Derwent Park later in the season. A Meeting in September under floodlights when the track is much more amenable to plenty of passing is a great spectacle. As I think I mentioned I'm in my 4th season of watching live Speedway now and it really is a fabulous family spectacle. Quite how it's all gone wrong from the heyday of the 40s would I'm sure cover many volumes. Having been a lifelong Burnley fan who has been to Hell and back watching the Clarets over the years (Stockport on an open terrace in the pouring rain on a February Friday night in the fourth division.... I could go on!) I never thought that I'd be taking my son to Speedway meetings over visits to Turf Moor...Strange how things pan out. Matches/Meetings so far= Burnley FC visits 3, Workington Speedway visits 34!!!
My tips for taking boys to speedway meetings as follows:
1. Play I Spy in the car on the way to the meeting.
2. Visit McDonald's once near the track
3. Buy a badge at the track shop (Pennies Permitting) and try and stick on Cap (which now weighs about 2 stone!!)
4. Buy a bagful of sweets and scoff said items between heats.
5. Tickle said son repeatedly between heats but only when he's least expecting it!!!
6. Guess who's going to win each heat and scream your head off for approximately 65 seconds!
Quality Time with son...PRICELESS!!
POSITIVE MEMORIES WHICH HOPEFULLY WILL REMAIN WITH HIM FOREVER.

copy for her hubby Derek, "It's a belated Father's Day gift. He'll enjoy it and it'll shut him up for a bit so there's an ulterior motive! He used to ride and speedway is number one for him, I'm a speedway widow!" One Glasgow fan is pleased that the club have booked the capable Steve Johnston as a guest but, nonetheless, is still disappointed their talismanic Australian Shane Parker's absent through injury. "Shane's out with his back after Adrian Rymel's bike hit him at the Pairs!" Sales at the trackshop seem steady but, once the bulk of the fans have come through the turnstiles, the most popular outlet is the programme stall where the fans are greeted in friendly fashion by Paula Denham and her colleague. The programme has a variety of entertaining columns written by promoter J. K. Denham , promoter and team manager, I. Thomas, announcer J. Walsh and club captain K. Doolan. Disappointingly there isn't any space given over to the thoughts and opinions of club chaplain Canon B. Rowe. In the manner of old-fashioned cricket scorebooks when the cricket world was split into gentlemen and players, the Workington programme lists its 2009 officials somewhat formally using initial and surname except for their medical officers: the famous Doctor Butler plus his colleagues Doctor Bickerton and Doctor Gardner. Only the photographers have their first name revealed in the list of Officials in the programme (Dave Payne and Adrian Randall). Various columns contain some useful nuggets of information. For example, John Walsh reveals that Tony Mole officiated as Birmingham Brummies team manager in the absence of Graham (and Denise) Drury when they won the Pairs tournament at Somerset. He updates us on Charles Wright's medical woes ("he's still getting problems from his hand – not the scaphoid, more the outside of the right hand by the little finger and he was going for another X-ray. His heels, too, are still not completely healed") and the recovery of team manager Ian Thomas ("making significant progress after his horrible post-operative experience").

Speedway teams are inevitably made up of guests -tonight Glasgow have Justin Sedgmen and Steve Johnston – while both teams run rider replacement for Charles Wright and Josh Grajczonek respectively. Even the Comets programme columnists have guests, ex-Workington programme editor Tony Jackson steps in to write the "THIS IS IT with Ian Thomas" column. In the Workington speedway universe, if Keith Denham is the sun (as evidenced by Keith's "View from the Top" column) then, due to his absence, Ian Thomas must be a black hole. ("Thanks to Tony Jackson for stepping in to fill the void and helping us with managing the team in particularly at our way [*sic*] fixtures, it is much appreciated").

If one night Steve Johnston can ride for Somerset and another for Glasgow, then the same holds true in the world of speedway presentation since the man on the mic at Derwent Park Stadium is Michael Max. Every Sunday during the speedway season, Michael is in charge of the centre-green microphone for the Glasgow Tigers. Consequently, we really couldn't get a more expert insight into both teams than that provided by Michael. Ever the true professional, if you were a first-time visitor to speedway, then you would have absolutely no hint or indication that Mr Max might possibly hold split loyalties. In fact, if the Boys in Blue break off from their interactions with recalcitrant speedway riders and, instead, decide to quiz the fans about his loyalties, I'm sure that they'd swear under oath that Michael's a confirmed devotee of the mighty Comets. The subject of first-time visitors is something close to Michael's heart, if judged by his early scene-setting announcement over the public address system. "Well, for any of you along for the first time after seeing the Cardiff GP[3] well, it's very different from what you see there! That's an individual event and this is a team event!" Helpfully Michael proceeds to give a quick but extremely complex introduction to the rules and regulations of speedway that, though they make sense to a regular speedway fan like myself, inevitably sounded as straightforward as the rules of a game of three-dimensional chess with Mr Spock would be to a Ludo player. Keen to retain the interest of said (probably imaginary) speedway virgins about to be blooded at Derwent Park tonight, Michael closes with a rousing but easy to follow imprecation, "The important rule in a sport that has a lot of rules is – enjoy yourself and make a lot of noise!"

Stood outside the second-bend bar, pint in hand Craig Branney chats amiably with a fan who's enquired about the reasons behind his recent removal from the Newcastle Diamonds line-up. Craig answers philosophically, "I was the one to give way in the numbers game!" Luckily for Craig and this quizzical fan, there are no inquisitive first-time visitors on hand who require an explanation of speedway team averages. However, almost telepathically, Michael decides to delight the Workington speedway fraternity with some "hot off the press" information on the latest PL rider averages. "And, believe it or not, the highest averaged rider in the Premier League on the July green sheets is [pause] James

[3] Sounds like it could be their second time!

Grieves!" This shock news sets our collective imaginations alight but that's nothing compared to the excitement generated by the imminent arrival on track of a Suzuki Swift. This vehicle is busily emblazoned with vital information about Workington Speedway club. It's going to be used to step up the promotional campaign of the club and will also be driven to schools in the Workington area. "You're about to see our brand new Workington car which you'll see driving round the town from now on!" No sooner have the words echoed over the speaker system than the Suzuki Swift – which looks remarkably like a less stylish version of a Mini – goes on a warm-up lap round the Derwent Park stadium track with its hazard lights flashing, hugging the inside race line! A local garage provides this sponsored vehicle. They've made it all the more distinctive with images of each Comets rider imaginatively stuck on its windows. Given it's a small hatchback car and, even if you allow for the fact that some speedway riders can be rather diminutive in stature, the sight of seven faces staring out at you from any five-seater car would give fellow motorists or passing pedestrians pause for thought.[4]

Justin Sedgmen's evening gets off to a bad start when referee Stuart Wilson disqualifies him for a tape touching offence. Unable to shake off his laudable desire to educate the uninitiated, Michael Max provides an explanation-cum-clarification of what has just occurred, "It won't count towards his rides but it will count towards his number of rides!" Too complicated to discuss further, Glasgow's serial banana eater Mitchell Davey replaces Sedgmen for the rerun and proceeds to relegate the highly-regarded Craig Cook into last place. Mitchell's liking and aptitude for the Derwent Park track continues when he wins the reserve's race. In a manner of an illusionist, Michael Max decides to distract the Comets faithful from any anxieties they might harbour by highlighting a potentially greater anxiety in the near future, "Next week we have the Premier Trophy semi-final when King's Lynn are here and we'll be aiming to knock them out of their stride!" Initially I stand on the back straight and, despite the extensive watering the track received before the meeting, from the outset any spectator there gets repeatedly covered by a fine dust storm that drifts slowly over us all each and every time the riders lap the circuit. The third race of the night sees Richard Lawson rear massively as he transitions from the first to second bend and, though he remains on his bike, he ensures that he'll finish last even though the race is only a few yards old. On his way to a comfortable win, the Comets Adrian Rymel also encounters problems in roughly this same spot on the track on the next lap. The home crowd react in lukewarm fashion to this first Workington race win of the night, though this is understandable enough given they continue to trail the Tigers by 2 points. Michael solicits some reaction, "Our sustainable whistles – I haven't heard them much tonight!" Michael's fascination with the recently issued green-sheet averages helps continue our ongoing collective education, "Only four riders have a 9-point average in the Premier League – James Grieves, Darcy Ward, Tomas Topinka and Shane Parker." Apart from the absent Shane Parker, the rest of these 9-point riders are all at Derwent Park tonight since the King's Lynn team have stopped off en route to Glasgow for a reconnaissance of the track and their opposition ahead of next week's Premier Trophy semi-final meeting.

Michael Max invites me to the centre green for a brief interview to alert the crowd to the availability of my latest book. With trademark understated wit, he backhandedly introduces me as the "Enid Blyton of Speedway!" Though in my writing I might occasionally ironise some of the more banal things that speedway presenters utter, centre-green interviews are difficult to conduct skilfully and it's definitely not my cup of tea to take part in them. This is partly because though I'm happy to make spontaneous comments I worry that I might inadvertently use an obscenity or, perhaps, say something anodyne that, nonetheless, inadvertently inflames the ire of overly sensitive listeners (aka speedway promoters). Though I expect you soon get used to it with practice, I find the most disconcerting factor about any centre-green interview is that – as you speak – you can also hear yourself speaking over the public address system, albeit with a split-second delay. I have to admit that I've yet to master the ability to either not listen to myself a fraction of a second after I've just said something or have yet to master the skill required to speak over my own comments. If this were tennis then Michael Max's first question is the interview equivalent of a gentle lob that any half competent player should be able to smash away for victory. Unfortunately, since I'm so easily distracted by the

[4] The *Speedway Star* carries a photograph of the ceremonial presentation where Justin Edgar gave Keith Denham the keys to car. "Justin Edgar, who runs J. Edgar & Son Dunmail Park showroom on Maryport Road, has given a Suzuki Swift to Keith Denham and his team for the rest of the season. Edgar & Son sponsor the weekly Rider of the Night award at home matches. The riders will be using the car on trips to local schools and it will be a familiar sight all round West Cumbria in the coming months. The car has images of all seven Comets riders on the windows and further decoration on the bodywork. The face of captain Kevin Doolan appears in the driver's window, with John Branney behind. Richard Lawson and Adrian Rymel appear in the left-hand windows, with the other three riders in the back. The images are made out of a material that allows the driver to see out making the car road legal. Justin said: 'I used to ride motocross and have known John Branney, Richard Lawson and Craig Cook for many years.'"

sound of my own voice, I'm overcome with the interview equivalent of the yips – so repeatedly say in awful Paul Hardcastle stuttering fashion "I've visited every speedway in Britain during 2008, 2008, 2008, 2008." Something may have hinted to the crowd that my latest book covers 2008. However, I'm also distracted by the fact that Michael keeps moving the microphone in his hand downwards and away from my head. Unable to ask him what the goodness he's doing, I instead follow the microphone around with my mouth as he waves it hither and dither thereby creating the impression that I'm a stuttering ant eater afflicted by Saint Vitas Dance. Luckily the sound of the two-minute warning saves further embarrassment as the riders' pootle out onto the track and Michael need to get on with the formality of a run through the rider line-up for this race takes precedence.

While we're off-air Michael explains that the microphone movement isn't an example of his sense of humour but a technical matter, "The level's a bit high tonight so I kept moving the mic away from you and you kept following it!" Though you wouldn't be able tell from his presentation so far, Michael is under the weather, "I have a blocked ear and a sore throat – if that's swine flu – I have it!" Sensible risk management dictates that I leave the centre green as quickly as possible to protect my health but, since a speedway race is in progress, I can't. Ever-professional Michael remains keen to overcome my stutters sufficiently long enough to extract some notional nugget of insight. Whenever you meet the Queen, it's said she puts you at your ease with the question, "And how was your journey here today?" This simple opener enables some form of challenge free dialogue/conversation to ensue before the Queen quickly moves on to the next member of the public. If Michael's first question was a dolly drop then his second is a beamer, "What do you think speedway needs to do to improve?" This questions has baffled speedway experts for decades and probably could be the subject of a *War and Peace* sized treatise rather than a few quick sound bites on a Saturday night stood on a centre green in Workington. Worse still, the potential to say something too honest and, thereby, fall into a Grand Canyon sized pit of my own making is a real and present danger. Unfortunately I can't manufacture deliberate stutters sufficiently long enough until the two-minute warning for the next race sounds so, instead, I trot out a few of the canards and platitudes so wonderfully provided every week by the Sky Sports live speedway commentary team.

The thrill and the spectacle of a speedway race viewed from the centre green quickens my pulse and, as ever, it's a genuine privilege to watch a couple of races from this vantage point. Heat 4 sees the fast gating and, viewed from this angle, wildly speedy Andre Compton beat Tigers guest Steve Johnston comfortably. Heat 5 sees Adrian Rymel best top of the averages James Grieves in a race that looks equally breathtakingly fast. Though he notionally had the chance to acclimatise to the track in heat 2, on his second outing Lee Dicken again fails to trouble the scorer. Without a hint of a smile or any vocal clue to indicate possible irony, Michael Max informs me, "Lee Dicken got paid 18 last week [pause] against Newport [pause] at home!" Though he doubtless has many more questions, Michael kindly doesn't ask them but does allow me to linger and watch one more race from the centre green. This sees Steve Johnston trail in behind an impressively fast looking Kevin Doolan. While announcer John Walsh confirms the official race result, Michael answers his own difficult question about speedway, "There's quite a few issues but the main problem is that the management committee haven't stamped down on it [alleged averages manipulation] and that isn't sensible and sends a strange message! Birmingham have brought in Jay Herne so they're now building a team to different rules to the rest of the Premier League! They're now on 43.2 something or other! Apparently 'cause they were refused over Piszcz, it's okay this time!"

Though I made a total fool of myself on the centre green, Michael encourages the crowd to show their appreciation and, in the polite manner of kindly speedway people everywhere, they generously applaud. Once restored to the comparative safety, security and silence of the terraces, a Comets fan buttonholes me to tell me about his view of track developments at the stadium. "They've widened bend one, changed the shale – Keith Denham says it's so the spectators don't get sprayed in dirt – but the racing's not what it was. And there have been bumps on the second bend all season. That said, I'd come and watch monkeys race here every week!" As if to illustrate his point about the bumps, in heat 7 experienced rider and race leader Andre Compton completely loses control on the second bend. Thankfully Craig Cook reveals the speed of his reflexes and the value of his motocross experience, when he does extremely well to avoid the stricken Compton (let alone go on to win the race).

There's quite a delay in proceedings before heat 8 ("We've got a little delay, I don't know why!"). The relentlessly professional Michael Max efficiently fills this time with an interview King's Lynn team manager, Rob Lyon. With his

Team GB team manager hat firmly on, Rob gives good interview. Not only that but he answers Michael's quick-fire questions with a potent mix of honesty and political sophistry.

[Rob] "At the end of the day someone's got to do the job. I'm starting again with the kids as you can see. You have to give them the chance and they'll give their all!"

[Michael] "In British speedway, the last two or three years has been devoid of really top-end talent."

[Rob] "We all know that passion, pride and 100% commitment is what makes a top speedway rider and we've been lacking that!"

[Michael] "What exactly is the job of the England team manager?"

[Rob] "You could be here all night if I'm honest … doing lots of things off the track: nutrition, discipline and fitness, how they project themselves as speedway riders! It takes up three or four days a week – it's not just picking five riders and having them ride."

[Michael] "There are a lot of egos involved in speedway – as you know – what approach are you going to take to that?"

[Rob] "I can't be involved in egos! We're all human beings at the end of the day and have to treat each other well. In the Elite League, and at the higher echelons of speedway, some people think that they're better than everyone else but we're all human beings."

[Michael] "To put you on the spot, who will be the next British speedway world champion?"

[Rob] "Oh, I'm not going to start picking one here … if I had to pick one for racing and preparation, I'd say Tai Woffinden!"

In the riders' viewing area, the entire King's Lynn team crowd together to watch each race intently. They really do study their homework in preparation for their encounter with the Comets next weekend. Based on the first half of the meeting, the Comets don't look a team since only Doolan and Rymel have been really consistent. That said, it would be hard to miss that Craig Cook has given them good support. Adrian Rymel wins the rerun of heat 9 and with Richard Lawson third, the Comets extend their lead on the night to 6 points (30-24). Excitedly Michael Max notes, "That's three out of three for Adrian Rymel – fast out of the starts, sometimes too fast! I've just had a mobile phone call from Ian Thomas who says he can't get the score on his computer – he should try turning it on – and he wants to pass on his thanks and best wishes and says he hopes to be at Redcar on Thursday and here on Saturday. He has an appointment at hospital on Tuesday." Two St John Ambulance staff also stand in the pits-viewing area primed for action in their helmets with the visors already pulled down, possibly to stop the thin film of shale dust from coating their eyes and mouth. Just after 8 o'clock, it starts to drizzle. Not good news for rider visibility or those fans stood in the open air of the first corner but it should, at least, reduce dust levels. Tonight's crowd level isn't quite at the capacity of yesteryear (or as I remember it). One of the stewards explains, "The rain in the area has kept people away. Workington crowds are like Carlisle ones in that whoever is out there, they could do better than them no matter how difficult it is to ride a speedway bike or play football at a high level! And it is difficult when things aren't going well, numbers drop off yet they flood back when there's success! Human nature, I s'pose, but they're really critical round here, I dunno why!" It's an analysis I don't have enough information to comment upon except, of course, for the fact that Workington presently top the PL table! Kevin Doolan wins heat 10. It's a sight that prompts Michael to observe, "I can exclusively reveal that Kevin Doolan was spotted [pause] in Glasgow last Tuesday! He was not up having talks about signing for Glasgow but was up to see the AC/DC concert and had a fantastic time!" After 11 races the score is 36-30 and, wonderfully coincidentally for the Tigers ambitions to get back into the match through the use of the tactical ride rules and regulations, they immediately concede a 5-1 in heat 12 to take the scores to 41-31. With a gap of 10 points now opened up, Glasgow are able to utilise the black-and-white helmet option. They immediately send James Grieves out in this headgear. He proceeds to vie for the lead with Kevin Doolan before he emerges triumphant. The 2-7 heat result justifies the Tigers 'tactics' and also narrows the score to 43-38.

Before the final two races of the night I retreat to my table by the trackshop. This allows me to watch the goings on in the Glasgow section of the pits and, just as each race starts, to dash up the steps to watch the race action from the gravel banking that tops the first-bend terraces. Apparently in a world of his own, Mitchell Davey is chosen to replace his reserve teammate Lee Dicken (after he's rode to a five-race minimum) for the vital penultimate race of the night. With very little of the two-minute time allowance left, Glasgow Tigers team manager Stewart Dickson shouts at the young Australian, "Twenty seconds! Go straight to the tapes but not over the grass!" After they've spent most of the night unlikely to challenge for a league point, let alone victory, the Tigers challenge suddenly sparks into life. When Justin Sedgmen wins, ahead of Craig Cook, with Mitchell Davey third, the overall scores narrow to 45-42 and the sparks flare enough to hint strongly of flame. To get the fans back on a regular basis you need exciting races and some level of uncertainty about the final result (before the home team emerges victorious). Maximum heat advantage in the last race of the night would enable the Tigers to snatch an improbable victory while, if the Comets are to consolidate their challenge for League honours, they too need a last race 5-1 to maximise the number of league points from the meeting. Prior to the nominated race, there's a Brains Trust style conflab between James Grieves, Steve Johnston, Stewart Dickson and Alan Dick who huddle together conspiratorially at the far end of the pits. Stating the obvious and offering encouragement all in the same phrase, Stewart Dickson closes their conversation with a loud "We need a 5-1!" Ever the showman, Johno pulls a pantomime, theatrical wide-eyed look! Never afraid to play the joker, Johno then wins his first race of the night to fulfil his side of the bargain only for James Grieves to fail to score for the first time tonight. The drawn heat confirms the Comets win but still enables the Tigers to leave the stadium with an unlikely league point. Michael Max continues to rise above his own divided loyalties when he summarises enthusiastically as the meeting officially closes at 21.02, "It's a result that keeps both teams relatively happy!"

The crowd filters away quickly and, in the darkness close to the trackshop, fans can't see the books to buy them. I fold away my table and pack up my books. As I carry them back and forth through the quickly deserted pits Keith Denham and Kevin Doolan (still dressed in his kevlars) are deep in conversation about the task they have ahead racing King's Lynn in the Premier Trophy final next weekend. His success in business, never mind his reputation, suggests that what Keith Denham wants, Keith Denham gets. It's abundantly clear that he'd like (wants) Kevin to come up to Workington earlier than usual ("next Friday!") to help advise on the track and its preparation for this vitally important encounter for this rejuvenated and ambitious club. Kevin's known to take his team captaincy duties extremely seriously and appears genuinely sincere when he enthusiastically volunteers to help. "I'll do anything I can! I'll drive the tractor if that's what it takes! [pause] Someone will have to show me what buttons to press!" After Kevin departs, Keith Denham finds time to offer a few words. "It was close. I had someone here tonight with £5 million or £6 million with their friends and family and the last thing you want is lots of processional races! We wouldn't want to have meetings where we score 60 points every week. Who'd want to come and see that? Close meetings are what's needed! We had that tonight – too close, really! But we've spent a lot of money improving this place to entertain the fans and to keep them coming back! That's our plan."

The crowd disappears so quickly I assume many are on a promise in the town centre but, in fact, it appears that after the meeting many of them congregate in the bar under the home-straight grandstand. There's a fantastically vibrant atmosphere and the place is hot and crowded with staff, fans, friends, partners and children. The raffle (yet to be drawn) has a huge number of prizes and, at the crowded bar, I bump into Gary Reid. He tells me that his job is to "buy and sell antiques and collectables". There's no shortage of work in the area because of many "house clearances" brought on by bereavement or financial necessity. "There was a story in the paper about how a local tax inspector bought a 1958 Harley at auction in Wetherby for £1,200 'cause he loved to do bikes up as a hobby. It was from his era so that'll give you an idea of how old he is. When he took it apart he discovered a note saying 'Happy Birthday Elvis' from Johnny Cash. It was a present to celebrate their first time on tour together in '58 or '59. He checked the chassis number back and it was genuine! It sold at Sotheby's for £3.1 million!" One man's rubbish is another man's treasure and it's clear tonight that from the atmosphere in the grandstand bar many people genuinely treasure their Saturday nights watching Workington speedway!

4th July Workington v. Glasgow (Premier League) 48-45

CHAPTER 14

Glasgow

"He's a real speedway fan. Not a celebrity one – he fills in the programme! Unfortunately, his wife doesn't like speedway!"

5th July

As I arrive in the Ashfield Stadium car park three hours before the scheduled start time, it's a complete surprise to see that the only other fans in the car park are Eastbourne stalwart Sid Greatley and his son Rob. They're on a mini-northern tour that has already taken in Edinburgh and Berwick ("what fantastic people"). Rob's son Tim has been laid up in Swindon hospital with acute myeloid leukaemia and shortly will go into Brompton Hospital. "We wanted to thank them for their kindness with Tim in hospital that's just like we'll do here when they passed a 'get well' card round the crowd and so many people signed it!" The Berwick promotion and presentational team went out of their way to make Sid and Rob welcome. "They announced we were there over the speakers!" They're also impressed with the impact that the new promotional broom has had at the club, "There's been so many changes – new shale and everything!" [1]

Also on a northern tour – that takes in Edinburgh, Berwick and Glasgow – is Britain's youngest speedway referee, Dan Holt. When I arrive, he's already ensconced in the Saracen Park Speedway Office with Alan Dick and Michael Max. They say 'hello' but appear keen to carry on with their men's talk. Sat in the bar area, I study the programme. Glasgow are another speedway club to follow the programme price inflation trend, so theirs is also now priced at £2.50. The 'Up Front' column written by the promotional triumvirate of Alan C. Dick, Stewart Dickson and Gordon Pairman (accompanied by a side-on photograph of them) expresses contrition about the lamentable home performance against Berwick a fortnight previously. ("There is no denying we should be beating the Bandits at home and to fail to do so was quite annoying"). Last Sunday the Tigers lost at Rye House but the promotional trio take some comfort that the Tigers "put up a reasonable attempt". The injury update confirms that Shane Parker is now up and about but still unable to ride. This afternoon's guests for Glasgow are William Lawson and Steve Johnston. Some measure of satisfaction is taken from the news that temporary captain James Grieves tops the Premier League averages. However, the rider every Glasgow speedway fan wants to see this afternoon is Darcy Ward. The 'Meet the Visitors' section of the programme succinctly summarises his potential appeal. "The Premier League newcomer of the year will definitely be Darcy Ward. The 16-year-old from Australia has taken the northern hemisphere speedway world by storm. He's gone straight to the top of the averages with a 10-plus figure. For comparison, he is posting better figures than Leigh Adams and Jason Crump did in their debut seasons in the British second tier when they were 16. If he maintains this progress then he will be on the Grand Prix circuit in a couple of years and who wouldn't bet on him becoming world champion at some stage? Hopefully we can get to see him at Glasgow a few times but I suspect he won't be hanging around the Premier League for too long. Enjoy watching him race while you have the opportunity." Should he remain injury-free, available and picked for their team, Darcy Ward will draw crowds at every club King's Lynn visit this season.

Fresh from his meeting, Michael Max wanders past on his way to the pits. Usually before any meeting, professionalism dictates Michael continues with some vague vestige of optimism prior to tapes up but, this afternoon, his assessment is bluntly realistic, "We'll get hammered! It'll be interesting to see how Darcy Ward rides here, though." Shortly after,

[1] Tim had a stem cell transplant on 2nd October 2009. The operation went well and he spent Christmas at home. In January, a lump on his neck unfortunately indicated the leukaemia had returned and, sadly, a complication with his blood made his condition inoperable. Tim passed away on 13th February 2010.

Dan Holt leaves to undertake the necessary supervisory duties that are the lot of any SCB official prior to a speedway meeting. When Alan Dick emerges, he looks noticeably less youthful than the fresh-faced photograph that appears in this week's programme ("that's '92 or '93 at Fir Park"). Alan quickly lists the catalogue of misfortune and injury that dogs the club (again) this season. "We've a strong team on paper but, again this season, we've been decimated by injuries. The original one to seven last appeared on 12th April! Shane has hurt his back, Ross Brady has a broken wrist, Anders Andersen broke his leg (but we replaced him) and Josh has broken an ankle. We only have four of our riders this afternoon." Controversy off the track also dogs the sport this season. Though Alan has strong opinions on what the future could hold, he studiously limits himself to a brief comment. "The sport needs a major shake-up! Neil Machin is an articulate advocate for the lower league clubs."

King's Lynn track walk

Colin Mackie and his wife set out the merchandise at their trackshop located at the back of the covered home-straight standing terraces that overlook the fourth bend. Colin's wife greets me with an ironic, "Is it going to rain?" Colin reminds me that my previous visits to Ashfield Stadium haven't always been dry, "Every time you come here it rains." A short distance away, stood by the raffle and programme stalls, ex-rider Jimmy Tannock discusses the Cardiff Grand Prix. "The racing was great but the PA was terrible! I couldn't hear the race results and the camera work [on the giant screens] was not much better! Still, it was the best yet! Emil Sayfutdinov has a lot to learn. He's with the big boys now, no one is going to move aside and wave him through! They're going to block him. What Scott did was just racing. Imagine what Nicki would do? When it happens, and it will, he just needs to smile. Showing a reaction like that means it will only happen more!" Jimmy has brought a couple of black-and-white photos along – one from April 1949 ("the first ever meeting was held here on April the twenty-something in 1949") and the other features the 1950 vintage Glasgow Tigers.

Rider parade

Glasgow uber-fan and committed-smoker Jim Fleming is pleased to see William Lawson in the Tigers team. "William is a good guest – he got 14 (paid 16) here for Berwick last weekend." A passing fan interjects, "They sacked Lawson last night at Berwick. They told him to frick off! He'd done nothing from three rides and Newport got a draw. His home average is only 3. If he goes away, then they can bring Burza back!" Though Steve Johnston is a capable guest, Jim Fleming remains concerned at the continued absence of Shane Parker. "He's the most exciting rider round here! You can see him line them up and then pass them. His points are missed but his leadership is missed more!" Jim does alert me to the fact that there might well be celebrity sportsmen in attendance this afternoon. "Stephen Craigan – Motherwell captain and current Northern Ireland centre half – I wonder if he's here? He's a real speedway fan. Not a celebrity one – he fills in the programme! Unfortunately, his wife doesn't like speedway!"

Celebration wheelie from Darcy

Taxi driver Jim Brykajlo arrives with his son Steven whom he jokingly dubs "Britain's number one train photographer!" Jim's a knowledgeable speedway fan with an in-depth appreciation of every club and rider but, most importantly, is an enthusiastic advocate for all things Berwick speedway. He tells me that the size of the border town and its comparatively isolated geographic location means, "75% of Berwick speedway fans come from outside

Berwick – from places like Dunbar, Addington and Midlothian." In my experience it's not a proper Glasgow Speedway meeting unless, like so many other committed Tigers fans, Alison Chalmers and Ian Maclean are both in the stadium to watch the Tigers race. As usual, Alison's come along with her daughter Laura who's already left her mum to watch from elsewhere. "Laura has discovered the back straight [at the top of the bank by the riders' vans]. They say it's one of the best places to watch speedway from the UK!" Ian Maclean spent last weekend away on missionary work in England and Wales and saw his beloved Tigers visit Rye House at Hoddesdon. Though they lost 56-37, Ian's fascinated with the overall presentation there since he believes it's a significant component factor of the enjoyment of any speedway meeting. "At Rye House last Sunday afternoon, they provided a lesson in how to run a meeting efficiently – then you expect Len Silver to always be professional!"

Michael Max conducts the rider parade with smooth efficiency and even includes a polite mention for the referee, "Last time Dan [Holt] was up here it lasted about four and a half days – it just went on and on!" A Tigers fan claims there were 42 reruns, 16 crashes and four exclusions! The first race of the afternoon promises to be a corker since it features a duel between the number one rider in the Premier League averages [James Grieves] against the number two rider [Darcy Ward]. Darcy and his partner Linus Eklof are both debutants this afternoon at Saracen Park. On duty this afternoon at the start line is assistant start marshal Hugh McNeilly ably helped by his daughter, Heather. If our collective expectation is for a thrilling debut race for Darcy then, it's safe to say, even those fans with the most grandiose expectations have them massively exceeded by the sheer brilliance of the young Australian on his first ever Ashfield outing. The green-helmeted Ward lines up on gate 3 with the red-helmeted Grieves outside him on gate 4. As they zoom to the corner, the experienced James Grieves attempts to assert his dominance by leaning on the youngster but finds himself imperiously brushed aside by Ward who proceeds to flash round the track with breathtaking speed and brilliance before he wins by over a quarter of a lap! Over the public address system Michael Max exclaims, "Wow! That's quite a track debut!" Collectively I suspect all of us in the crowd take pride that we've witnessed such a spectacle. Darcy showcases his incredible speed in combination with raw natural ability though the choice of the word 'raw' distracts from his sheer grace, vitality and skilful composure on the bike. Even more amazingly, he equals Shane Parker's track record time of 56.5 seconds. Like so many others, Alison Chalmers is bowled over by what she's just seen, "He lost the track record when he slightly locked-up on the last bend! He elbowed Grieves at the start as well, which also would have caused a fractional delay. It's taken Shane seasons to set that record and he equals it in his first ever ride!" Co-promoter Alan Dick's also on the terraces (with his sister) and equally impressed by Darcy's performance, "That was phenomenal! It's the second meeting running the track record has been beaten."

Even before we learn the race time, everyone in the crowd knew that Darcy was disgracefully fast. Though the sport is called speedway, it's not always speed itself that provides the drama or excitement in a race. Often, for a thriller of a race to really happen, there needs to be a tussle between at least two riders. Doubtless, when he progresses up the speedway ladder, Darcy will get to truly test his gifts and ability against similarly talented other riders. Nonetheless, sight of Darcy is enough to raise the philosophical question: what is speed? Well, the English word speed derives from the old English spowan, meaning to succeed or prosper and we all know speeding has long had associations with wealth, sex and power. [2] However, at its most basic, clearly speed has something to do with velocity. That said, all quantification requires a scale of measurement. In any vehicle – whether a car or speedway bike – to really feel speed you need landmarks, things that are slower or stationary since the notion of speed is both variable and absolute. Unlike the riders, as fans the drama of each speedway race effectively takes place on a comparatively featureless canvas we know as a speedway track. While track sizes and shapes vary – and even shale colours – apart from the start/finish line, it's essentially a featureless environment enlivened by the competition amongst the riders that takes place upon it. There's a strong gladiatorial element to any speedway race, especially one under floodlights where the velocity of the bikes, the colour of the kevlars, sparkle of the chrome as the riders transition through

[2] In the mid-19th century, some medical experts argued for speed limits as they feared that trains would go faster than the human body could stand and people would suffocate. The psychoanalyst Michael Balint argues in his book Thrills & Regressions that speed is related to competitive struggles and races are 'symbolically related to erection and potency'. Balint also notes beating a slower opponent is only a 'second-order enjoyment'. Like all thrills, racing at speed is a heady mixture of pleasure, fear and hope. For Balint, speed is both transitive (an affirmation of social power and status) and intransitive (an intensely personal enjoyment). It's possible to agree that this does, in a small way, explain some of the philosophical appeal of speedway – since, for fans, the experience is mostly transitive, while the riders get to live the Full Monty of both states. For more information on the practicalities, history and philosophies behind our experience of twentieth century British roads and road building read the excellent *On Roads* by Joe Moran (or, indeed, his just as thoughtful *Queuing for Beginners*). For his discussions of speed and modernity see pp.166-168.

Glasgow : *"He's a real speedway fan. Not a celebrity one – he fills in the programme! Unfortunately, his wife doesn't like speedway!"*

darkness, shadow and light all contribute to its mesmeric effect. Helmet cams for riders show that a speedway rider's experience of any race is much more forward facing and goal oriented. Sure they need rivals to compete against but part of their battle is against g-force and physics, conditions and perception (of available space, speed, danger and trajectory), let alone the brute reality of their powerful, vibrating equipment. So though speed and a speedway race is something that can be measured with lap times – it is also always a matter of perception and, for both the rider and the spectator, an optical and sensory illusion dependent on your surroundings. According to the French cultural theorist, Paul Virilio (crazy name for a crazy guy), who's not to my knowledge a speedway fan, modern society is defined by a culture of speed and its ideology of competitive speed. Virilio suggests our conception of modernity is based on the social denial of human fragility and mortality – founded on the illusion that we have limitless capacities constrained only by available technologies. Though not quite the modernist superman this interpretation suggests, in this one race Darcy Ward confirms this thesis with his youth, vigour and speed.

The second race of the afternoon is bound to be an anti-climax and, whatever happens, always likely to look comparatively mundane. However, any race that features the King's Lynn 'Roger Warnes Transport' Stars reserve rider Kozza Smith is almost duty bound to contain a frisson of unpredictability as well as dramatic incident. After a false start, the rerun of heat 2 proceeds predictably until the third bend of the second lap when Kozza decides to execute a 360 degree turn on the track that would be the gymnastic highlight of the skilled choreography of a police motorcycle display team. However, during a speedway race, this isn't exactly what the doctor ordered. Trailed some distance behind the rest of the riders, Lee Dicken has all the time in the world to avoid the wild-riding Australian. Kozza's teammate Jan Graversen only has a split second to make an evasive manoeuvre and this prompts his own slow-motion fall on the next bend. Fresh-faced SCB official Dan Holt disqualifies Kozza Smith as the cause of the stoppage. In the rerun, Glasgow Tigers reserves Mitchell Davey and Lee Dicken make short work of Jan Graversen the sole (out of touch) Stars representative in the race. This Tigers 5-1 gives them a surprise early 2-point lead. They maintain this margin in the next race when, despite an Emiliano Sanchez race victory, Lawson and Davey pack the minor positions after the retirement of Chris Schramm. The difference between Lee Dicken's performance last night at Workington and his performance this afternoon at Ashfield Stadium is the comparison between night and day. This is duly emphasised in heat 4 when he again relegates Jan Graversen to the back of the field. More surprisingly still, Steve Johnston, beats the highly fancied Tomas Topinka to take the scoreline to a surprise 14-10 after four races. Michael Max hails the race win, "There's very few riders more popular than Steve Johnston apart from Shane Parker, of course!" Michael provides us with an update on Shane's medical – we learn his "sore back" continues to plague Shane after his crash in Somerset at the Premier League Pairs, "He hasn't ruled out riding next weekend but, to be honest, it does look very remote." Michael also kindly draws the attention of the crowd to my "annual pilgrimage" to Ashfield Stadium and recommends my "Irreverent book *Quantum of Solace*". I'm appreciative that Michael not only promotes my book but also obliquely links me to the exciting world of James Bond. Michael manages to say "*Quantum of Solace*" three times in a matter of moments and this serves to remind Alison Chalmers that Michael's failed to name check the Growlers Kids Club.

The fifth race of the afternoon causes another buzz of anticipation to again surge through the stadium as Darcy Ward once more lines up at the start line. Apart from his great natural ability on the bike, another aspect of Darcy's appeal is the fact that he hasn't yet mastered the ability to gate consistently. As a case in point, Darcy completely fails to gate so arrives into the first bend placed in third place. William Lawson leads and, familiar with the circuit, proceeds to race fast and intelligently round the track. However, he soon has Darcy on his back wheel but, because of the determination shown by Lawson as well as Ward's lack of experience at Saracen Park, the Aussie appears unable to find a way past his rival. By the third bend of the third lap, Darcy backs off from racing tyre-to-tyre on Lawson's back wheel. However, Darcy's clearly used the previous three laps to weigh up his options as well as the performance level and racing lines taken by Lawson. Just as they enter the first bend of the last lap, Darcy suddenly blasts incredibly wide (on this narrow circuit) to ride round by the fence. He draws parallel with the Scotsman before he zooms through a slight to almost nonexistent gap as they exit the second bend together. At last ahead, Ward accelerates down the length of the back straight at breakneck speed and, thereby, enters the final corner much too quickly. Somehow his reflexes, balance and natural elegance ensures he remains on his machine and takes the chequered flag to the deserved adulation of the crowd. Again the speedway fan in Michael Max overcomes the usually professional presenter, "I've got to say I thought William Lawson had ridden a perfect race but that was awesome! Thank goodness he doesn't

Glasgow : *"He's a real speedway fan. Not a celebrity one – he fills in the programme! Unfortunately, his wife doesn't like speedway!"*

come out again until heat 11!"

Though he tops the green-sheet averages, James Grieves's second race of the afternoon (heat 6) sees him beaten by a visiting heat leader for the second time this afternoon (in this instance, Tomas Topinka). Though we're treated to the odd wild manoeuvre, Kozza Smith manages to complete four laps without the complete loss of control of his machinery and he deserves his third place ahead of Rusty Harrison. With the cumulative scores now level, Steve Johnston wins his second race of the afternoon in another drawn heat. If there'd been any chance to bet before the meeting, few people would have predicted 21 points each after seven races. Michael Max praises Glasgow guest Steve Johnston for his second win, "He looks very assured but he's still got to come up against Darcy!" Alison Chalmers is much more concerned with Mitchell Davey who, with each race of the afternoon, scores fewer points per outing. "Mitchell Davey is missing his pal Josh [Grajczonek]. They live together and drive to meetings together but he's injured and has had to go back to Australia. Mitchell started the season with some big scores but, everyone can see, his scores have fallen off. With all the extra rides 'cause of Ross Brady's absence, he's got very tired and, of course, often with seven rides a meeting his engines are wearing out and need costly services more often!" I tell Alison about my observations last night of Mitchell in the Workington pits. "Last night Mitchell ate bananas quietly and then checked the bin lid instructions before he disposed of his litter, while Lee Dicken regaled Johno with various stories of booze, birds and mayhem!" Alison reacts with incredulity, "What to Johno? He could write a book himself!"

With the scores level, Michael Max confidently "bigs up" the power Glasgow pairing apparently about to take to the track for heat 8, "It's Rusty Harrison and Lee Dicken!!!" Unfortunately for Tigers fans, Linus Eklof's third ever race at Ashfield Stadium results in a race win closely followed home by Kozza Smith whom Rob Lyon cunningly sends out in place of Jan Graversen. This maximum heat advantage gives the Stars their first lead since heat 1. After the first race the stadium announcer (either Jim Coyle MBE or Gordon Baillie) advised of Darcy's track record with an understandable note of extreme surprise in their tone of voice. Though no one has subsequently come close to that time or level of drama, nonetheless the announcer somehow finds himself trapped in a state of perpetual astonishment after every race when he relates the race time.

Michael Max conducts his second interview in 20 hours with England team manager Rob Lyon. Impressively, Michael poses completely different questions. "Why is it that the Danes and Swedes have so many promising young riders – is it the facilities?"
[Rob] "It's something we're working on in the background. The structure needs putting in place – we need to change the culture and the way we bring the youngsters through. My long-term goal is to have a five-year plan. Meanwhile, we'll have to make the best of what we have and get the best out of those. I've gone out of my way to select the youngsters and the message to the older riders is that they have to want it as much as the kids! They have to really want to ride for their country too!"

Darcy Ward's virtuoso performance on his bike appears to compel all riders to up their performance levels. Already with a known liking and aptitude for the Saracen Park track, William Lawson tracks Tomas Topinka for all four laps of heat 9 as he probes for the ideal opportunity to pass. Lawson bides his time until the final bend only to find his last gasp burst along the fence towards the finish line expertly repelled when Topinka firmly shuts the door on him. Though their transport is wheeled, we all understand what Michael Max means when he says that the riders matched each other "stride for stride!" Before heat 10, Alison Chalmers identifies the possible guilty parties should, by chance, the Glasgow Tigers suffer a home defeat, "Rusty Harrison has cost us this today. Every race he's been in we've lost: 2-4, 2-4, 1-5." Though scheduled in the programme to compete in heat 10, Mitchell Davey replaces Rusty who then unfortunately, seemingly channelling the spirit of the rider he replaces, finishes a comprehensive last. Fortunately for the Tigers, James Grieves shakes off the comparative torpor of his successive second places to finally win the rerun of heat 10.

We all bathe in our collective air of expectation before a heat 11 that notionally pitches Steve Johnston of the Glasgow Tigers against Darcy Ward of the King's Lynn Stars. The brute reality of their contest is really a race that pits an Australian of yesteryear against a youthful whippersnapper fellow countryman destined for success tomorrow. From an entertainment point of view, once again we get good value since Darcy continues to show a marked reluctance to leave the start line efficiently. Having missed the gate again, Ward proceeds to track behind Johnston until the third

Glasgow : *"He's a real speedway fan. Not a celebrity one – he fills in the programme! Unfortunately, his wife doesn't like speedway!"*

bend of the third lap when, with the close-shaven Australian straining every sinew and muscle to ring extra performance from his bike, Darcy effortlessly passes Johno with a magnificent blast round the outside through the proverbial non-existent gap to again ensure that he gets first sight of the chequered flag. Even though he travels past Johno with incredible velocity, Darcy still has enough time and confidence to make some sort of weird hand signal to his rival. Impressed though she is with his performance Alison Chalmers wonders, "What's the thing with the hand gestures? It's dangerous! I dunno what he's riding but it's like a rocket!" Quite how to describe the calibre of his racing is a struggle and on my notepad I scrawl down the words: fearless, peerless, exhilarating. Michael Max is seized with *faux* anxiety: "I dread to think what he'd be like at 17 'cause he's not bad at 16!" If this were a court of law, then Alison Chalmers has an objection: "Michael's got it wrong – he's already 17!" Though highly skilled themselves, every other rider here this afternoon lives in Darcy's shadow and suffers from comparisons to his nonchalant brilliance. That said, one rider who also impresses is William Lawson. He wins heat 12 so comfortably by a positively Darcyesque margin of victory of well over a quarter of a lap. Though given to understatement rather than hyperbole today, Michael Max notes, "William Lawson has ridden his socks off this afternoon."

If by the end of any of his races we think Darcy Ward's mounted on the speedway equivalent of a rocket then, in each race, he adds to the entertainment and spectacle when he leaves the start line on the speedway equivalent of a donkey. However he rides his equipment, the individual race-by-race nature of speedway life dictates Darcy would struggle to catch James Grieves in heat 13 since he leaps from the tape like the proverbial scalded cat. Predictably enough, Ward departs with the speed of a tortoise. Though the teenager immediately gives chase, he's held back from possible contention for a couple of laps by his own teammate Tomas Topinka. By the time the riders race towards the chequered flag, the extent of his delay is indicated by the fact that Johno has built up sufficient head of steam to nearly catch Darcy at the finish line and deprive him of his third (paid second) place. As Alan Dick walks past the grandstand terraces, a Tigers fan shares a team-building suggestion, namely that he immediately sign William Lawson and drop Rusty Harrison. Talk of equipment rather than skill rages in the crowd. "It wasn't a slow bike! From his first outing in heat 2, Lee Dicken's bike sounded throaty – I suggest that Darcy might finish fourth if you put him on Lee's bike!" Another fan retorts, "Unfortunately the reverse isn't true if you put Lee on Darcy's bike!" Alison Chalmers thanks her lucky stars for the "selfishness" of the Stars Czech heat leader, "I thought Topinka did us a big favour in that heat keeping Darcy behind them!" My book display attracts good attention and the best sales I achieve at any league meeting during 2009. As usual, it also attracts fans keen to talk about their speedway memories. One of these is David McDermott. "I first went to speedway with Robert Bamford 31 years ago! I'm 46 now. We used to go all over the country together [from Swindon]. Rob could drive and I couldn't!"

Before the penultimate heat gets underway, the Glasgow curatorial team employ their secret weapon and give the shale surface an extensive water. Jim Fleming's impressed with this afternoon's dust control, "They've kept the dust down today – not too bad. Against Newport it was dreadful – blowing all over you!" While we wait for the dousing to finish I let Jim know that Kozza (by his own reckoning) fell off 73 times during the 2008 season. Jim is amazed, "That's more than Steve Lawson crashed in his whole career! I only saw Steve Lawson fall three times! Amazing"! There's a Lawson namesake off the outside gate in heat 14. When it finally gets underway this Lawson fails to get any further than the first bend because, even though he was round and past Kozza Smith (off gate 3), the Australian fails to broadside into the corner and, instead, arrows onwards homing in on Lawson like an unwanted shadow to splatter him into the safety fence. For a few moments, feelings run high among fans, track staff, mechanics and riders. A track staff member holds Jan Graversen back as he tries to rush from the King's Lynn section of the pits to console Kozza after the crash. Alison Chalmers points out, "That track curator Danny Gibb has lifted Lawson's bike in his arms and carried it [easily] single-handedly back to the pits". To widespread incredulity, referee Dan Holt rules the incident an unsatisfactory start. His decision is greeted with loud disapproval from the crowd below and around him (throughout the stadium, actually). Though sympathetic to the plight of fallen riders, Michael Max loves nothing more than to stand with his head cocked to one side, like a predatory bird, closely observing the ministrations of the medical team while he offers a running commentary. "Kozza Smith is now sitting up and complaining about his right ankle." Ian Maclean can't believe that it's already five to six, let alone that the meeting hasn't yet been completed. "It's all this going round and round with the tractor." If laborious track work can cause delays, then wayward decision-making by officials can equally infuriate knowledgeable fans like Ian. "Bad refereeing decisions can ruin meetings! That wasn't an unsatisfactory start – you could see what would happen before it did!" Alison Chalmers is equally vehement in

her interpretation, "Kozza took him out! William was ahead. That's really poor letting him go back in – no way that's an unsatisfactory start!" Some angry Tigers fans try to run up the stairs that lead to the referee's box to remonstrate with Dan at even closer quarters. Alison doesn't join them but, instead, returns to the theme of her disappointment with Rusty Harrison this afternoon, "It's disappointing! We expected to get hammered but, if Harrison had scored a point rather than two duck eggs, we could have had the thriller of a last-heat decider!" With the rerun of heat 14 yet to get under orders, this possibility still remains – particularly since the Stars will track the lesser lights of Schramm and Smith to fight their corner. To pass the time while we wait for the rerun, on the centre green Michael Max quizzes Glasgow co-promoter and team manager Stewart Dickson, "King's Lynn are many people's favourites, can you see them getting beaten this season?"
[Stewart] "They looked pretty solid all the way through – nonetheless we've got about them. I can't say I was happy with that decision! That was a stonewall exclusion but, sometimes, the ref sees it different to everyone else in the stadium."
[Alison] "That's a fine! He's a Glasgow fan first and a Tigers manager second!"
[Stewart] "It's obvious Kozza was told by the King's Lynn management to go straight and right through him rather than round him!"
[Alison] "Oh! He's obviously really rattled to say that!"

When the two-minute warning finally sounds, Kozza Smith is serenaded to the start line with the kind of theatrical boos usually reserved for a pantomime villain (or Derek Sneddon). Though unfancied, Chris Schramm gates and potentially could have led William Lawson further than the exit from the second bend if he hadn't betrayed his lack of confidence with a quick backwards glance over his shoulder. The error of that fractional delay and hesitation is all that Lawson needs to blast round the outside and power onwards to a comfortable race win. With the score still comparatively poised at 40-44, a last-heat maximum for Glasgow will ensure a drawn meeting. The nominated race line-up that everyone in the stadium wishes to see arrives when William Lawson and James Grieves come to the tapes to race against Tomas Topinka and Darcy Ward. Predictably, Darcy again fails to gate but, by the third bend, he has cut under Grieves and passes him like he's practically stationary. Like the proverbial knife through butter, the youngster accelerates to the front of the field. Topinka and Ward cross the finish line almost side-by-side and, in synchronised fashion, they raise their left arms in celebration. Sportingly the Glasgow faithful applaud the victors with some abandon. Alison Chalmers basks in the glow of the Tigers sportsmanship, "What I like about the Glasgow fans is, that when Darcy walks across the centre green later to get changed, those here will applaud him! I like that! You never see the Edinburgh fans do that!" The entire King's Lynn team come back out on the truck for their victory parade to be greeted with warm applause throughout the stadium as they circle the track. There's enough applause to indicate some of them should linger on the centre green for a post-meeting debrief with Michael Max. Darcy Ward must have a different kind of debrief on his mind since he winks at Heather McNeilly. Their eyes can do no more than meet across a crowded centre green because, at that very moment, Michael Max advances with his microphone to interview Darcy only then for their interview to be interrupted by Stewart Dickson whispering in Michael's ear. "Could the owner of the caravanette blocking the pits gate please move it! Darcy, for your first time here you had an exceptional meeting."
[Darcy] "We all had a good meeting."
[Michael] "Have you been surprised by how things have gone this season?"
[Darcy] "Definitely, I'm just trying to get the experience and move forward."
[Michael] "Do you have any plans in mind for 2010?"
[Darcy] "No! I'm still concentrating on King's Lynn and things are going just fine!"
[Michael] "Are you looking forward to the World Under-21 Final?"
[Darcy] "That's still some time away, I'm not thinking about it as it's a while off yet.
Though they've been soundly beaten, Alison Chalmers takes nationalistic pride in the line-up for the Glasgow Tigers, "When was the last time two Scots last rode for Glasgow in Heat 15?" This afternoon we've all been privileged to see Darcy in his teenage pomp. Some fans have even got more lasting mementos than just their memories, "Laura's got Darcy's autograph – so she's happy!"

5th July Glasgow v. King's Lynn (Premier League) 41-49

Glasgow : *"He's a real speedway fan. Not a celebrity one – he fills in the programme! Unfortunately, his wife doesn't like speedway!"*

CHAPTER 15

Belle Vue

"He's so professional and hardworking. You should see his pits area and his lift!"

6th July

Dark clouds and a threat of forecast rain aren't the ideal climatic conditions to stage a speedway meeting in even a city with the population size of Manchester. If wavering neutrals question whether to go, diehard Belle Vue fans, like speedway fans everywhere, will know that the visit of the Elite League pre-season favourites the Swindon Robins strengthened by the arrival of Matej Zagar should provide excitement and entertainment. Already hard at work on the Kirkmanshulme Lane track two and a half hours before the scheduled start time is ex-Aces rider and current Belle Vue co-promoter Chris Morton MBE. Few fans get to see or appreciate the unglamorous side of speedway promotion which, in this case, sees Chris doing the fiddly but necessary pre-meeting task of securing the air-fence with cable ties. "I'm doing all the last-minute jobs other people should have done!" I enquire about attendance levels, "Our crowds aren't what we'd like! We put in a lot of effort promoting the club to the local area but I'm not quite sure what else we can do? I don't think it's any different elsewhere!"[1] To the uninformed neutral, it appears that Belle Vue have suffered both with injuries as well as with up and down performances from some of their key riders. More fundamentally, the team they have built for their pursuit of honours during the 2009 season doesn't have the strength in depth of some of the more so-called "glamour" clubs. A glance at the Belle Vue team sheet indicates that the line-up has sensibly been built to a predetermined budget level (that, apparently, is less than that of clubs like, say, Poole, Swindon or Coventry). It also indicates that the Aces regular Monday race night isn't exactly ideal if they are to attract the more feckless members of the upper tier of speedway talent who also compete in Poland on a Sunday and Sweden on a Tuesday. None of these obstacles are insurmountable but the chicken and egg situation – also faced by many other speedway clubs – is that success on the track is required to boost attendance levels through the turnstiles, while the calibre of team needed to ensure success out on track invariably requires robust gate receipts (or a sugar daddy).

Most of the Belle Vue team would be out-and-out heat leaders in the Premier League but, since they compete in the Elite League, only the Aces number 1 Krzysztof Kasprzak really qualifies as an internationally renowned top-tier rider. Someone of his calibre should really record a double-figure score every time they ride for the club. Both times Belle Vue have visited Eastbourne this season (for Elite League fixtures) to my eyes Krzysztof has looked exceptionally fast, exceptionally talented and, apparently, in a different class to everyone else on show. However, he has nonetheless stuttered at home – only recording 4 points against Wolverhampton, paid 4 points against Peterborough and eight against Poole – while away he's had a 7 at Swindon and paid 9 at Coventry. Chris Morton diplomatically summarises Krzysztof's season to date, "He hasn't been quite as consistent as a rider of his standard should be." His understated demeanour masks Chris Morton's determination to succeed as a promoter at Belle Vue. It's particularly important for some that he does, given the extent of his success as a rider. On the Aces most recent visit to Arlington, Chris rushed out on the track and did something that very few people have the courage to consider – had a vehement public disagreement with Bob Dugard. "I was having a word with Bob not him having a word with me! I told him to stop intimidating our riders! I've been around – and used to be a rider in the olden days – so I know what he was doing!

[1] In the programme Belle Vue co-promoter Gordon Pairman comments, "There is no doubt that David [Gordon] and Chris [Morton] put far more into working with sponsors, schools and other contacts than the previous promotions. And they couldn't do it without the help of Steve Casey and Ged Blake. David and Chris are also active in trying to work with Manchester City Council to make sure we are not forgotten. But these things all take time and results cannot truly be judged in just a couple of years. As far as the team is concerned, this is a tough old league and we do not have the asset base or the contact list that some of the others do. Despite that, we are largely holding our own this year, although the manner of the defeat by Peterborough still hurts. New promotions cannot waltz into British speedway and expect to win everything. But we are working on that too."

It was nothing to do with Charlie [Gjedde] – it's all part of the game with them." There is a school of thought that insists if there were more fights between riders on the track (whether genuine or feigned) then media interest created – along with the conversational buzz on the terraces this generates – would, necessarily, result in much greater numbers through the turnstiles. Unfortunately, times have changed since the heyday of swift automatic retribution among riders. Adrenalin levels remain heightened but, because of the close-knit touring-circus nature of the speedway riding community, many more riders are aware that their shared need for a continuing revenue stream of earnings dictates, if not demands, more professional standards of behaviour. Needless animosity is also inadvisable, given that they have to rub along together in many different countries each and every day of the week. Also, the modern regulatory regime dictates that SCB officials won't hesitate to dish out significant fines for what, not so long ago, would be deemed as either a minor infraction or, else, completely unnoteworthy. [2]

Like everywhere I visit, I already have the permission of the promoter (and trackshop franchisee) to display and sell my books prior to my visit. Nonetheless, I still double check with Chris if it's okay to stand just inside the Kirkmanshulme Lane entrance turnstiles so every fan that enters will (at least) see my books before they head off upstairs to watch from behind glass or trundle through the double doors via the bar area to get out onto the open-air terraces of the home-straight grandstand (or its environs). Even though it's a piffling matter to bother Chris with – given some of my previous encounters at the club with irate trackshop staff – I still make sure to double check. "I've never been over there so don't know what he [Nick Barber] does but make sure that you have a word with him and tell him what you're doing!"

Inside the reception area of the tall building that dominates the length of the home straight at the stadium, Buxton co-promoter Jayne Moss busily supervises the cash floats for each of the limited number of turnstiles that will actually open this evening. Though they have a choice of four possible entrances, predicted crowd levels dictate that only the two central turnstiles (numbers 2 and 3) will open tonight. This season I've invested in book-display holders that enable face-out presentation of a sub-set of my books on the small round table that I've temporarily borrowed from the bar area. One of the security men looks quizzically at a copy of *Quantum of Shale* and asks, "What's all that about then?" My table is off to the side of the vestibule area that fans enter after they've paid and come through the turnstiles. Directly opposite them as they enter is Belle Vue's friendly programme seller, John Thomas. Every time I visit the club, there's a noticeably high level of demand for the programme or, as we should call it in these more politically correct days, "the official raceday magazine of the Belle Vue Aces." The 2009 version of said official raceday magazine is nowadays a glossy affair called *Vue*. From a tactile point of view it feels smoothly substantial and, from a presentational point of view, I'd be astonished if there's a better programme in British speedway during 2009. You can't ignore that the content is generally excellent: thoughtful and up-to-date along with an appropriate use of photographs, paragraph indentation and all the other minutiae that obsess Howard Jones as key criteria for his annual programme reviews provided by the *Speedway Star*. Even more importantly, it's sensibly priced at £2! When I praise the quality of the 2009 Belle Vue programme to Jayne Moss, I'm told, "I don't really look at it. It's just your own programme, isn't it? I went to King's Lynn on Saturday – it's the first time I've been there and it's been warm – and they were charging £1 for their programme! It's two sheets of paper folded. It must have only cost them 10p to produce. At Sheffield, you accept that 'cause it's free!"

The official raceday magazine is packed with genuinely interesting articles and columns. It's an impressive overall package drawn together by programme editor Eddy Garvey, that reflects extremely well upon the club since it mixes wit with information, detail with flamboyance and, if I can continue to dare over-analyse it, combines honest opinion with photographic and presentational élan. It's also very readable. For example, the regular interview column ("Sixty seconds with ...") this week quizzes club co-promoter and "Scottish accountant" Gordon Pairman. The questions are

[2] Steve Casey in his "Anoraknaphobia" column in the Aces official raceday magazine *Vue* comments excitedly about the contretemps between Scott and Emil at the recent Cardiff Grand Prix. After he's trotted out the traditional canard-cum-caveat that the "events that took place after heat 5 cannot be condoned", Steve goes on to highlight the brute reality of our era of instantaneous communication in the modern media age. "Our sport will get more exposure because of these events than we would get than if it hadn't happened. Riders have always had explosive moments at all levels of the sport. The world championship is on another planet when it comes to pressure and when the stakes are high, you have to stand up and be counted." From the tone of his analysis Steve doesn't exactly sound a fan of FIM referee Frank Ziegler ("Frankie Z"). He's an official Steve deems too "quick to dish out hefty fines and a stern warning." Things have not always been this way, "I wonder how he would have coped in the days when promoters warned riders about the odd bout of fisticuffs in the pits. They were told in no uncertain terms that IF they were going to fight in the pits, when no one could see them, they were better doing it out on the track where everyone COULD see them! Those were the days, eh?"

far from anodyne and don't bother to beat about the bush. When asked, "In terms of the credit crunch, how much has it affected the gates at Kirkmanshulme Lane?" Gordon bluntly responds, "We budgeted for a big drop and, unfortunately, we were right. This is a year to hang on tight and hope that we come out safely. But we knew what was likely to happen, so the responsibility falls squarely on the shoulders of David, Chris and me." Another of these "Have you stopped beating your wife yet?" style questions asks, "How does today's Elite League compare to Premier League racing and could you see a time when there could be a place for Belle Vue in the lower league?" Gordon's reply is a master-class in diplomacy and plain speaking that still also requires some reading between the lines. "What a question! Some people have an aversion to the Premier League, thinking that it is inferior. And it certainly doesn't have the top riders (but then the Elite League doesn't have them all either). The support from Sky is very important to us – not just the money we receive, but also the exposure it gives the sport – and we would be likely to lose that if we dropped a league. On the other hand, we would gain many more derby meetings with the likes of Sheffield and Stoke and we wouldn't have to avoid Sunday racing as we do now due to rider availability. I think it is a debate that may come up sooner rather than later, but it is not something I would contemplate if I thought it would alienate the loyal supporters of the Aces."

Programme vendor John Thomas

Start line

Home straight crowd

Programme vendor, John Thomas, has followed speedway for years. He remains Belle Vue through and through so understands the outlook of both the fans and riders. "People will trickle in when the weather is good but today, they'll all come in a rush after 7, if they come at all! I don't care about winning. I'm much more interested in the fans getting entertained so that they come back in the future! We could win or we could get thrashed – it just depends on which of our teams turn up! On paper we should do really well but not everyone fires together. One night, Gjedde and Kasprzak only got 3 points between them. When Coventry came here they had four heat leaders, three of whom had a higher average than our number 1! That can't be right, can it? When that happens, it's not going to be any fun for the fans, is it? Swindon have got rider replacement tonight for Pavlic and they've also got Richard Sweetman. I haven't seen them here and, the first time riders come here, they often get unstuck on the first corner. It catches all of them out 'cause you really have to turn it in the corners to get round. If you don't, you shoot out to the fence. It used to be worse when John Perrin was here 'cause there was a ridge and, once you went over it, you were in the fence for sure! The other corner is the opposite, so it takes a bit of getting used to. The odd rider gets it first time but hardly any! Is Richard Sweetman related to Tommy Sweetman, do you know? There's more similar names in speedway nowadays [nods over to the turnstiles where Lynn Wright and Jayne Moss chatter] James's granddad Jim [Yacoby] used to ride at reserve with Bill Powell who must be the closest ever rider for living near to a track. From his house to the actual track was about 20 yards walk. He used to live at the back of Forth Street off Hunter's Lane – when we were at Hyde Road. That was a popular side then! Still, so long as it's close, then fans will come back to watch the speedway here in future! Hopefully Ulrich [Ostergaard] will go better tonight, he hasn't gone so well since he damaged his bike. Charlie [Gjedde] is improving each week."

Since Jayne Moss is here I enquire about the whereabouts of the Buxton mascot – her energetic and enthusiastic son Josh. "Since Steady and James left Josh hasn't really had anyone to identify with so he doesn't come as much. I know James is back, but he stays at home and watches it on Sky. He's nearly 10 now. They don't have a football team at Josh's junior school. Nowadays it's bad to be competitive at school! No wonder we don't produce the sportsmen and women we used to! I teach him it's a competition and it's good to be competitive! Everything is a competition – sports, jobs, Yearbooks. If you sell one it's winning!" Josh appears in a photograph in my latest book, "He's showing everyone who'll look! Dave Rat said to him, 'That book's just about you!'"

Forty minutes before the off, the dark clouds overhead finally carry out their threat and it begins to rain. John Thomas looks morosely out of the glass doors adjacent to his programme stall at the carpark, "When I got here they were watering the track!" There's not exactly a rush to get through the turnstiles. However, there is a noticeably high incidence of Aces replica tops, enough to indicate that worshippers at this particular speedway church are regular members of the congregation. Mariusz Dubielewicz from Poland arrives at the entrance turnstiles and flashes his Polish speedway press pass. This causes almost as much consternation as the £100 Scottish note that someone tried to spend here recently ("Scottish notes are so easy to forge that's why people are reluctant. But I checked with Gordon Pairman and he thought it wasn't legal tender. Who would come to a speedway meeting with £100 note?") The wet English summer weather has occasionally intruded upon the enjoyment of Mariusz's nationwide speedway tour. Last night he expected to see the Premier League clash between Newcastle and Sheffield. Though it had been, according to press reports, "a gloriously sunny day up to 5 p.m.", shortly afterwards, "torrential rain, accompanied by thunder and lightning quickly flooded the track making referee Stuart Wilson's decision to postpone the meeting a formality." In light drizzle, I expect Mariusz's heart sank when staff on the pits gate refused him entry with his press pass and sent him off to the turnstiles. No sooner does the rain start than it stops. While Mariusz waits, Jayne answers her mobile to reassure an anxious caller, "It's not raining, it's dark but it's dry!" After a brief explanation, Jayne is only too happy to grant Mariusz entry to the stadium with his press pass and he immediately heads off outside to the Kirkmanshulme terraces. "They should let him at the pits gate. It's not good customer service to send him away. And you don't want to treat the press badly, no matter where they come from!" Like many promoters, Jayne has a sensible attitude towards the press but there are still some tracks where hostility towards members of the fourth estate ensures that the sport remains a well-kept secret, even locally! Aces fan Kenneth Brown, 71, arrives, "You were supposed to be here last week!" That's not the case but Kenneth won't have it. He's accompanied by his friend Colin, "He's getting so forgetful, he was searching earlier for two lost library books – he's probably left them in a hotel somewhere. The other week, he lost his keys." By way of introduction Colin explains, "I'm a speedway friend of Kenneth's. We catch the same bus to Rawtenstall. I used to walk two miles home in one direction and he walked six miles in the other to Accrington. I give him a lift now." The casual freemasonry of the speedway community frequently dictates like-minded people help others out with small acts of generosity. Kenneth is a determined traveller to speedway meetings all around the country, though often he has to leave before the meeting ends, due to the inadequacy of public transport services and timetables. At the recent PL Pairs meeting at the Oak Tree Arena, half way through proceedings Kenneth walked past my table on his long trudge back to Highbridge railway station to catch his train on to Wales.

Any anxiety Belle Vue Aces fans might feel over which version of Krzysztof Kasprzak would turn up to this meeting is quickly dispelled when Krzysztof and James Wright combine to race to a first-heat race maximum against Leigh Adams and Ryan Fisher. If the first race 5-1 is a surprise, then the joy for Aces fans continues unabated when Kevin Doolan and Ulrich Ostergaard combine to record yet another maximum heat advantage in heat 2 to, thereby, take the score to a dramatic and unexpected 10-2. Prior to the meeting, averages dictated that Travis McGowan move up into the main body of the Swindon team while, in exchange, Ryan Fisher drops down to reserve. Given that Ryan Fisher is one of the top dogs of the Premier League, his return to the reserve berth for the Swindon Robins should give them much needed tactical flexibility until the next green-sheet averages are published. In the *Speedway Star* the regular Belle Vue match reporter noted, "Fisher's British career had seemed at the crossroads when he and the Aces parted company in the middle of the 2007 season and he may have felt that he had a point to prove on his return to Kirkmanshulme Lane." Another Aces old boy with a point to prove this evening is Swindon's number 4, Simon Stead, who first time out contents himself with a second place behind Morten Risager. Heat 4 sees Matej Zagar look a class apart from the Aces duo of Gjedde and Ostergaard. Charlie Gjedde rides creditably to finish third, despite the loss of his steel shoe on the first lap (something he'd also managed to do a few weeks previously). While two successive drawn heats wouldn't usually count as a fightback, 16-8 after four heats looks and sounds much better than a disastrous 10-2 after two heats.

Pound for pound and rider for rider, a casual glance at the racecard indicates that Swindon still have greater strength in depth in comparison to the Belle Vue line-up – something that still could tell as the meeting progresses. The notional advantage gained through any mastery or understanding of the peculiarities of the Kirkmanshulme Lane circuit is minimal, given that Richard Sweetman is the only rider in the Robins line-up who doesn't already have a significant number of laps at this circuit under his belt. The fifth race of the night sees the Robins halve their points deficit when Leigh Adams and Simon Stead comprehensively best their erstwhile rivals Patrick Hougaard and Morten Risager. No sooner has the Robins fightback flared into life than it subsides again. The team nature of league speedway dictates that Matej Zagar's win is effectively nullified Richard Sweetman's last place. Heat 7 sees ex-Swindon rider Charlie Gjedde skilfully battle his way from the back through the field and into the lead by the second bend of the last lap. A schoolboy error by Travis McGowan then enables Kevin Doolan to sneak past him and convert another drawn heat into an Aces 4-2. Before the meeting, the Belle Vue promotion would have definitely settled for a 24-18 scoreline after seven heats. The turning point of the meeting is, arguably, heat 8 when a battling James Wright fails to get the luck he deserves after he's nipped past McGowan to take second place behind Fisher. It's a position he holds until his throttle jams as he rounds bends 3 and 4 of the last lap. This unexpected and peculiar mechanical problem causes him to lock-up in mid track, fall from his bike and then have his leg run over by teammate Ulrich Ostergaard (who then splatters into the air-fence). Referee Graham Flint – with trainee official Darren Hartley by his side – disqualifies Wright and awards the race as a 5-1 to the Robins. From this point onwards, Belle Vue would only provide one further race winner. Nor would they have any answer to the onslaught of the top-end talent of the Swindon Robins.

Stood on the first step of the terraces close to the start line and below the ref's box is Sheffield co-promoter Dave Hoggart. He enthuses about Sheffield's trip to the Oak Tree Arena last Friday. "Our meeting at Somerset was cracking! Brilliant racing! Great atmosphere but we lost Richard [Hall] – he thought he'd broken a metatarsal but he hadn't – he got a point from the meeting. It was a brilliant advert for speedway!" Next to him in a replica Birmingham Brummies top is an unobtrusive Jason Lyons stood, just like any other fan, with a pint in one hand and a cigarette in the other. While we wait for the ninth race of the evening to start, it's clear from the shake of his head that Jason is less than impressed at the sight of the bowser spray equipment slowly circling the track. "It's as bald as frick in the corner [bend 3] and he's spraying all that on it! The surface will be slimy – someone will fall off there shortly!" Once the bowser departs, a member of track staff comes out with a hose and starts to douse the first bend, "Look at that bloke – frickin' using the hose!"

Like Jason, Dave Hoggart also has the night off but he too is ineluctably drawn to watch speedway. He's also here to conduct some unscientific market research on the state of Elite League speedway in Lancashire. Though there's a good-sized crowd, yet another race win for Matej Zagar in heat 9 – along with third place for Ryan Fisher – ensures that the meeting is now tied. Understandably the fightback by the Robins garners an underwhelmed, muted reaction from an already remarkably quiet crowd. Dave Hoggart reviews the situation with a practised eye, "Have a look round during the racing – there's little or no reaction from the crowd!" In considerable pain from Ulrich running over his foot, James Wright appears in his last programmed ride in heat 10 and creditably manages to finish third ahead of Simon Stead. With Kasprzak taking the chequered flag for his second race win of the night, Belle Vue lurch back into the lead by 2 points. We're then treated to a sudden impromptu five-minute interval. Jason has no doubt about its cause, "That'll be while the track dries out!" My impression of Jason as he chats in a low voice with Dave Hoggart about various speedway matters is that he is a modest and affable chain-smoking man. Completely shockingly, Jason asks if he can buy me a drink when he goes to the bar! My understanding of the usual order of things dictates that fans try to buy speedway riders drinks not the other way round! Dave Hoggart confirms my impression of Jason while he's away at the bar, "He's a nice man – totally straight." Dick Barrie has also just left a lasting impression with Dave, "I was at Edinburgh doing 5-10 mph by the grandstand 'cause of the fans and, just as I pass a car, he opens the passenger door and causes £600 worth of damage to the door and knocked off the wing mirror. He suggested we settle it on a knock-by-knock basis! That's enough to make you want to say Dick by name and Dick by nature but you have to remember his work. I think there are only two really good presenters in speedway – Dick Barrie and Mike Bennett. Mike's brilliant and his only fault is he's not impartial. For clarity and flow, you can't fault him nor can you say you can't understand him! He's also a tireless worker – charity work – the things Mike does: fits in all his work, does odd jobs and fits all this in around his speedway work while fitting in filming King's Lynn away and produces DVDs. I really rate the guy! Of course, he gets away with murder with the referees with some of the things he says."

Dave asks about my recent track visits and I tell him Kevin Doolan was very keen to help Keith Denham prepare the ideal track for their forthcoming meeting with King's Lynn. "Kevin Doolan is a journeyman but he's so professional and hardworking. You should see his pits area and his lift! He loves being captain at Workington, he's really into it! The thing with the track work and team selection – it doesn't surprise me that he'd want to do all those things. He's really nice and totally committed! He's always trying to learn and always trying to help." We discuss the Darcy Ward phenomenon and I ask Dave if Stewart Dickson will be fined for his outburst over the public address system at Glasgow yesterday. "Who was the referee? [Dan Holt] Dan wouldn't have fined Stewart 'cause he really likes to work with the managers. He's very good!"

Jason returns with the beers in time to see Ryan Fisher twitch and move at the line before the start of heat 11 and, thereby, relegate himself to the rear of the race as the riders enter the first corner. Though he didn't move, Leigh Adams also makes a poor start. The decision by referee Graham Flint to stop the race and order a rerun (with Belle Vue already notionally on a 5-1) does finally stir the crowd into a vocal reaction, albeit a negative one. Granted a reprieve, the Robins seize the invitation to make amends and ram home a maximum heat advantage to give them their first lead of the night. Some of the fans around us are apoplectic with rage and shout vainly up at the referee's box above with helpful comments like "What's the difference?" and "Did you sleep with Rosco?" Jason chain-smokes thoughtfully while the fans rage around us. He doesn't have any criticism of Graham Flint's frequent superfast release of the tapes (after the green light signals the riders are under starter's orders), "At least he doesn't leave you revving the fuck out of your engine like lots of them do!" Heat 12 features a lightning start by Ryan Fisher that prompts Dave Hoggart to exclaim, "How can they let that happen?" After a patchy start, Ryan now has the bit between his teeth. He rides with grace, determination and what looks like considerable speed to win easily. With McGowan third ahead of Ulrich Ostergaard, Swindon are in control even though their cumulative advantage is only 4 points. Dave Hoggart is in no doubt about Ryan's motivation, "It's payback time since they binned him!" Jason and Dave discuss Birmingham's defeat a few days ago at Loomer Road. Torrential rain exposed the quality of the fixtures and fittings on the away side of the pits – so much so that the Brummies had to relocate themselves. "We were at Stoke and it was frickin' leaking in through the roof. It was a joke! I had my first ever ride at Stoke in 1990 and it's the same now as then! Except grass now grows through the dog track 'cause the dogs don't run any more. They need someone who loves speedway with a lot of money to invest. The basics are all there – you've got the banking where people can watch in their cars or you could put seating in. The potential is really there! It's a nice track but tight in the corner, like here – well, it's not quite as tight as here – that's why there's so many incidents!" Talk of the potential for future greatness at Loomer Road is cut short by an incredibly ragged start to heat 13, "That was the worst frickin' start I've seen!" The ugliness of the start experience doesn't hamper Leigh Adams since he wins with ease. However, it does handicap Matej Zagar who, after three successive wins, blots his copybook with a last place. Sadly for the Aces fans, this drawn heat isn't the signal for a Belle Vue fightback and is only a temporary reprieve prior to another Robins heat advantage that ensures they win this meeting. Nonetheless, the new points scoring system implemented in 2009 provides additional zest for the last race of the night since Swindon's impressive Adams/Zagar partnership still require yet another heat advantage to ensure the Robins depart with all of the 4 points that are possibly available to them. Rediscovering his gating gloves, Zagar shoots from the tapes but, with a leaden Adams at the rear, it looks as if the fourth point will elude them until the Australian imperiously sweeps underneath Gjedde and Kasprzak just before the end of the first lap. Though it would make no difference to the outcome, Krzysztof Kasprzak nibbles away at Adams's back wheel like a hungry goldfish without ever finding enough momentum to pass him.

Incredibly, Belle Vue have somehow managed to fritter away the 8-point lead they held after two races (and still maintained after four) to suffer another home defeat by 40-50. Speedway expert and passionate Aces fan Charles McKay steps over for a few words with Dave Hoggart and myself before he leaves the stadium. Charles has a bee in his bonnet about the unorthodox and differential nature of British speedway regulations that effectively appears to endorse a two-tier system – with one set of rules for the 'in crowd' and another set that apply to those without backdoor influence. For Charles, symbolic of all that is wrong with the administration and transparency of the sport at the Elite League level is the mid-season inclusion of Matej Zagar in the Swindon side. Though initially this was supposedly only for a month while Troy Batchelor recovered from injury, it somehow then transmogrified into a permanent team change. Charles brandishes some papers he's taken out of his satchel and says with some vehemence to the only representative of the speedway authorities he can find within earshot in the stadium [Dave Hoggart], "That defeat was down to the rules not being administered properly! Making mid-season changes shouldn't be allowed! The rules should be agreed before the start of the season and they should be stuck to! [Waves his copy of the rulebook for emphasis] Where exactly are the rules in here that allow these changes to be made?" Dave nods sympathetically, "The Speedway Control Bureau is in charge, not me. There have been more rule changes this season than any other. They don't publish the supplementaries [rule changes made during the season] so it's impossible for interested fans, like yourself, to have all the information in front of you!" It's a diplomatic answer that doesn't apportion blame but implies room for improvement. Charles's dander remains up as he disappears inside the stadium building.

Back in the pits I'd expect the Belle Vue promotional team to feel both rueful and aggrieved at their failure to get the rub of the green in a meeting again plagued with accidents, injuries and contentious refereeing decisions. Afterwards the *Speedway Star* quotes David Gordon in a remarkably philosophical frame of mind, "We took a 10-2 lead against Swindon but they came back and their big guns sank us in the later races. We only had five heat winners and we looked brittle as the meeting wore on." Understandably the Robins co-owner, Gary Patchett left Kirkmanshulme Lane with a greater spring in his step. "I thought the wheels were coming off at the start but then we got our gating heads on and I'm a very happy man with the final result." Robins reserve Ryan Fisher scored 11 points and – with Swindon number 8, Richard Sweetman (in place of Paul Hurry) failing score – their cumulative points total was matched by the Aces reserves, Doolan and Ostergaard. In the final analysis the top-end strength of the Robins, particularly their powerhouse duo of Adams and Zagar with 12 apiece (along with Stead's useful 9) easily vanquished the Aces top five for whom Kasprzak top-scored with 11 points from five races. Building an attractive speedway team and then maintaining it throughout the season is an art, not a science. Tonight's meeting proved again that better finance and a regulatory fair wind behind you can also make a significant difference between failure and success.

6th July Belle Vue v. Swindon (Elite League) 40-50

CHAPTER 16

Stoke

"The forum has links to about seven different forecasts. Some of them say that and some of them don't!"

11th July

After a hit and run temporarily wrecked my car, I expensively hire another in order to not miss the book signing I'd arranged wth Mrs C. Tattum at Loomer Road during their Premier League meeting versus Glasgow meeting. Before I set off on my 250-mile drive from Brighton, as a sensible precaution I check various meteorological websites where the consensus suggests a slight chance of early evening drizzle before the likelihood of torrential overnight rain. Since I'd previously seen speedway meetings at Loomer Road conducted in heavy drizzle, I fully expect the meeting will go ahead. Because of recent controversy, I also had confidence that Phil Morris wouldn't ride because of 'injury' in this meeting against Glasgow. After a grunky drive via Wolverhampton (to pick up speedway reporter Tim Hamblin), we arrive on the Loomer Road industrial estate and park up outside the conspicuously locked entrance gates at 10 to 5. Usually I'd expect to see one or more members of "Stoke Speedway (promoted by Crewsline Ltd)" always welcoming entrance gate team already hard at work. They're all conspicuous by their absence while, behind the locked gates, nothing stirs. Nevertheless, speedway fans are notoriously a patient bunch before, during and after a meeting so – under cloudless skies – we sit in sunshine to wait for Stoke staff to arrive and unlock the gates. Shortly afterwards a white van parks up behind us. We patiently queue with slowly rising levels of anticipation for some form of action. Over recent seasons "Stoke Speedway (promoted by Crewsline Ltd)" have endured more than their fair share of weather-related postponements. I don't for a minute imagine that tonight's fixture will be imperilled. Looked at dispassionately, given that a fine line exists between a crowd size that is financially viable and one that is not, perhaps any club would have already postponed this fixture if they held any anxiety about stay-at-home speedway fans tempted to stay away and watch the speedway F.I.M. World Team Cup final live on the television. Personally, since I've yet to see a bad meeting at Loomer Road, so the lure of this meeting would trump any televised world team cup action every time.

Though probably not most people's idea of ideal surroundings to relax in the late afternoon sunshine, we sit peacefully in the car and continue to wait for some sign of life. Finally, at 5.30 p.m., a family on bikes (that I surmise to be father, mother and son) cycle up to where we're parked. In an England shirt, the bloke on the pushbike turns out to be Phil – webmaster of the recently created Stoke Speedway website. The Potters arrival on the Internet superhighway has been a long time in coming. Until just recently, should you have enough interest to click on their link on the BSPA website you would, slightly bizarrely, find your enquiry directed to the sports pages of the BBC Radio Staffordshire website. This web page would then provide absolutely no insight or information about "Stoke Speedway (promoted by Crewsline Ltd)", let alone its forthcoming meetings. The woman on the pushbike pulls alongside my open car window to ask rhetorically, "Are you waiting for the speedway?" Before I can even offer a hint of a reply, she continues, "It's off!" Phil explains, "It was called off at 1.02 p.m. 'cause of the weather forecast for tonight. Heavy rain!"
[Jeff] "It didn't say that on any of the websites I looked at."
[Phil] "The forum has links to about seven different forecasts. Some of them say that and some of them don't!"

Given the unpredictability of a British 'summer', the idea that speedway clubs would pre-emptorily postpone meetings due to a poor forecast is preposterous. Particularly since it would quickly decimate the fixture lists and hasten the further possible decline of the sport in this country. It's stating the obvious to say that weather forecasting isn't exactly an exact science. All regular speedway fans can instantly remember meetings where actual, recent or threatened torrential rain hasn't stopped promoters thundering through enough heats to ensure that admission tickets can't be used for readmission. When any speedway meeting is called off early it should save unnecessary travel expenses for fans, riders and promoters alike. If the postponement happens up to two hours before the arrival of the referee within the stadium, the decision can be taken at the discretion of the home promoter. However, once the referee arrives, any decision about the raceability or otherwise of the track surface or compliance against the SCB regulations is the responsibility of this official, albeit taken in consultation with interested parties like team captains, clerk of course, team managers, track curator and, of course, the promoter. (The one exception being Sky TV meetings, where the overall decision in taken by the additionally appointed TV Co-ordinator/TV Steward.)

Phil is only the messenger. It's nice that he and his family have taken the trouble to come out to advise us of the situation. Given that not all speedway fans have access to the Internet and might not use the premium-rate club hotline, after the track inspection that led to the postponement decision it would be a simple cost-effective customer service gesture to place a printed or handwritten notice on the locked club gates to announce the postponement. With Stoke presently fifth in the Premier League table, to an uninformed observer like myself, future possibilities for "Stoke Speedway (promoted by Crewsline Ltd)" look favourable. "Are you going to win the Premier League this season!? It could be your year!"
[Phil] "[laughs] Nah, we've got about 10 away meetings to race still! Lots of tracks including King's Lynn, Workington, Scunthorpe and Glasgow."
[Jeff] "Shame it's not on tonight. I always enjoy the racing here."
[Phil] "We have a very fair track with no home advantage!"
[Jeff] "You'd have beaten Glasgow."
[Phil] "Yeah, despite our two passengers!"
[Jeff] "Who?"
[Phil] "Morris and Tom P. Madsen. They're both past their best. Their careers are on the decline. Tom has dropped down to reserve and he can't score any points. [Another car pulls up] That tells you all you need to know about the communication here – he works in the pits!" [Car turns round before it pulls alongside our car]
[Man in car] "I finished work early and no one told me and I do the pits gate! [Doesn't look wonderfully happy] "Do you want a cup of tea? I only live round the corner – you're very welcome to come round if you want to." [Leaves]
[Tim] "You have the two Danes – Kristiansen and Jakobsen is it?
[Phil] "I like the tall one best, Kristiansen. He looks too tall to be on a speedway bike, let alone good on one. But he is! He's not as naturally talented as Jakobsen but he always really gives his all. When Jakobsen doesn't gate, he doesn't always try."
[Jeff] "Do you still have Buzz?"
[Phil] "No we have Lee Smart at reserve."
[Jeff] "Is he riding the long way round thinking Loomer Road is Bydgoszcz?"
[Phil] "He's done a job for us at reserve."
[Jeff] "You have a website now? I didn't know that."
[Phil] "Yeh, only 'cause we done it! Next time you come, click on the Potters Power contact button and you can have access to the forums and see the weather forecast or send me some info about your book and I'll promote it!"

Disappointed that we won't get to see a meeting we both looked forward to, as we drive away our conversation moves on to other matters. After many years in newspapers, Tim agrees that everyone judges a book by its cover but, perhaps, an even more significant factor behind a book's initial appeal lies in its choice of title. Famous American football commentator John Madden actually has two of my favourite book titles and also uses parentheses for his sub-titles with great élan. There's his memoir *Hey, Wait a Minute! (I Wrote a Book!)* and the much more obscure *One Knee Equals Two Feet (and everything else you need to know about football)*. Douglas Adams is obviously another genius when it comes to book titles and sub-titles. There's his *Long Dark Tea-time of the Soul* but also the fourth book in the Hitchhiker's trilogy *So Long, and Thanks for All the Fish*". Tim tells me about a Cold War spoof with the fantastic title *And to My Nephew Albert I Leave the Island What I Won Off Fatty Hagan in a Poker Game*. Tonight's meeting postponement merits a book title but, sadly, both my wit and ingenuity fail me.

11th July Stoke v Glasgow (Premier League) Postponed

CHAPTER 17

Birmingham

"If any rules are being broken – and I'm not saying they are – then they're not going to enforce them are they?"

12th July

One of the early arrivals inside the impressive grandstand that dominates the home straight at Perry Barr Stadium is Wolverhampton's Speedway Clerk of the Course Kevin Davies. Many fans and officials within speedway know Kevin has the memorabilia bug. His particular specialisation is to collect tabards, "I've got a few more Wolves jackets since I saw you last!" Kevin is keen to hurry over to the pits where he sometimes covers as Clerk of the Course (since Joe Thurley passed away). If you glance down the track officials listing inside the Birmingham Brummies programme it's like a Who's Who of speedway. Kevin and Wendy Jedrzejakski are both listed as a pits marshal while David Lucas is identified as Clerk of the Course. There are other august names on the Brummies roll call of responsibility. These include esteemed Track Curator Gareth Chrabaszcz, high-flying sports commentator Nigel Pearson is the Press Officer, Andy Povey is the club's website designer and also manages the Brummies Internet offerings, while man of many hats, David Rowe breaks off from his Coventry speedway and talkSPORT reporting duties to be both the Announcer and the Programme Editor. Denise Drury, wife of the promoter Graham, holds the unusual speedway job title of Child Welfare Officer. Arguably, the most significant job responsibilities (for the long-term future of the club) are those held by Brian Buck – who deals with Environmental and Community Liaison – and Adrian Guest who is Environmental Noise Consultant. Even though Perry Barr Stadium is located close by busy main roads including a dual carriageway, locally some questions have been raised about noise levels that intermittently emanate from the stadium on speedway race nights. Consequently, the modern way of the world dictates that club has had to jump through various administrative hoops in order to be licensed by the local council to run speedway at this venue. The club have been more than happy to fulfil the legislative requirements and to act responsibly within the community (ignoring that it is also in their commercial interests to do so). Unfortunately, planning approval isn't a one-off deal. Adherence by the club to the noise specification standards set by Birmingham City Council appears, if judged by reports in the and notices dotted throughout the stadium, to be a negotiable, on-going process. Bright yellow posters placed throughout the stadium (including the gents' toilet door) implore home fans and visitors to "Write your letter of support – save Birmingham Speedway". In order to maximise the impact this support behind the campaign for the continuation of Birmingham Speedway, it's far more effective to send individual letters of advocacy rather than sign a petition since many UK councils choose to count a petition as only one document of support! Throughout the duration of the meeting fans are directed upstairs to the grandstand bar. It's a space which not only provides panoramic views of the race track but is also where the Supporters' Club are happy to provide you with a pre-addressed envelope (stamp required) and a sheet of paper with the planning management address and planning application number (N/02660/09/FUL) already printed upon it. Even more helpfully, for each fan that wishes to write in with their own letter, there's a photocopied sheet that suggests some points that could be raised. [1]

1 "As a Birmingham Speedway supporter, I wish to submit my support for the above application and URGE THE Planning Department to approve this, on the grounds of:
Speedway in Birmingham has more paying attendees than any other regular sporting fixture in the city, other than football.
There is no police presence at any of the events, which have taken place over the past three years, and no segregation of rival supporters.
The club has over the past three years maintained each of the planning conditions placed upon it and has endeavoured to excel where practical.
The club is licensed by ACU, which is the National Governing Body for Speedway and if found negligent on any planning condition would have been severely fined, as this body wishes to encourage speedway, rather than create animosity amongst its clubs neighbours.
The applicant has publicly stated that if approval were granted then better sound baffles would be installed around the stadium perimeter in addition to a much tighter control by the RAC on vehicle silencers from March 2010.
The Department of Culture, Media and Sports recognise this sport.
The club has taken upon itself to have Birmingham Children's Hospital as its "bib" sponsored name and has built a good relationship with this hospital.
The club and its supporters over the past three years has raised nearly £7,500 for numerous worthy causes.

This advocacy document identifies – and it's worth stressing – Birmingham speedway is the second most popular sport in the city. If the number of people who talk about the possible demise of the club in 2010 is any indicator, the City Council will be deluged with letters of support. Quite what the truth of it is I don't know, but some fans mention that students (or more likely their representatives) from the Halls of Residence based on the opposite side of the main road from the stadium have objected on the grounds that their studies are interrupted by speedway noise! Though obviously the lead up to exams requires much study and revision during the months of April and May, this complaint (if it exists) flies in the face of the fact that the majority of the rooms in a University Hall of Residence remain free of full-time students during the key speedway summer months from June to September. On the club's regular Wednesday race night (with occasional Sundays, like this evening) not only is there a strictly observed time curfew but, apart from warm-ups and reruns, speedway bikes only really create intermittent noise for approximately a duration of 60 seconds 15 times during any speedway evening. Traffic noise in the area is appreciable and constant. However, questions of ambient noise remains something all speedway clubs throughout the country have to address with their local authorities, irrespective of their specific geographic location.

Ian & Dot Thomas

Petition notice

Panoramic view from upstairs

Nick Barber's trackshop at Birmingham comprises two outlets close to each other within the home-straight grandstand. His sister Bev runs one stall and Nick runs the other. He's just about finished setting out the books, DVDs, programmes and other printed memorabilia that forms the merchandise focus of his stall. Son of a speedway promoter with a lifetime's involvement in the sport, Nick is concerned about the future. "I honestly believe that, if someone said speedway was fixed and gave us some instances of that, then it might well collapse! The vested interests in speedway need to be swept away! So long as the promoters always do what's in their interest or, when things don't go as they want, threaten to pull the plug – then speedway isn't going to improve its image and have a long-term future. We need to have an independent five-man body grade every rider there is – even those who no longer ride or don't ride that season – into ten-men squads and pay the riders less but supply their engines and tyres, so that the only advantage they have is with the little bits and pieces! There's always going to be fiddles with averages and riders riding to orders. Poole at Swindon was booed as the fans could see what was going on. The Speedway Control Bureau ruling on that was predictable – all they need to do is to ask Rerun to film in the pits, if they want a record of what's going on. What's that with the Russians winning last night about then? They say Carl Blomfeldt must be doing all their engines! IMG are businessmen so they just want what will boost the crowds, get people talking and increase the interest. If any rules are being broken – and I'm not saying they are – then they're not going to enforce them are they? I think we can safely say Scott Nicholls isn't cheating! Really, everyone needs to be on a more equal footing. With my new [local government] responsibilities I'll have to have a really good think about which tracks I continue to do!" Though these questions potentially indicate general future uncertainty for the sport, from a practical perspective Nick believes it would be, "Very sensible for Birmingham to switch to a Thursday. Not only is it payday but the football really hits the gate. They can lose 400 at a meeting, if Villa are playing at home. It's only two miles up the road and lots of people are season ticket holders. Plus, during March, April and May I'm always hearing Villa are on the telly – or Man U – or whoever, so if they run on Thursdays they'll avoid that."

Workington is a proper speedway town and, consequently, a good number of fans travel to support them, wherever they ride in the country. Some Comets fans see each other regularly whereas others, because of the Workington Diaspora, only renew acquaintance intermittently at away meetings. Whatever their club allegiance, someone everyone is delighted to see back at tonight's Birmingham meeting is Comets club promoter Ian Thomas who, recently, was on the critical list in intensive care after a minor operation went awry. His irascible character, quick wit and enquiring mind indicate that he would probably be a fighter and, fortunately, this proves to be the case. Dressed for the occasion in a garish multi-coloured Wulfsport Workington Comets anorak – when I ask for a photo of Ian and charming wife Dot he tells me, "Let me take my jacket off so I don't look like a Christmas tree!" – Ian looks fit and remarkably youthful. So much so that you half suspect the talk of intensive care is really a smoke screen to disguise cosmetic surgery! As he comes out of the gents' toilet he proffers his hand and greets me with the words, "It's only water!" Like many other people within speedway I worried for him and tell him so. He bats off such concerns in a typically self-deprecating manner, "I wasn't too pleased at it either! When I was awake that is – the rest of the time, I didn't care! Three people died in intensive care when I was there! It was a nothing operation that turned into a something operation! I'm going in on Wednesday again – I couldn't be that unlucky twice! How did you do at Workington? [five copies sold] That's better than you used to do!"
[Jeff] "Well to put it in context, I did ten at Glasgow and two at Belle Vue."
[Ian] "They don't buy books at Belle Vue. I did 50 or 60 in a season and even Chris Morton didn't do well and, if he can't sell them at Belle Vue, who can? Jason Crump was disappointed at his sales and he was top of the world then! You picked a terrible meeting to go to [Workington v. Glasgow]. Last night's was brilliant! We beat King's Lynn by the biggest number of points anyone has beaten them by."
[Jeff] "They didn't have Ward though!"
[Ian] "They had Proctor and he's pretty good."
[Jeff] "But not as good."
[Ian] "He's a real talent. I haven't seen Ward ride yet. Topinka had a bad night last night and he usually goes very well round our place. Based on last night, they won't win the Four's and neither will our lot! What does *Quantum of Shale* mean?"
[Jeff] "Quantum means small like the amount of shale on some tracks."
[Ian] "There's tons of shale on my track! Next year call your book something I can understand!"
[Jeff] "Methanol and Mayhem."
[Dot Thomas] "That's good."
[Ian] "Mayhem and Worse."
[Jeff] "I can't call it that, some promoters don't like what I write anyway."
[Dot] "Only 'cause they're trying to put words in your mouth."
[Ian] "Call it what you want – write what you like!"
Ian and Dot move off to meet and greet with the gaggle of Workington fans who mill about the bar refreshment and trackshop kiosk area. Ever the entertainer and always 'on', Ian is engaged and affable with everyone he meets. He definitely looks much fresher faced.

Man about speedway and this evening's announcer David Rowe arrives and checks in at the trackshop to discover what new items of merchandise they'd like him to mention. He also takes the information sheet on my latest book, "If this year's book is hard hitting and controversial what will next year's be after all that's gone on?" Out on the shale of the Perry Barr track, one of the fastest tractors in speedway hurtles round the circuit, possibly grading it but definitely watering, despite the forecast of rain at 7 p.m. You expect speedway bikes to look fast out on the track but it's highly unusual to see such incredible speed from a tractor. After a 15-minute virtuoso display of high-speed tractor driving, said vehicle retires back to the pits (possibly for some mechanical repairs). Speedway is a sport peopled with fanatical collectors and, as Tom Jones identified, it's not unusual to see gentlemen of a certain age proudly dressed in items of clothing that are a history lesson in and of themselves. During the season I see many impressively badge laden jackets but that's nothing compared to the garment worn by a Comets fan with enough metal badges to start a scrap yard. Where space has historically permitted, he's also festooned this garment with sewn on badges. Luckily Workington speedway aficionado Tim Hamblin hasn't forgotten his roots during his many years away in the West Midlands. "That's Mel Pettit. He used to be Mayor of Workington! When I first went to Workington Speedway he was there then. That round tyre tread [sewn on] badge is the famous Workington badge from 1978." You only have to briefly lurk around downstairs in the grandstand this afternoon to quickly form the impression that pretty well everybody in Workington knows everybody else. Tim drops into conversation with Mel, who confirms that he was Mayor of Workington in 2001, "Yes, I had a civic reception for Ian Thomas and the team in the Mayor's parlour!" Tim and Mel then proceed to have an animated conversation before Mel moves off in the direction of the trackshop where Nick Barber hopefully suggests, "You should think about getting another jacket?" I tell Tim, "Nick should tell him he's banned from ever buying any more badges!" The sight of Mel takes Tim down memory lane, "Mel said it's 40 years since Workington opened. He's got a grip like iron for a bloke who's walking round with a stick. I was counting them when he let go! I first started going in 1975, when I was 17, and I wonder if Mel still sits where he used to by the referee's box? He used to shout a little bit but it was more the gimlet, laser stare that was the killer! He'd turn round slowly and didn't need to say any words! He'd just give them the stare, harrumph to himself and sit down. I wonder if John Walsh is here. He was my first chief reporter – he was a mover and a shaker when I started at the *Times & Star*!" When I ask when Tim started as a reporter on the *Times & Star*, he's not quite sure, "It's got to be '77 or '78? [wife] Patricia would know." The avuncular Comets temporary team manager Tony Jackson arrives and it's hardly a surprise to find that Tim and Tony know each other. Tony learns of Ian Thomas's earlier prediction that Workington won't win the Four-Team tournament (even though it'll be held at the Derwent Park Stadium). "I'd agree with that! I'm team manager at King's Lynn on Wednesday while Ian goes back in for an op – so, if we lose, it'll be my fault. I reckon we'll lose by 8 points. The way King's Lynn are riding, I said to Ian 'You're going into hospital and I'm going to King's Lynn. I reckon you're getting the better of that deal!'"

[Tim] "I've come here to see the Comets, more in hope than expectation."

[Tony] "There's a fine line between hope and expectation, it's called reality! It depends where you set your expectations too!"

[Nick Barber] "They'll get thrashed, Birmingham are going well!"

[Tony] "You need all the bad matches to appreciate the good ones. Your mam used to work with my mam. Everyone in Workington is related in some way and then you have speedway as a micro-community within a macro-community!"

[Jeff] "Why do the people from Workington have the best tans?"

[Tony] "I work at Sellafield so we won't talk about that!"

After the Tony departs, Tim comments, "I always have to remind myself that Workington is at the end of the line and miles away from anywhere, so it's going to remain a monoculture. I have a feeling Tony's [Jackson] distantly related to Patricia. As he said, everyone in Workington is distantly related. I've known Tony since the mid '70s." Another fan called Mike wanders up to my display table with a distinctive and really impressive glitter-covered programme board that I compliment him upon ("I'm just showing my age."). By speedway standards, Perry Barr Stadium this evening is comparatively thronged with away fans and it's a loyalty that's not lost on 'Glitter Board' Mike, "Reading the *Star* this week you can see that many people want the best for the sport and others just want the money! I see Dave Tattum is complaining that Stoke haven't been invited to the Four-Team tournament but, maybe, the fact they never take any fans away has some bearing on things! They were here last week and only brought six and they're local! Whereas we take many fans to theirs. So, if promoters have to think who to invite, it's not going to be a big gate if you have to rely on the Stoke fans!" Despite the forecast of rain, sunshine bursts through the clouds and I warn Mike, "If your board catches the sun the glare from the glitter could blind the riders!"

As speedway reporter for the Wolverhampton *Express & Star*, Tim Hamblin knows a lot about the riders, management and fans at Monmore Green. Thoughtful and modest, Tim always looks to the positive and is strenuously confidential. While he reports impartially, many things about the Monmore Green setup impress him, particularly the curatorial work of Alan 'Doc' Bridgett. "He has a philosophy to produce a track that riders have confidence in – no matter where they are on it! The racing comes from that philosophy rather than from specific racing lines. The racing at Monmore these past three or four seasons has been spectacular! I know Alan takes, obviously enough, the weather into account but also where the sun falls and where the shade is at any particular time in the day at different times in the year." Not all riders take advantage of these conditions, "The last time Lewis Bridger was at Wolves, I thought he was going to end with an alphabet not a score! With a few more vowels he could have been on

Countdown!"

Comets programme editor Barry Stephenson, though he follows the Comets all round the country to see them race, won't be going to the Norfolk Arena. "There's no bloody way on earth I am going to King's Lynn. We had a great meeting against them last night. What worried us was Darcy Ward – who was hobbling along on crutches – he made three trips to the burger van! What he was doing, I'll leave you to find out! He would have scored many more points than Proctor who only got 6 but he was a good last-minute replacement." With the racing about to get underway, the crowd disperses from the bar, refreshment kiosk and trackshop area out onto the open-air terrace that runs the length of the home straight. Where space permits, some fans also congregate on the covered and decked terraced area on the first bend, while others drink in the spectacle from the comfort of the stepped rows of seats and tables they have in the plush upstairs area of the main grandstand. During the meeting itself only those who are at work still remain in situ: Nick Barber at his stall, his sister Bev at hers, the Rerun Productions DVD man, myself, various staff behind the bar and those at the refreshment kiosk. Just before each race starts, Nick, Bev and I briefly rush outside and stand in the vicinity of the start gate area to watch the action. The height of the safety fence dictates that we can't uninterruptedly overlook the on-track action. If a panoramic view is required, then that's best found upstairs in the main grandstand. The rider parade and introductions pass off without incident, although the Thomas Armstrong Comets heat leader with the number 5 race tabard is rechristened "Andrew Compton".

The first race of the evening sees the Comets operate rider replacement for the injured Charles Wright while the Brummies operate rider replacement for Manuel Hauzinger. He's a rider I gathered earlier from Tim Hamblin, Birmingham let go. "Poor old Hauzinger. I saw him at Workington and, if races were decided over 40 metres, he'd have an 11-point average but, sadly, they're not and he was swallowed up by turn three every time!"[2] Clearly keen to establish a quick psychological advantage, Graham Drury sends out club captain Jason Lyons to partner the Brummies number 1 Tomasz Piszcz. The Comets track highly regarded reserve rider, Craig Cook, who moves dramatically at the start-line before the tapes go up. Though the Birmingham riders fire away from the start line, quite rightly, SCB official Chris Durno slams on the red lights. News that the adjudication is all four riders back for a rerun, garners yelps of "Wot?!" and similar but less polite comments. Lyons wins the rerun but, since Piszcz suffers an engine failure, the heat is drawn. Bathed in bright sunshine (but no glitter board glare) at the start of the second lap of heat 2 Jay Herne falls while third and, luckily for him, John Branney exhibits wonderful reactions (hitting the fence) to avoid him but, subsequently, falls and damages his hand. Herne's disqualification is a formality. Referee Chris Durno instructs the announcer to "Thank John Branney for his avoiding action". The varied nature of an English summer's evening is illustrated when the first attempt to run this race takes place in bright sunshine while they race the rerun under threatening dark clouds.

During an extended delay for John Branney to receive medical attention to his hand (once the Clerk of the Course has collected a medical staff member from the centre green to treat him), announcer Dave Rowe fills the time with an update on how fans can involve themselves in the planning application. "Every vote counts in this business: whether letters, phone calls or e-mails. So, we'd urge you to get in touch with Birmingham City Council." Richard Sweetman becomes the second Brummies rider to win a race, good news given he's the only Birmingham representative in the rerun of heat 2. The run of drawn heats looks likely to continue in the next race until Adrian Rymel – under no pressure at the front with an easy lead – suddenly decides on the last lap to ride an adventurous wide line round the third and fourth bends that ends dramatically when he somehow contrives to strike the board at the bottom of the safety fence at the exit of the fourth bend. It's a bizarre incident and a painful one for the rider who finds himself face-down in the shale. [3] In the blink of an eye 3-3 becomes 5-1 for the Brummies and their fans understandably celebrate enthusiastically. Watching on the apex of the first turn, Tim Hamblin unfortunately finds himself, "Standing near the

[2] The *Star* reported Manuel Hauzinger was given two meetings to save his team place after a poor run of form since returning to the club in May – but instead he sent a text message to Drury asking to stand down after the Berwick [home] meeting. Graham Drury commented, "Manuel sent me a text apologising for the fact it hasn't worked out for him back at Birmingham and asking to be released after Wednesday. I don't know for certain, but I suspect he wanted to miss the Workington meeting on Sunday because he had a Polish fixture. That's just not good enough for me. I've always said I won't let riders pick their meetings, when a rider signs for me, he has to be totally committed and I'm not sure that was the case with him. It's a shame it didn't work out because he's shown in a previous spell with us just what he can do and he was a pleasure to deal with, no problems whatsoever last time he was here."

[3] Dave Rowe in the *Speedway Star* subsequently reports, "The fence on the exit of turn 4 appeared like a magnet at times ... [Rymel] appeared set for an untroubled win in heat 3 but ended up off his machine yards from the flag."

most knuckle-dragging Neanderthal I've ever come across at a speedway match". On previous visits to see the Brummies, Tim has found Perry Barr "very welcoming" but, on this visit, finds himself next to the proverbial bad apple. Apparently said fan is a fatter, balder Neil Middleditch look-alike, further distinguished by his foul language, blinkered opinions and "chequered Grand Prix cap – think it was from 2007." Fortunately, he's the exception that proves the rule of usual Brummie bon homie. After he's expressed sympathy for John Branney, Dave Rowe enquires about the damage sustained to the stadium fixtures and fittings, "Can the Clerk of the Course give us a wave to let us know that the safety fence is alright?" When the tide turns against you further aggravation often ensues and, for the Comets, this arrives next race in the form of another maximum heat disadvantage that Dave Rowe hails as "Your first 5-1 of the evening!" In fact, successive 5-1s have seen the scoreline balloon from 6-6 to 16-8 in the space of two races.

All four riders for heat 5 make their way out to the start line – where, unusually for a Premier League club, from their first meeting Birmingham installed the innovative double set of tapes they favour for prestigious speedway meetings and also at the Speedway Grand Prix – before they're sent back again because the paramedic has again been called to the pits to attend to a still under the weather John Branney. Once the medical officer has pronounced Branney's hand tickety-boo, the fifth race finally gets underway but ends prematurely when Robert Ksiezak falls and is disqualified (with the race awarded as a 4-2 to the Comets). A Workington fightback looks a possibility when Compton gates with alacrity but, then, ends when he's swiftly overtaken on the second bend by Brummies super reserve Richard Sweetman who then accelerates away to win the race comfortably (for paid 9 from three rides). Andrew Compton, as we now have learnt to call him, holds on to second place until the start of the last lap where Tomasz Piszcz overtakes him. This gives the Brummies their third 5-1 in four heats. No Comets rider has yet to see the first wave of the chequered flag in any race so far (although Doolan was awarded a win in heat 5). To try to make amends, Ian Thomas gives Adrian Rymel the black-and-white helmet colour for heat 7 only for him to finish second behind Jason Lyons.

Theme music from *Red Dwarf* plays over the tannoy system while the track staff try to keep down the dust with yet more watering. You can appreciate their efforts when Nick Barber reveals, "The trouble with a Sunday is that the Dogs don't finish until 2.06 p.m. The trackman can't get out onto a bone-dry track until four hours before the meeting. Usually it's at 8 a.m. and he can soak the track. Whereas, on a dry day like today, although he soaks it at 2.07 p.m. it's always going to be patchy!" With the Brummies ahead by 8 points, we're then treated to a slew of drawn races. Powerhouse reserve Richard Sweetman wins again (heat 8) while Andre Compton rouses himself from his evening of torpor to snatch a win in the next race with a burst to the finish line. The initial running of the 10th race only lasts as far as the fourth bend when second-placed Tomasz Piszcz accelerates dramatically down the back straight, blasts thrillingly round the third bend only to come to grief when roughly thrown from his machine as he exits the fourth bend. Piszcz not only suffers dented pride but also shoulder ligament damage in this fall (and takes no further part in the meeting). With some understatement, Nick Barber observes, "It's not the track! He came into that about 15 mph too fast! He tried to do a Rickardsson. He could have shut off and waited but he tried to do it all in the first lap. He'd passed one; he could have waited to pass the second on another lap!"

The rerun of heat 10 sees Adrian Rymel hold the lead until the very last corner where Richard Sweetman – who'd stalked him throughout – blasts magnificently round bends three to four to pass him on the run in to the finish line. Heat 11 is just another normal day at the office for Jason Lyons with a run-of-the-mill victory in his Clash of the Captains with Kevin Doolan. Having seen and passed the chequered flag, Doolan then appears keen to win the consolation fifth lap if judged by his massive acceleration towards the corner (with a jammed throttle). Kevin manages to fling himself from his bike a fraction of a second before it smashes into the first-bend safety fence and nearly climbs it! The sheer impact causes the bike to bounce back from the fence with its back wheel spinning exponentially fast towards the flag marshal (who couldn't move that quickly because he'd only just come back out of hospital after an operation) stood stock still on the centre green. With speed of thought to match the wildly spinning back wheel of his bike, Kevin Doolan rises Lazarus-like from the shale, rushes over to his writhing machine, flings himself onto the floor next to it and, without the aid of his by now redundant cut-out, reaches out to disable the bike with a quick pull (of the spark plug cap). The prone Doolan suffers a mild form of electrocution and, understandably, appears shocked but then staggers to his feet and bows to an appreciative crowd. [4] Over the public address system, Dave Rowe ignores possible comment about whether a speedway bike lying on the centre green thrashing away pointlessly is a symbolic metaphor for British speedway and, instead, contents himself with the observation, "We've seen it all here this season but that just about tops it all!"

While we wait for the 12th race of the evening, Nick Barber revisits the virtues of the new grading system he's devised for British speedway in 2010. "Last night I graded all the riders in British speedway. It would be easy to do the same for riders who used to ride here but no longer do so or those that might. The grades could be agreed and released at the Annual Conference and would apply for the next year with no exemptions! That would be fair. A five-man committee could be set up to agree all these gradings so they'd be fair and impartially agreed. At the moment, promoters want it both ways! For example, Darcy Ward comes in as a 3-point rider and becomes a 10-point rider – so, when he's injured, they have a double benefit both ways 'cause they can bring in a 10-point rider! Whereas, if there were gradings, Darcy would be, say, a grade 4 rider then, if he was injured, King's Lynn could replace him with another grade 4 rider 'cause they'd already had the benefit of a high calibre rider at reserve."

There's a walking-wounded element to the Comets line-up for heat 12 after Rymel withdraws because of the after-effects of his heat 3 crash. John Branney who'd selflessly injured himself earlier (heat 2) replaces him. With Richard Sweetman also at the start-line, like many others in the stadium, Nick Barber has little doubt about who the likely race winner will be, "Sweetman's unbeaten here for three meetings now, I think!" Though Richard Sweetman duly wins and, thereby, takes his points tally to paid 18 from six rides, a subsection of the Brummies faithful around me demonstrate high expectations and tough love when they brand Robert Ksiezak as "useless" and "a waste of time" because he fails to pass either of the Comets reserves. While Sweetman scores for fun at reserve, it's all too easy to overlook the unobtrusive but significant contribution made by Brummies skipper Jason Lyons. He takes the chequered flag for the fifth successive time in heat 13, though all the drama is behind him in a duel for third between Andre Compton and Jay Herne. To gain the third place point, Andre Compton rides his rival really hard on the second bend of the last lap but then he's forced to drift really wide during the race from the fourth bend to the line in order to prevent the embarrassment of conceding a position to a rider who's previously failed to win a point all night. Though we're only mid-way through July, Nick Barber tells me that Jason Lyons is already on his third engine tuner of the season. Just like the magic he used to work on the track, Michael Lee must also have great skill in the workshop. Brummies reserve Richard Sweetman completes a hugely impressive night on the bike when he wins heat 14 to complete his seven-ride paid maximum (21 points). It's the first ever 21-pointer in the history of Birmingham Speedway. The nominated race sees Jason Lyons complete the formality of his six-ride maximum (18 points). The Brummies run-out easy victors at 53-39, though their racecard has a lopsided appearance since, aside from their maximum men, the remaining four riders only score 15 points between them.

12th July Birmingham v. Workington (Premier League) 53-39

[4] The initial impact of Kevin's bike on the safety fence destroyed his cut out and so it failed to isolate the ignition. This incident is precisely why the BSPA pushed for the new FIM cut outs to be imposed in 2009 but, subsequently, backed down after rider pressure.

CHAPTER 18

Weymouth

"I think she only comes down here 'cause she thinks you're flirting with her."

15th July

On Saturdays during the summer months every road to Weymouth is choked with holiday traffic keen to get to the seafront, the shops or their holiday accommodation and, hopefully, the speedway track. Possibly connected to the arrival of the 2012 Olympics in Weymouth apparently there are welcome proposals for a relief road to ease the congestion and reduce journey times. On the more circuitous cross-country route I use to get into town, in heavy rain a car crash completely blocks the road near Bere Regis and, after the Police turns us all round to take an alternative route, roadworks combine with an accident on the A354 Dorchester road to make it painfully slow but, thankfully, not impassable. Despite rain, in the lead up to the eagerly anticipated Wildcats versus Plymouth Devils National League fixture, I'm told by club photographer and press officer Julie Martin that, barring monsoon-like rain, the meeting is highly likely to go ahead. In the Elite League or even the Premier League (particularly at Stoke, where even a forecast of rain can apparently cause premature postponement), the drizzle and a sodden track would most likely put paid to the prospect of any racing. However, since this is the grass roots of British speedway, the make-do-and-mend attitude that is one of its hallmarks comes to the fore. When I arrive, riders, mechanics and officials from both teams already shelter from the drizzle in the pits as they wait for conditions to improve. At the Weymouth end of the pits, team manager and track curator, Jem Dicken, banters with Julie Martin who's not happy with the attitude of pits gate man, John Thorner, "He needs to go on a PR course!"
[Jem] "He's right though, isn't he? You know what they say, once a silly sausage, always a silly sausage!"
No sooner have the words left Jem's mouth than, at that very moment, the Plymouth promoter Weymouth like to pretend they love to hate, Mike Bowden, suddenly appears round the corner. The Wildcats section of the pits collapses in laughter and a bemused Mike glances up momentarily at the sound of this hilarity and talk of sausages. Discussion turns to who will be in charge of this evening's meeting. The identities of many SCB officials haven't registered with Julie Martin. "Paul Carrington, which one's he? I don't know many of the refs: Mr ZZ Top, Margaret, Chris Durno."
[Jem] "You must know Tony Steele."
[Julie] "Yeah. Oh, and Christina Turnbull. I think she only comes down here 'cause she thinks you're flirting with her."
[Jem] "Maybe I am."
[Julie] "If we get in the semi-finals, maybe you should, er ... invite her down the night before – oh, ah, actually maybe not – all the decisions will go against us!"
[Jem] "She's got a funny accent!" When reminded that he's also got a funny accent to some ears, Jem responds defensively, "I speak the Queen's English!"

Talk of the weather [drizzle] soon reveals that everyone has their own favoured meteorological website to consult and, even if you pay for your forecast, it's not exactly reliable. The Met Office famously forecast a barbeque summer, something that still tends to undermine some people's faith in its accuracy. Metcheck has easy to understand graphics and incredible specificity but, even within an exact postcode, often offers wildly improbable information. Unfortunately named, Accuweather completely fail to live up to their moniker because "they said at 11 there would be drizzle at 2!" Some riders are already unpacked and in the pits, while others wait parked up on the rough-hewn sloped ground adjacent to the pits. They occasionally scurry over to shelter in the pits with their colleagues but, conspicuously, don't unload their equipment. Plymouth's Seemond Stephens bucks the contemporary trend when he arrives in a completely unmarked van! It's apparently an immutable law of speedway that every rider demonstrate their pride in their chosen form of employment by emblazoning their names along with the additional phrase "Speedway Rider" or, its much more impressive variant, "International Speedway Rider" on every available surface of their vehicles (except the roof). Seemond has reached the age where he doesn't need this reassurance. Julie approves of his will to anonymity, "I dunno why they put their names on the outside unless it's for the sponsors 'cause it just attracts the thieves!"

The rain has stopped and, right on the imaginary border that separates the Plymouth section of the pits from the Weymouth one, Wildcats number 2 Tim Webster industriously sweeps an impressively sized puddle toward the Devils section. Plymouth team manager, Gary Spiller reacts playfully, "Hey, you dirty devil Webster, don't you sweep it up our end!" Jem moves out from under the cover of the roof, expertly sniffs the air and says with authority, "This will definitely be on! Even if it's off, it'll be too late for the World Cup!" Flamboyant speedway rider Lewis Bridger took his first real steps in the sport at Radipole Lane. His daredevil magnificence on a bike in Dorset is fondly recalled by many and burnishes more brightly with the passage of time. Judged by his score it could be said that Lewis had a poor night in the Play-off semi-final of the World Team Cup in Poland. Jem disagrees, "Not really! He had a chain snap, he touched the tapes and then his head went down! The difference between success and failure is so thin at that level." A notable feature of the Weymouth section of the pits is – on the wall above each rider's stall – there is an impressively large photo of each rider provided by club photographer, Julie Martin, "Yeah, obviously I have to Photoshop them quite a bit!" Sat on the pits wall, Wildcats reserve James White Williams takes the bait, "You didn't have to Photoshop mine!" Julie calls out some advice to a [nameless] Wildcats rider, "When you get out in front, can you stay there? [pause] So I can get a decent photo of you looking clean!" After the recent away meeting (2nd July) at Bournemouth in a KO Cup, Lee Smart suddenly left the Wildcats team. He's in bad enough odour with his ex-colleagues for his poster to be subsequently customised. "We super-glued a dummy and a clown's nose onto the Lee Smart poster and then we took it to all the night clubs!"

Plymouth's taciturn but friendly team manager, Gary Spiller, finds time for a few words. "I started six years ago watching at Trelawney in the Premier League and got hooked from there!" He's been out onto the Radipole Lane circuit, "The track is completely soaked and feels squidgy when you walk on it. There's not much they can do now!" Now that the National League has been in existence for a few months, Gary has started to put it into some sort of context. "The National League started so well. The extra teams – Bournemouth, Isle of Wight and Mildenhall – and the introduction of CMA [calculated meeting averages] but, then, they didn't publish the fixtures quickly but let them dribble out. Peter Morrish is a lovely bloke and you can talk to him but he doesn't own a computer, which you kind of think he might need to run things properly! Now it's ended up as the Conference League dressed up as the National League, just with the introduction of CMAs!" [1]

Plymouth promoter Mike Bowden can justifiably take huge satisfaction from the ongoing success of his club. Some originally pooh-poohed his plans for a speedway track in a rugby field but how many people (except Rob Godfrey) can claim in recent times that they have planned, built and made a success of a new speedway club? Though the smallest track in Britain, crowds at the St Boniface Arena still remain relatively robust compared to their rival. The team has enjoyed success on the track albeit, despite repeatedly making the Play-offs, significant silverware has continued to elude them. Local derby meetings with rivals Weymouth are always popular and tonight will already be the fourth time they've met during 2009. Never one to undervalue the entertainment levels of the product served up at the St Boniface Arena, Mike is particularly enthused with the Under-21s Test Match he recently had the honour to stage. "We had a brilliant meeting at ours last night between Great Britain and Australia! There were only a few points in it all night. Richard Sweetman got 18 – he's something, what a talent! Lee Smart didn't turn up. He called and said he was double booked. I don't think he'll be getting another chance [from team manager Laurence Rogers]. Everyone knows everyone in speedway and what goes on. He thinks he's bigger than speedway but nobody is and, I'm sure, he'll learn that! Are you coming to ours this season? Next week we have Bournemouth. They have Jerran

[1] During the close season Gary Spiller would reflect on his first season of team management for Plymouth. "I must admit I found the job mentally hard, but it was a good challenge. I know that I made a few mistakes during the past season, but I will learn from them and I now have more idea of what the job is all about." It's a job that has both its joys and demands. Gary makes a 130-mile round trip for every home meeting. He paid tribute to the support he's received from his boss (Len Brokenshire, of Kernow Coatings in Penryn) who allows Gary flexible use of his holidays so he can take time off for mid-week away meetings but, most importantly, also still keep his job as a forklift driver.

Hart at reserve – he's riding in the Elite League, Premier League and National League: all at reserve – it ain't right is it? The averages change shortly and then he'll have to go up into the team and Aaron Baseby or Kyle Newman will drop down and they're not the same! Dave Robinson was down last night. Looking smart [and clean shaven]. When he's down he don't say nothing but always, in the ref's report afterwards, it says the ref's box windows need a clean! They don't but he always says they do!" Mike offers no comment when I remark, "Fans often say referees have poor eyesight."

Wildcats promoter Phil Bartlett is quick to offer suggestions for my next book. "You can put down I'm a solo safe sex practitioner! After seven years of being told I am, I'm starting to believe it!" It's not an image to conjure with and, anyway, I understood that this particular lifetime achievement award has keen competition. It would be an understatement to say that the sudden departure of Lee Smart from the Weymouth team didn't thrill Phil. "With Lee Smart, I can take him throwing his race jacket at me at the end of the meeting and saying the track's shit! But doing it half way through the meeting when we're only 6 points down, well! He'd packed up all his stuff and loaded the van before he remembered to get signed out sick. We all know that really he walked out and cost his teammates some more pay packets and, probably, us four more meetings. He won't be riding for Weymouth again! He spat his dummy out once too often! [In the *Star*] One person is telling the truth and the other is full of bullshit. Telling me to f-off. He's not going to say that in print or admit it, is he?" [2] Phil Bartlett then asks, "Does signing them [my books] make you feel important? I wouldn't bother, you're nothing – like me!"
[Jeff] "Oh, you are something."
[Phil] "I'm not, I'm nothing!"

Wildcats announcer Alan Hodder (who used to be Director of Operations [3] of the National League in the late '80s) adds his two-penn'orth about the Lee Smart situation, "He told everyone on Facebook 'I've just been sacked, ha ha!' That's really unprofessional! Still, give Julie a bottle of wine, let her work three-quarters of the way through it and it all comes out and goes on Facebook! [nods towards start marshal Carl Price] Have you met Cat Flap – he swings both ways?"
[Carl] "Not Cat Flap! I don't want that reputation."
[Alan, laughs] "You fell over last week on the start-line!"
[Carl] "Oh no, don't put that in!"
[Alan, nods towards jet black clouds in the distance] "As Jem says, 'the sun shines on the righteous'." I ask Alan why there's long queue of track staff at the burger van, "They all get a free meal. I'm sure you could if you asked!"

Sometimes people claim (usually promoters) that the definition of an optimist is someone who hopes to make money from running a speedway club. Jem Dicken demonstrates that he's definitely an optimist when, three-quarters of an hour before the scheduled 7.15 p.m. start time, he takes to the track on a tractor and proceeds to grade it. He also selectively uses the ripper to rough up the shale surface. I don't have any curatorial expertise but, to my untrained eye, the Radipole Lane track looks to have a top surface of sludge. Pits marshal Arthur Greenway helps out the track work with frequent attempts to brush the puddles from the fourth bend. Phil Bartlett looks on dispassionately, "It's exhausting being a promoter. At one point, you can't wait for it [the season] to start and, then, you get so you can't wait for it to end! If I had my way I'd lock up the pits gate completely and I'd charge everyone £10 for getting in –

[2] Confusion reigned with competing interpretations of events after Lee Smart's abrupt departure. Lee noted he remained in Weymouth's one to seven until Phil Bartlett sacked him while Phil fulminated that Lee left the club. "Lee Smart walked out on us after heat 11 when he got excluded and acted like a child. He did not take his exclusion like a man. He told me where I could stick the club, and where speedway could be stuck too. That shows no respect to me as a promoter; it shows no respect to his teammates, and shows an absolute lack of respect to the fans who pay to come and watch speedway and pay his wages. It is a totally unacceptable and embarrassing situation that he has created for himself. It was an important meeting and it was a total, total embarrassment to me, the club, the fans, everybody. He has done it load of times before but I have ignored it. When Lee Smart isn't winning, he isn't happy. If he gets beaten by anyone, he's as miserable as sin. You can't expect to win every race you go out in and he needs to learn to grow up." Away from the National League, Lee Smart remains highly regarded enough to be recalled by his parent club Birmingham – replacing Manuel Hauzinger – from the Stoke 'Easy Rider' Potters where he'd been on loan. Lee Smart noted, "The bottom line is that I want to ride and will always give my all once the tapes go up."

[3] Dick Barrie recalls Alan's work during that period fondly: "Alan firmly but fairly guided the-then National League (nowadays, the Premier League) through a hugely-successful period, when it was quite independent of the British (now Elite) League, and he should have greater recognition for his efforts. He was a full-time employee, running an 18-club League in a manner so efficient it has never since been equalled. As a promoter myself (at Glasgow, then Berwick) during this period, I can vouch for his excellence in administration."

riders, mechanics, track staff, refs – and give them all a ticket. I'd stand in the refund booth afterwards and they could all come up and get a refund. I know it sounds daft but I'd say 'Yeah', or 'No' depending. I'd enjoy doing it! It might not be popular – but, anyway, I don't care – but it would soon sort things out!" Julie Martin stops to relate the tale of a missing track member. Phil listens, tuts and shakes his head, "I prefer to do everything myself then I know where I stand!" During the close season, it's reported that Weymouth's average crowd fell from 380 in 2008 to 320 in 2009.

Life off the track is rarely dull for those involved at Weymouth Speedway. Everyone has scrapes that everyone else remembers and, apparently, everyone has a story. Jem has recently embarrassed the Wildcats presenter with tales of his off-track shenanigans. "Paul Shackleton complained about my mentioning the pole dancing – at a lap dancing club visit – in the programme! He said, 'That's not what happened!' and I said 'Well, it's my version and it must be true 'cause it's the one that appears in the programme!'" Before the meeting starts, I take some of my pile of unsold books back to the car (to avoid them getting wet) still leaving a healthy stock in the trackshop. The studiously polite gentleman who works on the pits gate, Ian, worries about the weather. "I just wish it would really rain heavily or stay fine. Today, it's neither one nor the other. Last time, we shouldn't have even started but the riders said that they wanted too. They fell off lots!"

Prior to the meeting a minute's silence in honour of the late Kenny Smith is perfectly observed. It's almost completely silent, except for the squawk of a passing bird and the distant sound of the generator. Kenny was a passionate man with a love of speedway who made a significant contribution to the success of the Conference League. Sociable, knowledgeable and friendly, Kenny was known by all and sundry and will genuinely be sadly missed. With last respects studiously observed, Paul Shackleton cracks on with the rider parade. Dressed in kevlars that look that they have been designed by Sacha Baron Cohen's comic alter ego Bruno, Weymouth's "Number four and new Wildcats captain – James Cockle!" waves to the crowd. Veteran speedway rider and acknowledged entertainer at the Conference/National League level, Mark 'Buzz' Burrows "the original Mr Entertainer'" acknowledges his warm reception. The departure of Lee Smart still irks, though Julie Martin reassures me, "Jem says team spirit in the pits is much better! I'm not there, so I don't know, but that's what he says – so it must be true! We've got Jay Herne as a guest tonight. People have been ribbing him because his two bikes are taking up lots of space, 'Do you want the whole of the pits?'"

After the warm-up laps, the riders retreat back to the pits and presenter, Paul Shackleton, advises any first-time visitors in search of greater noise, "The Cat's Whiskers corner by the bar [fourth bend] is traditionally the noisiest corner in the stadium! If any of you have set your recorder for the World Team Cup Final on Sky tonight, it's been cancelled! Don't forget if you want to see the video of our start marshal, Carl Price, falling over at the Australian Test Match – it's on the website!" With the chitchat over – at much higher volume – a pre-recorded message blares out over the public address system, "Are you ready for the most exciting sport in the world?!" With hyperbole ratcheted higher than the volume, Paul makes a virtue of the sodden racing conditions, "I can tell you I've had a look at the track tonight and the best thing to say is that it looks exciting!" From the tentative way Jay Herne rides in the first race of the night, either he's reached similar conclusions on his track walk or else he's been influenced by Paul's concern. He starts spectacularly poorly, gets completely filled-in on the first corner and then proceeds to look tentative and underpowered as he lurks at the back for the rest of the race! Despite this shocking display in his first race, most people in the crowd were completely unaware that Plymouth chairman and promoter Mike Bowden would, afterwards, lodge a complaint about Weymouth's use of Jay Herne as a guest for Lee Smart in tonight's meeting. [4] Not quite so convinced that the world of speedway as we know it is at an end, Paul Shackleton takes a phlegmatic view of Jay's first run out. "Jay's looking like he has a few adjustments to make to his machinery before he comes out again!" Helpful advice over, Paul addresses the much more serious matter of the prominent out-of-order sign displayed on one of the portaloos inside the Radipole Stadium. "Just to let you know, there are reserve toilets in Weymouth footie ground!" Personally I hope that the football ground toilets lighting has improved. On my first ever

4 Graham Hambly subsequently reported comments from a disgruntled Mike Bowden. "Weymouth have gone on the record, making it public that they were parting company with Smart after he walked out on them in their knock-out cup match at Bournemouth. I do not believe they should be allowed a guest facility for a rider who has been sacked. It is no wonder the sport is treated as a joke in some quarters when this kind of situation is allowed. I've written to the Speedway Control Bureau and the British Speedway Promoters' Association seeking clarification of the rule, so I can try and explain it to our supporters."

visit to said toilets (at the end of a meeting), I found myself inside a room with a level of pitch darkness that you pay good money to find in a flotation tank (they smell a tad sweeter too). Manoeuvring myself around in the darkness by touch (on the walls), it was fortunate that my heightened sense of hearing alerted me that the bloke – who'd followed me in there – was less exacting in his spatial awareness.

Tim Webster in the pits

Fourth bend tlc

Though he's not scheduled to ride until the fourth heat, Seemond Stephens studies the action on the track with an intensity of a man checking the numbers on a winning lottery ticket. I'd like to think that I have good familiarity with the riders who ply their trade in the National League. However, tonight's Plymouth reserve partnership of Ritchie Andrews and David Gough haven't yet quite achieved household name status at Methanol Press. Nonetheless, I did note that Ritchie Andrews temporarily joins Seemond Stephens in his study of the track and possible the racing lines during heat 1. Ritchie is the only Devils rider (apart from Marks Simmonds and Seemond) to avail himself of this opportunity. Seemond makes up for this collective disinterest since he continually revisits the mound that overlooks the start gate and bend 1, whenever his preparations between his races allow. Sadly, Ritchie's research fails to pay any dividends during his first time out on the track (or in his second and third races). Nonetheless, you have to applaud his application and forethought. Without prior research, David Gough tracks James White Williams – who looks underpowered – for three laps before he determinedly blasts underneath him at the start of the final lap. Terry Day wins the race and, with James White Williams in third, the Wildcats establish a narrow lead that they wouldn't lose over the remainder of the meeting.

The third race produces the third Wildcat winner, this time James Cockle, though the heat is drawn since Weymouth heat leader Matt Wright retires from the race under the watchful eye of his mother Lorna [aka Doris] stood by the open doorway of the trackshop she manages on race day. Out of their earshot, the heat 4 clash between Mark Burrows and Seemond Stephens is dubbed the Battle of the Pensioners and, first time out, until the race stops because of James White Williams's movement at the line, Seemond comprehensively out-gates Buzz to lead him into the first bend. With Buzz outside him on gate 4, second time out a noticeably determined Seemond again comprehensively beats his erstwhile rival to the first bend. A chastened Buzz retires at the start of the second lap. Seemond cruises away up front towards an untroubled victory that's suddenly nearly denied him when (on the last bend) James White Williams has the temerity to power underneath the always exotically kevlared Stephens. At the second of asking, heat 5 sees the power Wildcats partnership of Wright and Cockle hammer home an imperious 5-1, while Devils number 1 Mark Simmonds becomes the third rider to retire in three heats. With his bike adjusted since his first outing, Jay Herne gates and wins heat 6 with ease. Seemond Stephens arrives second into the first bend, but then again elects to ride safely on the inside line of the sodden track. Throughout this race, Seemond rides his bike like he's going over bumps or, in the style of a struggling learner driver, kangaroos forwards in the manner of someone with a problematic clutch. On the centre green with headphones that make him look like a refugee from a call centre, or like a wannabe air traffic controller, Paul Shackleton is ecstatic about Weymouth's choice of guest. "That's the Jay Herne we know and love and like to see riding round here like that [pause] when he does it for us that is!"

Wildcats clerk of the course, Martyn Hepworth, enjoys a busy night. He watches from the centre green, while between races he either lurks in the vicinity of the pits or, optimistically, sweeps excess surface water off the track. The sight of Buzz Burrows at the start line sends a frisson of anticipation through the crowd. Paul Shackleton sincerely hopes he's put his mechanical difficulties behind him, "Gremlins last time out – let's hope he's fixed those!" While his bike might be fully functional, Buzz appears to labour under some psychological anxiety about the state of the track if judged by the careful way he glides into the first corner (from the inside gate). Consequently, he finds himself out-gated and then out-muscled by a confident Kyle Hughes. Referee Paul Carrington runs the first half of the meeting in super-quick fashion in case of later difficulty with the forecast rain. So much so that the two-minute warning for heat 8 sounds before 8 o'clock, less than 45 minutes into the meeting! Radipole Lane is one of those proudly unreconstituted British speedway tracks that continues to believe in the entertainment value of start-line girls. The Clifton Hotel in Portland (call them on 01305-820473) sponsor heat 7 but also sponsor the Weymouth start-line girls, aka The Kittens. Wildcats start marshal Carl Price enjoys their presence more than most since he frequently ostentatiously flirts with the red start-line girl. Notionally he holds the tapes up for the riders to adjust their gate position but really his focus is to exchange *bons mots* or smile broadly at the object of his attention. Tim Webster wins the eighth race (to take his points tally to paid 9 from three races) to show he's as accomplished on a speedway bike as he's a dab hand with puddles in pit lane.

Before heat 9, Paul Shackleton provides a public service announcement when he alerts fans inside the stadium to the dangers posed by itinerant authors. "The great speedway author Jeff Scott is here tonight. Be careful what you tell him as he's making notes! I can confirm he's already taken notes. For more information on our start marshal Carl – known affectionately as Banana Man and Cat Flap – go to the website, click on the forum where discussions get a bit lively at times. Say what you like about us, we don't care!" Before the tapes rise for each race, trackshop supervisor Lorna Wright rushes from the trackshop doorway to see the first two laps or so, albeit with one eye on the seven-eighths shut trackshop door before she moves back to wait for the sales rush that never materialises. Out on the track, Carl is oblivious to all around him as he concentratedly flirts and chats with the red start-line girl. He eventually has to draw his eyes away from the object of his desire in order to try to persuade Matt Wright (after an earlier refusal when asked by Seemond Stephens) to adjust his gate 3 start position and allow Seemond enough space to get alongside him in gate 2. When the tapes rise, Seemond provides the meat for the first bend Cockle/Wright sandwich and, with a rich repertoire of hard-won speedway experience, sensibly backs off. The Wildcats need no second invitation to zoom away to win. Club photographer Julie Martin has been notable by her absence from the centre green for many of this evening's races. Mostly she's based herself on the parade truck, parked close by to the exit of the fourth bend, which doubles as the riders' viewing platform during the meeting. Between his scheduled races, it's also a vantage point Mark 'Buzz' Burrows enjoys.

With his side 10 points behind, Devils team manager Gary Spiller gives the black-and-white helmet colour to Kyle Hughes to wear in heat 10. Along with Paul Starke, Kyle is to race the rejuvenated Jay Herne and also against Tim Webster. The transformed Herne suddenly finds untouchable status and duly completes the formality of an effortless race win. Behind him, Tim Webster feels the ministrations of a determined Kyle Hughes though he's unable to find his way past. We're then treated to a lengthy track grade that, to my untutored eye, merely slushes the shale from one damp section of the track to another. Stood on his mound, Seemond keeps a close eye on curatorial proceedings. As the Wildcats tractor circuits, he also conducts an animated discussion with the woman next to him. With flamboyant arm movements, Seemond is either an animated conversationalist or else he's exaggeratedly highlighting, in Hercule Poirot fashion, a previously hidden but vitally important clue in a bizarre unsolved murder mystery. Seemond points intently to a spot on the shale surface midway between the start gate and bend 1 and loudly exclaims, "Look at that!" Whether the impediment Seemond identifies is real or imaginary, it would appear from the tentative way that Buzz Burrows leaves the start-line for heat 11 that he's received news about these concerns about the existence of the aforesaid dangerous track elements. They say forewarned is forearmed. Buzz rides with such circumspection that you could half believe that it's a shale-covered bottomless pit rather than a rough patch of track. It's left to Terry Day to push the black-and-white helmeted Mark Simmonds throughout the race, albeit to no avail. However, since the Wildcats pack the minor placings, Weymouth retain a handsome 40-29 lead. Hardworking *Speedway Star* reporter

Paul Burbidge stops by at my table to reveals the surprise news that Emil Sayfutdinov's success in the speedway Grand Prix is due to help from Big Suze from the popular television programme Peep Show. "I really enjoyed my interview with Sayfutdinov. His manager Susi [Tomasz Suskiewicz] is very important to his team and can articulate his vision for him very well. It was interesting what his mechanic – Ashley Holloway – did to Scott before the race [at Cardiff]. You could see it on the TV pictures and I put it in my report that, before the race, he barged into Scott to get a rise out of him!"

Buzz mends his bike

Heat 12 features a performance from Kyle Hughes that, despite the cliché, is well worth the admission money alone. Weymouth riders' Matt Wright and James White Williams initially lead until Kyle battles his way past them in turn – on laps two and three – with flamboyant riding that suggests the track is bone dry! His all-action style draws the eye. Kyle's overtaking technique appears to require he enters the bend much too fast before he then uses the additional speed to imperiously blast round his rivals. Given how more experienced riders ride the sodden track extremely tentatively, Kyle's performance takes on even greater lustre. The arrival of the interval heralds the news that "unfortunately track conditions are too poor for the kids' race tonight which has disappointed our start marshal Carl." On the centre green, Paul Shackleton interviews star guest rider Jay Herne. He starts with a self-referential question, "I'd describe track conditions tonight as entertaining – how are you finding them?" Jay turns out to be a reluctant interviewee who requires a forced confession to give any reply beyond a few brief words. Paul changes tactics to ask a much more surreal question, "How many chapters of Jeff Scott's books are you in then?"
[Jay] "Oh, I'm not sure at all."
[Paul] "I'm sure you are – you better get over to his table and find out!"

Carl Price chats

After this interview, Phil Bartlett speaks movingly about the late Kenny Smith. "Kenny made it to the meeting last Saturday, typical of him, but unfortunately cancer worked its way right through him. Unfortunately when you get cancer, I've been there myself, you know what happens!" In the crowd, exiled Wimbledon fan Allen Boon – who regularly watches Weymouth and Bournemouth with his son Allen Boon – remains sceptical that Matt Ford will carry through with his threat to abandon the Elite League. "He says he's going to go Premier League or only run the National League team but that's just talk!" A new rider at the recent Under-21 Test Match caught Allen senior's eye, "Todd Kurtz – not a name I'm overly familiar with – but he made all the difference to their team!" Like many people Allen had been upset by Kenny Smith's death and also moved by Phil's comments from the centre green, "Did you hear Phil talk about Kenny Smith? That was hard for him! You could see he was quite upset." Paul Burbidge again roves past my table so I introduce him to Allen senior as the *Speedway Star*'s latest ace reporter. Allen's amazed, "I didn't realise you were so young!" Unable to hide his age, Paul replies, "Not being funny and that, but some of the older speedway journalists prefer to write about the stats whereas people want to know the man beneath the helmet and understand their character and outlook!" With Mark Burrows and Seemond Stephens about to renew their own special Battle of the Pensioners in heat 13, Allen believes track conditions have definitely influenced their level of application, "Seemond Stephens doesn't want to know but, then, he knows there's always another day!" A disappointing and expensive night for Buzz Burrows continues when he endures an engine failure on the start-line. Mark Simmonds makes light of the heavy conditions to streak away up front. On the third bend of the second lap Jay Herne gets massively out of shape but, luckily for him, Seemond is so far behind he's got ample time to recover and still manage to nearly catch Mark Simmonds on the run-in to the finish line. Seemond continues to race the track conditions warily so finishes well over half a lap behind the other riders.

Heat 14 sees James Cockle, Paul Starke and Terry Day arrive into the third bend three abreast. At the apex of the bend, on the outside of the triumvirate, Terry Day loses control and strikes Cockle's back wheel whose bike then smashes into the fourth bend as it throws him heavily onto the shale and into the fence. Plymouth chairman Mike Bowden easily outsprints the paramedics and Wildcats team manager Jem Dicken to be first on the scene. Paul Shackleton ventures an early medical opinion, "It looks like James Cockle has twisted his knee very badly." After a few minutes delay the use of the magic sponge or its Weymouth paramedical equivalent sees "Captain Cockle" rise from the shale surface serenaded over the loudspeaker system with the Can-Can ("I'm not sure the Can-Can is the most appropriate choice of music!"). James Cockle walks away from this bad crash. Terry Day is disqualified, Cockle repairs and remounts his equipment to wins the rerun and, thereby, ensures the vague mathematical outside chance of a Plymouth victory finally ends. By the start line, throughout the meeting speedway veteran Lew Coffin has stood and watched intently. "I've been watching speedway for some time. I used to go when the track is where the football is now. I did the training school for 20 or so years. I had Wiggy, Steve Schofield – I trained them all! Wiggy was always the same. He never changed! Neither did Steve Schofield. Neither has Briggo. Well, he might have got tighter – then he didn't have anything to start with! Ivan didn't either! He went away and came back, of course. He was super professional whereas Briggo was hit and miss. His equipment could be really terrible but he'd still win!"

Though the Wildcats win is assured, they've not yet secured all three league points on offer. Team manager Jem Dicken's decision to select Buzz Burrows for the nominated race (instead of Tim Webster or the battered James Cockle) draws audible exasperation from some members of the crowd. "Maybe he'll get round four laps this time!" If this selection news caused gasps then Buzz's earlier attempt to repair his seized engine caused yelps of terror in the pits amongst the riders. Paul Burbidge saw the funny side of the incident, "They tied it to the post and nearly pulled the pits down! As it wobbled, it was funny to see all the riders run out!" Sadly the gamble to use Buzz Burrows backfires when sparks fly from his bike and maroon him at the start-line at the very moment the tapes rise. With Buzz unable to promptly clear the track, Paul Carrington has no choice but to stop the race and disqualify the stricken Buzz. With Jay Herne now the sole Weymouth representative in the race, he gambles and fails to get flier from the tapes but, luckily, immediately finds the red lights lit since Paul Carrington deems it an unsatisfactory start. Jay proceeds to make it third time lucky with a lightning start on a track surface that is now so dry that his back wheel almost creates a hint of shale dust. It's a win that puts Weymouth back on top of the table ("I'm sure that'll please his Bournemouth teammates") and, though the fans celebrate, it's notable that the Weymouth side of the pits was almost completely cleared of bikes and toolboxes before heat 15 even started. Though they've already put most of their equipment away in their vans, still in their kevlars the Wildcats riders take to the parade truck for a victory lap. As they receive the applause of the home faithful, Paul Shackleton says optimistically, "I'm sure you Plymouth fans will put your hands together!" In the *Speedway Star* Mike Bowden would afterwards complain about the loss of an away point – which they could have gained if they'd taken a 5-1 in heat 15 – because of "a couple of very debatable refereeing decisions". [5] A couple of older generation Plymouth fans linger by my book display table dissatisfied at the outcome of the meeting.
[Fan 1, William] "What did you think of the track?"
[Fan 2] "Crap! That race we had a 5-1 until they stopped it because of Burrows not clearing the track!"

5 "The race was eventually completed at the third attempt, having been stopped twice when, each time, our two riders made the gate. In the first instance, we were on a 5-1 against Jay Herne when the race was stopped because Mark Burrows had machine failure at the start. The referee ruled that Burrows was still in a dangerous position, but I was near the starting gate and Burrows had moved his bike over a metre inside the track. That was backed up by the video evidence, which clearly showed that Burrows had got his bike off the track. In the first rerun, Hughes and Simmonds were again away ahead of Herne even though he tried to gain an advantage at the start. But the referee stopped the race to warn Herne about the rolling. At the third time, Herne eventually beat our riders and went on to secure the 3-3, which denied us a consolation point even though we'd made the gate twice. I feel so sorry for our supporters who had travelled to the meeting were denied seeing us gain any reward in such controversial circumstances."

[William] "That was frickin' terrible! The manager couldn't win a frickin' raffle! What was he doing with his tacticals? I've been coming 60-odd years and they're a shower!"

Post-race interviews completed, Paul Burbidge provides a brief review of the meeting. "What a tough competitor James Cockle is! That was one of the worst I've seen – yet, he was still back out in the rerun and won it! Quite what they were doing putting Buzz out in 15, when they still hadn't got all the points, I don't know? It didn't make sense to me! Did you hear that Jem is gonna become a co-promoter from next season? Every club has to have a co-promoter 'cause of what happened to Tim Stone! This is a great little track! They've really worked on it to make it what it has become. The racing here is always good. I always say I don't support anyone, I'm just a journalist. That said, Poole was where I saw my first speedway and so that's always special!" As I fold away my table, a photographer makes a point to come up to stress the entertainment value regularly provided by the third tier of British speedway. "So many people don't appreciate how good the riders are in the National League and how exciting the racing is!"

15th July Weymouth v. Plymouth (National League) 51-42

Weymouth Speedway
Wessex Stadium, Radipole Lane, Weymouth, Dorset DT4 9XJ
Start time: 7.15 p.m.

CHAPTER 19

Wolverhampton

"CVS once said to me if he could order it to rain the night before – or in the morning – he would, as it really helps the track bind together properly!"

20th July

At Monmore Green Stadium, Dave Rattenberry – the prosperous owner of the speedway Trackshop Empire that dominates the centre of the country – fiddles with his apron and asks, "How much do you think I'm worth?" Usually it's rude to talk politics, religion or money. Though I've heard rumour of a substantial stocks and shares windfall, Dave's usually very keen to play down the financial rewards of his entrepreneurial acumen in the world of memorabilia, collectables and embroidery. My guess that he's *Six Million Dollar Man* is dismissed as wildly wide off the mark. "More like half a million!" Last time I visited Monmore, Dave 'the Hat' Haddon owned 7,037 baseball caps in his collection, primarily speedway related. "I've got 8,022 hats now! I just bought 12 at the Isle of Man TT." If Wolverhampton continue their recent form, it's likely that Dave will soon have one emblazoned with the words "Elite League Champions 2009" to add to his burgeoning collection. Dave 'the Hat' dismisses talk of later season glory as premature, "I've been coming to speedway long enough to know that fortunes change! We're the best team to watch in the league. We have the most exciting racing every week but that's 'cause we got the fairest track in the country! Anyone can do well here."

[Jeff] "Are Coventry gonna win tonight?"

[Dave Rat] "Nah!

[Bill Gimbeth] "No way! Unless Durno or Margaret Vardy are referees."

[Karl Van Straaten] "Stichauer is injured. Wan is riding."

[Dave Rat] "He's Chris's eldest."

[Karl] "Have you got the autograph books for Graham Drury?"

[Dave Rat] "They'll be here on Wednesday."

[Karl] "Good, he's driving my dad mad!

[John Rich, holding up a Freddie Lindgren car window sticker that he claims lacks glue] "I want to stick it in my car so people can see it."

[Dave Rat] "You can."

[John] "No, no, I want people to be able to see it!"

[Dave Rat] "It's self-adhesive! They will be able to see it! You can't see the glue 'cause there is no glue – it's self-adhesive."

Chris Van Straaten [arrives to speak to his son] "I told the school if they wanted to come tonight there's no chance of going on the centre green." [Departs]

[Jeff] "What on earth is *Sludge on Speedway*?"

[Dave 'the Hat'] "It's crap – the worst DVD I've ever seen."

[Jeff] "What's wrong with it?"

[Dave Rat] "Watch it and see."

[Jeff] "It says 50 minutes of hilarity."

[Dave Rat] "If ever you can't sleep – put it on! Take one home and see what I mean."

Restlessly curious, Dave Rat intently studies tonight's programme (cost £2.50). He's turned to one of his favourite regular features: the "Black & Gold Scoring Legends" column. It has the strapline, "every week, John Hendley and

Mark Sawbridge countdown the top 25 riders in Wolves' history." Dave Rat looks wistful, "Tommy Sweetman! He was my hero when I first started coming!" Dave's reverie is interrupted when a fan comes up and starts fingering the Wolves' pyjamas set ("age 2 years") available for a bargain £20. Though pyjamas fell out of fashion in the same way duvets supersede blankets, Dave Rattenberry is the kind of old-fashioned clothing entrepreneur who continues to offer these garments for sale. Sadly, the fan decides against this highly recommended purchase and, thereby, implicitly raises the question – if you can't sell old-fashioned garments to speedway fans then who on earth can you sell them to? Dave remains taciturn in the face of rejection and continues to show no reaction when I let him know about the *Sun* reported findings by university teams in Oxford and London that claims "scientists believe" that "hunky men may produce fewer sperm during sex than ugly ones". Dave doubts the both methodology and evidential basis for these conclusions, particularly since these "scientists" chose to observe birds rather than humans. However, Dave concedes there may be some basis in truth for the *Sun*'s summary of the situation, ("unattractive ones know they won't get many chances – so they give it all they've got").

Lights, camera, action

Picture of concentration

Wolves Start Girls

Wolverhampton's speedway success on the track has bathed the club in the warm glow of celebrity as evidenced by the arrival of local media personality Ian Winter from BBC Midlands. "He's Mr Football – he's like Pat what's his name on BBC WM – he's excellent! He does Wolves, Villa and Birmingham, phone-ins and everything!" To add some much needed colour to his feature on Wolverhampton speedway, the cameraman films Ian while he's stood between Dave 'the Hat' Haddon and Keith Fletcher (with the trackshop behind them as a backdrop). Ian needs three takes in order to say, "Tonight I'm here with two model Wolves speedway fans!" Any local derby meeting against the Coventry Bees attracts a big crowd to the Monmore Green Stadium and tonight's Elite League B fixture clash is no exception. Outside in the car park, there's an impressive convoy of speedway rider owned white vans stood idle in a queue as they wait for the pits gate to open at 5:40. Close by them, an impressively long queue of fans also wait patiently between intermittent showers for the turnstiles to open. The rain gets much steadier when the ice-cream van arrives and inches carefully through the car park to its regular position overlooking the first bend. Dave Rattenberry patiently slots Adam Skornicki photos into a pile of yellow programme boards. With a captive audience, I ask him, "What is the future of British speedway?" "God only knows!" Round the corner from the trackshop, Pete Blackwell arrives in the red *Express & Star* van with tonight's edition of the paper. He flings open the side doors of the vehicle and briefly unloads a bright red metal stool from inside but soon puts it back because of the intense drizzle. Pete can't wait for October when he'll go on a month's holiday Down Under to visit his ex-speedway rider son Scott. Tireless behind-the-scenes organiser of many riders' testimonial meetings (along with Julie Reading), Stephanie Babb arrives laden with an impressively large bunch of flowers, "It's my birthday!"

No sooner do the Wolves riders park up than they go off for a team meeting with their manager, Peter Adams. Along with pre-season bonding sessions, the Wolverhampton speedway management set great store by these meetings prior to every fixture and, with Wolverhampton riding high in the table, this attention to detail appears to be yet another factor behind their ongoing success. The team meeting ends at 6:20. After it has finished, bespectacled talismanic Wolverhampton captain, Peter Karlsson – smartly dressed in immaculately ironed jeans and collared shirt – mingles with the fans, only too happy to pose for photographs, exchange a few words or sign autographs. There are a lot more children here this evening because of a speedway-wide initiative organised by the BSPA to celebrate the 80th anniversary of the arrival of speedway in Britain. Many more than usual of these children also clutch autograph books since they've just picked them up from a specially installed pasting table located just inside the turnstiles entrance supervised by Chris Van Straaten. Not only do all children (aged under 15) gain free admission to every speedway track in the country this season between July 19th and July 25th but the lucky first 250 youngsters at each speedway meeting also get "presented with a specially commissioned autograph book and there will be opportunities to get the riders to sign them". Along with the autograph book, the children are also given a pen along with a sheet of stickers printed up with the name of every team. The young people who've come along tonight to see Wolverhampton race against Coventry will, hopefully, have their imaginations sufficiently fired to, thereafter, become lifelong devotees to the shale. Though they're probably unaware of his status at the club or, indeed, his importance within the sport, all these children also get to meet a slightly awkward Chris Van Straaten as he stands dutifully by the pasting table. Chris has a fixed smile as he hands out the goodies to each child, often in double-quick fashion rather than the more elaborate ceremonies often reserved for the presentation of Gideon Bibles at a Sunday school. For a brief part of one evening only, Chris studiedly welcomes the children in a warm but slightly stilted manner that effortlessly mixes the child-friendly skills and outlook of the Pied Piper of Hamelin and King Herod. Although a large number of young people funnel through the turnstiles not all of them head to his table and this forces Chris to go in search of random children. Like a smartly dressed Fagin (albeit without the fingerless gloves or beard), Chris hunts the kiddies down to press a surprise speedway gift pack into their mostly grateful hands. [1]

Wolverhampton Speedway club historian, Mark Sawbridge, is too old to receive a gift pack from Chris Van Straaten but, given his love of all things Wolverhampton speedway, I half suspect he would if he could. "I've just got back from Poland at 5 a.m. this morning. I love trips abroad! Everyone has a different flavour. It was great! The Poles are mental about speedway, of course! Because the WTC Final was delayed, we couldn't get to a team meeting but it was still fantastic! [Glances up at the dark clouds overhead] CVS once said to me if he could order it to rain the night before – or in the morning – he would, as it really helps the track bind together properly!" Mark is here tonight as club historian and a fan but also as a speedway reporter. He reports every meeting on a Monday night for BBC WM. When there's no professional football played, Mark is often invited to the BBC WM studio on a Tuesday. "Once the football season starts, they cover Walsall away at Brentford rather than the speedway! Still, they give us fantastic coverage during the summer when the football's not on!"

Any speedway meeting inevitably provides a rich tapestry of comment upon past, present and future meetings. Mr I.C.A. Crook (aka 'Mushy Pea') didn't get to see any speedway yesterday afternoon at Buxton, "The meeting was called off at quarter to 10 yesterday. I reckon Wolves'll get 50 tonight. I've looked at heat 13 in the paper and its Frampton and Olly Allen versus PK and Freddie! That's a 4-pointer as is heat 15! It's kids free tonight – look at the queue for the autograph books!" Dyed-in-the-wool Cradley fan, Andy faces a dilemma common to increasing numbers of speedway fans after their favourite/local team goes defunct. "I used to love going to Cradley and, obviously, I switched to Coventry when Hancock and Hamill went there – but it's not the same, is it? The atmosphere used to be unique but this is a dog track that also has speedway! Cradley was a stadium made for speedway! Sure it did stage the dogs but it was a proper speedway club. I used to love the old Belle Vue and going to the funfair beforehand. The new Belle Vue is nothing like it and the feeling has gone! Fair play to them for carrying on speedway, of course, and we have to respect that – but, it's no longer the same."

Mildenhall team manager Laurence Rogers is a man whose intensive travel schedule mirrors that of many in demand speedway riders. "Let's see – a week ago Friday it was King's Lynn, Saturday Weymouth, Sunday Newport, Monday

[1] On its website, BSPA Chairman Peter Toogood comments positively on the 80th anniversary celebration project to try to tempt a new generation of fans into a love of the sport. "It's a great week to stage the celebrations because there are some terrific fixtures. The week includes the Premier League 4-Team tournament on July 25th plus a host of mouth-watering League fixtures. We have a great advertising tool in Sky Sports who do a fantastic job promoting the sport. It would be nice to see new fans coming along to our tracks and sample the sport in person. We are quite rightly proud of the fact that we are celebrating 80 years of league racing in the UK. It's something we wanted to mark in a special way and we hope to see plenty of youngsters visiting speedway tracks up and down the country throughout the week."

Wolverhampton : *"CVS once said to me if he could order it to rain the night before – or in the morning – he would, as it really helps the track bind together properly!"*

I watched the World Team Cup, Tuesday Isle of Wight, then I was ill for a day and a half, Thursday Sheffield, Friday Plymouth via Newport, Saturday at home (in Wolverhampton), Sunday Newcastle but it was off because of the rain, tonight here, Tuesday at Kenny Smith's funeral, Wednesday at Birmingham, Thursday at Poole, Friday at Weymouth, Saturday at Buxton for the Under-15s and then back to Newport on Sunday. In between, I'll try to run my business – which is mortgage broking, which is difficult at the moment! I'm here tonight watching my flock so I'm spectating Jordan [Frampton] on one side and Chris [Kerr] on the other. Oh, I could have gone to Swindon on Thursday and Friday with Jonas [Andersson] for the Under-21s." Laurence introduces me to Shelly-Ann Willetts from Stourbridge who adds some much needed glamour to the cover of my book *Concrete for Breakfast*. Shelly is "Super7evens start girls organiser" so is clearly well used to the limelight and, I suspect, unwanted attention. Shelly's also appeared in the *Sun* so her appearance on my book cover is only small beer, "It's only a photo, isn't it!?" First and foremost, Shelly is a speedway fan happy to be just another member of the Wolves faithful who gather on the stepped terraces that overlook the first bend. Margaret Vardy's partner, Steve Davies, has had a slow trip to the stadium, "The car park is completely full – we had to park in the street!" An off duty slim-line Chris Durno arrives to soak up the race action. "Me and Dave Watters are on a diet. When we go to Tesco's we get wraps and salads and that now. He's lost tons of weight, you should see him!"

Close racing on a well-prepared circuit is a hallmark of the Wolverhampton Speedway experience and another, though less celebrated, component of a night out at Monmore Green is the unique approach taken to speedway presentational matters by their centre-green man with the microphone, Ian 'Porky' Jones. Love him or loathe him, included in the price of speedway admission at Monmore is free entry to 'Porky-world'. It's a strange place! Some would claim it's a parallel universe where relentless enthusiasm and badinage leads some to believe the primary focus of every speedway fan's evening isn't the racing but this voluble Master of Ceremonies. One foible of his commentary is the way he talks the riders home throughout the last lap of each race. Convinced that none of us is able interpret the evidence of our own eyes, Porky must feel that it's his duty to provide us with his stream of consciousness in the manner of a horse-racing commentator.

Before the meeting starts, a minute's silence for the late Kenny Smith is immaculately observed (except for a slight noise from the far end of the grandstand). Freddie Lindgren and Nicolai Klindt then set the stage for the night ahead when they comprehensively dismiss the challenge of Chris Harris in the first race. Porky immediately observes, "It's a 5-1 and you all know what that means". Though regular attendees might well have the full SP, some in the crowd (like myself) aren't exactly sure what he means? Maybe 'Bomber' will be sent to the naughty step or, perhaps, Porky will dance a celebratory hula-hula? In fact, "what that means" is an exuberant wheelie celebration from Freddie Lindgren that he conducts in a matter-of-fact going through the motions manner rather than in virtuoso style. [2] Filip Sitera temporarily kindles a brief flicker of hope amongst those Bees fans safely inside the Monmore perimeter security fences when he manages to lead Chris Kerr and Ty Proctor to the second bend of heat 2. However, by the time they reach bend 3, both overtake him and proceed to win with some ease. With slightly over a lap to go Porky squeals, "It's a 5-1 and you know what that means, don't you!?" I expect to see more wheelies but in fact we're instead treated to loud feedback that plays over some badly distorted celebratory music. If Porky tails each race last lap commentary with afterthoughts, then he tops each race with notional insight from a vast but benign repertoire of ready-drafted phrases and slogans. One favourite gets an early run-out before heat 3. It combines a paean to speedway with talk of flatulence, "Let's go pass some gas! It's super-speedway!" Wolves wily pony-tailed Polish rider Adam Skornicki locks-up in almost every bend for the first three laps of this race and, thereby, repeatedly frustrates Coventry's Edward Kennett as they vie for the consolation place behind the lightning-quick Tai Woffinden. Also not short of savvy or knowledge about the Monmore Green track, on the last lap Edward powers down the back straight in order to blast under Adam Skornicki on the third bend. Adam, in my opinion, then "falls" theatrically in the hope of an exclusion from referee, Dale Entwistle. Behind them Jordan Frampton gets tangled with and thrown from his bucking bronco of a bike onto the shale surface of the fourth bend. Afterwards, when Peter Morrish relays the official result, we learn that Adam Skornicki and Jordan Frampton have both been disqualified. It's a decision that the crowd boo nearly as loudly as they did when they held Edward responsible for Adam's tumble from his equipment. Porky remains

[2] I'm later told "You know what that means" is the prelude to a musical sound bite used to signal any home 5-1. Apparently recorded by the Piranhas, it prompts many Wolves fans to sing and punch the air in synch. It's become a "spoons" tradition!

philosophical. "Well, a bit of a talking point in the third race – it passes the time!" The riders definitely harbour no animosity towards each other since Edward gives Adam a lift back to the pits on his bike (as the Pole's mechanic drags his battered machine away).

Something that's off the menu tonight are dad-dancing celebrations from Porky. It's a sight I've described elsewhere as exhibiting a style reminiscent of a bare-footed man as he steps out of the shower onto an exposed electric wire. "I must apologise to Coventry Bees fans – I can't do any dancing for a few weeks until the plaster's off." Always a showman, when Porky sustained the injury during a speedway meeting, some members of the crowd naturally assumed that his exaggerated writhe on the floor was all part of his act. [3] While we wait for the riders to come to the line for heat 4, Porky gives full rein to his inner pornographer leavened with a dash of obsequious lechery, "Hello girls! Why don't you kiss the camera like the Polish birds do?" When the fourth race gets underway, we're treated to the shock sight of a Coventry rider still in the lead past the second bend, albeit only for a fraction of a second, when Filip Sitera passes Ty Proctor along the back straight. His glory is short-lived since PK then blasts at huge speed up inside him and, without a touch, his mere presence is enough to frighten Filip and prompt him to leap into the air-fence. Predictably Sitera gets disqualified and Porky double underlines his chagrin, "Well, he's not happy! He's not a happy chap! It's a long walk back [pause] you gotta smile ain't ya?" While we wait for the rerun, 'Porky' reprises his earlier priapic observation, "You don't see those birds kissing anything at Wolves, do you?" With PK soon back up at the tapes Porky chants another of his well-used slogans in the hypnotic manner of a Buddhist incantation, "Super Trouper! Super Swede!" We're then told, PK "has more cylinders than a Volvo!" (albeit one that sometimes gates slowly). For two laps, PK is caught in traffic behind his teammate Ty Proctor until, finally, he's able to pass and properly pursue race leader Olly Allen. As they go into the last lap, Porky tries to enthuse about the Swede but also simultaneously manage our expectations, "PK! PK trying to find the PK racing line". PK is the Master of Monmore in the same way that Tomasz Gollob is Master of the ZKS Polonia Stadium in Bydgoszcz. As if to illustrate his brilliance round this particular track, PK gives us all a master-class in how to exploit the peculiar topography of the last bend at Monmore. Initially PK goes wide to the fence on bend 3 where he executes a weird manoeuvre that's part lockup to cut the corner and part carefully planned dive-cum-blast down the inside line. It's a trajectory that, almost inevitably, snatches the win from a startled Olly Allen at the finish line. Back at the trackshop, they don't share my amazement at this virtuoso exhibition of riding skill, "Is the Pope German?"

It's always a pleasure to see speedway intelligence in action. For the first two laps of heat 5 Chris 'Bomber' Harris holds up his third-placed teammate Edward Kennett. On the last lap of the race, 'Bomber' blasts round the outside to draw level with race leader Tai Woffinden then – as they enter the third bend at speed – he cuts back and appears to deliberately lock up (but does so in the PK manner) in order to blast down the inside line to snatch the race win on the finish line! This manoeuvre is all the more exciting since it's almost an exact replica of what he'd just seen PK do the race before. Before the start of heat 6, Porky reiterates one of his favourite slogans, "Let's blast the gas!" Freddie Lindgren wins the race by a country mile in a fashion that highlights his smooth racing style and draws the eye. His teammate Nicolai Klindt rears on the second bend to relegate himself from contention. It's a reality that Porky chooses to ignore after the race with a handy circumlocution, "Nicolai Klindt not looking happy there – he seemed to have machine problems big style! He'll go back to the pits and sort them out!"

Opposite the sun-kissed back straight, high up in the referee's box of the shaded grandstand, Peter Morrish reads my publicity material and, since he doesn't own a computer, he's touchingly unaware of the functionality available in any Word document, "250,000 words – I wonder who counted them?" Porky suggests that we might like to "get some photos of Peter Morrish – the Terry Wogan of speedway!" The start of heat 7 once again finds Jordan Frampton in the wars when he falls on the apex of the first bend. As a result, Jordan retires from the race and, subsequently, withdraws from the meeting with a broken wrist. PK's suddenly finally found his mislaid gating gloves and, although Edward Kennett stays close to him, there's no danger that he'll pass. Messrs Allen, Klindt and Proctor serve up a competitive battle in heat 8 that meets with Porky's approval, "What a great ride from all three riders at the front!" During his last lap commentary, Porky inadvertently lambasts Ty Proctor when he fails to pass the black-and-white

[3] At the time of the incident, Porky was dressed in a wig mocking Susan Boyle, while Shaun Leigh played 'river dance' over the PA. It was a display that must have irked the gods since Porky's ankle tendon then snapped to deliver more pain than usually provided by Susan's singing. Porky had to be treated by the paramedics whilst everyone jeered him. It turned out to be a very serious injury and, as is the modern way, ended up on YouTube.

helmeted Olly Allen as they exit the second bend on the final lap ("He's thrown it away!"). Before the start of heat 9, the apparently perpetually priapic Porky tries to induct Peter Morrish into a shared obsession. "You're missing all the action, Peter! There's a lovey-dovey couple kissing down at the front of the grandstand totally oblivious to the action. Well, I don't know!" On the terraces, even though Wolves lead comfortably 30-19, club historian Mark Sawbridge straight facedly advises me, "You can never take anything for granted in local derbies!" The 80th anniversary gift pack discombobulates Laurence Rogers, "I must see CVS and ask him what we're supposed to do with all the stickers?" When I suggest they should be given out, Laurence replies, "There's not been enough sent to do that!"

After Tai Woffinden blasts up inside Olly Allen and frightens him into second place, the ninth race of the night effectively ends as a contest. While he charms us with his thoughts over the public address system, with his foot encased in plaster, Porky limps about in discomfort on the centre green. With three riders already at the start line, the two-minute warning is cancelled and we learn, "the paramedic is in the pits checking on Jordan Frampton." After this medical examination, Ricky Wells replaces Frampton. The initial attempt to run this race gets nowhere and, after it's called back, the rider in blue (Nicolai Klindt) is warned by the referee to stay still at the start line. The rerun of the race lasts until Ricky Wells bursts through the third-bend air-fence and is disqualified. Immobile over at the start line, Porky updates us on the situation with the benefit of some X-ray vision that somehow allows him to see through an air-fence, "He's gone through the fence but looks to be moving around!" The *Express & Star*'s Tim Hamblin later suggests a generous explanation for this perspicacity, "Maybe he saw the air-fence fluttering?" When finally run to a conclusion, Freddie Lindgren comfortably bests Edward Kennett and, with the scores at 37-24, the interval is taken. Tim Hamblin, stops by my display table for a chat. "The track's a bit heavy; they probably prepared it that way for Coventry as they have Olly Allen returning from injury. They always prepare it a bit heavy for Lakeside as they're a team of gaters!" My admiration for PK's skill and cunning round the circuit in heat 4 overlooks the consequences of his bizarre trajectory for his teammate, "PK certainly stuffed Tai, anyway, by taking that peculiar line. Chris Harris was obviously watching as he took that line in the very next race! Did you hear the disturbance at the far end of the grandstand during the minute's silence? Someone had collapsed and they were trying to attract attention [from the stood-to-attention St John Ambulance staff]. Porky demanded help [for an OAP with a cracked skull] and pointed there immediately." The mystery of the night for Tim is the start-line enigma that is Peter Karlsson tonight. "PK has had a couple of shocking starts tonight – very unlike him!"

The first race after the interval features a good battle for third place between Chris Kerr and Ricky Wells until Kerr goes too wide on the last corner, loses position and theatrically admonishes himself with some severe shakes of his head. A tough first corner at the start of heat 12 sees Ty Proctor blast underneath Filip Sitera to prompt his fall and an excursion over the bend 2 air-fence. Porky ruminates cogently upon the newest word in the 2009 speedway vocabulary, "Disqualified – I don't like that word! 'Excluded' sounds better!" The rerun (without Sitera) indicates that Ty Proctor also closely watches PK in action and, though he doesn't need to pass a rival, Ty continually experiments with (but doesn't quite manage to emulate) the unique PK angle into bend 3. The third 5-1 of the night enables Porky to resume his rhetorical questioning, "5-1, you know what that means – do ya?" On this occasion it means the race winner Tai Woffinden provides a lap and a half of wheelie celebrations. Though frequently praised for their positive impact upon British speedway, the country's number one sports satellite broadcaster isn't everyone's cup of tea. "Hell will freeze over before I subscribe to Sky. In football, it's the big bully changing fixtures without any thought of the fans! Look at the cricket – all those old people who like to watch the Ashes – now can't! All the students who enjoyed 'Lost' on Channel 4 now can't see it. OAPs can't afford Sky, I can but I refuse!"

Porky identifies heat 13 as "one to watch" since it pits Freddie and PK against 'Bomber' and Olly, ("this is not one to be missed!"). For three and a half laps, the Coventry pair team ride up front until Freddie exploits the PK cut-back to snatch second place from Olly on the line. Cunning as a fox, PK follows in his slipstream and also nearly sneaks past Olly for the third-place point. The penultimate race of the night features a massive lock-up from Filip Sitera on the fourth bend that causes Chris Kerr to lay down and Edward Kennett to take swift evasive action that sees him to crash into the air-fence. Porky informs us, "The ref's gonna take a look at the replay to decide – all interesting stuff". Quick as a flash, a girl in the crowd retorts, "I'll make it easy for yah – yellah!" This judgement is confirmed seconds later. In the rerun, Adam Skornicki enjoys a tapes-to-line victory and, after a prompt from Porky, he does some celebration donuts in front of the grandstand. Such fripperies don't impress the OAP I'm stood next to, "It don't win races, do it?!" The business year to date in the Rattenberry Trackshop Empire has fallen short of Dave's expectations. "It's been really hard this year! No matter what you do you can't win. It's okay if one track isn't so good but, if it's all six ... [trails off] well, I can't complain about Redcar." Though over as a contest much earlier, the last race of the night is a thriller. PK again fails to gate but blasts past the Coventry pair on the second lap. Chris Harris refuses to give up or be intimidated. He shows determination and nerve to ride side by side with the Monmore maestro until he again takes the PK racing line in the last corner to seize another win at the finish line. Mark Sawbridge is generous in his praise, "Chris Harris was superb [his mobile rings] can you excuse me, it's the local radio station." After Mark provides them with an enthusiastic and insightful report on tonight's meeting, he allows himself to briefly luxuriate in the victory, "It's the biggest crowd we've seen here all season!" When notional championship rivals the Coventry Bees are swept aside so easily it's hard to see what the programme optimistically describes as the "revamped and revitalised with Scott Nicholls" Ipswich Witches will do at Monmore next Monday night to halt this Wolverhampton juggernaut.

20th July Wolverhampton v. Coventry (Elite League) 54-39

Wolverhampton : *"CVS once said to me if he could order it to rain the night before – or in the morning – he would, as it really helps the track bind together properly!"*

CHAPTER 20

Peterborough

"There's no shale on the GP tracks 'cause they don't want to obscure the adverts! It's mad but true!"

23rd July

On the drive to Peterborough, I hear on the radio that it's National Cuddle Day. Meanwhile 9 million people panic and try to call or log onto the Swine Flu hotline in its first hour! On the northbound A1 they have a large sign readable by passing motorists that proclaims "Adult Pit Stop". You can understand that there might be demand for food and refreshments but a garage and sex shop is, surely, a unique business combination! Similarly, when there is merchandise available at the Peterborough trackshop nowadays a large sign outside it proudly says it's "Open for Business"! When the Queen resides at Buckingham Palace or Windsor Castle, the flag is raised. The dawn of the Rick Frost era at Peterborough Speedway has seen many positive changes to the speedway infrastructure, fixtures and fittings at the East of England Showground. Just as significantly, Rick demands standards of professionalism backed by strict codes of behaviour from all staff. No area or department within the club has been neglected and this holds true, even for the trackshop run by Andy Griggs. With the added advantage of his revamped large and bold signage, inside the shop there are also huge presentational changes that require Andy to arrive much earlier than previously in order to dress his shop to the standards and specifications requested by Rick Frost. By the time I arrive, Andy has covered all the display tables with tablecloths in the Panthers team colours of red and black. The white walls of the glass windowed space that serves as the track shop premises within the rear of the main home-straight grandstand are also covered with impressive and appropriately team-coloured drapes! On one table a mannequin's head sports a Peterborough Panthers baseball cap complete with the vaguely heraldic new era double-headed Panthers logo. There's also the upper body of a larger mannequin on display dressed in a rather snazzy long-sleeved rugby shirt in the club colours. With the concentration and attention to detail you'd usually associate with Aspergers, Andy lines up the miniature model riders for sale on the table top with geometric precision. One falls to the floor, "Oh no, Hans Andersen has crashed!"

Amongst the cornucopia of Panthers merchandise on sale tonight, pride of place is given to a large glass-fronted black frame that, on closer examination, contains 40 images of some of the key riders who've raced Peterborough Speedway during the last 40 seasons. Each week inside the programme two cards are given away free. They're the type that commonly used to be given away with tea, cigarettes and sweet cigarettes. However, the photographs these cards use of the riders are more reminiscent of the soccer stars' stickers whose heyday was the '60s and '70s. Inside tonight's programme for the Elite League B meeting against Wolverhampton, every fan gets an image of a stern-looking Ales Dryml (2004-05 & 2009) and a youthful Gary Havelock (2003-04) with a Europress era Panthers logo on his kevlars that he clutches in the manner of a child who wishes to go to the toilet. Posters on the trackshop door and windows succinctly proclaim, "Frame your collector's cards! Reserve your custom made frame now! You've collected the cards, why not mount them in a professionally custom made black frame with a burgundy matted mount? Peterborough Speedway have commissioned a number of frames for supporters to mount the collector's cards that have been given away free in the match day programme during the 2009 season. The cost of the black frame with burgundy mount is just – £19.99." Given speedway attracts so many obsessive people, let alone memorabilia collectors, it's highly likely that there will be demand from people keen to order their custom-made frames (that "will be available for collection at the last meeting of 2009 season"). Fresh from the entrepreneurial triumph of selling a 20p on eBay for £170, Panthers' promoter and commercial director Mick Bratley is delighted with the success of the rider cards initiative. "They only cost 1p per card and I get 600 done. In a recession people might have thought of not buying them but our programme sales have gone up. You only need to sell three extra programmes to cover the cost of the print run of a card! If people are missing cards, they have to buy the programme for £2. We sell several online each week. The quality of our programme has gone up and I hate seeing programmes sell for 10p, 50p or whatever. I think it's one of the best ideas I've ever had! Next season we'll do more cards and sell a completed framed version as a collector's item.

[Jeff] "Who'll be on the cards?"

[Mick] "Hans Andersen, Zabik, Zengota – that might be misinformation or that might be true! I've been reading what Jon Cook has to say in the *Star* and I agree with him that we should price Elite League speedway meetings at £20, at least! But only so long as we run on two nights each week. I also agree that we have to work with BSI. They're the future and we can fight against them but that's only going to go one way. We need to work with them to survive and thrive! We had the World Team Cup here and gave them their best ever meeting! Heat 20 had passing and re-passing. It was all that you could ever ask for! Ole Olsen was going mental though! And I finally figured out why – there's no shale on the GP tracks 'cause they don't want to obscure the adverts! It's mad but true! With all the dirt that was sprayed on them here, Ole was really going mental. And with Buster [Chapman] ripping the frick out of the track it wasn't what they wanted. We had a day of practice and a fantastic meeting. What better advert could there be? 5,068 people attended, there were 400 odd guests and with staff we had nearly 6,000 here. BSI now have their own shale here [stored in Wales] as they have done for three or four years in Copenhagen. But, then, those two [Cardiff and Copenhagen] are the meetings that make their Series! Quite what they're doing with the rest of them, I don't know? Look at Prague, they had no one there at all!

[Andy] "Can you put down that Torben Olsen is a twit, I insist."

[Mick] "No he's a panicker! We need more fights! That got more attention than speedway has had in years. We need thrills, spills and controversy. In my press releases, I try and say something quirky. People, let alone the media, don't want to hear the usual platitudes. They want quirky! The weekly roundup [issued by the BSPA] always picks up on what I say and use it! Excuse me, I must go and chat to our so-called team manager [Trevor Swales]."

Poole Pirates haven't exactly torn up the trees this season but, though they're one of the Elite League's basement clubs in 2009, last night they punctured the play-off ambitions of the Panthers when they dismissed them 52-41. There was a 40-minute team meeting afterwards. These frank discussions allowed everyone to foreground matters of concern and identify possible means to their solution. When the going gets tough everyone can stick together or, alternatively, blamestorm in the search for a scapegoat. Panthers fans and, it is rumoured, the team manager have allegedly expressed some dissatisfaction with the commitment and performances of their diminutive Danish heat leader Kenneth Bjerre. According to this week's *Speedway Star*, after 25 meetings Kenneth's average is 8.24 [8.73 at home and 7.49 away]. This presently finds him ranked 16th in the Elite League averages. Despite what on the surface looks like a pretty creditable average, in some quarters there are grumbles that the quality of Kenneth's performances in Poland, Sweden and for Denmark outstrip this and indicate that he's not riding to his full potential in Britain. In a short space of time, many visitors to the trackshop reveal their opinions on the subject. "We threw it away last night. Kenneth Bjerre wins first time out then has two zeros and beat Holder who was on fire! What's that about? He's scoring loads of points abroad too. Trevor's joked before that he should wear his Danish kevlars when he rides here!" [1] Bjerre's patriotism is a popular theme, "He's only a Conference League rider here – we need to get some Danish kevlars made to see him ride properly!" If there's anxiety amongst the fans about performances and the possibility of qualification for the Elite League Play-offs, then tension also wracks the team as the pressure of heightened expectation about obtaining a lucrative top-four place mounts. Unsubstantiated rumours fly that Trevor Swales and Kenneth Bjerre had a passionate exchange in the Poole pits last night that allegedly concluded with Kenneth's suggestion, "Go on frickin' sack me then!" Things often get said in the heat of the moment and forgotten about later. Whatever was or wasn't said, late-season changes to the Panthers team wouldn't be practicable, "No one would want to come in for the amount of meetings we have left. If they brought Crumpie in, for example, they'd have to rearrange the whole team!" If their Play-off ambitions are to be realised, the only real solution is for the Panthers to take maximum points from all their remaining home fixtures, starting with Wolverhampton tonight followed by Belle Vue and Swindon in future weeks. Points on the road are also a possibility with meetings still to be raced at Ipswich, Wolverhampton (twice), Poole and Belle Vue.

[1] Kenneth Bjerre was actually second top scorer with 8 points from five rides. He finished second, first, last, last and first.

Always professional and invariably an early arrival to confirm the veracity of his meticulously pre-prepared notes with riders, officials and others, Craig 'Mr Potassium' Saul arrives clutching his regulation two bananas. Peterborough will ride as per programme except they'll operate rider replacement for Kenneth Hansen who's won the unwanted accolade of being the "first Elite League rider to get Swine Flu!" [2] Unlike some, Craig likes to read my books before he offers an opinion. "My favourite chapter was the Glyn Taylor one. You went there at the right time after the Gary Havelock thing and learning about the costs was really interesting!" Like Top Cat, Craig is busy, busy, busy so, after he's consulted Andy about what trackshop goodies to promote, he rushes off to the Panthers pits area. My display table positioned in front of the trackshop doesn't have the furnishings or presentational élan to be found through the glass window behind me but, nonetheless, many passers-by stop for a conversation. From the faded tattoo on his arm I gather that Chris is a Crewe fan, "I only ever went to a training school there once but, at least, I saw it with bikes on the track! Once it's gone, it's gone! I can't wait for the Crewe book [*When They Were Kings*] to arrive in the post. I collect race jackets. My dream is to have an original Crewe one. I have a replica but that's not the same. My big regret is throwing out my Ivan Mauger books. I have his Hull race jacket and I'd like to still be able to look at photos of it."

Mounted cards

Once again, the BSPA's 80th Anniversary celebration initiative successfully draws many more youngsters than usual to the stadium this evening. 6-year-old William and his friend Jack both clutch autograph books and, when William buys a discounted copy of *Shale Britannia*, he rather sweetly asks, "Which helmet do you wear?" Debbie – the Peterborough and Scunthorpe texter for the Speedway Updates website – still remains moved days after Kenny Smith's funeral ceremony at Scunthorpe Speedway's Normanby Road stadium. "Kenny's funeral was special. I haven't been to many – thank goodness. It was really personal! There were two bikes revving up as the hearse came in. Kenny was one of those lovely people! Everyone liked him! He had time for everyone and, of course, was very genuine!" Well-connected speedway fan Brian Oldham picks up on the thread of this conversation (while his wife Celia kindly goes off to buy us both a doughnut), "Speedway's full of genuine 'salt of the earth' people. I think it has more than most! Sure there's others, of course – like there are in every walk of life – but speedway has lots of wonderful people and it's one of the pleasures of it!" Brian is delighted that his eldest son recently really caught the speedway bug but his happiness is tinged by his son's choice of favourite speedway club. "My eldest son has really started to follow speedway – the only problem is who his favourite riders are and who his team is! [pause] Lewis Bridger, Lukas Dryml and Eastbourne! It's terrible!"

Rainbow over the home pits

The collegiate nature of the speedway community has been further underlined by the punctilious observation of a minute's silence at speedway tracks throughout the country to commemorate the life and contribution of the late Kenny Smith. Peterborough Speedway club are fortunate to actually have a club chaplain, the Reverend Michael Whawell who conducts tonight's

Henning Bager & a quizzical Craig Saul

[2] Kenneth Hansen confirmed to the *Speedway Star*, "The doctors told me I am showing all the symptoms of Swine Flu and I'm not feeling good at all. I've got a runny nose, my muscles are sore and my temperature is over 40 degrees." Where exactly he contracted the illness is uncertain since – during a two-week break from racing – Kenneth went on holiday to Spain and also travelled to Poland.

brief ceremony and address. The stadium hushes to listen studiously while Michael reprises the life, career and outstanding contribution made to British Speedway by the recently departed Scunthorpe team manager. "Kenneth Ian Smith enjoyed a brief career for Doncaster ... known affectionately as third-bend Kenny ... he's most remembered for his team management at Newcastle and his promotional work at Scunthorpe ... Kenny had an exceptional talent for identifying, nurturing and enthusing young talent! ... May he rest in peace." Respects were then paid with a minute's silence. Keen runner and veteran of many marathons, afterwards Michael reveals he brought his stopwatch to ensure accuracy in remembrance, "It ought to be noted that the minute's silence overran by 20/100ths of a second!" It's a small but symbolic difference but somehow appropriate given that Kenny always freely contributed more than his formal responsibilities and, thereby, touched so many with his understated but genuine humanity.

This season business commitments have meant that regular Panthers meeting presenter Craig Saul hasn't been able to entertain, enlighten and engage the East of England Showground crowds so often as usual. Kevin Moore has deputised instead and tonight he fills in as announcer in place of Edwin Overland who's away on holiday. Conscientious presenters like Craig Saul go out of their way – in BBC World Service fashion – to consult with exotically named foreign riders about how exactly their names should be pronounced. Given we have so few British riders on the modern speedway scene, you'd have thought that this would be common practice. Some announcers we hear over stadium public address systems or live on the Sky Sports speedway coverage frequently persist with their own idiosyncratic pronunciations. Thoughtlessly and overconfidently getting someone's name wrong when you're paid to do otherwise can be irksome, while for others these linguistic foibles instil affection. Michael laments Edwin's absence, "Edwin is on his way back from his holiday in Ireland so we haven't got Alice Dribble [Ales Dryml] – which is a shame!" In the heat of the moment words can get mangled, or phrases jumbled or even lost. Some presenters struggle with foreign names but not Kevin Moore who treats us with his own special pronunciation ("Wolverhampden") to effortlessly twin the visitors linguistically with Queen's Park football club. On balance, the speedway world would be a duller place without these ideosyncracies.

Even before a wheel turns, most speedway fans understand the chalk and cheese comparison between size, speed and dimensions of the Monmore Green and East of England Showground tracks make it highly unlikely that Wolverhampton will gain an away victory. That said, Wolves have a team in form and, this season, Lakeside have already emerged triumphant at the Showground. One definite thrill of this 336-metre track is the exhilarating speed that riders achieve. The first heat of the night pits Niels-Kristian Iversen [17th in the Elite League averages] against Wolves high-flying number 1 Fredrik Lindgren [second in the Elite League averages]. Iversen attacks the track with gusto and his victory is never in doubt. Though appearances can be deceptive, he looks tremendously fast. Indeed, he is tremendously fast! Iversen's time of 59.8 is only 0.7 seconds outside the track record set by Hans Andersen in April 2007. The second race sees Wolverhampton's Chris Kerr and Lee Complin fire into the first bend ahead of their Panthers rivals. It's an unexpected sight that prompts Coventry team manager Peter Oakes to observe, "I didn't think the Wolves reserves would get a point!" Moments later they're easily overtaken, "Oh, I was right!" In heat 3, Ales Dryml takes the first rider replacement ride of the night for Kenneth Hansen ("nine weeks projected absence") and, out for the second time in three races, wins comfortably. The Reverend Michael Whawell marks up the racecard in his programme approvingly, "He let that second place go in his first ride. I'm pleased to see he went to the front and stayed there!" It takes Peter Karlsson until the third bend to hit the front in heat 4, Michael exclaims gleefully, "The old boy's good, in't he? He knows too much!" Michael's naturally good company. He's lived a full and varied life and though learned, perceptive and wise, he wears this lightly. Michael has so many strings to his bow, he requires a second bow. He asks if I'm staying the night or going home before I go to Coventry tomorrow. News I'll be in the city centre at the Travelodge where even their website warns "may suffer from nightclub noise" gains the quick as a flash retort, "That's the whole of Peterborough actually."[3] Conversation is always wide ranging with Michael. Between the races, in a short space of time we touch upon his beloved Paris (he recommends the "Place du Contrescarpe near the Place du Pantheon"), health and safety in the modern church ("We have some new silly rules on chalices – we can't pass them round any more apparently!"), wall construction ("I've never heard of bungaroosh"), speedway

[3] The website warning doesn't do the night-time environment round this particular Travelodge justice since there are three night clubs together – thankfully only two of them are open – and a lap dancing club. The area also specialises in a selection of user unfriendly car parks that only allow you to purchase a £1.50 ticket valid until 3 a.m. All aforementioned car parks are helpfully festooned with notices that your car will be clamped unless you display a valid ticket when they re-open again at 7 a.m.! I doubt they make reference to this unique circumstance in the Peterborough Tourist Information office.

("Freddie's obviously changed his gearing") and the weather ("Look at that rainbow over Yaxley"). Michael turns to Yaxley resident Peter Oakes, "There'll be a pot of gold in your back garden when you get home." Rain in the distance and black clouds overhead prompt Mick Bratley to comment, "We haven't had one rain-off this season!" Though Michael has many skills, Mick probably slightly overestimates them when he nods towards the jet black cloud and rainbow, "Can you move those over and away from here?"

Freddie Lindgren completes the formality of his fifth race win and, with Nicolai Klindt third, the scores narrow to 17-13. Mads Korneliussen isn't happy with his second place in heat 5 as he comes back to the pits shouting. Michael isn't surprised, "Doh – he always shouts when he comes back." The green shoots of a Wolverhampton recovery last until the exit from the second bend of the next race when the outstretched hand of Peter Karlsson indicates he's suffered an engine failure ("I thought it was the old 'I am turning left' from the Highway Code"). When he gets back to the pits, the usually taciturn Peter Karlsson looks 'in high dudgeon'. Since it's National Cuddle Day, PK might benefit from a consolation cuddle but there are no ready volunteers. Craig Saul decides against an interview, "I was just lining PK up for an interview but I think I'll leave him for a bit. For a man with glasses he's getting very steamed up!" Niels-Kristian Iversen (with Ales Dryml in support) duly beat Chris Kerr in the rerun closely watched from the pits-viewing area by his mechanics Ray Blackwell and his son, Mark. Kenneth Bjerre comfortably wins heat 7 while Skornicki and Woffinden fill the minor places to keep the Panthers in the lead at a comfortable 8 points.

Team spirit in the Wolverhampton camp remains high despite their collective difficulties this evening during the first half of the meeting. Before the start of heat 8, Lee Complin's bike packs up and, without hesitation, Tai Woffinden sprints across the pits to immediately rush out his bike while the two-minute time allowance ticks down. The Reverend Whawell notes phlegmatically, "Two little fellows, not much to choose between them. Still it's a bit of drama." The replacement bike ensures Lee Complin isn't excluded under the time allowance but, nonetheless, he finishes last, "Tai's bike doesn't look so quick when ridden by Lee Complin!" The race is won by Ales Dryml who now has paid 10 points from four rides. Michael is pleased on his behalf, "I'm so pleased after how he was treated, saying 'we don't want you' and then, 'you can come back again'. He's such a nice chap – always so polite and always happy to speak. It's good to see him doing well because he can get easily discouraged." With the deficit now 10 points, Peter Adams explores his tactical options in heat 9 and sends Peter Karlsson out in the black-and-white helmet colour. Whatever difficulties plagued his machinery have subsided since PK proceeds to win the race in imperious fashion. When the interval arrives, the usually phlegmatic PK is happy to answer Craig's questions in his distinctive Black Country influenced English accent. Craig quickly establishes that PK's 'flabber' hasn't been 'gasted' by the Wolverhampton performance so far this evening. "Yes, of course, Peterborough have some good riders round here ... it ain't over till the fat lady sings!" Craig leavens the interview with some technical enquiries that prompt PK to confirm, "We've changed the ignition system now."

While the interval raffle prize of £81.50 is being won by someone with a sky-blue ticket, Brian and Celia Oldham stop by my bookstall for another brief conversation. Brian can't understand the pricing policy that operates at the East of England Showground, "It was £10 as a concession for the World Team Cup and tonight it's £12 to get in for an Elite League meeting!" After the interval, the meeting runs to its predictable conclusion. Craig dutifully tries to talk-up the possibility of a fightback from the visitors, "Wolves hoping to still get a bonus point by pulling back some points." After a drawn heat 11 with the scores less than poised at 40-29 Craig concedes, "The fat lady is definitely warming up!" The fourth Panthers 5-1 of the night in heat 12 prompts announcer Kevin Moore to close his summary of the race results with joyous news delivered in his trademark monotone, "the Panthers put the meeting beyond doubt!"

Though victory eludes them, canny Wolverhampton team manager Peter Adams hasn't given up hope of a bonus point. His decision to hand Freddie Lindgren the black-and-white helmet colour comes up trumps when PK follows him home for a 1-8 heat result that has Craig Saul purr in almost Porky-like fashion about the "speedy Swedes!" The penultimate race of the night sees Henning Bager delay his impatience to pass partner Mads Korneliussen for nearly three laps. Once he's got the run of the track, Mads then rides a very wide fast line that generates such high speed down the back straight and round the final bend that he nearly snatches victory on the finish line from a surprised Adam Skornicki. Andy Griggs and I watch the last race of the night from the grassy area adjacent to the bar that overlooks the first bend. Up front, PK races to untroubled victory while behind him Ales Dryml and Freddie Lindgren duel breathtakingly for second place. Andy remains appreciative throughout. "Whoa, whoa, what a great race!" The full-blooded nature of the last lap provides a snapshot of why – even when beset by off-track scandal and intrigue – a fast and furious speedway race for the chequered flag can exhilarate new and experienced fans alike. The gladiatorial glamour of their tactical, dander-up battle for supremacy where neither yields an inch on high-powered bikes without brakes is a sight to behold. Inevitably, heat-of-the-moment reactions and fractional measurements separate the heady bouquet of victory from reminders of the human frailty so often cruelly exposed by the brute reality of the hard shale surface upon which they race provides an additional patina of glamour to this contest. Trackshop man Andy Griggs, who could be forgiven if he'd become inured and careworn to the spectacle of speedway riders in full flight, talks to himself or, possibly, to an invisible audience throughout the last lap: "He'll try the outside swoop [Ales blocks] and now the inside [without a backwards glance Ales again blocks] ah another swoop [repelled] now down the inside [Freddie fails to snatch second place on the line by the proverbial tyre tread]".

Before the formality of the victory parade, many of the Panthers faithful rush through the darkness to the car parks. On just another day at the Elite League office for many of the frequent flier riders on display, the fast nature of the track has again served up a reminder of why we're drawn to speedway in the first place. The result is irrelevant to Wolverhampton's qualification for the Play-offs but the dropped home point could be a significant fly in the ointment for the Panthers and a further dent to their silverware credentials. After he's fulfilled his presentational responsibilities, Craig effortlessly networks with friends, acquaintances and staff on his wander back through the stadium en route towards his car. "We won but, quite how we didn't take all 3 points, I don't know! We really needed to do so to have any chance of the Play-offs!"

23rd July Peterborough v. Wolverhampton (Elite League) 51-45

Peterborough: *"There's no shale on the GP tracks 'cause they don't want to obscure the adverts! It's mad but true!"*

CHAPTER 21

Coventry

"Ben Wilson is like Filip Sitera. Once he gates, out in front he's happy to block anyone no matter who they are!"

24th July

Blocked roads and torrential rain make for a slow journey from Peterborough to Coventry for the Elite League B clash between the Bees and the Pirates. Though the journey is enlivened by a speeding black van that displays the Colourful Coffins (www.colourfulcoffins.com) livery and contact information. Poole Pirates hopes of 2009 Elite League glory already seem buried, despite a side that now boasts Hans Andersen, Bjarne Pedersen and Chris Holder. Tonight they'll face a reinvigorated Coventry boosted by the return of Ben Barker from injury and the reintroduction of their popular German rider Martin Smolinski in place of broken collarbone victim Rory Schlein. Inside the Bees trackshop there's the usual cornucopia of well-chosen yellow-and-black merchandise available for purchase including eye-catching colourful hand-painted programme boards that can be made to order for a bargain price of £12.50. There's also a prominently displayed advert for a 192-page book on the complete history of pre-war speedway in Coventry (*The Story of Lythalls Lane and Brandon Speedways From 1928-39* written by Colin Parker) exclusive to the trackshop priced at £14.99 with all proceeds going to the Speedway Riders' Benevolent Fund. Taped underneath the poster is a photo of Chris 'Bomber' Harris rather self-consciously signing copies of the book in what – if judged by the trophy cabinet behind him – could be the Coventry Speedway Office. Chris has contributed a Foreword to the book and, as a further incentive to purchase, has signed the first 50 copies!

The friendly and knowledgeable husband-and-wife team who run the trackshop, Joyce and Malcolm Blythe, have already been on site for several hours to ensure that, by the time the public come through the entrance turnstiles, the shop is dressed professionally and its many items presented attractively. First impressions count in any business and Coventry speedway are fortunate to have Malcolm and Joyce on hand to welcome any visitors who happen to pop into their premises. Both long-time employees, Joyce is more than happy to be one of the public faces of the speedway club or the stadium in general. "The trackshop is the first port of call for fans wanting to talk about anything. Whether people want to complain or praise, we're often the first to find out what the fans think, want or notice! They come in here for all sorts of things. If they want their glasses repaired – I have a little screwdriver specially for that – or want me to order a taxi for them for the end of the meeting or if they don't feel well, whatever! Even to borrow a chair. We like to help as we're the public face – or one of them – of the club. We would anyway but you know what I mean." Malcolm echoes this theme, "They ask why have we signed this person or haven't signed that person when Colin [Pratt] is always available in his office or on the gate for them to talk to!? It's not as if we know or decide!" Evidenced by the number of puddles outside the shop, they've clearly already had some rain in the area. Malcolm's confident that the renowned drainage at Brandon Stadium will prove more than adequate to cope with the recent rain or any forthcoming downpours. "I've been to look at the track. It's a bit damp on turns one and two but it'll be alright if we don't have any more rain! The track blokes say they've looked at the forecast for Birmingham Airport and it'll be showers this afternoon and fine tonight. If that's correct, that'll be good." Injuries are part and parcel of the sport but, according to Joyce, Coventry have had their unfair share this season. "We haven't got any team photos here in the trackshop because, since the first meeting this season, there's always been someone injured. Bob Dugard had the cheek to complain when we used our own rider for a month. What he said was disgusting! I think he'll notice when Coventry don't take a coach load down to the next meeting at Eastbourne!" Later on riders' merchandise stall supervisor Jodie Lowry echoes this theme and highlights the outrage felt by many Coventry fans about Bob's comments over the loudspeaker system at Arlington. "What was Dugard on about? I couldn't believe it! Mr Sandhu is one of the most modest men you could meet in speedway. Sure he's a multi-millionaire but he doesn't show-off and throw his money around! He considers things from the business point of view. If a young rider shows promise, he might help him and say 'pay me back later'. He's very unassuming and doesn't deserve to be spoken about like that!"

Talk of journeys inevitably excites Malcolm's inner Sat Nav. He quickly identifies and reels off five different routes that I could have taken this afternoon from Peterborough to Coventry. ("She don't need sat nav 'cause she's got me!"). One rider Malcolm's pleased has found his way back to the club is Martin Smolinski. Joyce is also happy at the return of the well-mannered German. "We still let Martin stock his stuff at the shop even though he doesn't ride for us. He's brought us more stock 'cause he knows it's a good thing! In all my time here, only two riders have come and collected the money for their merchandise [sales] and thought to put their hand in their pocket to give something to Jodie [who sells these items from a separate counter within the trackshop]. Scott gave her a tenner and Martin did too! Martin was delighted to see his posters were still up in his workshop. All the riders have their own workshop here round the back. Do you want to see them? Mr Sandhu knows how to look after his riders! Even when Scott was just here for the month, Mr Sandhu gave him all the Bees gear – anoraks, sweatshirts, pit shirts, the lot!" Given the amount of maintenance, let alone cleaning, required for just one speedway bike – workshop space is a vital aspect of any speedway rider's armoury if they're to do well on the track on a regular basis. It's a truism of speedway that workshop hours invariably translate into points on the track. This time spent in the workshop helps to eliminate mechanical gremlins as well as giving the opportunity for experiment and/fine tuning. Not every speedway club has a rider-friendly owner like Mr Sandhu or, indeed, sufficient grounds within their own stadium to invest in such facilities (later I learn there have been speedway workshops at Brandon Stadium since it re-opened in 1948). Joyce takes me round the back of the trackshop and proudly waves her arm towards a collection of sea-containers that serve as the heated and lit individual workshop spaces for each Coventry Bees rider. 'Bomber' Harris's mechanic Ted (former Mr Bear mascot at Bradford in the early 1990s) is already hard at work with the power washer, albeit he uses it to spray clean 'Bomber's' silver BMW. Chris supervises whilst stood nonchalantly sufficient distance away to avoid any unnecessary dampness. Colin Pratt walks determinedly past us to enter one of the substantial doored sea-container workshops to ask of whoever is inside, "What are the crowds like in Germany then?" Back at the trackshop Joyce draws my attention to the good value to be had there. "Look how many things we've got on sale at bargain prices! I bought one of Edward Kennett's hoodies – that grey one up there – 'cause it looks nice and the badge is nice and small and subtle. It doesn't shout out at you so you can wear it elsewhere easily!" Malcolm's surprised that I have chosen to come and see Poole, "Why do you come and watch the cheats rather than Eastbourne?" Alleged sharp practice elsewhere slightly disillusions Joyce, "If I didn't work here with all the shenanigans that's gone on this season, I'd have to think whether I'd come to speedway!"

With dark clouds overhead and rumbles of thunder off in the distance, while I wait to drop off a copy of my book for Colin Pratt, Sheila Hewitt answers the phone in the Coventry speedway office and states accurately, "It's not raining here, it's fine." By 6.15 p.m. the skies are still bright but there's heavy rain and thunder. Malcolm still takes an optimistic view, "this ain't rain, it's just water!" His positive outlook appears misplaced when, for five minutes around 6.35 p.m., the heavy rain turns into a torrential downpour. Dry under the shelter of the passageway (with snack-bar kiosk and toilets) that bisects either side of the home-straight grandstand, this rain lashes down with such velocity it ricochets back upwards! The severity of the rain is almost biblical but, since it stops as quickly as it starts, the stadium staff are able to work zealously to make all the stadium surfaces safely usable. Brushes in hand they sluice the puddles towards the drains from the grey-painted surface that surrounds the entrance turnstiles and programme booth. The staff efficiently set about their pre-arranged tasks, while a supervisor with a walkie-talkie inspects their handiwork and refuses to give permission for the turnstiles to open until everything is completely to his satisfaction. "We just need to get rid of the excess water [by the turnstiles] – it's like a paddling pool at the minute!" Behind his race-day satellite trackshop stall (used for the sale of speedway magazines and selected books), Malcolm surveys the scene. "They had this rain at Swindon yesterday and their first race wasn't until half-past 8!" Though over an hour still remains before the scheduled start time and with the public still patiently queuing outside the stadium, a lady staff member in a fluorescent jacket chats to her colleague as they pass, "Chris Harris says it's on!" Her younger colleague remains sceptical, "It is until they all fall off on the first bend anyway!" Two minutes later the turnstiles open and a phalanx of

Coventry: *"Ben Wilson is like Filip Sitera. Once he gates, out in front he's happy to block anyone no matter who they are!"*

old age pensioners head the initial sprint-cum-trot towards the grandstand to bagsy their favourite seats ("I wonder what the track is like?"). Karl Roberts from WildKaRD and Meth Designsz (inventor of the rights delayed 5-1 speedway computer game) arrives early with his son Alec, whose hooded anorak is complemented by his junior-sized golden race tabard. While they've waited in the queue outside they caught up on the gossip about tonight's meeting. "Davidsson hasn't got here from Stansted and Ben Wilson isn't here either! Karl turns to his son, 'What about Martin [Smolinski]?'" Alec remains silent but smiles broadly.
[Jeff] "He's everyone's favourite German speedway rider!"
[Karl] "Are there any others then?"

Painted Bomber programme board

When you consider the cloudburst, the weather forecast of showers and the dark clouds overhead – the sheer volume of people who come through the turnstiles in the 70 minutes before the scheduled start time of 8 p.m. is a testament to the popularity of the team and speedway they serve up at Brandon Stadium. Various people stop for a chat including Alan Sampson whom I recently met in the Sheffield Speedway Office during his track tour with Canadian Roger Stevens. "Neil [Machin] is one of the most honest men in speedway! Speedway is going downhill in my opinion!" Alan's keen to savour his speedway and makes light of his own medical ailments, ("I'm having chemo for a sort of rare sclerosis") and that of his parents ("they've both got cancer"). He remains optimistically philosophical, "It's best to get on with life and enjoy it!"

Hi vis jackets make ready at the turnstiles

Though the shale is dark and damp, the meeting starts as scheduled under the watchful eye of experienced referee Jim Lawrence. Coventry make a suboptimal start to the meeting and, stood together in the pits, Peter Oakes, Allen Trump and Mr Sandhu look on in stony silence as the Poole pair of Hans Andersen and Joe Screen race away to a comfortable 5-1 ahead of Chris 'Bomber' Harris. The second race of the night only gets to the third bend before Ben Barker blasts up inside race leader Ben Wilson who's just made it to the stadium only to be unseated from his equipment before he's even completed a lap. We've all seen the same incident. Two Coventry fans in front of me disagree about events – one says, "He nearly took his front wheel off huh huh" while the other retorts, "Nah, he wasn't anywhere near him!" Jim Lawrence makes his own adjudication and disqualifies Ben Barker. Actually it's a double disqualification since filled-in Pirates reserve Steve Boxall abandoned his race win ambitions on the first bend and, therefore, is also disqualified for not being under power at the time of the stoppage. In the rerun, Ben Wilson again shows good speed from the start line to beat Ricky Wells in a match race. Rumours that Daniel Davidsson has been delayed en route from the airport to Coventry appear well-founded when he fails to line up with the rest of the riders for heat 3 and is soon disqualified under the two-minute time allowance. His hard-working replacement Ben Wilson proceeds to hold off Edward Kennett for three laps in their battle for second place until the Bees rider finally overhauls him. This Coventry maximum gives the scoreline an odd look at 8-9 but, of greater worry for Poole, is a lacklustre Bjarne Pedersen hugely trailed off at the back of the race. Along with the team he captains, Bjarne hasn't enjoyed the best of seasons so far. More shockingly, a fickle section of the Wimborne Road faithful now boo him on his home patch. Tonight, fortunately, the Pirates are on the road so this debacle is treated with silence except for

Alec Roberts

Coventry: *"Ben Wilson is like Filip Sitera. Once he gates, out in front he's happy to block anyone no matter who they are!"*

the ecstasy of Martin Horsley (who's presenter tonight in place of Peter York), "My, oh, my, wasn't that superb!" Martin Smolinski returns for the Bees at number 5 and, immediately, finds himself wheel to wheel with the gifted Australian rider Chris Holder for the Pirates in heat 4. Race rusty but determined, nonetheless the result is predictable. Steve Boxall takes third and the Pirates inch back into a surprise 3-point lead. Three successive drawn heats follow. In heat 6, Chris Harris finishes ahead of Ben Wilson and, with Chris Holder relegated to a surprise third, memories stir among the more suspicious Coventry fans around me about average manipulation allegations that dogged the Pirates team earlier in the season. Finally inside the stadium, Daniel Davidsson makes a spectacularly slow start from the tapes at the start of heat 7 and proceeds to fail to showcase his ability on a speedway bike. Bjarne Pedersen shakes off the torpor of his first ride while behind him Ben Barker wins his first home point since his return from injury.

On the centre green, the multi-talented Mike Bennett films the race action while, over the public address system, Martin Horsley advises parents that the autograph books – given to the first 250 youngsters through the turnstiles as part of the 80th anniversary celebrations of British speedway – could have some use well past many children's bedtime. "Riders will be in the under-stand bar 20 minutes after the finish of the meeting to sign autographs!" One of the children admitted free with an accompanying adult as part of these celebrations screams psychotically every time the tapes rise and soon forces me to move elsewhere. Whether it's the conditions, lack of concentration or fatigue – terrible gates seem to be the order of the night. Chris Holder lumbers away at the start of heat 9 but a somnambulant Olly Allen still gifts him a third-place point. Fast-paced Ben Wilson leads until, to the ecstatic delight of the home crowd, Edward Kennett overhauls him near the end of the third lap. Karl Roberts appreciates his efforts, "Ben Wilson is like Filip Sitera. Once he gates, out in front he's happy to block anyone no matter who they are!" The conundrum that is the quixotic Bjarne Pedersen continues with a tapes-to-flag win in heat 10. Daniel Davidsson's gating gloves remain stuck either on the luggage carousel at Stansted Airport or at home in Weymouth. Nonetheless, he still entertains the crowd with a last-bend pirouette when safely marooned at the back of the race. Hans Andersen makes it three wins out of three when he races to victory in heat 11 ahead of Ben Barker. Martin Smolinski won't have far to take his bike for an examination after an engine failure cuts short his challenge close to the pits. Karl Roberts is far from happy at how the meeting has gone so far, "The only good thing we've got is there's no Peter York. Do you want me to talk for the last two laps of each heat for you?" Daniel Davidsson's untimely dash to the stadium is finally rewarded with a point when he is gifted third place in heat 12 after his impressive, hard-riding teammate Ben Wilson tries to muscle aside Ricky Wells and falls instead. With the 5-1, what had looked an uncomfortable scoreline suddenly and undeservedly narrows to 34-37. The sign of a fightback from his beloved Coventry convinces Karl that heat 12 is the "best race of the meeting. Wilson tried leaning on Ricky but got nowhere and fell off. I was waiting for Ricky to come off but he didn't!"

The nascent Bees fightback looks likely to stall until second-placed Chris Holder contrives to fall after he's nearly run into his race partner Hans Andersen on the third bend of heat 13. Until that moment, the Pirates were on a possible 5-1 that would have taken the scoreline to a probably insurmountable 35-42. After the disqualification of Holder, while we wait for the riders to re-examine their equipment for the rerun, Martin Horsley issues some justifiable praise, "After the heavy downpour I think you'll agree the riders have put on a good show against the conditions!" Understated Wolverhampton Speedway club historian, Mark Sawbridge, reveals a recent brush with celebrity, "I went on one of the marches against Iraq in my Wolves jacket and chatted to some bloke in a woolly hat for 15 minutes – then I realised it was Robert Plant!" Poole get the best that they can from the rerun of heat 13 when Hans Andersen races to his fourth win in four races. With the score now 37-40, the permutations indicate Poole require a second place from Bjarne Pedersen in heat 14 and a win from Hans Andersen in heat 15 to ensure that they win the meeting. However, when referee Jim Lawrence holds the tapes for a fraction of a second longer than usual at the start of penultimate race of the night, Bjarne twitches and touches the tapes – something that the Coventry fans in the home-straight grandstand greet with loud cheers. Poole team manager Neil Middleditch elects to send Bjarne Pedersen back out again off 15 metres rather than send out impressive reserve Ben Wilson to deputise. To a neutral, this appears mistaken; particularly given Wilson's all-action style on the wet surface has already often nearly paid dividends. Edward Kennett and Ben Barker give Steve Boxall short shrift in the first corner before they proceed to hammer home the maximum race advantage that sends many Coventry fans into rapture and the Bees into a lead (42-41) for the first time in the meeting.

There's a helpful explanatory note on the racecard adjacent to where we'll enter the riders' names the team managers nominate to contest the last race. [1] In the full knowledge that a drawn heat will result in a victory that looked highly improbable after 11 heats, Coventry send out Chris Harris and Edward Kennett to race Hans Andersen and Chris Holder. Edward Kennett effectively kills the race and the meeting as a contest when he gates brilliantly to streak away to victory. Like many Coventry fans, Karl Roberts is ecstatic, "What an excellent, excellent end to a meeting! What a fantastic end to a meeting!" Rather than confirm the results, announcer Dave Hammond confirms the official closure of the meeting at 22.05 and then says, "I'll let you enjoy the moment … certainly speedway is unpredictable!" An enervated Malcolm Blythe is positively exuberant, "What a team! We've done that three or four times this season when we've looked dead and buried!" Demand should be high at the Edward Kennett merchandise stall for Jodie Lowry. "My dad said Edward had both wheels off the ground when he was in the dirt on the second bend. When he came here, I wasn't so keen but he's been brilliant since he moved away from Eastbourne! You never know, next year we might have Lewis Bridger – he goes very well round here." Panthers fans Graham and Hilary Rouse enjoyed the meeting. Hilary identifies Bjarne Petersen as the key factor behind the Coventry win. "It was Bjarne who cost them touching the tapes – though I would have put him out in 15 rather than Chris Holder too!"

24th July Coventry v. Poole (Elite League) 46-43

[1] "Eligibility for Heat 15 is restricted to the meeting's three top scorers [from programmed rides] or a rider in the club's top three on current Green Sheet averages."

CHAPTER 22

Eastbourne

"I think we have to go to two nights a week every fortnight. All the riders would want to ride then."

25th July

Speedway in Poland enjoys a level of popularity that British speedway promoters can only marvel at enviously. The importance of the sport and the prominence of its coverage in the Polish media ensures that, along with healthy revenues through the turnstiles, Polish speedway clubs are blessed with much more lucrative sponsorships than their British counterparts. Not only is the top tier of Polish speedway the most competitive in the world but, in order to attract the best, the rates for individual riders are similarly lucrative. When the Polish Speedway Federation or a Polish speedway club demands action or attendance, very few riders will take the career-limiting decision to ignore them. In addition, Polish speedway clubs and authorities are prepared to act unilaterally in their own best interests without thought of the ramifications or consequences for speedway clubs, leagues or authorities beyond their borders. Like a death star in science fiction draws everything within its orbit into a black hole, whether it wants to admit it or not British speedway (particularly at the Elite League level) is inextricably and disadvantageously shackled to the rhythm and rhyme of its schedule.

There have been tangible signs of this influence during recent weeks for both Eastbourne and Lakeside who race tonight in the Elite League for the second time this season at Arlington. Ostensibly entirely unconnected with the travel schedules and Polish commitments of their riders, the scheduled Elite League meeting at Lakeside between the Hammers and Swindon was called off the previous (Thursday) evening. [1] One of the first Lakeside fans through the turnstiles agrees with the postponement decision. "We called off early 'cause of the forecast. They said seven hours of torrential rain but all we got was a couple of showers. That said, the stockcar track was two foot under water and the car park and roads were totally flooded. In Dartford 120,000 people haven't had any power since Monday 'cause some kids set fire to an electrical cable and then threw it into the river!" More significantly for the Eastbourne Eagles, Lewis Bridger's complicated failure to return from Poland for last Monday's away trip to Belle Vue has stoked controversy about the relationship between British and Polish speedway. It's also seen Eagles promoter Bob Dugard fine Lewis £5,000 and ban him from two meetings – Thursday night's meeting at Ipswich and tonight's against Lakeside. [2] Though Lewis's absence

[1] Jon Cook bluntly dismissed Internet conspiracy theories. "The press release was issued in haste so that everyone would have maximum notice. Whenever there was likely to be a meeting with the rain issue associated with it, we do contact the opposition promotion the day before just to alert them of the situation. We are mindful of the travelling undertaken by many riders from both teams and, of course, the fans and we want to do our best to avoid everyone making any unnecessary journey. To consider travelling costs, not only for our own riders but also the opposition, I spoke to Terry Russell on Thursday and he agreed that if a call-off was announced, it would not be the end of the world as far as Swindon were concerned. Both teams had riders involved with extremely difficult travelling schedules although that was not my major concern to be frank, but the postponement decision was based entirely on the extremely poor weather forecast. As far as we were concerned, and given the information that we had, there was no reason to delay a call-off until Friday because there was no likely improvement in the weather predicted and that proved just so. As it happens, we had a practice arranged for 3 p.m. on the Friday and that would have been cancelled because of the rainstorm at the raceway at that time and there was further rain between then and the intended start time of the meeting including the 7 o'clock deluge. If we had left the postponement decision till Friday, nobody would have questioned it because there was a lot of rain around the country. We had the best of intentions in trying to assist people but there has been criticism of our actions."

[2] Lewis stayed in Poland after his World Cup race-off appearance to practise ahead of his Polish club Czestochowa's home meeting against Wroclaw. After this meeting was called off, Lewis went to a restaurant with other riders and unfortunately left his jacket there. This was unlucky since this jacket contained his passport. By the time Lewis had been reunited with his passport, he'd missed the 05.50 flight he required to make sure he was back in time to make the Eagles trip to Kirkmanshulme Lane. Lewis explained to the *Speedway Star*, "I know that you just can't miss an Elite League meeting because you want to race in Poland. Marian [Maslanka, Czestochowa promoter] said as I was there, I may as well ride but I didn't even think we would get start permission. I phoned the English Federation about the lost passport. I had no way to get back to England and I told Trevor Geer at about half-past 2 or 3 in the afternoon. I haven't any idea why people said I was ill." In the heat of the moment after Eastbourne had lost 48-41 at Belle Vue, Trevor Geer commented, "I'm livid with Lewis. I expect him to be banned and I expect the BSPA to make an example of this." Bob Dugard expressed scepticism about the 'lost passport' incident but took a pragmatic view despite his disappointment. "People should realise how much pressure riders came under to ride in that meeting. Lewis is in debt and probably saw a chance to wipe 25% of it out."

contributed to defeat at Belle Vue and ensured his absence from two further Eagles fixtures, many hail Bob Dugard's decision to immediately issue a fine and a ban as a shrewd one since the BSPA then wouldn't be able to impose their usual 28-day ban. Unofficial club statistician Sid Shine isn't bothered about this storm in a teacup but does have anxieties about the future of the club. "I don't think we'll be here next year! I don't think Bob wants anything to do with speedway any more the way it's going. When Floppy got injured, they knew he wasn't coming back but ran rider replacement 'cause they didn't want to pay someone else! If the crowd's down, you can see their point." Over at the trackshop, ReRun Productions DVD supremo Steve Girdwood also has anxieties about the economic and demographic environment in which British speedway now operates. "It's worrying for people who earn a living from the sport. The people who started coming 20 or 30 years ago are dying off! The crowds are dying off. We're not getting any youngsters. It can only go one way! Money is tight! Though [the suggestion of] putting prices up 25% – unless there's some big dramatic changes, and I don't know what they'd be exactly – isn't probably gonna work!"

[Nick Barber] "I think we have to go to two nights a week every fortnight. All the riders would want to ride then."

[Jeff] "Three years ago we had all the superstars and it was £12-£13 per meeting. Maybe bringing Holta, Gollob, Pedersen, Hancock, Gizatulin and Sayfutdinov would be a draw but it's not guaranteed that people would want to pay £20 to see that."

[Steve] "Without the superstars this season and last, the speedway racing itself hasn't suffered! Crumpie used to win by half a lap; Nicki Pedersen is good box office, full stop, and exciting to see – when he misses the gate occasionally. Whatever the answer is: I don't have it! But something needs to be done! It's all changed since I started out watching at Canterbury."

Nick Barber is so anxious about the long-term future of the sport that he's taken the decision to diversify and become a local councillor for the Conservative Party in Felixstowe. The demands of local government and his own conscientiousness will inevitably place considerable demands upon Nick's time. "One of the reasons I done it is 'cause of what's going on in speedway! I saw the opportunity and went for it!"

One of the bright spots of the 2009 season has been the enthusiastic adoption of Lukas Dryml by the Arlington crowd, especially those that base themselves in the home-straight grandstand. Each week the Jones family festoon the fences with flags in his honour, fans acclaim his every appearance on the track and Lukas has responded in kind with showman-like warmth to their adulation. Still with some time before the riders need to get changed, Lukas has come over from the pits to see Nick Barber about the possibility of cooperation about the sale of his merchandise.

[Lukas] "Would you be interested to sell it here? Some people have the clothes but maybe more want? I have a box! Would you be interested? We can talk some prices, if it's legal. Is it legal or illegal?"

[Nick] "It's illegal [smiles] no it's legal! I already sell some and we'd like to sell some more. The problem is your T-shirts are very expensive. £22.50 but your manager says they cost you £15 each."

[Lukas] "What is a good price to sell a T-shirt for?"

[Nick] "£16."

Lukas Dryml & Nick Barber

Tribute flags

Home straight fans

[Lukas] "£16! Because £16 is nearly the price I pay. Ladies polo's, I think, are £18."
[Nick] "£20 is easier."
[Lukas] "£19.50?"
[Nick] "£20 is easier."
[Lukas] "Some is better quality. £19.50 sounds better! £19.50 men's polo – I buy them for £19.50. Is £22 too much?"
[Nick] [Blows out cheeks expressively in Dave Rattenberry fashion] "£22.50?"
[Lukas] "Vests for £15 or £14.50?"
[Nick] "£15. I could do with some caps if you have some."
[Lukas] "Ok. Is it too late yes? I make some next year but not specially."
[Nick] "Where do you get them done?"
[Lukas] "England."
[Nick] "You're paying way too much! So, talk to me at the end of the season."
[Lukas] "Really! You make them, the Eastbourne clothes, you buy them and then you put on the badges?"
[Nick] "Yes."
[Lukas] "Good."
[Nick] "You pay too much! Speak to me at the end of the season!"

The notoriously unreliable speedway rumour mill has it that a British rider – say, like Lewis – might be paid 400 euros per point when they ride in Poland. This would be fantastic money if you were guaranteed significant points every week but, given the competitive nature of the league, it's rare breed of rider who consistently scores double figures in Poland. In Lewis's case, he shares a team place. So, not only is he not guaranteed to ride every meeting but his optional status also dictates he won't get as many races as a highly regarded heat leader. Indeed, the Wlokniarz Czestochowa website shows that Lewis is rarely called on to ride. [3] No matter how many rides are granted, it's a difficult circle to square but clearly still isn't one where British speedway obligations will come first. Nick Barber has every sympathy with his dilemma, "If you had a job that paid you £500 or one that paid you £5 that was a flight away, what would you do? Of course, it's the money! Why can't they just be honest? Poland can get 25,000 people going so they can afford to pay more! If you're a fringe rider anywhere – Poland, Grand Prix or Elite League – your general sharpness drops. For Jason Crump that's no problem but for a Scott Nicholls or a Lewis Bridger, they forget that their sharpness disappears when they don't get the rides. You know there's gonna come a time when there's a big meeting in Poland and five riders aren't gonna turn up and all get 28-day bans. We need a squad system. Look at that rearranged meeting in Poland on the Friday – Leigh Adams and some other riders were going to ride in Poland. If Leigh Adams had ridden there and missed a meeting, he'd have got a 28-day ban. I reckon Terry Russell said we're not going to ride!"

Whatever the issues are in Poland, closer to home Bob Dugard has endured a season of frustration with attendance levels, transfer disputes and a sense of injustice at the greater impact the Saturday staging of the SGP has upon Eastbourne in comparison to any other Elite League club. Eastbourne fan Nigel has every sympathy, "I fully understand Bob's reasons for wanting to give up! I just hope someone else comes in. I don't care what league we race in so long as there's racing! If we were winning or in the top two, there'd be 500 more each meeting but, when we're not, people won't come! If it was Premier League we'd see a different team every week rather than seeing the same few teams all the time." If gauged by the number of Eastbourne Eagles replica tops worn this evening, you could be forgiven for the assumption that trackshop merchandise sales were robust. Martin Dadswell disabuses me of that idea, "Yeah, but they're all last season's or the season before, or before that!" My suggestion that it should be a close meeting tonight gets short shrift from Nick, "Nah, Lakeside should thrash them! The crowd could be terrible here tonight. If you could say it was any one thing, then they could put it better. Nicki was brilliant here but also he was the one that murdered it that season when he kept not turning up half the season. It's never really recovered since then, has it? Scott didn't really replace him – he was half the rider and half the money! When you think of the team Eastbourne had [last season] – Richardson, Woodward, Bridger, Nicholls, Simon Gustafsson – you have to wonder why they didn't do better?"

[3] During 2009, Lewis rode in just four Extra League meetings where he scored 18 points.

Eastbourne's south-coast derby rivals have traditionally been the Poole Pirates but, over recent years, meetings with Lakeside have assumed great significance but also tension. This is partly due to the acrimonious departure of Jon Cook and Adam Shields but also while Eastbourne' s star has waned, Lakeside have thrown off the shackles of their wooden-spoon reputation to emerge as a much stronger mid-ranking club who can nowadays actually challenge for silverware. Last season, Lee Richardson didn't always live up to the exacting standards of some sections of the Arlington crowd. This season his 2009 rejuvenation at Lakeside is another bone of contention and possible cause of uber-fan resentment. Tonight Bjarne Pedersen replaces the injured Adam Shields so, any members of the Eastbourne congregation keen to vocalise their disgruntlement, only have Lee Richardson to direct their ire towards. In the opening race, Eagles guest Travis McGowan holds off Richardson for three laps until Rico bustles past with a shimmy and a quick burst of speed that allows him to take the chequered flag. Presenter Kevin Coombes chortles, "It's all about throttle and balance to ride these machines – okay, and of course, you have to be mad!" Eastbourne reserve Ricky Kling also notionally has a point to prove against his former club Lakeside but he's beaten in the race for third place by game-show stalwart and much-travelled speedway rider, Phil Morris (after his first-heat rider replacement ride for fourth acclimatises him to the vagaries of tonight's Arlington track).

A merry-go-round of team changes dictated by averages, injuries and loan agreements dictates that many riders often race against their previous employers on a very regular basis. One such is ex-Eagle Hammer Joonas Kylmakorpi. Kevin Coombes suspects he'll enjoy improved motivation this evening. "Joonas had a bit of a dressing down by Jon Cook after the Sky meeting where he only scored 2 points [against Poole]. He's now switched to his Swedish bikes – and they're done by Trevor's son, Chris, from nearby here – so it'll be interesting to see how he goes." The rough-and-tumble nature of speedway has given Joonas shoulder problems aggravated by a horror crash at Edinburgh that left him with what Jon Cook describes as an "elbow held together by nuts though eventually it fell apart on him". Heat 3 pits Eastbourne's two Australians against Lakeside's two Finns. When the men from Down Under emerge victorious, Kevin Coombes joyfully embraces his inner fan, "Arlington let us rejoice – we got a win and we're in the lead!" Cameron Woodward's parents alternate the year in which they come over to visit their son in England. Last year Cameron's father Ross visited and, tonight, his proud mum Jenny is on hand to watch her son in his fourth season at Eastbourne ("Cameron – mummy's boy – got second"). The start of heat 4 sees a fired-up Lukas Dryml really constrict the space available to Bjarne Pedersen on an ongoing continuous basis until the Dane encounters the bend 2 air-fence. Kevin glosses over this example of hard riding as "showing a bit of Eagles aggression" Trackside by the start line, Eagles fan Dave Rice notes approvingly, "He needs to show a bit of bite – which he did there!" With Dryml disqualified from the rerun, it's now Ricky Kling's turn to ride with aggression into the first corner where he barges Sunderland-born Stuart Robson wide and, thereby, nearly takes off the previously shaken Pedersen. Everyone just about remains on their bikes but, though Pedersen chases, Kling seizes his advantage to win. A rumble of discontent greets Lee Richardson onto the track for heat 5. Oblivious beneath his helmet, Lee only has to pass Davey Watt in the first corner to win with ease and confidence.

Chosen for a rider replacement ride in heat 6, Lukas Dryml lines up on gate 1 with Bjarne Pedersen once again beside him on gate 2. Lukas fires from the tapes, Bjarne blasts round the outside of the second bend before the riders rush neck and neck down the back straight into the third bend where – dependent upon your allegiance – Lukas either drifts wide, "picks up drive" and pins Bjarne to the bend 4 air-fence. Or, on the basis that Lukas has been hired as a hit man by persons unknown to eliminate Lakeside guest Pedersen, appears to spear side on into Bjarne and smash him into the air-fence. His exertions also prompt Lukas to fall but he's immediately up from the shale to rush over and check on his stricken rival. Various members of the Lakeside pits crew sprint across the centre green – including team manager Alan Sargent and promoter Jon Cook – to join the medical staff clustered round the groggy fallen guest rider. Kevin Coombes also joins the throng to study the situation, "Bjarne – making sure everything is in the right place, as you do!" There's a lengthy delay for Bjarne to clear his head that also allows his bike to be repaired. In the rerun, Eagles guest Travis McGowan gates with great acceleration closely pursued by Bjarne. The Dane is initially second until his teammate Phil Morris apparently misunderstands the nature of speedway team riding and battles past Bjarne only to then proceed to successfully block his every attempt at a passing manoeuvre. Both Lakeside riders slowly slip further and further from contention. Widely seen as no slouch in the toughness department himself, heat 7 then sees Kauko Nieminen give Lukas a massive elbow (as they race into the first corner) albeit without any noticeable effect before Dryml heads off away into the distance to win the race. In fact, the effort and velocity distracts Kauko so much it relegates him to last place. Ahead of him, Simon Gustafsson chases Joonas Kylmakorpi until, on the last lap, he generates sufficient speed for a blast round the outside of the pits bend. Instead of fresh air, Simon nearly clatters into the fence but shows great skill and presence of mind to stay on his bike.

A comfortable 5-1 for McGowan and Kling in heat 8 doubles the Eagles advantage to 8 points (28-20). Between races Kevin Coombes trails his forthcoming centre-green heart-to-heart with Eastbourne team manager, Trevor Geer. This interview will cover the whys and wherefores of the Lewis Bridger suspension. In true vox-pop fashion, Kevin consults the crowd for their reaction, "Oh, er, well, what do we think? Hero or villain?" If Arlington were suddenly a Roman amphitheatre then it's a definite thumbs down for Lewis. "We'll speak to Trevor later about the whole debacle ... I bet he's sick of the whole thing – poor ol' Trev!" The two-minute time allowance for heat 9 is suddenly cancelled, "while a paramedic attends to someone in pit lane". Jon Cook would subsequently comment, "We went there full of anticipation but realistically, when our guest Bjarne Pedersen was injured by Lukas Dryml, it ended our hopes of getting a win. I'm sure that Lukas doesn't mean to have these sort of accidents but it did for our chances because we believed that Bjarne was going to be a key figure for us." When the ninth race eventually gets underway Stuart Robson (in place of the disqualified Pedersen) manages to elude the attentions of his teammate Phil Morris but can make no impression on the Eastbourne Australian combination of Watt and Woodward as they ride to a comfortable 5-1 to extend the Eagles interval lead to 12 points.

Questioned by Kevin Coombes, Trevor Geer recaps recent events. "Lewis rang with the lost passport and that. We did tell him he must not ride that evening, otherwise he'd be in big trouble. Please do not ride! Trouble is with Lewis and any rider in Poland, they're put under so much pressure to ride out there and Lewis succumbed to it! I don't know whether he lost the passport or not, he shouldn't ride out there and should be at Belle Vue. I went through and tried every Elite League rider that wasn't riding to get a guest. Lee Complin came down from Yorkshire, did the parade and that and, before he was going out in heat 1, we had to tell him Lewis had rode three rides in Poland so he couldn't ride!" [4]
Lewis's granddad Tony Thompson joins the centre-green interview.
[Kevin] "Obviously Lewis is your grandson, the Czestochowa team manager has questioned his desire to be a speedway rider."
[Granddad] "He's totally committed. Trouble is, the rules and regulations of speedway, Lewis didn't understand it! And I don't! Lewis thought you could use rider replacement, Lewis thought it was a rearranged meeting. He was put under an awful lot of pressure to ride. I'm sure he didn't know all the trouble he'd be in."
[Kevin] "Does that tell us something about Lewis?"
[Granddad, frostily] "In what way?! [pause] Lewis shouldn't have ridden – no question about it! But there's no question about his commitment to Eastbourne and speedway. He will come back as the same Lewis."
[Trevor] "Lewis is still the hottest property in speedway and we need him here at Eastbourne and we need him to win."
[Granddad] "He didn't do it for the money. Whether it was £10,000 or £3 million, he would have done the same. Lewis thought he was letting Poland down and the pressure was too much."
[Kevin] "I think we'll reserve judgement until we can speak to him."
Granddad walks back to the pits in his Lewis Bridger Racing team shirt.
[Kevin] "Lewis isn't the first speedway rider to have gone slightly wayward."
[Trevor] "We've seen so many riders in speedway, 'cause they're young and that, they go a bit wayward! We need Lewis back in the team."
[Kevin] "It's frustration around Arlington, I love Eastbourne but the frustration is out there. What with slipping down the table and ongoing rider replacement – can you understand that?"
[Trevor] "I can!"

During the break in proceedings I bump into Alex Raby who nowadays enjoys a swathe of responsibilities for various

[4] In fact, Lee Complin was barred from racing that night at Belle Vue since he was ineligible. The only covering facility for a no-show rider in the Elite League is with a Premier League rider with a CMA of 6.00 or below. Lee Complin was close to 8.00 so was correctly prevented from riding by the referee Graham Flint. This decision is nothing to do with whether Lewis Bridger had actually ridden in Poland or not.

forms of media content at Eastbourne Speedway club. To all intents and purposes, the politely spoken Alex is a one-man media production company. He films the meetings, conducts interviews, edits the film and has recently "edited 17 programmes for the Motors TV channel on speedway." Alex's second year at the prestigious University of Durham – where he studies Modern Languages and Cultures – has just ended and will be followed by a spell abroad in Northern France (October 2009-April 2010) that he's "chosen to coincide with the speedway close season!" When the racing resumes, Davey Watt leads heat 10 by a country mile until his bike splutters at the start of lap 4 and then grinds to a halt a few yards later. These mechanical failures gift other riders endless points – Joonas Kylmakorpi is the latest beneficiary with 6 points since he sports the black-and-white helmet colour. In the trackshop Martin Dadswell isn't pleased with the obscured view he now receives because of four Czech flags pinned on the wire fence by love-struck Eagles fans keen to celebrate Lukas Dryml's native background. "Frickin' flags, I can't see the frickin' first corner now!"

Everyone is curious about Lukas Dryml. Mason, Dave Rice's inquisitive grandson, has been brought along to the speedway to, hopefully, have his imagination fired and his future loyalties captured. His indoctrination proceeds well since he points to Lukas Dryml and asks, "Is he the one who always knocks off riders?" When the tapes rise Lee Richardson gives Lukas little chance jostle him because he immediately zooms off for a comfortable race win. His always competitively combative teammate, Stuart Robson, wins his third-place battle with Simon Gustafsson to narrow the score to 36-33. Davey Watt gates and easily wins heat 12 and also manages to evade further mechanical difficulty. Phil Morris struggles in pit-bend traffic while Ricky Kling goes round the outside. When they get to bend 4, Morris tries a manoeuvre that is part drift wide and part rough house. Sadly, he's no longer fast enough for it to have any impact (and retires from the sport shortly afterwards). While there is no 'I' in team, payment for third place requires that Phil holds an out-of-form Kauko Nieminen behind him. Mason explains the appeal of speedway, "It's exciting and I just like the bikes – they're pretty cool!" Alex Raby has been granted permission to record events at Arlington and stands on the roof of the referee's box to do so. However, Kevin Coombes pointedly reminds other patrons to desist from such activities or risk expulsion. "Arlington, can I remind you if you have digital recording equipment and do not have a permit and are caught using it, you will be escorted from the stadium! It's not big and it's not clever! So please, no flash photography or digital recording equipment."

Before the riders take to the shale for heat 13, we learn that Bjarne Pedersen has withdrawn from the meeting.[5] Stuart Robson takes his place and, although he doesn't gain any points, he once again impresses with his speed and whole-hearted determination for Lakeside. Lee Richardson once more comfortably bests Lukas Dryml to record his fourth win in four races. Though Bob Dugard is away on holiday in Spain, there's something about Lukas Dryml that, according to Dave Rice, echoes him, "Bob Dugard was always a hard bastard when he rode for Wimbledon – and outspoken!" The penultimate race of the night initially ends in anti-climax when Stuart Robson falls on the second bend of the second lap. This prompts referee Dave Robinson to award the race. This Eagles 5-1 takes the scores to an ungainly looking 49-38 until Jon Cook sensibly appeals the decision on the basis that – since all four riders hadn't completed two laps – under present speedway regulations the race couldn't actually be awarded. With a harrumph, Kevin explains why there will be a rerun before (without a hint of his trademark irony) he identifies this decision as a possible threat to the fabric of society, "If speedway can't stick to its rules, anarchy will reign!" Joonas Kylmakorpi takes full advantage of the reprieve to battle past both Eastbourne riders. After some delay behind Simon Gustafsson, Cameron Woodward gives lusty chase but is unable to turn his challenge into a race win. The sacrilege of completely messed-up programmes raises a collective mutter throughout the stadium as we collectively "correct" the result on our race cards!

Under the 2009 innovative league points structure, this drawn heat 14 still gives Lakeside an outside possibility to snatch a point provided they take a 5-1 from heat 15. Either unaware of this possibility or insouciant about it, Trevor Geer nominates Ricky Kling instead of Lukas Dryml or Travis McGowan, while the main responsibility for Lakeside rests upon the injury-prone shoulder of Joonas Kylmakorpi. Predictably enough, Lee Richardson completes an

[5] Bjarne Pedersen suffers memory loss for the first time in his career after his heat 6 fall. "It's the first time I have experienced not being able to remember being in a race. After I came in the pits [after the rerun] I couldn't remember it. It was so strange when I think about it now because when I went for a sit down I couldn't remember what I had done in my second race. I had no memory of how many points I had scored, I had to ask my mechanic. It's the first time it's happened to me. I have had a few hard falls, but nothing like this – loss of memory. I can remember they pushed me out for the re-start, but I can't remember what happened in the heat."

imperious 15-point maximum with yet another untroubled race win. Behind him Lakeside's late challenge ends in an anti-climax when Joonas nearly falls on the third bend to relegate himself to the rear of the race. After three consecutive home defeats, the Eagles team enjoy a victory parade for the first time since they vanquished Coventry in early June. After the relatively exuberant adulation has died down, Kevin Coombes catches a few words with Davey Watt in the pits who, with a hint of understatement, concedes, "We let a few meetings go this season." Kevin decides to accentuate the positive ("we showed what we're capable off") and this enables Davey Watt to name-check the fabled Arlington pits camaraderie, "A lot of people gloss over the fact that we are a team! We just don't put on the blue race suits – we have true team spirit!" Davey's heat 10 mechanical failure isn't discussed. Afterwards, unofficial club statistician and back gate supervisor Sid Shine provides some insight, "Davey Watt's mechanic didn't put any fuel in his bike and that's why he stopped, 'cause he ran out!" Over at the trackshop, Nick Barber has a rhetorical question, "Guess who won the 4s at Workington? [Workington] I dunno why they hold it there every year? All the other shared events get moved about the country. Why not go to a neutral track? Workington's out of the way and slick! Why not go to a Midlands track like Coventry or Stoke? Maybe, even, Ipswich? Anywhere that's neutral!" Jon Cook issues some post-meeting praise for Sussex-based rider, Lee Richardson. "The performance from Lee Richardson was out of this world and was as good a 15-point maximum as I've ever seen in my time. It was unbelievable and right up there in the class of Andreas Jonsson. I believe that Lee is currently riding as well as he's ever done."

25th July Eastbourne v. Lakeside (Elite League) 50-43

CHAPTER 23

Ipswich

"My husband said 'I've got a surprise' and Chris Schramm walked in in his kevlars and presented me with some flowers!"

30th July

In the inner sanctum of the Ipswich Speedway Office, John Louis sits behind his desk with a cup of coffee beside him and a fruitcake to hand made by Chris Ellis. "Chris is the trackman's wife – she makes one every week. They're delicious! Everyone looks forward to them." John looks youthful, smartly attired in a grey jumper, collared shirt and tie. There's a hint of school uniform about it. He's in an affable mood. There's an article in the *Speedway Star* that says he's going to retire at the end of the season and in tonight's *Evening Star* there's another article by Elvin King that confirms John Louis has definitely made up his mind to retire. John smiles, "Do you believe that? Elvin just makes it up sometimes!" Chris Ellis's fruitcake is completely moreish and I quickly accept John's invitation to have a second piece, "You liked that, didn't you?"

When I arrived, the trackshop was deserted but, on my return, Bev Barber arrives but only to leave a message for her brothers Nick and Johnny to say she can't come along tonight because of complications at work. Almost as soon as Johnny Barber arrives, John Louis pops by with a request, "I want the Ipswich versus Belle Vue programme of the 28th May."
[Johnny] "What, the one with the yellow cover for the rain-off?"
[John] "We did an insert."

They chitchat for a few minutes and then John wanders over to my table.
[John] "Is this your annual visit to Foxhall? It'll be your last chance to see the track before they change it. They're going to widen the bends by 15 metres and widen the straight. Ipswich has always been a fast track 'cause of the straights but, since they put in the air-fence, we've had no accidents. [1] Here's a track that would be better without it and just leave the old air-fence. I know we have to have it but the airbag sections sit on where the riders used to race! Right by the fence is the old Gollob line. He would sit there all night from the first race! Now he couldn't 'cause of the air-fence! The riders have to cut back and, as they go down the straight, they have to move across. Before they were already on the correct line as they exited the second bend and they didn't have to move across."

There's a make-do-and-mend appearance about the teams programmed to race for Ipswich and Poole this evening. Partly because of injuries but also because they've both been affected by the Latvian GP. The Pirates are without Hans Andersen and the Witches are without Scott Nicholls. Due to an 'agreement' between the promotions of both clubs, they will both save costs when they run rider replacement for these travelling GP stars rather than find guests. Other changes to the line-ups are prompted by recent injuries – Bjarne Pedersen has headaches from a spill at Eastbourne ("and memory loss for the first time in his career") while Danny King cracked a sternum in his first race in Sweden on Tuesday night. The net result is that Simon Stead will replace Danny King and Piotr Swiderski will replace Bjarne Pedersen. Lou Hood stops for a chat. Afterwards Nick Barber tells me, "He's the chairman of the Sports Club and also writes in the programme – he's a very nice man. You don't know his wife June, she's very nice too. She's got Swine Flu tonight, unfortunately or fortunately, given what the teams look like!" After Lou bats away jovial suggestions that tonight a Poole select races against an Ipswich select, he notes that the Pirates choice of Piotr Swiderski could be

[1] Mark Loram, Leigh Lanham and Kozza Smith's accidents at the track in the past couple of years spring to mind.

a shrewd move. "Bjarne Pedersen isn't so good at the moment. He's a gater. If he doesn't gate, he looks ordinary! Look at Leigh Adams in the GPs, he's gone down dramatically all of a sudden. If you're a gater, when you get older – your reactions go! It's alright for riders who can fight their way through the field. Chris Louis was a gater but, since he had his last injury in Sweden, he's had to fight his way through again. It's exciting to watch him pick people off 'cause I don't know anyone who knows the track better than him!" Peter Thorpe passes by with a roll of re-admission tickets in his hand.
[Lou] "I see you got them in case."
[Peter] "Got what exactly?"
[Lou] "The tickets."
[Peter] "What kind of tickets?"
[Lou] "The rain-off tickets."
[Peter] "They're not rain-off tickets – there's no such thing! They're re-admission tickets. There could be a power failure or a bad accident or the paramedic doesn't turn up, so the meeting has to be abandoned."
[Lou] "You're full of the joys of life."
[Peter] "Well it could happen!"

Johnny Barber has some strong opinions about postponement due to the weather. "I think in these times of recession they should call the meetings off as soon as possible before people travel! I think Jon Cook should be applauded for that. Look at King's Lynn yesterday, they called it off at 3 and, minutes later, on the forums people claimed it summed up all that was wrong with speedway. Yet, at 5, it rained torrentially – as forecast – until 11.30. If promoters know it's really gonna chuck it down, it's the responsible thing to do. Tonight it might shower or it might not, so you can't say!"

Seventy-five minutes before the scheduled start time, Nick Barber spots the bowser at work on the track, "Oh, hello, look – water!" His brother, Johnny, gleefully lets me know about some sweaty bottomed reactions *Quantum of Shale* provokes elsewhere. "Like Mike Bennett, Kevin Moore won't be promoting your book. He told Mike Moseley you'd disparaged him. The next week [at Mildenhall] when he came and said, 'Is there anything you specifically want promoting?' I said, '*Quantum of Shale*' and he refused saying he'd been disparaged. I said, 'That's not disparaged! You should see what he's written about Mike Bennett!'"

Someone who hasn't featured in any of my previous books and wouldn't in any future ones arrives at my table with a surprise request. "Can I ask not to feature in your chapter on [name redacted].
[Jeff] "Did I put you in then?"
[xxx] "I dunno but you were standing there with your pen scribbling away and I don't want to be."
One young Ipswich fan clutches one of the BSPA 80th Anniversary free autograph books and, as they queue for a programme, asks his dad "Why are there blank pages?" Without a blink, his dad replies, "'Cause you've got to get the autographs yet!"

Recently retired Ipswich and Mildenhall presenter, Kevin Long arrives at the stadium with his mum Joyce and his friend Debbie Nevell. "She can go in your book of speedway folk with no personality – write that down!"

[Jeff] "Who is she?"
[Kevin] "Debs, formerly Mrs Long (no relation)!"
Debs is in charge of a Facebook campaign entitled "Get Kevin Long back on the Mic".
[Kevin] "Really?"
[Debbie] "Johnny's joined."
[Kevin] "He spends all his time on there."
[Debbie] "I've invited you as a friend and sent you a personal message saying, 'Are you going to Brighton [Gay Pride] for a stick of rock this weekend!'
[Kevin affects not to understand the inference] "I'm going to Sidmouth for a Folk Festival not Gay Pride. I was getting my bike tyres fixed ("I'd like proper ones like they have on cars"). This engineer said 'I'll have to drill your rim' and I said something back but you could see the tumbleweed blowing."
[Debbie] "I'm Debbie Nevell, formerly Long (no relation)."

Ipswich: *"My husband said 'I've got a surprise' and Chris Schramm walked in in his kevlars and presented me with some flowers!"*

[Jeff] "He said that."
[Debbie] "I put a photo on Facebook of Kevin – in a woolly hat ["I look a right Muppet"] – of the 1976 civic reception. I can't remember what happened in '76. Oh, we won the cup and league! I'm at the civic reception. Anyway Johnny replied saying I need a new scarf!"
Kevin briefly studies tonight's racecard, "Why would you have Matej Zagar when you can have frickin' Simon Stead? Why have Matej Zagar score 18 when you can have Simon Stead score 2 plus 1?" These are Zen conundrums without answer.

Photo display

Colleen Wilkin (51) stops at my display table with her father Colin Howlett (71). They've both recently been re-bitten by the speedway bug. Colleen reminisces, "I used to come in 1975. When I watched, John Louis rode and Chris Louis was 6! I used to babysit him while John rode. I knew Malcolm Simmons, Billy Sanders and that. I used to be good friends with all the promoters! I've been round the track here – with Terry Betts on the back of his bike. I came to the Bank Holiday meeting against Lakeside and got the bug again." Colin has an equally illustrious speedway pedigree, "I knew [former King's Lynn promoter] Maurice Littlechild. I went everywhere with him. Buster Chapman used to be on the turnstiles at King's Lynn back then. Michael Lee was just world champion as I finished going. I got the bug again recently and went to Bydgoszcz. We flew out with Nicki Pedersen and Kenneth Bjerre. We went at the last minute and got a slightly more expensive hotel in the centre of town. It had a private bar and, when we were in there at 1 a.m., Tomasz Gollob and all his team came in. Everyone was looking for them but he was with us! Maurice Littlechild was a brilliant man – my best friend outside our family! I don't cry when people die usually but I did when he died, I did cry."
[Colleen] "We've met a lot of the old-timers. Buster used to be on the turnstiles – he and his wife [Cheryl] treated us like royalty when we went back to King's Lynn. I used to look after Chris [Louis] in the '70s. Dad used to say Jenny [his wife] used to say to Chris, 'Are you gonna do this when you grow up?' And Chris used to say 'I'm not going to!'

Two Johns – Barber & Louis

[Colin] "I came back to speedway after Maurice Littlechild died. Cyril Crane was with him. We had a few bad words and I said, 'Cyril, you can keep speedway!' And I never went again. I saw it on the telly and that but, then, we went to Peterborough and Ipswich. The smell of the bikes and meeting the riders like Hans Andersen – who's charming – got us the bug and I haven't missed a meeting since. She [Colleen] would like to be a promoter again. She used to promote stockcars. Did she tell you that? I started Swaffham Raceway and then Colleen took over!"
[Colleen] "Speedway is like a family. There's so many old-timers. We didn't go for years and now we travel all over to see it everywhere!"

Joyce & Kevin Long with Debbie Nevell

The extended Ipswich speedway family reconvenes next Monday at Chantry Park (in Ipswich) for a 20/20 cricket match staged in aid of the Kim Jansson Fund. Though entry is free, there will be a raffle and auction to raise money for Kim whose injuries forced him to retire from the sport. The Witches Select 11 will represent the speedway club and they will take on a Media 11 drawn from the staff of the *Evening Star* and *East Anglian Daily Times.* Though John Louis told me, "I might go but I won't play!" According to team manager Pete Simmons's column in the programme, "as many of the current squad that are available" will play along with "Jeremy Doncaster, Mark Loram, John Louis, Jason Gillingham (track medic) Steve Smith (track electrician) and even Mike Smillie's dog Omar has been drafted in as 12th man (or 12th dog)." Interviewed by Stephen Foster, after Ipswich have lost the toss for gate position, Pete Simmons reveals he's had a word with the injured Danny King, "I spoke to him today and he'll be coming along to the cricket match … Tobi, yeah, he's captain. He's lost the toss but I'm sure he'll make up for it!" Immediately after said coin toss, Stephen Foster also quizzes Poole Pirates team manager Neil 'Middlo' Middleditch, "You're at the bottom of the league – do you want to avoid the wooden spoon?" Middlo replies *sotto voce*, "Yeah, obviously, every meeting we go to we wanna win!" Super brief interview over, and keen to try to bump up the atmosphere, Stephen Foster exclaims, "Let's go racing!"

The first attempt to run heat 1 only lasts as far as lap two, more than long enough for Poole's guest Piotr Swiderski to lock up on the first bend. Behind him Tobi Kroner lays down with alacrity while Joe Screen demonstrates a delayed reaction to the crash. Kroner finds himself disqualified (by referee Paul Carrington) as the prime cause of the stoppage. Security man Lee isn't impressed with Joe Screen, "He did it deliberately to get a rerun and to get him excluded!" Swiderski wins the rerun chased hard by the Witches reinvigorated Australian, Troy Batchelor. Trailed way off at the back, Joe Screen rides the last lap with his bike upright and doesn't even attempt to slide into any of the corners. Johnny Barber shrugs, "It's been a bit lacklustre this season. Whether it's the credit crunch, I don't know? One thing is for sure, if you have a losing team it's never very good for sales!" Dawid Stachyra – pronounced by Stephen Foster as "Dawid Sty-hear-rah"- wins heat 2 and draws the eye with his distinctive racing style characterised by weird late, jumpy broadsides into each corner.

Nick Barber's impressed by the size of the crowd inside Foxhall Stadium tonight, "There must be 1,500 here. There's not many other clubs where the top two are missing and you get a crowd like this! If they go fortnightly next year, which I think they will, I said to John [Louis] he should run a junior team. They'll get 600 or so, like they do at Poole. John complained, 'I still have to pay all the rent'. But people are so keen here and like their speedway!" Heat 3 sees Ipswich race to successive 5-1s, this time through Robert Miskowiak and guest Simon Stead. Just before the tapes rise for the fourth race, Nick Barber prophecies, "Easy win for Holder? [Batchelor gates] Oh!" The Pirates could steady the ship with a drawn heat if only their reserve Steve Boxall maintains concentration but, instead, he loses third place after a determined Carl Wilkinson catches him just prior to the finish line. Nick's mystified, "What has happened to Steve Boxall? You know where he'll be next season, don't you? [pauses] Hoddesdon!" Speedway fans generally need no second invitation to take a trip down memory lane, Stephen Foster is no exception, "It was 34 years ago today that John Louis won the British final at Coventry." Last season, Kevin Long and the late Kenny Smith had a contretemps in the pits in Mildenhall. It's an afternoon that's covered in the chapter on Mildenhall in my book *Quantum of Shale*. Kevin reminisces, "I enjoyed the bit about Kenny Smith where we discussed our differing points of view. He was in remission at the time – full of life and very passionate! That's how he was and that's how I'd like to remember him!" Over the loudspeakers before heat 6, Kevin's replacement as Ipswich presenter, Stephen Foster, tells us, "Simon Stead – so far unbeaten for the Witches tonight!" It's the kiss of death for Stead who finishes third behind teammate Tobi Kroner. Neither get close to black-and-white helmeted Chris Holder. His victory narrows the scores to 34-15. A bloke in a Poole Pirates jacket asks politely, "Can I put my food down [on your table] while I fill in my programme?" While this Poole fan eats his sausage and chips with gusto, we chitchat between the next couple of heats. The Pirates have been on the road for the past week and this gentleman follows them everywhere. "We've had Coventry and Belle Vue – Joe Screen was awful – and then the rain-off last night and now we're here. It hasn't been the best season. It's amazing how our crowds have fallen off! We can't believe it! You'd never have thought it. Lots of them have defected over to the National League. If they go there they pay £10 whereas, for the Elite League, they pay £15. Still everyone is struggling – that said Coventry had a big crowd." [2]
[Jeff] "It's amazing Coventry got it on, given the rain just before."
[Bloke] "Dunno how we lost it. I dunno if you remember but the announcer said before heat 13 'stand up if you think we can win it' and no one stood up! It just didn't go our way though. I've never seen Bjarne touch the tapes!"
[Jeff] "You'd have thought he'd been told to touch them."
[Bloke] "You would have thought so!"
[Jeff] "I admire you for coming here and for watching them so often."
[Bloke] "I have to, I co-promote it!"

[2] It's said that Bournemouth's first crowd was 550, but subsequent reports placed their average reported attendance at 310.

During our conversation, the Witches get a 4-2 and follow it in heat 8 with a 5-1. Giles Hartwell strides off towards the pits to help further steady the Pirates ship while, out on the track, Robert Miskowiak easily wins heat 9 (ahead of Chris Holder) to take his points tally for the night to paid 9 from three rides. Security man Lee looks on approvingly, "Miskowiak has looked a different rider since he came back!" With his confidence lifted, Miskowiak wins his heat 10 rider replacement ride by an absolute street to nullify Neil Middleditch's second use of the tactical black-and-white helmet colour. Heat 11 starts dramatically. Chris Holder is fractionally ahead of Troy Batchelor into the first corner. On the outside, Troy falls theatrically to win the all-four-back adjudication he'd hoped to engineer. Chris then sportingly stops to pick Batchelor up who refuses and, instead, offers some passionately gestural words before he stomps off. Johnny comments sardonically, "Oh dear, Holder's coming back and Troy gives him the finger!" They say size isn't everything but Ipswich fan Chris has found comparisons can sometimes be invidious. "We went to Somerset and we thought it was fantastic. Poole looks huge on the telly but when we got there we thought 'is that it?' It's about the same length as here – 300 metres – but looks much smaller!" Comparatively newly-wed Debbie and Andy enjoyed a memorable wedding last November ("it was my second and his third"), "My husband said 'I've got a surprise' and Chris Schramm walked in in his kevlars and presented me with some flowers! He put off a trip to Manchester to come to our do – has was supposed to be going to his own engagement party!" On the centre green, Stephen Foster conducts the raffle though he needs assistance to do so, "I'm colour blind as you know by now!" What is it about speedway presentational work that attracts colour blind people? While we all know the difficulties colour causes in snooker ("for those of you watching in black-and-white, the green is next to the pink"), both Shaun Leigh (at Scunthorpe) and Stephen must surely recognise speedway riders by their gait and demeanour on their equipment (along with their kevlar design) rather than orient themselves in the traditional manner by the riders helmet colours!

If Ipswich were a crocodile and Poole its prey then, much earlier in the meeting, the beast locked its jaws and dragged the Pirates on a twirling death dive to the bottom of the river. All night the only real sign of life from the Pirates is shown by temporary team captain Chris Holder and their guest, ex-Ipswich rider Piotr Swiderski. Heat 13 promises potential fireworks with a rematch scheduled between the laidback Chris Holder and the occasionally animus-driven Troy Batchelor. While Tobi Kroner rears massively at the gate and the young Aussies enter the first bend, I confidently tell referee Chris Gay, "We've really got a race on our hands!" Chris is unconvinced, "Have we?" By the start of lap two, Chris Holder leads by the proverbial country mile ("See!"). Chris Gay's injury has kept him away from the speedway circuit recuperating but, like speedway riders everywhere, he's keen to make a comeback as quickly as possible. "It's four weeks since I left so I had to come!" He's driven over to Ipswich from Southend with his father Gordon because it's possible to drive his car to the far side of the Foxhall Stadium (bend two) and watch from there. Chris can also hobble around the track perimeter, if the inclination strikes. "It's nice to get close to the people and be part of it again! There's some lovely people in speedway! I still love it – that's why I do it! [Nods down to his injury] At five-a-side. I'm very competitive at everything I do – I have to give 100% and do my best to try and win! We've gelled as a team and, even though we were the underdogs, we were getting on top and that's how it happened!" Another win for Swiderski enables the Pirates to massage the scoreline with a second successive heat advantage (helped along by a Dawid Stachyra who falls and fails to finish).

The make-do-and-mend line-up assembled for this particular Elite League meeting stars Robert Miskowiak and he closes with a win to complete a paid maximum from six rides. With Swiderski second, Troy Batchelor finally bests Chris Holder, albeit in a meaningless battle for third place. Ipswich run out comfortable winners 57-38 and, thereby, swop places with the Poole Pirates who now drop down to second from bottom. Each Ipswich rider won at least one race while, from the visitors, only Swiderski and Holder provide any real opposition. The Pirates third-highest points scorer (with 4 points), Joe Screen fails to beat any finishing Witches rider. Some of the crowd head for the exits while others stop to watch the second-halfers ("that can't be Leigh as they're going too quick"). It seems pretty well everyone I speak to at the club tonight has some previous notable connection with John Louis. Wheelchair-bound Ruby is no exception. "I used to clean John Louis's leathers! [Pause] I lent the Barry Briggs book I bought for my husband – while he was ill in hospital with cancer – and my John Louis book – I lent them to someone but I never got them back!"

30th July Ipswich v. Poole (Elite League) 57-38

CHAPTER 24

Mildenhall

"The atmosphere is better than last year and the track looks much better than last year too!"

2nd August

Smart in a white collared shirt and tie, Plymouth team manager Gary Spiller stands in the uncovered section of the Mildenhall pits as he watches his riders start to prepare their machines for their National League meeting against the Funky Catering Fen Tigers. "I had a good journey here – we went round Birmingham on the 42 and then down the A14 with no problems. We're running rider replacement for Matt Bates this afternoon. Paul [Starke], Kyle Hughes and the two reserves [Josh Dingle and David Gough] can all take a ride. The averages in the programme are the July averages. They should be higher but, as previously explained, the electronic era hasn't yet hit the National League coordinator [Peter Morrish] who still uses quill pens and pigeon post!"

The trackshop at Mildenhall is located adjacent to the Fenman Bar at the top of the terraced stairs in a roofed grandstand that overlooks bends one and two of the West Row track. The shop is dressed and ready for action and so is Johnny in trademark casual style as he luxuriates behind a table laden with merchandise. His chair is strategically placed so he can serve the customers, have an uninterrupted view of the action on the track and also look down towards the pits or the main home-straight grandstand. "Did I tell you about Thursday? You know when you think that everything that could happen to you at speedway has already happened, probably many times? Well this kid kept coming in and out, lots of times, during the interval he said 'Excuse me – I don't want to buy anything I just want to give you this'. He hands over a piece of paper with J A Thomas written on it! I said 'What's this?' And he said 'my autograph!' His name must be John Thomas!"

After I'd made a few journeys to lug my stock from the car park to my stall (and chatted to the charming young girl who helps supervise riders and officials to sign in), I'm so absorbed in an article in the *Observer* about the German sex industry; I miss the arrival of Mildenhall presenter Kevin Moore. Previously buoyant, the industry now struggles because the recession's caused a precipitous drop in demand for prostitutes. So much so that the nation's brothels have been forced to come up with some creative cross-promotions. A number have introduced bogofs, flat-rate all-you-can-sleep-with deals or, for the sex seeker worried about his carbon emissions, there's a reduction if you arrive on bike or by public transport. For the UK, this apparently indicates that if legalised and subjected to VAT, the German model suggests price increases will lead to a fall-off in demand. So, contrary to popular opinion it turns out that sex with a prostitute is a price-sensitive commodity and a luxury item vulnerable to recessionary pressures. Interestingly, though speedway also suffers from falling demand, it has traditionally responded with less promotion, limited innovation and/or price increases. Even the laziest business school MBA student could identify this approach as 'brave'.

Mildenhall announcer Kevin Moore has a reputation among some Tigers fans for a presentational style modelled on the flamboyance of a Speak Your Weight machine. Johnny alerts me to my loss. "While you were reading, Kevin has been and left. He asked what I wanted promoting this afternoon but didn't ask you." Innocently I wonder, "Did he see me?" only for Johnny to chortle, "He could hardly miss you, could he?!" Since he read about himself in *Quantum of Shale* Kevin Moore has – in the words of Rye House, Peterborough and Somerset trackshop franchisee Andy Griggs, "copped a snot!" Though Kevin has whined to all and sundry on a regular basis that he'd been "disparaged", he hasn't said anything directly to me but, instead, adopts the belligerent aggressive stare of a hormonal teenager whenever our paths cross at various tracks around the country. In fact, whenever he's in the vicinity of my display table, I'd say he seems to adopt a distinctive gait – almost as if he's tucked his vest too tightly into a chaffing pair of two sizes too-small Simon Lambert Racing Y-Fronts and perhaps, at the same time, is on a sponsored charity walk to transport ice cubes between his buttock cheeks without them melting. At pretty well every track in the country, except for King's Lynn, when Mike Bennett controls the microphone – they're only happy to make some brief informational announcement about my books. If the Fen Tigers faithful who don't frequent the trackshop or Fenman Bar are to be advised I'm here, then I've no choice but to search out Kevin, (if this were a film would it be called *Desperately Seeking Kevin*?) in order to lance the boil of his ongoing passive-aggressive noncooperation. He's pretty easy to find close to the pit lane dressed with a vague hint of fashion like a Sunday school teacher in charge of a church hall disco that mixes faithful parishioners and recalcitrant teenagers much keener to snog or smoke surreptitiously in the graveyard. Schooled in his own ministry of silly walks, Kevin initially tries to totter away clutching his clipboard authoritatively as if en route to help with some important pre-meeting executive decision-making body. But, when faced with the emptiness of the referee's box ahead of him, he instead stops, raises himself to his full height and glares.

[Jeff] "Would you announce my book this afternoon?"

[Kevin] [Pulls a facial expression that indicates he's just come across a noxious gas or drank a particularly bitter draft of prune juice] "I won't be! Unless you have permission from the Promotion and I'm instructed to do so!"

[Jeff] "The promotion know I'm here and so imagine that means they're happy for it to be promoted."

[Kevin] "Do you have <u>specific</u> permission from the promoter Ray Mascall?"

[Jeff] "Er, no, I don't."

[Kevin] "Well until I have formal permission that's the procedure I always stick to!" Taps clipboard authoritatively, possibly indicating it holds an approval document within that requires many signatures in triplicate and a watermark date stamp.

[Jeff] "Which one is Ray then?"

[Kevin] [Nods to a family group stood at the edge of the grandstand close to bend 4] "He's the one in the BSPA jacket."

Kevin then initially heads off in the opposite direction before he changes his mind and follows at an apparently deferential, three or so steps behind me.

[Jeff] "Kevin tells me that I need your formal permission to mention my book over the tannoy! Can I have that?"

[Ray] "That's fine by me."

[Jeff] "Kevin, Ray has given his formal permission!"

[Kevin] "I'm now happy to do that now that I have formal instruction to do so!" Kevin executes a parade ground turn, modelled on the military service he was too young to serve, and stalks off purposefully in order to find something to do before the turnstiles open, possible cleaning stray hairs from his deluxe padded Simon Lambert Racing anorak.

Ray has the demeanour of a polite but diffident man.

[Jeff] "How's the season been for you so far?"

[Ray] "Okay. It could have been better. Two of the riders haven't performed as we expected them to!

[Jeff] "Is it always the same two riders?"

[Ray] "It is always the same two – you can only be patient for so long!"

[Jeff] "The writing sounds like it's on the wall."

Tiger transport

Plymouth section of the pits

Mike Moseley poses with banana

[Ray] "It is! We've had a few home defeats recently that we shouldn't have done, possibly. The crowds were very good to start with! But, now, they've dropped off, which is understandable as people like to see a winning team. I would. We all would!"
[Jeff] "What's it like becoming a promoter?"
[Ray] "I'm not the promoter, I'm the Club Chairman! The BSPA know that, I've told everyone but everyone still calls me the promoter – when I'm the Club Chairman! What can you do when you've told people lots of times already? As Club Chairman I'd have liked things to have been better! We'll see what happens this afternoon."
[Jeff] "Do you think you'll beat Plymouth this afternoon?"
[Ray] "I don't know. I think they'll find it a bit different here. I haven't been to Plymouth but it's supposed to be quite small!"

With formal permission attained, from a polite man my sixth sense tells me might be the Club Chairman, I confidently return to my trackshop table safe in the knowledge that Kevin will actually read out the preprepared statement on book details I've handed him. Most likely he will adopt his famous train announcer "after the death of a beloved family pet" tone of voice rather than the exuberant "barely able to control his orgasmic joy" version that he's rumoured to reserve for any Simon Lambert mention that he regularly crowbars into random speedway meetings on a countrywide basis.

Well-travelled and keen speedway fans Graham and Hilary Rouse stop by my table to conduct a post-mortem on the recent home meeting we all saw that pitted their beloved Peterborough against Wolverhampton.
[Hilary] "Someone [Kenneth Bjerre] needs to improve on Thursday night!"
[Jeff] "Maybe it's a question of motivation? He's motivated everywhere but for the Panthers."
[Hilary] "Did you see the GP last night? He looked a different rider! He needs to do something – if he doesn't he'll get some stick!"
[Graham] "Trevor [Swales] has started to get some stick. Though I don't know so much about speedway management, even I can see he's been missing some tricks. I wonder how long before Rick [Frost] gets discontented with him?"
[Hilary] "Watch what you say or he'll write it down."

Full-time police officer and part-time highly regarded photographer Phil Hilton points to the grader that circles the West Row track. "We got here at 5 or 10 past 2 and the track hadn't been touched! It's lucky we've had a lot of rain, otherwise it would be a dustbowl! It's a disgrace! They make Ipswich look professional and that's saying something." At 3.25 p.m., all the speedway bikes in the pits together roar into life at ear-splitting volume. The wall of sound they create is amplified by the enclosed space and the adjacent grandstands. As soon as the bikes fire into life there's a muted, barely audible sound of an indistinguishable announcement that rumbles incoherently over the tannoy closest to me in the grandstand. Kevin could be telling us to evacuate the stadium due to fire, the arrival of a supermodel in the Fenman Bar, exciting news on ice-cube-related charity events or recent Simon Lambert news. Whatever it is, we would have no idea whether we were about to burnt alive, meet the love of our lives, benefit a charity or obtain a valuable, much-needed update. In some ways loud speedway bike engine noise is a perfect accompaniment to the monotone information free twitter that's the hallmark of Kevin's speedway presentational vocabulary. Johnny laughs triumphantly, "That's your plug!" To be fair to Kevin, now he's been granted permission from the promotion he's actually giving the complete text of my publicity material the full speaking-clock treatment or, at least, I assume he is judged by the length of his peroration. Sadly it's an incomprehensible gabble to the decent-sized gaggle of us stood in this section of the grandstand while we patiently wait for the on-track action to get underway. In order to savour the only time this season Kevin will deign to include announcements about my work as part of his presenter's job description, I run the length of the grandstand and briefly loiter by the steps that lead up from the turnstiles to savour these *bons mots*. Even there I can barely just about make out what Kevin says (and only then because I'm so familiar with my own promotional text). I think he says, "The promotional material claims there's one controversial chapter on Mildenhall." Even here with my ears on full strain and without the full amplifying effects of the enclosed space of the roofed grandstand, the insistent choreographed roar of the bikes as they warm up drown the rest of these words of wisdom out! Throughout the rest of the afternoon, Kevin's always heard clearly over the public address system mainly because, sensibly, he times his announcements to take place during lulls in the action. The much more measured use of their equipment by the riders (to actually race) rather than this one-off full-throated roar of 13 speedway bikes suddenly springing into urgent life also helps.

Wherever speedway fans go there's the usual concatenation of opinions. Some consider that the speedway Grand Prix has peaked and now may potentially decline. Last night's Grand Prix in Latvia wasn't the easiest for the ordinary fans to even get to and, even if you ignore its obscure location, it was raced on a track inappropriate to the calibre of competition that the World Championship nowadays still claims to be. To my mind, live National League speedway at Mildenhall is infinitely more appealing. Other fans think similarly, "Did you see the GP last night? It was so dull! I can't recall the last time I saw an exciting one. Not this year or last. If they carry on like that they'll kill it!" Diehard Mildenhall fan Jason has turned detective about the identity of the club's title sponsor, Funky Catering. "When you get home tell me if you can find a telephone number or a website for Funky Catering? Usually advertisers like to advertise. It's probably a friend of the sister of the promoter." Even if it's also not clear who exactly these sponsors are, their support is to be applauded. I also don't know who runs the catering franchise at West Row Stadium but nowadays, according to the programme on BBC Radio 4 I heard as I drove through Suffolk, stadium catering is big business. Half a billion pounds a year is spent at sport stadiums. Analysts segment the UK market into football, cricket, rugby and 'the rest'. This latter category includes horseracing and, of course, speedway. Radio 4 reports Compass are the biggest stadium catering company in the country. They not only provide the food but also have to deal with business issues like ethics, sustainability and local sourcing. Compass also do the catering at the Cardiff Millennium Stadium. The jewel in the crown of contract catering – apart from that provided at speedway tracks, of course – is the Olympics where 3.5 million meals were served in the Olympic Village when the event was last staged. With volumes of over 100,000 meals a day in the Olympic Village alone, the costs, revenues and profits involved are immense. Aramark have catered the last 13 Olympics and, for their sins, also do this at St James's Park. The exception to the rule of contract catering remains Lords since it does its own and even has its own patisserie manufacturing capability. Surprisingly, this programme didn't mention food at speedway tracks and with this afternoon's revenues (excluding ice cream) somewhere in the region of £57.56 this is completely understandable.

Also out and about this afternoon is Arnie Gibbons official club historian of the now defunct Reading Racers and author of the widely acclaimed *Tears and Glory*. Compared to many other lifelong speedway fans, Arnie takes a philosophical attitude to meeting selection and the weather. "If I don't travel and it's on, there's always another one to go to! If I do travel and it's off, I've wasted a lot of time and sat in traffic!" On the centre green, Kevin Moore has taken us one step collectively closer to catatonia with a turgid series of uninspired rider introductions. Freed from the speedway equivalent of after-school detention the riders are finally able to have a few practice laps. Plymouth 'GT Motorcycles Silverline' Devils reserve Josh Dingle takes a heavy tumble on the back straight during his first warm-up lap. Arnie gazes on insouciantly, "Despite what they say about Rye House – you can see good racing there!" Arnie recommends another reason to visit the West Country in addition to the speedway meetings they stage at the St Boniface Arena, "When you go down to Plymouth you'll see one of their sponsors is Dingles Fairground Museum – it sounds absolutely fascinating!" Ahead of the recent fashion in speedway of political involvement, Arnie wears his Lib Dem allegiance lightly but with pride (he played a key role in Nick Clegg's 1999 election as an MEP). Lib Dem Poster Politician, Vince Cable, this morning spurred Arnie into further party political action before his trip to the speedway. "When I saw Vince Cable was on Andrew Marr today – there was only one thing to do – go leafleting my local area! So a nice morning's leafleting and then a boring drive here!" Johnny Barber wonders what will happen when his brother Nick (who now represents his local Conservative Party in Felixstowe) engages with the electorate and enjoys political success, "You can call Nick 'Sir' from now on rather than Councillor. When he becomes Prime Minister, we'll all have to bow to him!"

Last season at Mildenhall, the dapper and knowledgeable Kevin Long handled presentational duties. He's got an engaging way with people, a love of words and speedway. It's a style that comes across as both effortless and natural that engages regulars and newcomers alike. Kevin's famous for his double entendres – some believe he's got the speed of thought and wit to work as a stand up comedian. Inevitably there are delays and tedious longueurs that requires any speedway presenter worth their salt to think on their feet in order to entertain the crowd. Kevin Long could make the delivery schedule for Poundland sound like the Oscars, his 2009 replacement at West Row effortless achieves the opposite. Faced with dull goings on, Kevin Long realises he must Pimp Our Ride; faced with excitement; Kevin Moore's default setting is to Crimp Our Ride. True to form, over the stadium loudspeaker system Kevin Moore

– for a few brief moments speedway's answer to gangsta rap – gets carried away with the ersatz lyricism of his own verbiage, "This afternoon's championship racing challenge." Arnie pretends to be impressed, "Oh, listen to that alliteration!" A sudden burst of poetry can't hide the fact that although Kevin gets paid to "entertain" us with facts, comments and insight throughout the afternoon, you'd expect he'd consistently have greater general knowledge of speedway rules and regulations. Any first-time visitors inside the stadium depend on his guidance but would be misled by his analysis of the rider replacement facility Plymouth enjoy for the absent Matt Bates, "Even Seemond Stephens can take a ride!" In the shaded lee of the grandstand adjacent to the Fenman Bar, Arnie immediately corrects this statement, "Previous years in the Conference League, any rider could take a ride but – now they use averages – they can only use Kyle! Still, you can't say anything with absolute authority in speedway! Speedway isn't the only sport to tie itself in knots. Look at that Twenty20 cricket game this week where they had three days of rain-offs and then ended up bowling at one stump." If you position yourself correctly in this West Row grandstand, you can see the cricket on the television screen inside the Fenman Bar and also watch the speedway racing. News that it's now 311 for 7 doesn't excite Arnie, "It's cricket – it doesn't matter! They've had rain for three days. When speedway fans turn up at seven for a 7.30 meeting that's delayed till 8.30 they complain like mad but the cricket fans all sit there and watch the roller more patiently than we watch tractors grade the track!" Kevin Moore counts down the moments until the first race lifts off, "Less than sixty seconds remaining." He announces this in morose fashion, as if suddenly aware we're all 60 seconds closer to death but also reminiscent of Eeyore on his birthday, waving his tail at nothing, "look at all the presents I've had!"
[Arnie] "There's only one rider out there, such enthusiasm!"
[Kevin] "Less than 30 seconds remaining"
[Arnie] "There's still only two out there!
[Kevin] "The two-minute time allowance has expired and I'm sorry to say that means disqualification for Oliver Rayson."
[Arnie] "Did you see on the forums after one of the [U21] test matches where Great Britain only had five riders someone posted on Oliver's behalf saying 'Why wasn't I picked as I'm better than a lot of the riders who were?' Apparently it turned out that [team manager] Dave Croucher didn't have his mobile number so rang someone whose number he did have!"

Joe Jacobs replaces Oliver and gains third place ahead of Paul Starke in a drawn heat won by Devils Mark Simmonds. Joe Jacobs is immediately out again for his schedule ride in heat 2 but, sadly, only gets to the second bend before he falls. Plymouth reserve Josh Dingle hasn't quite mastered the back straight yet so follows his practice lap fall with another on the third bend. This latest mishap prompts referee Mick Bates to put on the red lights. Arnie's in no doubt that Josh will be excluded, "Crucially blue [Jacobs] was under power when it was stopped!" Less than subtly, Kevin Moore tries to influence the referee's decision, "JJ was back on his bike when the race was stopped but we'll wait for a decision on that one." Arnie raises a verbal eyebrow at the choice of this afternoon's referee, "I'm surprised Mick Bates can ref Mildenhall meetings given he rode so many years [1976-1982] here!" Arnie also has his own take on the Lewis Bridger 'lost passport' conundrum, "At Czestochowa, they have Jonas Davidsson who rode for Lakeside as one reserve while Tai and Lewis share a place. Tai rode at Wolves [Monday] night so I'm sure Lewis was under a lot of pressure. Lewis Bridger is such a trustworthy character that everyone immediately believed the 'lost passport' story. Though, interestingly, Trevor Geer said he was ill for a while. Either he was covering up or, more likely, it's what he'd been told! Lewis scored a pitiful 3 from five rides and one of those was a gift – it was a Scott Nicholls in Poland score. There's an interesting post on the Ostrow Riot thread that lists what the riders have been paid this year so far in zlotys, euros and pounds!"

There's no shortage of drama on the track and usually in the National League you would say that a combination of inexperience, high-powered machines and track surface were all contributory factors. However, third-race fallers Luke Priest and Dean 'Fuzzy' Felton have both been around speedway for quite some time. When third behind Plymouth reserve David Gough, Luke Priest falls on the second bend of lap three while, still further behind, his race partner Dean 'Fuzzy' Felton (despite considerable distance and time to evade him), is drawn black-hole-like towards disaster. Fuzzy bangs into Luke before he leisurely idles onwards into the bend-two safety fence. Johnny Barber takes some positives from the situation, "If 'Fuzzy' had been going any quicker, he'd have hurt himself! He laid his bike down there and you don't want that at his age!" Maybe 'Fuzzy' is one of the mystery under-performing riders obliquely identified by Mildenhall Club Chairman? I decide to quiz Johnny, "Ray Mascall said 'two riders have consistently underperformed', which ones are they?" Quick as a flash I'm told, "Dave Mason and Dean Felton but I don't agree with 'Fuzzy'. Admittedly he hasn't scored the points but he's been consistent throughout his career not scoring the points!" A few minutes pass with little sign of action on the track before – in a distinctive presenter's voice that mixes bored clarity with a hint of irked metalwork teacher – Kevin Moore informs us, "There'll be a slight delay as David Gough has three rides." This is notionally helpful information but, when the riders eventually take to the track, Josh Dingle in fact partners persistent race winner Kyle Hughes. These Devils are separated at the start line by one of speedway's power-users of hair gel – Mildenhall captain, David Mason. Nonetheless, they race away and gain Plymouth's second heat advantage of the afternoon to extend the Devils' aggregate lead to 4 points (10-14).

Luke Priest's fall looks to have been a mere blip when he proceeds to win heat 5 though fellow crashee, Dean 'Fuzzy' Felton, finishes comprehensively last. Johnny Barber affects concern, "He's still feeling the after effects of his crash. It's a big shock for old people when they fall down!" Heat 6 sees Barrie Evans beat the highly regarded Kyle Hughes and, with Oliver Rayson third, the Tigers' deficit narrows to 2 points. It's a short-lived recovery since Kyle Hughes wins the next heat partnered home by Seemond Stephens with a lacklustre David Mason trailed off in third. Heat wins for Gough (heat 8) followed by another win for Kyle Hughes (heat 9) fire Plymouth into a comfortable 23-31 lead. During the interval there's intensive work on the track and Kevin rather unnecessarily informs us, "The track grade continues during the interval." Planes fly overhead from the nearby airbase and perhaps vehicles on display this afternoon could inspire a speedway-based film entitled, *Tractors, Bikes and Planes*. Stood close to the trackshop, a Milton Keynes fan watches on with incredulous dismay at the frequent curatorial work. "Why do they do the track grade practically between every race? If you were to bring someone here for the first time, they wouldn't be entertained! There's a fine line between charming and amateur and they've fallen completely over the edge." Personally I think Mildenhall definitely remain on the charm side of the equation.

After four successive home defeats in the National League, fans of the Tigers no longer have to pretend to be disconcerted by another poor performance served up at headquarters. During the interval, demand remains tepid for my book. There's much written material available on hand to buy or study. On the trackshop table, there's a copy of the evocatively entitled *Mike Patrick's World of Speedway*. Johnny tells me, "It's produced by Howard Jones and packed with lots of exciting photos you've seen before in the *Speedway Star* – well, except, of course, for those of Ronnie Moore and Mike Patrick himself!" The Tigers programme is well worth a read and particularly taken the two-page spread given over to much-travelled programme contributor, Derek Barclay, who "casts his thoughts on this afternoon's West Row visitors from South Devon – that's Francis Drake's country." Derek's hard work (at his keyboard) typifies the volunteer labour upon which so many speedway clubs depend in order to survive and, hopefully, thrive. He's held a variety of responsibilities – including announcer, press officer and programme editor – at a number of clubs. In fact, he changes clubs with dizzying speed – recent years have seen him at Wimbledon, Sittingbourne and Stoke as well as this season's glamour clubs: Bournemouth and Mildenhall. After the inevitable departure, his vituperative Internet alter ego 'Parsloes 1928 nearly', invariably then lambasts – or hints at dark undiscovered secrets and strategic management errors (except at the fabulous CL version of Wimbledon, of course) – those whose interest he'd only so recently zealously advocated.It rather brings to mind Javier Marías's great Spanish novel "*Tu Rostro Mañana*" ("your face tomorrow") which is about betrayals during the Spanish Civil War.[1] Unusually for a Barclay programme piece, in this particular Tigers programme there are absolutely no irrelevant mentions of either Wimbledon or Crayford. There's actually even a new and interesting fact about Kyle Hughes ("Kyle's first cousin is highly-ranked international snooker star, Steven Lee") that raises this team overview above the platitudinous norm.

Just before heat 10 Michael Lee dashes out of the Fenman Bar (pint in hand) in time to see the tapes rise. His reward

[1] Then Scunthorpe team manager, Malcolm Vasey bravely engages and critiques some of Derek's Internet postings as "ridiculous spin" characterises his pretentions to management influence as "laughable". Unkindly, Malcolm suggests Derek should be viewed as "really just a supporter who puts a few odds and ends in programmes". Malcolm Vasey continued, "Parsloes problem is that he becomes infatuated with the cause of his many teams and has almost reached the stage where everyone in speedway has been at one of them. Soon you won't know where to turn. He attempts to justify the unjustifiable and it goes on for years. At last he has pitched up somewhere that has achieved a degree of success and insists on justifying all parts of it. I congratulate Bournemouth on their achievements, they have done very well and I hope that they retain a presence at this level. There is not much else to say. The Parsloes claim to be part of Bournemouth makes me laugh. Garry May, Neil Vatcher and the promoter are the ones to revel in any success not a programme columnist who fails to mention his similar efforts at Mildenhall. And why would that be after 2009 I wonder? Claims for reflected glory I suspect."

is sight of Barrie Evans and Oliver Rayson as they combine to hammer home a 5-1. The nature of this maximum heat advantage temporarily sweeps me up in the excitement and causes me to exclaim, "The fightback has begun!" Arnie remains studiedly sceptical, "Yes [doubtfully] ask me again in two minutes. Seemond Stephens was in the bar chatting during heat 9 which, I imagine, is ideal preparation for his third place in heat 10!" The Tigers resurgence continues into heat 11 when, after the completion of one lap, Mildenhall find themselves on the cusp another 5-1. No sooner does Arnie pull a theatrical shocked expression than Mark Simmonds negotiates the often tricky second bend to gain a lead that he holds to the chequered flag. Before the start of heat 12, Kevin Moore conducts a stadium-wide master-class in how to get us all to pointlessly scribble in our programmes when he announces, "Plymouth have David Gough in yellow and Josh Dingle in green". Josh Dingle is programmed to appear in the yellow helmet colour and, no sooner have I written his name next to the green helmet colour (as Kevin Moore advises) than Arnie tells me that Josh remains in yellow as originally programmed. Perhaps this type of thing is difficult for Kevin to see or interpret when he's stood only yards away on the centre green from the riders on the start line? If Kevin did attempt to correct his error – above the noise of the bikes as they attain the high revs required to exit powerfully from the start-line – the meaning of exact import of his chatter cum inaudible announcement is lost in the West Row equivalent of Phil Spector's Wall of Sound. Yellow-helmeted Josh Dingle proceeds to finish third. Joe Jacobs and Luke Priest combine to achieve the Tigers second maximum heat advantage in three races to level the score at 36 apiece.

With the Tigers collective dander up, heat 13 represents the ideal opportunity for David Mason to gainsay the naysayers who question his hunger for points and track success. Sadly these naysayers remain unanswered although David's teammate, Barrie Evans, at least manages to gate and briefly leads (until the third bend) before both Plymouth riders easily swoop past him. Kyle Hughes and Mark Simmonds provide their own interpretation of the teamwork required to block out – in this instance – an invisible opponent. They flit hither and dither about the track as if they're the outriders for a renegade police formation display team. Though somewhat wild, they nonetheless combine to extract a deserved maximum heat advantage and get the reward of a tut from Arnie, "Despite that inept team riding, it's still a 5-1!" One young rider who improves as the meeting progresses is young Tigers reserve, Joe Jacobs. His resurgence continues on the first lap of heat 14 when, along the back straight, he battles past a visibly surprised Seemond Stephens. With fellow reserve Nick Laurence third as the lap ends, the Tigers look set fair for a 4-2. However, with the Tigers set fair, Nick Laurence bizarrely decides to ride a very wide, almost Tomasz Gollobesque outside line for the remainder of the race that comprehensively relegates him into last place!

With the scores comparatively poised at 40-44, Mildenhall can still snatch a draw from the "last heat decider" that Kevin whittles on about in a way others discuss a dental check up. When it finally gets underway, the race ends strangely. With the Devils set for a 5-1, Mark Simmonds falls on the third lap in the West Row Bermuda Triangle – aka the second bend. Rather than stop the race, referee Mick Bates strangely allows the riders to progress with varying degrees of application – the Mildenhall riders race while Karl Hughes doesn't – before he finally stops it and awards the race as a 5-1 to the home team. This ensures a draw that sends loyal Tigers fans into something that approaches the ecstasy of muted celebration. Kevin Moore burbles into his microphone about, "A dramatic meeting that has had just about everything!" Johnny Barber remains unconvinced, "Yeah, except good racing! That said, the atmosphere is better than last year and the track looks much better than last year too!"

The meeting has taken less than two hours to run. While we wait for whatever the victory parade is called after a drawn meeting, I quiz Arnie about what the future might hold for Dean 'Fuzzy' Felton? "I think he's a very likable chap. I saw him in '93 with Long Eaton and I was far from impressed then and in subsequent years so, I have to say, yes – it's time for Felton to retire!" After the celebrations subside almost as quickly as they begin, Ray Mascall refuses to get carried away, "That was better. We still have to make changes!" Pleased that I've figured out who he might have been talking about I confess, "I put two and two together!" Like any Zen master Ray replies, "Two plus two makes four plus five!" With no likelihood of a rush to purchase my books, I decide it's finally time to get an ice cream. As I head in one direction Hilary Rouse heads in the other, possibly to see Trevor Swales in the pits to complain about the curious incident of Kenneth Bjerre's variable scores. Sadly the ice-cream man has already left but King's Lynn fan Julie Neal (here with her daughter) tells me, "You were lucky – he's so rude – no please; no thank you!" West Row Stadium was one of many possible speedway destinations they could have visited this Sunday afternoon. "We could have gone to Buxton or Newport but we came here. It's 20 minutes away. It became a good meeting at the end but I heard they didn't start work on the track till 2 o'clock. They should be named and shamed in your book. We thought about going to see the Barracudas at Buxton but we're pleased we didn't 'cause we're losing 17-13 and the tracks not very good!"

Even at this stage of the season, the partial resurgence Ray Mascall has achieved at Mildenhall Speedway is already significant. Many have tried and failed to make a success of the club in recent years. Ray appears to have an effective approach that could lead to success. Indeed, the former announcer has literally put his life savings into saving the club – at great risk to the rest of his retirement life – and has brought a refreshing upbeat turnaround there after a number of years in the doldrums. The arrival of Taylor Poole shortly after this meeting symbolises Ray's ambition but also how one sincere person can have a great impact and start to re-energise a club. Obviously, Ray Mascall is too modest to make such claims for himself, though it doesn't make it any less true. Hopefully, speedway in Suffolk will continue its resurgence under his leadership.

2nd August Mildenhall v. Plymouth (National League) 45-45

Mildenhall: *"The atmosphere is better than last year and the track looks much better than last year too!"*

CHAPTER 25

Edinburgh

"You just know that when he finishes second when he gets back to the pits the tool boxes go flying!"

7th August

One of the speedway tracks you can (with some effort) get to by public transport in this country is the Edinburgh Monarchs Armadale Stadium. The modern commuter experience requires we constantly receive instructions or apologies. At Gatwick a power-crazed security man located *after* passport control repeatedly tells passengers to "put your passports and boarding passes away, you don't need them!" They must have a better class of well-travelled benefit fraudster at Edinburgh Airport because, moments after you step off the walkway up from the plane, you're confronted with the sign "We're closing in on you." When I arrive at the gates of Armadale Stadium, promoter John Campbell is busy with the various hidden speedway management tasks needed to be completed on race day. He readies the entrance kiosk, unloads his car of programmes and then, close to the season ticket holders' entrance, patiently proceeds to tie various notices to the green-painted wire of the stadium fence with black plastic tie pins. One notice advises of admission prices – Adult £14, OAPs £10.50, child £5 (if unaccompanied under 12 or aged between 12 and 15) – while another sign advises where to go for cash entry, plus there is a sign headed "Warning". It reads, "If you have parked across the road from the stadium and your car is blocking the pavement to pedestrians then please go and move your car to the car park before entering the stadium or you may regret it." Quite what will happen (or you'll regret) isn't specified but it certainly sounds ominous. Perhaps the cars are clamped, towed away or doused in paint stripper? Whatever exactly happens, the management of Edinburgh Speedway club sensibly seek to maintain good relations with the residents that surround the stadium. While he works John is happy to chat.

[Jeff] "Will there be a big crowd tonight?"

[John] "No, not for Sheffield!"

[Jeff] "Don't they have that exciting kiddie at reserve now?"

[John] "Hugh Skidmore, you mean. They also have Paul Cooper who struggles to find his way round here. It'll be closer now because Andrew Tully is injured. The result still isn't in doubt!"

[Jeff] "At one point, I thought you'd changed this fixture to be against King's Lynn?"

[John] "Rye House you mean. We didn't because Len [Silver] thinks speedway is his so we couldn't agree dates. He said he'd come tonight so long as we could race soon afterwards to preserve the tension. Then he came back with a suggested date of 19th September! There wouldn't be much tension left by then so we changed back to Sheffield."

[Jeff] "Will it rain tonight?"

[John] "There were definitely a few spots as I drove over here and it's forecast for showers."

[Jeff] "Maybe you need the Lakeside weather promise."

[John] "What's that?"

[Jeff] "Giving a commitment to their fans to always get the meetings on unless the weather is totally awful or, so it now seems if you look in the small print, also postpone it if Leigh Adams needs to ride in Poland."

[John] "I don't know about that but Lakeside certainly change their team all the time. Recently they redeclared their team and redeclared it again before they had even ridden!"

[Jeff] "Does it cost to do that?"

[John] "Not if you do it right! We're trying to get this on tonight. We've got a fixture backlog so we'll keep trying until we have a postponement and then we'll have to say we're not going to complete all our meetings before the [Premier League] cut-off date. Last Friday it rained at 6, stopped at half-6 before it started again and Jim McGregor abandoned it at quarter-past 7 saying we had to consider the riders' safety! Sixteen professional riders ready to race and he says he's thinking of their safety! They ride speedway for goodness sake! I didn't mind 'cause, if we'd put it on, it would've been an awful meeting anyway. But, talking about safety and speedway isn't something you want to happen is it? [John rips off a large plastic poster from the railings of the two hospitality units] Last weekend at the Fours [in Workington] – which could have been run over two bends rather than four laps – I said to Malcolm Vasey that there wouldn't be racing at Glasgow because the forecast was so bad. But it passed over by 2 o'clock so you just can't rely on the forecasts. All week the forecast has been wonderful for tonight but, last night, it started to say it'll rain between 4 and 7. We've had some really awful meetings against Sheffield when it's rained – they struggle enough without that anyway!"

[Jeff] "Surely the new spirit at Sheffield means they'll do better this time."

[John] "I don't know about that. They lost at Stoke last weekend. Some got on the Internet and said they threw it away and Neil [Machin] responded saying there were factors they didn't know about. It's best not to respond to these people on the Internet. It's not worth the trouble and a few can influence opinions. Some people got on the Internet last week to criticise the £18 admission price for the Scottish Open. I don't respond but when asked [in person] I say we always set our admission prices to cover our costs! Sure, we operate in a competitive environment. We usually charge £14, Glasgow £13.50, Berwick £13.50 or maybe £13. It's a club decision based on the costs and attendances. For the Ashfield Classic, Glasgow got their admission price wrong at £15 because they need dry weather to ensure they definitely covered their costs."

[Man] "Will there be any Sheffield supporters' coaches tonight?"

[John] "No! I've had people ring up this week to ask if they can use their ticket to get into this week's meeting. Of course they can! One of them didn't want a refund of the difference [£4] and said I should put it towards the losses we made. It was probably the wonderful entertainment we put on."

[Jeff] "What was that?"

[John] "Nothing! I came at the same time as normal and got home at the usual time and forgot I hadn't worked! I stayed and chatted to people. There were probably more drunks in the bar than normal. The BSPA rules say we can't give cash refunds anyway. People can use them [readmission tickets] at another meeting. It's best to avoid refunding the difference at the turnstiles as that just makes it tricky for them. I did say to the crowd if they wanted to hand the tickets in to Margaret in the programme stall with their names and addresses written on the back, I'd send a refund. There weren't many given in. What surprised me was how far they'd come to see it! Normally we don't even get people to travel 25 miles from Glasgow for a Premier League meeting. We'll definitely run it at the end of the season. Probably as the last meeting at the end of October – with fireworks because people say they like those. We got a big crowd last year anyway!"

One of the early arrivals and regular attendees at Edinburgh Monarchs home meetings is experienced speedway professional and Berwick presenter Dick Barrie. "I'll roll out the red carpet when you come along tomorrow. I'll tell everyone how good the book is [which Dick has already read] and interview you!"

[Jeff] "I don't like the sound of my own voice. I didn't when Michael Max interviewed me."

Trophy

One of the hospitality suites

Margaret searches for Monster merchandise

[Dick] "Well Michael likes the sound of his own voice."
[Jeff] "Michael asked what speedway should do in the future but I didn't know."
[Dick] "What should be done? Now that you've had the time to think of your answer?"
[Jeff] "Dunno. It's beaten better brains than mine! Jon Cook probably has a new plan in the *Star*."
[Dick] "He has lots of good ideas; you just need to sift through them all to find the good ones! Have you met Allan McDade? He's the best commercial artist in speedway."
[Allan] "I started doing Glasgow programme covers in 1984 and I've done them ever since. And, now, I do Edinburgh ones and some big meetings like the Ben Fund. Have you seen our bike? [Points to speedway bike on the decking outside one of the hospitality areas] At the end of the meeting we have a 'test your reactions' competition. What I like about it is that it's not just the guys but the wives and the kids. The riders come up at the end and the guests try to beat them! We have had two beat them which is pretty embarrassing for the riders but good fun for everyone else!"

Outside the stadium, the new-build residential estate appears to have moved even closer to the stadium perimeter. Inside Armadale, the stadium infrastructure changes appear to be minimal to the naked eye. There's a new slightly frosted window above the gents urinals so the inquisitive can check on activities outside. For some time now Internet forums have claimed that the stadium will be demolished to make way for a Sainsbury's superstore. John Campbell tells me that the area will change when the railway line gets extended onwards from Armadale to Glasgow. When I buy my programme the stallholder tells me about an exciting new Monarchs signing, "Max Dilger is our new German who still hasn't ridden for us yet!"
[Jeff] "Maybe you can fire him before he does!"
[John] "What, do a Glasgow, you mean?!"

It's 6.30 p.m., an hour before the scheduled start time when the loudspeaker crackles into life and at deafening volume with a pre-recorded announcement to informs us: "Ladies and Gentlemen, welcome to the Scotwaste Arena home of the Premier League champions for the meeting between Edinburgh and Sheffield which is only 16 minutes away!"John Campbell passes and is clearly inured to public service announcements. "In this nation of cricket haters, there's Margaret sat in the [programme] booth smoking away and listening to the radio. They're getting slaughtered – 102 all out!"
[Margaret] "We were 102 all out and they're 180 for 4. It's strange so it is, isn't it? They do well and we get the new ball and can't do nothing with it! Still, that's why we like it – 'cause it's unpredictable!"
[John] "We have the Monster Energy [drink] people here tonight. It's a caffeine drink like Red Bull."
[Jeff] "Will that attract a crowd?"
[John] "It could, of course, but I doubt it 'cause no one knows about it! I only remembered when my wife reminded me they were coming. You'll enjoy them though! I can't think our fans will like their drinks. They prefer tea or coffee!"

John's comment that I would enjoy a Monster Energy drink when he doesn't even know my beverage preferences mystifies me until an over-sized 4x4 US style truck decorated with snazzy green graphics pulls up alongside my table. Shortly after a bloke in a cap jumps out from its cab dressed in the sub-standard European approximation of a super surfer dude favoured in European provincial cities. He's accompanied by a woman with bottle blonde hair who emerges from the passenger side door of the truck dressed in true rock-chick fashion and wearing muffin-top jeans. To further confirm their self-conscious rock image, almost straight away they switch on some unknown but tritely derivative heavy metal music that they play at ear-splitting volume making rational thought, let alone light conversation, difficult. John passes and, with a smirk on his face, says, "I said you'd enjoy it."
[Jeff] "I hope they don't stay long."
[John] "So do they! They say they have to get off quickly, that's what they told me. The girl said they have some event in Newcastle."

Margaret temporarily abandons her booth and the cricket commentary in order to inspect the rear of the truck and peer curiously at the cases of free Monster Energy drink piled there. She inspects the goods extremely suspiciously. In a media-saturated age, product placement and brand association are key components for any publicity campaign. At the top end of the glamour scale, Formula I Champion Jenson Button sports the distinctive Monster green claw marks on his crash helmet and, after he'd become champion, he was happy to have his privacy invaded in Dubai

while he stagily smooched with his Japanese model girlfriend – Jessica Michibata – on a speedboat. [1] In speedway circles, Greg Hancock is the most exalted rider to receive the benefit of sponsorship from whatever company is behind the Monster Energy drink brand. Whenever possible, Greg holds cans of their drink, draws attention to their logo or wears an appropriately branded baseball cap. While theoretically you can understand that Jenson might appreciate the jolt to his concentration that a can of the Monster Energy drink might provide (although, even if you ignore he's a triathlete, I somehow doubt this) then the logic of Greg Hancock's consumption is much harder to fathom. Should he avail himself of his sponsors' drink prior to a Grand Prix meeting then the calm steady nerves he requires along with exceptional hand/eye coordination at the start line would count for nought – if he clumsily or accidentally released his clutch prematurely. Appropriately enough, the heavy metal played celebrates delirium tremens or its equivalent with the mantra "Shaking like a leaf"! While, stood on the back of his pick-up truck, the Monster surfer dude in the cap sings tunelessly along. If something is gratis then people usually feel like they shouldn't miss out. However, it's very noticeable that few adults stop to pick up a complimentary can of Monster Energy drink. Perhaps they're driven back by the volume of the "music" or, perhaps, they'd previously tasted this liquid? Among the youngsters in the stadium, the brand clearly has cache and some inspirational appeal, particularly since they're frequently refused a can when they ask since the age restriction on its consumption is scrupulously adhered to by the Monster surfer dude in charge of handing them out. Demand among adults remains so pitiful that the girl takes a case to the back-straight grandstand in search of anoraked punters. Smartly dressed in his replica Sheffield Wednesday football top, Gary Lough isn't inclined to savour this beverage, "That's that shite that Greg Hancock tries to sell!" Gary prefers to bemoan the ongoing serial use of rider replacement by the Edinburgh Monarchs (this evening for Andrew Tully). "We're running RR – it's okay at home but not so good away."
[Jeff] "Who's this Max Dilger then?"
[Gary] "I've seen him on YouTube."
[Jeff] "Any player Sunderland sign that looks brilliant on YouTube is usually hopeless on the pitch."
[Gary] "I'd seen him from the Under-21 reports too!"

Gary's helper Regan looks covetously towards the Monster Energy drinks but, though the music blares, both servers have temporarily disappeared. The ongoing histrionics of the music and its volume further dampens the low levels of interest in my bookstall but does attract people convinced that anything in the vicinity of this grotesquely sized truck will be available without charge this evening. Shortly afterwards a young man in what looks like the terminal stages of acne asks, "What are you selling here?"
[Jeff] "Books."
[Young man] "Oh!"
[Jeff] "You can get a free Energy drink over there."
[Young man] "What, if I just ask for one?"

The Sheffield Tigers supporting Brown family have come up to Armadale to watch the Tigers roar at the Scotwaste Arena this evening. They've purchased all my books. Not only do they read them but they also provide honest feedback. The younger Mr Brown (Philip) summarises the development of the œuvre. "You're much more ingrained in the sport now. It's not better or worse. When you did the first book, you were new and described what we knew or had already gone through but described some things we hadn't noticed. Now you've been back a few times, inevitably, that has changed and it's not something we hear so much about anymore. I'm not bored with the format or the subject – I expect it could go on for a while!" After Philip has admired my wheelie case ("I like your case"), which the quaint cobbles of Edinburgh city centre earlier damaged beyond repair, he lets me know he also reads my blog but has no real time or sympathy with my perspective on the iniquities of the speedway Grand Prix organisers, boosters or events. "It's not like Pinegen hid the fact that they designed the programmes. It was there for all to see if you looked! They're in a difficult position that I think they manage very well. They have a commercial relationship but they have their journalistic integrity to preserve – which they do! They make critical comments and, also, they report well and extensively on the sport. They do a good job for speedway and that's something to be proud of."

[1] The *Sun* headline above the accompanying photographs was: "Jenson: I want kids (but not as much as I want you to see my sponsors' fizzy drink)". The article continued in mock outraged fashion, "he held a can of the Red Bull-style drink from the base so its logo was visible AND wore a baseball cap bearing the symbol."

Indeed, like many people in the sport, I have the utmost respect for the integrity of its journalists, the quality of the material it produces as well as their extensive reporting of all matters speedway. Doubtless it's true that there's no conflict that anyone could concretely identify but, as with so much in life (let alone the goldfish bowl of the media), perceptions often count more than reality. It's hard to imagine a situation where, for example, the Channel 4 managing editor responsible for Channel 4 News could simultaneously hold the position of press officer for one of the major political parties or station advertisers they regularly cover. It appears that these common standards of transparency aren't really applicable to the world of speedway.

Dennis Wallace – who writes under the nom de plume of Merlin on the speedway forums – stops by at my display table. "I want to buy a copy as I'm in it! But, I've come out with a chequebook with no cheques! Speedway's such a friendly sport. Where else could you meet so many nice people and form such good friendships? The forums help – sure there's anonymity but everyone gets to know who you are eventually. We're all enthusiasts – we'd have to be to put up with the inferior stadium facilities they have at some places. Why else would you stand in the cold and wet and put up with it if you didn't like it?" Our conversation is briefly interrupted by the dulcet tones of Scott Wilson drifting over the public address system as he takes a metaphorical onion from his pocket to massage our expectations of tonight's contest. "Welcome to the meeting between Sheffield and a weakened Monarchs team!" Dennis gets on well with the Somerset Rebels massive [Ian Belcher and Aron Whiting]. "It's become a tradition they come and stay with me. It's nice to do and they've given me a lot of pleasure. I live on my own with a cat who's not such a good conversationalist!" Scott continues to wax lyrical about both the forthcoming entertainment and the meteorological conditions in the local area, "Hope you have a wonderful evening with us here at a sun-kissed Armadale!" Promoter John Campbell walks by. He's been impressed with the level of attention that the Monster truck has demanded and praises the studied exoticism of their staff. "I think they even try to speak with American accents!" The terms and conditions under which the speedway club operate at Armadale Stadium dictates that they have to adhere to a curfew ("all meetings officially have to be over by 21.35 p.m.") and as a result, there will be no opportunity for me to sell my books during the meeting, "Why would we have an interval when we can make no money from it?"

My trips to Armadale would feel incomplete if I were unable to watch the action from my usual vantage point between the raised base of one of the hospitality portacabins and the first-bend grandstand. Stood there you can see the majority of the track (except where the wooden safety fence obscures it) and, even better, it also offers the opportunity to enjoy watching with knowledgeable and passionate Monarchs fans, Dougie Copland and his father Bill. The first race sees Ryan Fisher establish psychological advantage over his opposite number Ricky Ashworth in the battle of the number 1s. The second race of the night takes several attempts to complete because of fallers. The first time out Byron Bekker falls on the first bend and Paul Cooper falls on the second. Referee Dale Entwhistle orders all four back but when, Cooper falls under pressure from the South African on the third bend of the rerun, he's disqualified by Dale Entwhistle. Dougie notes the strategic method in Byron's flamboyant racing style, "That's Byron's new tactic – he dives under them on bend 3 and they fall off!"

Scott Wilson roams with his Mic and finds Sheffield co-promoter Neil Machin for a few words. The Tigers are comfortably third placed in the table though Neil's understated approach wouldn't hint they'd arrived anywhere near at that position, "We started the Premier League season with four very tough Aways." Scott decides to get to the bottom of the "psychological advantage of Owlerton" but only learns "Well, that's part of it, people come to Sheffield and know we're a solid team throughout the order." The third attempt to run the second race again sees Byron Bekker fall (this time on the first bend) though he remounts to finish third in a three-man race. The two previous attempts to run the race have seen Hugh Skidmore gate with alacrity but, when it really matters, he's beaten away from the tapes by Aaron Summers. For the duration of heat 3, Richard Hall decides to ride an extremely wide line. It's an experiment encouraged by his position at the rear of the field. Richard's attempt to establish a new route round Armadale ends he nearly comes to grief on the third bend of lap two. Somehow, he remains on his equipment and still manages to beat German debutant Max Dilger at the finish line to snatch an unlikely third place. Dilger looks stylish enough during his first ever competitive run-out on the Armadale circuit though, understandably, he rides within himself. Dougie's keen that he's set achievable ambitions, "Beat Chris Mills in heat 5 – that's his target!" Paul Cooper appears to have overcome his historic under-performances at the Scotwaste Arena when he leads the field as the riders exit the second bend of heat 4. However, by the time they reach the third bend – not a great distance on this track – Paul falls back into last place! Michal Rajkowski always looks likely to win the race until Josh Auty snatches it from him on the line. This dash for the flag prompts some praise from Scott Wilson for the opposition ("the tenacity of Josh Auty"). While we wait for the next race, Scott interviews possible hot speedway prospect of the future, 13-year-old Arthur Sissis.

[Arthur] "Yeah, I started racing speedway when I was 7 and I'm still at it!"

[Scott] "I take it you're Australian – how did you get into speedway?"

[Arthur] "My dad took me to a race meeting."

[Scott] "You're a long way from home – shouldn't you be at school?"

[Dougie] "He could put a few reserves to shame. He wants to be a road racer and he's a very talented speedway rider. He's very, very stylish. I'm surprised you haven't come across him riding second halves. He races on his own 'cause of his age!" [2]

Off gate 2, in the second Armadale race of his career, Max Dilger finds Chris Mills intervene in his apprenticeship with a bit of bump and grind as they race towards the first corner ("Chris Mills got a wee nudge on him"). Sensibly enough, 'once bitten twice shy' is the safety-first motto adopted by Dilger in the rerun. Max again enters the corner stylishly but also slowly to avoid any further knocks from fellow riders. Matthew Wethers charges round the last bend of the last lap only to find his progress to the line blocked by the Tigers number 2, ("Chris Mills's lock-up put an end to that!"). With Ashworth the victor, Sheffield's maximum heat advantage gives them a narrow 14-16 lead. Dougie still remains guardedly optimistic about the likely future progression of Max Dilger, "He said he'd never seen a track as small as this! Wait till he sees Redcar, that's a gater's paradise. Germany has big tracks so he might get 15 at Berwick!" Of greater concern to Dougie is the present fragility of the Monarchs line-up in the context of their fixture pile-up before the end of the season. "This [meeting] could be a bit tight. We don't look so good this season. Tully's injured and he's worth 11 points round here. Fisher always gives a hundred per cent and you just know that when he finishes second when he gets back to the pits the tool boxes go flying! I'd always rather have him in my side. Matthew Wethers is another who also gives a hundred per cent."

If Chris Mills gave Max Dilger a slight nudge then, comparatively, Ryan Fisher barges his teammate Michal Rajkowski on the second bend of heat 6. Luckily, a Hugh Skidmore fall ensures that the Monarchs take a 4-2 to regain the lead. In the next race, Ryan Fisher repeats the race-win medicine and, this time, doesn't impede his teammate Byron Bekker who, nonetheless, still manages to finish last under his own volition. Rejuvenated by giving the "new kid on the block" a lesson, Chris Mills leads heat 8 closely pursued by Aaron Summers. The Australian's failure to venture off his favoured racing line frustrates Dougie, "Try something else man – don't just stick to the same line!" With Paul Cooper marooned in last place ("Paul Cooper is dreadful"), a drawn heat is the inevitable conclusion. Chris Mills's victory is loudly booed by a small section of fans that cluster close to my vantage point. When I ask Dougie, "Why are they booing Mills?" He replies, "'Cause they're idiots! There's six of them who've been coming the last year and a half. They sing football songs. Ask around and everyone will say that about them! They boo them 'cause they're wearing the wrong body colours!" Though not in action here tonight, the present Premier League leaders don't inspire affection from Dougie. "You should have been here for the King's Lynn meeting to see the latest tricks they pull. I still remember when Buster Chapman faked a heart attack 'cause Davey Watt or Trevor Harding or someone wasn't here. It was disgusting – particularly with his daughter – Tom P. Madsen's wife – seven months pregnant and worried in the crowd. He did thank me once for going to King's Lynn but I still think he's a tosser! I know you like them!"

Possible anxiety about experiencing another rough bend again sees Max Dilger adopt his stately safety-first entry into the first corner, well behind the possible tangle of men and machines that potentially lies ahead of him. Though built for storms, boats that remain in the harbour definitely don't sink and, so it is with Dilger, who again finishes last in a race won by Matthew Wethers. Ryan Fisher makes it four wins out of four when he triumphs in heat 10. The sequence of four successive drawn heats is broken when Summers and Wethers combine for a 5-1 to take the

[2] During the winter the excellent *Keep Turning Left* blog (www.keep-turning-left.blogspot.com) features photos of the now 14-year-old Arthur in his road racing leathers under the headline, "The New Slide King". Judged by this article, Arthur's speedway career might be over before it has begun because of the attraction and lure of a future potential Moto GP career. "By the looks of it he may well be lost to the shale sport, as he has made the recent switch to tarmac, having won a place in the prestigious Red Bull Rookies Cup which aims to unearth the future stars of Moto GP. He raced in the competition in 2009 and he's on the provisional entry list for 2010. Sissis wouldn't be the first Aussie to make such a switch, as Casey Stoner raced junior speedway and dirt track and Gary McCoy also started out in speedway."

Monarchs into a lead (35-31) that they then don't relinquish for the rest of the meeting. Dougie savours the moment, "It's easy when you gate properly – I think Edinburgh must be the worst gaters in the Premier League!" Heat 12 enables Max Dilger to reach an important personal milestone – he records his first ever point in British speedway! When combined with Aaron Summers's race win, the heat advantage extends the Edinburgh lead to 6 points. Back in the pits, Monarchs team manager Alan Bridgett shuffles his six rider pack to cover the rider replacement rides of Andrew Tully. Byron Bekker does the honours in heat 13. Like many other people in the stadium, I expect Ryan Fisher will emerge victorious from this clash of the heat leaders. However, Byron falls, Ryan finishes second and Josh Auty wins to leave the meeting comparatively poised with only two races left. Before heat 14, Dougie Copeland thoroughly reviews the scorecard to consider the various options, "Dilger has 1 point, Bekker has 1 point, rider replacement has 7 points! With Cooper out in this Sheffield must know something we don't! If Edinburgh get a 5-1, you'd have to ask why they put out Cooper and not Skidmore." Quite what permutations or scenario could develop with Paul Cooper's fellow reserve in the race is open to question. One thing is for sure, on the third bend of the second lap Paul Cooper knocks into the safety fence to accidently break it and, thereby, stop the race! Ahead when the race stopped, Richard Hall doesn't do so well second time out, since he falls on the second bend when placed second. Dougie has seen enough to issue judgement, "That's why Richard Hall won't make a decent speedway rider 'cause he ain't thinking! It's slick so you don't need to ride like you're at Sheffield!" Though he remounts, Hall can only chase home behind Wethers and Summers (second despite the fact that he blew his engine before heat 14 and so rides on Byron Bekker's bike) for the third-place point. The maximum heat advantage ensures Edinburgh win the meeting. They massage the scoreline further in the final race of the night when Ryan Fisher resumes normal service to finish with 17 points from six rides.

Facing the frosted window in the toilets, a Monarch's fan pronounces the meeting "awesome". Unlikely ever to use the word awesome, even if the Monarchs had swept all before them in every available trophy, John Campbell reflects on recent events prompted by the ever-curious Edinburgh presenter Scott Wilson. John identifies a silver lining about the postponement of the Scottish Open ("it turned into a good social occasion") before he ponders the club's response to the Andrew Tully injury. "We need to get in a rider to replace Andrew Tully as rider replacement makes it hard. That said, in July and August it is very, very difficult to get someone in!" The great and the good of Scottish speedway have come along to watch tonight's encounter. Glasgow co-promoter Alan Dick enjoyed what he's seen ("It was a good meeting!"). Shortly afterwards, Sheffield co-promoter Dave Hoggart looks back over the meeting philosophically, "It's typical of this season, we get ahead and then we don't win! As I've walked down here [along the back-straight grandstand] many Edinburgh fans have said thank you for a great meeting. One said our riders really had to go all out to ensure victory! It made for a good contest. Lack of top-end strength – we know that's our problem! Summers has been cheating like frick all evening! We let two of them [rolling starts] go but then we kicked up when it was his fourth or fifth ride before he was called back. Ricky Ashworth got pulled back twice for doing that here. Then got warned and fined! We don't mind it happening if it applies to everyone equally all the time!" Our chat is interrupted by a fan who accosts Dave to ask, "Why was Paul Cooper in Heat 14?" Dave gives a polite roundabout explanation that concludes with the phrase "Bekker knew what happened but the ref didn't want to know!" After the fan has moved off Dave is less phlegmatic, "That's what we have to put up with – the hindsight brigade! The reason Paul Cooper was in Heat 14 is 'cause he's the only one who could get among them and do a job!"

Without any transport to the railway station, the casual freemasonry of the speedway community intervenes when Alan Walker kindly volunteers to take me there. He's enjoyed the meeting and, despite the fixture backlog, contrary to expert Internet opinion (and the management's determination to pour cold water on such suggestions), he believes that Edinburgh could still be 2009 Premier League champions!

7th August Edinburgh v. Sheffield (Premier League) 51-39

CHAPTER 26

Berwick

"The surface has now gone from motocross to smooth. The riders say it's excellent – not just our riders either!"

8th August

When I walk from the town centre towards Shielfield Park – home of Berwick Rangers Football Club and the Berwick F1 Finance (Scotland) Bandits – I get a vague sense of what it might feel like to be a salmon keen to spawn upstream. Though not exactly a flood, there's a good volume of Berwick Rangers fans walking away from the stadium. Their team have beaten Annan 2-1 to go top of the league since all their rivals drew. It's noticeable that there are almost no female fans amongst this stream of football supporters. Another contrast to a 'typical' Berwick speedway crowd is the noticeable number of overweight fans – some of them in tight-fitting replica tops – and a higher incidence of scarves. At the open gates by the turnstiles a man of few words barks, "Pit Gate!" It's a short distance away down the road that runs parallel to the length of the home-straight grandstand. A small queue of riders, mechanics and others wait patiently to enter the stadium. Since my last visit there's been a quiet revolution at the club. Long-time promoter Peter Waite has left and a new era dawned under ex-club sponsor John Anderson (of Anderson's Quality Butchers fame) and his business partner Lynda Waite (no relation to Peter). According to press reports and club evangelist Dick Barrie, the new management team have changed the organisation, infrastructure and attitude. Most significantly, John and Lynda retained many of the loyal volunteer staff that, along with Peter Waite, made Berwick speedway so welcoming in the past. They have also brought in ex-referee and ex-Hull co-promoter Dave Peet as team manager, appointed Ian Rae as track curator and kept the services of always helpful Dennis McCleary. He's got so many responsibilities for the Berwick Bandits (and Berwick Rangers) Dennis would need a sheaf of business cards if he attempted list all his job titles.

Talk of a new spirit and culture around the club is reflected in the much more spick and span first impression created by the pits area, the track and stadium in general. A helpful and chatty man in the pits extols the virtues of some of these changes. "The track isn't any wider – it just looks that way 'cause things have been smartened up!" The lush pristine football pitch that forms the centre green at Shielfield Park adds to the lustre of the uniquely coloured shale track that surrounds it. "The Edinburgh photographer [Jack Cupido] was here last week – 'cause he was on holiday – and he said the Hearts and Hibs pitches don't look so good!" While we talk, we also admire a new-looking tractor as it magic wheels (also a new investment) the light brown coloured shale on bend four before it continues slowly round the track hugging the inside line. "The farmer five minutes down the road lends us a tractor for the meetings. When we were at the old track and things went wrong with the tractors, he'd rush home for parts. He supports the local community as he sponsors the speedway and the football clubs." To the casual glance of someone untutored in the specifics of the stadium infrastructure changes, there's some new plastic seating in the home-straight grandstand, the safety fencing looks more robust, orange and white plastic crash barriers demarcate the pits-viewing area and, over by the turnstiles, there's a rather swish new programme booth positioned to overlook the first bend of the track. Though the wooden hut she used to occupy has been swept away by the tide of change, friendly programme seller Davina Johnston remains in situ and now sells a much more reasonably priced programme, "Aye, they're £2 now!"

The lure of tonight's clash between the Bandits and the Monarchs means I haven't seen the (comparatively nearby) friendly between Hearts and Sunderland at Tynecastle nor the Elite League Pairs staged at Eastbourne. With just over an hour and a half to go before the scheduled 7 p.m. start time, the bowser takes to the Shielfield Park shale to douse the surface. Stood by the referee's box at the back of the home-straight grandstand is tonight's SCB official, Dale Entwistle (who officiated last night at the Scotwaste Arena) in the company of trainee referee, Michael Breckon. Dale

and Michael will shortly head off to the pits to conduct the vital pre-meeting checks that form a key part of every SCB official's pre-meeting repertoire. Dale hasn't been to the Borders area for quite a while. "I stayed in Falkirk last night. It's my first Northern Tour in a few years and that's convenient for all three meetings. I'm not reffing tonight, it's Michael."
[Jeff] "I'm sure you'll both sort them out."
[Dale] "There's the added pressure that Dave Peet used to be a referee! He'll ring up and say 'Why don't you think of this?' and 'Why don't you think of that?' Of course, he used to be an assessor too – so that makes it all the more fun!"
[Michael] "I'm just here tonight and going to Peterborough on Thursday to see Graham Reeve and hopefully get rubber-stamped. Then I can get paid and get some petrol money. I haven't been able to do so many meetings as family and other things have come first. Darren Hartley [newly qualified referee] did a lot of meetings in succession."

While we talk, speedway turnstile operatives Muriel Ennis and Lacey Louden, scamper along the now obstruction-free ginnel that separates the grandstand from the safety fence. They nod to the impressive spray from the approaching bowser, "We can't stop 'cause we don't want a shower from the wetter!" When not studying or practising his new trade, Michael Breckon is a Middlesbrough Football Club fan. "I didn't renew my season ticket this season. I'm sick of it! Last night we drew 0-0 and there were all the usual excuses from Southgate. I haven't been enjoying it for years, if I'm honest. Even under McClaren we supposedly had our best ever years but the football was so dull and boring!" Dale interjects, "Have you heard about Norwich? My wife rang to say they were 4-0 down at half time. Fans were tearing up their season tickets in front of [manager] Bryan Gunn [in the dug-out] even some of the directors came down from the box to tell him what to do and had to be escorted away by the security! Amazing!" Dale is a long way away from his home in Colchester, "As we're there, we have to support them! They've got a new ground now but Layer Road still hasn't been built on – the recession hit, so it's not likely at the moment."

Berwick Bandits Speedway Club Limited director and co-promoter John Anderson arrives to survey the pre-meeting scene stood by the plastic security barriers that separate the pits from the public viewing area. Even these barriers are a sign of change at Shielfield since Linda and John spotted these on their travels to other tracks and, as soon as they held the reins of power at the club, they introduced this popular feature to the Berwick spectating experience. In one direction, there's the bustle of activity in the pits as riders and mechanics prepare and, in the other, the Bandits curatorial team continue to tend to the track surface. John's business is located in North Berwick, which always surprises southerners like myself to learn is some distance from Berwick-upon-Tweed. "12,000 people were in North Berwick for the Highland Games. It was pandemonium! August is our harvest so it's very, very busy. I started going to speedway way back in the Meadowbank days almost 50 years ago (I was 60 on Wednesday). I've been to speedway more or less continuously over that period of time. When I stopped going to Meadowbank, I followed Edinburgh to Coatbridge but it didn't have the same appeal to me. I had a bad accident in 1974 to my head and had concussion and this arm got all messed up. I spent six weeks in the house and I was frightened to go in the car and a friends said 'Come on, I'll take you out – come on, you're coming with me to the speedway'. The very first person I seen – the first rider – was my hero from Meadowbank days, Dougie Templeton![1] I've been every year since '74, except when we were at Barrow [track sharing in 1981]. For two years we were the main sponsor [Anderson's Quality Butchers]. Since we started, we've made some changes! We're aware but had no big insight into professional speedway, except things that were visible to the eye. Some nights the track was like a motocross, the place was uncared for and unloved. We've renewed all the [wooden safety] boards, the riders complained about the lights, well that's what they said to Lynda, and we've sorted that. We got 150 tons of shale! We got Ian Rae in as a track curator – one of the best – so the surface has now gone from motocross to smooth. The riders say it's excellent – not just our riders either! We've spent £4,000 upgrading the lighting system. We've got a new pole on the fourth bend with double lighting and we've got a new pole on the second bend. Each other pole now has an extra light. There's been lots of painting [points to the safety fence], we spent the whole weekend digging up roots and rubbish and we've added a new

[1] A glance at the racecard in the centre of the Bandits programme reveals every heat has a sponsor. The text by heat 13 reads, "Dougie Templeton – Thanks Berwick for the Memories."

Berwick: *"The surface has now gone from motocross to smooth. The riders say it's excellent – not just our riders either!"*

fence. We've thrown away bricks."[2]

"Our initial plan was to renew things and replace everything that's needed replacing. Our overall plan is, well, it would be nice to think we could bring a trophy to Berwick! Not short-term but long-term. We rent the ground from the Berwick Rangers supporters club. Peter never had a good relationship with them but we have a fantastic one! It's worked in our favour – they're so passionate to keep speedway, the people have been fantastic everyone has helped who could help. People have pulled together. The first day we asked for help with the boards, we had 30 people came along the next day and we had an average of 20 people from then on. I've been to every meeting this year, except King's Lynn, it was closer than the score [65-25] suggests. We made it quite clear that Ian Rae and Dennis McCleary – a referee for 10 years, fantastic man! – are the backbones. Dennis is also club secretary and on race nights, announcer, timekeeper and incident recorder. They know so much of the history and have the experience. Nothing's a bother to them. Without them life would have been more difficult. Along with Dave Peet, we reckon we've got the best team in the business. What Dave doesn't know about running a speedway team isn't worth knowing. He had 10 years as a ref too and 2 years as an assessor. A lot of the success is down to them. Okay, we came in with the finance and kept the place going but all these other guys have kept the place going too. Have you spoken to Lynda? She's brilliant, so enthusiastic. I couldn't pick a more brilliant business partner! The amount of time and effort she puts in behind the scenes is unbelievable! I promised I'd never go into a partnership but this is good! And, of course, Dick Barrie is our wordsmith on the centre green. Is there anyone better?" [3]

Ex club owner Peter Waite enjoyed a fascination with Poland and property investments there. He's not the only one with this inclination. Indeed, the rider in the Bandits number 4 race tabard tonight, Stanislaw Burza helped build John Anderson's house near Tarnow in Poland. Before I can ask, "Do you have to own at least one house in Poland to qualify to promote at Berwick?", John walks off to warmly greet some new arrivals.

Smooth as a baby's bottom

John Anderson

Start line

[2] Club captain Paul Clews offers his informed assessment of the situation via the pages of the *Speedway Star*. "Having joined Berwick midway through 2008, I noticed a few differences this year and made everything work for me. The promoters, John Anderson and Lynda Waite, were absolutely first-rate and there was a family atmosphere about the place. They were always looking at ways to encourage new people through the gates and it seems to have worked from what I can see. What we as a team gave back to the promoters and the supporters, was entertainment and a lot of winning ways I'd say. In truth, the track changed quite a lot this year and a lot of riders really rate it. Under Peter Waite last year, the track was wet and heavy and quite hard to ride, though I didn't think it was too bad. This year, though, it was smoother and slicker but with the dirt line on the outside. Not everyone liked that high line but that's a huge part of my game."

[3] John Anderson echoes some of these comments in an interview with Peter Oakes in the *Speedway Star*. "When we were involved as sponsors I tried to help Peter to do things to try and give a little to make things better. I could see where the downfalls were, the track was like a ploughed field some nights. I thought at times the track was dangerous, especially the second bend. Ian's changed all that, although he's still not happy with it yet, he keeps telling us it's still not finished! If you see the track now you wouldn't believe it's the same track. We've had people like Gary Havelock saying they like coming to Berwick ... Peter was a deep guy, you never really got to know much, he was very much a one-man band – we'll try to give it back to the community. I liken it to a merry-go-round. If some of the cogs are not working properly, you can sometimes have a rough ride. The things that had to be attended to first was the track, the safety fence and lighting. We couldn't have entertainment if the track was like a ploughed field. I'm not a millionaire or anything but I said to Lynda the extra money we had should be spent on lights ... if the product isn't right, you can't sell it. I think we are getting the product right but that's not down to me and Lynda it's because of other people – [names] Ian Rae, Dennis McCleary, Dick Barrie, Lawrence Heppell, Dave Peet and Phil and Julie Newton.

When the turnstiles open there's quite a rush to the main home-straight grandstand to find favoured seats. There's also quite a large contingent of Edinburgh fans who've come along to enjoy the rejuvenated Shielfield Park experience. The consensus sounds somewhat pessimistic about the Monarchs prospects for success this evening. "We don't go to so many away meetings anymore. The Sheffield fans by us [last night] got very excited at one point thinking that Sheffield were going to win! Especially when Edinburgh had so many passengers: Byron Bekker and Max Dilger – though he might go well here this evening as they have big tracks in Germany. I bet Armadale is a bit of a shock to the system! Why was Paul Cooper in Heat 14? [I explain the plan]. Whatever the plan was, knocking into the fence on bend three and stopping the race to turn a 3-3 into a 5-1 wasn't what was needed!"

Over the speaker system the dulcet tones of Dick Barrie welcome fans to the stadium and treat us to a number of housekeeping announcements. "When you come through the gate, you can buy the best value speedway programme in Britain!" All British speedway clubs depend upon their sponsorship as well as their gate revenues to survive. Ever professional, Dick decides to name-check the complete range of products and services provided by Bandits heat sponsors [4] along with tonight's meeting sponsor: Gary Young and Friends. The only heat sponsors who don't have a product to sell are Maureen and Peter Blackie and, of course, the aforementioned Dougie Templeton who "Thanks Berwick for the Memories". If cleanliness is next to godliness then tidiness still ranks pretty highly, "If you have any rubbish tonight, please put it in the receptacles because it's a condition of our use of the stadium and, picking it up at quarter to 11, isn't much fun!" Announcements over, though in his 60th summer of speedway Dick still exudes vim, vigour and enthusiasm for what he does. Initial announcements completed, Dick bounds up to my display table, "Here I am panting up to see you."
[Jeff] "The crowds look appreciably bigger."
[Dick] "But are they any happier though?"
[Jeff] "I couldn't say!"
[Dick rejects a prepared sheet I tried to hand him on *Quantum of Shale*] "I don't need that I've read it."
[Jeff] "You're one of the few!"
[Dick] "If you can come and talk to me later that would be nice – if not, you'll get a bad review next year!"

No meeting at Shielfield Park would truly be complete without the presence of Edinburgh taxi driver, Berwick Bandits fan and speedway obsessive Jim Brykajlo who's here tonight without his son Steven ("He's away with the trains on a four-day jaunt to Scunthorpe and Doncaster"). Similarly to the Edinburgh fans, Jim downplays the strength of the Berwick Bandits line-up. "Carl Wilkinson got 3 last night which is crap and he's our guest tonight 'cause [Josef] Franc's away riding in a Czech Best Pairs Championship better known as the Czech Hoover Championship." Edinburgh fan Maurice (pronounced More-reece) reports in to say, "I didn't read any of your book last night; I was watching the cricket highlights."
[Jim] "Australia is 300 ahead and England 80 for 4."
[Maurice] "80 for 5!" [both laugh]
[Jim] "The crowds have been up here all season."
[Matthew Platten] "The local derby always gets four-figure crowds."
[Maurice] "Who's going to win the battle of the Germans tonight?"
Dick Barrie announces over the tannoy that a "silver Peugeot is blocking a nearby driveway".
[Maurice] "I know how mad I would be if I came out to find my driveway blocked!"
[Jim] "I can tell you exclusively that Thomas Jonasson [who recently left the Monarchs to return to his native Sweden] will sign for a mid-week Elite League track next season. Who'd want to go to Edinburgh on a Friday night when you can be on the Continent?!"

[4] There's quite a selection of sponsors and these include: Nissan-Suzuki-Vauxhall in Berwick and Alnwick; there's Blackshaws Garages. You could do worse than to 'check out Cara House' for bed and breakfast or the Berwick Wedding Parlour in Castlegate. A1 Cabs offer a 'Prompt Reliable Service'; Cameron Lowrie is definitely yer man for 'All Types of Fencing'. You can 'Travel in Style' with Waits Coaches. If the renowned fish and chips at the always Robert Smith 'Quality Takeaway' aren't for you (it would be silly to deny yourself) after the meeting then there's always the 'authentic' Hong Kong Chop Suey House Chinese Takeaway. John and Tricia can help you become much more proficient at the City School of Motorcycling. For a rare example of sponsor synergy, you could go to Ideal Carpets and get the 'Best Choice at Best Prices (WE SELL BEDS NOW)' and then later call into the 'Specialist Carpentry and Upholstery Cleaning Technicians' at Dry Fusion. In fact you're completely spoilt for choice on the carpet front since Jim Youngman Carpets have 'Carpets and Beds for Every Budget'. You can hire unspecified machines and get your 'Groundworks Priced' at AGF Plant (Drew Fiddes).

Berwick: *"The surface has now gone from motocross to smooth. The riders say it's excellent – not just our riders either!"*

Away on the centre green, close by the start line, both sets of riders line up next to their bikes. Dick Barrie does the rider-parade introductions, "Let's meet the victims, the Premier League champions – the Scotwaste Monarchs!" He greets the riders in descending race tabard order and it's not long before you can almost visualise tanks and barbed wire, "Another one! This is getting like Poland in 1939. Meet Max Dilger!" A few moments later, sight of Monarchs reserve Byron Bekker fails to prompt any thoughts of apartheid or Nelson Mandela's prison food for Dick, so he contents himself with a more traditional observation, "A rider who always gives of his best!" Edinburgh have also brought along their number 8 this evening, Johnny Grey (though he doesn't get to ride). When I express concern to Jim Brykajlo that, with Andrew Tully injured, the Monarchs line-up has a slightly weakened look, he retorts, "I don't care, they have no sympathy for us!" With his enviable knowledge of the sport, Jim is more obsessed with records. "Michal Makovsky needs 122 points to become the all-time top points scorer for Berwick, overtaking Steve McDermott who's presently the all-time top scorer. Steve's got something like 3,200 points."

By the start/finish line, Dick Barrie conducts the ceremonial toss of the coin for gate positions between team captains Paul Clews and Matthew Wethers with the levity usually reserved for a pantomime, "Wake up, Matty, wake up!" "Heads" "That's a tail, Matty!" Berwick choose gates one and three. Jim notes resignedly, "Dick Barrie's in time warp!" Monarchs number 1 Ryan Fisher comfortably sees off Bandits guest Carl Wilkinson to win heat 1 with ease. Dick's pleased with what is probably speedway's equivalent of a quick flash of knicker by a can-can girl, "and, for me, the real pleasure of that win for Ryan is that his green helmet slipped to reveal a white helmet! Why can't we have white helmet colours anymore?" The Bandits immediately hit back with a 4-2 to tie the scores at 6 each after an impressive Tero Aarnio rode with aggression into the first corner to emerge in the lead. Stan Burza wins the third race and, with Paul Clews ahead of big track-expert-in-waiting, Max Dilger, the Bandits enjoy a narrow lead. One pleasure of speedway at Shielfield Park is the opportunity to stand on the grass and concrete banked terraces that overlook the exit of the second bend. Not only does it provide an excellent panoramic view of the whole vista of the circuit but you're ideally positioned to watch the start-line and the vital first-bend action. After three races without hint of a pass, I ask evangelical Bandits fan Jim Brykajlo, "Will we see any overtaking tonight?" He believes there is some probability, "We might see Clews try a couple – the track's too slick!" In his report on the meeting for the *Speedway Star* Keith Hamblin would remark, "The racing was fast and furious, but passing was virtually impossible".

At the start of the fourth race the riders get no further than the first bend before trainee referee Michael Breckon slaps on the red lights to stop the race. It's a decision that appears to exasperate presenter Dick Barrie, if judged by the exagerated way he holds his arms out wide (then, again, he might be a keen angler). The rerun sees Tero Aarnio and Michal Rajkowski alongside each other as they exit the second bend until Rajkowski tries an attempted shove. It's one of the dark arts of speedway gamesmanship or, would be, except Aarnio refuses to be shoved aside. Encountering an immovable object and, probably, not anticipating this rebuff, the effort involved causes Rajkowski to fall peculiarly on the banked incline of the third bend. The manner of Tero Aarnio's rebuff certainly impressed the Berwick fans in my section, almost as much as they enjoy the sight of Michal Makovsky cross the finish line closely followed by Aarnio. After 12 meetings without a win against the Monarchs, joyous celebration is understandable but somewhat premature. Ryan Fisher wins the next race (heat 5) comfortably, while behind him a fascinating battle rages between Stan Burza and Michal Rajkowski. Third-placed Burza repeatedly threatens an overtake on the fourth bend of each lap. First time round the threat is there but poses no danger. On the second lap, Rajkowski looks inside as he exits the bend and the fractional loss of momentum this causes nearly proves costly. Another fourth-bend charge is repelled on the third lap and, just when it looks like we'll see Burza again fail to swoop past Rajkowski, he finally manages to win their dash to the line and, thereby, deprives Edinburgh of their maximum heat advantage by the width of a wheel. If the loss of the second-place point isn't quite enough to make a grown man weep it, nonetheless, provokes one of the Monarchs fans to gloomily claim, "Only Fisher will win a race here tonight!" Though with some possible merit, this forecast only lasts until the second bend of heat 6 when the yellow-helmeted Aaron Summers overtakes Carl Wilkinson at the very same moment that his green-helmeted teammate Mathew Wethers executes a similar manoeuvre on the inside. It's the turn of another exasperated fan (this time from Berwick) to cry out, "Why pick Wilkinson? He can't gate against a team of gaters!" I don't like to intrude on private grief, but can't help myself so have to point out that he did gate, "Wilkinson actually led". Though factually correct it's not a point of view that gains favour, "He was mid-track when he should be by the fence to block them!" [5] Another Berwick fan disagrees, "If he'd moved across he'd have had them off!" Clearly unable to concede any argument, even when wrong, he retorts, "Phil Morris would!"

While the Bandits fans bicker amongst themselves and contemplate how a 6-point lead after four races fritters away by the sixth, Jim Brykajlo has Paul Cooper on his mind. "He'll come here and be brilliant, he'll do well at Glasgow but all he does at Armadale is fall on his arse!" One of life's great pleasures is to remind others of their misfortune. Some enjoy it silently but not the Monarchs fan with the theatrically loud voice, "I think they [Berwick] were conned by William Lawson who wanted to go to Glasgow but he had too high an average for them to fit him in!" If overtakes are a rarity at Shielfield Park tonight, then there's no lack of entertainment from the bump and grind. Heat 7 is a case in point when Max Dilger shows trackcraft and aggression as he changes racing line to block Luke Priest's blast round the outside. Priest suddenly finds himself pinched up against the fence as they exit the second bend and, forced to shut off momentarily, Dilger escapes to claim his first ever away point (paid 2) in a Monarchs tabard. The Bandits German national Frankie Facher looks off the pace and out of sorts but, luckily for the Bandits, their tungsten-tough, hard-riding reserve Tero Aarnio races to his third (full or paid) win of the night. If modesty, pessimism, and gamesmanship dictates that Monarchs fans play down their chances of yet another victory at Shielfield Park, then heat 9 confirms that it might well not be their night. Stan Burza rides an aggressive first and second bend to streak away for a comfortable win by over half a lap and, thereby, equals the second fastest time ever round Shielfield Park (only 0.2 of a second outside the record set by Sean Wilson in 1999). Surprisingly for a non-informed neutral like me, Bandits captain Paul Clews also gives no quarter on the first bend and proceeds to dominate the often rambunctious Ryan Fisher. Despite the continued lack of overtaking, this was the race of the night (so far)! The much-heralded "Battle of the Germans" completely fails to materialise in heat 10 when Tero Aarnio replaces Frankie Facher. Carl Wilkinson again shoots from the tapes and continues up front to justify his selection as a guest with a race win. Behind him, Tero Aarnio zooms through an extremely small gap as he exits the second bend and holds off Matthew Wethers for the rest of the race.

Another joy of my book promotion tours is that, occasionally, I'm invited to the centre green. I'm not so keen on the interviews but the chance to watch any speedway race from there is truly exhilarating and wonderful! I'm privileged to be able to witness tonight's heat 11 duel between Michal Makovsky (off gate 1) and Ryan Fisher (gate 2) from this unique vantage point and enjoy the different perspective it gives on the race action. Dick Barrie tees up the likely lively action beforehand, "Fisher and Makovsky, they're at each other like Rangers and Celtic. They're sporting in their own way however, although their jousts usually involve elbows and might even end up with one or the other down and out -- they'll come and pick each other up, and always, always shake hands after their races!" Watched from the centre green, the race is brilliantly exciting. Makovsky rides his bike in a manner that suggests he's a cross between a gymnast and a jockey. Michal frequently alters his body position to change his weight distribution on the bike to ring out the maximum speed from his machine. His manoeuvre round the banked third and fourth bends (on the third lap) stands out for its potent mix of daring and skill. Michal initially tries to blast round the top of the banking but, when he finds that avenue past blocked, he shuts off dramatically and so has to suddenly throw out his leg to counterbalance the g-force of this sudden manoeuvre to steady himself enough to stay on his bike. It's poetry in motion. The bare facts of the race are that he finishes third behind race winner Ryan Fisher and his teammate Michal Rajkowski but, that said, the speed he generates while he gymnastically dances-cum-glides around his bike is poetic to witness. People often claim to me that they have the best job in speedway but, surely, anyone who gets to watch the racing from the centre green on a regular basis does really enjoys a privilege that must be hard to ever become jaundiced about!

Not only has 2009 seen a 20 per cent reduction in the price of the Berwick programme but expectations about the quality of said product have changed dramatically too. Dennis McCleary draws everyone's attention to tonight's collection for the Speedway Riders' Benevolent Fund and then follows it with a statement on behalf of the club, "We apologise for the resolution of the printing on page 2 of the programme." Dick Barrie concludes his centre-green interview with the recommendation that everyone purchase my latest book, something he renames as "*Quantum of Speedway*". If the result of heat 11 suggests a possible Monarchs fightback, then the team, management and fans are quickly disabused of this idea in heat 12 by another win from Tero Aarnio (to take his points tally to paid 15 from five

[5] So, he should have shouted, "Why pick Wilkinson? He rides mid track against a team of riders who can pass on the inside or outside!". This doesn't quite have the same ring about it.

rides). He's closely followed home by Paul Clews, while Max Dilger gets a consolation point for the Monarchs to further extend his personal points tally to paid 3 from four rides. After four successive 5-1s (three of them for the Bandits), the 40-32 scoreline still offers possible hope of a Monarchs fightback. However, the choice of Edinburgh pair for heat 13 – Ryan Fisher with Byron Bekker – either indicates all hope is lost or, from a more cynical/tactical point of view, that Edinburgh wish to 'fall' enough points behind to use a tactical option. When Ryan Fisher finishes behind Michal Makovsky, their 10 point deficit allows Monarchs wily co-promoter and team manager, John Campbell, to send out Matthew Wethers in the black-and-white helmet colour for the penultimate race of the night. Mathematically a 8-1 heat advantage followed by a 5-1 could give Edinburgh an unlikely 46-47 win but this possible scenario is immediately wrecked when Stan Burza wins his third race of the night.

So many changes have been wrought at Shielfield Park Stadium that even the catering vehicle has undergone a significant make-over. As a steady stream of satisfied customers departs to the burger van, one man with a burger and a chop advises, "That's my idea of a balanced diet!" GRT Media supremo, Bob Tasker draws my attention to something I might have otherwise missed, "You will notice a big difference here – there might not be tons of overtaking but there's many less crashes!!" Preparations for the last race of the Premier League meeting are put on hold after the wonder-wheel jumps off the back of the tractor about five yards ahead of gate three. Dick Barrie makes a virtue of this mechanical failure, "What about that? A wonder-wheel that can jump off the tractor by itself!" Davina Johnston takes a phlegmatic view, "I like to see overtaking, there's not so much of that! Some of these southern boys come out of the gate – like Ben Barker last week – and they're gone! That's not racing when they're off and away! It's much better here but I like to see overtaking." While the track staff struggle with the beached wonder-wheel Dick Barrie takes it upon himself to explain the miracle of speedway scoring (one race from the end of the meeting) and concludes his analysis, "It's a bit like cricket, actually!" Somewhat obsessed with the recent record of the Monarchs ("we race our bogey team – you read the programme, it's in there!"), Dick excitedly shares his joy that the Bandits finally win their first home fixture against the Monarchs since their 52-38 Premier Trophy victory in March 2007. "It's the first time the Bandits have beaten the Monarchs in 12 meetings!" When heat 15 eventually gets underway, Ryan Fisher wins but the heat is drawn. Second-placed Stan Burza demonstrates his donuting ability afterwards, while Dick Barrie chortles, "For the Monarchs fans on the back straight, you must be gritting your teeth and Stan's got a small celebration for you!" Moments after, Dennis McCleary runs through the final racecard. The Bandits stars of the night are Tero Aarnio [paid 16], Stan Burza [paid 13] and Michal Makovsky [paid 12]. Ryan Fisher top scores for the Monarchs ably supported by Matthew Wethers [paid 12]. A man of generous spirit who believes praise should be given where praise is due, Dennis McCleary informs us, "In fact the whole meeting was controlled by Michael Breacons – a probationary referee – and what a good job he did!" Predictably enough Tero Aarnio is nominated as the "most entertaining" rider of the night. On the centre green Dick Barrie speaks to the person next to him but accidentally broadcasts his ruminations over the stadium loudspeaker system, "And what's the presenter's name? Jevon? Oh, yes, Jevon!"

Far away in Hertfordshire, Rye House stage a double-header fixture against King's Lynn and Birmingham. Dennis McCleary leaves us in no doubt that he's bemused, "That match at Rye House versus Birmingham will be starting at 5 past 9. Goodness me! You'll be home before the result of that one!" Graham Platten's son Matthew provides me with a matter-of-fact update on his dad's Motor Neurone Disease. "Oh, he's alright! [then, in a way it says he's definitely not] he has his good days and his bad days. He struggles to walk and get up and down stairs. He has a stick now and he's more confident with that. He loves coming here and he's desperate to go to Scunthorpe [with Bob Tasker]." [6]

Monarchs fan Karen Kelly discounts the significance of tonight's defeat in the context of tomorrow's local derby fixture

[6] Sadly Graham lost his fight against Motor Neurone Disease on 10th December 2009. Graham was track photographer at Shielfield from 2000 until the end of the 2008 season when he gave up his familiar role on the centre green and that of trackshop franchisee due to his illness. Dennis McCleary officially commented: "On behalf of everyone involved with Berwick, from the promotion to the riders, officials and staff we express our sincere condolences to Christine and all the family following Graham's passing today. We all knew he was not in the best of health and only yesterday Colin Poole and Michal Makovsky visited Graham in hospital at South Tyneside. To receive news of his death today was a hammer blow. Those who had the pleasure to know Graham Platten as a friend and to work with him through speedway will know what we mean when we say he was a gentleman, a genuine family man who loved his sport, particularly Berwick speedway. In all my years of being involved in the sport at Shielfield I can honestly say I have not met a more decent man." Tributes poured into the electronic Book of Condolence on the club website. Graham's niece Natalie Platten posts a message in response to the many respondents: "My Uncle Graham was a great man, I always knew that, though what I didn't know was how many lives he had touched. He was a very talented photographer but, more importantly, he was a real family man. Nothing was ever too much trouble for him. My heart is with his five children who he should be so proud off and Christine his loving wife who he was so happy with. Everyone always says the best ones go first. This really was the case with Graham."

with the Glasgow Tigers. "You can carry one rider but not two! I'm not looking forward to going to Glasgow for tomorrow. That's one place I hate to go to and lose! We looked through the back issues of the *Speedway Star* and saw Dilger has scored quite well in Poland!" Mike Hunter's primary concern is with the ongoing deleterious impact the late season fixture pile up inflicts upon man and machine. "The team's falling apart due to circumstances – it's become an endurance test! The German's [Dilger] not up to much. Dunno how riders can beat Elite League riders in Germany and look so out of sorts here? It can't be that different!"

Despite the strict time curfew at Shielfield Park Stadium, nonetheless, the Berwick promotion stage a Berwick Borderers versus Edinburgh Wildcats Junior Challenge meeting over six heats (that the programme advertises as Berwick Borderers v. Team Viking). The home side run out comprehensive victors 20-10. It transpires that Johnny Grey isn't really the Edinburgh number 8 (or, then again since this is speedway, actually might be) but rides for Berwick. Either way, he definitely wears the number 2 race tabard for the Berwick Borderers. In the number 3 tabard is the exotically named Hungarian Tamas Sike, whose surname is bound to cause pronunciation problems when his career takes off (pronounced Si-Kay). Not only does the junior challenge provide harum scarum entertainment and give valuable track time for the youngsters but it also gives trainee referee Michael Breckon further opportunity to hone his judicial decision-making. "This ref is very strict, I dunno who he is, but before the start he made all the stewards clear the kids from by the start gate before he would allow the meeting to start! We've never had a ref do that!"

8th August Berwick v. Edinburgh (Premier League) 51-41

CHAPTER 27

Glasgow

"It's one of the safest safety fences in Britain but, now, we'll go to some music!"

9th August

The dark clouds in an otherwise bright sky over Saracen Park visibly signals that the forecast of later showers probably will dampen the eagerly awaited Premier League clash between the Glasgow Tigers and the Edinburgh Scotwaste Monarchs. Tigers co-promoter Alan Dick is in upbeat mood, "Last time you were here [versus King's Lynn] we had two guests and rider replacement. This time we're stronger! Edinburgh aren't at their best but they do have Ryan Fisher, Michal Rajkowski and Matty Wethers who all go well round here. I'm not so sure about Byron Bekker or their German rider!" Friendly programme seller Adam Stokes also takes comfort from the Monarchs line-up this afternoon. "Andrew Tully did badly the first time he ever rode here but, every time he's come since, he's got better and better so I don't think rider replacement is so good for them."

The turnstiles won't open for at least another hour so those already inside Ashfield Stadium are here to work. Invariably the first rider to arrive in the pits prior to almost any Tigers meeting is their popular 39-year-old Australian captain Shane Parker. Shane's a man who leads by example and deservedly enjoys great respect from the Glasgow faithful for his approach both on and off the track. After the meeting he would tell Dennis McQuade, "I got there early, as I always do, and I go round the track to see if there're any subtle changes we can make to help with the entertainment level and then all the focus goes on the meeting." Everyone has their particular race-day tasks to complete so I retreat to sit out of the way in the completely empty home-straight grandstand that overlooks the start line. It's the ideal vantage point from which to observe the various comings and goings within the stadium. After a run of meetings when the Monarchs have been far stronger on their visits to Saracen Park, there's a genuine air of anticipation and even a couple of frisky Husky dogs need to be calmed down when they arrive. With the turnstiles still closed, the first person to arrive in the 400-seater grandstand is a man who says, "Excuse me, you're in my seat!" Down below us, Glasgow co-promoter Gordon Pairman passes in deep earnest mobile phone conversation. When Gordon returns, he shares the theoretical template of a made-to-measure speedway rider. "We all know the ideal anatomical shape of a speedway rider – small head and big balls to give them balance and fire power! As they get older, it reverses and they get bigger heads to do more thinking and smaller balls. It's not a good combination! In Paul Bentley's last season he changed his bikes, engine tuners, set-ups, everything! It wasn't the machine – it was his head where the problem was! You can see it in a rider. He'd be in the corner and he'll just have throttled off a fraction. They should retire then! It's not a good approach for anyone. There comes a point when a rider needs to think clearly about their future and whether they still really want to ride speedway. What was Berwick like last night?"
[Jeff] "I saw an amazing race from the centre green and the acrobatic skill on his bike from Makovsky was really something!"
[Gordon] "Yes, it's a totally different perspective! You notice lots of things you don't see from the terraces. How close they get, the speed and the skill on the bike!"

Gordon departs towards the Speedway Office that's housed in a white-walled building adjacent to the third and fourth bends. Men diligently clean its shale-splattered windows to ensure that there's an uninterrupted view from the bar and seating areas during later. The red warning light klaxon is tested and emits a sound like a bagpipe. Presenter and PR guru Michael Max is clearly well schooled in the Coarse Art of Speedway Gamesmanship if judged by the additional psychological pressure he subtly tries to pile upon the Monarchs Ashfield German debutant Max Dilger during the rider parade. "So 3 points in three days for Max Dilger!" Though we can't be sure if Max Dilger suffers from any self-doubt prior to his second ever Premier League away meeting, Michael Max definitely obliquely places a finger on his psychological scales. Due to Derek Sneddon's absence from the 2009 version of the Edinburgh Monarchs, the mantle of this afternoon's pantomime villain for the home faithful passes to their combative, talismanic number 1, Ryan Fisher. Michael introduces Ryan in the full knowledge of his box office impact, "One of the most entertaining and hardest riders around. He's always good to watch!" The crowd need no first invitation to greet him with boos.

The Shane Parker track tweaks pay immediate dividends when he wins heat 1 by an absolute street to set a new track record of 56.2 seconds! Behind him the Monarchs pack the minor places. Heat 2 sees Aaron Summers emerge victorious ahead of Lee Dicken and Mitchell Davey in another shared heat to keep the scores tied. Michael Max decides to double underline the nature of Shane's achievement, "This season Shane Parker has taken 0.9 seconds off the track record!" It's a milestone that deserves some form of additional celebration and, fortunately at this afternoon's meeting (and next weekend's A-Plant Classic), selected members of the Blok Professional Dance Troupe are on hand to commemorate Shane's record with a few nifty moves. They also double up as start-line girls. The Stars Supporters Group extended the invitation to the Blok Professional Dance Troupe. It's impossible not to notice them stood by the start line before the first race and, in a noncommittal voice Michael Max, tells us they'll be "Doubling up as start-line girls and also giving us some dance moves this week and next week." There's a brief silence before announcer Jim Coyle MBE – who has a soothing voice that deserves extensive radio work – chivvies the centre-green announcer from his vantage point in the referee's box, "Michael Max, oh come on, you can give them a bigger welcome than that!" Oblivious to this banter, the girls stand expectantly in formation poised in readiness for the music to start. Over the stadium loudspeaker system, Jim Coyle explains the delay to them, "Girls, I've been advised that the DJ isn't actually gonna play the music unless you're on the grass!" Keen to showcase their dance moves to the crowd (and the close by, vigilant Michael Max) even when the rain and next race starts, the dance troupe absentmindedly forget their start-line duties as they're lost in their flamboyant choreography. Indeed, they continue to dance long after the music stops and the third heat is well underway. They eventually break off their performance because Matthew Wethers provides a natural pause when he comes to grief on the fourth bend with the Tigers apparently set fair for maximum heat advantage. Whenever there's a crash, Michael Max is always a keen bystander and loves to temporarily don his imaginary white coat. With the rain in evidence (15 minutes into the meeting), Michael seamlessly adds some meteorological expertise to his phantom repertoire of medical skills, "It's raining at the moment but the sky looks bright!" With Matthew Wethers disqualified by referee Dale Entwistle as the primary cause of the stoppage, the three remaining riders come back to the start line in light drizzle. Slightly undermining his meteorological expertise, Michael sounds a note of misplaced optimism, "The rain has just about ceased in its entirety," and, as if keenest to convince himself, he then immediately erroneously adds, "there are bright skies!" Speedway's version of Sod's Law for once doesn't apply because the Tigers take up where they left off to record a comfortable maximum ahead of the lone Monarch, Max Dilger. A moist shale surface makes their collective progress much more of a struggle than usual as they slip and slither round the circuit. Massively experienced as a presenter, Michael has a ready-drafted euphemism on the tip of his tongue, "Riding conditions look a little difficult as the shale moves about and the riders go from wet to dry!" Quite what the Blok Professional Dance Troupe make of their first three heats of speedway remains unasked but, with no brollies and only one fleece between them, they adhere to a commendable 'the show must go on' ethos as they dance through the heavy drizzle only Michael believes has ceased. In these conditions, riders with greater experience and/or load-weight ratios usually cope better with slippery conditions. In spite of drizzle-induced poor visibility, James Grieves ignores the conditions to vanquish Aaron Summers in the fourth race. Behind them on the last bend of the third lap, Lee Dicken looks over his shoulders in both directions but can't find any sign of South African Monarch Byron Bekker who's three-quarters of a lap away after a slithering fall and remount.

With the meeting 13 minutes old, the rain stops but the track's already altered dramatically from the almost pristine conditions that enabled Shane Parker to set a new track record in heat 1. The first attempt to run heat 5 sees William Lawson move at the start but manage not to touch the tapes while, moments later, Ryan Fisher takes a spectacular tumble that Dale Entwistle adjudicates as first-bend bunching. Given a second chance to compete, Ryan Fisher makes no mistake in the rerun. Behind him Lawson pressures Rajkowski for three laps but, despite his best efforts, can't pass to confirm that overtaking will be at a premium this afternoon now that the track has taken on water. If rain can be talked away, Michael Max is the man to do it. Just as it starts to slightly spit on again Michael tells us, "Okay, ladies and gentlemen, the weather has now passed and it looks brighter in the distance!" Between races Michael conducts the Glasgow Tigers equivalent of the World Cup draw to randomly decide which riders will be supported by which sponsor for next weekend's Ashfield Classic. "James Grieves will be sponsored by James Grieves senior – that's appropriate!" Eking out the mystery and drama of the situation, Michael prefaces each draw with theatrical aplomb, "A good friend of Glasgow's speedway [pause] not, Andre Compton!" Speedway still awards bonus points in order to encourage team riding between riders (when they finish behind a colleague who's either won the race or finished second). Sadly, though a financial incentive exists for cooperation, the old-fashioned art of team riding no longer appears to have the coherency it once did in this contemporary era of slick tracks with its highly tuned "race for the flag" modern style of speedway bikes. Nonetheless, Shane Parker gives a master-class in this neglected art after he allows his teammate Josh Grajczonek to pass him on the exit of the second bend of heat 6 and proceeds to shepherd him home for the next three and a half laps.[1] Michael Max delights in this display of skill as well as the 5-1 heat advantage. Though yet to get a confirmed place in the programme schedules, we learn that the BBC's Gaelic language television station have chosen this afternoon to visit Saracen Park. "BBC Alba are doing quite a bit of filming this afternoon which will hopefully get a slot so we can see it soon!"

Blok Professional Dance Troupe

Heat 7 features a win for James Grieves and a second successive third place for Max Dilger who, this time, actually beats an opponent in order to gain his point. It's another small step in his speedway apprenticeship. Rain sprinkles the track for five minutes before it stops again. I've moved to watch the action from the back straight. It's too slippy to venture up the steep grass slope to watch from where the riders' vans park so, instead, I stand on the grass banking that overlooks the slightly worn section of concrete terracing and the safety stanchions. Before the eighth race of the afternoon, Michael Max explains the purpose of this afternoon's pending Speedway Riders' Benevolent Fund collection, ("for riders who've fallen on bad times or injury"). He then effortlessly segues into a name check for sponsors of heat 8 – David McAllen Spares and Service – "that's a case in point, a rider out through injury due to actions of [pause] I'm not going there!" Without a point to his name, Byron Bekker must have misunderstood all this talk of "fallen" speedway riders because he immediately showcases a virtuoso slow-motion fall on the apex of the third and fourth bend. Attracted by the grace of his encounter with the shale, I nearly don't notice that the Huskies try to eat my food! Heat 9 starts with great drama between the Monarchs partnership of Ryan Fisher and Aaron Summers. Aaron is first into the bend and drifts wide while, behind him, Ryan Fisher suddenly decides to attempt to dash round the outside of his partner through a completely nonexistent gap. Immediately finding nowhere to go, Ryan uses all his skill to stay on his bike as it bumps and bores as though he's riding over speed bumps. The loss of speed this near-miss encounter causes instantly creates a huge second bend gap for William Lawson and Mitchell Davey to exploit. They need no second invitation to hit fresh air ahead of their rivals. Completely and comprehensively fourth, Ryan indulges in a few

Riders viewing area

Shane Parker & fallen boy

[1] Afterwards Shane would tell the *Speedway Star*, "I've always prided myself in doing my bit for the team and it was good to be able to help Josh round. He is not quite right after his fall last week and he possibly has a broken finger, so he was not as quick as he usually is, so I decided to settle in behind him and ensure we got the maximum points from that heat."

theatrical glances down at his machine in a manner that would definitely pass an examination at mime school. We all clearly get the signal that Ryan is about to have a real or imaginary mechanical interlude with his bike and so it proves. After the race, when Aaron arrives at the pit lane gate at the edge of the slope that leads up towards the Ashfield Stadium pits area, he discovers Ryan Fisher spontaneously forms his own unofficial one-man welcome committee. This involves briefly going helmet to helmet with his teammate before Ryan thinks better of it! Barely able to keep the glee from his voice, like everyone else in the stadium, Michael watches the Monarchs square up and realises that the team spirit required for a fightback has, just possibly, taken a fatal dent. "Well, Ryan's got a difference of opinion with Aaron over that one – but, it's a living!" Quite what manoeuvre Ryan thought he was about to pull off when Aaron clearly already clearly occupied the outside line, is open to conjecture but, by his actions, Ryan again demonstrates the passionate approach he takes to his successful speedway career. Few would agree with his allocation blame in this instance but no one would gainsay Ryan's robust desire for success. [2]

Until the second bend of Heat 10 Matthew Wethers looks as if he might best Shane Parker until the Australian overtakes with imperious ease and wins by well over a quarter of a lap. If people wagered on the outcome of heat 11, they probably wouldn't predict that Michal Rajkowski would telepathically block the repeated charges of James Grieves round the outside of bends one and two on laps two, three and four. In a black-and-white helmet colour, Ryan Fisher's also keen to overtake James Grieves. Ryan champs at the bit until – on the transition from bend one to bend two on the last lap – he rides a very, very wide line that, consequently, as the track narrows after the exit from the bend, causes him to clatter into the safety fence with massive impact. The fence stops Ryan but the velocity of his acceleration and its impact flings the bike rag doll-like toward the crowd. Mercifully, his bike stops short of the fans when it hits a wall and then lies forlornly on the steps. Shane Parker easily wins the sprint to Ryan's side. The incident looks serious. Ryan's wife Daelyn and baby are quickly out there along with fellow riders, track staff and medics. Anji Parker is also dashes there quickly to offer advice and support to Daelyn. The damaged bike is retrieved from over the safety fence and carried back single-handedly by trackman Danny Gibb. [3] Tigers fan Jim Fleming isn't surprised by the crash, "Fisher took a real one there! He tries too hard – he does that all the time!" Announcer Jim Coyle informs the crowd, "It shows you the safety fence does its job and it's one of the safest safety fences in Britain but, now, we'll go to some music!"

Because of this crash, the interval arrives one heat early though the SRBF collection continues as planned. The Blok Professional Dance Troupe are interviewed and reveal that the troupe comprises 14 girls in all. They dance at an extensive list of events much too mysterious to list at length here as well as a slew of charity events ("most of us combine it with other jobs!"). The girls come from many different parts of Scotland (and Sunderland). Kerry, Nicola, Laura and Samantha dance for the crowd this weekend, while next a different four members from the troupe will entertain. Michael asks the girls one of his trademark closed questions that already presumes its answer. "What do you think of these nutcases?" prompts the reply, "It's been fantastic! It's speedway, I actually love speedway!" The steel shoe-shod riders wander throughout the stadium crowd with assorted helmet covers that serve as their collection buckets. Shane works his way pitwards picking his way carefully through the crowd on the weed-strewn back-straight terraces with his blue helmet cover in hand. A young boy runs past him oblivious but, an instant later, painfully falls full length onto the unforgiving concrete surface. Without hesitation Shane dashes alongside him – again he's first to the fallen – picks the young boy up, kneels next to him and holds him. Shane ostentatiously inspects his arms for injuries to calm and comfort the boy. What a man! Consideration and common humanity is clearly intuitive for Shane. It's subsequently no surprise to learn that he takes the boy to the pits to ensure the signatures of the riders of both teams fill his autograph book. How many other speedway riders would immediately think to do this?

On the centre green in front of the home-straight grandstand Michael apologises for his interjection ("as the Ronettes were singing some beautiful music!") before he conducts another interview – this time with Tigers co-promoter and

[2] Mike Hunter's race reports in the *Speedway Star* and on the Edinburgh Monarchs website are always characterised by the eloquence of their writing, the measured subtexts of his descriptions and the pithiness of his point of view. Mike describes this incident as follows: "A mix up between Ryan Fisher and Aaron Summers on the first bend of heat 9 cost them a likely 5-1 there and descended into embarrassment when they had a public disagreement after the race."

[3] Robin Goodall describes this incident in his *Speedway Star* report, "In an effort to better his position, [Ryan Fisher] went too fast round the first and second bends. He was pulled towards the fence and crashed spectacularly coming off the second turn. He was sent tumbling to the ground while his machine was catapulted over the fence, being stopped by the retaining wall from reaching the crowd. It was a frightening looking spill but Fisher walked back to the pit although he was ruled out for the rest of the match."

team manager, Stewart Dickson.
[Michael] "I reckon teams will want to avoid us 'cause we're getting stronger!"
[Stewart] "We are getting stronger – we need a couple of away wins to get into the Young Shield and, I think, an away banker at Armadale."
[Michael] "Well, I dunno about that! Let's look further ahead?"
[Stewart] "Next year there'll be no experimenting, no carrying about – we'll have our strongest team on the track. We have a lot of competition at the lower end. Look at Trent whose on about a 4½ average – we'd be silly not to have a look at him as he's one of ours. Anders [Andersen] is such a nice boy as everyone will tell you. He's flown over a couple of time just to watch us ride!" [4]

The rerun of heat 11 after the interval starts promisingly for Max Dilger when he gates but soon finds himself passed remarkably easily by William Lawson as they enter the first bend. Lee Dicken also tracks the young German before he blasts round him on the fourth bend. The Tigers 5-1 takes the score to 43-21 and, if a Monarchs fightback looked unlikely at this point, then it definitively ended with the announcement of Ryan Fisher's withdrawal from the meeting. He's replaced in heat 13 by Byron Bekker who's unable to stop the Grieves/Parker partnership registering the second successive Tigers 5-1 that stretches their lead to 48-30. "Well done to James and Shane, who were up against the most impressive Monarch this afternoon [pause] Michal Rajkowski!" Like many Tigers fans, Jim Fleming savours the triumph, "It's good to beat Edinburgh 'cause we've taken too many beatings here! Shame about the rain though!"

Children are everywhere in the stadium this afternoon and a young girl runs past in ear defenders while her father calls instructions to her without response. On principle rather than in real expectation, Monarchs team manager Alex Harkess uses his last tactical option to give Matthew Wethers the black-and-white helmet colour for heat 14. Until the third bend of the second lap, it looks unlikely to have any impact until Aaron Summers overtakes Mitchell Davey with a manoeuvre that shocks the Tiger so much that he drifts so wide it also allows Matthew Wethers through. Track conditions are such that the riders really only stick to one racing line and, up front, this is already comfortably occupied by William Lawson. However, to the chagrin of some brightly kilted Tigers fans on the third bend, Matty Wethers snatches an unlikely win in his race to the finish line with Lawson. The Monarchs 2-7 heat advantage comes too late to do anything other than massage the scoreline to a more acceptable 50-37. Heat 15 sees James Grieves gate with alacrity and then power onwards to take the chequered flag. Behind him Shane Parker completely fails to gate and finds himself in fourth. However, with a brilliant exhibition of speed, trackcraft and guile Shane proceeds to pass Matthew Wethers round bends one and two of the second lap. Shane then repeats the medicine in almost the identical place on the next lap to dash past Michal Rajkowski. Shane celebrates with donuts in front of the Edinburgh fans packed together on the fourth bend before he heads off to the pits to receive some well-deserved ceremonial bumps from his fellow riders, assorted mechanics and track staff. To commemorate his paid maximum as well as his track record breaking exploits, Shane is thrown surprisingly high into the air – so high that I suspect that Danny Gibb (the trackstaff member who picks up speedway bikes single-handedly) must be involved! Glasgow fans celebrate their 55-38 win in exuberant fashion while, sensibly, many Monarchs fans make an early dash to the exits including a woman in a pink/purple cocktail dress who totters away in her high heels, possibly in search of the wedding reception her attire suggests. Tigers fan Ian Maclean speaks in his usual measured understated way albeit with a bit of a gleam in his eyes that hints of his exaltation. "What a cracker of a meeting! The last race was fantastic, of course, but that race with James Grieves, Michal Rajkowski and Fisher where they pushed and shoved each other was something else!" Maximum man Shane Parker relives selected highlights of his earlier exploits in a centre-green interview. Michael Max asks half rhetorically and half pleadingly, "You can't possibly retire?" Ever the diplomat, Shane evades a definitive

[4] Difficult decisions are made during the close season by the Tigers management. After they sign Travis McGowan they are, thereby, left with only two places and a choice of Mitchell Davey, Lee Dicken and Anders Andersen. Co-promoter Alan Dick explains that the choice of Mitchell was relatively straightforward, given that he'd continued to ride over the winter in Australia and would make "some significant changes to his off-track set up". More significantly, the management had "noticed a huge change in his mental approach to things." Alan continues, "The second spot proved much closer in its selection. Obviously Anders was having a fine season at the start of last year until his leg injury but when he came back at the tail end of the year he didn't quite seem the same Anders. That is not to say that he isn't fit, it is just that when it came down to it we were more comfortable with Lee's fitness than Anders. I also believe Lee has been working very hard over the winter with a view to getting himself into better shape and is prepared to make some significant investment in his machinery, so that was a plus point. The other factor was in the team positioning. If we signed Anders, then he would have started at reserve with Mitchell in the main body, while it would be at reserve for Mitchell if Lee signs so again we felt that the balance of the team is better suited with Lee ... Anders is certainly very much in our thoughts for the future." The sudden withdrawal of Nick Simmons from the Berwick team two weeks before the start of the season for a shoulder operation subsequently provides Anders with a Premier League team place.

response, "Well, it would be a nice way to go out!"

The Edinburgh fans I encounter are in reflective mood, Davey believes that the outcome could have been different, "I think we could have got a point if 'Fish' hadn't totalled himself! Why he tried to get round the outside of Aaron when Aaron was on the outside I don't know?" Margaret, the Edinburgh trackshop manager, takes a philosophical view. "After last night, I was depressed and dreading this but, though we lost, which I don't like, I'm pretty happy with the result. With the luck we've had, the injuries and everything plus the riders who've left, it's not too bad! We've run rider replacement for so long I think the riders and their machines have got worn out! Aaron blew an engine this weekend and Byron has blown two! I didn't know that until his girlfriend told me this morning. He's had the most expensive weekend of his speedway career and hasn't earned a penny!" Always observant and insightful about so many things as well as speedway, Ian Maclean tells me, "I've noticed over the years that slightly built people don't do well in the wet compared to the heavier ones who do well! Grieves and, of course, Dicken got stuck in – no talent or finesse but lots of guts!"

9th August Glasgow v. Edinburgh (Premier League) 55-38

Glasgow: *"It's one of the safest safety fences in Britain but, now, we'll go to some music!"*

CHAPTER 28

Isle of Wight

"You see it all, simple children, people from Macclesfield who cut short their holiday in the South West due to the death of their guinea pig."

18th August

The reception area of the Portsmouth Wightlink Ferry office serves as a temporary administration centre for Dave Pavitt of the Isle of Wight on speedway race day. Outside in the car park many riders who'll complete in this evening's National League Best Pairs Championship final at Smallbrook Stadium patiently wait in their vans for the signal to start to board. While the ferry off-loads, Pav deals with a stream of last-minute arrivals before he heads out on the next sailing to Ryde. One half of the Weymouth pair, Mark 'Buzz' Burrows pops in for his ferry tickets ("I like old Buzz") before he pops out to rejoin his van parked in the queue outside. Dave is filled with optimism about the night ahead, "There's no reason why we shouldn't have a big crowd – the weather's nice, it's the holidays and it's a great meeting in prospect!"

Though now no longer formally associated with the Island club, Somerset's Dave Croucher has kindly volunteered to give me a lift to the stadium. Because of his work in the motor trade, Crouch has an endless stream of different invariably exotic cars to drive. This afternoon he's excelled himself with a large white American car that I can only describe as a *Dukes of Hazzard* US style police car, though, technically, it's really an imported Crown Victoria manufactured in the United States by Ford. It's big and, given it's festooned in the distinctive Confederate Flag livery of the Somerset Rebels, it's also clever since wherever it's driven or parked it'll attract significant attention. Crouch is rather pleased with his wheels and, true to form and intention, a small knot of interested bystanders stand round for a gawp, amongst them the always charming Dave Johnson, father of Brendan. Its sheer size and decoration (but probably not its petrol consumption) are a source of pride for Crouch. "When I went to Sheffield they said 'Are you sure it's subtle enough?' and I said 'I ain't finished it yet!'" Dave banters with many of those around him. With Buzz Burrows's van parked in the next lane, Crouch jovially engages him, "You're looking a bit radiant, mate!" They exchange a few words and, when out of earshot, Crouch refers to the wimbledon press releases of years gone by, "Buzz – the most exciting speedway rider in British speedway!" As befits such a car, its interior is plush, the wood finish deluxe and the range of options and accessories excessive. So much so that it appears to have everything but an inside toilet. While he fumbles for his fags, Dave turns on the industrial strength air conditioning, "You'll have icicles hanging off your plumbs in here!" The cigarettes come in a distinctive box and have a pungent aroma, "They're Double Happiness cigarettes from China – they're the best you can buy! Light them and it's like a roman candle – three puffs and it's gone!" Given his vehicle would look like a police car to other motorists when they see it from a distance, I ask Crouch if it's attracted more attention from the Boys in Blue than his previous prestige vehicles. "I'm not a big fan of the police being able to issue fixed notice penalties for traffic offences. I think being judge, jury and executioner is open to abuse! The trouble is we don't establish discipline in schools any longer – so it's anarchy when they get older! We pretty well need martial law just to look after the parking." The itinerant life of a speedway promoter and team manager during the speedway season wouldn't be for everyone but it's lifestyle that Crouch relishes. "Pav said to me once 'I'd hate to be normal!' He's right. I'd hate to be normal too! I do this 'cause I love it! Well, let's be honest – a lot of the time it's a pain and not enjoyable. All the travel, the haggling, all the aggravations but, when you stand in the middle of a field in Hungary – as I did this season – with Rob Woffinden, as the National Anthem plays, and we see Tai with a golden sash! Or when I see 11-year-old Robert Lambert win two 250cc races – well it's something special! It's what you do it for!"

After all the vehicles have been carefully parked under the guidance of the ferry staff and we've set sail, Pav and Crouch rendezvous on the outside platform at the stern of the ferry to watch a sun-dappled Portsmouth recede in the distance behind the white frothing wake of the boat. It's a journey they've done countless times before. Crouch smokes his fast burn cigarettes while a reflective Pav considers the present state of speedway. "Nowadays there's a new speedway fan! They get their fix in front of the telly on a Monday night and then, if they want to, they chose what speedway meeting they're going to go to. At the big events – Pairs, World Team Cup, Cardiff, 4TT – crowds are up 'cause the fans know they're going to see a good meeting with the best riders. The old speedway fan used to go and watch their team home and away – well, home at least! But now they don't! If they still go they pick and choose."

[Jeff] "But there have been some dreadful meetings on the telly!"

[Pav] "And some very good ones! The new fan gets their fix on a Monday."

[Jeff] "Sky seem to go to the same clubs all the time."

[Pav] "It's alright now they get a good wedge. They didn't used to but they do now! The Play-offs work well – Wolves v. Swindon could be something special."

[Jeff] "Shame they can't stage it as the semi-final too!"

[Pav] "In the Premier League, they have champions and then they have the Play-off winners who ride to see if they can get promotion."

[Jeff] "Lucky for you they don't have it in the National League."

[Pav] "We've done that already [Premier League] and we wouldn't want it!"

[Jeff] "The Premier League meetings have looked good on Sky."

[Pav] "It's something special! The Premier League crowds are up for those meeting 'cause it's something different. When we had one at Somerset, we made a big effort and went out and really sold it to the fans, the local area, the media and the sponsors! But, when you get it four or five times a season, you get blasé. It's human nature. Is the winner of the National League Play-offs the champions?"

[Jeff] "I dunno, I suppose so. You should know the rules, you wrote them!"

[Pav] "Yeah, but I forget. I'll ask Peter Morrish later, he's gonna be there and he'll know. You know I've promoted in all three leagues and I've never been happier 'cause the National League is the best! And you know why that is? 'Cause the riders really want to ride! They can't wait to ride for £10 or £15 [a point]. In other leagues, you can pay them £50-60-70-80-90, a £100 per point and all they do is moan! In the National League, they just can't wait! It's hard to lose money in the National League."

[Jeff] "Why?"

[Pav] "'Cause the costs are so low! Since the summer has started we've had good crowds. Twice a week! We survive on the summer and other events like the scooter rally over the Bank Holiday weekend when we have 2,000 scooters. The rest of the time, it's pretty empty. Can you do me a favour? Can you take me some photos of the crowd tonight? I love photos of crowds! I love photos of queues too! Get as many photos of queues as you can."

[Jeff] "And, I seem to remember, you also like full car parks too!"

[Pav] "I love them! Seeing big crowds makes it all worthwhile. Most of the time, there's no one around but when it's busy that makes it special!"

Pav asks how my books are doing and what reactions I get. I tell him it's mostly positive but there are some people who aren't big fans. Crouch interjects, "Lots of people tell us we're wankers but it hasn't stopped us!" I leave the two Daves to discuss important matters of state and wander to the upstairs outside seating area. Even on a summer's day the speed of the ferry means that it's quite breezy and, most times of the year, it would only appeal to die-hard smokers. This afternoon there's a crowd of young riders gathered round a table where Buzz Burrows and his partner Samantha Knight sit. There's animated debate about the race format and the tactics you need to employ. Discussions are led by Sam, "It's a 20-heat format – it's four in each group, hold on, there's five in each group – there's 10 teams overall!" She lowers her voice so her exact words of wisdom are lost on the wind.

Back in his car the size of a spaceship, while Crouch drives us to Smallbrook Stadium he animatedly tells me a complicated story about the culture and goings on at the guesthouse he stays in near Somerset speedway. "It's like a soap opera – not the owners, they're alright but the guests! You see it all, simple children, people from Macclesfield who cut short their holiday in the South West due to the death of their guinea pig; a grumpy petrol pump attendant who hates mobile phones. He shook my hand when I said he was the grumpiest man I'd met in Somerset! Or the

Isle of Wight: *"You see it all, simple children, people from Macclesfield who cut short their holiday in the South West due to the death of their guinea pig."*

hugely well-informed MOT man who knew all about this Crown Victoria. It's a US car that's been imported from Saudi but he knew everything about it. But, if you take it to a normal Ford garage, just to change a spark plug, they pretty well run off!" Every different person whose conversation Crouch relates requires that he speaks in another accent for each. He's got a virtuoso range of voices and has a keen ear for their linguistic idiosyncrasies. I tell him "You should be on the stage". "My dad used to say that – either painting it or sweeping it!" Though an alternative career might beckon treading the boards, Crouch certainly won't be mistaken for an environmentalist or an advocate of a sustainable planet. "I'm a consumer – so I consume! The carbon footprint I have must be the size of America. I go to 70-75 meetings here and 8 or 10 abroad in the season that runs from March to October. I wouldn't have it any other way!" When we pull up outside the Smallbrook Stadium turnstiles, Crouch has barely parked the car on the stony surface when he's engaged in conversation by a fretful member of the volunteer workers who ensure that the Island club runs its meeting professionally. "Are you happy, Ken?"

Rebel yell

[Ken] "No, I'm frickin' not!" That Barrie frickin' Evans has just driven round the car park and sprayed stones everywhere! I said to Pav he should send him back on the next boat."

Crouch makes sympathetic noises but stops short of a promise to rusticate one half of the Mildenhall Tigers Best Pair. The Smallbrook Stadium clubhouse houses a gymnasium, bar and sufficient deluxe tables and chairs to stage a large wedding reception. Dave Pavitt isn't to be found in his usual lair of the Speedway Office with its flickering computer monitor and impressive piles of folders and paperwork. Instead he's at the far end of the clubhouse stood on the balcony that overlooks the second bend and provides an excellent view down the back straight. "The track looks a bit mucky but it's early yet!"

[Man] "There's plenty of dirt on it."

[Pav] "Good! I'm just gonna text Crouch to ask him where the donuts are."

Tactics

Almost telepathically, Crouch arrives on the balcony clutching two bags with a different type of donut in each. Pav hungrily opens the bags and then daintily eats half of each donut before he replaces them for Crouch to eat later. Crouch has the contented look of a man with sufficient willpower to resist the joy of this snack, albeit in the full knowledge that that time isn't too far away. "It was a good idea – oh great and wise one – to get them bags to keep them fresh!" Instead of a snack, Crouch slurps on his tea, "I'm just doing what I said I'd never do – drinking out of a Chris Johnson mug." He nods to my open file and the notes I've taken, "A bunch of cunts has a capital C!" Brendan Johnson has joined us on the balcony and Pav tells him paternally, "Don't go without your cheque tonight! It's a small one and there's another one on Thursday. Don't forget! If you do, there'll be two of them on Thursday." Though three days still remain until Somerset's next meeting at the Oak Tree Arena against the Workington Comets, Crouch frets about manpower levels, "I'm still short of a rider for Friday!"

[Jeff] "I thought you said it was going to rain."

Programme queue

[Crouch] "It probably will but you need a rider in case it doesn't! We're missing Tom Brown 'cause he fell off and got some sort of hairline compound fracture. It was his own doing, he was on his own – in fourth – I shouldn't laugh 'cause it's not funny and at the end of the day, he was only trying to get that extra point! It never ceases to amaze me that some Riders have an almighty crash, perform acrobatics the like of the Moscow State Circus and get up and walk away. Tom falls off, on his own, in last place and he's buggered for the rest of the season."

The two Daves then have an animated discussion about Jodie's [Tom Brown's girlfriend] breast implants. "If I could only have one thing for Christmas, I'd have them because they're magnificent! Between the races all Tom wants to talk about is the puppies – 'we lost another one!' – between heats four and five, it isn't quite what you want to talk about!" The administrative chores that make up the life of a speedway promoter temporarily obscure in Dave Croucher's mind the compensations of pride in a job well done or tangible evidence of young rider development. Whatever the trials, tribulations or awards, Crouch remains adamant, "I'm not doing it for the money!"

With more riders on display than usual tonight, there's a hustle and a bustle in the pits as well as a premium on space. Highly regarded Poole speedway press officer Gordon Day has just left the pits to stand next to the referee's box that overlooks the start line in one direction and is adjacent to the all-important staff tearoom in the other. Islanders announcer Bryn Williams has stepped outside the referee's box to have yet another well-deserved cigarette. Unlike some people Gordon doesn't hold with the idea that the best riders produce the best speedway, he prefers to evangelise for the sport of speedway in general. "People don't care what league they're watching so long as all four riders are together and racing each other! I asked some of the Poole fans why they don't come and watch the [Bournemouth] Buccaneers and they say 'but it's five seconds a race slower!' They just aren't convinced about how exciting it really is! [To Bryn] They need to throw out all the foreign riders and all the GP stars and have one big league, sort of Premier League standard and split it into north and south. It's the only way! I see they're forecasting petrol at £1.20 a litre by December so it'll make even more sense then! Whatever the [NL] crowd size is, they always put its 400 or 500 in the *Bournemouth Echo*. We've had some Elite League meetings where we could have put them all in the grandstand and still had room left! That grandstand can hold up to 1,200!"

In the always shaded stony passageway that runs behind the main home-straight grandstand, Weymouth photographer and press officer Julie Martin is en route to the pits. She has a keen interest in speedway and her new boyfriend has pretty good shale credentials since he's Grant Tregoning's mechanic. Julie affects to take a philosophical approach to affairs of the heart, "Luke Priest's mum told me 'when you go to the library you don't have to buy the book, just take it back if you don't like it!' I'm going to take her advice!" She's youthful enough to laugh off my anxiety, "this is a good philosophy until you find the library is suddenly unexpectedly shut!"

In old money, this event would be the Conference League Pairs but, since speedway's equivalent of decimalisation, in the new funny money it's become the National League Pairs. Whatever the meeting is called, you can be certain that Oxford uber-fan Rob Peasley will attend. Rob is understated but passionate about his speedway. When he's not trackside he often to be found posting on the British speedway forum. "Did you see that bit from Derek [Barclay] on the BSF where he was boasting that there's five ex-Wimbledon riders in the meeting tonight? I posted that we only had one – we have two actually Chris Johnson and Kyle Hughes – because ours have progressed into the Premier League or, in Ben Barker's case, the Elite League! Rather than go around in the third tier just beating the youngsters." It's only a few short years since the Conference League Pairs were staged by the plc that ran speedway at Plough Lane. That particular staging continued at interminable length on an incredibly sultry afternoon, "I'm sure it was a complete coincidence that people fell off on the first bend whenever Buzz was off the inside gate."

On the subject of gates, Dave Pavitt is stood close by to the entrance turnstiles on the walkway adjacent to the apex of the first and second bend. He warmly meets and greets passing fans with the practised, friendly manner of an usher. "I'm just standing here getting the horn watching all these cars arrive – I love it! Promise me you'll take a photo when there's a big queue!" Bryn Williams' long-time partner in crime in the referee's box is incident recorder Chris Golding. "That Kevin Moore is a big fan of yours judged by the way he went on about you for 10 minutes [at King's Lynn]! You haven't arrived as a writer until someone has hit you. Has anyone hit you yet? It's only a matter of time!" We're interrupted by a kerfuffle at the programme stall where an older fan loudly exclaims, "When I go to Poole, it's never £2.50! It's the dearest programme in the country!" Though his anger is righteous, his claims are not founded on accurate evidence. The increasingly highly regarded and hard-working speedway reporter Paul Burbidge is on his second ever trip to the Island to watch the speedway. This season he's ventured widely on his speedway travels to tracks he's previously not visited. "The announcer at Buxton told me the track slopes so that you learn to ride the different corners differently! I suppose it makes sense when you think about it. Have you seen Craig Cook ride yet?

Isle of Wight: *"You see it all, simple children, people from Macclesfield who cut short their holiday in the South West due to the death of their guinea pig."*

[I have – in the Premier League for Workington] You're in for a treat tonight! He scored 19 paid 21 at Buxton to pretty well beat Bournemouth single-handedly. It was their first defeat in the league! I heard Grant Tregoning is taking it seriously [tonight] – he's had an engine done specially and has brought four mechanics!"

Without prior arrangement, Reading club historian Arnie Gibbons serendipitously arrives at Smallbrook Stadium at the same time as itinerant speedway programme editor and regular BSF contributor, Derek Barclay. Even more spookily coincidental, both clutch matching Leicester programme boards. If I were an anthropologist keen to decode the meaning of sacred objects, it would be little trouble to identify that these distinctive bright yellow boards mark out their owners as exulted speedway aficionados with many decades following their beloved sport and also simultaneously identifies that – given the likely return of the Leicester Lions to speedway action in the near future – they remain open to historic winds of change. If I didn't know better or wished to badly misjudge Arnie's taste, I could jump to the conclusion that Derek was Arnie's long-time partner. ("I have much better taste than that"). Instead I content myself with the observation that "Arnie has an authentic battered one!" Arnie wipes an imaginary stain from the slightly discoloured and battered board and recalls his Leicester Lions pedigree, "I became a regular at Leicester when I got my first job there in 1982." Though I gather Derek is a graduate – probably from a polytechnic, correspondence course or the evening class school of life, he immediately reposts, "I cleaned mine up! I first went when I was a student at the University of Leicester from 1978-1981." Any regular reader of the British speedway forum could be forgiven if they suspected Derek had taken a literature degree since his posts often veer towards fiction. Or, perhaps, it was a politics degree given his Citizen Smith-like espousal of what – in the right-leaning, monocultural world of speedway – counts as revolutionary and/or left wing opinion. Though he criticised *Quantum of Shale* prior to its publication (without apparent irony) for its narcissism, as far as I'm aware Derek has yet to extricate a £20 note from the pocket of his slightly too tight trousers to purchase a copy. "I've looked at the book and there aren't too many disparaging comments about me!" Talk of higher education prompts Derek to grumble about the youth of today. His son studies in the highly regarded chemistry department at the University of Sussex on a four-year degree. "I'm not sure what the world is coming to nowadays. I'm 49 and I'm at a hot sweaty gig in Camden, while he's dining at a posh restaurant in Brighton with his girlfriend Chelsy. They still live in the same student squalor but have much more expensive tastes!" In his hot little hand Derek holds tonight's programme and is desperately keen to know if the racecard – specially designed by Kandysoft (run by Dave Gambrill – a Coventry fan, speedway journalist and a consultant to the SCB) – requires any amendment. I tell him what I know. Namely, "There are some changes but I don't know what they are." Quick as a flash, Derek retorts, "That's 'cause Bryn will be mumbling!"

All 10 teams that comprise the National League in 2009 are represented in the Best Pairs Championship. They're split into two groups and the usual Pairs scoring format is in use – 4 points for a win, 3 points for second, 2 points for third – supposedly to encourage both team riding and canny tactics. Somewhat in contradiction to the concept that the National League will help develop young riders, the first race of the night is won by Tony Atkin of Newport (closely followed home by his race partner Grant Tregoning) who is one of two 43-year-olds racing tonight. The second of these veteran riders, Mark 'Buzz' Burrows appears in heat 2 and finishes third. More significantly for the Weymouth Wildcats pursuit of this particular item of silverware, his partner James Cockle retires from the race with mechanical difficulties to leave the Dorset partnership with much to do during the remainder of the meeting. On the third bend of the second lap of heat 3, King's Lynn's Adam Allott and Darren Mallett provide their own unique interpretation of what it means to team ride. While placed second, Darren signals he's had an engine failure. Sadly it's a sign that his teammate Adam Allott misinterprets and so temporarily slows down to escort his teammate almost to a halt before he realises the error of his ways. By which time, Rye House's Lee Strudwick and David Mason are way off ahead in the distance. The highly regarded National League incarnation of Craig Cook is welcomed onto the track by Bryn Williams ("and Craig Cook who scored a mere 22 points last time he was here") before he duly wins comfortably. Although, once again, the team nature of this event dictates that – because of his partner Scott James's engine failure – second and third places for Mildenhall's Barrie Evans and Luke Priest gives them the heat 5-4. Indeed, it's a night of hard first bends, high-speed racing and repeated mechanical difficulties. An engine failure for Chris Johnson dents the Isle of Wight's championship ambitions less than they could have because his partner Nick Simmons roars to victory ahead of Scunthorpe's Simon Lambert and Ashley Morris.

Just in time for the sixth race of the night, I'm stood in my favourite part of the stadium – on the elevated section of rough ground that overlooks the third and fourth bend – since it provides a panoramic view of the track and the race to the finish line. It's the ideal spot to witness the close contest on the fourth bend between Mark Simmonds and Mark Baseby that results in the exclusion of the Bournemouth rider, after he falls from his machine. Mark Baseby's dad is quickly out on the rack to tend to his stricken son but, when Mark Simmonds sportingly returns to check on Mark Baseby's health, he's told to go away in no uncertain terms by Mark Baseby's dad. "You had him off straightaway – go on – frick off!" The prestige and importance of tonight's Pairs championship prompts an invite for ex-Reading presenter Dave Stallworthy who (for one night only) shares microphone duties with regular stadium incumbent Bryn Williams. Dave places occasional adverts in the *Speedway Star* to highlight his availability to work as a Master of Ceremonies, something he illustrates with a photo of himself apparently dressed as the Mayor of London or, perhaps, an uninjured pirate. Whenever his duties tonight cause his dulcet tones echo over the speaker system, it orally (if not visually) transports me back to speedway nights of yore at the much missed and occasionally lamented Smallmead Stadium. The rerun of the sixth race results in a win for Jay Herne and, in the process, he sets a new National League track record of 68 seconds (a second and a half outside the time set when Premier League racing was held at this track).

Heat 7 requires three attempts to complete and almost becomes a mini-meeting in itself. Bryn Williams relays a warning to King's Lynn's Adam Allott from referee Paul Carrington, "The rider in green will be admonished for moving at the start. The marshal will have a word in his ear – he's probably heard a few of those already over the years has young Adam!" After the next abortive attempt to run the heat there's some additional delay, "Extra time has been allowed there for Darren to sort his bike out or, rather, his dad to sort the machine out!" Bryn fills the time with talk of the Islander's easily audible raffle operative, "Happy 54th is it? Oh, er, Happy 45th birthday next Monday to sexy Sue, our raffle ticket seller!" At the third attempt, heat 7 finally reaches its conclusion and provides the second successive maximum heat advantage for the Newport pair of Tony Atkin and Grant Tregoning. Though they win easily, all the action is behind them when Adam Allott and Darren Mallett showcase yet another unique variation on their interpretation of what it means to team ride together. They vie intensely for third place until a hard fourth bend on the penultimate lap immediately followed up by a hard first bend on the last lap allows Darren to fire off and win their own mini race within a race. Another retirement for James Cockle – this time in heat 8 – further undermines the Weymouth Wildcats silverware credentials and, although Buzz Burrows finishes second, their chances of victory get reduced to infinitesimal. There's a slight delay before the start of heat 9 that Bryn patiently explains to us, "The Rye House riders have the wrong helmet colours on [pause] according to the programme." Quite what the programme advises or its significance, I will leave to other expert commentators. [1]

I must say that along with the racing itself, helmet colouration is also a contributory factor in the entertainment provided. David Mason rides with a white helmet colour while his teammate Lee Strudwick wore a loosely fitting green helmet colour that by the second bend had flapped aside to reveal his dark red helmet. Therefore, the order of helmet colours at the finish was: blue, red, red, white though the programme would record this as: blue, green,

1 Personally I found the 2009 National League Best Pairs Championship programme racecard to be user-friendly, despite the minor inconvenience that the helmet colours weren't identified in print. As a long-time spectator I could quickly grasp that the first two named riders in any race would sport the red and blue helmet colours. However, not all speedway fans are created equal, let alone that many speedway followers are known to be obsessive about their love (and tabulation) of arcane detail. However, without the specific instructions beloved of so many people to exonerate their behaviour, three times during the meeting riders came up to the start line in the wrong helmet colours. The programme did also contain a couple of gate errors in heats 9 and 10 that were easy to resolve. Drinking deep on the milk of human kindness after the meeting Derek Barclay's online alter ego 'Parsloes 1928 nearly' would demand a *mea culpa* from Bryn Williams, "Ah right, so there were a couple (at least…) of heats printed in the prog with incorrect gate positions…considering the person responsible for the prog last night is the same person who made such a fuss (and hasn't stopped repeating this fuss for FOUR years) when in the 2005 Pairs prog there was one mistake and that was in helmet colours NOT gate positions by the way) ALSO..then may we expect to see a FULL apology from that person right now..I trust when you got your munchies for the long journey home last night, Bryn, it was good old humble pie you had to eat..!!" Rob Peasley's much more avuncular online alter ego Lucifer Sam was quick to goad the righteousness of this post. "Still, carry on Parsoles [*sic*] I like a good laugh, and you trying to compare last night's two-second repair job to the proggie to the mini-Chernobyl tippex-feast of 2005 (including the complete lack of individual score charts for the second half of that infamous proggie) is making me chuckle." With the righteousness of a victim of apartheid or an industrial injury, 'Parsloes 1928 nearly' continues to demand an apology and comment from Bryn Williams. Bryn's online alter ego is undramatically called "Bryn" eventually responds. "Before saying anything else here, my only apologies in this posting go to the forum moderators in advance of what is to follow and I'm hoping they realise that indeed in respect of what follows below, it is meant and intended to conform to this forum's basic principle of "attack the post not the poster". So Mr Barclay: 1. I am not responding to the gibberish you've been posting on this thread but I've left it to you to make a bigger twerp of yourself through what you have been adding each time you have posted and you've done a pretty good job in my humble opinion. 2. I've had far more important things to worry about and deal with [Brendan's Johnson's nearly fatal crash] as will become clear here and through other sources no doubt later today than concern myself with trying to add any form of credence to what appears to be the ramblings of a very bitter person, the reasons for such bitterness have been totally unclear to myself. 3. I cannot and will not apologise for something I have absolutely no reason to apologise for. Bryn Williams."

Isle of Wight: *"You see it all, simple children, people from Macclesfield who cut short their holiday in the South West due to the death of their guinea pig."*

red, yellow. Speedway's equivalent of pass the parcel as applied to helmet colours continues before the start of heat 10, though this time it stars the Buxton riders. Bryn interprets the pre-race action for the crowd, "They're just swapping the helmet colours [green and yellow] over – the right riders are on the correct gates but the helmet colours are wrong. Anyway, we got there in the end; it's only these two heats [that are affected]". A disembodied male voice (that's too deep pitched to be Derek Barclay's) shouts from the crowd, "They should know what they're doing!" The 11th race of the night sees Adam Allott finally have intense battle for position with a rival rider, namely Simon Lambert. They duel for position over four exciting laps before Allott emerges victorious. Helped into the groove by some earlier high-speed manoeuvres in the car park, Barrie Evans wins heat 12 but, because his partner Luke Priest falls [then remounts], Mildenhall fail to capitalise on a position that sees them amass 11 points after two races. The interval is taken and I stand forlornly with my books by the start line directly in front of the referee's box in the home-straight grandstand awaiting an announcement from Bryn Williams that never comes. He jovially mentions a runaway gorilla ("Is that Dave Pavitt?") and a forthcoming birthday ("I won't mention it's her 45th birthday this month!") before he departs the microphone for yet another well-deserved cigarette.

Entered in a competition with a sensible meeting format that doesn't require a protracted finale, each team knows they have to win their group in order to qualify for the grand final. With the option of qualification or nothing, heat 13 proves decisive when Newport take their third successive maximum heat advantage while successive retirements for David Mason fatally flaws Rye House's hopes of qualification. As they race for supremacy on the first bend of heat 14, Scott James appears to knock into an already fishtailing Buzz Burrows to send him flying from his bike. Full of sympathy, Bryn notes, "That's not something you want to do when you're 43! One of the great servants of British speedway has given great entertainment for many, many years. That's not something we like to see!" Though Buzz is back on his feet, it's clear his equipment is completely wrecked by that first-bend bunching incident. "He'd prefer to ride back on his bike but he won't be riding back on that one!" It's ymbolic of his evening. In the rerun, meeting reserve Ben Hopwood replaces Buzz and, with Weymouth's challenge at an end, Buzz also wouldn't appear in his final race of the night.

Highly fancied Smallbrook track experts, Chris Johnson and Nick Simmons romp home in heat 15 to give themselves a mathematical chance of qualification in what has effectively become a sudden death play-off for qualification with Newport in heat 19. Pre-meeting favourites Jay Herne and Mark Baseby take the Bournemouth Buccaneers a step closer to qualification with a maximum heat advantage in heat 16, albeit one that requires Mark Baseby to snatch second place on the finish line from Barrie Evans. Over the loudspeaker system, Bryn Williams offers congratulations to the Islander's club photographer, "Congratulations to Jean and Dave Valentine who've become grandparents today for the fourth time. Jean tells me it's a baby boy who's only four hours old. Dave is our resident flasher with his big one." The Islanders qualification for the final looks in hand after Chris Johnson gates and his partner Nick Simmons occupies the all-important second place. However, the heat comes to a sudden dramatic end when, up front and untroubled, Chris Johnson loses control of his bike and falls heavily to prematurely end the race. His disqualification means the race is awarded and this ensures that Newport progress to a final where it still isn't clear whether they will face Plymouth, Buxton or Bournemouth. No stranger to severe injury, Johnson spends some time on the shale before he limps back to the pits. With undefeated Jay Herne at the tapes for the Bournemouth Buccaneers, the 4 points they need to ensure qualification always looks likely to come from this rider alone but, with Mark Baseby third, they qualify with ease to disappoint the fans of Plymouth and Buxton, for whom Craig Cook amasses 15 out of their 20 points. However, Pairs speedway is a team event and this is clearly illustrated when Newport's Tony Atkin (43) and Grant Tregoning (21) let Jay Herne remain unbeaten round this 385-metre track. However, since they both finish ahead of Mark Baseby, it guarantees them the trophy under a points scoring system that enables them to win the heat 5-4.

For riders and fans alike, the option remains to stay at the track and celebrate Newport's unlikely triumph or race like madmen to get to the ferry.[2] On the ferry back to the mainland, Roy Collins detects that Bryn hasn't quite been his usual ebullient self, "He was a bit put out by Dave Stallworthy being there!" Also together on the ferry are John Strudwick and his brother, proud speedway fathers of cousins Niall ("He's away on a lifesaving course tonight") and

[2] In grandiloquent fashion Bryn Williams would wear his Welsh patriotism on his sleeve in his meeting report penned for the *Speedway Star*. Alluding to a history of military triumphs mysteriously absent from the hegemonic accounts that appear in the history books, Bryn chooses to portray Bournemouth versus Newport as symbolic of previous battles between England and Wales, "but, as it was in ancient times, the minnows stood their ground with veteran Atkin and youngster Tregoning richly deserving their title success."

Lee who rode with some élan tonight. They're accompanied by Rye House team manager John Sampford. I used to stand with the Strudwicks at Eastbourne Speedway so I've always followed the progress of Niall and Lee. Recent months have seen Lee return to form and his dad takes the view that ability alone, unless coupled with belief, won't ever get results. In recent months, Lee's run of high scores indicates that his confidence is high – during the 2009 season he wins more races away than at home and also fails to run a last at Hoddesdon – but modesty ensures that he remains understated, smiles and acknowledges my congratulations with a simple "Thank you". By his usual scrupulously taciturn standards, John Sampford is positively voluble. "Lee wasn't even supposed to be here tonight. I rang them up and said they should include him but they insisted it had to be the top two even though we knew Lee would perform much, much better than the rider they wanted. So it proved! They started well as a pair in the first race but then we faded a bit. Lee got a win, two seconds and a third so more than justified his inclusion!"

18th August National League Best Pairs Championship Winners: Newport

Isle of Wight: *"You see it all, simple children, people from Macclesfield who cut short their holiday in the South West due to the death of their guinea pig."*

CHAPTER 29

Redcar

"The riders here tonight at this level earn a living from speedway but, without Sky, it would become an amateur sport or semi-professional, at best!"

24th August

When I ask for directions to the South Tees Motorsports Park at the reception desk of the new Travelodge they've built in Middlesbrough on the site of the old hospital, the bloke behind the counter says, "Never heard of it!" When I clarify that is where they race speedway, he retorts, "What's that?" Though I already know where it is, instead he gives me directions to the nearby large bus station. Middlesbrough's bus station is an example of one of those municipal spaces notionally designed for passenger comfort that requires everyone to queue inside the building for their bus. It's not much fun in the summer but, then again, the Costa del Teesside isn't known for its heatwaves. For the first-time visitor, there's no obvious entrance into the bus station when approached from the direction I arrive from. When I finally find my way inside, I head to the grandly named Arriva Information Centre to enquire exactly what bus I need to get to the speedway. The lady behind the desk begrudgingly breaks off her conversation with her colleagues and is adamant that, "We don't have one anymore! The one we had was up the road and it shut down years ago!" You have to have every sympathy with Brian Havelock or Chris Van Straaten and Glyn Taylor about the local lack of knowledge or awareness of the existence of Redcar speedway within the city. Admittedly my straw poll isn't scientific. I must have spoken to people who also don't read the local newspaper (*Evening Gazette*) since, on a regular basis, this gives good support to the activities of the club. The words that flow from the keyboard of the *Gazette's* knowledgeable and hardworking reporter Martin Neal must communicate the excitement of speedway mainly to those who are already converts or aficionados. One of the information lady's chatty colleagues manages to explain to her roughly where the STMP is located. I'm then sent off to the correct bus stand for a particular bus with instructions to ask the driver where exactly to get off. Though the important landmarks remain the same whether you travel by car or public transport, though he passes it every day on his bus, the driver doesn't quite know where the stadium is located. He does know the whereabouts of the nearby McDonald's so, unfortunately, I get off a stop or two earlier than I should. With my trusty three-wheeled travel case, the extra walk isn't a problem except, no sooner does the bus pull off, than the jet black sky overhead empties. Such heavy rain on any normal race night would give you justifiable anxiety about whether the meeting would go ahead but, since I'm here on a Monday (rather than the traditional Thursday) because the Sky Sports cameras are in town to capture the speedway race action on this well-regarded banked circuit, I'm certain that the meeting will go ahead no matter what!

In heavy rain, my trip from the bus stop past some derelict buildings and across the rough-hewn land that serves as the speedway car park feels like a long distance. All the paraphernalia you'd expect for a live Sky outside broadcast is already on display: from the giant trucks to the various camera gantries. Highly praised in their own publicity, the Meccano-like structure built from chrome-plated scaffolding poles that's the distinctive commentary booth regularly used by Sky's duo of pundit commentators – Kelvin Tatum and Nigel Pearson – stands in damp pride of place in the vicinity of the first corner. This location provides them with a panoramic view of the tight banked 266 metre track. Transported to Teesside and stood in the rain, it looks incongruously shiny compared to the stadium surroundings or the unseasonal darkness of this late August afternoon. It catches the eye like a religious monument or sacred artefact, albeit one without any worshippers prepared to brave the downpour.

Since my last visit Redcar speedway, STMP has gained a clubhouse and I head straight there to shelter from the rain. Though the clubhouse is a new addition to the emergent infrastructure of the STMP, it's previously loved and appears to have seen sterling service elsewhere. Inside it's filled with warm damp bodies that mist the windows. A few minutes later, the arrival of glamorous, blonde Sky Sports speedway pits presenter Charlie Webster causes conversation to temporarily completely stop. Despite the downpour outside, Charlie doesn't sport the bedraggled look favoured by everyone else. She hasn't exactly dressed for these climactic conditions. Instead she wears a stylish leather jacket and faded grey jeans though, in her choice of footwear, she's made some concession to the night's work ahead when she'll scramble around the pits in search of cutting-edge and insightful interviews. Though she doesn't have an umbrella or a hat, her blonde hair looks dry and artfully casual. She smiles broadly, "I'm jinxed! I hope it's not raining later!" After a lengthy visit to powder her nose in the ladies toilets located on the far side of the clubhouse adjacent to the refreshment kiosk, Charlie emerges and unaffectedly agrees to my request, "Can I take a photo of you with the trackshop guys?" She stands patiently, happy to pose between the two trackshop thorns of John Rich and Bill Gimbeth who've independently perfected a shared expression somewhere between glazed and awkward. To break the ice Bill jokes, "You owe him a fiver now, John!" With further pre-meeting preparations to complete, Charlie walks off and, is still only about three yards away, when John Rich says much too loudly, "She's not as attractive as the other girl!" Bill and I shush him and simultaneously dive into the nearby room that houses the trackshop in an attempt to hide our embarrassment. Unrepentant about his unsubtle opinion, John protests, "But she's not! The Welsh girl was more attractive!" It's one of the immutable laws of life that any judgment on the attractiveness of the opposite sex is made without any reflection about your own appearance or the basis for your judgement.

A damp but cheerful Gareth Rogers arrives and has the manners to think about some introductions, "I'll introduce you to Brian Havelock. He won't say much. He'll be brusque." The few hours before the start of any race night isn't the ideal time to try to snatch a meaningful in-depth conversation with any speedway promoter, let alone on a night that's billed as the biggest night in the club's history! National exposure on satellite television is a much-needed publicity boost for any sports organisation but, particularly, one under new management. Brian's got understandably obsessed with meteorology. "It's forecast to go away by 10 to 7 according to the satellite. We've only put three bowsers full on it [the track] today. I'm sure we can still start but the damage may have already been done and it could be fricked. The [standing] water will drain off but it might be fricked!" Even if you can't stop the rain, like Top Cat, Brian is keen to mingle with the newcomers and various regulars attracted to the STMP for tonight's satellite broadcast. Though it presently rains on his potential parade, Gareth has a strong sense of homecoming. "I feel quite nostalgic today. I wouldn't usually be commentating but Martin [Neal] is in Ecuador [Estonia]. I can remember standing on the hill over there [gestures towards the back-straight banking] when it was a rubbish tip saying 'I'm sure that I can get the local media along and maybe, even one day, Sky!' And here they are! It's unbelievable how far things have come!" Stood only a few yards away Brian's conversations are interrupted by his mobile phone. It trills incessantly. He's brief and to the point. To each caller he repeats the mantra, "At the moment, it's still on!"

At one of the many clubhouse windows that overlook the track, John Rich sits with a lady and surveys the damp scene. Various track and television staff continue with their duties in the downpour. Unobservable to human eyes, (except his) John claims, "It's brightening up!" The lady next to him looks disconsolately out but remains unconvinced, "Is it? Look at that water [impressive, large-sized puddles] on the bends!" With just over two hours to go before the scheduled start time of tonight's Sky Sports broadcast, the rain appears even heavier. Out on the second bend, apparently King Canute-like, track staff industriously sweep the shale surface and, industriously but hopefully, repeatedly prod the second bend drain. A bedraggled man notes gloomily, "If it carries on like this for another hour, it'll be off!" The sky changes from jet black to merely dark so I say to Gareth, "It's getting brighter."
[Gareth] "It is but, the trouble is, it's coming straight down!"
[Man on mobile] "It's the nightmare scenario!"
[Colin Meredith] "It'll drain okay; it just needs to stop raining first!"
[Man on mobile to second caller] "It's terrible – the rain – and it's forced Charlie to change out of her shorts into her jeans!"
[Brian Havelock, on mobile] "It is! It is raining heavy but the forecast is that it's going to be okay!"

Redcar: *"The riders here tonight at this level earn a living from speedway but, without Sky, it would become an amateur sport or semi-professional, at best!"*

[Steve Harland, on mobile] "It's got to be on 'cause that Jeff Scott is here, you know the one who writes the literary books that get reviewed in the *Guardian* and that. It's stopped now!"

Though it won't take long, Gareth Rogers proudly gives me a proprietorial tour of the new facilities. "It was a rugby clubhouse. It makes a big difference! There's a sponsors' and corporate hospitality area, catering, a bar, lots of seating and tables, the trackshop and an office for Brian!" We walk into the trackshop just as John Rich holds forth with an explanation of the likely structure of a speedway race night when Sky are in town for a live broadcast. "It'll be 15 minutes of chat, then they'll have four races, a break, then four, a break, then four, a break and then four [realises that's 16 races] no, four-four-three plus one or, er, no four-four-four, two plus one." I show Gareth the photo with Charlie and this prompts John to abandon his educational outline of the likely structure of Sky broadcasts to defend his 'the Welsh girl or Sophie Blake is better [looking] than Charlie Webster' point of view. "She was nice then she buggered off with Scottie and started the hanky-panky!" Gareth isn't really fussed either way, "I'm in Brighton next week for the 100th Anniversary of the School of Education. I didn't go when it opened!"
[Bill] "I'm trying to figure out how I can display your books better."
[Jeff] "It would be hard to do worse."
[Bill] "I've only got one left now!"
[Jeff] "How many did you have to start with?"
[Bill] "At the start of the season [pause] two! It's been a poor year this season. People don't have much money to spend."
[Jeff] "At least it's been exciting to watch Wolves."
[Bill] "I only see the first bend 'cause I'm minding the shop. At Scunthorpe, 'cause we're right by the start line, I get to see it all!"

Though part of the same clubhouse, the sponsors' and corporate hospitality area is roped off from the general public inside and also outside on the sodden wooden observation deck. No speedway club can depend for its survival on season ticket sales and turnstile revenues alone. A successful commercial department is a prerequisite for any speedway club to approach financial viability. Close to where hard-working and enthusiastic commercial manager Steve Harland makes yet another mobile telephone call, there's a table that prominently displays Redcar's 'corporate' brochure. Its entitled "Speedway Racing Advertising and Sponsorship Menu" (written by Steve and Gareth Rogers). Not quite at the same deluxe specification levels of the Lakeside corporate brochure, though produced at a fraction of the cost it's still snappily written, clearly laid out and condenses a substantial amount of information into a very small space. Copy on the front of the brochure informs would-be sponsors and advertisers, "The League is one of the most cosmopolitan in sport with clubs based as far apart as Edinburgh and Glasgow in the North, Workington in the West and competing against the likes of Newport, Rye House and Somerset in the South. Local derbies are maintained against Newcastle and Sheffield (a Yorkshire derby!). There is a large free car park, a clubhouse with catering and drinks: alcohol, soft drinks and beverages. We invite local businesses to become involved in the fast and exciting sport of speedway racing." Inside there's a helpful description of

Charlie Webster & friends

Jan Harland gets ready

Brolly weather

speedway racing. [1]

The affable man responsible for this brochure and conscientious liaison with the advertisers and sponsors of Redcar Speedway is serial mobile phone user Steve Harland. Away from the track, his full-time work requires he travel widely around Middlesbrough as a Community Protection Officer. After his work is completed, Steve's a tireless, dedicated networker on behalf of the Bears. Every club should have a Steve Harland figure rustling the bushes for the commercial department. Typically, he's too modest to blow his own trumpet and prefers to reminisce or talk about the hard work and lives of others. "Do you remember Ron Wilson in the '70s? He used to put straw down – oh, that's right, sawdust – imagine them doing that now!" In the brief respite between phone calls I snatch a conversation. "I've been to every single meeting this season – I think we've had 22 and they've all been sponsored. Tonight we have three sponsors! [phone rings] It's nowt to do with me, Baz – I've been overruled on everything [ends call]. Obviously with having the old Boro Bears connection and developing it when speedway came back to Middlesbrough and being a point of contact and going out to visit the companies and to speak to them – things have gone well! I want Redcar speedway to win but people just want to see good racing and you get that here! We don't have a greyhound track in the way and it's usually fast and furious! Well, not tonight. People complain about Sky but, before we had Sky to promote the sport, many people had forgotten about it. Simon Wigg was a great ambassador for speedway, of course. He'd been long-tracking abroad and brought back a lot of good ideas like race suits. People like him and Peter Collins could have been great ambassadors for speedway but they've been so underused, it's criminal. As you know, when speedway's good it's good but, when it's bad, it's bloody awful!" Steve's wife Jan also helps out at the club (every Thursday) with the refreshments in the sponsors' and corporate hospitality area. On the tables of the hospitality area, there's already an impressive array of sandwiches and snacks laid out, albeit covered in cling film. Jan also busies herself preparing hot drinks. Steve says proudly, "There's 12 big pies to come from a local butchers [Alastair Jackson] later. He's from Ruswarp near Whitby. He does these lovely pork and stilton pies. The sandwiches are done by Nice & Tasty catering who've got five stars awarded by Redcar and Cleveland Borough Council. We've been pleased with the interest we've had to sponsor the club or to advertise but I don't take anything for granted, so we've even sold the boards on the back straight. A lot of people in Middlesbrough and Redcar have got behind it. One of our sponsors – Darren from Practical Car & Van Rental said their head office in Birmingham wasn't keen but, they say, they've had a lot of new business from it. They've renewed next year already and that's what I want to mature! We have a contract with Total Fitness – starting now – for all seven riders to use their facilities whenever they want in Thornaby." With 75 minutes to go until the lights, sound, razzmatazz and cameras of Sky flare into life, outside the rain still comes down heavily. Jan Harland isn't optimistic, "Brian just said on the phone 'It's on but doubtful!'"

[1] "The sport is acclaimed as the Number One family entertainment where the fans out on the terraces range from babes in arms to great grandmas and great granddads!! Its origins are from Australia with the pioneers of dirt track racing establishing the sport in the UK in about 1928 with High Beech in the Epping Forest renowned as the birth place of British Speedway Racing.

The sport has had its real boom times with crowds of 40,000 to 100,000 flocking to the likes of Wembley, White City, Birmingham, Manchester, Glasgow etc to witness the action. Television has captured the thrills, spills and kill throttle action over the years with Sky Sports now televising weekly meetings from the Elite League plus giving full worldwide coverage of the World Championship Grand Prix Series.

The format for league racing involves four leather clad racers battling it out over four laps for points on brakeless 500cc methanol powered bikes on circuits ranging from 240 to 400 plus metre ovals throughout the UK. The excitement is breathtaking and the sport proudly has some 35 plus tracks from Scotland to the Isle of Wight.

Sponsorship & Advertising go hand in hand with the sport. Being a family sport the speedway fan is very loyal to those who back their sport. The support is found from multi-national companies to local tradesmen, one man bands and the fans themselves! The sport certainly lends itself to sponsors and advertisers who get full value for their money. Some have even become so involved that they have gone on to become speedway promoters themselves the sport is so infectious.

The use of "SUPPORT THOSE WHO SUPPORT US" is widely used and the two way involvement is plain to see. Testimony of this [is] the continuation of regular backing at each and every track in the country from their local sponsors and advertisers. No one can predict the outcome of any advertising undertaken but history shows that this form of backing at low-rate costs does pay for itself.

At Redcar Bears Speedway we offer the opportunity of backing YOUR local club. We will tailor your involvement to a package that suits both you and us. We have a "menu" of available methods of backing from a simple advertising square in the match day programme to full backing of the team itself with national identity and exposure for your firm. We hope that we can interest you in becoming involved with the Bears and that you will take up our invitation of joining us at one of our Thursday night meetings at The South Tees Motorsport Park."

The Redcar Bears Advertising & Sponsorship Menu offers an exciting range of opportunities: "Meeting sponsorship: £350; Guest sponsorship: £150; Programme sponsorship: (rates start from £125 for an eighth of a page for 26 meetings building up to a full page at £1,000; Heat sponsorship: £250 for the season and Tyre Fund sponsorship: (£10 a month). There's also the possibility of Advertising Board sponsorship on the back straight or on the clubhouse with prices from £250 for a smaller type board to £500 for a "larger". The brochure also reveals that "attendances average between 800/1500 for speedway meetings at STMP."

Though the rain is heavy and constant it doesn't appear to bother BSPA press officer, Sky speedway commentator and sports journalist Nigel Pearson. He stands by the Sky commentary booth to chat amiably with fans, sponsors and assorted other speedway folk. Many of these have umbrellas but Nigel stands there stoically without a hat with his dramatically receding hairline exposed to the elements. Nigel ignores the strange bloke in the hooded anorak stood patiently next to him waiting for a word until he eventually says, "I didn't recognise you with your cagoule on! Fifteen minutes ago it was brightening but this looks bad news. What are you doing here? You'll have a crowd of 200 and not many sales!"
[Jeff] "It's a big night for the club and I wanted to be here to record that. Commercially it's not sensible but it's a good story that shows how quickly the club has developed."
[Nigel] "I've renegotiated my talkSPORT contract so that when speedway and football cross over I can take one Saturday a month to do speedway – well the GPs. Without Sky, this would be the highest level of sport in this country. People want to think about that! The riders here tonight at this level earn a living from speedway but, without Sky, it would become an amateur sport or semi-professional, at best! They'd all still ride speedway but they'd also have to work and fit in speedway around that! Without Sky, where would we be as a sport? It's an interesting question for us all to ponder!"

Back in the dry warmth of the clubhouse, the Redcar start-line girls arrive with their large multi-coloured umbrellas. These will actually be useful tonight rather than just held as props. The brolly girls rush off en masse to the loos where, shortly afterwards, Charlie joins them. Also stood just inside the clubhouse doorway is the Edinburgh Monarchs Mike Hunter who's absorbed using his Apple iPhone. More common than the Blackberry, in speedway circles to own such a sleek piece of equipment signals that you're on trend but also that you have a will to technology geekishness. I briefly think that I might christen Mike the Stephen Fry of speedway, mainly because they both have sharp intelligence, dry wit and elegant writing styles. They clearly also share a love of technology/gadgets but then I recall that Stephen has been on a dramatic diet and Mike's not remotely thespian or gay. "I like gadgets! It's great for sending messages and storing addresses but not good as a phone! It looks like it's brightening up! It's a shame 'cause this could have been an evenly matched contest between two average teams! Sky likes to complete their matches – once they start them – so, I expect, they'll slither about until it's completed! We've had three of our last five meeting rained-off. Last Friday, we stopped at heat 12 and we've had three away meetings called off – that's why we have 10 meetings in 12 days or so to race! A normal meeting would have been off by now but – with Sky here – they want a show!" Brian Havelock breaks off from the myriad of tasks and competing demands for his time to kindly take the trouble to position my mini book display by the condiments table adjacent to the burger bar also located close to both the ladies and gents toilets. "Everyone will walk past or come in for something to eat or drink" he tells me helpfully and apparently confident that everyone washes their hands after a visit to the facilities. Frustratingly for Brian, there's a huge queue of fans outside the entrance turnstiles who (sensibly) stand patiently in the rain, prepared to wait and rather reluctant to part with their money to come in until they see if the meeting is definitely on. With or without the reflected glory provided by the cameras, home and away Redcar fans have a real passion for their club. In fact, there's invariably a strong sense of theatre and circus, almost pantomime, amongst some sections of their fans. Innovative fancy dress is definitely the order of the night for some. Of the characters I can recognise, the STMP has attracted the scarecrow from the Wizard of Oz, Scooby-Doo and, in a fancy dress I can't quite place, there's a lady obscurely dressed in her version of a serving wench. Redcar Bears announcer Keith McGhie isn't in fancy dress. He tells those inside (and outside) the stadium over the loudspeaker system, "You can see it looks like it's brightening up! So, we're going to wait and delay the start of the meeting until 7.45 p.m."

Like many other people, Colin Meredith passes my table but doesn't purchase a book. Colin's here tonight as SCB Meeting coordinator. He also works at the Cardiff Grand Prix, is formally charged with inspection responsibilities to ensure that all British speedway tracks come up to specification and adhere to the regulations of the SCB as well as advising Sky in some curatorial capacity about each Elite League meeting they televise. Nonetheless, he still finds time to look for more work. "I've put my bid in to run Leicester but they need to find a promoter first!" The pies made by butcher Alastair Jackson arrive and my only comment is that they're completely delicious! They must surely be the best pies in speedway? I could eat Alastair's pies all day. They melt in the mouth. It's definitely the best food I've ever had at a speedway meeting. My location doesn't attract sales but does attract conversation or, sometimes, complaints about bar prices, ("It's £2.50 a pint – which is crap for what it's like – or £3 a bottle!") While some customers might

have concerns, the bar remains hugely popular all night and the service delivered by Bob Pope and Roberta Bowman is efficient and friendly. Nobody ever speaks quietly on their mobile phone in public nowadays and a young boy stood a few yards away is no exception, "They say there's good weather over the transporter bridge but we need it here – it's still raining hard!" David Howells stops to buy a discounted copy of *Shale Britannia* and our initial casual conversation about the city centre Travelodge I'll stay in tonight quickly morphs into something like speedway's version of the Antiques Road Show. "Where you are is where the old Infirmary used to be. It was a listed building but, while they hummed and hawed, there were some back-handers – probably – and it got demolished. It took nine weeks. I used to drink in the Speedway Hotel on West Lane in Middlesbrough. I'm 52 and I used to drink in there when I was 17. Do you know anything about this picture? [Shows me a photograph] It was above the fireplace till they knocked it down three years ago. I used that pub from 1975 and it's been hung over the fireplace since I started going there. It's six foot by four foot. I want to find out all about it. It's signed by Alfred Common. I wrote to the *Speedway Star* but haven't heard. [Brandishes photograph] They don't have full face helmets."
[Other Man] "What's that?"
[David] "I'm on about this picture I have signed – Alfred Common has signed it."
[Other Man] "He was a footballer – the first £1,000 footballer to be transferred for £1,000."
It's a distinctive representation of a speedway race. I suggest that David might have much more success with his *ad hoc* investigation if he contacts Allan Melville – webmaster of the excellent and justifiably highly respected *Speedway Plus* website – so that he can appeal to his readers for information about its exact provenance. [2]

Edinburgh fan Norrie Tait is mystified why Sky have chosen Redcar as the location for their live broadcast this evening, "There's Wolverhampton v. Swindon and they're at this tonight!" Outside the rain stops and, as he surveys the damp scene before him from the wooden terrace of the clubhouse, Mike Hunter's confident we're going to see some action. "They're not gonna call it off now after they've made us stand through all the rain!" A Redcar fan stood close by comments morosely, "We never ride well when it's raining! If you put sawdust down, it'll ruin the track for future weeks – we've just had a lot of new shale delivered in the last few weeks – so I don't think Brian would want the expense!"

It's not clear how much rain there would have to be for announcer Keith McGhie to use the 'W' word (wet), "A warm but slightly damp welcome to the South Tees Motorsports Park!" Back on the microphone for one night only, Gareth Rogers slips effortlessly into his presentational mode, "Thank you for your patience. Just to tell you Redcar have won the toss and will be taking gates one and three. Hopefully, that's a good omen!" Edinburgh track all seven riders listed in the programme while the Redcar Bears operate rider replacement for Robbie Kessler. Gareth informs us "Robbie is missing with a Michael Schumacher injury – a pain in the neck." As it starts to drizzle again, all four riders line up for heat 1 while Keith again praises the crowd on behalf of the management, "Thank you for your tremendous patience!" The illuminated green light signals that the riders have come under orders and, when referee Graham Flint presses the button to release the start-gate mechanism, the tapes immediately malfunction (on live television). Well, the tapes do rise sufficiently to release the riders on the outside gates, though they trap the blue-helmeted Carl Stonehewer on the inside. Keith McGhie is quick to offer reassurance, "As you can see the water has seeped into everything! Well, Ladies and Gentlemen, do you ever think that we might be fated?" After the inside start-gate mechanism is examined by many but touched by few, it's soon pronounced fully functional. The rerun of heat 1 gets no further because the tapes this time catch on Carl Stonehewer's helmet. John Rich issues some advice on the content of this book, "Get it in your book, Jeff – two tape malfunctions!" When the first race finally gets properly underway, it's processional but meets with acclaim from the Redcar faithful since Ty Proctor and Carl Stonehewer combine to gain a 5-1 and relegate Ryan Fisher into third place in the process. Stuart Swales and Aaron Summers battle for supremacy on the first and second bend of heat 2 before it settles into another processional race that, once again, sees the Bears partnership race to a 5-1 to give them a cumulative 8-point lead. Norrie Tait is exasperated, "It's déjà vu all over again! Like the Edinburgh meeting last year [on Sky] it was 15-3 after three heats before Workington woke up. Edinburgh is a team that can't gate and come from the back, so we're snookered on this!"

[2] Though the appeal garners many replies, Allan is unable to definitively uncover the exact origins of the painting. The consensus of knowledgeable visitors who frequent the *Speedway Plus* website indicates that the picture "Shows Barry Briggs falling in heat 5 of the 1972 World final in which he lost a finger. Bernie Persson is the rider leading the race and Valeri Gordeev from the USSR is about to hit Briggs. The fourth rider in the race is Grigori Chlynovski."

Redcar: *"The riders here tonight at this level earn a living from speedway but, without Sky, it would become an amateur sport or semi-professional, at best!"*

Every speedway team comprises riders from many different nations and, at the STMP, they have announcer Keith McGhie who – with the producers from Sky Sports on site – is suddenly a man of a million 'Allo 'Allo style accents. Gareth Rogers his guest partner in crime for tonight only develops a brief obsession with all things German, "Max Dilger's the German Under-21 Champion," he informs us before Max races to a third place in heat 3. Fortunately from the Sky producer's perspective, the third heat of the night also produces an Edinburgh winner. Keith is quick to verbally pat everyone on the back about the generosity of the Bears fans response, "A sporting round of applause for Edinburgh's first race winner – Matthew Wethers." Gareth's German theme continues before the start of heat 4, "Kevin Wolbert is the German Champion – scoring 14 last night for the Monarchs at Newcastle – let's see what he can do on his first visit to the South Tees Motorsports Park!" Kevin only gets as far as the first bend before his teammate Aaron Summers knocks him off. Another peculiarity of any Sky live broadcast is the opportunity it provides for the referee to consider television replays to help make, confirm or clarify his/her decision. To my mind, this hints at the stealth introduction of technology by the backdoor (nor am I sufficiently *au fait* with the rulebook to know whether this is really allowed under present speedway regulations). Some incidents would lead you to divergent conclusions if viewed from one camera angle in isolation from another. Quite whether it's the analytical boon it's portrayed to be remains open to debate. Given the track conditions, the clash between Wolbert and Summers has the novelty factor that they're teammates but 'all four back' is the decision most fans would anticipate. Keith explains the delay, "The wonders of technology means that our referee Graham Flint can review the incident on screen so, we'll have a brief delay, while he does that!" It's some time since any British speedway team tracked two German heat leaders. Perhaps, it's this rare occurrence or the two towel-covered bays within the Monarchs pits that fires Gareth's fascination. In the commentary box, to pass the time Keith is happy to read any piece of paper that's put in front of him. "It says here to say 'Hello' to Lauren Shanks who's at her last meeting here tonight. She's been over from Canada and has become a massive Bears fan and it says 'she can't wait to come back to see it all again next year'. We'll be pleased to see you back next year Lauren – Or [effects French accent] Law-erh- [clears throat sound] wren – Shanks!" Kevin Wolbert ignores track conditions in the rerun of heat 4 to really give chase to Gary 'Havvy' Havelock throughout all four laps, albeit without success. Strangely reticent to pronounce his name with a German accent, Keith plays detective, "You suspect Edinburgh have got themselves quite a find!" With suboptimal conditions created by the rain, the Monarchs need Ryan Fisher to ride with his traditional dominance but, instead, the fifth race delivers a race win for Ben Wilson in another processional race. Judged by his determination first time out, Kevin Wolbert looks most likely to be the rider (from either team) who makes light of conditions and so it proves when he overtakes 'Stoney' on the first bend of the second lap of heat 6. Though it only gains him second place, we have to take our kicks where we can. Still, it's a manoeuvre notable as the first overtake of the night but also, more significantly, for the fact that 'Stoney' sportingly leaves Kevin room to execute it. Gareth glories in the thrilled delight that he surmises must have overwhelmed living rooms across the country immediately they set their eyes upon this first overtaking manoeuvre, "Great TV viewing I should imagine!" With the official race result to announce, Keith McGhie can no longer resist the desire to speak in Tongues. Though he intones Ty Proctor's name without a faux Strine accent, Kevin [*Dad's Army* German accent] Voll-Bert proves much too hard to resist.

More inside-gate gremlins strike to delay the start of heat 7. The tune *Howzat* tinkles over the speaker system and prompts Keith to observe, "I think we're playing this for the Australian cricket team." Already 10 points down, John Campbell nominates Matthew Wethers to wear the black-and-white helmet colour. After the tapes almost rise in regulation fashion, stuck back in third Matty is unable to make any impression since Bears captain Gary Havelock has let Arlo Bugeja through to the front (technically the second overtake of the night) and then proceeds to team ride him home. Keith gurgles, "That's put a spanner in John Campbell's plans!" There's a suspicion that the start-line tapes continue to rise unevenly throughout heats 7 to 10. Viewed from the terrace outside the sponsors' and corporate hospitality area, the racing wafts us with an evocative smell – drifts of methanol. Overtakes on damp shale must be a German speciality evidenced by the style and aggression with which Kevin Wolbert powers past Arlo Bugeja on the fourth bend of the first lap of heat 9. Somewhat synchronistically Max Dilger manages to pass 'Stoney' round the banked third and fourth bends on the first lap of the next race. Edinburgh look likely to stage a mini revival until the last bend of heat 11 when Michal Rajkowski makes the strange decision to ride the inside line for the only time in the race and, thereby, gifts second place to Gary Havelock. His decision converts a maximum heat advantage into a much less satisfactory 2-4 and exasperates Norrie Tait, "When I see things like that I think someone has been given a handful.

Redcar: *"The riders here tonight at this level earn a living from speedway but, without Sky, it would become an amateur sport or semi-professional, at best!"*

He leads by a mile and then he starts riding the kerb!" There's a brief delay before Keith McGhie announces the race results, possibly so he can practise his American accent because Ryan Fisher's finally won his first race of the night. However, it turns out that although 'Havvy' easily grabs second place, for some obscure reason TV replays have to be examined. They say if the technology is there, it should be used. Whatever the reason, it hasn't taken Graham Flint long to become obsessional. The third bend of heat 12 sees Stuart Swales come together with Max Dilger who's flung from his machine. To the naked eye, it looks like Dilger has been come off under pressure (rather than contact) from Stuart Swales. The refrain, "and the referee's reviewing the TV replays" once again echoes like a Buddhist incantation over the public address system. To my neutral eye, whether rightly or wrongly, Swales is always likely to be the rider disqualified. However, the technology induced delay leads some Bears fans to imagine a different outcome so, when the disappointing news eventually arrives, it's greeted as a much more controversial decision than it really is. A more restrained Redcar fan on the terraces shouts, "Rubbish!" Norrie Tait isn't so sure, "He's seen the TV replays – without them I'd have excluded Dilger." Stood close by to us is a generously sized woman with a bust to match who sports a T-shirt emblazoned in large but stretched letters with the phrase "Kelvin says whoa!" In fact Kelvin says nothing in the Sky commentary booth because Sam Ermolenko's here instead. Interesting notes arrive thick and fast on Keith's desk in the commentary box, "There's an captivating request here for a birthday for Steve Wilcox, I wonder if it's THE Steve Wilcox?" Norrie tuts, "its Wilcock." With Swales no longer in the mix, Wilson flies from the tapes and, with overtaking at a premium, Max Dilger and Aaron Summers potter around for the formality of a drawn heat. That was definitely the case until – with Wilson ahead by nearly half a lap – he frustratingly slithers from his machine to gift the Monarchs a maximum heat advantage. Though they'd previously used both of their tactical options, suddenly the Monarchs can still mathematically snatch an unlikely victory, if (only) they gain 5-1s in each of the remaining three heats of the meeting.

For drama and unpredictability, heat 13 is worth the proverbial admission money alone, never mind it indicates how quickly the STMP surface recovers from torrential rain! Gary Havelock gates and leads down the back straight until Ryan Fisher passes him around bends three and four with a manoeuvre that mixes skill and bravery but lacks common sense. It also allows Kevin Wolbert to pass. The possibility of a Monarchs maximum heat advantage only lasts as long as it takes Ty Proctor to get fired up and blast past Kevin Wolbert as a prelude to chasing down race leader Ryan Fisher. The heat nearly ends dramatically until Fisher (cunningly) uses trackcraft and experience to drift wide after he exits bend four to block Proctor's anticipated run to the line. Without need for affectation or accent, Keith McGhie justifiably gets excited, "When you consider what the track was like a couple of hours ago – what a race!" On the terrace there's a ripple of appreciation, "They daren't show that on Sky 'cause it'll embarrass the Elite League!"

With two races to go Edinburgh have mathematically lost their chance to win the meeting but, if they get two maximum heat advantages, they could still snatch a draw. This looks unlikely when Ben Wilson again gates with alacrity to lead down the back straight. However, his next visit to the fourth bend – after his previous fall there only two races previously – again undoes him. Ben totally loses his grip of his machine in almost the identical spot and, worryingly, remains prostrate on the damp surface of the track. Like many other Redcar fans in the stadium, Keith McGhie can't quite believe that Ben has again gated but then fell, "He is having a certain amount of trouble negotiating the fourth bend and, my word, we hope and pray he's okay!" With easier access and a roving microphone, Gareth Rogers is soon alongside the medical staff while they treat Ben. He's able to update us on the impact Ben's encounter with the track fence has wrought on his body, "First thought, Ben says he's having enormous pain in his right ankle and, at the speed he went in there, that's understandable!" In the toilets a man dressed as a scarecrow (or possibly the Mad Hatter) describes the crash and concludes with the claim, "He was doing 55-60 mph when he went into the fence!" When I question if that was really the speed he achieved on the damp compact STMP circuit, the scarecrow (or Mad Hatter) demands, "How long have you been going to speedway?" [34 years] "Well you know how they speed up in the corners and slow down on the straights – so it was definitely 55 mph!" Ben's exact speed as he exited the fourth bend remains a mystery but he definitely hit the fence with great velocity. In the rerun, Matthew Wethers looks certain to gain his second race win of the night until the third bend of the second lap when an inspired manoeuvre by the blue-helmeted Arlo Bugeja sees him swoop past with bravery and skill. [3]

[3] After the 2009 season ends, the Bears Supporters' Group nominate this as their "Race of the Season"! They also have a number of other less traditional awards. Nothing illustrates this better than by the BSG decision to award the "Best Supporter's Costume" to the Ostrich worn by Mark Smith.

Redcar: *"The riders here tonight at this level earn a living from speedway but, without Sky, it would become an amateur sport or semi-professional, at best!"*

With only one race to go, a drawn heat will give Redcar maximum league points from the meeting and this looks likely, given the Bears nomination of Ty Proctor and Gary Havelock. Keith still finds the time to give us one last German accent, "Kevin Vo-oh-but". With the earlier mechanical gremlins a thing of the past, the tapes rise evenly and Proctor enters the first bend a fraction ahead of Fisher [from gate 2] and Havelock [from gate 3]. As they jockey for position, Fisher and Havelock's bikes lock together to fling men and machines into the safety fence. Although Ryan's quickly back onto his feet, Gary's condition remains a cause for concern. Though surrounded by paramedics and track staff, Gareth's still able to update us, "He's complaining of pain in the lower back and upper right leg – I will keep you updated."[4]

Back in the trackshop John Rich declares the meeting over, at least from a merchandise sales point of view, "We're packing up after the night we've had – worse than normal! Tell you what, they're all wringing wet outside there and they're going to go straight home!" Bill Gimbeth's thoughts are elsewhere, "I wonder how Wolves have got on? They've probably lost! That'll really make the night!" With staff, paramedics and the stricken Gary Havelock still on the track, proceedings can't continue. Keith McGhie updates us, "Of course, the doctors are attending to Havvy, Gary, so the racing can't go on! But thank you, you have all been extremely patient. Thank you for that!" Quite what the situation is we don't formally know but we can all guess. Gareth Rogers advises, "With Ben and Gary en route to the hospital, it's not been the best of nights for the Bears!" Shortly after this, word comes through to those inside the stadium that the meeting has been abandoned due to a lack of ambulances but also because of the 10 p.m. curfew. More significantly, the Sky Sports viewers learn – before we all do – that the meeting has been abandoned. Norrie Tait isn't impressed, "Everyone on the television knew it was abandoned before we did!" There's a mass exodus to an extremely full car park where, in almost total darkness, drivers jockey for fractional position to ease their swift departure. In the clubhouse, one fan is delighted to see Gareth Rogers, "Nice to see you back tonight. Why aren't you doing it this season?"
[Gareth] "The shareholders voted that I shouldn't continue [I lose the train of the conversation …] Brian was away and one of the directors claimed I was swanning about – I never swan about!" [5]
[Fan] "Martin [Neal] has got better as he's gone along."
[Gareth] "I think tonight would have been a test."
[Fan] "That's where experience comes in!"

Once the crush of fans finally ebbs away from the car park, Gareth kindly gives me a lift to Middlesbrough town centre in a car recently owned by Dave Rattenberry that's now surplus to his fleet. "Usually I've left by quarter to 10. I've learnt over the years, never to rush when you leave late! It was great to be here when Sky came to Redcar speedway. I always knew it would happen!"

24th August Redcar v. Edinburgh (Premier League) 47-39

[4] X-rays would reveal Gary cracked four vertebrae in his lower back in this crash.

[5] The consortium in charge of Redcar reconsidered their decision over the close season and, by popular demand, Gareth Rogers returns to his centre green duties for the 2010 season.

CHAPTER 30

Plymouth

"Speedway isn't so much of a rich tapestry, nowadays it's more like a shabby carpet!"

28th August

Severe delays caused by the Bank Holiday traffic ensure I arrive late at the St Boniface Arena. Though I've visited quite a few times, I somehow take a wrong turn and end up in the nearby complimentary car park rather than by the entrance gates where I'd like to be. When I ask some fans in Plymouth GT Motorcycles Silverline Devils scarves for directions, they tell me they don't know how to get there by car! Luckily Kirsty from the Supporters' Club passes and helpfully provides directions. When I get there, she even carries in some of my books! On my next journey from my car, I bump into Mike Bowden junior who's initially not at all keen to let me inside the hallowed portals of the arena, "Which press are you then?" While I set up my display table, friendly Devils team manager Gary Spiller stops for a few words. For tonight's clash against the top of the table Bournemouth Buccaneers, it's been a struggle to find a suitable replacement for last-minute absentee and Devils number 1, Mark Simmonds. "Mark has swine flu and, as of yesterday, he's now in quarantine for five days! Under the 180 hour [8-Day] rule I couldn't get anyone from the Isle of Wight, Bournemouth, Weymouth or Mildenhall. I did look through Rye House, Scunthorpe and Newport but obviously Grant Tregoning is here [as a guest for Bournemouth] and Craig Cook is riding tonight and tomorrow. We are pretty much in the Play-offs! The misfortune at the Isle of Wight with Brendan created team shuffles and, along with injuries to Chris Johnson and Tom Hill, restricted their options. Buxton and Newport are still in it mathematically but they need to win at home and also away. Buxton need 4 points from the 7 they have left to go for. Perhaps the absence of their top two riders will affect the crowd? Jay Herne is having an excellent season and Jerran Hart got 21 from seven rides the last time he was here! At least the weather is good. They've got a good rider guesting – Grant Tregoning." The Buccaneers definitely have an altered line-up from usual since they track Grant (instead of Jay Herne) and also call up John Resch to fill one of their reserve team places.

With a good-sized crowd already inside the arena, there's still a substantial queue of fans keen to make their way through the entrance turnstiles. I'm situated next to promoter Mike Bowden's grandson, 16-year-old Adam. He enthusiastically engages passersby in conversation in an attempt to interest them in a purchase of the *Speedway Star*. Between possible purchasers, Adam chats amiably. The idea of the chance to travel to every British speedway track in the country, like I do, appeals to him. "Do you know all the top riders then? Do you know Darcy Ward – he's an amazing rider!" Our conversation is interrupted when Adam optimistically tries to sell a *Speedway Star* to the Bournemouth Buccaneers team manager Garry May. "Nah, thanks!" Smartly attired in his Buccaneers team anorak, Garry strides determinedly towards the pits and, once he's out of earshot, I explain to Adam what I believe to be his error, "That's the Bournemouth team manager!" "I know! I was going to say to him – next week it'll have you losing in here! Do you know Taylor Poole of Mildenhall? Jason Crump mechanics for him! He got 8 points for Mildenhall the first time he rode." The sheer volume of fans means that Adam can't entice everyone with the offer of a purchase. Nonetheless, he definitely speaks to all the girls as they pass. "Do you wanna buy the *Speedway Star*, I say to them all?! I only sell them to beautiful girls! It's great for talking to them. I hate the way some people just ignore you and say nothing."

All good salesmen know their customers but they also know their product. Adam brushes up on his product knowledge with a quick glance through this week's *Speedway Star*. He isn't impressed with the team photograph of the Weymouth Wildcats on the back page, "Why is Cockle holding a teddy?" It's a good question but, perhaps, an even better one would be "Why has James Cockle chosen kevlars that make him look like Borat?" Our philosophising is interrupted by the arrival of the Sittingbourne Massive in the form of Graham Arnold and Dick Jarvis. I'm surprised to see them but the avuncular Dick retorts, "We have a bit of interest in Bournemouth – 'cause it's the Sittingbourne B." I just can't compute what he's told me. "B?" Patiently, "Yes! You know, B team, 'cause they have so many of our riders. It's a joke!" In reality they're here to "look after" and "look out for" speedway brothers Mark and Aaron Baseby, who both ride tonight for Bournemouth. The advent of the National League saw Conference League stalwarts Sittingbourne decide not to track a team during 2009. Consequently, many riders they discovered now ply their trade elsewhere. Some relatively recent Sittingbourne 'discoveries' have even progressed to the extent that they now grace the Premier League. Though they don't formally have any National League fixtures, the club continues to develop the grassroots riders with practice days and, of course, a variety of team and individual meetings. "It was supposed to be a Dragons meeting but, if they've a meeting on the 20th at Newport, it'll be a practice. On 18th October we have a credit crunch meeting and, on 15th November, we've got a load of Belgians coming over – they go mad for it!" Graham Arnold holds his cards close to his chest as to whether Sittingbourne might possibly return to the National League. "We might be back next season, you never know! They'll all have to learn to ride the track again if we do! You won't recognise it when you come – from a racing point of view anyway!" I'm surprised to learn of Graham's disappointment that ex-Wimbledon Plc chairman Ian Perkin floundered with his attempt to bring speedway to another stadium within Sittingbourne. "I think it's a shame! He tried. I think he had Robert Heath in the background! I said to him 'You know they call you Dorothy'. He said, 'I know they do but I don't know why?' I had to explain to him that it's from Dorothy Perkins." It's a moniker chosen with the kind of wit usually associated with footballers. Graham and Dick laugh at what a "Dorothy" can colloquially mean in Brighton. Graham is a fund of information, "They've an auction here tonight. I dunno what for. They tried to hold it in a pub but only eight people turned up so they're doing it here." Like myself, Dick Jarvis will be at Stoke tomorrow night, though his evening in Plymouth is tinged with disappointment, "It's a shame there's no Marc Andrews here tonight."

Dick Jarvis studies the form

Bathed in sunlight

Keen Plymouth Devils fan Julie Rickard arrives with her daughter Laura. They're hoping for a Devils win but they're not absolutely confident. Laura's Egyptology and Ancient History degree interrupts her speedway, "I might miss the Play-offs 'cause I'll be back at Uni in Swansea. It's the same as Plymouth really except they've got a beach and we've got a cliff! I've wrangled a flat on campus again [next year] with my mates."

[Jeff] "Have you seen the stained glass window in the Taliesin Arts Centre?"

[Laura] "I have. It says 'In memory of' but there's always something blocking it.

[Jeff] "It's a memorial window for my best friend Edwin's first wife, Stephanie MacLeod, who died in 1996." [1]

[Laura] "That's nice!"

Grizzly & *Plymouth Herald* photographer Lucy Blake

[1] Designed by Catrin Jones. She's also installed some lovely "cultural" windows in Carmarthen, Newport, Sheffield, Haverhill, Sunderland and Caernarfon. Catrin's work with glass is highly skilled specialist work but has numerous beautiful applications – churches, schools, hospitals, businesses, housing – and enlivens buildings throughout Great Britain. Go to http://www.catrinjones.co.uk/culture.html to see her work.

There's quite an outbreak of photographers at the St Boniface Arena tonight. Official track photographer Nick Truscott kindly says to let him know if I need any Devils photos in future, "The sun's gonna be a pain tonight – it's low and bright as you look towards bend two. Anyway, usually after three heats it gets so dark. This should be one of the biggest crowds of the season!" Also here tonight is the glamorous but slightly flustered sports photographer from the *Plymouth Herald*, Lucy Blake. I must be infected by Adam's chattiness because I ask, "Do you come here often?" She's a regular at the St Boniface Arena, "I've been coming since it started but not every week, though. Whoever's on late shift gets to go to the speedway for the Herald on a Friday night. We always have other things to go to so I'll probably only stay for the first few races." David Hawking ("or Big D is my trade name") runs the DVD stall adjacent to my table and his company – DL Actionsports – produce a DVD of each and every Plymouth home meeting. "Things are slow – there's a recession. Luckily this isn't a living for me. [nods to my notepad] I hope you're writing something good! Last time you were here there was a punch-up!" There was certainly a rumpus but I only heard shouts and didn't know punches were thrown. We're unable to carry on our conversation because a bloke comes up. Dave gives a barely perceptible nod and asks him, "You alright?"
[Bloke] "No I'm not, I've got cancer."
[Dave] "What, on your elbow?"
[Bloke] "No [points to lump by his eye/eyebrow] I've had it bloody months and kept knocking the scab off when I washed it. It's a sad job, for sure. I've got to go to the hospital on 9th September."
I'm distracted from their conversation by Adam's latest encounter with the opposite sex which, unusually, hasn't been initiated by him.
[Girl] "I like your shorts."
[Adam] "They're beautiful, like you! [laughs and says to me] What a line!"
[Jeff] "Yes, corny."
[Adam] "It's one of my best."

Even when you're ill, life goes on around you and, as the gentleman explains to Dave the ins and outs of his appointment schedule, I take some photographs. Adam Bowden joins in, "Actually, I'll take a photo of you too!" Adam's photography experiment is short-lived since a blonde lady, possibly in her fifties, approaches his table.
[Adam] "*Speedway Star*?"
[Lady] "Yes please."
[Adam] "You're looking very nice today."
[Lady, smiles] "Thank you!"
Adam brightens this lady's night and, stood with him, it's easy to enjoy his natural interest in people and good-natured bonhomie. "It's not usually this busy for me! Bournemouth are a good team, I mean, they have good supporters. Usually it's really slow but tonight I've only three left out of twenty-five!"

Paul Adams [aka Grizzly] latterly *Western Morning News* speedway correspondent, brother of Julie and uncle of Laura, arrives at my display table just at the moment Mike Bowden announces that next season there will be a Testimonial meeting for the Plymouth Devils Seemond Stephens. Though it's likely to be an individual meeting, Grizzly would like the Testimonial to be a team affair. "I suggested Cornwall versus the Rest of the World. It would be easy to raise seven Cornish or pseudo Cornish riders. There's Seemond of course, who sort of got the [speedway] bug off Mark Loram. Mark wanted to do trials and Seemond wanted to do speedway and they met. Trelawny was in Cornwall, of course. We could have Matej Zagar – I used to interview him for the paper, he wasn't the easiest to speak to – Chris Harris, Mark Simmonds, Jason Prynne, Wayne Barrett, Gary and Roger Lobb, Tim Webster from Saltash and, of course, Seemond himself." Grizzly refuses the opportunity to purchase my latest book ("my staff have already got me one"). On my last visit, he took the time and trouble to explain some aspects of the water table and drainage as it affects the land upon which the speedway track of the St Boniface Arena rests. "It's my old school playing fields – circa 1970s – when I was at grammar school no less – I can't stay away from the place!" Grizzly points into the distance, "See that hill that the sun's going behind, there was a ford there. The ford was owned by a bloke called Ebb so it became Ebb's Ford. At one time, the only way to get across to here was when the tide went out. All this is reclaimed land from about the 1300s onwards. Believe it or not, at Plympton St Maurice they used to berth the galleons there! This was all sea water. This was a large inlet, but a big part of the river Plym is all silted up now – there used to be a china clays works (at Coypool) which was a major contributor to that problem. It still gets a bit murky and damp that end [on bends three and four] when the tide's in and it rains. There aren't many houses near here but it's a peculiar place because some of the residents are still up in arms! Despite the track being next to the A38 and having been there three or four years now."

Our history-cum-geography lesson is interrupted by the sound of the first race. It's won easily by Kyle Hughes ably supported by his teammate Paul Starke and fires Plymouth into an early 5-1 lead. Bournemouth's choice of Grant Tregoning as their guest doesn't look so clever when he finishes last. Many people expressed doubts about whether Devils owner Mike Bowden could turn a rugby field into a fully functioning speedway club, let alone one that consistently challenges for league honours. He's proved these naysayers wrong, albeit that despite two table-topping campaigns somehow the club hasn't yet quite managed to obtain any notable silverware. Mike's an enthusiast for both speedway and his club. There are lots of telltale signs. Every race night, he stands smart and proud in his dark BSPA jacket with the Association crest on its pocket. Mike prefers to watch the races from the centre green since it's a position from which he can dash back to supervise affairs in the pits and also go out on the track, until the race action starts. When the riders come under orders, traditionally Mike watches the start-line intently until his body jerks (almost jumps) immediately the tapes begin to rise. Some of his riders (but more of the Bournemouth ones) could do with his sense of anticipation at the tapes. Though David Gough easily wins the second race, the Buccaneers reserve partnership of Aaron Baseby and John Resch combines to take the minor places and ensure a drawn heat. While in horseracing it's possible to win by a short head, on the shale it's possible to win by a margin as small as the knobble of a tyre. However, before you cross the line it's important that man and machine remain in concert. Unfortunately for Devils heat leader Matt Bates, this technicality disqualifies him prior to the end of heat 3. In a race won easily by Seemond Stephens, second-placed red-helmeted Matt Bates races energetically for the line slightly ahead of the green-helmeted Kyle Newman who's in close pursuit on the inside. Unfortunately, Matt's determination to reach the finish line ahead of his rival causes him to smash into the safety fence fractionally before the chequered flag. To compound matters, Kyle Newman then runs over his head. In fact, Matt's head does cross the finish line but he's still disqualified because he fails to finish the race in contact with his bike. Grizzly is downcast at his misfortune, "Once Matt started wobbling it was only going to end one way!" Still under the weather, Matt Bates doesn't appear for his scheduled ride two heats later. His place is taken by Josh Dingle. It's a race the evergreen Seemond Stephens wins easily in a time of 53.38 seconds. It's a triumph that excites announcer Graham Hambly enough to rechristen Seemond, "Mark" Stephens. After this race I spot *Plymouth Herald* photographer Lucy already en route to the car park, "I have to go to another job in town." When I make small talk and stupidly chatter, "Back to work then?" Lucy retorts, "This is work! I always leave around now. We only use two or three shots and I have what I want!"

When the tapes rise for the seventh race Josh Dingle makes an early bid for the Wheelie of the Night competition. Sadly for him, it quickly becomes a sudden and immediate dismount. It's of limited consequence for the Devils since the battle of the Kyles sees Plymouth's Hughes beat Bournemouth's Newman. When not fixing start tapes or the referee with his gimlet gaze, Mike Bowden rushes from the centre green to the pits to oversee the work of team manager Gary Spiller. Mike also likes to take to the airwaves. With a voice reminiscent of Jesse from the Fast Show when he emerges unshaven from the toilet to impart some words of wisdom ("this week I have mainly been eating pop-tarts"), Mike admonishes a mystery photographer, "I have been told there's someone using flash photography on bend 3, please do not do this as the riders may mistake it for a red light. Thank you." Adam Bowden is close by, so I tell him, "I like your granddad's accent." "He loves doing announcements! He really does!" Before heat 9 we're told that Matt Bates has withdrawn from the meeting with a hand injury before announcer Graham Hambly continues, "I want to apologise that there's a slight delay because David Gough has two rides on the trot!" So far the whole meeting has been run at frightening speed and, although it's only 35 minutes old, we've already seen eight races! Rather than step from the centre green over to the pits to ask, microphone in hand Mike Bowden says over the public address system, "Can I have our 15-year-old reserve Josh Dingle onto the centre green please? After this race we're going to make a wish for the Wish Foundation. We'll do the draw for the model of the lovely sailing ship. At this draw we're going to have the oldest (Allen Trump) and the youngest (Josh Dingle)!"

After a restart prompted by the fall and disqualification of Buccaneers reserve John Resch, Seemond Stephens rides to his third straight win of the night accompanied by David Gough for a 5-1 to take the cumulative scores to 33-21. Delighted by events, Mike Bowden instructs the crowd, "Put your hands together for Seemond and David!" Two disabled fans sat in their wheelchairs on the raised platform close by the bend 1 safety fence applaud enthusiastically. Given their proximity to the track, the disabled viewing platform guarantees they'll definitely get showered in shale. Tonight's trackshop lady, Donna Jones agrees, "I think that disabled people should have a glass screen. We had three girls and their carers but they weren't so active, so didn't see the shale coming. Even if they had, I don't think they'd have been ones to have moved!" The lovely sailing ship is won by Zak (1) and Hayley (5), "Allen Trump the Elite League co-promoter will present the prize." Mike evangelises about the Wish Foundation as well as the draw generously organised by the Indian Inn, "It's an absolutely brilliant, fantastic charity! They cater for permanently ill children who wish to do something in their remaining days." After the draw but before the start of heat 10, I half hear Graham Hambly mention a "travelling insect circus" and immediately I feel itchy. This turns out to be a travelling insect circus museum they display at Dingles Fairground located in the Heritage Centre at Lifton (they also sponsor heat 13).

With the Buccaneers 11 points behind after nine races, their joint team managers, Garry May and Neil Vatcher, send out Mark Baseby in the black-and-white helmet colour. When the tapes rise, Seemond Stephens sweeps to the front from the outside unbothered by the bumpy track. The first two laps see Kyle Newman and Paul Starke really battle for supremacy with Mark Baseby last. He continues to unsuccessfully harry and attempt to catch Paul Starke until, on the final lap, Mark rears, struggles for control, just about regains it only to then tumble in a heap just before the third bend. Despite the virtuosity of this fall, Mark's disqualified from the race by referee Jim Lawrence, who also awards the race. Five minutes later Mark gets back to his feet to generous applause. On the shoulders of his father a small boy asks, "Why are they clapping?" Patiently his dad explains, "He's the one who crashed." This exposes there are still some gaps in his son's knowledge, "Did he win?"

The interval is taken early while Mark Baseby is seen by the paramedic in the pits. With a pause in proceedings, Mike Bowden needs no second invitation to take to the public address system with some housekeeping announcements. "For our older patrons – from next week for the colder evenings – 20 or so can sit in the bus! Come along early and you can sit there out of the cold." With his distinctive burr, Mike describes some of the 40 items we can bid for in the forthcoming charity auction, "A Sunderland Premier League shirt signed by Marcus Stewart, a Bolton Wanderers pennant and autobiographies by Ian Botham and Lewis Hamilton." Though there are still five races left, Devils heat leader Kyle Hughes is prematurely invited out onto the centre green, "Kyle – you are the Silverline fastest rider of the night, at the moment. Come out and collect your award – a series of cooling drinks for after the meeting!" We're again told about the Seemond Stephens Testimonial to be held next season, "I'm delighted to say that Seemond has been granted a 10- year testimonial! It will be our first meeting of 2010!" Mike lists likely participants and lingers over each lustrous name. These include Ben Barker, Matej Zagar, Jason Bunyan and "Chris Harris our Cornish GP star". There's a special offer, "I've just been told by Seemond that anyone aged over 65 who can bring both parents here can get in free!" Seemond receives positive news too, "Allen Trump, who owns LCD Publishing in Exeter, has kindly volunteered to print Seemond Stephen's programme completely free of charge – give Allen Trump a round of applause!" When Mike eventually falls silent, Graham Hambly carries on with the barrage of announcements. We learn, "Tonight is our last National League meeting of the season" and that Mark Baseby has become the second rider to withdraw from the meeting, in his case with a back injury.

Bargain sweet prices in the trackshop (30p for jelly love hearts) allied to an impressively wide selection causes near anarchy among the kids crowded inside as they try to make their choice. Though we're not yet in September, temperatures fall noticeably, enough to prompt the sale of two Plymouth Devils scarves to some German speakers. After they've left, Donna Jones ("it's usually Diana here") highlights the run of scarf sales to foreign visitors, "We had some Poles earlier buying scarves – I've sold three now!" Like the temperature, darkness also falls, though I optimistically hope for interest in my display of books in the gloom. Soon the action resumes. The very bright spotlights dotted at roughly 20-foot intervals around the track perimeter create a mottled effect that accentuates the speed of the riders as they zoom from one pool of light to the next via a short dark stretch of shade. Consistent race wins by Seemond Stephens provide the backbone for Plymouth's third-tier successes over the past five seasons. Tonight he's matched for verve and point-scoring ability by Kyle Hughes who wins heat 11 to record his third successive victory. A win for Kyle Newman in the black-and-white helmet colour sees the Buccaneers riders and pits crew make a meal of their 8-1 celebrations in the 12th race sponsored by Camerons Catering. Fascinated by the

punches thrown in the air, the boy on his father's shoulders asks, "Daddy, why aren't you clapping?"
[Dad] "'Cause we lost big time there!"
[Boy] "Can I come another day?"
[Dad] "Do you want to?"
[Boy] "Yeah!!"

Though their lead has diminished, Grizzly comes over specifically to highlight the quality of the Plymouth speedway product. "We always have "bums off seats" entertainment here! It's a phrase coined by Dave Smith Scottish ex-Plymouth Argyle manager – affectionately known as Ciderman (eccentric in a nice way) – to describe when you involuntarily lean forward to see the excitement." Grizzly has an understated but sharp wit. "Speedway isn't so much of a rich tapestry, nowadays it's more like a shabby carpet! Many speedway promoters seem to reach for the stars and get the nearest lamp post by mistake!" If the Buccaneers fightback is to maintain its momentum they need their guest, Grant Tregoning, to gate in the next race. Grant does briefly lead until Kyle Hughes battles ferociously round the outside of him as they travel from the second to the third bend. Further drama ensues on the last lap when third-placed Paul Starke hits the mogul run of the second-bend bumps, rears massively to fall dramatically and, thereby, gift Danny Warwick a third-placed point in an awarded race.

The penultimate race of the night takes a couple of attempts to complete. First time out, John Resch brings down David Gough and is disqualified for his trouble. In the rerun, Seemond Stephens leads Bournemouth's sole remaining representative, Adam Baseby, until his chain snaps and throws him from his bike to also earn him a disqualification. Third-placed David Gough shows great reactions to lay down his machine swiftly and so avoids compounding Seemond's mechanical agonies. Since they were already on their fourth lap, Jim Lawrence awards the race for an ungainly 2-3 heat result that confirms – irrespective of the outcome of the last race – Plymouth will emerge victorious. However, the Devils meagre 6-point lead also means that a draw or better could still gain the table-topping Buccaneers a valuable league point. Prior to the race Mike Bowden rails against the dangers of new technology disseminating inaccurate information that could well commercially damage his business: namely, the erroneous claim that this is the last Plymouth speedway meeting of the season! Quite how such a misconception has arisen is surreal, particularly given that – even without the possible additional Play-off fixtures – the club still have a further six home meetings scheduled! "As I've said before, don't take any notice of people on the Internet! Phone me, I'm down here seven days a week!" Kyle Hughes wins the last race of the night to complete his impeccable five-race 15-point maximum. Behind him, Grant Tregoning and Kyle Newman combine to ensure the race is drawn and, as the riders cross the line, Bournemouth staff in the pits celebrate their away point ecstatically! Mike Bowden immediately takes to the microphone to issue a heartfelt retort, "Well, we actually beat Bournemouth Buccaneers! It goes to show that without Jay Herne and Jerran Hart, they're just an average team!"

In the pitch darkness sensibly prepared older fans pick their way across the uneven surfaces armed with torches. The meeting is officially closed at 21.16 and perhaps, conclusive proof that I'm a serial optimist, I stand in the dark and wait for sales that never materialise. Grizzly takes heart from the news that Seemond's Testimonial will be an individual meeting rather than his initial preference for Cornwall versus the Rest of the World, "as Cornwall would get a bit of a battering!"

28th August Plymouth v. Bournemouth (National League) 49-43

CHAPTER 31

Stoke

"It's so scary and exciting! They just keep going till they stop"

29th August

Though there's a forecast of rain, the Premier League meeting between Stoke and Rye House isn't called off. Indeed, the entrance gates are open ready to receive riders, mechanics, officials, track staff and fans although it's a couple of hours before the scheduled start time. I'm soon told what we can expect, "They won last time they were here but they won't this time! We've had some bloody good meetings here recently against Redcar and Sheffield – where it went to a last heat decider."

Inside the home-straight grandstand bar and hospitality area that overlooks the home straight at Loomer Road, I base myself down the far end of the clubhouse by the doorway that leads to the stepped terraces that overlook the fourth bend. My book display is arguably symbolic of the tenor of speedway infrastructure investments in this country. Last season I comfortably destroyed three bargain priced B&Q versions so, over the close season, I invested in a notional upgrade of my equipment but though this promised well, the table hasn't been as robust as expected when frequently used. It also requires specialist equipment. Shockingly, I've travelled to the Midlands without a Phillips screwdriver. This is very remiss of me but luckily a kindly member of staff is able to help.

Back at my bookstall a Wolverhampton fan joins me, "Were you at Eastbourne last night when they lost to Poole? It's not a surprise when they've got four heat leaders – Bjarne Pedersen, Chris Holder, Hans Andersen and Joe Screen. None of the teams want to come up [to the Elite League] 'cause they know what goes on! Wolves are the only clean side in the Elite League – well, along with Eastbourne, Ipswich and Belle Vue, though they had to get rid of two riders to bring in Jason Crump. Look at Swindon; once Troy Batchelor was fit again they should have got rid of Zagar. They'll pull a stroke in the Play-offs. Paul Hurry will declare himself injured and they'll bring in Cory Gathercole. Just you watch! I can read promoters like a book!"

Steve Davies arrives ready to watch the action along with his partner, off-duty speedway referee Margaret Vardy. Out on the centre green a woman fusses about tieing ribbons on a trophy. "Stoke and trophy aren't words you hear in the same sentence that often!" This statement ignores distant past triumphs, notably the Pairs (1984, 1988 & 1989), Four Team (1990) and, of course, who can forget that the Conference League Fours victory in 2006?Earlier today Steve saw his beloved Walsall draw 0-0. "I nearly fell asleep this afternoon. We had 3,300 – we only really get a big crowd for dirty Leeds and that was last week!" I can sympathise since I'd also seen two unimaginative Premier League teams (Stoke and Sunderland) play – barely separated by a rare Dave Kitson goal that he cunningly smashed into the pitch to ensure it bounced through a crowd of players and into the net. There were scuffles at half-time during the match in the home end outside the Gents toilets, "There was a Stoke fan laid out on the floor with a paramedic treating him and two lots of Stoke fans were being held apart from hitting each other." There's a strong desire for a quick fag and a chippy sense of victimhood that leads some football fans to be under the impression that the toilets have been designated an unofficial smoking area. Many speedway clubs don't have the surface, sheen or modernity of the Britannia Stadium whereas, at speedway, we enjoy bonhomie and civility in spades. Outside the bar, on the open-air terracing, two ladies enjoy a cigarette.

The Stoke speedway programme is included in the admission price for the majority of fans who pass through the turnstiles. Inside it says it has a value of £2.75. Within its pages there's a hard-hitting column by promoter Mr D. Tattum that expresses unhappiness with the nature of last week's 33-57 home defeat to the King's Lynn Stars. "At the end of the night I was fuming to say the least and told the riders in no uncertain terms how I felt." The best-laid team building plans can go awry and Mr. D. Tattum's column highlights Stoke have suffered from "an imbalance of first home matches, and now away matches". Out on the track the distinctive Stoke speedway approach to the rider parade is underway. In Noah's Ark fashion, the teams ride number by number, side by side without helmets in race tabard order. The mere thought of Noah's Ark dictates that rain spits on at about 19.32 but won't interrupt our enjoyment. The recent postponed meeting against the Glasgow Tigers has been rescheduled for next Saturday and the programme bigs up the challenge that this clash of the titans presents.

Potters meeting presenter, George Andrews, introduces the six-man Rockets team and explains all the changes we'll have to make to their section of the racecard ("it's rider replacement for Linus Sundstrom as he has the highest average"). The Easy-Rider Potters ride as per programme. Unlike some presenters George doesn't introduce them with a litany of tenuously invented monikers nor does he affect any faux matiness. His presentational approach is characterised by enthusiasm, trademark bluster and a repertoire of ready-made phrases designed to excite the fans. With the riders up at the tapes and just about to be placed under the orders of referee Craig Ackroyd, George cries: "Let's go racing! Let's shift the shale!" Rockets number 1 Robert Mear takes George's advice to heart and wins the first race of the night ahead of Jason Bunyan who's often difficult to defeat at Loomer Road. In the trackshop, John Rich hasn't quite recovered from his recent encounter with Sky's Charlie Webster. "If you're looking for an attractive woman to take a photo of here – you'll have to get one of Tom P. Madsen's wife!" Tom P. fails to get to the start-line promptly from the pits and is disqualified under the two minute time allowance. He still takes part in the rerun handicapped by 15 metres and, although he catches up with Tommy Allen easily, he fails to find a way to pass though a lady on the terraces repeatedly cries encouragement: "Go on Tom!" The race winner of heat 2 was never in doubt after Andrew Silver gates from the outside berth with great speed to win with some ease. Andrew Silver is credited in the programme as the holder of the "fastest track record", the only sub-minute four laps ever ridden at Loomer Road (59.1 seconds for Arena Essex on the 8th August 1987). Ty Proctor holds the "current track record" with a more modest 60.5 seconds. With a weird synchronicity that would look implausible if it was to appear in a novel, Ty also set his record on the 8th August – albeit in 2009. Almost as quick from the tapes and equally comfortable up front, Ludvig Lindgren wins heat 3 to give the Rockets their second successive heat advantage and progress the score to 7-11. Before anxiety that another home defeat takes firm hold, Robert Ksiezak and Tom P. Madsen romp to a maximum heat win for the Potters to level the score. They are helped in no small part by Tommy Allen of the Rockets, who holds up Andrew Silver for the first two laps. Once he'd cut free, Silver rode with some dash and verve but was unable to make up the lost ground.

During the delay for a track grade, a man arrives at my book display, points to *Quantum of Shale* and smiles proudly, "I'm in there!" "You are?" It's Peter Oliver. "I'm the chap who had a fit when Redcar came down! You got some of the facts wrong." I apologise and tell Peter, "I can only go on what I see." He's phlegmatic, "Or what you're told and, if that's not right, you can't help it. It's no problem! I bet I know who told you too! It's too complicated to explain. If I'm Dave Rattenberry's best customer, then I deserve a big discount! I think I'm helping him. He can smell me coming – I like to buy all the DVDs and pile them up for the winter. I'm doing the garden at the moment – I've tons of muck and I'm clearing out the rhododendrons 'cause I'm a roses man."

After the track grade ends, the realigned shale must suit the Rockets setup since Robert Mear gates closely followed by his team mate Joe Haines into the first bend. However, Lee Complin uses his track knowledge and composure on the bike to get between them on the second bend. Lee then accelerates down the back straight in pursuit of the Rye House number 1. At maximum speed as they enter the third bend, the Potter loses control, falls cum slides and his momentum causes him to clatter into Robert Mear and throw the unprepared Rocket from his machine. Joe Haines avoids the carnage by a whisker. Though both riders are soon on their feet, their crash punctures the air fence. During the delay, smartly dressed in suit, tie and collared shirt George Andrews comes up from the centre green to my stall to note down all the details of my books so he can meaningfully promote them throughout the rest of the meeting. He's not overly optimistic about the Potters chances, "I don't fancy us getting much out of this!" His verbal dexterity and skill on the microphone means that George is in demand. "I'm exhausted from all the motorways! I've been at Blackburn today for the West Ham game."
[Jeff] "What? Do you commentate?"
[George] "No. I do all the interviews for Signal, BRMB and across the Midlands and also across Cheshire. We're part

of the Sky Group. Of course, I do all the interviews for the Potters website too and CVS has asked me to present at Monmore on Monday 'cause Porky is away on holiday or someint."

Before heat 5 resumes, George tells the crowd, "Unfortunately Robert Mear has withdrawn from the meeting with a damaged right hand." The withdrawal of the Rye House number 1 is a big blow for the visitors' chances of victory. Not only will he miss the rerun but his absence from his programmed rides – including the vital heat 13 (and possible candidacy for the nominated heat 15) – won't be adequately covered by the Rockets reserves. Tonight, however, most of the Rockets actually live up to their team nickname. At least so far as their departure from the start-line ("these can really gate!"). In the rerun fifth race, Joe Haines showcases his lightning reflexes as the tapes rise. After a lengthy absence from the sport, Andrew Silver has lost none of his old liking for the Loomer Road circuit. It's no surprise he starts heat 6 with yet another lightning-fast departure from the tapes. When Ludvig Lindgren rides aggressively to power past Jesper Kristiansen on the second lap, the Rockets look set fair for a maximum heat advantage. Though fourth at the end of the second lap, Jason Bunyan has other ideas. Second-placed Ludvig Lindgren impedes his own progress when he locks up on the last bend of the penultimate lap to provide Jason with the fractional opportunity he needs to accelerate and dive underneath Ludvig on the first bend of lap 4. With momentum and surprise on his side, Bunyan then cuts up inside Andrew Silver who immediately and very noticeably backs off rather than attempt to match Jason's aggressive charge down the back straight. It's a race that's worth the proverbial admission money alone and, to my mind, is a signature Loomer Road race since it combines dramatic speed with sufficient variety of racing lines to ensure that passing continuously remains a clear and present danger. Bunyan's charge from fourth to first results in a drawn heat and alters what could have been a 15-21 scoreline into a far more manageable 2-point Potter's deficit.

The Stoke revival looks likely to continue when reserve Craig Branney leads heat 7 but, unfortunately, he falls on the third bend. After his disqualification, the Rockets regroup. Chris Neath wins to become their fifth different heat winner in seven races closely followed home by his race partner, Ludvig Lindgren. It's an almost immutable law of speedway start marshalship that, if they decide to be fastidious about any rider's pre-race position, then you can safely bet that the rider won't wear a red or blue helmet colour. The ninth race is under orders when the start marshal leaves his central position to go over towards gate 1 to hassle Joe Haines for not lining up at the tapes correctly. He returns to his usual central position and, as the riders rev their bikes ever louder, the start marshal again moves over to correct Haines's position. The riders jet away from the tapes and Joe Haines exits bend two in second place. However, by the end of the lap, Lee Complin blasts past the youngster to join Potters race leader Klaus Jakobsen up front. The Potters second 5-1 of the meeting that manages their deficit back to 2 points. The home riders' reluctance to consistently win races continues in the tenth heat when Lindgren sees off Bunyan. With Haines back out on track for heat 11, the start marshal again subjects him to some over-fastidious attention. Whether you see this as good practice or gamesmanship usually depends on your allegiance. Either way, the start marshal stands between gates three and four for this race (rather than between gates two and there where he's content to stand for other heats) to give Joe Haines on the outside gate the full benefit of his attention. Usually there's rider movement at the start-line but, from my vantage point, the riders appear to sit stock still so the only real movement comes from the start marshal as he makes pernickety miniscule changes to Joe Haines' start position. Haines remains unmoved by this aspect of his speedway education and again answers in the best way possible when he gates with electric speed to win the race. Fourth placed Craig Branney falls on the first bend but, with the Rockets placed in first and third, his only thought is to immediately remount when, tactically, the Potters team management would probably prefer he stays down in the hope of a disqualification for Andrew Silver or, alternatively a rerun. Joe Haines really looks remarkably quick round the Loomer Road track. It's an effect emphasised by his finish half a lap ahead of Robert Ksiezak. The low hum of incipient Stoke fan dissatisfaction ramps up when Ludvig Lindgren gates to win heat 12. There are shouts of disgruntlement as this race ends and the Potters fall 6 points behind with three races to go. An OAP mutters to his friend, "It looks like we're going to lose another one!"

The interval provides a welcome chance for the Stoke management to regroup and re-motivate their riders. For the mechanics, it provides the chance to tinker with or repair the bikes under their charge. The mystery of the centre green silverware is solved. It's a memorial trophy to remember John Jarvis that's awarded to the most exciting rider of the night (along with a cheque). Birmingham fan Paul won't be going to see the Brummies against King's Lynn tomorrow evening. "We're going to Buxton tomorrow 'cause we don't want to give any money to Tony Mole. I like to go in at the interval for free when the turnstiles are closed and the gates are open. Tony Mole caught me sneaking in last week and gave me a filthy look. When the published accounts appeared for the first season, it turned out that Tony took half of the raffle proceeds that the Supporters' Club ran. Like most people, I expect, I buy a ticket and try and win a prize and take satisfaction from half the money going to the riders – but not to Tony Mole! The next season, sales fell dramatically and the Supporters' Club couldn't figure out why! The season tickets weren't that well priced either. It worked out that you only got one meeting free if you paid up front! Some people like to support the club, of course. If you buy a football season ticket, you get five or six matches free. They gave away 100 tickets in the paper some weeks so you could end up losing out through your loyalty! This season they gave a 10% discount, I think." I offer no comment but do say how much I enjoyed my recent trip because of my belated discovery of the panoramic views available from upstairs in the home-straight grandstand. "The view is good but you're behind glass and still so far from the track. They say the facilities are great – here might be a bit dilapidated but the atmosphere is fantastic 'cause you're so close to the track! We came here for the King's Lynn meeting and the scoreline wasn't close but it was a great meeting!"

After a rejuvenating cuppa, the riders approach the start-line and Stoke speedway's mantra man George Andrews tries to revive the crowd with one of his chants, "Your riders! Your colours! Your gate positions!" Perhaps George should have added "His engine failure" after Andrew Silver's mechanical gremlins reduce the Rockets heat 13 reserve rider spearhead to the sole efforts of Tommy Allen. Sadly for the visitors, he's completely unable to make any impression upon Jason Bunyan and Robert Ksiezak as they romp to a maximum heat advantage. George savours the Potters nascent fight-back, "Come on – let's hear it!" he implores the still mostly silent crowd. Prior to the penultimate race of the night, George remains in excitable form, "Let's go racing! Let's shift the shale!" It's a message that finds some approval from the on-track audience of Lee Complin and Tom P. Madsen who combine to vanquish Neath and Silver of the Rockets to the minor places. George savours the turnaround in Potters fortunes with wild abandon, "Hit me! Hit me! Woo! Hit me!" With Stoke 2 points to the good for the first time tonight, they only need to draw the last heat to emerge victorious. Given, the widely acknowledged fair nature of the Loomer Road track let alone its multiple racing lines, even if you discount the often electric gating skills of the Rockets, it's not beyond the bounds of possibility that Rye House could still win the meeting. George adds to the anticipatory tension – while the riders attentively garden their gates – with his confident statement that there will be "No quarter asked, no quarter given!" From the point of view of fast-flowing action on the track, the meeting ends in anti-climax with an engine failure for Joe Haines at the start line that's greeted with great almost rapturous jubilation by the home-straight crowd. Potters captain Lee Complin wins and, with Jason Bunyan second, three consecutive 5-1s massage the final scoreline to 48-42 (though, under the 2009 revised league points allocation system, the Rockets do gain one league point for their efforts). After a short delay, the Stoke riders come out to receive the warm celebration of the crowd. First out on the victory lap is a helmetless Jason Bunyan with a jubilant Dave Tattum as his pillion rider – the rest of the team take part in this victory parade on the club tractor. While the tractor wends its way back to the pits, Jason Bunyan stops off at the start-line to receive the John Jones Memorial Trophy he's been awarded for being the most exciting rider of the night. With Jason otherwise engaged, Dave Tattum pootles off on Jason's bike until he gets to the back straight where temptation overcomes him and he opens up the throttle to feel the wind blow through his hair.

Two young women arrive at my table with some questions about speedway. Sian and Lauren have both never been to speedway before and only came in during the interval because the entrance gates were open. They'd seen the last three races from the second bend.
[Sian] "Don't you get scared watching them – they get so close and go so fast!"
[Jeff] "It's always like that."
[Sian] "Do they have it on again soon?"
[Jeff] "Next Saturday."
[Sian] "Are you sure? Do you promise? How much is it to get in?"
[Jeff] "How old are you?"
[Sian] "We're 15 – I'm 16 soon."
[Jeff] "I'll ask." [It's £4 if they're 15 and accompanied by an adult.]
[Sian] "Are you sure it's on every week?"

[Lauren] "It's so scary and exciting! They just keep going till they stop."
[Jeff] "Did you know they don't have brakes?"
[Lauren] "Why? How do they stop?"
[Jeff] "They take their hand off the throttle and slow it down."
[Lauren] "Do they have crashes?"
[Jeff] "Yes."
[Lauren] "Did they have any tonight?"
[Jeff] "Yes."
[Sian] "Are you sure it's on next Saturday?"
[Jeff "It's definitely on. You can watch it at many other places in the Midlands too." [lists tracks]
[Sian] "We live very close by."
[Jeff] "Well, unless the rain is torrential, you'll find they'll race. Come at 7 p.m. and see the parade."
[Sian] "Can we get to meet the riders?"
[Jeff] "They'll be in the bar afterwards."
[Sian] "Can we buy a drink here?"
[Jeff] "Yes, but it can't be alcoholic if you say you're 15!"

George Andrews is old enough to have a drink at the bar but prefers to meet and greet the fans. He tells me, "That's what it's all about, getting the crowd excited!" George then greets an OAP with loud enthusiasm, "What about that then?!"
[OAP] "It was alright."\
[George] "Alright?!! It was great!"

29th August Stoke v. Rye House (Premier League) 48-42

CHAPTER 32

Buxton

"Speedway rule changes and general strangeness have always gone together."

30th August

After a less than restful night at the Travelodge in Talke, [1] on the comparatively short trip from Talke to Buxton in Leek a newspaper headline I pass proudly proclaims "Brett Applies for 100 jobs". Buxton is a hilly attractive spa town crowded with Bank Holiday visitors. It's the kind of place that's posh enough to have a Marks & Spencer and a Waitrose only 20 yards apart. Outside of the town centre on the winding hilly road to Dale Head, I'm soon on the cross-country cattle-gridded single-track road that appears to lead towards the wilderness but, after nearly two miles, brings you to the stockcar stadium. Down a slightly rocky slope at the far end of the stockcar stadium perimeter is the entrance gate to Buxton Speedway. I'm so early that co-promoter and club chairman Jayne Moss has yet to open up. Rather than stop to chat, instead I drive down to the seated area outside the trackshop adjacent to both the pits and the track itself. With dark clouds overhead, I decide it's not sensible to set up my book display just yet. Out on the track, members of the curatorial team busy themselves setting out assorted centre-green paraphernalia and, of course, the flags that are the essential equipment at any speedway meeting.

By the time I return to the entrance, inside the booth that serves as the admissions nerve centre prior to each meeting at Buxton, Jayne Moss busies herself with administrative matters in between greeting early arrivals. Everyone arrives in a vehicle, whether they're riders, fans or officials. Jade Mudgway has come on foot from the pits keen to collect his

[1] The start of a bizarre night was signalled in the car park when what looked like a bride (or bridesmaid) and her groom got out of the car that had just parked up next to mine. I chose the Travelodge at Talke for its convenient location to Stoke Speedway, though it still doesn't strike me as your ideal wedding night location. When I arrived at reception shortly after half-past 10, I was asked to wait for a few minutes while the receptionist consulted the manager. After 15 minutes delay, I was told that the Travelodge was full except for my room that they hadn't yet serviced. Though, clearly on my own, they checked with me their computer reservation that said I also required a child's cot. Desperate for a cup of tea, the receptionist agreed that I could go to my room on the understanding that the Travelodge manager would shortly be along to service it. The word "unserviced" didn't prepare me for the poor treatment the room had received from the previous occupant. This included distressed bedding, an unflushed toilet and an abandoned but impressively long fluorescent tube that had been removed from above the bathroom mirror but then abandoned. Without a significant clean and disinfection, most people would have second thoughts about sitting on the sofa let alone making a cup of tea! However, the Travelodge hotel manager was charming and diligent, plus the news that they wouldn't charge me for my stay brightened the situation. Nearly an hour after I arrived, I was finally alone in my newly serviced room complete with a working fluorescent light in the bathroom capably fitted by the receptionist. Just after midnight, I was woken up by a commotion in the corridor that I put down to people coming back from a night out. Approximately an hour later, further commotion in the corridor woke me again and, this time, I decided to investigate. The hallway outside my room was crowded with people – almost as if a silent fire alarm had sounded to summon everyone from their bedrooms. After some to-ing and fro-ing, doors shut noisily and the corridor fell back into silence. Little over an hour later I was again woken by a commotion in the corridor and, amazed at the further disruption, I again found the corridor similarly crowded. Doors opened and shut loudly at regular intervals throughout the night. As Charlie Rich famously noted, what people get up to in the privacy of their own bedrooms (or houses) is unknown and entirely up to them. Obviously, I'll never know exactly who these people were or where they came from. They weren't the sexiest-looking crowd. All the usual problems of middle age were in evidence: receding hairlines, poor fashion sense, weight gain, and the like. There was the odd young one, with emphasis on the word odd. An atmosphere of determined but frantic joylessness prevailed, at least in the public spaces. When I checked out the next day I reconfirmed that I wouldn't be paying for my room and queried whether this level of regular disruption was a special feature of the Travelodge at Talke. The receptionist apologised and said that she suspected that there had been a 'swingers' party (wife swap party in old money) held there last night. She hadn't been on night duty so couldn't definitively say. Rather naively I was astonished at the news. "You'd be amazed at what goes on!" When you use the online reservation on the Travelodge website, you're asked whether your stay will be for business or leisure - there is no functionality to specify your intended leisure activity as 'swinging'! Understandably, the staff would have no idea of the residents' planned activities unless they draw unnecessary attention to themselves. Even then, with limited staff on duty, it must be hard to police the situation. Interestingly, in October the *Sun* carried an article about Julia Sinclair (48) who worked as personal assistant to Rear Admiral Stephen Lloyd at the Abbey Wood MoD base near Bristol. The Rear Admiral is in charge of procurement and delivery of nuclear submarines and, as a consequence, his assistant would have high-level security clearance and access to strategic documents including Trident missiles. The *Sun* alleged that "MoD swinger Julia Sinclair enjoyed sordid sex" when she "romped with a group of men at a Travelodge". The entrance to the Travelodge was pictured but unnamed. Julia's "sleazy hobby" potentially exposed her to "blackmail". An unnamed expert was quoted "she is likely to have access to the Admiral's emails, his diary and details of all personnel in that department. Those details could be used in a terrorist plot. Her swinging could have had serious implications. It's a threat to national security." I don't know if nuclear secrets were exchanged in Talke but, when swinging takes place in the early hours, it's certainly a threat to a good night's sleep whether you're a frisky participant or not.

purple pits wristband and meeting racecard for this afternoon's National League/National Trophy double header with the Weymouth Wildcats. He looms large in the doorway of the hut. Each Buxton rider has a personalised racecard. Jane double confirms the idiosyncrasies of the team management's plans for this afternoon directly with Jade, "You'll have an R/R in heat 14." Jade recalls, "I was winning heat 14 all the time until I fell last week." Jayne explains today's situation, "We've had to change the line-ups around today to cope." Jade is a politely spoken young man with a soothing New Zealand accent. He's tall and thin with a Spandau Ballet style '80s haircut. Trackshop worker John Rich also now hovers by the doorway and offers him some words of encouragement, albeit disguised as a rhetorical question, "You gonna go well today?" Though laidback, Jade is quietly confident that his performance this afternoon will be more than up to scratch. While Jade heads back to the pits, John chews over some gossip with Jayne before their discussions move on to Simon Lambert. Jayne praises his development, outlook and status "Simon's the number 1 in the National League this season – he's a nice lad and a good rider!" Belle Vue fan Charles McKay arrives and buys seven programmes. I can't quite place my finger on it but I suspect he may have a programme collection at home. Unfailingly polite speedway referee Chris Gay arrives with passengers in his Mercedes, "I've brought my mum with me today so I'd like to pay for her!" Jayne is having none of it, "No need, it's okay." The next fan in the traffic queue queries the increased cost of admission for this afternoon's meeting until he learns that it's a double header. He then suddenly decides it's extremely good value. The weather isn't exactly optimal but cool and windswept is perhaps traditional August Bank Holiday weather in this part of the country? Away on the hills that dominate the near horizon, drizzle and mist look like they are blowing in our direction, "I hope that's not rain coming!"

Charles McKay has wandered down to the converted metal sea container that serves as the trackshop at Buxton Speedway. At this stage of the season, it's unlikely that this outpost of the Dave Rattenberry's souvenir empire will have any new merchandise on sale (though, with Dave in charge of stock, you wouldn't bet against the arrival of some previously unseen limited edition badges). Charles has an extensive knowledge of speedway along with a keen insight into the specific vagaries of the ongoing iterations of the rules and regulations of the sport. "Certain teams have it in their contracts that the National League takes preference over the Premier League, which they've never done before! The fact that Bournemouth are in the league has nothing to do with it – that's cynical."
[John Rich] "Could King's Lynn beat Poole or Belle Vue? [pause] No, it's a waste of time!"
[Charles] "The Elite League teams have to wait for a month to find out who they ride in the relegation Play-offs, while the Premier League sorts out who'll race them."

Wherever speedway fans congregate, meteorology is rarely off the agenda. John takes a phlegmatic view, "The rain is good for the track!" Another frequently discussed topic of the 2009 Elite League campaign is the mid-season decision to alter the number of teams that could qualify for the Play-offs (reduced from the original six to four). "If you finish fourth, and you win both legs of the Play-offs, you could still not progress to the final because of the points handicap (depending on the points you get)." Though many people believe arbitrary mid-season changes to rules and regulations to only be a feature of the 21st century speedway world, Charles points out that it has always been thus – even from the first year that speedway was raced in this country. "It started in '29 – half way through the season they changed the number of heats from six to eight! Speedway rule changes and general strangeness have always gone together. 1959 was the year that the number of heats in a meeting was changed from 15 to 18, after 22 league matches had already taken place! 1962 was the year that they had a handicap system with different handicaps when you rode home and away. Changes were made to the handicaps on a regular basis throughout the season. They also had supplementary reserves who were in the team and they had other rules about who could replace the reserves. Another time there was a meeting between Wimbledon and Coventry. Wimbledon signed Vic Huxley and the *News of the World*, who sponsored the meeting, they didn't like it 'cause they didn't want any foreigners – only British stars! But, then, they also accepted Aussies – so they got in Jack Parker. You could say that very little has changed in speedway but, at the same time, you could say that very little has stayed the same. In 1929 the scoring was 4 points for a win, 2 points for a second and 1 point for third. There was a rules cock-up in 2000 in the Conference League. In 1999, the rules allowed a team to run a minimum of six home and six away meetings (with a maximum of two home fixtures against the same team but the second meeting had to be in addition to the minimum six meetings). This was okay when there were only seven teams in the league. The same rules applied in 2000, the only problem was that the number of teams had increased to ten. So how would you work out league positions if teams had raced different numbers of fixtures? The rules gave no clues. Was the rule for 1999 left in by mistake? They changed it mid-season

Buxton: *"Speedway rule changes and general strangeness have always gone together."*

but the problem was made worse because each team did, in fact, intend to race against each other but, in the end, the weather won and Mildenhall didn't ride their home fixture against St Austell and the BSPA wouldn't allow them to extend the season. And so, Sheffield and Mildenhall finished level on points and Sheffield became league champions on having a better points average. It's a decision which still upsets the Mildenhall fans! In 2001 they introduced new rules that, if the start gate goes wrong, you have to use a bit of elastic. But when the gate went wrong after heat 2 at Belle Vue last week, they didn't think they had a piece of elastic in the stadium! I must check the rules to see if they have to have that as a part of the equipment they mandatorily need to run a meeting!" Our conversation about the enduring nature of the mad world of speedway rules and regulation changes and the iniquities that ensue as a result is interrupted by the loud screech of tyres from the stockcar track next door. Charles owns a perpetually questioning mind, even away from his detailed consideration of the minutiae of the speedway world, "What's the difference between driftcars and stockcars then?" Part of the audience that has listened to his peroration is an OAP who answers, "He's had an argument with his missus, I reckon." Further debate is put on hold when club co-chairman (and son of the man who founded the club) Richard Moss arrives in the trackshop to ask, "How many Buxton fleeces do you have left?"
[John] "I think we've got six. What sizes do you want?"
[Richard] "Extra large."
[John] "You don't want that, they're not that big!"

Jem Dicken learns the latest

Graham Tagg enjoys the view

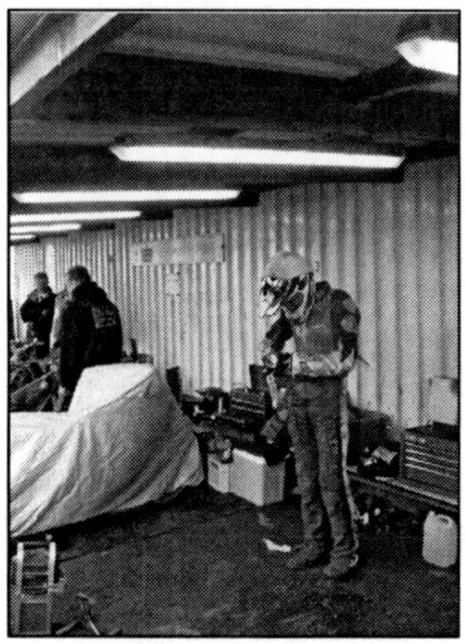

Muddy

There's a sudden brief surge in demand from speedway fans based in the Weymouth area keen to read speedway books that include mention of red undergarments. Despite my studied veil of secrecy, *Concrete for Breakfast* and *Quantum of Shale* apparently enjoy brief infamy, notoriety or something similar amongst the speedway cognoscenti based in or around the Dorset coast. One of the bubbly Weymouth start-line girls (aka the Kittens), Hannah Coventry purchases a signed copy of Concrete but I soon gather she could fill a much more exciting book based on her own recent experiences of the speedway world.

Under darkening skies stood by the entrance gate to the pits, Wildcats team manager Jem Dicken has an outlook to match. He tells me that recent events off the track have impinged on the riders' outlook and motivation. "I'm just looking at it from the team manager's point of view. I'm just interested in what goes on on the track and I don't care what goes on off it! Team spirit is a delicate thing and they will all think like a team so, anything that upsets one of them will upset all of them! There are no secrets in speedway!" Inside the compact referee's box, smartly dressed Buxton announcer Graham Tagg ignores the view and instead prepares for the afternoon's work ahead. This afternoon's programme is open at the racecard. Next to it, Graham has a sheaf of notes, some spare pens and two unopened cans of full-fat Coca-Cola. When you look out of these windows, you have the ideal vantage point to look out over the sloped dark shale240-metre track. Away in the distance, it's mainly hills and clouds apart from a number of large but nondescript buildings grouped together in the valley below. I ask the amiable Graham how long he's worked at the club. "Time goes by that quick it must be eight or nine years by now. Most of all I enjoy the involvement with the fans and the riders. Especially with the fans 'cause we have a good laff here, 'cause we do make mistakes and they're quick to pull me up on it. Sometimes I drop them in deliberate to see if they notice! We're small but, yer know, we're a really good family club and the riders get on well together. I first went in 1968 to Sheffield – they're me club that's where I started going 41 years ago! I used to come here as a supporter when they first opened and I saw an advert in the *Speedway Star* over the winter and applied. Ken Moss was here then – I had a trial and I've been doing it ever since! I don't do this for a living. I'm a volunteer who does it for a hobby. I'm not professional – I do it 'cause I want to! I ain't had no training. I've listened to other presenters and have me own style – at least, I think I do. Some have worked on radio and have a media background, I ain't got that! The main thing is I enjoy it – otherwise, I wouldn't do it. I suppose at Premier League, it's more professional. I tek it as fun and I try to entertain people in me own little way! I enjoy every minute of it!" Graham also enjoys his proximity to the referees every week. Proximity is the right word given the confines of the referee's box. During the meeting, Graham stands next to the control panel that the officials operate from this booth. "Chris [Gay] is a nice ref. They're all brilliant! They've got a job to do. When you look from up here, you get a totally different view. At Sheffield, I might dispute the odd decision. Before this wasn't as high as this. It was just above ground level and before, when the ref made what we thought was a wrong decision, we used to have quite a bit of fun. Not many of the fans come from Buxton. There's a few away fans and they [Hitmen fans] mostly come from Sheffield, Belle Vue and Stoke. Since Scunthorpe opened, there's less of them 'cause they go 20 miles away rather than come here. We still have some Sheffield fans – there's a couple that sponsor the riders, Mr and Mrs Shepherd, and they follow them home and away. It's these kinds of people who are the grassroots of the sport!"

In the unlikely event that this afternoon's referee Chris Gay needs to consult anyone about the specifics of the 2009 speedway rules and regulations as issued by the SCB prior to the season, then he'll have to look no further than in Charles McKay's bag for a copy. "On page 39, Rule 16.4.1 says that the play-off for promotion/relegation will be between the bottom placed [Elite League speedway club] versus the winner of the top placed four [Premier League] teams. On page 40, it says the winner in the Premier League is 'to compete against the Elite League relegation Play-off winners'. Surely that implies that there's a relegation play-off? Maybe that's been changed but, as usual, we [the fans] haven't been told about it!" Earlier Charles worried about the availability of elastic and now he's anxious about the light. "I think referees have a need for a light meter for tracks where you don't have floodlights! But, maybe, it doesn't translate for Welsh? Stoke has a curfew at half 9 unless an ambulance comes out onto the track and, then, it's 10. That doesn't sound like a planning curfew! It says in the rulebook a ref should know of any local restrictions. Imagine if a new track wants to open and an objector says that they know of tracks where the curfew isn't adhered to! It's lucky that objectors don't coordinate their objections!" Charles has many questions. "How come Swindon have [Morten] Risager riding for them? He's their asset but it's the first time he's ever ridden for them!" Another *bête noire* for Charles is the IMG/BSI Speedway Grand Prix series. "In the GP, if the result of the first [2009] GP had been repeated for every GP, the Russian [Sayfutdinov] would not be world champion even though he'd won all the individual GP rounds. I emailed Nicola Sands [IMG/BSI Press spokesperson] saying I'm doing an article on the success of the GPs over recent years and, one method, would be to look at the GP attendances. I don't have these for 2008 but she hasn't replied, so far. I'll give her some time before I write back to say that, obviously, by this measure it isn't a success!" [2] Charles prefers team meetings to individual meetings as well as competitive events to friendlies. Select team meetings aren't his cup of tea but he jokingly wonders if there would be a market for "a Jailbird 7 for drugs, allegedly, versus a Jailbird 7 for motor offences, allegedly?" Discussion of quite who would appear in such line-ups is interrupted before it starts by the arrival of Peterborough programme editor, Steve Miles, "We're not competing for the top four to get into the Elite League Play-offs, we're in the Midlands League where we hope to finish third!" According to Charles, the recent staging of the Team GB versus Australia Under-21 Test Match Series at the Norfolk Arena wasn't speedway's finest hour. "There were 75 on the first bend, 30 on the third and fourth and whatever was in that shed you pay to get into. There were no flags on the centre green and there was no presentations. They gave you that posh ticket and then, 20 yards later, they ripped it up! An ex-rider whose son rides told me the Barracudas had a meeting where they didn't have a promoter in attendance and the ref said 'well you can't have a meeting' so they deputised someone for the meeting." John Rich reveals that there won't be any photos of the Weymouth team on sale in the trackshop following this meeting, "Ian Charles [Buxton track photographer] was going to take a team photo of Weymouth on the centre green but he couldn't 'cause only four of them turned up ("there was only four of them so I couldn't be bothered!") I have five of

[2] Charles didn't get the information he requested from Nicola but, after he contacted head honcho Paul Bellamy, the information was soon forthcoming after Charles agrees to supply Paul with the GP attendance figures for years previous to 2008!

them [team photos] every week. It'll cost him 'cause he makes his money that way!"

One of the yet to be resolved tensions of the 2009 National League structure is that stand-alone teams invariably have a different business philosophy to other clubs with a parent team in a higher division. Those for whom National League racing is the sole source of club income (for example, Weymouth and Plymouth) sometimes have a tendency to attract slightly older and/or more experienced riders. Ostensibly to provide their fans with entertainment but also to give the team a sufficiently solid backbone upon which to try to build results and, thereby, challenge for honours. The stand-alone/parent club tension is far from a hard-and-fast rule – particularly since Buxton operate differently as a stand-alone team and, for many years, have pursued a policy that bloods youngsters with the primary aim of track experience in mind rather than silverware. Although, that said, this season the performances of Craig Cook have thrust Buxton into what by their recent standards is the nosebleed territory of the upper echelons of the National League table. Whatever the rule of thumb, there's always an exception. Nonetheless, it's safe to say that Charles McKay isn't impressed with the Wildcats philosophy that, on balance, is weighted slightly more in favour of success than rider development (even though, this 'criticism' ignores some previous sterling work in that respect). With the rider parade over and the brief practice lap session underway, Charles remarks ironically, "Look at Weymouth with all their good young prospects for the future!" Just in time for the start of the meeting, fine Peaks drizzle that quickly soaks starts to slather riders and fans alike. "I'm retiring to the grandstand otherwise known as my Nissan Micra!" James Cockle also retires from the first race (after a fall) while the Buxton partnership of Craig Cook and Scott James make light of the slippery track (and opposition) to record a 5-1. If this is a bad start for the Wildcats then things immediately get much worse when the Hitmen repeat the medicine in successive subsequent heats to take the score, after three races, to an already unforgiving 15-3. Buzz Burrows then steadies the ship when he gates determinedly at the start of heat 4. He calls upon his considerable speedway experience to vanquish the other three riders in the first bend and becomes the first Wildcat race winner of the afternoon. After he's confirmed the results, announcer Graham Tagg lists an impressive number of items for sale in the trackshop before he concludes pragmatically, "I don't think they're going to sell many T-shirts this afternoon!" Well, not unless they're wind and water resistant!

Heat 5 starts brightly for the Wildcats who are on a 5-1 until the third bend when a tentative Terry Day decides to approach track conditions with extreme care and, thereby, relegates himself from contention. Jade Mudgway rides with passion and some control to hammer home his second win in two outings. Stood by the start-line a Buxton fan morosely comments, "There's only going to be one winner today and that's the weather!" In the pits, there's a 'show must go on' attitude exemplified by the riders' determination to ignore meteorological and curatorial conditions out on the track. However, residual psychological issues are harder to ignore. Buxton club chairman Jayne Moss shrugs, "This is annoying but what can you do? I dunno if we'll manage to finish!" Tim Webster doesn't even manage to start heat 6 after referee Chris Gay disqualifies him for delaying the start when he's actually at the start line! Lurking outside the trackshop door I.C.A. Crook (aka Mushy Pea) always has a positive outlook on life so definitely isn't irked by a bit of drizzle, "At least this has kept the dust down!" Back out at the start-line, Buzz Burrows on a tactical ride now has a new partner for the sixth race – James White Williams – who sadly doesn't complete all four laps before he retires. However, Buzz treats the spectators and also gives Craig Cook a masterclass in trackcraft (round his own circuit) when he eases up inside him on the third bend of the first lap. Like many speedway riders, despite his experience, Buzz sometimes lets his throttle hand rule his head but not in this race. Because of JWW's retirement, the full benefit of Buzz's second win of the afternoon isn't reflected in the heat score (3-6), though the Wildcats deficit does narrow slightly. The sea container that serves as the trackshop is positioned in such a way that it provides an outlet for the souvenir sales but, also, I suspect one side also serves as the pits wall. That must be the explanation since, whenever the two-minute warning sounds in the pits, the signal vibrates in the trackshop like a farting bee. Having worked at Buxton for some time, John Rich is oblivious to the sound and uninterruptedly carries on his conversation. "Scunthorpe didn't have a good crowd Friday – the first time I've seen such low numbers there! It was £20 a ticket for a Friday and the double-header on [Bank Holiday] Monday [tomorrow] but most people must have decided to go then, if at all! People just don't have the money." Though the Wildcats track one of their more experienced partnerships (Lee Smethills and James Cockle), it's the Hitmen's Ben Taylor who emerges victorious from the seventh race. If a fight-back is to happen then it will have to materialise soon for Weymouth. Unfortunately for the visitors, heat 8 sees Lewis Dallaway win closely followed home by his partner Scott James for the fourth Buxton maximum heat advantage, so far, in the first part of this afternoon's planned double header.

If Axe Edge had an airport (an unlikely prospect), poor visibility caused by low cloud would ensure that computer auto-pilot would land most planes. As it is, even the riders who've won races find their kevlars and machines absolutely clarted in sticky shale. When it's dry, shale flies into the crowd but, when they get home tonight, each rider is going to have a substantial part of the Buxton race surface back in their workshops. James White Williams makes particularly heavy weather of the second bend at the start of heat 9. He rides in mid-track in the manner of someone whose bike has unexpectedly found itself in a swamp. Up front Jade Mudgway looks untroubled and leads Buzz Burrows until he tries to exit bend two second time round and then the swamp wreaks its own revenge since heavy slop unseats him from his bike. Gifted the lead, Buzz needs no second invitation to ram home this unexpected advantage, albeit he rides with care and controlled speed. Without any real time to do anything other than refuel and vaguely sluice his bike down, Buzz is back out again in the next race on a rider replacement ride for the Wildcats absent number 4, Benji Compton. Craig Cook is also out in this race so it's a clash to potentially savour for the fans. Once it begins, Craig rides hard under Buzz on the third bend and the veteran rider again showcases his experience to cope with this manoeuvre and remain on his bike, though he loses the lead. The swamp-like conditions of the second bend soon prompt Craig to lock-up and, thereby, enable Buzz to regain the lead. However, the steady throttle hand of his earlier outing now deserts Buzz. It's been replaced by the twitchy grip of his inner boy racer. Consequently on the opening bend of the third lap Buzz, to his own great dissatisfaction, slithers off to gift the lead back to Craig Cook.

Sat behind his table in the trackshop, John Rich looks out of the rain-splattered window towards the start-line and the third and fourth bends. From this vantage point he doesn't get wet but, equally, he can't see the first and second bends where, for the most part this afternoon, all the action is. Nonetheless he's got strong opinions on what should happen, "If it gets to heat 12 and Buxton have enough, they should go on to the next one! I tell you this rain's gonna hang about until the end of the meeting and it'll clear then." For heat 11, Wildcats team manager Jem Dicken hands the black-and-white helmet colour to Wildcats number 1, James Cockle, who wins but only after he's shaken off the close attentions of Ben Taylor during the first half of the last lap. With Ben's last-ditch challenge repelled and Terry Day third, the 2-7 heat result reduces the Wildcats deficit to only 10 points. Jem expresses satisfaction but still has half an eye towards ongoing personnel issues possibly affecting his team. The possibility of a Weymouth resurgence then all but mathematically disappears after Jade Mudgway wins heat 12 to retain his record of race wins in every heat that he manages to remain on his bike. If the visitors close out the meeting with three successive maximum heat advantages they'll snatch an unlikely draw. Unfortunately track, meteorological and psychological conditions combine to frustrate Buzz who hits the berm of the swamp on the second bend and then suddenly finds himself trapped under the safety fence (after a less than elegant slow-motion fall). Already irked by his disqualification, Buzz drags his bike back out from underneath the fence only to find his back wheel locked completely solid! Second-bend Weymouth-rider slow-motion falls suddenly become the order of the afternoon. On the second lap of the rerun, James Cockle executes a similar dismount but, since he avoids the attentions of the fence, is able to remount for a consolation third-place point that will boost his earnings but leaves the scoreline beyond the reach of the Wildcats.

Steve Miles is impressed with the determined enthusiasm of the riders but also the quality of the racing surface. "It holds up really well! I think they need a plough not a grader – it's about six inches deep! It's funny how a rider can be crap all afternoon but give them a black-and-white helmet colour and it all changes! James Cockle's a case in point." James White Williams fires from the gate in heat 14 only to dramatically slow after two yards and then, when relegated to fourth, speed up again. Luckily for him the race is called back but, disappointingly for the riders and fans at Axe Edge, the drizzle turns into heavy rain. In the rerun though James White Williams is again fourth into the corner helped in no small part by a huge elbow from Jade Mudgway on the way there. Steve Miles likes what he sees, "That Mudgway doesn't give a shit!" Without a win to his name all afternoon, Lee Smethills decides to make light of the inclement weather and cloying track conditions to race to victory ahead of the always combative but big-hearted Jade Mudgway. For the final race of the National League fixture, Jem Dicken bizarrely [3] sends out Wildcats reserve Tim Webster who, until that point, has raced to an unspectacular four-ride minimum. The previous two heats have both had to be rerun and, to continue the sequence, this race is no exception. While we wait for the riders to return to the tapes I suddenly

[3] Jem later explains: "It was quite simple really. We were due to race in both legs of the double header, meaning (as we were using rider replacement) that some of the boys would have had six rides per meeting equalling twelve. I started sharing the rides around after it became apparent that we were not going to win any points, so that we would get through the afternoon. Luckily it got rained off."

realise that there aren't any rakers out on the centre green. Steve Miles isn't surprised, "They'd need shovels today, anyway!" At the second time of asking, Buzz Burrows makes no mistake to again emerge victorious from his third head to head encounter with Craig Cook. It's a win founded upon sheer determination and experience. Something a small knot of dedicated Weymouth fans (that includes Wildcat Kitten Hannah Coventry) greet ecstatically with a rush to the safety fence to salute him.

The interval between the National League and National Trophy meetings arrives at 16.45. Almost everyone who has the option retreats to the dry. Fans go to their cars or the refreshment portacabin that overlooks the first and second bend. The riders lurk disconsolately in the pits. Some fans finger the merchandise in the trackshop but don't make a purchase. Chris Gay leaves the warmth of the referee's box to have discussions in the pits. "The meeting is on a knife edge! I'm pleased Buzz (i.e. as he's on the losing side) won the last one as I've already had a phone call from the pits to say there's rumblings, which I can understand! It's all very well me telling the riders to ride but the rain affects visibility!"
[Jeff] "Why did Tim Webster ride in heat 15?"
[Chris] "He's probably the only one who wanted to ride!"

Given the cloud cover and the ferocity of the downpour, only an optimist would believe that the second half of the meeting would still take place. Announcer Graham Tagg confirms that before any abandonment decision is made, we'll definitely go through the motions. "At quarter past 5, there'll be a track inspection and we'll see what the track looks like then!" If anything, no sooner have these words echoed away over the surrounding hills than the rain gets heavier. Boggy conditions on the second bend have already consistently caught out the riders of both teams – irrespective of their track knowledge or experience. Some now treat that part of the track with such circumspection that you could half-believe that stories swept through the pits of a rider-hungry monster snatching prey into its swamp. Stood in the downpour by the start-line – albeit slightly sheltered in the lee of the referee's box, some Buxton fans express satisfaction at the three league points gained for their win. "I reckon the racing's been better today than it has been for some time this season."

30th August Buxton v. Weymouth (National League) 56-40

CHAPTER 33

Lakeside

"There's a lot behind the scenarios and that."

11th September

The sunshine Jon Cook forecast would bathe the stadium for the Ipswich meeting fails to materialise. Low clouds hover over Lakeside and the Queen Elizabeth Bridge. The early afternoon Friday night traffic queue started six miles before the tunnel but moved steadily. On the radio the ubiquitous Stephen Fry promotes his latest television programme on animals facing extinction. It's a topic he examines by various trips to jungles and other assorted obscure locations. Unconnected to these geographic excursions, Fry has also gone from 22 stone to 15½, "I think intuitively we all know there is no magic formula other than eating less!" The first programme in the series deals with the white rhino that is, now, "functionally extinct". The technical definition of functional extinction is that there are no "breeding pairs" in captivity or the wild. Even though new British speedway tracks have emerged over recent years, this has been counter-balanced by the demise of other locations. Though its popularity and attendances have declined since its heydays, speedway isn't functionally extinct but, nonetheless, continues to flirt dangerously with the possibility of further contraction. British speedway at all levels would probably be much more buoyant if every club were like the Lakeside Hammers.

The Lakeside Hammers local derby in geographic and possibly emotional terms is with the Ipswich Witches who visit tonight for their Elite League B clash. If the rules on the Play-off qualification criteria hadn't changed mid-season, then Ipswich would still have a chance to qualify for the original version of these by virtue of their likely sixth-placed finish. However, though the possibility of qualification is no longer an option for the Witches, the Hammers continue their renaissance, inspired by Stuart Douglas and Jon Cook, and have already assured themselves of qualification. Under the terms of this process, the top two Elite League teams – Swindon and Wolverhampton – effectively choose who they initially compete against, the order of the home and away meetings as well as enjoy varying degrees of points advantage. In his programme notes Jon Cook comments, "Rumours say we will not be picked by Swindon and that's fine as they can wait until the final". The Play-off clash with Wolverhampton could certainly be one to savour. This season, though Lakeside (like so many other teams) lost at Monmore Green they kept the scores close and only went down by 9 and 7 points respectively. Jon Cook is in bullish mood about the Play-offs but also about recent changes seen at Lakeside and the attitude towards achievement that's ensued. "Everything we've achieved so far has only been a victory for positivity! Speedway can be a very annoying sport and, at times, it's been on its hands and knees. However, our crowds are up. We have 1,800 on average – and the amount of new people we've attracted shows that the product we provide fits well in the normal everyday world. We had a good crowd for Belle Vue, a bigger one for Swindon and more again the next week for Belle Vue again, which must mean we're serving up a product the public likes! The extra numbers aren't lapsed speedway fans but the normal general public who've been curious enough to come along and give it a go! We've been taking care over all our outside communications. You look at the promoter's notes in some away programmes and see they've only changed a few words from the week before. We're positive to the outside world and, if we have to, we sort out our issues behind closed doors. We've weeded out negative people from ours. If you're with us, you're with us completely. Sounds Stalinistic but it works! We won't compromise our Friday speedway for any rider. Those days are over! To run on every Friday you can't have GP riders. Ours know if they qualify [for the SGP] they're out of the team! The changes we've made here you wouldn't believe and, if we can turn a profit, it would be the proudest achievement of my whole career – including winning leagues at other clubs! CVS admits he's worried by Lakeside. We can win big here and let's see what we can do at theirs! We've had to compromise our principles [in track preparation] so it'll be tried and tested Arena – slick and hard at the start!"

Bryn Williams hunches over the computer keyboard one finger typing in the outer office of the Lakeside Speedway Office. While he guards the empty inner sanctum, he's also their impromptu webmaster, "I'm just updating the website with the weather forecast."
[Jeff] "What is it?"
[Bryn] "It's sunny – isn't it?"
[Jeff] "There's some big dark clouds."
[Bryn] "Well, it's dry and it was sunny when I looked earlier and the forecast is no rain!"

The always affable Zimbabwean (Rhodesia in old money) Lakeside track curator Gerald Richter pops into the office. He's tanned and svelte. It's the first time I've seen him since some early season medical matters prompted him to take some time off from his relentless curatorial schedule at Swindon and Lakeside. I skirt around any mention of a heart attack, "Nice to see you back".
[Gerald] "Why, where have I been?"
[Jeff] "Off!"
[Gerald] "I only took a month off and was back by the end of May. However, it was long enough for Swindon to get rid of me citing fears about my health and worrying for me that I might have another heart attack. Never mind the stress of only having half the work and half the money would give anyone a heart attack! "

No sooner does Gerald arrive than he leaves again to take the bowser out onto the track. Tonight's fixture against Ipswich should have already taken place but was abandoned by referee Phil Griffin one hour after the first race – following a downpour and subsequent track work – in consultation with the captains of both teams. With a good crowd already inside the stadium, possible fixture congestion pending and with remedial track work they considered satisfactory enough to permit the meeting to continue, the promotional duo of Stuart Douglas and Jon Cook weren't happy with the decision. [1] As usual on a Lakeside Friday race night, locally based Bryn Williams was at the track. "There was a monsoon. I've never seen rain like it! The track was flooded but Jon was convinced he could get the meeting on. The refs – Frank Ebdon was there 'cause he was invigilating that night – just sat chatting in the box for half an hour and then they went down to the track with the two team captains – not the team managers – walked to the far end of the track and, both said, it was unraceable. You've been in the referee's box. They can only make decisions

No smoking

Track curator Gerald Richter

Clean shaven Dave Robinson

[1] The abandonment decision was lamented by Stuart Douglas in the *Speedway Star*. "We have worked tirelessly over the past three seasons to build a club to be proud of and this is potentially our most damaging night, all from circumstances beyond our control. The combined attendance for last night's match and our meeting the previous week against Coventry was just short of 4,000 people. That is the kind of figures we could only have dreamt about in the past and I hope our terrific fans will understand that nights like this are not the fault of this club and they will continue to support us over these exciting weeks ahead." Jon Cook spoke about that evening even more bluntly. "We have to respect the decisions taken but that doesn't mean we are happy with them and I can only again place on record my thanks to the fans for their patience in waiting and to our quite brilliant team of track staff for their efforts. Both were deserving, at the very least, of seeing a couple of heats run but just before the track inspection the referee told me that's what would happen and he went back on what he said. He claims his decision was based on a conversation that he had with both captains. I wasn't privy to that conversation but I've since been led to believe from my clerk of the course, who was privy to the conversation, that the only request from our captain Lee Richardson was to blade the track to be consistent all over. The referee was told it would take five laps which would take approximately five minutes but apparently he said we had waited long enough and called the meeting off. We have raced in far worse track conditions than that this season and, as a team that has taken its fair share of injuries over the years, I would have been the first to say if that track was dangerous. I don't believe it was at all."

on what they see or what they think they see! Everyone can always see perfectly, no matter how far they are away. And everyone on the Internet can always see perfectly too! At the Isle of Wight, you can't see if the riders touch on the third bend from the box – so how are you supposed to know for sure? They make the decisions based on knowledge, experience, the rules and what they see. That's all you can ask!" During the British speedway close season, Bryn likes to get some sun on his back and Bundy in his hand during his trips to Australia. Doctors express some doubts about the advisability of such long journeys but Bryn believes their diagnosis to be flawed, "I keep having blackouts – they reckon it's epilepsy but I think it's just 'cause I'm tired!"

For speedway workers (riders and referees), their travel schedules dictate each night it's a different track (often in a different country for the riders). Phil Griffin won't officiate at the restaging of the Elite League B fixture he abandoned. His place on the buttons is taken by Dave Robinson who's almost unrecognisable nowadays since he's clean shaven and also in a tie! "It makes you look much younger!"
[Dave] "Yeah, lots of people say that."
[Jeff] "Why did you get rid of it?"
[Dave] "I was made redundant and, if you turn up looking like that, [a roadie from ZZ Top] it ain't gonna happen! I had fun with it – I don't think I'll ever grow it again!"
As a concession to the Beard Liberation Front, Dave retains his moustache. "Having it shaved off raised £400 for the Speedway Riders' Benevolent Fund. I took a form round with me everywhere and got sponsored. It's the second time I've shaved it off! Last time raised £850 for Armando Castagna's Testimonial. His first one! I forget when it was! He's had so many of them! He's had more comebacks that Frank Sinatra!"

On any trip to Lakeside it's hard to miss tireless fund raiser and die-hard Lakeside fan 'Scary' Sheila Le-Sage. An optimist at the best of times, in the pink cowboy hat purchased at the Cardiff GP ("in the Dagenham Pound Shops they're a pound but in Cardiff it was a fiver – I was a little bit tipsy!") she's even harder to miss, "I haven't organised a coach to the Play-offs at Wolverhampton. It's too short a notice to arrange a coach. It always is. I've got a coach going to Coventry for the GP qualifier but I can't get it full. Have you seen how much it is? £25 to get in! And £5 for a programme! If I'd known that, I wouldn't have organised it. Who can afford that? Have you heard the rumours that Jon Cook is going to Eastbourne?"
[Jeff] "Yes – but Jon Cook specifically denied this to me when we spoke. I think it's because wild talk and speculation that here will become a car park for the Olympics and will be compulsory purchased, or whatever, that prompts two and two to equal five."
[Scary] "There's no work going on here! The whole place is riddled with rabbits so there's tunnels, warrens and holes everywhere!"
[Jeff] "You mean I might come back and find my car fallen into a hole?"
[Scary] "Yeah, with a rabbit sat on the seat! I've got to go down the pits and get the mascot's photo signed. I didn't think it would take off but it really did. It cost £60 and they get in free with an adult. They're mascot, watch three races from the centre green and the rest of the meeting from the track wall. It was Tracy's idea!"

Tracy Manning is the blond bubbly manageress of the renowned First Place Diner situated on the ground floor of the main grandstand. The food and drink served there is sensibly priced. You can consume it sat down at their tables or take it out. The atmosphere, like the staff, is warm and welcoming. When I walk up to the counter, Tracy isn't available to speak, "We're having a competition to see who can make the best omelette!" Tracy goes head-to-head with one of her male colleagues. The title of Best Thurrock Omelette Chef will be decided after a blind tasting – Tracy tastes defeat shortly afterwards.

Speedway photographer legend Alf Weedon arrives in the passenger seat of his car driven over from his home by Paco. Scary is pleased to see he's not behind the wheel, "He's a liability when he arrives himself. He's gonna retire this season – that's what his son [Paco] tells him 'cause he's the one that does the driving!" Alf is dressed smartly for the trip and, ever the salesman, sports the new-style Lakeside black anorak that has enough fashion about it that you could think about wearing it away from the track. Though tieless, he also has a collared shirt that matches his cream coloured jumper and white Velcro-fastened trainers. Nowadays Alf's default setting is frustrated – usually at the gradual infirmity you suffer as you age or that results from operations to notionally improve the quality of your life. "Can you pull my leg out? You can't frickin' hurt it 'cause there ain't any frickin' feeling there! Go on – pull! Thank you. Could you get the crutches out of the back too?" Once on his feet and with crutches to aid him, Alf makes rapid progress over to the trackshop where, shortly afterwards, strong language is expressed about the fact that the shutters will only open half way, thereby shielding the cornucopia of merchandise inside from potential purchasers. Even though everything isn't visible to prospective punters, written in black marker pen on a bright yellow fluorescent card is the 2009 price list for "Banger racing/ Stockcars" and "Speedway". Lakeside polo tops and T-shirts have already sold out but, nonetheless, there's still a healthy selection of other options including waterproof jacket tops (£27.50); fleece jackets (£22.50); woolly hats (£5.95); programme boards (£5.95); autograph books (£3.95); pens (£50p/£2.50); air horns small (£3.95); air horns large (£7.20 – previously £6.50!); sew-on badges (3.50); badges pin (indecipherable could be £3.15 or £8.15?) and model speedway riders remain a bargain £3.95.

Pink cowboy hat

Rye House pits marshal 51-year-old Steve Webb (aka Webby) stops by my table for a chat. "I'm legendary! Rye House is my track and I come [to work] here on my day off. Most probably, I've been to over 10,000 meetings. I've seen some fairly good meetings. I've only missed six meetings in 25 years [at Lakeside/Arena] and I've missed none at Rye House in 28 years. There's a lot behind the scenarios and that. I work in the pits. We are in the pits. We are related. I've known Len since I was five years old. *Confessions of a Speedway Supporter* would be the title of my book. I'm not criticising any book but you don't get enough from the pits side of things. [Len Silver] He's 78 and he gets up at 7 in the morning and he still does his own track! He's one of the few to still do his own track! I've been here since 8 this morning. They'd a new kid this morning, 14, and I taught him how the air-fence goes up and how to put all the kick boards in and that. He's a speedway supporter and it's nice to have a speedway supporter and that. One of the most legendary things we went to was Farewell to Wembley Stadium – 50 years of world champions! Twelve of us from Rye House who helped set it up. I'm a scrubber – I did the cleaning and all the work behind the scenes. They look after me like I'm one of their sons!"

Crowded balcony

Keith Taylor and his wife Linda stop for a chat. Keith wears a Cradley Heath speedway blue sweatshirt but identifies himself as a lapsed Rye House fan. The recent Birmingham versus King's Lynn meeting didn't impress him. "They couldn't get round the first bend was the trouble. They reran heat 15 four times. To give you an idea of how bad it was – only three heats finished with all four riders! It rained throughout. After we fell out with Len, we followed Newport for the whole season in 2004. We had a green Vauxhall Senator unmarked ex-police car. We used to get there in 2¾ hours. We lost all our home meetings. They wanted to ban me 'cause of all the accidents! I can't do the accent 'I think it must be Christmas here today – we're getting a right stuffing!' Tim Stone was a lovely man. He used to shake my hand as soon as I walked in the pits." Some questions defy philosophical analysis and Keith has one in search of an answer. "Why has Leigh Adams turned into a dirty rider this season? He had a coming together with Piotr Swiderski and Scott Nicholls!"

With the stadium turnstiles open, Alf's frustrations at his half-shut trackshop because of a mislaid key increase, "It should be on top of the telly!" In Alf's mind things haven't changed for the better in the speedway world. "We used

to do 130 *Speedway Stars* – it used to pay the rent! Now it would be good if we did half that."
[Jeff] "Still at least you saw the golden age!"
[Alf] "I did! Wembley, White City, West Ham – were all licenses to print money! Real money earners!"
Alf then randomly hobbles up to a family of Ipswich supporters who've just walked up the slope from the turnstiles to survey the panorama that is the Lakeside bowl and track. For Alf they suddenly embody all that has changed and is wrong, "Speedway fans get me down!"
[Man] "We don't get you down do we – we're Ipswich fans?!"
[Lady] "Last time we came here two weeks ago, the rain was unbelievable!"

Co-editor of the Peterborough Panthers speedway programme, Sarah Miles isn't keen to be quoted, "I'm keeping my mouth shut!" Honey-coloured Jon Cook stands just inside the entrance turnstiles happy to meet and greet fans as they arrive at the stadium. He gratefully receives a copy of *Quantum of Shale*, "Oh, it's Ashley [Wooler] on the cover! Thank you. I'll look forward to reading that." The jovial Lakeside presentational team of Geoff Cox (presenter) and Bob Miller (announcer) arrive ready for duty. I can't quite put my finger on it but I think Geoff finds it interesting that the Robins allegedly won't choose Lakeside to race against them in the Elite League Play-off semi-final, "Interesting that Swindon didn't want to race against us! That is interesting, isn't it?" Bob has a wild theory to explain the situation, "I reckon that's down to our music man Steve [Gobey] who's tapped them up and told them how good we are here!" I'm sure that Geoff and Bob both recall that Lakeside have already won twice at Blunsdon this season. Justine the trackshop lady arrives and immediately finds herself in Alf's bad books. However, she's more concerned about my book, "Am I in this book? [she is but not pictured] I'm never gonna be famous! Did you notice I was in the doghouse when I arrived? [Bollocked by Paco] Usually I leave the key but, the shutters wouldn't lock after the stockcars on Sunday, so I was worried it might get broken into – so I took all the cash home with me to be safe. I don't start till 8 but, apparently, I was late. I'm the mother of three teenagers and your family has to come first! Next time, I'm just not going to care. I won't have a job next year anyway 'cause Alf is retiring!" Calmer now his shop is fully open, Alf pops out to survey my stock display and ever the salesman asks, "Have you broke the ice yet?"

It's always fun to dress up *Schadenfreude* as information provision and this is a skill that Bob Miller masters effortlessly, "I know there's some Rye House fans in the crowd tonight. As you know they're up at Edinburgh this evening. It's not good news I'm afraid! After four heats – Edinburgh 19, Rye House 5!" Obsessive collector and speedway fan Roger Adams arrives, "I love pylons! There's a disabled woman in a wheelchair who takes photos of every pylon in the country. Her two favourite ones are near here in Braintree! I dunno why they're her favourites." Belle Vue co-promoter and Glasgow speedway investor Gordon Pairman is here along with his personable daughter Amy (who's on a break from Cambridge and her foundation course in fine arts and special effects make-up). Gordon still hasn't quite recovered from the shock triumph by the Aces the previous evening at Wimborne Road. "It was fantastic to win at Poole last night! I spoke to Matt Ford this morning and he wasn't too happy that we had a facility for Jason Crump. But we did! Otherwise, we'd have had to have a 6-point Premier League rider. It was such a brilliant victory that Nigel Pearson rang me up – which he never does! He misquoted me, of course, but never mind."

You can't often say that there's a carnival atmosphere at a speedway meeting but, above me on the balcony in the main grandstand, the Lakeside faithful immediately find a party mood to match the panoramic view when Lee Richardson and Joonas Kylmakorpi combine to hammer home their first heat maximum advantage. Over the stadium speaker system, *Hey Rock 'n' Roll* plays loudly as the race ends. Air horns parp in time to the rhythm of the music while, on the crowded balcony, fans enthusiastically sing along with the chorus. It's a reaction that typifies the tone set throughout the night at Lakeside speedway. There's a pumped-up crowd led onwards by a slick presentation – Geoff Cox and Bob Miller combine comment, results and banter – and, encouraged by the sheer volume of the loudspeakers, the mood is buoyant and the atmosphere carnival like. With the club on the up over recent years, it's natural for enthusiasm levels to be high anyway. In five heats, the Hammers hammer home three 5-1s (and draw two others) to lead by 21-9 and, nowadays, their "Hammer time jingle" is in danger of excessive wear after multiple repeat plays. If the Witches fightback is to happen, then black-and-white helmeted Scott Nicholls has to vanquish the Lakeside power partnership of Richardson and Kylmakorpi. Sadly he fails to gate and the Hammers pair proceed to ram home another 5-1 – the fourth Lakeside maximum heat advantage in six heats. While Geoff Cox formally announces the race result, exuberant fans above me on the crowded balcony shout "Who!" at the mention of Scott

Nicholls's name. Up in the commentary box perched above the start-line Bob Miller struggles to promote my books. "I can't read his writing! I hope he's printed the books 'cause his writing is impossible to read! It looks like *Concrete and Prayers* – I can't read his writing!"

Heat 7 sees Lakeside's talismanic but quietly modest Australian, Adam Shields, take to the track to go head to head with the Witches headstrong younger Australian rider Troy Batchelor whose modesty chip has been permanently disabled. Adam goes about his work at the club in a professional but understated manner that belies his skill and, where necessary, his aggression on the bike. Adam excels at Lakeside, even though, as Jon Cook describes it, he "puts up with his dislike of our track" to "genuinely enjoy riding at this club". [2] Apparently able to have an argument on his own in a phone box, Troy Batchelor often attracts strong feelings from his fellow riders both during and after his races. The start of heat 7 sees Adam Shields ride Troy so close to the air-fence (round bends one and two) that he crashes. Troy immediately leaps to his feet, kicks the fence, removes the advertising banner with so much force that you'd be forgiven if you thought he'd an intense dislike of that sponsor before he then leaps over the air-fence. A nearby Hammers fan tuts at Adam Shields's combative race technique: "So unnecessary to put him in the fence. There must be something behind it! Is he shagging his wife or something?" The air-fence panel punctures but the delay for its repair fails to deflate the party atmosphere inside the stadium, particularly amongst those members of the Lakeside faithful on the balcony (whom Bryn Williams describes as the "Brains Trust"). When the riders do eventually come back to the line, Lakeside only have one representative in the race because of the disqualification of Adam Shields. In the absence of any announcement, you can only assume that Hammers reserve Rusty Harrison – who took part in the initial attempt to run the race – has been abducted by aliens since his place on the track has been taken by fellow reserve Stuart Robson. Given Rusty is a guest reserve and Stuart a regular round the technical contours of the Lakeside track, this smacks of sharp practice and, arguably, proves to be so when Robson races to second place. In a three-rider race, should he finish, Harrison would have been guaranteed at least a point. In effect, a potential Witches 1-5 thereby changes to 2-4. It's definitely something Ipswich team manager Pete Simmons should have queried. An aggrieved Ipswich fan wants to know what's going on, "How come Rusty Harrison can come out the first time they run the race and yet Stuart Robson comes out in the rerun, when Rusty Harrison wasn't injured or nothing?" My understanding is that Rusty was legally replaced under the two-minutes exclusion rule. This rule can be invoked for legitimate reasons or misused. Any rider can identify that his bike has mechanical problems, get timed out and replaced by the other reserve. Potentially, it's a risky practice if Stuart Robson then touches the tapes, since Rusty Harrison couldn't then be returned into a race that he has already been replaced in.

A short distance along from the trackshop, Lakeside boasts arguably the best sweet shop in British speedway. There's an incredible selection and, predictably enough, it's a magnet for youngsters of all ages. Though he has a stream of regular prospective customers keen to buy, the man who runs the stall always appears reluctant to serve if he can manage to busy himself with stock replenishment instead. Obviously, he's there to sell and does that but, nonetheless, he fusses endlessly in sweet-filled stock boxes that, after he searches them, strangely doesn't put stock out from them to sell. Fully engaged again, Ipswich team manager Pete Simmons sends out Troy Batchelor in a black-and-white helmet colour in heat 8 on a rider replacement in place of Tobias Kroner. It's a shrewd decision and, with guest Chris Kerr third across the line, the Witches second consecutive heat advantage of the night reduces their deficit to 9 points

[2] Reticent on live television and sincerely reluctant to ever come across as the 'Big I Am', 32-year-old Adam is nonetheless plainly spoken when asked his specific opinions. During the close season when interviewed by Paul Hiscock, Adam has some blunt thoughts about the British track conditions that pertain to his choice of livelihood. "I think the tracks in England are quite terrible and it's almost a novelty when you arrive at a track that has been well prepared." He identifies Wolverhampton ("pretty good"), Peterborough ("okay") and Coventry ("alright although I missed the one that was really bad") but apart from these three Elite tracks, Adam concludes, "I can't really think of a track that had done a really good job with the preparation. I suppose I can kind of understand why the tracks aren't as good as they could be. Basically, I believe there's not enough [effort] put into them but that's probably because it costs a lot of money to get the right equipment needed, and also pay someone a decent wage to do the job properly. As a rider and a racer, you can only do what you can on the surface you've been given to work with. I wouldn't actually argue the bad tracks make the speedway more dangerous because riders are aware of the conditions and probably ride with a more sensible note of caution and within their limitations a little bit, but what it does do is detract from the spectacle of the sport. If you are going to watch a meeting and there are riders shutting off half way up the back straight to avoid a hole, then for me, that can't be very entertaining. But that's what the fans are having to contend with a lot of the time. Whilst it might be fun to see the bikes careering all over the place, what I think is really entertaining is the sight of riders going into corners flat out, able to feel confident and comfortable on the track whilst able to switch their racing lines, mix it up and race very hard … I haven't been too reticent in delivering my thoughts on the Lakeside track since I joined them and I've voiced my opinions with the problems I have with it. I'll agree that it's always very smooth and nicely prepared, but it's always also so very slick. It's no surprise that it's kept like that because it does work to give the team home advantage, but for me personally, I feel I'm a racer and as someone who always wants to be trying my hardest, it makes it difficult to get too excited about just going round the white lines. The one thing about it though is that it is always very smooth and safe but, for me, its slickness does limit the opportunities to make any kind of manoeuvres that give me any kind of home track advantage."

overall (30-21). Perhaps more relevantly to claims of sharp practice in the rerun of the previous heat, Rusty Harrison "officially" replaces Stuart Robson in the race but finishes last (and ends the meeting with a four-race minimum of zero points). The Witches fightback stalls as soon as it starts, despite a comfortable race win for Scott Nicholls in heat 9. Boisterous celebrations continue on the balcony and, before heat 10, lager falls from the sky to splash my head, writing pad, books and table. A speedway fan from yesteryear chooses this moment to share his reaction to the modern version of the sport. "I've just started coming again with my son. I used to watch Hackney in the mid-'70s and early '80s. When we went to Coventry a few weeks ago, every time the race was over the riders came round and celebrated and really milked it! So why are they just going straight back to the pits tonight after each race?" I'm at a loss to provide an explanation but advise that the gentleman comes back with his son for the Play-offs ("you'll see them celebrate every race win"). The 10th race of the night takes some time to get underway. First time out, referee Dave Robinson isn't happy with the start and "asks the rider in green – Troy Batchelor – to sit still at the start!" On the second bend of the second lap of the rerun, Lee Richardson takes Daniel King for a close inspection of the air-fence. It's a manoeuvre that finds Danny tucked up and discombobulated to the extent that he clatters into the air-fence as he exits from bend two. On the balcony they chant gleefully (and rhythmically), "Can't stay on! Can't stay on!" Joy quickly turns to strongly worded expressions of disbelief when – quite rightly – Lee Richardson's disqualified by the referee. At the third time of asking combative Troy Batchelor leads the race until the second lap at which point Joonas Kylmakorpi passes him effortlessly. Perhaps indicative of the Ipswich riders' attitude about the likelihood of their potential fight-back, it's a disappointment to see two of their best three riders – Troy Batchelor and Danny King – immediately decide to settle into their comfort zone and just ride the race out for second and third place respectively.

The sequence of drawn heats continues during the 11th and 12th races but, with three heats to go, Ipswich could still mathematically snatch an unlikely victory. This slim chance of an upset ends when Adam Shields and Lee Richardson finally snuff out their challenge. Though derided by the Lakeside faithful who gain their speedway kicks on the grandstand balcony, not only does Scott Nicholls deserve praise for the fact that he's ridden here tonight when many of his contemporaries wouldn't have done so if, like him, they're due to ride in a Slovenian Grand Prix tomorrow night. But, also, Scott never stops trying. Third placed from the first corner, Scott repeatedly rides a wide outside line in an attempt to generate sufficient speed to try and overtake on the short straights that characterise the Lakeside track and restrict the possibility of such a manoeuvre. Almost worn smooth by over-repetition, Scott's name is again greeted with loud cries of "Who?" when Geoff Cox announces the race result. Eastbourne fan Tom Edwards isn't impressed, "That gets boring after the first time!" Equally the fact that I take my notes in longhand doesn't pass muster, "You're not a proper writer then – you can't do shorthand!" Though Danny King wins the penultimate race of the night, even with Chris Kerr in third place the heat advantage does little other than massage the result. Tom Edwards identifies what he believes to be the root cause of their difficulties, "Ipswich are another team that builds their teams on the cheap! A few Poles and see what happens!" Tom is anxious about the future of speedway at Arlington. "A season ticket holder – an OAP lady – who complained to Bob about having to pay £1 for the grandstand [seat] Bob [Dugard] said to her, 'You won't have to worry about it in a few weeks when I shut the club'. The whole season has been depressing. It seems all everyone has done is complain about cheating!" Without even the possibility of a face-saving match point for Ipswich, Lakeside team manager Jon Cook safely sends out tonight's unlikely Lakeside top scorers for heat 15: Joonas Kylmakorpi and Kauko Nieminen. They go head to head with the Witches Nicholls/Batchelor partnership. Scott wins his third race of the night but fails to blunt the derision he receives from the alcohol-fuelled fans on the balcony who are also in confident voice about their eagerness to face and vanquish tougher opposition in the Play-offs. Even with nothing to really race for (other than to avoid injury), Lakeside ease to victory and the large crowd enjoys the atmosphere manufactured and promoted by the club. It's a bubbly attitude provoked by Lakeside's positive on-track results and further boosted by their ongoing transformation from also-rans into genuine contenders.

11th September Lakeside v. Ipswich (Elite League) 51-42

CHAPTER 34

Sittingbourne

"The first time I ever ran here was in late '94. We had 65 riders and we ran 89 races in one afternoon in December! Tim Mount had 12 rides that day."

13th September

The inaugural season of the National League suffers from the glaring absence of one of the stalwart clubs of the Conference League incarnation that preceded it: Sittingbourne. Speedway at the Old Gun Site is always a hand-to-mouth existence founded upon the hard work of volunteers as well as the regular paid use of its training tracks. Justifiably, they pride themselves on the development of riders irrespective of their age, ability or gender. Rider improvement and progression is their raison d'être and, despite the absence of the imprimatur of league racing, this continues! Some people lament their absence, others criticise, but the brute fact remains that though they are notionally far from the madding crowd in geographic and formal league terms, the club is still in good health. Indeed like a swan serenely gliding along the river, Sittingbourne speedway remains nonchalantly aloof and continues its support of a thriving speedway community, albeit it on a wholly amateur rather than part professional, part amateur basis. This afternoon sees a packed schedule of racing and, according to the programme (price £1), the "Dragons Amateur Speedway Club" intend to stage an incredible 42 races! Affable club trainer Paul Heller explains business is booming. "There's supposed to be a recession but the Speedway Experience days are getting more and more popular! It's £120 and, for that, they get to ride all day plus it covers the insurance, the bikes, all the gear and the food, of course. New riders are always welcome – especially women riders – as we don't get too many of them!"

Inside the terrapin hut that overlooks the first bend of the main track and serves as the tearoom cum tuck shop, there's already quite a crowd of volunteers. Some are crowded round a television watching a DVD of some unidentifiable meeting. It sounds like a tinny angry wasp is caught inside the confined space of the hut. Behind the service counter but in front of the kitchen area, Arsenal fan Alison surveys the scene, "I started the Kenny Carter book yesterday at 3 and when I put it down at 11 I'd got to chapter 12." I joke, "I won't tell you how it ends" but Alison clearly isn't quite *au fait* with the details of Kenny's life, "No don't!"

Sittingbourne start marshal Ian Glover – he of multi-coloured checked trousers fame – is keen to provide some context about the club's decision to forego membership of the National League tier of British speedway. "If we'd gone into the National League, we'd have been out of business by now! Some people have complained but why would we cut our own throats? Survival is the key – we've continued to do what we've always done: running amateur meetings and speedway experience days!" I enquire who will be the referee today. "John Strong will be in the box. As it's an amateur meeting, we don't need the expense of a proper ref."
[Jeff] "Do they come along and help?"
[Ian] "Not during the season 'cause they're travelling about so much and, when they have some time off, they want to rest. During the winter, they sometimes come over and help out."
[Jeff] "How long will it go on today?"
[Ian] "I reckon until about 4. We have 20 riders in the Pairs and we'll do 40-odd races."

Graham Arnold tears himself away from the angry wasp vision for a brief stroll down memory lane. "The first time I ever ran here was in late '94. We had 65 riders and we ran 89 races in one afternoon in December! Tim Mount had 12 rides that day. He rode in the Southern track meeting and then he rode in our meeting. He was knackered after that! How we got it all done, I don't know! We ran the last four races in the dark. We ran the Under-19s final in '99 in the dark. People wouldn't do that now!" ["Why's that?"] "The track wouldn't allow it, people would take longer to get out there and, then, it was more of an enthusiast's thing. You always remember your first meeting don't you! 89 races!" Dressed like an extra from St. Elsewhere or possibly Scrubs, Graham fingers his baseball cap as he drifts back in time to Old Gun Site meetings of yesteryear. "I've got a photo of Chris Gay on the centre green presenting the trophies with a lovely sunset behind him!"

If this were a detective story, the tried and tested narrative approach is to follow the money and see who benefits. Judged by the hive of activity in the pits, amateur speedway is a hobby pursued with passion and, even if money and time are tight, application outstrips ambition but always burnishes dreams. Up in the referee's box that perches upon one of the substantial fortifications that gave this location its romantic name, John Strong takes time over his appearance – putting on a tie that will complete the professional look his white collared shirt already ensures – before he starts to prepare for his presentational and refereeing duties. The social glue that unites strangers the world over (and also within the speedway community) are discussions about present or forthcoming meteorological conditions. It's a cold day and the exposed nature of the track in this flat area of Kent marshland always exaggerates the felt experience of the weather – whether it's hot or cold. Today "it's a bit fresh." John can see nothing but positives, "It was sunny when I left Stansted. It's ideal Sittingbourne weather, though. There's a wind – the track shouldn't dry out too much so it won't need watering, so often. Have you noticed all the changes to the track? They've got rid of the banking on the first bend and, on the other corner; they've pushed it back six or eight feet. There used to be only one line into the bend – on the inside – the riders used to end up hitting the fence there [points to the fourth bend] but now they have a choice of lines and can go much deeper!" I hand over the information sheet on my book and ask if John would be so kind as to announce my attendance. "I hope you're not slagging me off in this one? When I glanced at Bryn's copy, I didn't think so!" I confess John does get a slightly critical mention. "In your last book [*Concrete for Breakfast*], when you highlighted my conversation approach, you thought I was in the ref's box but I was down on the track with the riders so I could chat with them!" I've barely climbed down the stairs that lead back to the pits area before over the speaker system, John runs through some information on the book before he notes, "He has me stumbling over riders' names so we should be in for a good afternoon, if I'm doing that. So, Jeff, whatever his name is, is in the tearoom."

Out on the track the first race of the afternoon is about to get underway. According to the programme the format of this afternoon's meeting – subject to change – will feature three Club Pairs races followed by a Junior race, then two Support Pairs races and finally a Training race before this order events is repeated a further five times. Traditional Pairs scoring will apply (4 points for a win, 3 points for second and 2 points for third). Mark Bibby and Lee Harris race unopposed in the first race of the afternoon because the Mark Baldock and Steve Edwards combination fails to compete in this or any other of their programmed races. The back inside page of the programme contains various important items of information including a disclaimer, confirmation that "THE REFEREE'S DECISION IS FINAL" and, pretty significantly, an underlined instruction "YOU MUST BE READY FOR YOUR HEATS OR THEY WILL START WITHOUT YOU". The scorecards are split into two sections – Club Pairs and Support Pairs – though the rules advise "In the Club Pairs event, all riders will take 5 program rides to determine their place in heats 36 to 38. Trophies will be awarded to the top 3 points scoring pairings. In the Support Pairs event, all riders will take 6 program rides and plaques will be awarded 1st to 4th in order of points scored". It quickly becomes clear that the race order schedule of the programme is more flexible than listed and can be subject to dramatic alteration at any time due to rider absences as well as equipment failure brought on by the wear and tear of so many races in succession. The programmed junior races and training races don't take place at all this afternoon. While the track is graded ahead of the fourth race of the afternoon (aka heat 5, otherwise known as the first Support Pairs race of the afternoon) I study news, views and scandal that are one of the joys of the News of the World. Russell Brand's spurned ex-lover Christy Peterson spills the beans, "Russell buys XL condoms but normal size would do him just fine." If that wasn't news enough we're also informed, "The warning signs were there. He even offered me a freshly-laundered woman's underwear that he kept in his [bed] room! I ought to have realised he wasn't going to be the most faithful guy in the world."

Sarah Cook is the only woman racing this afternoon and, after a slow start to heat 5, she fights her way through to third place but, in the short distance from the wider last bend to the finish line, Martin Brown suddenly decides to race to restore his male pride and, just about, snatches third place by a proverbial tyre knobble. I temporarily

Sittingbourne: *"The first time I ever ran here was in late '94. We had 65 riders and we ran 89 races in one afternoon in December! Tim Mount had 12 rides that day."*

abandon my table by the tearoom window to watch heat 6 from outside on the concrete slope that provides wheelchair access to the refreshment service counter. Stood with a group of friends, many of whom smoke roll-up cigarettes, Mark Bibby shouts words of encouragement throughout ("follow your teammate!") to a rider whose identity I fail to establish. On the fourth bend of the third lap, Russell Tooley appears to lose traction and, in the blink of an eye, transitions from upright into a serenely gentle fall and, then, into the fence. During a track-grade break prior to the next round of races, start marshal Ian Glover expresses approval about the new look smoother and wider circuit, "The track's riding well – there's many more racing lines for them to use!"

Alison

After the track TLC, heat 8 gets underway (aka the sixth race of the afternoon) featuring the absent Baldock/Edwards partnership against the champagne partnership of Daniel I'Anson and Adam Sheppard. Given the race stars only one pairing, no sooner do the tapes rise than events take a surreal turn when one half of the partnership, Adam Sheppard, fails to get off the start-line. Since he's got a machine that exhibits all the liveliness of the famous Monty Python parrot, Adam rushes his bike onto the centre green and flings himself down onto its grassy surface. Back on his feet, Adam parades another slow-motion loss of temper when he strips off his gloves exasperatedly one by one in the manner of an angry burlesque dancer before he throws his crash helmet to the floor. From behind her counter in the tearoom, Alison throws a casual glance out of the window at the shenanigans on the turf, "Is he alright?" On the track, his partner Daniel I'Anson races unopposed to victory. Though it's a race that lasts only 69.5 seconds, nonetheless, it captures part of the joy, appeal and emotional appeal of amateur speedway in all its fragile human glory. Presenter John Strong kindly decides to gloss over Adam's centre-green tantrum, "Well, bit of a strange one there! The winner and only finisher Daniel I'Anson."

Dragons tabards

Heat 9 requires a few attempts to start. When it finally gets underway, this afternoon's most stylish rider Mark Bibby (29), son of ex-Crayford Kestrel Jack Bibby, starts off 15 metres but has the lead by the time he exits the second bend. His father watches from the disabled ramp and, after Mark takes the chequered flag, comments, "He thought he was Jason Crump in that last race!" Mark rejoins his father shortly after to explain his race, "They'd blocked the inside but, they'd left such a big gap on the outside, I could go round them. Over the last two laps, I got slower and slower 'cause I didn't want to fall off. I've had three years of falling off so I don't need to do any more of that!" Jack is happy to recall his own speedway past, "It was 1980, I think it must have been, Roy Barwick used to hold the track record here. I took it off him and Barry Thomas took it off me! Barry Thomas – it was his track, weren't it? I beat Gordon Kennett round here and he told Les Rumsey and he came down here and gave me a beating. There used to be some really good races here! Not today, they're at different standards and there's health and safety!" Out on the track heat 10 is underway. Josh Pickering blasts under race leader Jim Wannell on the second bend and then races away to victory. While he insouciantly makes yet another roll-up, Jack continues, "The wife left about 10 years ago and Mark came back 10 years later and said he wanted to ride. He's the best here today but he's got no competition!" Jack doesn't respond to my observation, "He's following in your tyre treads."

Refresing cuppa

Sittingbourne: *"The first time I ever ran here was in late '94. We had 65 riders and we ran 89 races in one afternoon in December! Tim Mount had 12 rides that day."*

Apparently Mark and Jack's shared fascination with bikes extends beyond shale to the road. Jack wistfully recalls, "a 350cc AJS road bike and then a 650cc Bonneville and then a Jap. The parts are so expensive nowadays if they fall off you practically need a new bike!" Jack's work takes him down to Brighton, "Do you know the Pig in Paradise pub there? I did it out like I did the nightclub under the Arches. They're both really nice. I used to fish down there too! We've stayed down when we did. A bit of a queer place, though."

Sarah Cook has gained the measure of the track and her opponents if judged by heat 12 (aka race 9) where she finishes behind her race partner Tony Venables but vanquishes both Craig Whitehead and Alan Pierson. When Alan comes into the tearoom for a rest between races while they grade the track, only to have his wife Jan exasperatedly ask him, "Why didn't you overtake her?" Alan's explanation ("I was too tired") cuts little ice ("It don't matter"). Another Support Pairs competitor (rider number 20) with a small ginger moustache, Chriss Shallcross, also comes in for some much-needed refreshment, "I've only been doing it a year a couple of times a month but it's brilliant! I should be pushing them, really, but I'm out there riding!" Chriss is too modest about his progress on the bike since he rides well all afternoon and never finishes lower than second. When the racing resumes, Jack and Mark Bibby scope out some of their later race opposition. Though I don't catch exactly which rider we're supposed to watch out for, Jack advises his son, "Keep your eye on him." Mark's already aware of the threat, "He's the fastest up-and-coming youngster here. If I gate ahead of him, I'll beat him! He's only 17 or 19 – only young."

Mark Bibby easily wins heat 17. After he announces the race results John Strong informs us, "There's no time there 'cause Claire forgot to stop her stopwatch!" After two wins in his previous outings, Josh Pickering falls in this race and is then replaced throughout the rest of the meeting by Dan Bibby. There are more Bibbys on display than there used to be ships in the Merchant fleet of the Bibby line. In my opinion, though the cold wind makes it unpleasant to sit out, Mick Corby seems content to watch the action from his wheelchair parked on the grass in the lee of the gun placement wall. From this position, Mick overlooks the slight uphill slope of the fourth bend with a plate of food on his lap and a cup of tea close at hand. Despite the sparse crowd, Sod's Law invariably dictates that any rogue bike that flies over the fence will, ineluctably, be drawn towards the nearest handy spectator. Russell Tooley decides to test the robustness of the safety equipment on the penultimate lap of heat 19 when he plays ducks and drakes with the fourth-bend wooden safety fence. Mick Corby laughs off my suggestion, "I thought he was going to come and join you!" Indeed, Mick remains impassive throughout the incident with his plate of food resting on his legs, "I'd get out of the way quicker than you!" Before the interval I catch a few words with paramedic lookalike Graham Arnold, "The track's holding up well. Better than I thought! The sun not being out helps."

The lengthier interval allows all the track staff to retreat from the centre green to the tearoom for some refreshments. Those fans without bikes to prepare on behalf of family members also repair to the warm and pleasantly crowded terrapin hut. Lakeside fan Michelle Saveall (mother of teenage Cameron) evangelises on behalf of the Thurrock-based club. "When you think where we've gone in the few last years – from wooden spoonists to fifth, to second and this year third! In the Play-offs two years running and the KO final two years running! I love Jonas Davidsson and Kauko Nieminen to death, I don't think they'll qualify from the GP qualifier but, if they do, they'll have to choose between individual success and team speedway! A lot of riders want to come and ride at Lakeside now – it's not just a question of who's left anymore! It's the place to be! And that's all because of Stuart [Douglas] and Jon [Cook]." Out on the track, Team Baseby (Mark and Aaron) treat us to some high-powered demonstration rides. Compared to what has gone before, they make it look a completely different track. Behind her counter Alison can't contain her admiration, "They're brilliant them two, they're absolutely awesome!" Ian Glover explains the huge visual difference we can all now clearly see, "It's the sort of track you have to really attack!"

Like so many speedway clubs, Sittingbourne's success is built on the goodwill and hard work of its volunteers. Many have also voluntarily given good service at other speedway tracks. Brian and Terry fondly recall their time at Plough Lane, how "charming" Plc director Perry Attwood was. They wish the club still existed. "There was one night when the track staff didn't get their programmes 'cause there wasn't enough of them – so they left the fence up after the meeting. It had to come down as a condition of racing there [Plough Lane]. To be fair to him, Ian Perkin got down there and helped us take it down. He had to, of course. We used to have to take the start gate down after the meeting and carry it to the far side of the car park. It was quite a way!" Dick Jarvis also has his own fond memories of the brief era of Conference League speedway staged in South London. "You weren't there at the meeting where all the second

Sittingbourne: *"The first time I ever ran here was in late '94. We had 65 riders and we ran 89 races in one afternoon in December! Tim Mount had 12 rides that day."*

halfers went out to the centre green to complain to Ian Perkin that, if he didn't talk so much, they'd be able to get some racing in! They got there early enough to ride but he used to go on and on and use up all the available time. There was the time Newcastle – that George English and Kenny Smith – got him banned by the ref from his own centre green. If you're there [on centre green], you can't really comment on something and he did, so they complained to the ref."

The joy of the day is in the participation as much as the competition. Without the junior and training races there are still 30 races rather than the scheduled 42! Heat 31 (aka race 23) sees Mark Bibby rear at the start-line and fall off. His dad Jack laughs loudly, "Such is life! He'll have to go off 15 metres!" In the rerun, Mark doesn't gate well and, caught in traffic, finds himself fourth as the riders exit the second corner. However, he's soon third and then team rides behind his race partner Lee Harris and block off the yellow-helmeted Adam Sheppard. Though a Pairs competition, many individual riders stand out. In the Club Pairs competition Mark Bibby and Lee Harris both score well to emerge victorious. However, individual plaudits also go to Daniel I'Anson who remains undefeated in his six races. Jim Wannell also scores highly (20 points) and Steve Lockyer deserves recognition for his consistency, since he finishes second in all his races. In the Support Pairs event, Kieron Davidson (undefeated) and his partner Martin Brown are head and shoulders above their rivals. Sarah Cook scores 11 points from her six races and, thereby, ensures that with her partner Tony Venables (16 points) they finish second overall. However, once again at Sittingbourne, the real winner is speedway! The back page of the programme advertises that the next Dragons event will take place at Newport speedway next Sunday ("Please confirm your intention to attend, with Julie") while the next training/practice session at the Old Gun Site would be in four weeks' time. Persistence, resilience and enthusiasm are required by volunteers and riders alike to ensure that speedway remains active in this corner of Kent. However, no one rests on their laurels and the back page of the programme contains an important message if it is to continue to do so. "Please support our events in order for the club to continue. Thank you."

13th September Dragons Amateur Speedway Club (Sittingbourne)
Club Pairs Winners: Mark Bibby/Lee Harris
Support Pairs Winners: Kieron Davidson/Martin Brown

Sittingbourne: *"The first time I ever ran here was in late '94. We had 65 riders and we ran 89 races in one afternoon in December! Tim Mount had 12 rides that day."*

CHAPTER 35

Swindon

"You have to admire Adam Shields – he's had so many injuries but still races like he never has had!"

17th September

When the Four-Team Tournament between Swindon, Reading, Oxford and Cradley Heath was postponed due to lack of suitable rider availability on 30th July, many fans thought it unlikely that the meeting would ever get re-staged at Blunsdon. While some of the team line-ups have altered in the interim, the doubters have been proved wrong. This evening's meeting is the brainchild of Swindon co-owner Gary Patchett and his commitment ensures that the supporters of the three illustrious, yet sadly without a track, speedway clubs will – for one night only – see their side race and, once again, be able to reminisce with fellow devotees at a meeting. One sniff of methanol doesn't make a summer but, for the fans of Oxford, Reading and Cradley Heath, representative sides competing on shale in their name signals that their plight has not been completely forgotten, even if they all still remain homeless.

With many hours still to go before the meeting, in the still pristine Swindon pits area track volunteer and founder of the *Blunsdon Blog*, Graham Cooke has, like many others of the curatorial team, already spent many hours at the track. Track preparation at Swindon doesn't happen without the hard work and dedication of a loyal band of volunteers whose pride in their work and camaraderie is regularly revealed on the *Blunsdon Blog*. It's also very much in evidence on any personal visit to the club. Until recently Gerard Richter managed the curatorial team though, in recent months, they've been under the supervision of the avuncular Ronnie Russell, brother of Swindon co-owner Terry. After he ceased to run the then-named Arena-Essex, Ronnie took a sabbatical from the sport but now appears to have returned with even greater vigour, bonhomie and, as always, fluently expressed strong cogent opinions leavened with quick wit. Dressed in a blue boiler-suit, Ronnie sports a deep honey-coloured tan similar to his Lakeside successor Jon Cook. He also is noticeably slim line compared to a few years previously. Ronnie greets me with a warm handshake and alludes to his super-tanned face, "We've a special micro-climate here as you can see from my colour!"
[Jeff] "Is it me, or have you lost some weight?"
[Ronnie] "Yeah, I've lost six stone on my special diet – cancer, it's called!"
[Jeff] "That's a bit drastic!"
[Ronnie] "Well, it's okay providing you recover from it, like I have!"

Ronnie's proprietorial pride in the changes he's wrought at Blunsdon tumble out while Graham, Ronnie and I stand together on the hallowed shale adjacent to the pits gate. "We got the Olson mix from Breedon, Derbyshire – it's the way they mix the clay into it! When I first reshaped the track here, Leigh Adams said 'you've done great but I can't break the track records here. When I broke the track record it had pulled before and they scraped it and I road rallied round and smashed the track record by a second. But now you've taken the banking away, there's no chance!' Leigh still holds the track record [63.86 seconds established on the 31 August 2009]. When Freddie Lindgren came here he broke the old track record in heat 1." Graham Cooke takes similar pride in these changes, "We made it lower and level, plus there's a hell of a lot more grip in the track!" Ronnie waves his hand in the general direction of the bend and continues, "When I came here the turning point was [points] and they had to scrub all the speed off. Whereas now, it's a few yards back."

En route back to number 96 (aka the Swindon track staff staffroom), Graham highlights some of the many changes to the pits area. "The reserves now have a separate stall – possibly the most spacious reserves' area in Elite League speedway! We're going to get rid of the jinxed end of the pits which we'll use as a store for the air pumps." Given its not so long ago that there was anguished talk of the closure and demolition of Blunsdon stadium, such small infrastructure development must, surely, bode well for the future of the club. As ever, the staffroom is as cosy and welcoming. A large television is the most noticeable addition ("the DVD has stopped working") to the facilities complete with an oversized outside television aerial that looks incongruously out of place indoors. Since there are so few buildings at this end of the stadium, it's something of a mystery to me why the staffroom is known as number 96. "It's the number on the door that Punch [aka Rod Ford] found by the side of the road. We became number 96 and everyone re-numbered themselves so the shower room is number 92, Mike Hunt's office number 90 and Karen Pantry's room is number 94. One of our track staff sent a postcard from holiday to number 96 Abbey Stadium and it arrived!" Though everyone brings their own sandwiches, the staffroom is famous for the delicious cakes baked by sports therapist Karen Pantry, as well as the seasonal range of produce from Punch's garden. "The back seat of Punch's car every week is filled with an enormous selection of vegetables: tomatoes, cucumbers, pretty well everything that's in season." Punch sees great similarities between the rain required by a verdant allotment and that needed to create the ideal track, ("same as everything, if you get a couple of good days of rain before, you just have to top it up!")

Graham Cooke takes pride in the Nurdin sponsorship

On the worldwide web the work of the track staff as represented by Graham in his *Blunsdon Blog* continues to prove popular ("this year, so far, we've had 240,000 visitors!"). Graham now includes news from Armadale in Scotland, "Ian Hawkins up at Edinburgh is a great contributor. I've never met the guy but I'd like to go up and meet him, as he's such a brilliant contributor! That people enjoy the blog is a pleasure in itself and I know that we have some very important regular readers because Terry Russell got in touch with Ronnie about the saga of the Ford that fails to start. He told Ronnie, 'I'm sick of hearing about the faulty equipment' and Ronnie asked him 'Where do you hear about it?' [Graham permits himself a wry smile] and Terry said, 'On the blog, I read it every week!'" The season so far has been successful for Swindon Speedway but, as you'd expect from such an articulate and intelligent man, Graham has concerns about others in the wider community. "The recession has really hit Swindon. The percentage of 16–24-year-olds out of work is higher than any other city in the country! Until the late '80s, Swindon was one of the fastest growing towns in Europe. It grew tremendously quickly but, slowly over the years, Swindon's been contracting but nobody noticed! Honda put people on paid holiday. When they reopened, there was a very complicated arrangement where you had to work extra hours to pay for the holiday that they'd given you! The kind of people who took redundancy and golden handshakes where those with 10 years' service so, suddenly, they have a big skills shortage!" Graham's sporting worries also aren't solely confined to the rarefied world of speedway. "I'm worried and don't quite know what is going on with the world. In the week we hear about the Renault crash, the rugby farce, and footballers diving we also had the infamous Swindon/Poole match. It was nothing I could put my finger on, but it was a very odd experience." Understandably enough, like the rest of the curatorial team, Graham takes great pride in the performance and appearance of their track handiwork, particularly when it appears live on satellite television. "It is nice when it looks good. The last televised match looked great! It's sad when I look at the tape of the meeting – I'm not looking at the racing but the air safety barrier, the banner, those bloody weeds growing in the sand down the front straight on the other side of the

Dave & Brendan Johnson

Once a Racer always a Racer!

kickboards. While the riders race, I think to myself things like 'we must re-seed that bit of the centre green!' When I watch meetings from other tracks, I say 'they haven't cleaned the kickboards' and the kids say 'Dad! Just watch the racing!'" Rex Woodroffe (67) chips in, "Terry [Russell] doesn't like daisies! Rosco brought his home mower up and I ran up and down before the meeting. Mind you, I like some daisies in a lawn. I think they come up at 7 o'clock to annoy Terry." I ask Rex what he does at the track, "All sorts of things! I drive the Chevrolet for the parade lap and winner's lap, I just brought the programmes up and I operate the pits gate on to the track. I've been coming up for 51 years – working about half of that and, the rest, just supporting. I used to live just round the corner so that was easy but, now, I live in Cheltenham. I've been lucky enough to be invited to help at Cardiff. That's wonderful! I'm very grateful! I enjoy everything! The company, the speedway and, of course, you feel you've put something back for all the pleasure you've taken!" Graham tells me, "I know if Rex is doing it, everything will be fine!"

If it's not daisies on the centre green, then another ongoing obsession for the track staff are dust levels. "On the ref's questionnaire meeting report, the referee has to put in, in which heat dust appears. On Monday night when I watched Poole versus Peterborough, there was dust swirling as they made their way to the tapes – while Kelvin [Tatum] chuntered on about superb track preparation! Then we saw them skate across the bumps of turn 1, across the smooth of bend 2 and then chase the dirt on the back straight." Graham is another person proud to help out each year at the Cardiff Grand Prix they stage inside the impressive Millennium Stadium. It's a couple of days of hard work but this goes unnoticed because of the pleasure of his involvement and, of course, the behind-the-scenes access. Graham's proximity to the Scott Nicholls/Emil Sayfutdinov contretemps unexpectedly threw Graham (with his mouth open in surprise) into the international spotlight. "It was on the telly, it's on YouTube and was in the *Daily Mirror*, the *Mail*, the *Sun*: even my mother rang up to say, 'Why are you on page 23 of my newspaper?' The track was superb this year – there was only one small rut on turn 1. Ole Olsen brought across this awfully great big blade with two wings on it that open out. The blade guy drives it incredibly slowly. It's so hi-tech that it has a computerised set-up that has a laser to measure and accurately grade the surface within one millimetre. There's amazing control of the blade that can be moved up and down. You could have played marbles on the track it was so smooth and stone hard before they put the top dressing down. Greater clay content – from Breedon, Punch will know for definite – made all the difference. Shale isn't that expensive, it's the cost of transportation and, nowadays, storage. Ironically, people have complained about the track, but now they're going on about how it took away the drama and the theatre!"

Given Graham's honorary membership of Team Holta any talk of the 2009 SGP Series brings up the question of who exactly will occupy fifth to ninth place in the final table and, thereby, qualify (or not qualify) for the 2010 Series. As the SGP again boringly grinds to its denouement you could argue that the only real thrill you can derive from the regular routine of meetings comes from the very last event and the dramatic uncertainty about who exactly will fail to automatically re-qualify (at least until the organisers seed their discretionary 'picks', shortly afterwards). "There's a 7-point spread between Holta, Pedersen, Lindgren, Bjerre and Jonsson where you start thinking there's a possibility that Rune will have to be a pick for next year. Hans Andersen will have to be a pick. If you said a short while ago that Rune would be in the last two finals [he was second in Vojens], they'd have got the men in white coats. The last meeting is at Bydgoszcz where he used to be the track record holder!" Clerk of the course Mike Hunt arrives in number 96 ahead of his duties for tonight's meeting, "I do think Chris Holder deserves to get in the GPs, I've been coming here for years and, no disrespect to Leigh Adams, his time has gone. We need some fresh blood! As the top Englishman, Lee Richardson should definitely get one of the picks based on his riding this season and, not that I'm that keen, but Tai Woffinden should, too. All the Englishmen have gone in and been given a chance, but flunked and not made the top ten." Graham interjects, "Since Loram." Mike and deputy clerk of the course Andy Reynolds are known on the *Blunsdon Blog* as the 'Men in Black' "because of their dark glasses and attire." Graham rouses himself from his seat to return back to his curatorial duties, "It's quarter past 4 and I've still got to put those big bloody banners up 'cause it's windy and I've got to paint the white line!" News that Lewis Bridger will replace Niels-Kristian Iversen in the Oxford Cheetahs side provides further anxiety, "I'm just worried about the air-fence – we don't have any spare panels – or kickboards, at the moment!"

Tonight the Swindon pits split into four discreet areas demarcated by club tabards hung on the pits wall. Skilled, but laidback mechanic Ashley Wooler is hard at work on Cameron Woodward's bike in the Heathens section of the pits. "We're one of the main attractions tonight! [nods to the empty berths around him] We're the Cradley team. I never thought I'd ever be spannering for Cradley! Funnily enough, Cameron was asked to ride a few nights ago for a rider that had dropped out [Darcy Ward] and then they rang back to ask if Cameron really wanted to ride 'cause he could now. He told them he wanted to ride." The Eastbourne Eagles end-of- season Dinner Dance won't take place in the clubhouse at Arlington Stadium this year, but has been transferred to a posh hotel in Eastbourne. "It's a step up from what we've had before! It was gonna be on the Saturday, but a lot of the riders would be away for the [Pardubice] Golden Helmet. So, when Trevor [Geer] and Jayne [Wooler] sat down, if they wanted to get as many riders there as possible, it had to be that day, that Thursday night [8 October]."

Swindon co-owner Gary Patchett surveys the pits scene smartly attired in a red Robins anorak. The forecast is good and talk of a reasonable crowd offers no consolation for Gary who's irked by last-minute withdrawals from the line-up. "Niels-Kristian Iversen pulled out without so much as an explanation or a kiss my arse! He just sent a text saying 'I can't come'. He was supposed to fly back with Mads, but he's just stayed at home! Jason [Crump] has had to pull out [injured] but that's just speedway and, of course, there's Darcy! A month ago, I would have had a bet that he would pull out the day before – and so it's proved! I had Buster on the phone this morning saying he's not happy with what I put on the website. [1] Buster's effing and blinding and thinking he can get his way by bullying. Buster claimed they never said Darcy couldn't ride and he now says he can 'cause King's Lynn are champions, after Birmingham lost last night. That wasn't what Rob Lyon said. He said 'He can't ride!' He didn't say 'He might be able to ride'. He was clear that he couldn't! Looking after Darcy's health isn't the real issue – it's the contract in my pocket now for Troy [Batchelor]. There's a fixed formula for the transfer of foreign permit riders from the Premier League to the Elite League, which values them at £2,000 per point. Premier League promoters would prefer open market rates and, no doubt, will propose a rule change during the winter. But you can't make rules up to suit just one rider. The formula was agreed to ensure that the Premier League clubs can't stop the progression of foreign permit riders. They [Premier League clubs] didn't used to be able to have them [foreign permit riders], but now they can. They get to use them and then the riders move on! Troy went through all the correct procedures, but Buster refused to recognise it 'cause he didn't like the terms – the agreed formula – of the transfer. It's in the rules, but he was shouting that we'd stolen him! He's going to be even unhappier about Darcy 'cause he is going to move up to the Elite League next season and ride for someone, whoever that is, and the maximum he'll be able to get is £20,000. He would be worth more on the open market, but there isn't one! Darcy's an exceptional talent, but the formula works well enough already, so won't need changing. It's ironic that the rider that's replacing Jason is the one that knocked him off. He's replacing him tomorrow night at Mark's [Lemon] Testimonial. He is a Swindon asset, of course! The people who've been short changed tonight are the fans who've been deprived of seeing him ride. I haven't seen him ride yet! The idea was that this wasn't about Swindon, but all the other teams involved – Oxford, Reading and Cradley Heath. All we want to do is to try and break even and put on a good show! Fingers crossed we do get a good crowd!"

Almost no important speedway event in Britain is complete without Steve Girdwood from the highly regarded speedway DVD company, Re-Run Productions, in attendance. He has a request for me. "We always do messages from various people on the crashes and cock-ups video and it's your chance to make your Re-Run debut! Well, that's not true, I filmed you at Eastbourne the other week. Say whatever you want, just try and make it interesting!" For reasons that continue to escape me, whenever I'm presented with a microphone I either get tongue tied or distracted. This afternoon, I add catatonically uninterestingly to my repertoire.

After 1st attempt: "Let's try again!"

After 2nd attempt: "Best to look into the camera."

After 3rd attempt: "That was really boring – say something interesting! Scott said toodlepip at the end of his."

After 4th attempt: "Nah."

After 5th attempt: "Let's try with the track in the background instead."

[1] A statement on the Robins website dated 16 September informs us: "Regrettably, King's Lynn have refused to allow Darcy Ward permission to ride in Thursday's Four-Team Tournament." Co-promoter Gary Patchett adds: "I received a phone call from Rob Lyon earlier this evening advising me that Darcy riding tomorrow was against their wishes and that the rider was withdrawing on that basis. I cannot but think that this was part of a preconceived agenda on the part of the King's Lynn promotion after the protracted transfer of Troy Batchelor to Swindon. Considering Jonathan Chapman was sat opposite me all day yesterday at a promoters' meeting in Rugby, I would have thought he might have remembered to mention it to me then. What they clearly do not appreciate is that by doing this they are depriving the broader speedway public of the opportunity to see one of the sport's outstanding prospects. This meeting was never about Swindon, but about the plight of Cradley Heath, Oxford and Reading. Considering the Chapmans' involvement in the Leicester project, I would have thought that they would be sympathetic to the cause. Obviously not. Using a rider as a pawn in this way is disgraceful. Eastbourne's Australian star Cameron Woodward steps in and we are grateful to him for accepting our invitation at this late stage."

After 6th attempt: "Big yourself up – say you're speedway's No. 1 author extraordinaire."
After 7th attempt: "Try and promote yourself."
[Jeff] "This is why I write."
After 8th attempt: "I can see that now! It's only frickin' 10 seconds."
[Jeff] "It's harder than it looks."
[Steve] "You're certainly making it look hard."
After 9th attempt: "Well, thank you, Jeff. We nearly got there!"

Oxford uber-fan Robert Peasley arrives early at the stadium, "I have Reading down to finish fourth but, now we've had a few changes, I think we'll finish bottom now!" Rob has a column in tonight's programme that mixes fact, opinion ("I love the Eighties!") and insight in a manner that should entertain readers. However, the talking point about his page (and arguably the whole programme) is the photo of Rob that adorns the head of his column. If you didn't know better, sight of this mug shot would convince you that Rob was a mental patient intent on murder or the right-hand man of the Unabomber. "I look like a psycho-killer in the programme. Gary said 'Have you got any photos?' and all I had was a passport photo!" If this photo makes it into Rob's passport then I expect customs officials the world over are either going to fearfully wave him through or strip search him and impound his luggage.

The Swindon track-shop is another of the many outposts of the Nick Barber speedway track-shop empire. It's run on race-night by Swindon Robins fanatic Lucy Aubrey (daughter of Robins track photographer Les) and her partner, Lee. This season they have additional company in the form of speedway historian, best-selling author and obsessive Gary Numan/Morrissey fan, Robert Bamford. Most people that come through the entrance gates stop briefly at the track-shop en route to the bar, Legends' Lounge or the pits. Co-promoter Terry Russell's hardworking son, Wayne, dashes to-and-fro from the Speedway Office situated adjacent to the turnstiles to all points Blunsdon. Often many times throughout the evening on a typical race-night. Tonight is no exception. "The Play-offs are really exciting this year! Lakeside versus Wolves that's quite a meeting! I think whoever gets to the final – obviously, we hope it's us – it'll be really exciting and, of course, good for the sport which is, after all, what it's all about!" Speedway referee Graham Reeve has come to the track-shop with a foreign visitor who's fascinated by the cornucopia of speedway merchandise available. While his visitor feasts his eyes, Graham tells me, "He's written a book on the history of Slovenian speedway." Given Slovenia is a relatively new country, this book might possibly be on Yugoslav speedway? Either way, Graham's friend is Franci Tomazic and it's quickly clear from the way that Graham speaks to him – slowly and loudly – that his English mustn't be that good (or, perhaps, he has a hearing problem). "Come on! We've-got-to-go-and-see-Matej." At the sound of a word he can recognise, Franci breaks off from his concentrated study of the merchandise to exclaim, "Matej! Matej! [thumbs up] Won! [smiles broadly] Slovenia!" With this level of exuberance and articulacy I worry that Kelvin could lose his lucrative Sky Sports commentary work.

Patiently stood outside the stadium waiting to go through the turnstiles is Reading club historian, Arnie Gibbons. He's brought along with him a pile of his acclaimed history of the club *Tears and Glory: The Winged Wheel Story*. "I just can't get enthused. When I woke up this morning, I didn't think 'Oh my God I'm seeing Reading tonight' but I'm going to a meeting!" Arnie's magnum opus was published before the Reading Racers last season at Smallmead in 2008. Consequently, Arnie has produced and brought along a supplement for his book entitled "The Final Chapter?" Though his text states, "In all other respects the season could best be described as forgettable", once again his writing brings alive the facts, twists, turns and highlights of the season in engaging style. Arnie's supplement also provides a personal account of the End-of-an-Era meeting that formally brought speedway at Smallmead Stadium to a close. His account skilfully mixes events from the night itself along with memories and reminiscences from yesteryear. "I've usually kept my idols at arm's length. I was happy to watch their on-track heroics without trying to become their drinking buddy". Arnie also reveals he'd not "seen John Davis's seven incher for nearly 30 years". His supplement provides an opportunity for Arnie to express gratitude to a variety of people. "Mark Legg was another person I sought out during the day, to thank him for the extra one-and-a-half seasons that he had given us after the Bulldog implosion." However, nearly a year later Arnie was somewhat less than complimentary about Mr Legg's financial affairs. I fatuously enquire, "Does he owe you any money?" Arnie confirms, "£780, but I gather he owes many other people more money than me! The riders were owed money, but the BSPA pay them. My monies are owed by Aston Leisure Ltd. After all, Reading were losing money." The supplement updates the statistical appendices that delighted many readers of the book and Arnie also provides some errata. Amazingly, there are only four listed (and arguably only three of them are corrections), which illustrates – if it needed to be further emphasised – that the book was compiled with great love, care and fastidious attention to detail. That said, Arnie betrays his accountancy background when the quotation that opens this document re-christens the highly regarded American bank worker and poet as T.S. Elliot. Like many fans in attendance tonight, Arnie wears his club colours with pride. He sports a Reading Racers speedway team blue anorak and also a white T-shirt with a Racers logo positioned on his moob that states "Once a Racer always a Racer!"

It's also a delight to see that Brendan Johnson is at the meeting along with his dad, Dave. Only a short while back, Brendan's crash at Smallbrook Stadium on the Isle of Wight left him potentially at death's door in a critical condition in the intensive care unit of Southampton General Hospital. Always politely spoken and generally optimistic, Brendan makes light of the delight many people feel and express when they see him back on his feet again. "I wish I could ride now to be honest. It's really annoying 'cause I was having my best season but, I suppose, I can come back stronger!"[2]
[Dave] "Good thing it was at the end of the season not the start. Of course, you missed going to Australia."
[Brendan, looks grumpy] "I'm not happy about it."
[Dave] "Lucky I haven't brought it up then!"

Ex-Reading press officer and webmaster, the diminutive Andy Povey would have required wild horses to keep him away from this meeting. He misses his involvement with the club but, due to his burgeoning website empire along with his press duties for the BSPA, Andy has had little time to contemplate the full horror of the Racers demise. "I'm busier now than I ever was before, only I don't have any of the annoying half 7 in the morning phone calls from [Malcolm] Holloway or Jim Lynch!" Emma Lemon, wife of speedway rider Mark, is here to watch her husband captain the Reading team. She's accompanied by Mark's dad, Graeme (in a Reading Bulldogs jacket), who's over in the UK from Australia. Graeme has no time for anyone who grumbles about the absence of Bristol-born Jason Crump, "It's not like Crumpie has a minor injury – he's had to have a skin graft!" Emma nods, "Jason's regretting his decision to come back for Belle Vue now!" Though he's here tonight, tomorrow evening at the Oak Tree Arena (home of the Somerset Rebels) Mark will stage his testimonial. It will feature a 15-heat meeting between Australia and the Rest of the World, followed by a mini three-heat individual competition. There will be various guests of honour, including ex-Australian Test cricketer (and current Somerset captain) Justin Langer, Speedway World Champion Freddie Williams (1950 and 1953) and ex-Newcastle, Stoke and Hull speedway legend Tom Owen (father of Emma Lemon). Reports in the press indicate that there are also plans to stage a "gladiatorial" speedway match-race between Sam Ermolenko and Chris Louis. Mark's raced in Britain for nearly two decades since he arrived in this country as an inexperienced teenager in 1986, though he missed the 1993-1995 seasons because he couldn't get a work permit (because of an average 0.04 below the required benchmark). Since 1990, Mark has ridden for Poole, Middlesbrough, Long Eaton, Oxford, Eastbourne, Hull, Somerset, Belle Vue, Exeter, Stoke, Reading, Newport and, now, Newcastle. Graeme Lemon tells me proudly, "Justin Langer is going to the testimonial and Freddie Williams, too." He ignores my question ("Did Freddie play cricket for Australia then?"), but can't resist a flicker of patriot pride, "It's nice that you can have the Ashes for a change!"

The organisational stress of a testimonial is considerable. Emma now has first-hand experience of the last-minute details that require sudden attention – usually ranging from the sublime to the ridiculous. "Mark rang up Reading to get the mascot uniform and Andy [Povey] said, 'Sure you can have Rory!' I didn't think anything of it. When it came this week, it turned out to be a lion! I didn't want a lion, I wanted a Bulldog! Mark said 'Didn't the name Rory give you a clue?' I thought Rory was a nice name for a Bulldog. He said 'You know Rory is obviously a lion!' It wasn't to me and I wasn't happy. The lion is better than nothing, though I'd like a Bulldog." Given the Newcastle connections of Tom (and Joe) Owen, Mark's mid-season decision to join the Diamonds has a certain synchronicity. It's also worked out well. "It's amazing, Newcastle were bottom when Mark went there. It's a good place to be. Newport wasn't a happy place to be so it's a lot better at Newcastle! Mark saw how good all the riders were – Kingy, the two Danes – and said, 'I'm going to have to pick up my game to get in heat 15'. It's all extra and you really miss it if you're not getting

[2] Brendan would go to Australia to soak up the sunshine and practise extensively to help restore his speedway fitness. His parents let him go Down Under on the strict understanding that he wouldn't race competitively while there.

picked for that! The whole team has clicked and, now, touch wood they're in the Play-offs! Joan [English] is coming tomorrow, but George can't."

I set my table up in its traditional position at Blunsdon under the lee of the home-straight grandstand, adjacent to the yellow hash-marked floor that designates the fire escape access-way at the bottom of the steep stairs that lead down from the Legends' Lounge, grandstand bar and toilets. My appearance invariably causes an outbreak of deep sighs and various small passive-aggressive acts of resistance from the old age pensioners who usually stand in this position every week and, quite rightly, resent the unannounced arrival of an unwanted interloper. Harold Davies (89) is the most personable of these veteran Swindon speedway fans. "My father took me to speedway when I was 10 years old! I worked for the BBC doing the *Antiques Roadshow*. I used to put the set up. I worked for them for 32 years. I've broken me hip when I tripped over a cable in the bedroom." Harold is pictured in *Quantum of Shale* but questions my camerawork, "Why didn't you take a photo of all of me?" Harold's dad took him to see the speedway in Bristol. "It was the Bristol Bulldogs with Cordy Milne, Jack Milne, Lionel Van Praag – all the lot of them. They used to do leg-trailing, not foot forward like they do now! I watched Billy Hole and Johnny Hole after the war." I question Harold to find out the secret of how he's remained so alert and active, "Doing the job I was doing was the best job I ever had. I used to work at the chocolate factory when I was 14."

Speedway reporter from the Wolverhampton *Express & Star*, Tim Hamblin is here to watch the Cradley Heathens, hopefully, excel under the management guidance of their former promoter and team manager, Colin Pratt. Tomorrow night he'll go to the GP qualifier event staged at Brandon Stadium on the outskirts of Coventry. "It's an easy night for me tomorrow, Freddie [Lindgren] either makes it or he doesn't! They set the paper on a Friday afternoon for the Saturday so I only have a few lines anyway." The nearby refreshment kiosk does a roaring trade judging by the sheer number of people who walk by with food from there. They appear to specialise in chips with everything. Tim jokes, "It's what [son] David Hamblin always calls the two major food groups – carbon and salmonella!" Rob Peasley's quietly spoken but knowledgeable dad, Cliff, soaks up the pre-meeting atmosphere on the reasonably crowded home-straight terrace, "It doesn't matter who wins, it's just being here!" Tim Hamblin is never short of insight or subtle appreciation. "It's a nice touch getting Adam Shields to captain the Cradley side given his family connections [His uncle Dave Shields rode for Cradley in the 1981 Championship-winning team]. Will Pottinger – the usual team manager for the Club Cradley Academy team – is unbeaten on the road." Prior to his travel down from the West Midlands this afternoon, Tim (as usual) has done his research. "As luck would have it, I was on the Swindon website last night and I saw the Gary Patchett statement. I rang Rob Lyon and he said, 'I suppose Gary Patchett told you to call?' I said, 'Nah, I just looked on the website'. Rob's just the middleman, he told me 'I think there may be something more to it than that!' Nah, you don't say, I thought. Gary told me a lot when I rang him after but, sadly, the most quotable things couldn't go in!" Another fan has an artistic view of Swindon's co-promoter, "Have you noticed that Gary has a slightly off-shaped nose? If he was a painting, Picasso would do it!"

Traditionally, you'd expect an invitation meeting – what is in effect only really a friendly – to only have riders going through the motions. However, heat 1 starts with an aggressive battle between the blue-helmeted Hans Andersen and the yellow-helmeted Patrick Hougaard – representing Cradley and Reading, respectively. They look incredibly fast and no quarter is given until Hougaard smashes into the bend 3 air-fence and, thereby, earns a disqualification. In the rerun, Hans Andersen fails to gate and it takes him until the third bend of the third lap to overtake Paul Hurry. The Heathen then threatens to also go round the outside of Morten Risager on the third bend of the last lap, but is thwarted so cuts inside to race for the line – but is again held at bay by a super-fast and noticeably robust Morten. Graham Cooke has approvingly followed Morten's development with interest. "When he first came over here at 16 or 17 he was too young but, now, he's put on a few pounds. So, unlike before, when other riders gave him a shove, he just ignores it and isn't moved off the line!" The latter part of Matej Zagar's career at Reading (by then in their Bulldogs incarnation) didn't end satisfactorily for either the rider or the club. His reappearance in the Winged Wheeled tabard doesn't impress and, in fact, barely happens since he's quickly disqualified under the 2-minute time allowance. The announcer informs us that Matej can come back out in the rerun and start off 15 metres or, possibly, a reserve can come out in his place. A fan in a Reading jacket plaintively asks the crowd around him, "Is there a reserve?" The announcer then informs us that Justin Sedgmen will replace Zagar for the rerun but, when the riders arrive at the tapes, he corrects himself, "I didn't mean to mess up your programmes but, you may have noticed, it's

Richard Sweetman in yellow!" The easily disgruntled Racers fan exclaims, "This programme's a nightmare!" Mine certainly looks a mess, even if you ignore that the race-card design inadvertently fails to provide any column to record individual riders' results for each heat. Reading finally get off the mark in heat 3 when Travis McGowan finishes third. On the terraces rather than the centre green to savour the race action, Graham Cooke lingers with his blonde 18-year-old daughter, Steffie, "If there was a league for nice speedway riders, Travis would be top every time!" Another nice speedway rider is Cameron Woodward. He snatches third place for the Heathens in heat four, when he overtakes Mark Lemon on the second bend of lap 3. Ahead of them, Lewis Bridger chases Leigh Adams but is unable to make any impression. Even at this early stage of the evening, victory for any other team than Swindon looks highly unlikely. The meeting silverware (if there is actually any) looks destined for the cobwebbed Robins trophy cabinet unless, as is traditional, they somehow conspire to throw it away. With changes to the track shape already increasing speeds and reducing times around the 363-metre circuit, a healthy covering of shale tonight will also be an important contributory factor. Graham Cooke has kindly advised any mechanic who'll listen to set up their bikes accordingly. Matej Zagar's mechanic didn't want his advice, "I said there's a lot of material out there, there'll be lots of fast times. He said 'Nah, nah, it's slick! I'm taking a couple of teeth off his sprockets. See how he goes!' I saw how he went – he only just got to the line!"

With Reading only on a magnificent 2 points after six races, it doesn't take a genius to predict that team manager, Tim Sugar, will send out Matej Zagar in the black-and-white helmet colour for heat 7. The race fails to start auspiciously when the Slovenian finds himself marooned in fourth place only to get a reprieve when Paul Hurry has a sudden dramatic fall ("a mechanical problem – his bike appeared to stop underneath him") on the second bend. The small huddle of Racers fans in front of my table debate whether Zagar was under power at the time of the incident, "He looked to have given up!" Whenever he's interviewed live on television, Matej always speaks plainly and avoids the platitudes that are the lingua franca of so many other modern speedway riders. Graham Cooke has also noticed his articulacy, "Matej is much more articulate than most speedway riders and I always enjoy his interviews!" The rerun sees Simon Stead fly from the tapes and it takes Zagar until the third bend of the third lap to blast underneath him only for Stead to immediately return the favour on the next bend and then stay there to take the chequered flag. Matej Zagar's second-place points double to 4 but, even with an aggregate total boosted to 6 points, this only massages Reading's score rather than thrusts them back into contention. Patrick Hougaard's second successive race without troubling the scorer doubly underlines that the Racers challenge ebbs rather than flows and, even after eight races, they still have only 6 points, despite the early use of their tactical option. Oxford use their tactical option in heat 9, but Lewis Bridger can only finish second behind Matej Zagar! He'll be the Racers only race winner of the night. Troy Batchelor wins the next race for Oxford and, suddenly, they're level on points with Swindon and, thereby, illustrate the structural iniquity of differentially used tactical regulations.

The 11th race of the night takes two attempts to complete. Mark Lemon is disqualified from the initial attempt to race it and then, proof positive that referees can and do change their minds (in friendly meetings), Graham Reeve then reinstates the unfortunate Racer to widespread approval from the crowd ("I thought it was a bit harsh"). In the rerun, 'Lemo' gains a point and, by the standards of the earlier races, this counts as a renaissance for the Reading Racers. However, this is snuffed out in the next race when "Mr Nice Guy" Travis McGowan clatters into the bend 3 air-fence. Though unlucky for Travis, it represents good fortune for Oxford's Paul Hurry who falls but remounts by the time the referee calls the race to a halt. Speedway journalist Brian Burford has taken a rare night away from his mother's ongoing heart problems and osteoporosis to savour the distraction of some much-needed speedway action. "It's my first meeting since June. I'm looking after my mum and working, so I haven't had time to come." Typically, Brian is quick to praise the handlebar heroes who risk life and limb for our entertainment, "You have to admire Adam Shields – he's had so many injuries but still races like he never has had! I must say it's better than I expected. They're really racing rather than just going through the motions!" Brian nods towards Robert Bamford, who is taking things easy behind the relative safety of the track-shop tables. Despite this, Rob's luxuriant hair almost billows with the frenetic speed of his movements as he moves sideways to double-check his results with those of Lee Poole. Rod Ford (aka Punch) wanders past and proudly shows me his first-ever blisters at the track. Clearly, Punch has inadvertently ignored his own expert advice about the correct but delicate manner in which to grasp and use a shovel.

Before heat 14, Cradley trail Swindon by 6 points and, on the principle of use it or lose it, many in the crowd anticipate that their wily Heathens team manager, Colin Pratt, will send out Cameron Woodward in the black-and-white helmet colour. However, when the riders come to the line, Cameron resolutely remains in his programmed blue-helmet colour. Indeed, he wears it with some distinction to win the race and, thereby, preclude any use of their tactical by Cradley. Afterwards, the Racers team manager, Tim Sugar, sees the funny side, "Colin Pratt was funny. He was asking how many he had to be behind to use a tactical ride! Cam went out and won – so we all pissed ourselves laughing, saying 'How many years have you been doing this?'" Though the Heathens can still mathematically overtake the Robins, this appears an unlikely outcome with Simon Stead and Leigh Adams still to take their final races. While we wait, Robert Bamford tells me, "Your hair suits your face better." On the track, Adam Shields again rides determinedly to win heat 15, though most of the entertainment is behind him. Third-placed Simon Stead rears massively on the third bend of the second lap, but somehow has enough acrobatic ability to remain on board his bike. This race result means that should Hans Andersen win the last race and Leigh Adams finish last, then Cradley will emerge triumphant. Hans Andersen proceeds to gate with alacrity and leads as the riders exit the second bend but, by the third bend, finds himself relegated to fourth! Though he recovers position, second place behind Leigh Adams isn't going to be enough to wrest the silverware from the claws of the Robins. Matej Zagar snatches third place on the line from Oxford's Troy Batchelor but it's all too little too late for the Racers, who take the wooden spoon. Club historian Arnie Gibbons doesn't look pleased.

Tim Hamblin enjoyed the action, but is slightly disappointed that Cradley haven't won. "I blame Colin Pratt for not using the tactical in heat 14, saving it for heat 15 and, typically, young Woodward shot out and won. By my reckoning they would have tied!" Amazingly, some riders who've worn the Heathens race tabard tonight genuinely do appear to have some real passion for the club! Particularly Adam Shields ("there's the Shields connection") and Hans Andersen "'cause of the Gundersen thing – he would have worn white leathers if he could!"

17 September Four-Team Tournament: Swindon 32, Cradley 29, Oxford 20, Reading 19.

CHAPTER 36

Coventry

"You see the nerves in their eyes and in their faces."

18th September

The 2009 Grand Prix Challenge final actually takes place in Britain this season at Brandon Stadium in Coventry. Officially this is a meeting held under the Sporting Code of the FIM supervised by the BSPA. Sixteen riders compete throughout the summer to win the chance to gain one of the three prestigious qualification places on offer for next season's 2010 Speedway Grand Prix series. Despite the ongoing sick joke that is the grace-and-favour basis allocation of some places for the series by the organisers, last season the SGP Press Officer Philip Rising questioned the validity or need of this event both before and after the meeting. However, while it might irk IMG/BSI that they can't gerrymander every entrant in the SGP, for many fans this event is the closest we nowadays still get to the old-style one-off speedway final. Tonight's field all notionally have an equal chance of qualification, though it's anticipated that Coventry might (unconsciously) bear their rider Chris 'Bomber' Harris in mind during their track preparation. Nonetheless, once up at the tapes each rider will have five races to determine their own destiny, albeit they'll also require good fortune to avoid engine failures, falls and crashes. Given so much rests on qualification, the riders won't merely go through the motions but will give their all.

Since this is one of the biggest events of the 2009 British Speedway calendar, it's hardly a surprise that five hours before the scheduled start time of 8 p.m. there's already 20 or so cars in the sun-drenched car park. Some people have even started to queue but the majority sit and wait with their windows open with the radio on, paper open or in mid-sandwich. The selection of Brandon Stadium for this event is a testament to the hard work and commitment shown by all the volunteers and staff of Coventry speedway and, in particular, stadium owner and Chief Executive Avtar Sandhu. In the programme BSPA Chairman Peter Toogood waxes lyrical about Mr Sandhu's impact, "Brandon Stadium has enjoyed a new lease of life with some excellent corporate and spectator facilities in a perfect geographical location. We're delighted to see big-time world championship racing back here!" Everyone at the club definitely wants to put their best foot forward. Co-promoter Colin Pratt is no exception and, in the hours before the action gets underway, he prowls the stadium buildings, highways, byways and entrances to ensure that all housekeeping is in order and that everything looks ship shape. When I arrive at the entrance gate to the stadium, Colin also arrives from the other direction with a hand-written note of additions ("Craig Boyce and Beverley, Lol Hare") for the carefully controlled guest list. Colin surveys the scene and instructs the security man on the gate, "I don't want anyone round the gate area! I don't frickin' care if they're riders, promoters or who the goodness they are! They can blooming well stand round the corner! [Smiles] I'm after Ole Olson's job!" The security man hasn't heard of this person, "Who's he?" Colin enlightens us, "Director of Operations for the Grand Prix." Ben Barker strolls by dressed in a black T-shirt and black jeans. Colin accosts him, "Make sure you come back dressed smart later!" Ben looks nonplussed, "Why?" "'Cause it's an important meeting!" Instructions issued, Colin rushes off elsewhere within the stadium to check, double check or supervise.

More cars arrive in the car park and the queue outside starts to swell. The man on the riders' and officials' entrance gate surveys the scene, "If you let people free into speedway, you'd have 10,000 every week!"
[Jeff] "I thought that's what you got anyway?"
[Man] Take off a nought and double it, that's probably our average crowd. We get 2,300 at stockcars on a Saturday."
Malcolm Blythe wanders up from the trackshop located round the corner from the entrance gate clutching the autumn issue of *Classic Speedway* magazine that features a photograph of 'Little Boy Blue' Nigel Boocock on the cover. "I haven't looked into it until now. Tony McDonald told me they introduced it to replace *Vintage Speedway* magazine 'cause there were getting fewer and fewer of them [subscribers] and those that were left were getting hard to get

hold of." He theatrically opens the magazine and randomly finds an article about Bradford, "It's 20 years since Eric Gundersen was injured at Bradford. That was a dangerous track. It was square 'cause it went round the rugby league pitch and they had a number of bad injuries there!" Malcolm surveys the impressively sized car park bathed in late September sunshine. "In the old days, CO [Charles Ochiltree] would have had ice cream vans, parking attendants and temporary toilets in the car park already! Whereas, there's nothing out there, is there?" I've been invited here this evening by the BSPA as a member of the press and my liaison person at the club is Bees Press Officer David Rowe. Not all clubs enjoy Coventry speedway's on-track success or, like David, have to cope with the unquenchable media thirst for information about the club. "I can understand why some Premier League clubs' press officers have a fulltime job. But, at Coventry, the media demand for information is so high – across different mediums – that, if there's some breaking news, like they do at Manchester United, I can get the message out there within half an hour without delay!" It's David's fifth season as a press officer ("I started in 2005 after Mike Berry stopped doing it") and the staging of tonight's GP qualifier whets his appetite. "This will be a really good meeting that showcases Coventry speedway but, more importantly, British speedway in a favourable light! I wasn't the biggest fan of the old GP knock-out system where you could be out after two bad races but, nowadays, the GP is effectively a 20-heat qualifying meeting to decide the bottom eight riders, six or seven of whom finish at the bottom almost every week! It's only the last three races where there's a bit more cut and thrust! Tonight, if you have a third [in your opening ride] you're going to have to win all or most of your remaining races. 12 points is going to be a minimum to be on the podium. I don't think the field could really be any stronger – it's only really missing Matej Zagar – who's phenomenal round here and Lindback, I suppose, but I expect he'll get one of the wild card picks for the 2010 GP series anyway. No one is going to stop going for it all night! Two seconds and, unless you win the other three, it's all over!"

Up the blue-painted stairs of the grandstand located in the vicinity of the toilets and refreshment areas – guarded this evening by security – you soon arrive outside the impressive Brandon Stadium corporate hospitality entertainment area that comprises a suite of rooms and a private bar. Each room provides panoramic views of the track and stadium, Internet access, tables and chairs as well as ready access to the aforementioned private bar dedicated to the use of corporate patrons. At the far end of the corridor, the press are allocated a swishly furnished room filled with a selection of tables, chairs and stools designed in the modern contemporary style. Through the large windows you overlook the track in one direction and, in the other, there's a fantastic view of a large section of the pits as well as the pit lane. Two cases of bottled water stand unopened but ready for the crowd of print, broadcast and online media people from various speedway nations who'll later descend on this room to enjoy the racing and report on events. Presently, either they're otherwise occupied with rider interviews in the pits or they have yet to arrive at the stadium. David gives a proud wave of his hand and explains, "We have the media reception in this room after the [Coventry Bees] Press and Practice day at the start of the season. All the riders come here and sit down for interviews. I think here is better to watch the meeting from than, say, than by the start-line, 'cause you can see all the action and you can overlook the pits in case anything kicks off in there!" Another member of staff earlier sat behind the impressive control panel cum desk at the top of the stairs you climb to access the corporate hospitality area pops his head into the room, "Colin's just been along and said anyone who's standing at the top of the stairs is to be thrown out!" Speedway isn't the only string to David's sports journalism bow since he also regularly does football commentary for talkSPORT. "I think they like me 'cause I'll travel anywhere! Tomorrow I'm at Bristol City, the next day at Everton. There's the [speedway] Play-offs here on Monday, Leeds Tuesday, Preston Wednesday and I've got to do the [speedway] programmes in between! I only do premiership and championship and the cups – obviously, the two next week are league cup."

Close by the pits, speedway and grasstrack competition specialist, Geoff Collins' parked-up spares van is open for business. There's an impressive array of tyres laid out on display next to a board that proclaims "Notice to Riders: GP Challenge. All tyres fuel and spares to be paid for on collection. Card. Cash. Thank you." In case the message isn't received loud and clear or has been inadvertently forgotten by the time the riders stand at the back of his van that doubles as a serving area for the spares and equipment, Geoff has attached a notice to the van door that reiterates the payment terms policy "Cash or Card before release of goods. Simple technology. No Cash, No Goods!!" I can't quite place my finger on it but, something hints to me, that some people might expect to gain use of these virgin tyres on a complimentary basis. "It's cash or credit card only. I've done too many of these meetings to do otherwise! Some riders in the past have taken £200 worth of tyres and then gone off without paying for them. But that's speedway for you! Some of the home riders think it's a free service and, though I'm stood here every week, it still doesn't make any difference. One rider from last season, naming no names, still owes me thousands."

In an age of sports psychologists and nutritionists, nowadays speedway riders' bodies are often a temple still unransacked by the Goths. To illustrate the point, meeting reserve Morton Risager clutches a low-calorie chicken pasta salad as he walks past the van. Assuming that it's his, Morton clearly watches his figure and nutritional intake. Everyone who is anyone within British speedway – at least a good few of them – is here tonight. The great and the good are everywhere. One of the head honchos of BSI/IMG, Paul Bellamy, is also here. He's probably come along to witness the one SGP event each season where there's genuine fan anticipation beforehand as well as actual drama and excitement on track throughout the meeting. He's casually dressed and his executive lifestyle doesn't yet appear to have given him a midlife paunch. He chats amiably to Tony Briggs and Peter Toogood. A short distance away in the pits there's a slimline Kelvin Tatum. Close by Shane Parker (wearing gloves) helps out as part of the Chris Holder pits crew. Bees fan and rider merchandise sales woman Jodie Lowry has, like her father, arrived in good time before the turnstiles open.
[Jeff] "I've seen your dad – he's media tonight."
[Jodie] "Yeah, he's Mr Clean Cut Sports Steve Brandon."
[Jeff] "Surely not?"
[Jodie] "I hope not. I met him for the first time at Bydgoszcz last year when he came up and gobbed on my hand and said 'Do you know who I am?'"
[Jeff] "Why did he gob on your hand?"
[Jodie] "I think he went for an attempted kiss that was part slobber and part gob."
[Jeff] "Did you immediately ask others around you, 'Can you help? This man doesn't know who he is?'"
[Jodie] "No, I told him to go forth and multiply."

Inside the grandstand building, the man at the top of the stairs adjacent to the corporate hospitality area has another message for David Rowe from Colin Pratt. "You can't keep having the press guys go down and ask Sheila [in the Speedway Office] for a programme! Sheila and Colin are doing their nuts.
[David] "That was what I was told to do to stop people taking more than one and them all going at once before everyone's got here."
[Man] "Well, yeah, you'll have to sort out something different now!"

Back outside on the concourse, well-travelled speedway fan Brian Oldham provides some feedback on my written work. "You can still do better! Your book is ideal for reading short snippets in the toilet! Does anyone read them from cover to cover? What Jonathan Chapman said about your books is true. Compared to your previous book a lot more was correct in this one." His charming wife Celia looks forward to the meeting ahead with a confident prediction, "Freddie will win!" She also forecasts who else'll qualify but I'm distracted so miss the clues she provides. Even some of the photographers await the meeting with keen anticipation. "This is the meeting with the most emotion amongst the riders! Especially if they miss out just getting to the GPs – it's a big financial difference! Plus they can say they got there and that they qualified properly!" Newcastle Diamonds fan Steve has come down specially

Morten Risager & Dave Robinson

Paul Bellamy & Peter Toogood

Great atmosphere

(on public transport) to savour this event. "The riders will really go for it. This will be the top individual meeting of the season in this country! Better than the GPs, the riders know it's top three or a really good showing to get a wildcard!" After a slow start, the Diamonds are the dark horses of the Premier League season. "We're going to give King's Lynn a big surprise on Sunday. The two Davids are flying and Mark Lemon is riding out of his skin. They shouldn't underestimate us! I reckon we'll get Birmingham in the Play-off semi-final and we should have the beating of them. Topinka and Ward will go well at ours [on Sunday] but Schramm and the like could struggle. The worry is that Kenni Larsen has the World U21 final the day before in Croatia so it depends on the flights going okay."

Peter Toogood surveys the scene with satisfaction as an impressively large crowd mills about in the vicinity of the pits, trackshop and refreshment area. He meets and greets anyone who stops for a chat including myself. "These last two weeks the weather has got colder. It's dropping now and it's cold on a morning! Do you make any money doing this?"
[Jeff] "Nah, I've made a £x loss, at least, since I started. It's the travel [costs] that kills you!"
[Peter] "Oh, well, to some people that would be a lot of money and others wouldn't even notice! Keep up the good work!"
Well-travelled German speedway fan Jurgen Gilsdorf has travelled to Coventry without his mother ("has been ill"). Dressed in his usual manner, Jurgen wears his metaphorical press hat. "I am Press today as I write for a speedway magazine in Switzerland. This is an important meeting. I think BOMBB-BURR needs to do well , otherwise he will be out of the GP. Look at him last weekend [in Latvia], he has so much skill but it is his gating that is bad. If he gets that good, well, I hope so!"

Upstairs at the press bar, Tim Sugar and Andy Povey get in the early beers, "Has the drinking started already?" One slurp into his first pint Tim Sugar confirms, "Yes, it's a rare moment 'cause Andy has his money out and is buying!" Undertones admirer Andy Povey has his finger on the pulse when it comes to the latest Reading Racers gossip. In this instance about one of the members of the now defunct Racers commercial team, "Rob Bamford bumped into Ross Marks at a Gary Numan concert and he revealed that he'd been laid off!" Back in the trackshop, Jodie interrupts her conversation with another lady to provide some feedback upon my written work. "I read my bit in the book where you're criticising my salesmanship claiming I couldn't sell a Coventry DVD to Allen Trump when I did!" You can only report what you see, "I didn't know that you'd had. But, to be fair to me, I took out the bit where you said something uncomplimentary." The lady with Jodie is Jane from the acclaimed speedway DVD production company Clean Cut Sports. "Oh, you're the man whose book quoted our competitors about our work! [pause] My husband's Pete." Robert Peasley arrives clutching last night's Four Team programme (from Swindon) and, without much prompting, reveals the photograph that adorns his column. Jodie notes, "Is that your passport photo? I wouldn't let you in any country as you look so scary! Why did you use that one?"

Though I could watch proceedings from behind the glass in the press box, shortly before the rider parade, I'm doubly fortunate to be able to sit in a section of the grandstand that overlooks the bend and pit lane. There's a spare seat between Peterborough Panthers speedway fanatics Graham and Hilary Rouse. Hilary quickly intrigues me with the words, "Jason Crump came into our shop" before she then thinks better of it. Encounters with speedway riders away from the track always fascinate me. To protect Hilary and Jason's confidentiality, I volunteer to write the important details on to a piece of rice paper and eat it immediately after Hilary reveals all but she refuses. What could Jason be shopping for that is so damning? Hilary doesn't look the type of lady to work in a sex shop or, for that matter in Poundland where Jason, perhaps, likes to buy secret, forbidden snacks like a bumper eight-pack of Quavers specially manufactured for the Turkish market. Hilary coquettishly gives me some clues, "Where would you buy Australian honey?" My immediate thought would be Australia. Clearly Jason must hanker for a taste of his adopted home since I doubt that they manufacture much honey in his birthplace (Bristol). Australian honey is a specialist purchase so that can only really indicate that Hilary works at Holland & Barrett or perhaps one of the pricier notionally 'upmarket' supermarkets, like M&S or Waitrose. Given that Jason will soon be world champion again, I'd expect him to shop aspirationally and, indeed, would be disappointed if he didn't! Hilary still refuses to identify the location of the shop, let alone reveal its name, "We had a famous footballer in there as well! It's a top store!" I have to say that I didn't realise that Harrods now have franchises located in parts of the country known to be where speedway riders domicile themselves. Towns like Stevenage and Hemel Hempstead spring to mind but I gather Jason lives north of there, probably somewhere exotic like Oundle or Spalding. Hilary's definitely not going to help me with my detective work and news that "he used to be able to get an Olympic breakfast there" adds further confusion. Perhaps Jason is, after all, a man in pursuit of good value and use of a loyalty card? Possibly Tesco or Sainsbury's! I don't think Lidl or Aldi do breakfasts (though Hilary's store no longer does either). Perhaps, Hilary's secrecy is because she's seen Jason buy some foul-tasting caffeine jolt liquid abomination not actually manufactured by his top sponsor Red Bull? It definitely seems highly unlikely that he would slurp back any of the Monster products promoted by his great rival Greg Hancock. Though, perhaps, Hilary had seen him purchasing something innocuous but allegedly more 'nutritious' like a Sports Lucozade drink? Whatever the answer, Hilary's taken a vow of silence.

One man who definitely hasn't taken a vow of silence is Coventry presenter Peter York. It's such a significant night that the organisers celebrate in the only way possible – with the rider parade where all the riders get specially introduced to Peter Collins. While this goes on Peter York name-checks each of the competitors including reserves Ales Dryml and "Moor-han Reese-ha" like he's just seen them written down for the first time. Probably worried that he might meet her, Hilary notes, "Kenneth Bjerre is the only one to go on parade wearing his helmet." While the riders retreat to the pits to prepare, there's time for a bit of repartee between presenter and guest.
[Peter York] "Peter – where are you keeping yourself nowadays?"
[PC] "I don't go so much now. I've been this season quite a lot. I go to Belle Vue every Monday which is sometimes a little disappointing!"
[Peter York]"It's a big night."
[PC] "You see the nerves in their eyes and in their faces."
After a little more banter, Peter York signals that the action is about to start when he informs the packed Brandon stadium, "Everything is good to go!" Sight of Colin Pratt in the pits prompts Hilary to recall a trip to a rained-off meeting at Cradley Heath. "I said to Graham it was nice of the gateman to speak to us like that and Graham said, 'You do know who that is, don't you? It's not the gateman, it's Colin Pratt – he used to be a rider.' So, since then, we've known him as the gateman!" Heat 1 sees the riders pootle round to the line on a sodden-looking race track that some fans in the crowd claim has been specially prepared to that specification for home favourite Chris 'Bomber' Harris. His present position in the 2009 SGP standings dictate that a podium placing would definitely ensure his participation in the 2010 series. Though, luckily for him the size/importance of the lucrative UK television advertising market, dictates that his participation as a wild card pick remains a strong possibility, even if he doesn't formally qualify tonight.

Along with the sudden-death qualification format, it's a night to warm the hearts of speedway traditionalists since we'll also enjoy the treat of white helmet colour (use of which in recent years was suspended, allegedly to help the clarity of the television pictures). Given the importance of the meeting, it's widely anticipated that no quarter will be asked or given and so it proves in the first corner of the first race when Chris Holder and Jaroslaw Hampel immediately bump and grind for supremacy. The Australian demonstrates his gymnastic ability on the second bend before he stamps his authority on the race. Surprisingly, almost shockingly, Chris Harris finishes last and now most probably needs four wins to achieve his pre-meeting goal of qualification. Hilary is alive to the atmosphere and off-track action, "Don't the start girls look smart?" Riders, bikes and even mechanics all really look the part in the pits under floodlights that pick out but also dramatise the hustle and bustle of pit lane as well as the action on the track. Bikes glisten, kevlars glow and every available surface is logoed-up. Hilary spots a curious Freddie Lindgren pressed close to the fence to watch the first-corner action of heat 2. "Look, there's Freddie, he always waves his arms and keeps himself looking fit! He's a nice looking lad!" The race fails to progress beyond the first corner when Jonas Davidsson falls melodramatically (when fourth and already at the rear) after Grzegorz Walasek comes sharply across him. Graham's not impressed, "He could have stayed on, if he wanted to!" However, it was always worth a tumble and, in the rerun, Jonas gains a point that otherwise would've eluded him. The white-helmeted Peterborough rider Kenneth Bjerre gates brilliantly to lead heat 3 but, almost immediately, suffers an engine failure on the back straight that puts an immediate kink in his qualification ambitions and, most likely, psychologically undermines his campaign. Magnus Zetterstrom needs no second invitation to seize an unexpected advantage to win the race by a street. Adrian Miedzinski easily leads the fourth heat until the second bend of the third lap where he rears massively and looks likely to fall from his machine. Somehow he stays on but drops to second place behind eventual race winner Freddie Lindgren.

After each competitor has had their initial outing, it's a natural moment to give the track some attention. Peter York warns of this pending activity, "As I say, to get the shale back on the racing line." Back in the pressroom, the wonders of new technology aren't always a gift to efficiency, according to Paul Burbidge, "I've got connection problems!" The Poole speedway reporting massive are here in full force tonight on the tables found in the centre of the press lounge. Highly regarded Dorset-based speedway reporter, Phil Chard, repeatedly dashes the yard or so from his desk to the hospitality suite windows to watch the action and then back again to summarise what he's just seen on his laptop for his readers. It's definitely an object lesson in how to compile elegant prose under time-pressured conditions, "I'm fine. Sorry, I can't talk, I have a 10.30 deadline!" [1]

Freddie Lindgren rides twice in successive heats though, with the delay for the track grade, he's got more than enough time to conduct further gymnastic calisthenics. Freddie's up against the supremely laidback Australian Chris Holder – who confidently fires to his second successive win of the night. The diminutive Kenneth Bjerre eludes mechanical difficulties but, when he surrenders second place to Lindgren, effectively ends his chances of qualification continuing the inconsistent form that has dogged his 2009 speedway season on British shores. Jaroslaw Hampel wins heat 6 and with Zorro second, both riders find themselves nicely placed on 5 points. Heat 8 is make or break for Coventry's favourite Cornishman, something that Peter York labours over beforehand, "Mr Harris knows what he has to do – does he ever!" It takes three attempts to run this race to completion. Each time Grzegorz Walasek is centre stage. The initial attempt stops after Walasek moves at the tapes, the next attempt is recalled after he falls and, although Chris Harris battles throughout, he doesn't quite have the speed to overtake Walasek in the re-rerun. Only a catalogue of misfortune and complicated points arithmetic will now allow Chris Harris any outside chance of qualification for the GPs from tonight's meeting (via a third place run-off).

Chris Holder's third win of the night in heat 9 prompts Hilary to observe, "We always do better [at Peterborough] when we have Aussies in the team!" Tension, track conditions and a brief outbreak of dropsy sees Lukas Dryml fall on the second bend of heat 10 and Adrian Miedzinski tumble on the third bend and, thereby, wreck his chances. Kenneth Bjerre's run of misfortune continues in heat 11 when, from the inside gate, Walasek clatters into him to cause his bike to spectacularly somersault and careen at high speed away from its stricken owner. The bright farings on Kenneth's bike glint in the floodlights to add to the drama of the wild random somersaults of his equipment. Graham comments, "Bjerre's having a bad night. That's smashed that bike up and his other one's not working properly!" While the crowd wait for the riders to regroup and fine-tune their equipment for the rerun (with all four back), I venture off to watch some action from the luxury of the pressroom. Ben Barker pops in with a red anorak on but is immediately sent off on an errand by Colin Pratt, "Go downstairs and get the water from the office and bring it up here!" Hopefully, the cases of water bottles aren't too heavy since Ben told the *Speedway Star*, "I've separated my collarbone, and I've done some ligament damage around that area." Though the meeting is successfully underway, Colin refuses to rest

[1] If this were *Question of Sport*, Phil kindly explains what happened next. "The meeting finished about 11.15 p.m. (if my memory serves me right) and I think I emailed the final version of my copy to the sports desk sub-editor at the *Daily Echo* at about 11.20!Their final, final, deadline is 11.30! But I'd already sent over the full heat details and score chart, which we also carry, beforehand, so they just about had time to read through it, correct any errors, put my copy on the page, think up and tap-in a suitable headline, and send it away to meet our production team and printer's deadline of about 11.45 p.m. When I joined the *Daily Echo*, or *Bournemouth Evening Echo* as it was then called, in 1995, my deadline for a Wednesday night meeting at Poole was to file my copy by 6.45 a.m. in the morning. Up until about a month before the end of the 2008 speedway season, my deadline was still 1 a.m., with the sub-editor's deadline 2 a.m. What joy. I actually had time to conjure up and write two stories, a match report and a quotes-based report, that would be published in the next day's paper. In September of that year, my deadline suddenly became 10.30 p.m., although, at a push, I can go to 10.45 p.m., which is usually very strictly adhered too! That's so our newspaper can be printed earlier overnight, and, therefore, go on sale at the same time as the national newspapers in the morning. That way, the *Daily Echo* – which in the days of it being called the *Evening Echo* used to hit the newsstands late morning and/or early afternoon – has a longer time span on the newsagents' shelf. So, hopefully, we sell more copies. Fortunately, from my point of view as a reporter, there is a strict local government curfew in place at the town centre-based Poole track whereby they can't run meetings past 10 p.m. because of the noise factor, so very rarely does a meeting finish after 10 p.m. (In fact, it's probably only happened on a handful of occasions in my 15 years of covering Pirates.) It's great when meetings finish by 10 p.m. because I have to interview riders/team managers/promoters/referee, whoever, etc., post-meeting, write approximately 400 to 550 words, pick a rider of the night, write 50 to 100 words on them, check I've got the scorechart and heat details right, and send it all to the sub-editor in double-quick time. In special circumstances, and the night of the Grand Prix Challenge was definitely extremely special circumstances (thank you, Zorro!), the deadline can be edged back, but only to the ultimate point of no return, because if our complete paper doesn't meet the strict deadline for its print run, the overall editor of the *Daily Echo* gets fined! So it's a big challenge every time I cover a meeting. But an enjoyable challenge. And don't even mention our *Daily Echo* website (bournemouthecho.co.uk) deadlines! They're even earlier. Suffice to say, the 11.15 p.m. finish at Coventry was the latest for a meeting I've ever covered in Britain. But with Zorro and Noddy Holder getting through to the 2010 GP series, it was one where it was a privilege for me to actually be there and cover it, particularly as I have known Magnus since he first came over to Britain from Sweden and joined Poole in 1996. I was still in the pits interviewing Magnus at 1 a.m. when Poole owner Matt Ford rang to congratulate him for finishing second! Matt had thought Chris had won the meeting but that Zorro had also got through. He couldn't believe it when Zorro told him he'd actually won the whole thing. I wrote that interview up straight after I had finished a two-and-a-half hour drive home to Dorset and put it on our website myself, so nocturnal *Echo* readers could view it by about 4.30 a.m. Then I went to bed, trying not to wake up my lovely wife Jean at the same time."

on his laurels so continues to prowl territorially throughout the stadium to ensure that the club puts its best foot forward before, during and after the action. David Rowe is well used to his vigilant attention to detail. "Colin doesn't really do any team management any more. Peter does that and Colin makes sure everything is right with the track and all the stuff you need to have in order to run a speedway meeting properly! Colin was here all day yesterday. He wouldn't have left until late to go to Swindon and would have been here since first thing. He's not as young as he was so will be a bit tired and stressed!"

Symbolic of his inconsistency at Arlington throughout 2009, Davey Watt absolutely destroys the field in the rerun of heat 11 when he shoots past Kenneth Bjerre on the second bend. The 12th race of the night showcases the power and fluency of the riders until the fourth bend of the second lap when Piotr Protasiewicz locks up, Chris Harris clatters into him and, on the inside line, Freddie Lindgren gets caught up in the carnage when he tangles with Harris's runaway bike. Zorro's so far behind the trio that he easily avoids the conflagration of men and machines that explodes in front of him. Mistaking Chris Harris for George Davis or Nelson Mandela, a highly aggravated fan a few rows in front of me repeatedly screams, "Harris is innocent!" Apparently an expert authority on a split-second incident quite some considerable distance away from us, this fan vehemently claims to all and sundry that Freddie Lindgren knocked off Bomber – until replays contradict his account. He immediately changes his tune and, instead, blames Piotr Protasiewicz with equal vehemence. The endless looped replays of the incident showcases how quickly a speedway race can descend into the dodgems. Clearly not privy to sight of the replays, Peter York informs us, "We're told we've had the call on only three riders but we've not been told the excluded rider!" Given a massive reprieve from the poor position he occupied when the race stopped, Zorro makes no mistake in the rerun and finds himself in an unexpectedly strong position with 8 points after three races. Chris Harris finishes second but Peter York saves the triumphant note in his voice for tribal Midlands speedway matters, "Just a point for Freddie – that's gonna disappoint him!" Andy Povey takes a philosophical view the events of heat 12, "I think the bike just hit Lindgren's left side and winded him. He was third in the rerun but he was third first time anyway!"

Chris Holder wins heat 13 to take his total to 12 points out of a possible 12. Though Freddie Lindgren heads home Jaroslaw Hampel in heat 14, on aggregate Hampel still has 10 points to his rival's 9 and, therefore, a win in heat 18 should ensure his qualification. If Zorro kept out of the wars in heat 12 then the same couldn't be said of heat 15 where, on the first corner, Lukas Dryml locks up and Zorro can't avoid the tangle of men and machines that throws him over his handlebars. Phil Chard worries that this has prematurely ended his unlikely GP qualification charge, "If he gets up, he'll have another chance as it was Dryml that locked up in front of him." Like many in the stadium Paul Burbidge didn't even have Zorro down as a dark horse, "If I make one mistake this year – and that's underestimating Zorro – I won't mind!" Zorro spends a considerable amount of time prostrate on the track to heighten fears that he may be unable to continue. Predictably Lukas Dryml is disqualified as the primary cause of the incident. Tim Sugar identifies Kauko Nieminen as the real cause of the incident, "I thought blue had something to do with him coming off!" Replays at Brandon Stadium get shown before the riders get back to their feet. The replay footage shows Tim Sugar (rather than German FIM referee Christian Froschauer) is correct since Nieminen elbows Dryml (Andy Povey exclaims, "he's given him a nudge!") who, thereby, loses control and clatters into Zorro. Phil Chard is aghast, "The stretcher is coming out – oh frick, shite!" Paul Burbidge metaphorically has his fingers crossed, "If he can just get up and do two rides!" Peter York updates us, "I can tell you he's up on his knees – yeah, he's up!" The three-rider rerun more or less gets to the second bend before Kauko Nieminen rides aggressively for the outside line and dumps Zorro into the air-fence. Magnus's close inspection of the Brandon shale and another rendezvous with the medical team ensue. Eventually Zorro collects his thoughts – while, once again, his mechanical team work miracles in the pits as he lies prostrate upon the shale – and then comes out to beat Maksims Bogdanovs in their match race.

Amazingly a win in his last race will see Zorro qualify for the 2010 SGP series. But, with unbeaten Chris Holder in this race, second looks the likely realistic option. On the next week's Sky Sports live speedway broadcast, Kelvin Tatum would be critical of the meeting, "It was too wet that night – greasy and difficult!" He would also incorrectly state "gate 4 didn't work all night!" However, on a night when the form book has some sections rewritten, Zorro gates from the outside gate 4 in heat 17 to tear away to victory. Behind him Chris Holder's held up in traffic and takes some time to get past meeting reserve Morton Risager (riding in place of triple-broken collarbone victim Tobias Kroner). It's a result that ensures that both Chris Holder and Zorro automatically qualify. Jaroslaw Hampel must win heat 18 in order to ensure his progression into the 2010 SGP series. He proceeds to do so comfortably and, thereby, ends Freddie Lindgren's hope of automatic qualification (though many confidently expect he'll be awarded a wildcard by the organisers).

With Holder and Zetterstrom tied on 14 points apiece, we're treated to a run-off to decide who would leave with the commemorative silverware. Again, the consensus is that Holder will right the wrong that was the unexpected heat 17 result. However, though he no longer rides in this country, Zorro's liking for this damper version of the Brandon shale continues and, although he comes under pressure, Magnus triumphs to win the meeting! So many aspects of the BSI/IMG Speedway Grand Prix series devalue it as a serious competition – poor tracks, predictable format, too many rounds, capricious advertiser rather than talent-led wildcard selections, lack of transparency from the series organisers, ticket price increases and so forth. To that extensive list, some naysayers stupidly want to add the bizarre claim that Zorro's fair and square victory on the night somehow devalues the competition because he doesn't have a realistic chance of becoming world champion in 2010! Given that there's only been three world champions in the last nine seasons and that many riders never even get a sniff of semi-final qualification, this beggars belief. Zorro's win both re-animates and captures the spirit of the one-off World Championships. He showed skill and courage on the night, took advantage of his good fortune and, thereby, rightly is crowned the best man on the night! More importantly, he injects some much needed romance, albeit briefly, into a SGP series that manages to project all the lustre and excitement of a trip to the bottle bank.

18th September 2009 Grand Prix Challenge Winner: Magnus Zetterstrom

CHAPTER 37

Eastbourne

"Are you saying I'm small and appear to have no body strength?"

19th September

If the rules hadn't been changed half way through the season, Eastbourne's last Elite League meeting of 2009 against Ipswich would attract a bumper crowd keen to find out who exactly will claim sixth place in the Elite League table. However, the rules changed midway through the season and, rather than the top six clubs taking part in the Play-offs, this process now only applies to the top four. Consequently what could have been a significant fixture has now been reduced in status to one that will give the victors the full bragging rights naturally conferred on any team that finishes sixth(!), while the losers gain the consolation of a seventh-placed finish in a league that comprises nine teams. Another peculiar outcome of this rule change is that the rules and regulations that apply presently to the Elite League discriminate against any team that ends up placed between fifth and eighth place and instead, favours the most mediocre club (who finish last/ninth) since they'll be rewarded with promotion/relegation end-of-season fixtures that'll see bumper crowds flood through their respective turnstiles. In times of economic constraint, where clubs have to struggle to attract let alone retain every possible fan, the idea that the structure of the league ensures that failure is rewarded much more than inconsistency is a point for both club accountants and the promoters to ponder.

Those fans that have come along to see the last meaningful fixture of the season at Arlington enjoy the opportunity to buy (price 50p) a commemorative poster of Simon Gustafsson produced by the local Brighton-based newspaper, the *Argus*. On race night at Arlington the *Argus* press gang comprise the outgoing Lucy Cross and her fiancé, Kenny Penfold. Lucy's a big fan of Simon's, so much so that she even has a pet name for him: namely, "Smurfy". Kenny is prepared to indulge his future wife's obsessions, "With his blond hair and blue eyes, he looked like a Smurf. She likes him so much she named her hamster after him but, it turned out to be a female, so he had to call her Smurfette!" It's also possible to buy a complete set of the posters produced this season by the *Argus* for a bargain price of £3. Every Eagles rider features including David Norris whose season (and career) ended prematurely on 11th May during the meeting against Swindon. Lucy suggests to every fan that passes that they might like to buy a poster. This prompts one girl to ask, "Do you like Simon?" Quick as a flash Kenny retorts rhetorically, "Does she like him!?" The Pope is apparently catholic (and German) while bears, unless they're of the polar variety, like to use the woods for specific purposes. Kevin Ling the hardworking press officer for Eastbourne isn't here tonight (instead, Paul Watson will produce the meeting report sent out to the media) but his father and loyal Eastbourne Eagles fan, John, is. Like many Arlington regulars, oft-voiced concerns by the management about attendance numbers and gate receipts[1] has led to an undercurrent of anxiety about the exact nature of the club's future. "Bob has had an offer from Dean Barker backed by Matt Ford but, it would be in the Premier League, and we'd be a feeder club for Poole!" Such a thought would be heresy. "Bob rejected that! He's always said it should be top-flight or nothing! And, fair play to him, he's stuck by that. We haven't always done that well but he's been true to his word. Sure, if anyone came in, he'd have conditions but, if they put some money in too, he'd back them! "

In the trackshop Johnny Barber didn't attend the GP qualifier at Coventry last night but informs me that the consensus reached by attendees he's spoken to and posters on the British Speedway Forum is that it was "boring, slow but better than a GP!" Though it's nearly 10 months away, Johnny now can't wait for next year's Cardiff GP, "How I long to see the excitement of Magnus doing his dance and donuts at Cardiff after he's got his fifth nought and messes up the track even more!" Exceptional performances in athletics or cycling nowadays invariably raise doubts about their legitimacy and, such is the modern cynicism of the world, that any result that bucks the accepted formbook within speedway can be similarly tainted by wild and unfounded supposition. "Someone said to me 'Why didn't Scott

Nicholls qualify for the GP?' Someone else said, 'If he was on what Magnus Zetterstrom was on last night, he would have qualified!'"

Johnny shares trackshop duties at Eastbourne with his brother Nick and their regular Boy Saturday, Martin Dadswell. Johnny also works at Ipswich every Thursday during the season. Consequently, he meets and greets a huge number of fans as they pass by, even if he doesn't always sell them something. "I do know a juicy bit of gossip, [pause] Eastbourne are going to be favourites for [lengthier pause] the Suntrap Trophy!" No one yet knows what this particular piece of silverware actually looks like (or even if it's been manufactured). However, while it's not the Ashes, it does guarantee Poole's fourth appearance at Arlington this season and ensures that the stadium will resound to the roar of speedway bikes one last time before the season ends. Johnny has made his New Year's resolution for 2010 already. "When I lose all my weight, I know I've said that before, but I'm gonna come in wearing my 16th birthday present – a luminous Ian Walker goalkeeping shirt!" Keen Witches fan Adie has travelled down from Suffolk to Sussex. His burden in life is also to support Ipswich Town football club who are soon to be transformed under the innovative management of Roy Keane. He's already set about player motivation is his own inimitable style, plus he raids the Sunderland squad to buy Grant Leadbitter (sensible purchase) and Carlos Edwards (not so sensible purchase). Since Adie goes to the match quite often I ask, "Does Carlos Edwards still wear those tossy coloured boots?" It's hard to miss them but Adie has, "I was so bored it wouldn't have mattered if he'd run around naked!"

Johnny also looks after the King's Lynn speedway trackshop. Apart from the tension of their Premier League challenge, there were additional benefits to be had during the last meeting at the Norfolk Arena. "Unfortunately Edwin [Overland] was away so it was Mike Bennett with Kevin Moore in the box – the dream ticket! Mike Bennett said 'Is there anything you want me to do?' I said, 'Yeah, Workington are here and Simon Lambert is guesting for them – I

[1] Bob Dugard's masterclass in speedway finance has been almost a season-long feature of the pages of the *Speedway Star*. In late November 2008, prior to transfer requests, Brian Owen identified that the "'cut price' prospective team of Watt, Kennett, Bridger, Darkin, Woodward, Gustafsson and Mustonen" would cost £50,000 less than its 2008 predecessor. Revealing that the Eagles lost £30,000 in 2008, Owen informed us that Bob Dugard had "revised his breakeven attendance down to about 1,000 from 1,350." Prior to the start of the season, Bob considered the impact of live Sky Sports broadcasts upon the club. Brian Owen revealed the stark facts of the situation, "It costs Eastbourne at least £10,000 per meeting in lost gate revenue when they switch from Saturday to Monday for TV." Though it's rumoured that Sky Sports pay each Elite League team a base fee of £100,000 for the honour of broadcasting their meetings on the television, uncertainty about which track is covered and when, does lead to logistical complications for any club that wants to pre-book cheaper flights for their foreign-based riders. ("I've got 62 flights to arrange for riders"). The Dean Barker testimonial season opener at Arlington drew 1,600 fans but, when the club stage their next meeting – an Elite Shield encounter with Poole – only 970 paying customers come through the turnstiles. This figure includes season ticket holders but not the under-8s who get in free. Already surprised, though the season's barely underway, Bob Dugard comments, "For me the Elite Shield is a serious fixture but not for others it seems." The live Sky Sports meeting versus Swindon on a mid-May Monday night attracts a crowd of "about the 1,000 mark" and the Eagles management are quoted as "reasonably happy". To put this in context, later in the month of May, Poole Promoter Matt Ford reveals a poor start to their season has seen crowds at Wimborne Road average "in the region of 1,800-2,000". This is a situation that Ford noted ensures that the most successful top tier club of the past decade are "playing to our lowest crowd since 1998". Eastbourne's last home fixture with the lap-dancing start-line girls on show to entertain the crowd is their May 23rd meeting against Peterborough. Brian Owen subsequently reveals, "Saturday's gate was another disappointing one at 1,011." With the finances having fallen off the knife edge upon which they're poised, Brian Owen also notes that the budgeted £50,000 loss for the East Sussex club could prove an underestimate if "crowds hover around the 1,000 mark" throughout the remainder of the 2009 season. Bob fulminates, "Attendances are dismal. We have the lowest crowds in the League. Even Lakeside, who we used to be well ahead off, are getting 300 more people than us. We take an average of £13.20 per spectator, when you take into account children's tickets, so that extra 300 is worth almost £4,000 per meeting. Multiply that over a season and it's a lot of money. The level of entertainment has been so good and yet the crowds are falling away. How we overcome that I don't know." The 2009 trend towards attendance levels below club expectations is bucked by a "season's best crowd of just over 1,500" for the Elite League 'A' fixture against Coventry. Worryingly the decline in crowd numbers is, arguably, a sign of a wider malaise. A few weeks later *Speedway Star* managing editor (and SGP press officer) Philip Rising publishes a hard-hitting page 2 comment piece on the urgent need for dramatic changes in the administration and governance of the sport (as well as some pruning of the rulebook). Fulmination appeared to be the order of the day throughout May and June for practically everyone involved in speedway. As if it were possible, Philip Rising claims the credibility of the sport has suffered further. "Why is it that neither Poland nor Sweden, with successful domestic competitions, encounters the same problems as those that plague Britain? For someone who has dealt successfully with speedway bosses for over 40 years, I honestly don't think things have ever been as bad as they are right now. Make no mistake, the writing is on the wall and we all need the custodians of British Speedway to recognise the danger signals and take action to put it back on the rails before it crashes into the buffers." Saturday August 8th saw the biggest crowd of the season ("about 2,000 people") flood into Arlington. Sadly the 1,779 adults and 230 young children who turned up were there to watch a BSPA shared event (the Elite League Pairs) rather than an Eastbourne meeting. Bob Dugard wonders philosophically, "Why these people don't come to League matches, I don't know. It seemed to be mostly local people judging from the applause. They turned out in force and it was £20 to get in." Mid-season rule changes saw the number of play-off places for the Elite League qualifiers reduce from six to four, allied to rider injuries and some indifferent performances both home and away, the September Monday night live televised fixture against Coventry only attracts 800 fans. Bob's keen to yet again double underline the implications of this continued lack of support. "People need to be aware you cannot continue like that. To run in the Elite League you need an average crowd of 1,300 as a bare minimum or charge £20 for admission but that, of course, would drive people away." Local reporter Brian Owen identifies the speedway crowd is down by 22% though this is, apparently, offset by increased attendances at stockcar meetings at Arlington (up 8%). Brian also reveals that the 2009 season was "the first time the average crowd had dropped below 1,000, except for the time the club operated in a lower division." In a further word about the economics of Eastbourne Speedway Club in the pages of the *Speedway Star*, Bob notes, "Jon Cook in his last year got it making a small profit. He was a fulltime manager. I cannot do that. I have a fulltime job."

wondered if you could interview Simon Lambert first?' Mike Bennett smiled, 'Why?' I said 'I'm having withdrawals not knowing what Simon Lambert has done over the past six days!' Kevin Moore told me that a King's Lynn fan complained that he interviewed Simon Lambert too much! Apparently he said, 'I don't mind you interviewing him – so long as it's not first!' Kevin told me proudly, 'So I rebelled and interviewed him first!'" One item of merchandise – apart from *Quantum of Shale* – that fails to excite speedway fans at any track served by the Barber trackshop empire are the laudable but laughable eco-friendly air horns, "Jonathan Chapman invented these!" Out on the centre green Kevin Coombes buttonholes Niall Strudwick for one of his trademark interviews but also to award Niall with a prize from the 50/50 Club for his riding this season. "Have you progressed this year?" Niall quickly confirms, "I have!" Kevin then tries out one of his disco gig/event questions at Arlington, "How old are you?" "19." Unable to summon any further questions to mind, Kevin contents himself with, "You've been around for years!"

ipswichspeedway.eu van

There's an end-of-season sale at the trackshop that prompts one fan to try on a blue Wulfsport jacket. He twirls in true Anthea Redfern fashion with jacket held at arm's length to better aid his consideration, pulls the material to adjust it and then looks me in the eye, "It's really comfy but I dunno if I can wear it over a suit." Since I'm stood behind the trackshop merchandise table chatting to Johnny, he's mistaken me for a member of the Speedway Style police. Nonetheless, I still blurt out, "Why would you wear it over a suit?"
[Man] "'Cause that's why I need a jacket!"
[Jeff] "You look like a speedway rider in it."
[Man] "Are you saying I'm small and appear to have no body strength?"
Tired of my help but still wearing the jacket he can't quite decide whether to buy or not, the fan turns for a second opinion to the person who regularly brings his own brand of effortless Tourettes-type vocabulary to speedway trackshop customer service, Martin Dadswell. "Do you have a mirror?" Martin's heard this sort of silly question before, "You don't need a mirror! Put it on and, if we laugh, you'll know it doesn't look alright!" Back in pit lane Kevin Coombes buttonholes Bob Dugard for a few words but starts the interview rhetorically, "It's all about sixth place!" A hundred of yards away, Johnny Barber retorts, "My lips are dry with anticipation!" After Bob confirms the positional dynamics of tonight's mid-table battle, Kevin questions whether rumours that "Jon Cook is returning" have any foundation. "I've had no discussions with Jon Cook. I think it would be an enormous surprise for him! He was the right man for the job but he's very well settled where he is." Bob proceeds to sketch a few of the attributes required to manage Eastbourne speedway club before he, once again, reiterates why he is happy to relinquish the administrative banes that are the daily lot of any contemporary promoter. Bob also confesses, "I just don't want that day-to-day commitment of running a speedway club."
[Kevin] "You've been very vocal and honest that you have been carrying speedway at Eastbourne for nearly a year."
Many Eastbourne fans take great comfort in the knowledge of this generous financial backing after an anxious season stirred by frequent comment in the local and trade press about parlous fan numbers and revenues. Tonight, Bob is keen to correct misapprehensions about performance levels during 2009, "We haven't had a bad year, you know! We won the Elite Shield, we have the Under-21 British champion and Under-15 British champion in young Brandon

Ashley & Jane Wooller

Lucy Cross with poster of "Smurfy"

Freemantle [aged 13]. He won the seventh round of the Under-15 championship at Northside this afternoon. He's also won the most improved rider on a 250cc bike." The interview's soon over because Bob quickly reverts to his regular man of action rather than words persona. Kevin reemphasizes Bob's emotional, psychological and financial commitment to the Eastbourne Eagles, "He put his hand in his pocket and kept us afloat for many a year!" Talk of money prompts Johnny to recall, "Did you see you the press release from Gary Patchett on the Swindon website? I nearly had a tear in my eye when he said it wasn't about Swindon speedway but about the fans of Reading, Oxford and Cradley!"

When the speedway action finally gets underway, Davey Watt goes theatrically wide on the first bend from gate four for no apparent reason under absolutely no pressure. It's a manoeuvre that relegates him to the back of the field and, somehow, he manages to remain behind a lacklustre and ungainly looking Dawid Stachyra for four laps. As Watt pootles across the line a disgruntled Eastbourne fan calls out from the home-straight covered grandstand, "Bloody hell, Davey – you want a kick up the arse!" Johnny suspects that Watt might become Davey "Who" next season, "Anyone with a more cynical turn of mind, would think that Poole have been in touch with him about coming back next season!" Any more rides like the last one would see Davey's already diminished 2009 Elite League average fall further. Stood close to the start line Dave Rice takes pride in the improvement shown this season by some Eastbourne riders. "Simon [Gustafsson] is my Eastbourne rider of the year! He's really come on, shown commitment racing and he came back from injury!" Lukas Dryml's brother Ales rides at reserve for the Eagles and he shows an instant liking for the shape of the Arlington circuit to win heat 2 closely followed home by his teammate Ricky Kling for a 5-1 that gives the Eagles an 8-4 lead. Similarly peculiar to Davey Watt's extravagant first-heat first corner, Scott Nicholls hammers through the tapes at the start of heat 3 almost before the riders have even really come under the orders of referee Chris Gay. As a result of this tapes offence, Scott starts the rerun from 15 metres back and, consequently, fails to make any impression. His failure to score also has a small depressive statistical effect upon his 2009 Elite League average. Long-time Eagles fan John Hazleden's been exposed to some of the lurid rumours that uncertainty invariably prompts. "The two rumours I've heard this afternoon was that Eastbourne are only going to run the A fixtures [in the Elite League] next season. Why the riders would want to ride only eight times wasn't discussed. And the other rumour is that Lakeside is shutting and Stuart and Jon are going to buy the licence and move down here! Bob Dugard isn't going to stand out there and say 'We're selling out to Lakeside' is he? I've been coming here now for 27 years and every year I hear we ain't gonna run next year and we always do!"

Almost every rider on display tonight has his own unique but accidental way to seize the opportunity to reduce their average. Heat 4 sees Lukas Dryml lock up on the apex of the third and fourth bends (during lap one) and, as a result, he finishes last. Ales Dryml is again amongst the points, though his second place is sandwiched between Ipswich's Danny King and Carl Wilkinson. Eastbourne hit back with successive 4-2 heat advantages that feature wins for Lewis Bridger and Simon Gustafsson (with Davey Watt third ahead of Dawid Stachyra). The Witches track their power partnership of Batchelor and Nicholls for heat 7 but find themselves surprisingly vanquished by Eagles reserve, Ricky Kling, rather than his heat-leader teammate and more illustrious partner, Lukas Dryml (who finishes last for the second successive race). In rich vein of end-of-season form, Troy Batchelor comfortably wins heat 8 on a rider replacement for the injured Tobias Kroner. Judy Hazleden has some feedback for referee Christina Turnbull who officiated at the recent August Bank Holiday weekend home defeat against Poole. "Your friend was down here and got it all bloody wrong when she excluded Cameron! Everyone thought it was wrong! She's not here tonight. I asked her to come down but she didn't hear me. It was when Andrew Silver rode – and against Poole, that's what made it worse!" Cameron Woodward wins heat 9 while behind him there's a fierce battle for second place between promising British riders Danny King and Lewis Bridger. No quarter is asked or given ("he was desperate to beat Danny King"). With Eastbourne ahead 31-23, the interval is called early.

The press corps section of the referee/announcer's box is crowded with (some of) the cream of British speedway reporting in the form of methanol fume obsessed reporters Paul Watson (*Sussex Express*), Brian Owen (*Argus*) and Ben Findon (*Daily Telegraph*). In the room next door to them Chris Gay enjoys a brief break from his usual intense concentration and, alongside him, is Eagles soundman and musical maestro Barrie Geer (Kevin Coombes's long-time partner in presentational crime). Via their headphones, Barrie passes onto Kevin the key information that burnishes perceptions of his (undoubted) expertise about such matters as rider changes, referee's decisions, race times and, of course, the final race order. Eagles executive manager Mike Bellerby arrives in the referee's box with one of those oft-spoken about but rarely seen brown envelopes. It's for Barrie Geer not for Chris Gay but, nonetheless, he jokes, "I thought that was for me! [smiles] Thank goodness it's not like that for speedway refs! In all my career, I've never been offered anything like that and I've been in charge of some BIG meetings! I can't comment on the riders but it's not something that affects the refs." Chris has an interesting take on Magnus Zetterstrom's victory in the GP qualifier last night. "Obviously the mental strength is there – riders who do it in key meetings have that ability! Zorro is the Andy Smith of Swedish speedway! You know a 5- or 6-point rider who, then, wins the British final and goes on and qualifies from the GP qualifier. Magnus, of course, was the [2008] Swedish champion. People have underestimated the mental strength that is there!" Many of the top cadre of contemporary speedway riders compete in Britain, Poland and Sweden. For up-and-coming riders, invariably their ambition is to find clubs to ride for in European leagues. However, the grass isn't always greener, "I was speaking to Danny King earlier and he said he's asked around and everyone [riders] was being paid in Britain but some were and some weren't in Poland and Sweden!" When he's not officiating, Chris goes to as many meetings as possible as a speedway fan. His local track is Lakeside where he's overheard some grumbles. "Lakeside fans aren't that happy feeling there are less meetings this season. It ceases to be a weekly activity! Some have also commented that no one from Lakeside went to the Annual Conference. They are hard taskmasters but I think they do appreciate that Jon and Stuart are taking the Club forward and at quite a pace." Troy Batchelor rides tonight for Ipswich but is a Swindon asset and his transfer to the Elite League has left a sour taste in the mouth of his Premier League club, King's Lynn, "Buster told me in August that he wasn't happy with how the Troy Batchelor transfer had gone and the fee he received."

The press corps isn't immune from discussions about Eastbourne's future but they're no wiser than the fans on the specific details, if judged by what they tell me. The *Argus*'s Brian Owen enjoys access to most areas, "The talk of pit lane for the last few weeks has been a takeover by Jon Cook and Stuart Douglas but, as you've said, Bob isn't going to stand out there and say that! Away from Eastbourne, lots of the fans don't take Bob's threat to quit seriously but maybe they should!" Ben Findon sympathises with the sheer volume of administration the lot of a modern speedway promoter requires, "Bob can't be bothered with all the politics and the day-to-day running of a speedway club. He's used to being his own boss and saying how it is, or should be, rather than consulting!" The racing resumes and – with the Witches super-powerful combination of Troy Batchelor and Scott Nicholls (riding in the number 4 race tabard!) on track – it's no surprise they ride to a comfortable maximum heat advantage ahead of Simon Gustafsson. Davey Watt tootles around at the back of the field and retires at the end of lap two after no real attempt to pretend to even try. Understandably irked by a season of torpor and excuses, some Eagles fans understandably shout, "Get off the bloody track!" Theatrical boos greet the announcement of Scott Nicholls's win. Brian Owen's pleased with how successfully the *Argus* press team promote the Eastbourne speedway posters initiative. "I thought 50p a poster was a bit steep but Lucy [Cross] is to be congratulated for knowing the fans and the market and getting the pricing just right!" Brian covers many sports for the paper including Brighton & Hove Albion aka the Seagulls. "I'm not going to be here for the last meeting of the season 'cause I'll be at Yeovil. Even if I rush back from Somerset, I'll probably only make the last heat. It could be rained-off, of course! Brighton are going to finish mid-table, probably somewhere between sixth and twelfth."

The torrid night endured by Witches reserve Carl Wilkinson continues with a fall/retirement on the second bend for the second race in three outings (incidents separated by his engine failure in heat 8). However, since he scored 2 points in his first two outings, Carl ensures that Davey Watt remains the lowest scorer from either side with the same number of points as his race tabard number (1). Nonetheless, the heat's still drawn since Robert Miskowiak wins while, behind him but not close, Lukas Dryml scores his first points of the night. Kevin Coombes summarises the situation succinctly. "Four heats of Elite League speedway before the [Eagles] Elite League season ends – Ipswich are still in it at only 4 points behind!" Judy Hazleden isn't exactly impressed, "It's a bit of a joke when the top two riders [Watt and Dryml] have only got 3 points between them!" Heat 12 features an ebullient Troy Batchelor and he again easily vanquishes his ostensible home-track rival, Lewis Bridger, for the second time this evening. The young Australian looks irresistible all night as he powers to paid 14 from five rides, bizarrely dropping his only point to Ricky Kling! Kevin Coombes announces that Davey Watt's withdrawal from heat 13 (replaced by the aforementioned Kling) is due to previous exertion. "Apparently he didn't get home from Coventry until half 3 or 4 this morning and then it was straight into the workshop!" During March, Davey scored double figures in every meeting. Though he didn't lose that ability, he's been plagued by inconsistency and, up until tonight's meeting, rode in 16 subsequent meetings where he fails to get the double-figure scores you'd expect from your main heat leader. Watt's scores in Poland and Sweden have been consistent and also better than his Elite League form, so news that the GP qualifier takes priority doesn't sit well with many of the fans disgruntled at a lacklustre season characterised by loss of form and regular mechanical difficulty. With the Eagles lead narrowed to 2 points, a good performance from the Dryml/Kling partnership is imperative and duly arrives!

The penultimate race of the Eagles Elite League season is all important and, predictably enough, Scott Nicholls leads for Ipswich. Behind him Ricky Kling, Cameron Woodward and Dawid Stachyra fly into the third bend on the second lap alongside each other as they vie for fractional advantage. It's déjà vu all over again for Cameron. He's bumped on entry into the bend and, unlike heat 5 when he somehow manages to glide-cum-navigate round the corner, unfortunately for Eastbourne's hopes he clatters into the air-fence to earn a disqualification from referee Chris Gay. What looked like a match-winning drawn heat for the Eagles now has to be rerun. Next time out, Ricky Kling leads for the first three laps, tracked closely by Scott Nicholls who then exploits his Arlington track knowledge to power underneath his rival at the start of lap four taking Kling to the fence and out of contention. This Ipswich race advantage takes the scoreline to 44-40. Kevin Coombes praises Scott for "showing his class eventually" before he echoes the thoughts of many Eastbourne fans and notes, "Ipswich can still take away some points here tonight!" If the Witches gain a maximum heat advantage in heat 15, the meeting will be drawn and, under the 2009 scoring regime, Eastbourne will gain one league point and Ipswich two! Before the final race Kevin Coombes looks forward to the Suntrap Trophy challenge meeting against Poole that will bring the curtain down on the 2009 season. "I understand Bjarne Pedersen isn't riding 'cause he's just had a baby or, rather, has become a new father so he's taking a bit of time out and Poole will book some new rider. I can wish Barrie Geer and his lovely partner Mel all the best for their first baby! Their bundle of joy is due in eight or nine days. I'm going to be a dad as well in about six weeks' time. I know it's amazing it's worked! They don't know what they're having – we know that we're having a boy! So Kevin junior and Barrie junior have a ring about it. We're starting a crèche!" I'm sure they'll both be wonderful fathers.

Imagine the tension if this last race of the Elite League season at Arlington could decide who would finish sixth and thereby qualify for the Play-offs? On paper the Nicholls/Batchelor partnership look fractionally stronger than the Gustafsson/Bridger pair. However, Simon shoots from the gate and leads the Ipswich pair (until they both pass him on the second bend). Though Lewis Bridger gives chase, the race is already beyond redemption and, understandably, Ipswich riders and fans alike jubilantly celebrate their comeback. Tonight's result doubles Ipswich's tally of away points for the season. Though he enjoys double figures less often than Davey Watt (only 5 meetings out of 31), Lukas Dryml finds far greater affection from some sections of the Eastbourne fans, especially those located inside the covered home-straight grandstand. Kevin Coombes grabs him in the pit lane for an interview. "It has been my best ever season in British speedway! I would do even better if I came back. It just wasn't my night, I was a bit unlucky. I was excluded once, I dropped 3 points but there were riders better than me." Keen to test his commitment to all things Eastbourne, Kevin asks, "Will you be going to the dinner dance?" Lukas reveals more than he intends with his reply, "I would do everything with Oxf [catches himself] Eastbourne speedway!" Conversation over, Kevin provides a valedictory summary of the season, "The racing we've had this season has been exceptional! Last-heat deciders, close racing – everything. We must say thank you to the track staff, to the riders and, of course, the fans!"

19th September Eastbourne v. Ipswich (Elite League) 45-45

CHAPTER 38

Rye House

"I thought they were professionals and would laugh it off but Moggo had other ideas!"

26th September

It's a beautiful sunny September day with a hint of genuine warmth in the air. En route to the National League Riders Championship staged at Rye House via the endlessly changing Harlow Industrial Estate, they discuss the "Experiment in Capitalism" that is modern China on the radio. As I drive along Edinburgh Way past the previously award winning Edinburgh Gate building that houses Pearson Education (that they used to share with Tesco), this tiny Essex corner of rampant capitalism almost looks attractive. I arrive so early at the stadium that the car park's completely empty and the stadium gates locked. I now know where the doorbell is but, though it rings inaudibly elsewhere, it fails to get an answer. Trackshop owner Andy Griggs is running late. Hazal Silver's right-hand woman Lisa arrives in her car with her 14-year-old daughter. Their arrival has eddies of dust spiral across the deserted car park. Lisa kindly volunteers to check whether I'm allowed in the stadium prior to Andy's arrival, "I'll go and check with Hazal in her caravan if you can come in!" Lisa's gone for a few minutes probably searching for the caravan they sold four weeks previously. "Hazal says, 'Can you wait until Andy arrives?'" The next car to arrive in the car park belongs to a man who says he's the Belle Vue machine examiner (along with his wife). They've been to the Paradise Park Speedway Museum and, though they can't stay for the meeting, they've driven out of their way to try and just have a look at the Rye House speedway track. I volunteer to find out if they can have permission to come inside for a look. Lisa goes off to ask Hazal and soon comes back with an answer, "Tell them to come back at five and ask for Hazal." The stadium couldn't fail to create a good impression with any newcomer since it looks finely manicured ahead of tonight's National League Riders Championship meeting. I don't like to presume to know where to set up my table in case that spot has already been allocated to other yet-to-arrive stallholders. Since Hazal's not around to ask, I consult Andy.
[Andy] "It's not my decision. I'd ask Hazal."
[Pete] "I couldn't say, ask Lisa. Eh, Lisa, where should he go?"
[Lisa] "I dunno. Anywhere over there by that wall [overlooks fourth bend] will be fine. Can I have a look at your new book?"
[Jeff] "I believe I got the barmaid's name wrong."
[Lisa] "It wouldn't be so much of a problem but you confused her with mine and I don't like her! She don't work here any longer."

Understandably, Len Silver takes great pride in the track and stadium. Nothing illustrates this better than the gradual ongoing development of its infrastructure. Since my last visit, there's been yet more development. Sensibly enough, Len invests for the future – so much so that the club now satisfies the exacting standards the FIM require to stage meetings. Around the perimeter of the third and fourth bend, they've installed rows of red plastic chairs with fold-up seats (bought from Walthamstow Greyhound Stadium), they've upgraded the stadium track lighting significantly and the referee's box has been relocated to a position that now overlooks the start/finish line (rather than the previously disadvantageous position some yards in front of the tapes). At the top of the steps adjacent to the doors that lead either to the toilets or the home-straight grandstand bar, George and Linda Barclay patiently Blu-Tack speedway action photos to a large wooden board that they'll later display on the steps to advertise the increasingly popular Rye House Training Days. George explains, "It's a good way to let everyone know about the Rye House speedway tuition training dates. Tutors are Len Silver, Alan Mogridge and myself. With three of us, we can really give them the attention! We run them on many Sundays during the speedway season, every Saturday in November and the first two Saturdays of December. It's £40 if they bring their own bike and £80 if they don't for the bike – and that includes the dope and oil and everything! We get all ages and it's up to a maximum of 20. We find the big difference is that we offer tuition! There's no point having them go round and round making exactly the same mistakes again and again! Last year, we [George and Linda Barclay] did the corporate training days at Sittingbourne. It was £135 per person and that included everything. Linda did the sandwiches, I did the tuition. People used to say what good value it is. It's £500 for the day at Scunthorpe – as many can go as you like – and £195 at King's Lynn. We get some of the King's Lynn National League riders come here though 'cause they know they'll get the tuition! We're going to depend on young riders for the future. Look at that [photo] it's little Ben Morley. He's only 15. We saw his first time ever on a speedway bike at Sittingbourne on the practice track. You could see straight away that he was meant to ride and would do well. He's very nice and a nice family supports him. It's important to have that support given how expensive it is! His dad is particularly nice. Ben rides at reserve for our Cobras National League side. He rides flat out."

[Linda] "He's had a time of 59 seconds."

[George] "That's very good for his age, only 15."

[Linda] "He's smaller than me."

[George] "The National League's all about bringing on the youngsters! There are lots of riders in the league who are much older who've never gone anywhere and won't go anywhere!"

[Linda] "If Buzz had ridden here tonight he'd have made a difference to the average age."

[George] "I wonder what the average age is tonight and in the National League? There are some old ones. You have to call it our League Riders Championship as it's no longer just youngsters, as it should be! Some of the teams have many older riders!" George doesn't have the involvement with the current crop of speedway riders that he once had. "I don't get to chat to the riders much nowadays. They're so busy on race nights and have their minds on other things. I'm looking forward to seeing that Kyle Hughes tonight. Watch him. He's so smooth on the bike. Really stylish! He's always going in the right direction. Some of them [holds imaginary handlebars and makes jerky motions with his arms and upper body] struggle with the bike but he's effortless!"

When the turnstiles open, there's an initial rush of fans keen to grab their favoured spot within the stadium. They're equally quick to return to the undercroft of the home-straight grandstand to queue for the highly regarded fish and chips they serve at Rye House. From the patriotically decorated refreshment kiosk close to the start-line, Gaz passes, "I'm not speaking to you! [pause] Have you sold many then?" Everyone's been in too big a rush to even stop to chat, let alone linger long enough to think about any book purchases. Gaz isn't surprised about the lack of sales. "I think you tell them too much. Why don't you tell them what they want to hear?" The official for tonight's meeting, Margaret Vardy, arrives with her partner Steve. While Margaret heads off to the repositioned referee's box Steve stops to chat amiably. "Your lot [Sunderland] haven't lost today, at least! [we play Wolves tomorrow] That's what they say on talkSPORT anyway." Spoken like a true Walsall fan, Steve complains, "Three hours [drive] and all you hear about is the Premier League!" He surveys the track from our vantage point on the fourth bend. "It's a few years since I've been here and, looking round the stadium, they clearly don't sell it very well if you judge it by the number of advertisers' signs you can see!" I count six adverts on the back-straight fence and two on the first bend. Lisa rushes about like a mad thing but stops temporarily for a dawdle by my table so I strike up a conversation, "It's a nice day for it. Are you expecting a big crowd?"

[Lisa] "It is. I hope so! We have another [NL] meeting tomorrow."

[Jeff] "It's free isn't it?"

[Lisa] "Nah, it's not. Who said it was?"

[Jeff] "I'm sure I read it on the forums, I must have been wrong. Actually, one poster claimed it should have been staged before this meeting."

[Lisa] "That wouldn't be sensible."

Thinking about this suggestion, though the chance to see Rye House versus Weymouth is exciting, the track will cut up, never mind that the riders and their equipment would experience unnecessary wear and tear. Even if you ignore the shoestring finance of every National League club, any sensible business tries to maximise their revenues – in this case through gate receipts, programme sales and bar/refreshment kiosk takings. Rye House and Peterborough presenter, Craig 'Mr Potassium' Saul arrives with his regulation two bananas. He's researched, prepared and ready to entertain the crowd in his usual engaging and knowledgeable style. Craig started as a speedway presenter in 1993 at Peterborough's East of England Showground. "I was very naive. It was my first season in the sport. There I was throwing out quips and nicknames about the riders. I thought they were professionals and would laugh it off but, being the last night of the season, Moggo had other ideas! I didn't see it coming! I've never forgotten it, though. I expected the flour and water but there was an equestrian jump on the third – a water hazard – and they threw me in there. Alan Mogridge, I think was the ringleader, Paul Hurry too. It was very dark and they hid their faces so I don't really know. Into their mix of flour and water they'd also thrown an inordinate amount of curry powder. I was reeking of it. It was pungent for two or three days afterwards. I had lots of showers but it was up my nose. I had a change of clothes but, of course, they were in the car. I took it in good heart, as much as you can, when you're soaked – until I discovered I'd lost my car keys! You try searching for a set of black car keys on the centre green in the dark. It was hopeless! I went up to my promoter Peter Oakes and said 'I can't get home, what are you going to do about it?' and he said, 'take my wife's car'. I came back the next morning and there was a line of us searching the centre green carefully, as if we were part of a forensic examination. We found them after about 20 minutes." Craig heads off to continue with his preparations. Shortly afterwards Mildenhall presenter Kevin Moore walks past aloofly in clothing probably festooned with the distinctive Simon Lambert Racing logo. Kevin ostentatiously fails to stop for a chat at my bookstall nor does he frequent the trackshop. Andy Griggs doesn't have any Simon Lambert merchandise on sale and isn't bothered by the lack of conversation, "He's really copped a snot, hasn't he?"

Bathed in sunlight

A smooth style never leaves you

By 5.30 p.m., pretty well every fan who's in the stadium seems to be in the queue for the fish and chips from under the main grandstand. One fan who bucks that particular trend is hugely knowledgeable speedway obsessive, Charles McKay. He's worried how youngsters can be encouraged to take up the sport or how they'll get enough practice to gain sufficient ability to compete in what is, nowadays, called the National League. "There's no sense of direction from the BSPA or any sign of the promoters working hand-in-hand together to ensure that there's a base for the juniors! Look at the Under-15s. When it started, there were 16 at every meeting but, this year in the 500cc's, it was down to 10 at Northside! You'd have thought they'd have someone from the BSPA to present the trophies, wouldn't you? Rob Lyon was there 'cause King's Lynn were at Workington [as was Graham Reeve from the SCB]. The owner at Workington – Keith Denham – doesn't like Northside 'cause he's convinced it takes away from his crowd. I doubt it! At Northside, there were a few Belle Vue fans along with some Workington ones. If I was him, I'd base my juniors there and do it that way. If you're at Northside, you're going to go to Workington to watch, aren't you?" As he passes again, Gaz interrupts us in our conversation, "Oi Billy!"
[Jeff] Why Billy?"
[Gaz] "Billy Bullshitter! Have you noticed how this shirt makes me look fat? I see you called Tina 'Lisa'."
[Jeff] "It was the only thing I got wrong."
[Gaz] "I think you got a few things wrong!"

George Barclay

Charles McKay usually suspects that the BSPA have got it wrong. "It says in the rules – the printed rules that the fans can read – this season that the defending champion has to take part [in the NLRC]. How Benji [Compton] won it I just don't know! It was a poor crowd last year but, let's be honest, they don't promote it! Bloody hell, half an hour to go and there's no one here – it is a bit poor! What you've got to think is how long they've been riding. Benji Compton don't look that old but when you think how long he's been riding, it must be seven years. [1] Tomorrow at the PLRC, there's lots of old men too! Even more than here! Did you hear that Coventry wouldn't let the Super 7even girls use their umbrellas? Tony Jackson had to lend them the Workington brollies!"

Barry Matthews pops up to my book display table and informs me about his first ever meeting at Ipswich, "in '57 or was it '56? I knew Len Silver when I was 10. He fixed it for me to ride on the back of Barry Briggs's bike. I haven't seen Len since then. I hope I bump into him tonight! [fingers stock but doesn't purchase anything] I tell you a book you should do: *World Finals since 1972.* I have one called World Finals 1929-1972. It would really sell! I wrote a book on Fender guitars [*Fender Bass for Britain: The History of the 1966 Slab-Bodied Precision Bass*] published by Author House. They got a foreword by John Entwistle so it sold 'cause of that, not what I'd written inside!" Steve Davies clutches tonight's meeting programme, "Quite a novelty tonight, it's as per programme! All 18 of them! It's a bit traumatic for the ref [his partner, Margaret Vardy] 'cause she hasn't got it [an individual meeting format] loaded on the laptop so she's having to do it the old way with three programmes!" On the cover of the "Official Programme 2009" it states the event we are about to see is the "National League Riders Championship". The scorecard in the centre must have used last season's layout as a template since the header there states we're about to see the "Conference League Riders Championship". [2]

Peter Butcher the ex-sports editor of the *Romford Recorder* has ventured along to Hertfordshire tonight for his speedway kicks. He too admires the programme, "I see it is an "Official" programme tonight! How's it going?" ("I didn't know it at the time but it turns out last year was a golden age!") Peter spent his journalistic apprentice years working for the regional press and, inevitably, has his own fair share of snafus to report. "I used to work for the *Worthing Gazette*. When Steyning went to Hungerford for a FA Vase game they lost 8-1 so we tried to avoid all mentions of words like 'shot' or 'killed-off their hopes' – which we did. But the sub-editor was under pressure and put in the headline 'Hungerford Massacre'." No meeting at Rye House is complete without the media presence of the T2TV DVD production company run by Ken Burnett and his family. Their advert in the official programme states "The Professionals. Proud to be covering the Rockets and Cobras. Relive all the action, interviews, replays and full match commentary. Order you [*sic*] copy today. Only £10 including P&P!" The advert also advises potential would-be customers for "top quality DVDs" that they should "visit our stall on turn 4". As usual the DVD saleswoman in charge of their stall is Ken's daughter, Kirsty Burnett. She can barely contain her excitement, "Guess who we've got as co-commentator for tonight?" Before I can answer, Kirsty squeals, "Luke Bowen! Luke Bowen! It should be brilliant!" Though the stadium might not be quite as packed as the organisers would hope, various speedway personalities are here including Nigel 'Noddy' Fordham whose speedway meetings attendance record never fails to impress me. I wonder where he'll be when he sees his 5,000th meeting? "I'm not gonna have it at Ipswich! We might not have a club, John Louis is retiring and there's no one taking it over. He wants £100 grand for them! I'm gonna have it at Coventry where I've saw my first ever British league meeting. I've been to 16 Pardubice Czech golden helmets on the trot."

The demands of stadium rock, never mind macho pride, used to dictate that rock bands endlessly tried to escalate the volume at which they subjected their fans to their music. The golden age for such an outlook was arguably the 1970s (prior to modern health and safety regimes) and, given this decade is seen by many as the last speedway heyday, it's appropriate that Rye House sound like they've invested in the loudest public address speaker system in

[1] A glance at Robert Bamford's highly regarded and authoritative *2008 Speedway Yearbook* quickly confirms that it's Benji's eighth season in British speedway since he first rode in 2002.]

[2] In the spring 2010 edition of the always compulsively readable quarterly speedway magazine, *Voice: The Official Journal of Friends of Speedway*, Charles McKay provides a first-year report on the National League. "Only the cover of the Isle of Wight programme used the official title of the league, the National Development League, everyone else used the alternative name, the National League, apart from, of course, the score chart page of the programme for the League Riders Championship at Rye House which referred to the Conference League! This, of course, wasn't the only mistake in the programme. The score chart was set up for the traditional 20-heat format for an individual meeting and this was how the meeting was won by Craig Cook but the regulations stated that the championship should have been decided by the alternative format of a final featuring the top two scorers after 20 heats and the first and second from a race-off between the next four highest scoring riders as used in all other League Riders Championship finals in Britain in 2009." For a subscription to the *Voice* magazine contact Stuart.towner@blueyonder.co.uk or telephone (0208) 397 6599.

speedway. Though obviously they face stiff competition, particularly given the volume levels provided at the Norfolk Arena, it ensures that any noise-sensitive neighbours won't complain about the speedway bikes but, will instead, concentrate on the speaker volume. Fortunately for tonight's attendees, the only speedway presenter inside the stadium with access to the microphone is the always entertaining Craig Saul. Mark Simmonds (whose name is spelt incorrectly throughout in the centre-fold racecard) falls on the first bend of the first race and is shown no mercy by Margaret Vardy. His disqualification effectively ends any hope of his outright victory but, should the 38-year-old Plymouth rider win his last four races, there is still a chance that he might snatch a podium place. Defending champion Benji Compton leads the rerun until he reaches the back straight on the second lap where the highly fancied Jay Herne hammers past him to zoom away for victory. The next race features another Simmons – Nick – who hails, according to the programme, from "Island". His name is spelt correctly without a 'd' in the programme. However, he's soon fallen from his bike and, when he glances anxiously round to see who's about to smash into him, he instead sees 43-year-old Anthony Neville Atkin skilfully manoeuvre past him. Peter Butcher notes, "Not a good night for the Simmons family! Actually, I think that Mark Simmonds is spelt with a 'd'." Over the speakers Craig Saul informs us, "A note has been passed to me by Bryn Williams, here tonight next to me in the box, about a very special rider here tonight – Brendan Johnson!" Brendan's recovery from life-threatening injuries is splendid news and the crowd greets this news with a warm round of applause. After the disqualification of Nick Simmons, the rerun of heat 2 lasts until the second bend until Daniel Halsey locks up in front of James Cockle (who lays down with alacrity). Margaret Vardy ponders her decision, "Our referee is thinking long and hard about that. She's trying very hard to be fair to all the riders here this evening!" Margaret's adjudication is a rerun with all three riders. The re-rerun only lasts as long as it takes James Cockle to fall off. Peter's in no doubt about who should be disqualified, "Cockle just fell off in front and everyone else laid down." With so much drama early on, Craig Saul sympathises with *Speedway Star* reporter Pete Hill whose job it will be to capture the glory of tonight's NLRC. "Peter has a word limit of 800 words and a bumper double-page spread and, I expect, he's used quite a few already!" Before the rerun of the re-rerun Craig just can't quite get the Spice Girls lyrics out of his head. "Four has become three, has become two – both have led this heat at various stages tonight!" Once the race gets underway, it takes an even more peculiar twist after Daniel Halsey falls on the second bend of the second lap and is then unable to get his bike restarted. Through a protracted process of elimination, Tony Atkin becomes the only rider to evade disqualification and mechanical difficulty in this race. He marks the occasion by completing his four laps in the slowest time of the night. Craig hails the eccentricity of the situation, "One of the truly bizarre races at Rye House this season!"

Before the third heat gets underway we're treated to the formation tractor driving that characterises track grades at Rye House stadium. Peter Butcher has seen speedway action at quite a few venues this season, not always without embarrassment. "Did I tell you about putting my foot in my mouth with Terry Russell? When I said to him 'I've been round the country all season and it's a really good product but why the hell does it take two hours to run a 15-heat meeting?' Terry Russell glared at me, 'Well, at Swindon, we plan for two hours!' Did I feel stupid! Six minutes a race is surely enough!" The third race of the night features the rider described by Craig Saul as "World Under-21 competitor Simon Lambert". When the race starts, Simon entertains the crowd with a battle against his bike throughout all four of his circuits of the track. At the start of the last lap, Simon overtakes Barrie Evans on the home straight, concedes second place and looks set fair to hold onto that comfortably until, on the last bend, he executes a superb pirouette but, after a flirt with disaster, he still somehow finishes second. Craig knows his various rider championships and he introduces heat 4 with the words, "Starring Jerran Hart, British Under-18 champion!" This observation prompts Charles McKay to expand, "It can't be right that Joe Haines gets a five-ride maximum but isn't the winner!"

The regularity of track curatorial work at Rye House stadium is a constant at each and every meeting, particularly important ones. Some fans praise the fastidiousness while others are irked by the delay. Craig Saul suggests people visit my stall, "The Sage of the Age is back tonight. What you see is what you get – promoters, riders and fans all feature in Jeff Scott's true study of the sport which he covers warts and all ... go and see him now, you might at least get a mention in it ... go and see him, he doesn't bite!" Peter Butcher belongs to the school of the speedway fandom that appreciates fine shale surfaces but would relish greater haste along with the craftsmanship ("at this rate it'll be 10.45 p.m. before we finish!") Earlier Tommy Allen's bad crash here at the stadium where he hit the plastic stanchion 10 yards away from the fourth-bend safety fence was recalled. Peter Butcher sings the praises of the Hoddesdon safety furniture, "I think that this is the best safety fence in the country! There's nothing to hit and you can just go straight through it!" Later Reading Racers club historian Arnie Gibbons echoes Peter's praise of the safety fence. "We've been very lucky tonight 'cause they haven't had to rebuild the safety fence. The riders are rarely hurt! It's the rebuilding that takes all the time. There's an unusual amount of dirt tonight which is retarding the bikes as they fall." Why would you need an inflatable safety fence when you already have a tried and tested version – albeit one that, to the untutored eye, looks like the kind of thing you'd grow raspberries on – with a proven track record of safety success? On a fashion note, one fan here tonight wears a yellow T-shirt with an eye-catching slogan: Sex, Drugs and Sausage Rolls.

Heat 5 sees Benji Compton fall at the start of the last lap and, while he remounts, the red lights come on and Benji finds himself disqualified even though he's remounted so efficiently that Jade Mudgway has yet to catch up with him! While Craig Saul confirms that this race is awarded (after Benji's disqualification), fans around me provide their own *ad hoc* collective interpretation of events at the far end of the stadium. Stood where we all are on the fourth bend, it's easy to see and analyse events in front of us on bends three and four. However, away in the distance, there's definitely an element that the riders disappear into the background murk of the first and second bend. However, after some debate, these fans reconstruct their version of the chain of events and, armed with this interpretation, they try to fathom Margaret Vardy's decision. The consensus – without the vantage point let alone the authority of the referee – is that Benji Compton shouldn't be disqualified. Even if he'd been allowed to continue after he remounts, Benji would've only gained third place and his defence of the silverware would still be in tatters.

Kyle Hughes exhibits the smooth stylish figure on a speedway bike George Barclay earlier predicted. He employs this skill to good effect to win the sixth race of the night sponsored by Dave Jessup Racing. The meeting is already 76 minutes old before the seventh race of the night won by Darren Mallett begins. Based on predictions prior to the NLRC, heat 8 always looks likely to be a key encounter as it features Jay Herne, James Cockle, Simon Lambert and Jerran Hart. It's something of an anticlimax. Partly because it's awarded (after the disqualification of James Cockle) but also because the riders are strung out like a line of washing with Herne streets ahead of Hart who, in turn, rides streets ahead of Simon Lambert as he battles manfully with his bike. Arnie Gibbons likes to view any speedway meeting from a number of different vantage points. When he joins Peter Butcher and myself on the fourth bend he comments waspishly, "If only Buzz Burrows were here tonight we could restage the match race [with Barrie Evans] that you and I were so taken with!" [3] Like other fans with a keen eye for detail and a good knowledge of the sport, Arnie is taken with some of the errors contained in tonight's programme. "Interestingly I see we're watching the Conference League Riders Championship. Simmonds [M.] should be spelt with a 'd' and it appears Nick and Mark, if you read the rider biographies, have enjoyed similar careers!"[4] Arnie also closely studies "Lens Lines", promoter Len Silver's page 3 column in the programme. "The Elite League and Premier League Riders' Championships both have apostrophes whereas the National League or Conference League Riders Championship hasn't. When you're noting apostrophes in the programmes – it's rather sad!" As an ex-journalist, sub-editor errors are a topic close to Peter Butcher's heart. Predictably, Arnie's thought carefully about his opinion on his subject. "I have to say I have considered this at great length and "riders" is an adjective not a possessive noun. It doesn't belong to the riders." Peter Butcher makes a hummm noise that I can't quite fathom. Instead of further comment on the vexed issues of apostrophes and the word riders, Peter recalls his worst mistake, "We must sincerely apologise for describing X as a 'bottle scarred veteran" ' when it should have read "battle scared veteran!" An advert for Len Silver's autobiography in *Backtrack* excites Arnie, "Oh look, Len's written his book "personally"! I'm curious to read about Len's fallings out with Reg Fearman!"

[Peter] "Didn't he fall out with everyone?"

[3] 2nd June 2008 saw the management team of Wimbledon Speedway Plc commemorate the 80th anniversary of their club with a match race between Buzz Burrows and Barrie Evans for the Ronnie Moore Trophy at Reading's Smallmead Stadium. Dependent upon your point of view – this was either a fitting tribute to 80 years of speedway at Plough Lane that ended during the recent Conference League incarnation of the club. Or, alternatively, a sad spectacle of a race between two mismatched Premier League riders that failed to honour the tradition of the club.

[4] Logically the following text must be accurate for one of these two riders. "Now 38, the former Exeter captain returned to action last season after – a few challenge matches aside – a four year absence from the sport. He's been averaging out this term with a shade under 10, in the process helping the Devils to third place in the table and a consequent championship Play-offs spot."

[Arnie] "Reg can get quite upset when people write things that doesn't accord with his recollection!"

Jerran Hart rides successive heats but this doesn't cramp his style since he wins heat 9 ahead of Barrie Evans. Third place goes to the oldest rider on display tonight, 43-year-old Tony Atkin. The 10th race of the night is won in a time of 59.8 seconds by "the rider dubbed Lambo Rambo", Simon Lambert. Peter Butcher is much more concerned with the time it has taken to get to this point, "One hour and 22 minutes and we're only half way!" Arnie's made his mind up about his own red-hot favourite to win the NLRC, "I think Herne is a shoo-in. It's the fourth time I've seen him here this season and I only come every three weeks. I've seen him ride for Somerset, Birmingham and Bournemouth but, to be fair, they were teams he rode for not guest appearances! He has the sort of average that is good for Premier League number sixes." Peter worries that another pre-meeting favourite, Craig Cook, might struggle in heat 11, "It's very hard off gate two." This proves to be a prophetic observation since the race is won by Kyle Hughes off gate four (and is the only point Craig would drop all night).

Before Heat 12 Craig Saul decrees some unofficial motivational targets, "Adam Allott has yet to score – that's his mission here!" It's a tough race to try to break his duck because it also features Jay Herne and Jade Mudgway (who "looked good here for Buxton a few weeks back"). A nearby fan questions Adam's all-round capabilities as a speedway rider, "Allott is just a gating tart – a one track trick pony!" Adam's so keen to get a jump from the start line that he demolishes the tapes and also causes an electrical fault! Though reserve Daniel Blake takes his place in the line-up the result remains a foregone conclusion, "That's won by the rider they all have to beat – Jay Herne!" The 13th race of the night sees Simon Lambert again manfully battle his equipment, at least until the apex of the third bend where he would've crashed into the fence, except he's saved this indignity by the immediate loss of momentum his bike suffers when it digs into the thick shale of the Rye House circuit. With some understatement Arnie observes, "Lambert just doesn't look comfortable on this track!" Gaz again deserts his refreshment kiosk to stretch his legs, "Is this your living? I can't imagine it is. I reckon it's your writing that frickin' kills it! It's frickin' shit your writing. Personally I think it's the writing that's wrong. You didn't put that bit in about Harlow being frickin' shit – the best thing about it is the road out!"
[Man] "Are you doing the write-ups?"
[Gaz] "No his writing is shit! You don't actually do this for a living do you? Thank frick for that!"

The first attempt to run heat 14 ends after Mark Simmonds (with a 'd') falls. This prompts a 25-minute delay while for medical attention. Initially Peter Butcher thinks the worst, "I was terrified when I saw them run to the red box on the centre green!" After it becomes clear that Mark's injuries aren't life-threatening Peter joins the long queue for refreshments. While there he becomes aware that an ongoing decline in science educational standards means that the chemistry curriculum no longer extends to discussions of the saturation point of liquids. "The 15-year-old girl in front of me put 10 sugars in her tea!" During the enforced break my books get some attention but no sales. Lisa shows Hazal my Tina/Lisa error. I apologise for the inadvertent confusion, "There's a mistake in the book, Hazal!" Hazal isn't that fussed, "It's nothing to do with me!"

Keen photographer Keith Lilywhite buys a book and provides some feedback upon my photographic book *Shale Britannia*. "I have that one. I understand the effects you're trying to create by putting the object at the edge of the frame but, if I did that or entered it in a competition, I'd get nowhere!" Keith's a lapsed speedway fan who's only relatively recently rediscovered the sport. "I have come back to speedway after nearly 60 years by two coincidences. Having been a keen supporter of Walthamstow Wolves (1949-1951) I purchased on eBay a programme which, on opening it, had a picture of me looking over the pit wall at Archie Windmill in 1950. On a visit to my niece in Hoddesdon, I 'discovered' Rye House stadium and, after one visit, I was hooked again. I've been back to many meeting this year as a photographer and also supplying photos for the Southern Track Riders' website gallery. On the whole, I have found speedway folk very friendly and Rye House has a wonderful family feeling under Len Silver!"

Heat 16 provides strong guidance about the likely result of the NLRC as Craig Cook beats Jay Herne comfortably. No sooner does Peter utter the words, "it's cat among the pigeons time!" than five seconds later, over the tannoy, Craig Saul reiterates, "Well, that's certainly set the cat among the pigeons." After working through all possible permutations in the programme, Peter's only got one comment, "Tut tut – there's only space for one run-off in the programme!" In the trackshop Andy Griggs isn't enjoying a successful night, "This is terrible ain't it? [waves to seating area outside the bar and toilets] It used to be heaving round here!" As the meeting builds towards a crescendo, Craig gives a rough outline of the likely denouement, "Well, there are two races out of the final three to decide where the silverware will go." With podium places at stake, a hard-fought first corner in heat 18 sees Jerran Hart come to grief on the second bend and Craig Cook zoom away with the lead until referee Margaret Vardy lights the red bulbs to stop the race. "So, heat 18 lasting no further than the second bend and the referee has thought this one over and decided it's all four back!" Cook and Hart immediately resume their intense battle for the first couple of bends before Jerran Hart shuts off so dramatically that Daniel Halsey passes him, albeit only temporarily. By the end of the rerun, Jerran's back on terms with Craig but unable to quite catch him. Peter highlights that there's no love lost between these riders this evening, "the lack of a handshake at the end of that one, I notice!" The penultimate race (heat 19) of the qualification process won't influence the destination of the silverware. It's won by 43-year-old Tony Atkin who, thereby, finishes fifth in the NLRC with 8 points. Though it's his second win of the night, Peter Butcher is still surprised, "Where did he find that one from?" Always well researched and effortlessly but enjoyably encyclopaedic, Craig Saul drops in an arcane but relevant fact into our entertainment, "So the former World Longtrack finalist signs off with that one!" Kyle Hughes and Jay Herne both require a last-race win in order to tie with Craig Cook on 14 points. In fact, the race ends in victory for Kyle Hughes who, thereby, finishes ahead of Jay Herne. This means Hughes ties with Cook (on 14 points) while Herne ties with Jerran Hart on 13. Peter's amazed at his own perspicacity, "I think that's my most successful prediction of my life! Before the meeting I said Cook and Hughes and Herne and Hart with the proviso that Herne didn't go through the card. I'll have to take Cook [to win the first place run-off] as he rode for Rye House last week."

Three hours seven minutes into the meeting, Jay Herne beats Jerran Hart in their match race for third place. Three hours thirteen minutes after the scheduled start time, Kyle Hughes gates and successfully holds off the attentions of Craig Cook until the very last bend where he suffers a hugely unfortunate engine failure! Craig Saul can't quite believe it, "What cruel luck after what was an incredible match race!" One fan en route for the car park isn't happy with what he's seen, "There wasn't one overtake after heat 8! Unfortunately, it gets so slick!" If Kyle Hughes impressed neutral observers with his grace and fluency on the bike, his magnanimity and generosity when interviewed afterwards stands out even more, "He won on the night – good luck to him!"
[Craig] "You're the only rider in the top four here tonight without a Premier League place."
[Kyle] "Definitely, I need to move up. I can't progress any more at Conference League!"
Craig Cook is overcome with delight and proceeds to react to his victory in a manner that might invite ironic comment if it were heard at an Oscar ceremony. "I can't believe it! It's a dream come true just to be here! My heart goes out to Kyle … I haven't been riding a year and to come here and do this is amazing! I'd like to dedicate my win to mum and dad, me family, friends, Scott James who does me engines."

Charles McKay smiles broadly, "What a great night! Our fifth [NLRC] winner for Buxton! The only problem was there should have been a semi-final and a final." Ever appreciative of the subtle nuances, Craig Saul acknowledges Buxton Speedway club, "What an incredible record of success they're having at Hi-Edge. See you back here in a few hours' time for the Cobras versus Wildcats." Despite the fact that there's been drama until the last bend of the last race of the night, some of the Rye House fans still aren't happy, "The lighting on that first bend was crap. In the first race, she [Margaret Vardy] didn't put the lights on until they were on the back straight. They say a generator has gone. It was crap!" While I carry boxes to the car park, Craig Saul briefly joins me and, as ever, lives in a world where the cup is always at least half full, "That was a great advert for National League speedway!" He waves goodbye with the words, "I'll see you in Paradise!"

26th September National League Riders Championship Winner: Craig Cook

CHAPTER 39

Newcastle

"Whenever any rider falls off, he runs over and signals for the ambulance – whether they want it or not!"

4th October

Any visit to the UK's most sustainable city is always a delight. The mid-afternoon sunshine beats down on Newcastle Stadium (or Brough Park in old money) prior to the Diamonds Premier League Play-off semi-final (first leg) against the Edinburgh Monarchs. The wind makes it cold in the shade and, until mid-July, a chill wind had blown through the Diamonds fixture list to the extent that they had only won two of their nine Premier League meetings (albeit seven of these had been away). However, with the addition of the experienced Mark Lemon (unbelievably discarded by the bottom-placed Premier League club, Newport) into a Diamonds side that features the highly regarded Danes – Kenni Larsen and Rene Bach – adopted Geordie Jason King as well as the combative Derek Sneddon, the Diamonds suddenly clicked into gear to become the form team of the Premier League over the closing months of the speedway season. Both long-term favourites for the Premier League silverware – King's Lynn and Edinburgh – are suddenly keen to keep their tinder dry and avoid the high-flying Diamonds. In recent years that definitely wouldn't have been the case. Newcastle will provide a stiff test for the Monarchs, although their cause tonight is aided by the fact that the Diamonds track guest William Lawson in place of Kenni Larsen, who isn't available because he's competing in the World Under-21 final (staged in Croatia).

Three hours before the scheduled start time (at half-past 3 in the afternoon), Mark Lemon is the only rider to arrive on either side of the pits. Throughout the rest of the stadium, track staff and volunteers go about their work with diligence. Joan English, the always active and friendly mother of Diamond's co-owner George English busies herself in the Speedway Office. She tells me that the turnstiles will open at half 5 and, when I predict, "And then the big crowd will rush in!" She responds, "Well, if there's not, then there's something seriously wrong!" Mark Lemon cleans and prepares his bike for the meeting ahead closely watched by his father Graeme who's come over from Mildura (Australia) to visit for a month. The Diamonds section of the pits isn't in the sunlight and, although it offers some protection from the wind, Graeme's quickly forced to put on a Reading Bulldogs race jacket. "I've been here 33 days and I fly home tomorrow. Mark has been so busy that I'll be glad to get back to put my feet up again! Wednesday he rode for Birmingham [at King's Lynn]. He doesn't seem to get on so well there, either that or the home team is very strong. Last night we were at Workington – it was really freezing – Mark's father-in-law, Tom Owen, said it's the change in the seasons. Today we're here early so that Mark can clean the bikes. We need a big win here tonight 'cause Edinburgh are the form team and go well at their place. Wednesday he's riding for Birmingham again. He would have rode on Monday at Wolverhampton too but Swindon have brought in that other one [Ryan Fisher] who's riding here today. I reckon Swindon are going to have their work cut out to win. Wolves are very strong. Their only weak link is Peter Karlsson who's coming back from injury so soon but, then, he's very experienced so it'll make a difference in the pits. I suppose you were at Newport versus Newcastle? ["Nah."] They made the real mistake letting Mark go. It wasn't a commercial decision. I think they were listening to the fans too much! They don't have many of them – it was my first time there and it was empty! They get really good crowds here. ["Success attracts interest."] Yes, I suppose so. Mark tells me that last year at Poole they were getting huge crowds but, this season, it has fallen really dramatically. That's one of the wealthiest areas in the country too! I expect people have had to pull their horns in everywhere. Newport certainly didn't have many fans there. I wouldn't be surprised if they pull the pin. It's 2½ months since Mark left and he's still top of their averages! Still, he loves it here and things have gone well for him. He's been in demand all the time I've been here and I've had the best of your weather. The best of the summer, I hear. We've had 10 mm of rain [in Mildura] and we only get 39 in a year! It keeps the dust down. We've had four red dust storms while I've been away. When I was a kid, we used to get them every other day. You can see them moving towards you from the distance – it's a giant red cloud. We used to get them so badly that you couldn't see more than a foot in front of you. If it happened when you were coming home on the school bus, they'd pull over and you'd have to walk home. It's not great for you either. We have less of them 'cause they've changed the way they do agriculture. There's dust every day though. You can clean your car one day and the next there's a thin film on it!"

Mark's wife Emma pops round into the pits from Mark's van parked round the corner. She has strong Newcastle connections as the daughter of Diamonds speedway legend, Tom Owen. She's been applying Vicks for her chesty cold, possibly gained as a result of her recent run in a 10-kilometre race, completed in an impressive time of one hour three minutes. "We've only been doing it seven weeks so I was really pleased. I had some porridge before but Mark insisted I was properly hydrated. I just have to go and do his bottles in a minute. Makes him sound like a baby, doesn't it? It's a glucose drink – I add powder to water. He's been doing it for four years. It makes him quicker, he thinks. He drinks some before and some after. He swears by it. He's been doing very well so it must be working! We were at Workington last night, here tonight and Birmingham Wednesday, Edinburgh on Friday. If he's not doing anything on Saturday he might ride for Workington at Stoke in the Young Shield. It was the quarter-finals last night, wasn't it, Mark? And then maybe here again Sunday but maybe not. [1] Did you hear Tai [Woffinden] would have won last night [in the World Under-21 Championship in Croatia] if he hadn't touched the tapes in his first race?!" The last time I saw Tai was on Sky, "He was probably a bit tense – he was het up on the telly last Monday at Lakeside." Emma saw that too. "Yeah, he looked really mad like he was going to kill someone. Lee [Richardson] didn't touch him and he was probably just frustrated that he couldn't get past. You have to wonder what Michael Lee said to him. Probably, 'if you hit him you can definitely wave goodbye to getting in the GPs next year!' He'd done well all night till then. When that happens in heat 15, you should just think – 'well, I've done my best' and get on with it. Easy for me to say! Anyway I must do Mark's bottle for him!" Out of curiosity I follow Emma to the van. She opens its side door to produce a giant bright red container. If Newcastle stadium featured in Alice in Wonderland, there'd be a label on the bottle that said 'Drink me!' Instead there's a chequered flag motif either side of the phrase "winning ways". So there's absolutely no mistake about the container's contents, giant letters on the side of the bottle say "ENERGY BOOST" while underneath – making it sound all medical and scientific (and, doubtless, justifying the price) – the label notes in much smaller letters "complex carbohydrate drink with glucose polymers". It sounds like it's part drink, part decorating material. Whatever the specifics of the complex wonder-powder, there's two kilos of it. Unlike the infantilising strong strawberry milkshake smell given off by body-building drinks at the gym I go to, Mark's taste of choice is "orange flavour".

Last season Newcastle deservedly won the *Speedway Star* Programme of the Year award. Given its look, design and content, the club justifiably prefer to refer to their programme as a magazine. Though the number of adverts appear to have slightly increased this season, it remains a superb document and sets the standard many other clubs could do well to emulate. It would be a surprise if the club wasn't there or thereabouts when it comes to the decision about who will be the *Speedway Star* Programme of the Year in 2009 (in my opinion, Belle Vue looks to be their keenest rival). George English's two-page 'Cards on the Table' column provides news, insight and comment about the club, the Premier League and speedway generally. [2] George provides a succinct summary of the tale of two halves that's been the Newcastle Diamonds 2009 Premier League season. "For the Sapphire Engineering Diamonds to finish third in the Premier League after the poor start we made was a remarkable achievement. Everyone knew that with the lack of home matches ridden earlier in the season we were in a false position at the bottom of the league but it was clear at that point that we didn't have the right team to attack other sides at the top end of the table. A few changes were made both on and off the track and we came storming through to ride up the table and claim a Play-off place rounded off by the match here a fortnight ago when we sent the champions, King's Lynn, home with their tails between their legs. It was good that such a good crowd saw that meeting and that included some good friends of Newcastle Speedway from the political arena ... Councillors Margaret and David Wood were in attendance but they were also joined by another former regular supporter in the shape of Government Chief Whip and Minister for the

[1] The Premier League Play-off final will be in a fortnight on 18th October, if Newcastle qualify.

[2] "It's a bit of a surprise that Jeff is here today from his southern base as Sunderland are not at home this weekend, there you go Dalbers [Newcastle entertainment manager Andrew Dalby is also a Sunderland season ticket holder] you're not the only one after all!"

North East the Right Honourable Nick Brown MP who was a supporter of the Debmat Diamonds before other things got in the way."

The Newcastle promotional team kindly provide me with a table close to the walkway that every fan uses before they either head off to the home-straight terraces or towards the pits. My position is in the shade and in something of a wind tunnel. If George English was a female teenage Geordie then he'd dress in a crop top and mini skirt, instead, despite the refreshingly cool nature of the wind, he wears a short-sleeved collared white shirt (and no vest). "You look cold, Jeff – welcome to the sunny North!" Once the turnstiles open a young Newcastle fan pointedly informs me, "We should definitely make the semi-finals!" When I tell him, "You are in the semi-finals," he changes his tune, "Oh, okay, the finals!" He then identifies some of the factors that've contributed to the Diamonds success, "Once they made changes off the track early in the season things got better! Robbie [Best] came back to do the track – the riders started to do really well!" Monarchs fan and member of the Armadale race-night first aid staff, Derek Nimmo analyses the Monarchs line-up, "Andrew Tully isn't here tonight, he's hurt his back." Stating the obvious, I say, "You'll be weaker then?" only to learn, "Actually, we'll be stronger 'cause Andrew doesn't go well round here and everyone can take a ride!"

Pits berth

Bob Tasker & Graeme Lemon

Emma Lemon & energy drink

Shortly afterwards Monarchs fan and author, Gary Lough reconfirms the identity of the first aider. "That's Derek Nimmo, he's part of the first aid staff at Armadale. Whenever any rider falls off, he runs over and signals for the ambulance – whether they want it or not!" When I wonder where Derek Nimmo's cassock has got to Gary just looks blank since he's too young to recall Derek Nimmo's role as the Bishop's Chaplain – the Rev Mervyn Noote – in the ecclesiastical sitcom *All Gas and Gaiters* (shown on the BBC between 1966 and 1971). Actually, now that I think about it, Derek perhaps didn't wear a cassock around St Ogg's Cathedral, maybe that was Sean Connery in *The Name of the Rose*? Either way, the Edinburgh speedway supporting Derek Nimmo prefers to wear high-visibility clothing. It's quite a night for sitcoms since Gary's been touched by the spirit of Frazer from *Dad's Army*, "We're not going to win here tonight! I would hope it's 12 points at the worst." Graham Platten's son, Matthew, forecasts the score will be 47-43. Perpetually cigar-smoking Monarchs fan, Norrie Tait, brings the conversation back to the topic of ambulances. "Dick Barrie was telling me that the ambulance at Berwick doesn't have an MOT! What would have happened if one of their riders had been seriously injured in the junior meeting last night?" Another early arrival is Mike Hunter, "I'm never happy coming here!" when I ask why, I learn, "'Cause it's not a very good track!"

Speedway fan David Barnett has been on an odyssey round every track in Britain – travelling by public transport! "This is my final track. Probably 'cause of the people I met it's restored my faith in humanity. On the whole, everyone has been so super-nice to me. I was well looked after at Redcar. I drank in the bar after the meeting and Brian Havelock gave me a lift afterwards to the coach station. Another place I really liked was Berwick – great banking! I really liked Eastbourne – it seemed so close to the action and it was a beautiful sunny stereotypical south coast day. The one I went to last week was Glasgow – I liked the sound and the smell and being so close to the track. I'm getting them all mixed up now. I've been to one every weekend for the last three months.

Sometimes, getting the 9 o'clock coach back to get to London at 6.20 in the morning. I've been to a few abroad. Sweden three times, the Czech Republic, Denmark and Poland. It's involved long walks out in the forest. Living in London, I go to Rye House (eight times) and Lakeside. It all came out of a redundancy payment! I've had the time and money. I'm having some treatment on my back. People on the forums and some riders slag off the tracks but I'm going to form my own opinion. It's great to come to a track like this in the city centre and be able to get here on public transport so easily!"

After the rider parade and practice lap, Diamonds presenter Barry Wallace foreshadows the task ahead for the Diamonds, "14 points in four amazing days shows what we're up against tonight against the Monarchs!" The first race of the night sees an easy win for guest William Lawson from gate four. The key action of the race is the first-bend battle for third place where Derek Sneddon gives Michal Rajkowski a massive shove to completely no avail! Stood next to me on the terraces in his Reading Bulldogs anorak, Graeme Lemon comments, "Derek can be quite a combative rider!" Sunderland season ticket holder Andrew Dalby is so committed to the Newcastle Diamonds that he happily wears a Newcastle Wulfsport anorak to the speedway. A drawn heat doesn't lull Graeme Lemon into any false sense of complacency, "The Monarchs will be really flying tonight – don't you worry!" The second race is drawn and also won by the rider from gate four, in this case Aaron Summers for the Monarchs. Nonetheless, Graeme appreciates the performance of a fellow Australian, "He's riding good. Aaron is a good rider. He'll ride in the Elite League. Whether or not he goes next year, I don't know. He could do with another year in the Premier League." Graeme has brought all of his family up on two wheels, "All my kids rode motorbikes – girls and all!" Mark rode from the age of 3, "At the house, we built him a little speedway track. He actually started junior speedway at 12 and riding senior speedway at 16. He was little when he was younger but then grew like a mushroom at 15. Mark is my baby. My eldest is 45. We celebrated our 48th wedding anniversary before I came to the UK." Jason King wins heat 3 – again from gate four – accompanied home by his Diamonds race partner, Rene Bach, to give Newcastle their first maximum heat advantage of the night. Graeme looks on appreciatively, "This might be our first break-through!"

Another group of people looking on appreciatively are the sponsors gathered by the pits gate who, as soon as the race ends, rush out onto the centre green where (if my own experiences are anything to go by) they'll be amazed by the speed and vitality of the race action. Graeme's son Mark finally takes to the track and the omens look good since he'll start from the blessed fourth gate. "I used to get nervous when I watched him but not anymore! His mum still does. He was a bit nervous [at the start gate] once upon a time. They used to accept rollers but not now, you have to be stationary." Mark stamps his authority on the race from the start gate while Graeme looks on with quiet satisfaction. Behind Mark, the highly regarded Kevin Wolbert rides a tentative first lap before he gets the hang of the track and appears to ride each lap quicker and quicker. With Trent Leverington third, the Diamonds further extend their lead to 15-9. During the brief break between heats four and five, Barry Wallace talks up the commemorative cards mounted in a frame that's available from the merchandise department. "You can order a frame in the trackshop for £25. Forty cards. Very attractive – would look very nice on someone's bedroom wall or, even, their living-room wall!" When Barry's not suggesting home decoration possibilities, Andrew Dalby ranges widely to fill the time. Graeme notes sardonically, "He's never lost for words Andrew, is he?" Off gate four, Ryan Fisher wins heat 5 though he's chased hard over the last couple of laps by Rene Bach who, on the second bend of the last lap, briefly looks like he might snatch the lead ("Go on, Rene, you can do it!" shouts Graeme) before Fisher closes the metaphorical door to speed away to victory. With Michal Rajkowski last, it's another drawn heat. Barry Wallace prefaces confirmation of the race result with the observation, "Continuing the sequence of winners off gate four." Sad news that 27-year-old Newcastle fan George Scott has been killed temporarily quietens the crowd ("Donations to the Bobby Robson Cancer Fund can be brought to the announcer's box").

Famous psychologist Stanley Milgram conducted many influential experiments including one that popularised the concept that everyone in the world is connected by only "six degrees of separation". The myriad links that exist within the closed speedway community suggests even less separation than that implies. In the world of films, the six degrees of separation meme is known as the Bacon number. For example, if you worked in a film with Kevin Bacon then your Bacon number would be 1. If you knew a producer who once worked on a Kevin Bacon film then your Bacon number would be 2. If your agent knows an actor who knows the producer who worked on a film with Kevin Bacon then your Bacon number would be 3, and so on. Internet rumours claim there is an obscure 1920s Russian film that has a Kevin

Bacon number of 7!" In speedway, the equivalent would be the Street number. This analytical framework could be used to establish degrees of connectedness of anyone in the speedway world with the modest speedway legend Neil Street. This could easily apply to anyone within the sport but particularly young Australians who come to Britain to find their way within European speedway. "I've known Streetie for years. Mark stayed with him for three or four months when he first came over here. I know Phil Crump. His [former] wife Carol worked for me for three or four years. Nice lady!" Derek Sneddon starts heat 6 from the fourth gate and enjoys an early lead since Kevin Wolbert is caught in traffic. However, by the start of the second lap, Kevin catches and efficiently passes Derek. Kevin wins extremely easily and, thereby, shatters the sequence of five successive race victories from gate 4. Interested in every race, Graeme concentrates even more attentively when his son comes out onto the track. The seventh race has Mark line up on gate one next to Ryan Fisher of the Monarchs. The American gates quickly for the lead but, then, appears to stop suddenly on the second bend – this causes Mark Lemon to clatter into him. Graeme is less than impressed, "Fisher just turned left on him! Mark was on the inside and Fisher tried to shut the gate by turning left on him. I knew they'd be a bit competitive 'cause they're both competing for one place at Swindon." Making conversation, I suggest, "Mark seems a calm rider." Graeme is mentally elsewhere, "He's had to learn to be. Excuse me, I'm just going to see how he is!"

Referee Darren Hartley disqualifies Ryan Fisher from the rerun. Graeme remains in the pits with his son until the riders go back out on the track. He returns to our vantage point on the stepped section of the home-straight terrace that overlooks the first bend. "Mark is winded. Ryan turned left on him and spun him round. Fisher was stupid 'cause second would have been fine in a meeting this important! Even third is good when every point counts." Whether or not the lost points will prove significant isn't clear at this stage of proceedings. Mark Lemon wins the rerun ahead of Matthew Wethers and, with Adam McKinna third, Newcastle gain a 4-2 heat advantage that takes the cumulative score to 25-17. The Diamonds second 5-1 of the night – through Derek Sneddon and Trent Leverington – then fires the Diamonds into a 12-point lead (with eight races completed). Because of this deficit, Monarchs team manager John Campbell immediately hands Kevin Wolbert the black-and-white helmet colour. Aaron Summers replaces out-of-touch fellow Monarchs reserve Byron Bekker and storms to a race win from the favoured gate four. Behind him, there's a lusty battle between Kevin Wolbert and Rene Bach. On the second bend of the second lap Bach rides Wolbert hard to leave him beached by the fence. By the last lap, Wolbert's fought back into contention to ride a fast first and second bend before a blast round the outside of Bach on bend three. He then cuts back up the inside to race to the finish line only for Rene Bach to show an amazing late burst to retain second place at the chequered flag. It's an effort that restricts the impact of Edinburgh's use of the tactical option but, nonetheless, gives the visitors a 2-5 heat advantage. The most surprising aspect of the race is that Diamonds captain Jason King finishes last.

On walkabout in his Newcastle Wulfsport anorak, Andrew Dalby stops for a brief word and compares the young rider prospects within the Diamonds ranks. "Bach is the better prospect. Larsen is 21, whereas Bach is 19. He's not afraid to mix it and looks good on the bike. Wolbert looked very good when he came here a few weeks back and that was a great race between them in that last race, wasn't it?" Already with 7 points from three rides Wolbert further underlines his skill on a speedway bike with a comfortable win in heat 10 (from gate four) ahead of William Lawson. More significantly for the Diamonds, Matthew Wethers plays possum and completely out-thinks third-placed Derek Sneddon. At the end of laps two and three, the Monarch ostentatiously trails some distance off at the back and, possibly unconsciously, Sneddon relaxes only to suddenly find himself overtaken on the exit from bend two and, consequently, unable to make up the gap during the remainder of the last lap. Biggar-based Glasgow fan Jim Fleming kindly provided a taxi service for the Monarchs Michal Rajkowski to ensure he could take part in tonight's meeting against Newcastle. "I brought Michal from Glasgow Airport where he arrived at 4. His dad brought his bikes down. He was in Edinburgh on Friday night but he had to go back to Poland for a PE course!"

Heat 11 provides a rematch between Ryan Fisher and Mark Lemon, off gates one and two respectively. From the inside gate position, Fisher rides Lemon hard to the apex of the first and second bends. This prompts an aggrieved exclamation from Graeme Lemon, "He's taken him out to the fence again! Come on, Mark!" It's a hard speedway racing manoeuvre that establishes all the advantage that Fisher requires to ensure a race win and, with Summers third, Edinburgh record their third successive heat advantage to further reduce the Diamonds lead to a suboptimal 5 points. After the race Graeme suggests a wager, "Do you wanna bet now he won't beat him in 15?" Like many in the crowd,

Jim Fleming believes that the in-form Diamonds haven't done enough to ensure their progression to the Premier League Play-off final, "Newcastle need about 15 points to have a chance!" With ticket number 404, Lawrence Heppell wins the chance to choose the key that might unlock a door that inside contains untold riches. Lawrence chooses box number 15 and, instead, wins £10 to spend in the trackshop. He then calls tails in a double or quits toss of the coin and has to resign himself to the fact that tonight he won't gain the chance of early retirement or go home with anything from the trackshop.

Jason King rediscovers his form round Brough Park to win heat 12 and, with Trent Leverington third ahead of Matthew Wethers, Newcastle gain a 4-2 advantage to take them back into a 7-point lead. We don't have to wait until the last race of the night to see the next instalment of the Lemon/Fisher since their wheel-to-wheel battle reconvenes in heat 13. Before the race, Graeme Lemon is keen to emphasise that there's no real antipathy between the riders, "It's not that he dislikes him, he just thinks he's crazy!" Dust and the tapes almost rise together at the start of race as Kevin Wolbert hammers away to record the fastest time of the night (62.9). Graeme only has eyes for his son until he suddenly exclaims, "Is that Fisher out the back?" Rene Bach records his first race win of the night in heat 14 and, with Leverington third, Newcastle gain another heat advantage to further extend their lead to 9 points. Graeme Lemon comments, "A 5-1 would set it up nicely now!" Ryan Fisher sits out the last race of the night but his teammate Kevin Wolbert does the honours and, yet again, records the fastest heat time (62.6) of the night. Newcastle gain a 9-point lead to defend at Armadale. Andrew Dalby conducts some rider interviews on the centre green. Guest William Lawson scored paid 9, but still elicits Andrew's sympathy, "We put you in a strange position tonight – a Glasgow rider riding against Edinburgh!" Rene Bach makes light of his exciting heat 9 duel with Kevin Wolbert, "That's speedway!" Jason King answers anonymous slurs that he might not return to Newcastle next season, "I just wanted to say – I want to be back here next year!" Andrew also optimistically conducts a straw poll to find out who'll be going up to Armadale on Friday to watch the second leg, "Give us a wave if you're going to Edinburgh? Come on, there must be more of you than that!" Sheffield fan Paul Brown has, on reflection, enjoyed his night's speedway, "It was dire the first half of the meeting. The first seven or eight races were processional but, then, it livened up!" Kevin Wolbert at full tilt is definitely an exciting spectacle to behold. Jim Fleming praises the Newcastle race-day magazine, "Isn't this a good programme, don't you think? It's very informative and very helpful!" Many Monarchs fans express delight that they've only lost by 9 points. One visiting fan is so ecstatic he buys – possibly for his living room wall – the framed cards from the trackshop, "It's lovely, isn't it?!"

4th October Newcastle v. Edinburgh (Premier League Play-off semi-final, first leg) 50-41

CHAPTER 40

Wolverhampton

"Will Steve Johnston – who has Rosco's car keys – take them to the pits immediately!"

5th October

The success of the end of season Play-offs effectively means that the regular Elite League season is nothing more than a glorified qualification tournament to determine which four teams (or six) will enjoy the thrill and revenues of boosted gate receipts at the close of the season. Based on their season-long performances, most speedway fans from a fairness or entertainment point of view would select Wolves and Swindon as deserving finalists. Despite injury niggles, most neutral observers would also make Wolverhampton pre-meeting favourites to lift the trophy. However, one appeal of speedway is the manner in which random events, sudden loss of form or mechanical failure can undermine the likely success of even the most skilful rider. Outsiders with little knowledge of speedway would dismiss the idea of the possibility of psychological mind games in a sport often ignorantly characterised as premised on sheer speed away from the start-line. This naive but oft-cited opinion ignores the many nuances that can edge percentages in your favour and result in success. Pure chance is a factor but the shrewd rider, manager or promoter invariably plans for what appears to be the rub of the green. Indeed, Wolverhampton have defied the convention of recent years to opt to race the first leg of the final at home. The speedway trade press identifies the Wolverhampton strategic master plan as aiming to rack up a medium to big lead at Monmore that they then defend on the road. On the team-management front Wolverhampton pit their Brer Rabbit (Peter Adams) against the Swindon Robins Brer Fox (Alun Rossiter). Similarly, from a promotional point of view, Chris Van Straaten is probably Brer Rabbit to Terry Russell's Brer Fox. The commemorative programme produced for tonight's meeting at Monmore Green features full-colour passport photos of every rider, a frothy pint of Banks's beer and also provides information on each rider's birth sign. Whether horoscopes or astrological matters will play a part is a moot point but, even here, Wolverhampton appear to have the advantage as they line up as Virgo, Capricorn, Libra, Leo, Sagittarius, Cancer and Pisces against a less varied line-up of Taurus, Virgo, Capricorn, Taurus, Aries, Aries, Libra. Thankfully I'm no Russell Grant, though I have to say Ryan Fisher appears an unlikely Virgo in the same way that Paul Hurry seems an unlikely Aries.

When I invite every fan of either persuasion I meet to stare into the tea leaves, most Wolverhampton fans pointedly talk down my wild talk of an emphatic victory. Bucking this trend, ex Miss Fina Invader Wendy Jedrzejakski takes a surprisingly ebullient line, "I'm not sure! Speaking to one of the Swindon riders – who will have to remain nameless – they're worried about coming here tonight 'cause we're so good!" When space allows (and it's not the football season), the Wolverhampton *Express & Star* gives comprehensive coverage to Wolves and speedway generally. For tonight's meeting they've produced a "Play-off Final Special Edition" that completely occupies the front and back cover of the newspaper. Every single article is written by their fastidious, knowledgeable and hardworking speedway reporter Tim Hamblin whose photograph stares back at us from near the masthead of the paper. With his designer stubble and fashionable glasses, Tim looks like one of the millionaire investors from *Dragons' Den* or possibly a successful Celebrity Chef. His photo belies his investigative skill and enthusiasm for all things speedway. A casual glance at any of his articles quickly reveals the elegance of his writing, the economy of his word selection and his ability to coax thoughtful comment from pretty well anyone he interviews. Unkind Wolverhampton fans point to a mismatch between Peter Adams and Alun Rossiter that they characterise in film terms as Spock versus Forest Gump. Interviewed beforehand by Tim, Alun's military film connections appear to be much more 4077 MASH, thereby metaphorically possibly pitting his Frank Burns against Peter Adams's Hawkeye Pierce. Never afraid to play to the gallery, Rosco also isn't afraid to employ Derren Brown-like misdirection and double-think, "I spoke to the great Peter Adams; it's all about mind games". Rosco is also happy to make predictions. When asked about his target for the night, "draw or win!" falls from his lips before he concedes a more realistic position, "keep it close, 4 or 6 points, something like that would be a good result."

When I consult Tim about his thoughts on tonight's score he doesn't hesitate to play the Wolverhampton "I'm not sure" card, "I'm not sure! I think we'll win here but go down by 8 points overall!" It's understated pessimism gone mad! Wendy Jedrzejakski wouldn't indulge me with an aggregate prediction but is happy to say, "We need 6 or 8." Tim nods his agreement, "10 or 12 is a preference! The problem is Ty and PK aren't really fit!" These medical difficulties are the headline news of the *Express & Star* special issue: "No pain, no gain for Wolves duo". Peter Karlsson will race only a fortnight after he broke his collarbone in a crash with fallen Lakeside rider Stuart Robson. Ty Proctor pulled out of Redcar's (his Premier League team) meeting at Scunthorpe last Friday with a "combination of a kidney infection and back injury". Tim catalogues the injuries but – without the shorthand and keen ear of a professional reporter – I get them confused in my notes as "PK's collarbone rubbing on his kidneys". Like many other Wolverhampton fans, Wendy's seized by anxiety and anticipation at the same time, "I feel a bit nervous, you know – that's why I'm here early." Whether or not the Swindon riders, team management or promotional team read the local paper is unclear (but unlikely). However, Tim proudly tells me that – speedway or no speedway – the *Express & Star* has "140,000 circulation every night!" Whatever the outcome, the Play-off final special must surely massively boost awareness of Wolverhampton Speedway within its local community. Hopefully, this increased profile will attract new fans through the turnstiles in 2010 and, more importantly, motivate local businesses to want to be part of this success story. If the club had paid for a front and back double page, it would cost them many thousands of pounds!

Round at the trackshop, Bill, John and Rat stand ready for the turnstiles to open behind their perfectly set out stall. The cornucopia of Wolverhampton speedway merchandise on offer should cater for every need, age group and pocket. Dave Rattenberry even has an impressive display of the mugs with the peculiar colour photo resolution that in many ways is his trademark. On some of them, PK looks like he's suffered some sort of terrible poisoning that's caused his skin to go orange while on another his face is so red you could half suspect he'd been horrifically burnt in some form of hushed-up tanning salon accident. Ever the salesman, John Rich concedes, "They shouldn't be red, they should be gold!" Clean Cut Sports cameraman and supremo, Pete Ballinger arrives ahead of schedule to deliver 20 Wolverhampton versus Lakeside DVDs hot off the press. Rat rummages through them and demands, "Where's the GP Challenge?"
[Pete] Frick off, I'm just back from Gorican."
[Rat] "What about the, you know, the Sheffield meeting? [PLRC]"
[Pete] "Come on, come on I'll have them in a fortnight!"
[Rat] "A fortnight!?"
[Pete] "For the triumphant homecoming with the trophy and the Olympique."
[Rat] (pause) "The Lakeside DVDs?"

An impressive selection of rider photographs are available for sale – all expertly mounted and displayed. There's every conceivable permutation of photograph for every single Wolverhampton rider – headshot, bodyshot or distant, racing or stationary, stood alone or as a team, in their kevlars or normal clothes. Everything except topless. There's even a photograph of Scott Nicholls that prompts me to question Rat, "Does Scott Nicholls ride for Wolves?"
[Rat] "He has!"
[Jeff] "What's on sale tonight then Dave?"
[Rat] "There's nothing on discount!!"

At 17.45, with the turnstiles now open, sensible fans join the queue at the burger bar early so that they can avoid a long wait later and also ensure they still get to reserve their ideal spot on the terraces in front of the impressive grandstand building. Stepped terraces line most of the home straight. Tonight the club have installed temporary stands that overlook the apex of the third and fourth bend. At the front of the burger bar queue the Swindon management team of Terry Russell, Wayne Russell and Alun Rossiter prove that the early bird (Robin) catches the worm. They wear their corporate garments with pride – their anoraks look bright and box-fresh. The modern rider nowadays talks about body fat percentages as much as they discuss the teeth on their sprockets. International success on the speedway stage (allegedly) dictates that riders observe carefully constructed exercise programmes and follow a diet regime equally suited to jockeys or supermodels. Not only have Terry, Wayne and Rosco beaten the queue but they also have full choice from the complete range of hot and fried foodstuffs available from this mobile "Food Court". If they'd ever started, they certainly throw their macrobiotic diet to the wind with their man-of-the-people choice of burgers (and tea/coffee) that they scarf down barely yards from the stall – apparently blissfully unaware that such foodstuffs are notorious for the energy knock and concomitant lack of concentration they'll provide a couple of hours later (just when the race action is about to get really serious). Though he looks a stranger to tofu, sunflower seeds or cottage cheese, I expect Peter Adams's season-long preparations dictate that he'll have selected a diet over the past weeks, days and hours that ensures he's sated but alert, ready to concentrate but dietetically protected from the distraction of the adrenaline rush of his autoimmune system. Their possible collective dietary *faux pas* bothers me so much that I rush up to Nigel Pearson and blurt out, "Look at them! I worry about their blood sugar levels later!" Nigel glances over just as Rosco appears only to be having a cup of tea (seconds later he picks up some unidentified deep fried foodstuff), "Terry Russell strikes me as a burger man!"

Commemorative photos

Nigel probably isn't the best to consult since he also strikes me as burger man or, possibly, a pie, pint and chips bloke who, in an emergency, will settle for a liquid diet rather than soil the temple of his body with a quiche and salad. Though he's an experienced sports commentator who travels widely for his work, Nigel is clearly also in a "big night" mood. "You know I don't give you the PR bullshit I'm supposed to. Before the season, people said 'The Elite League is going to be shit without Crump, Pedersen and Nicholls' and the like but it hasn't been! It's been alright and they're all coming back now! Just recently with the Play-offs, it's been fantastic! Sky are very pleased with what we've been showing. If they have any frustration, it's the rag-arsed Sunday parks football approach of certain clubs but, 'cause of the product, they will live with that! Tonight, I'm here and then Wednesday I'm off to Dublin for the darts and then, the weekend after, it's Bydgoszcz. I love sports and, imagine, I get to work on speedway, football and darts! It's an ideal life – a good combination of sports too! When I have time off, I go to watch Worcester at New Road. I'm a member. It's the best ground in the country to watch cricket at. It hasn't been too clever on the field this year but still excellent. I just saw Tim Hamblin in the pits – did you see the *Express & Star* have done a speedway special tonight for the meeting? A two-page wraparound! He even called me up last Thursday – he's that thorough!"

PK Mugs plus cap selection

The Play-off final special edition of the *Express & Star* has certainly had an impact. Tim discusses it with characteristic modesty. "4,500 words. Good detail. If it sells well then they might do it more often! It took a bit of effort. None of this stripping stuff off the Internet. They're all face-to-face interviews or on the phone! I got lucky at the ELRC at Coventry on Friday. I caught Freddie and, then, I asked Leigh Adams and he said, 'Could you kindly come back at the end of the meeting?' And, though he was in a mad rush, he gave a thoughtful and intelligent piece. I caught PK in Sweden on Saturday, Adam Skornicki at Lakeside, Hynek Stichauer in the Czech Republic on the way to Pardubice and Ty Proctor in the doctors. I rang back after – once he'd emerged from the throes of medical attention – and CVS in the office for the website. If you ask nicely, riders rarely refuse! I've been turned down five times, three times by the same rider! I dunno where to stand tonight. On the grandstand but I do need to go down to the pits too!"

Early arrivals

Speedway Star photographer and circulation manager Dave Fairbrother refuses to make a prediction but does say, "If Swindon keep it to 6, they'll do alright!" On the section of the home-straight terraces that overlooks the start line and bend 1, Wolverhampton speedway club historian Mark Sawbridge answers by repeating the opinion of others, "Darren was saying we need 16."
[Jeff] "16!"
[Darren] "If it's 10 or less, we won't win!"
Reading Racers club historian Arnie Gibbons arrives, "I'm mentally preparing myself for a Swindon victory!"
[Jeff] "But you're a closet Swindon fan."
[Arnie] "I'm not!"

The last few weeks of any season see a slew of important meetings. This year is no different. Arnie takes a measured view of the outcome of the recent World Under-21 final held at Gorican in Croatia. "Tai didn't have to break the tapes. Look at Maciej Janowski he had a fall and exclusion in his first ride – if he hadn't, he might have had 14 and won! There's a head of steam behind Tai Woffinden being in the GP. I recall Jason Crump winning the Under-21 and going in the GP and struggling. It hasn't done Chris Holder any harm waiting an extra year and that probably applies to Tai too! I think Darcy must be the youngest ever Under-21 champ. He's barely 17." Arnie also has some news that could possibly indicate the basis for a flicker of optimism about the future of the Reading Racers. "I had an email out of the blue from Cheri Legg this week. I had a word with Andy Povey who's in a similar position. Apparently, there's rumblings from Stadia UK so, in order to have a promoter's licence to use or to sell, Mark Legg has to clear off outstanding debts – that the BSPA know about – plus there's the Zagar transfer fee that must be five figures." Press comment about the introduction of new silencers concerns Mark Sawbridge, "I don't understand the *Speedway Star* coverage. The *Star* was against noise reduction completely and now they're for it. I wish these things were a bit more intelligent. There have been noise problems at Exeter, Birmingham, Sittingbourne, Weymouth, Bodmin and Mildenhall!" Arnie has extensive experience behind the scenes in local government (and also national party politics) so understands their outlook. "The councillors are trying definitely as hard as they can to avoid coming down on either side of the fence. If travellers moved in, all the people who derided them would suddenly change their minds! When it comes to speedway tracks and noise, a cautious welcome with adequate restrictions is as much as you could expect. They want to get re-elected and aren't interested in the views of people who live outside the area."

The speaker system crackles into life since Shaun Leigh has some vitally important information to impart, "Ladies and Gentlemen, we do have a bar outside on the grandstand terracing!" Though Tim Hamblin is punctilious about his speedway reports, Mark Sawbridge relates that he can sometimes be let down by his co-workers. "I rang Tim last Thursday and said 'Have you seen the headline on your piece?' They'd spelt Tai as Thai even though it was spelt correctly in the third line! Tim swore and said he was going to kill the sub-editor!" Mark sympathises with the difficulty any speedway writer has if they have to produce work on a daily or weekly basis. "I used to do some history pieces in the programme. After a while you run out of interesting riders with Wolves connections. I did a piece on Mark Loram who doesn't really have any connections and didn't do well here. I said in the bar 'I'm not going to get so desperate that I'd do something on Steve Johnston!' And Julie Reading said, 'Have you met Mrs Johnston – Steve's mum?' who was stood next to us! She was very polite and handled it really well." Fuelling rumours that the Robins 'special' tactics for tonight's meeting have been written down on the back of a postage stamp locked in Rosco's car boot, the public address system again crackles back into life, "Steve Johnston – who has Rosco's car keys – can you take them to the pits immediately!" Away on the second bend, the Sky Sports commentary booth is lit up like an important monument in a tourist area. The grandstand is massively crowded, something you'd expect since this part of the world is full of passionate speedway fans. The man behind me is no exception, "I've been going for 66 years now. I first went when I was 10. I'm a Cradley fan. It broke my heart when they closed! I had to come here tonight!" With the car keys still urgently needed to retrieve the Swindon game plan, there's another appeal, "Will Steve Johnston – who has Rosco's car keys – take them to the pits immediately!" People ask me why I've come to the meeting, so I tell them, "I've only come to see Porky!" Ian 'Porky' Jones inspires strong feelings among some speedway fans. Tim Hamblin is quick to defend him. "When Edinburgh came here last year, there was a big crowd of them who hadn't heard it before and they knew they were going to lose – so had come out for a good time and he played off them brilliantly! When he has a knowledgeable crowd who hear him every week, it doesn't work so well."

For one night only, just like old times, Mr Wolf – the Monmore Green mascot of yesteryear – joins Porky on the centre green. Though his mascot's outfit shows some sign of age, wear and tear, nonetheless, it's somehow reassuring and more authentic that it isn't quite as bling or Disney as those you always see at football clubs nowadays. That said, Mr Wolf is an experienced pantomime performer and some fans claim they'd prefer it if Porky had his level of articulacy. The mascot uniform is worn by Spike (aka Colin Burton) who, when he doesn't cavort on the home-straight shale for the benefit of the fans, is a local teacher. Porky expresses delight at his return, "For one night only, the return of Mr Wolf! Would you like to see Mr Wolf at speedway [cheer] oh, he's teaching nowadays." Mr Wolf appears to an adulatory welcome and screams without the aid of a microphone, "Give us a W!" I half expect that he's about to retort to Porky but, instead, he spells out the word Wolves. Mr Wolf exhibits natural grace and rhythm as he bounds up and down the track trying to incite the crowd. Ever professional, Porky works with what he has – so wobbles his stomach in lieu of the age inappropriate hip shakes he continues to attempt but is no longer able to perform. Wolverhampton fans around me clearly hold Mr Wolf in some affection. More than can be said for the Swindon fans who – rather cruelly – deride his appearance during the meeting and afterwards.[1] Sight of Spike sends Mark Sawbridge down memory lane. "George Hunter's car always blew up on the way to Exeter and Newport. Wherever the Wolves team went, the junior team was sure to follow. In 1973, with George not there again, they promoted the top junior into the team and Spike rode in the reserves race. He was so far behind they'd announced the result before he'd finished!"

Swindon take first blood when they win the toss and choose gates 1 and 3. Meanwhile, Tim Hamblin sings the praises of Mr Wolf, "He's an outgoing inquisitive man! Likes people. Gets on well with everyone. I can imagine it's great to be taught by him!" The Mexican wave led and encouraged by Spike travels round the stadium but ends abruptly when it reaches the brightly lit Speedway Office on the first bend. Inside the blinds (unusually) aren't down and, with the lights ablaze, Chris Van Straaten is visible as he looks out towards the track – where Freddie Lindgren and Nicolai Klindt are about to line up against the Robins power partnership of Leigh Adams and Ryan Fisher. Interviewed recently in the *Express & Star*, Nicolai Klindt has the intuition of a tabloid reporter if judged by the phrase (that I don't quite understand) "Save the castle – screw the princess!" Seconds before the tapes rise Tim Hamblin makes his final carefully considered prediction, "a win by 6!" Freddie and Leigh battle for position until the third bend whereupon Lindgren establishes dominance and proceeds to win comfortably. Wolverhampton immediately follow-up this heat advantage with another that sees Chris Kerr win a close battling race. My section of the Wolverhampton terraces is amazed at sight of Kerr's triumph. Tim notes, "That has to be a worry if you're a Swindon fan, Chris Kerr winning a race! I can't remember the last time he won a race."
[Mark Sawbridge] "That's his first win for a long, long, long time."
[Tim] "I honestly can't remember when he last won a heat."
[Mark] "I dunno, probably early in the season?"
[Tim] "Maybe, if at all."
[Arnie] "Jeff, it's the sort of thing you expect Mark to know, isn't it?"

Arnie likes to dress up his barely disguised closet Swindon fandom as adulation for Travis McGowan, though he definitely gets funny looks when, just before the start of heat 3, he forgets his whereabouts and shouts, "Go on Travis! Go on Travis!" Ever the politician, Arnie then even-handedly tries to integrate himself back into the partisan crowd that surrounds him with a less loud but politically astute shout of, "Go on Wolves!" The unpredictable nature of any speedway race is part of its enduring appeal. This is re-emphasised by the third race of the night when with Adam Skornicki up front and Tai Woffinden second Wolverhampton appear to be cruising to a comfortable 5-1 that'll progress the score to an emphatic 13-5 when, on the very last bend of the race, Tai's slight tendency to override causes him to stutter, spin round and fall. Until that point, the only real contest was the battle for third place between teammates Simon Stead and Travis McGowan! Under no pressure at all, there's mystification in the crowd at Tai's fall, "I think he's a bit pumped up! He nearly put it down in the same place last time turning too hard!" Residual anxiety surges through the crowd with the disillusioning realisation that a possible 13-5 has changed in an instant into 11-7. More or less in the same place on the fourth bend where Tai Woffinden fell the heat before, his differently spelt

[1] Remind me again of the Swindon mascot? Though I stand to be corrected I can't recall ever seeing anyone in a Robin or for that matter, possibly even more appropriately, dressed as a Bridesmaid?

namesake Ty [Proctor] – who looks in genuine discomfort for the first two laps – executes a weird wiggly manoeuvre with his bike before he falls. His inevitable disqualification leaves Peter Karlsson as the sole Wolverhampton representative in the rerun and, thereby, prompts Tim's anxieties about the extent of his injuries to immediately resurface, "Let's hope PK knows what he's doing or it could all go horribly wrong!" On the first bend of the rerun Matej Zagar rides really hard under PK in the full knowledge of his debilitating injury. Understandably PK takes care to race with some (notional) reticence but, nonetheless, still finishes ahead of Robins reserve Morten Risager. Mark Sawbridge is downcast, "I can't believe its 13-11! He [PK] wasn't turning tight like he normally does!" Tim Hamblin also detects some understandable tentativeness from this widely admired veteran rider, "PK was taking a very wide line and riding as gently as he could! The momentum has dissipated. This is where [Peter] Adams steps in and marshals the troops!"

Out on the shale Mr Wolf rallies the Wolves fans with an "Oggie, Oggie, Oggie" chant that prompts Porky to (wittily) observe, "He speaks very posh for Wolves!" The start of heat 5 features a keenly contested first corner. Ryan Fisher is at the centre of the action and battles so much that he manages to relegate his teammate Leigh Adams to the rear of the field only to then find himself unable to capitalise upon his own aggression to the extent that he's immediately relegated to third by the time the Wolves riders exit the second bend. With Skornicki and Woffinden way out in front, it takes Leigh Adams until the third bend of the last lap to pass Fisher and even then he's only able to do so because he drives really hard underneath his race partner! With a 5-1 in the bag and the scoreline a much healthier 18-12, Mark Sawbridge revises his outlook, "There's only one team in this, so far!" Everyday common-or-garden Elite League meetings throughout the season definitely don't have the cut and thrust of tonight's first corners! Neither do they have the fantastic atmosphere that the really crowded terraces at Monmore Green generate. Tim Hamblin believes spatial awareness will become even more important as the meeting progresses and riders compete for fractional advantage, "My prediction still is that Ryan and Ty [Proctor] will scrabble over the same bit of track at some point." Princess botherer Nicolai Klindt is out in the next race off gate 4 (with Paul Hurry on the gate next to him). It's a situation that Tim views positively, "I don't want to fate him but Nicolai could do something special out of gate 4 here – he loves the outside!" No matter how special Nicolai could potentially be, it's always difficult to dominate any race where Matej Zagar starts off gate 1. However, Master of Monmore Freddie Lindgren brooks no argument and roars away to win with ease. With Nicolai third, this latest heat advantage extends Wolverhampton's lead to 8 points. If Wolves maintain this performance level, then it won't be long before Alun 'Rosco' Rossiter gets to explore his tactical options. Tim Hamblin predicts heat 11 for a possible Swindon use of the tacticals. Fans around him recall that during the Wolves pre-season discussions, Peter Adams commented on the strength of the Swindon team in gnomic fashion, "One thing to remember is that Swindon have Rosco as team manager!" It's an observation that's become so popular, it's almost a mantra nowadays. Just as importantly, none of the Wolves fans forget that, prior to the meeting, their own team manager will have assessed (and reassessed) almost every possible permutation of team line-up and gate position. Tim confirms this expectation, "Peter Adams had a careful plan at Lakeside for Skornicki to ride at number 5 to support the reserves. He'd also worked out the order of his rider-replacement rides based on gate positions and, if there was any, how the dirt would move out during the meeting!"

Peter Karlsson wins his first race of the night and the drawn seventh heat ensures that use of the Swindon tactical will remain on the back burner for at least one more race. Ryan Fisher makes amends for his earlier thoughtlessness (in heat 5) when, on the first lap of heat 8, he rides his bike like a rocket down the back straight to secure a lead he never looks likely to relinquish. Ty Proctor struggles to make any impression on second-placed Morten Risager as he apparently struggles to overcome both his kidney infection and vertebrae tissue problems. The peculiarly ridged Monmore Green fourth bend claims another victim on lap two when Nicolai Klindt gets into a tangle with himself and subsequently retires. This 5-1 to the Robins narrows the Wolves advantage and noticeably quietens the home-straight terrace crowd. Since I'm stood on the terraces close by to Tim Hamblin, I'm treated to the speedway equivalent of a 'listen again' pre-record of tomorrow afternoon's *Express & Star* report on tonight's meeting. "Ty looks sore and Nikolai keeps getting bogged down at the starts! Dunno whether it's a mechanical or mental thing?" Off gate two in heat 9, Matej Zagar lines up incredibly close to Tai Woffinden who's on the start gate inside him. Whether or not the psychology has any impact is difficult to estimate since Zagar makes a dream start to fire away from the start-line into a lead that he definitely never looks likely to relinquish. The 10th race of the night features an incredibly ragged start, so much so that members of the crowd around me express surprise that referee Peter

Clarke doesn't stop the race ("Come on, you've got to stop that one!"). Playing to the whistle (or red light), Nicolai Klindt makes good his escape as the other riders slow-mo in the expectation of a rerun that, when it doesn't materialise, stifles further complaints in the throats of the Wolverhampton fans since Freddie Lindgren reacts quickest and accelerates away to secure second ahead of his sleepier Robins rivals. Though Travis McGowan does put up some semblance of a fight, his dashes round the outside are predictable and repelled. Mark Sawbridge can't quite believe it: "I've never used 'intelligent' in the same sentence as 'Nicolai Klindt', but that was an intelligent race!"

Wolves 8-point lead subverts predictions that Swindon might use tacticals in heat 11, though the heat does effectively provide two match races in one when Peter Karlsson gates to defeat Leigh Adams (who nearly catches him on the line), while Ryan Fisher easily sees off the challenge of Chris Kerr. Another drawn heat maintains the Wolverhampton advantage. Adam Skornicki starts slowly out of the gate in heat 12 but somehow leads into the first bend ahead of McGowan and Risager by what I can only describe as sheer willpower. His race partner Ty Proctor escapes into second place as he exits the second bend closely follows Skornicki. The Wolverhampton partnership cruises away to hammer home the 5-1, which then enables Rosco to finally use the black-and-white helmet colour (Matej Zagar) in heat 13. If PK hadn't broken his collarbone only 11 days beforehand, then Lindgren and Karlsson versus Adams and Zagar would really be a contest to savour. Whether through nerves or gamesmanship, Zagar faffs about long enough to effectively delay the start of the race. When the tapes finally rise, Lindgren leads, PK gives no quarter to Leigh Adams and (just when the big race is required) the rejuvenated Zagar comes up massively short! Successive late meeting 5-1s destroy the Robins challenge and massively extend the Wolverhampton lead to a scoreline that reads 47-31. Mark Sawbridge is ecstatic, "I've died and gone to heaven!" In the excitement, even Tim Hamblin forgets to choose his words carefully, "I thought I'd seen it all!" To the backing sounds of *Hi Ho Silver Lining*, Porky leads the crowd in a rendition of "It's Hi Ho Wolverhampton!"

More on principle than expectation, Rosco sends Simon Stead out in the black-and-white helmet colour for the penultimate race of the night. It's won by Tai Woffinden ahead of Stead and, with Proctor third, the 4-4 drawn heat further nullifies the impact of the Swindon tactical rides (they only generate 2 additional points out of a possible 6). Freddie Lindgren closes out a successful night with a win in heat 15 ahead of Adams and Zagar. It leaves Wolverhampton poised on the edge of greatness with a ludicrously comfortable lead of 16 points. Porky celebrates over the public address system on behalf of the black-and-gold faithful. "Are you going to Swindon next week? Too right we are! Safe journey home, Swindon fans! You're lovely people." Porky conducts some post-meeting interviews with the Wolverhampton riders in joyful fashion. He tells Fredrik Lindgren, "Tell you what, we've just got to keep it tight and ride sensibly and the Elite League trophy will be on its way back to Wolves!" With his own brand of a Black Country accent, PK strikes a contemplative attitude, "We kind of gave away a few points to start with – but we fought back!" False modesty is a cloak that Porky is happy to cast off, "Tell you what, I'm sick of hearing people saying Swindon this and Swindon that, you want to take a look at Wolves!" BBC Radio Swindon presenter Richard Crowley is on duty tonight at Monmore Green but struggles to hide his disappointment. "It's hard to see us pulling that back next week. It's Leigh Adams I feel sorry for 'cause he's not going to be world champion and, I think, he'd really like to win the Elite League for Swindon this year or next! I've waited 42 years to see it and, I suppose, I can wait a bit longer!"

5th October Wolverhampton v. Swindon (Elite League Play-off Final, first leg) 54-38

CHAPTER 41

Swindon

"I'm not saying we can, but, if we can hold the two tacticals and win heat 15, then we can!"

12th October

The 2009 Elite League season formally closes at Blunsdon after the Swindon Robins take on the Wolverhampton Parrys International Wolves in the second leg of the Play-off final. In the attractive commemorative programme produced to celebrate the event, the Full Throttle Torque column by Alun 'Rosco' Rossiter brushes aside any understandable anxiety about the 16-point first-leg deficit Swindon have to recover from if they are to lift the Sky Sports Elite League trophy. "We won't be throwing in the towel because, as I've said before, this final has a fair distance to run yet, 15 heats is a long time in speedway." Rosco's ghost-written column doesn't state that speedway is raced on shale not paper, possibly keen to save the odd cliché until the press conference afterwards. When their Elite League campaign fell apart for the Robins in the 2007 Play-off final, Rosco was quick to highlight a lack of team spirit brought on by the language difficulties ostensibly caused by an outbreak of Polish riders in the Swindon side. And, after going out at Lakeside in the semi-final in 2008, this alleged lack of cohesion is something the club addressed during the 2009 pre-season, so motivation (along with tactical acumen) continues to be the key metric by which Rosco judges his performance as a team manager. "Understandably, immediately after the meeting the mood in the camp was subdued. In the changing rooms, I said to the boys that they need to re-focus and really concentrate on our gating for tonight's encounter. I'm confident they've taken that on board." Apparently the "most loyal and dedicated support bases in speedway" can also play their part in recouping this deficit, "We need you to be our eighth man here at Blunsdon this evening. With your help we really do need to make the Abbey Stadium an intimidating place to be for the Wolverhampton riders."

Over in the pits the always affable and extremely quotable Swindon track curator, Ronnie Russell, is in ebullient form. Ronnie's a natural communicator and motivator. Leaving nothing to chance, he too has discussed the task ahead with the team. "It's been building up since Tuesday. I said to them 'I'm going to split you into three teams 'cause you didn't frickin' turn up last Monday! Excluding bonus points, I told them the teams were as follows: Team 1 is Leigh Adams and Matej Zagar. You will get 24 points (that's two 12s). Team 2 will be Simon Stead, Ryan Fisher and Travis McGowan. You will get 20 points (that's 7, 7 and 6)!' Simon Stead said 'I'm going to get 12!' I told them, 'If you go over it, you score for your teammates. Team 3 will be Morten Risager and Cory Gathercole. You will get 10 points (that's 5 points each)'. Morten Risager liked that, he said, 'Without Team 3 you're fricked!' If you add the scores of the three teams together, that's 24+20+10 that's 54 points. Heat 1 will be a 4-2, heat 2 will be a 5-1. We'll have 6 points back, the crowd will be behind the team, the team will start to believe and the train will leave the station!" It's a compelling and motivating plan of action, but ignores the possibility that – under contemporary rules – Wolverhampton might use tactical rides (so, really, to be absolutely sure, 60 points should really be the target). Blunsdon blogger and volunteer trackman Graham Cooke sympathises about the expectations loaded upon the riders by a local community mad keen to enjoy trophy success at the highest level of speedway. "I think 42 years is an awful lot of pressure!" Over the past few days, the Swindon riders had a behind-closed-doors practice to hone their confidence, skills and tactics. Doubtless, though neither Ronnie nor Graham mention it, the track has also had special attention. Cory Gathercole's equipment has also had a significant overhaul, "Cory is on an Ashley Holloway tuned ex-Hans Andersen machine tonight."

Although there are still three hours until the tapes are due to rise for the first race, the pits are understandably a hive of activity. The riders are casually dressed as they walk out on the track in small groups or, along with their

mechanics, they prepare and adjust their equipment. Wolverhampton team manager Peter Adams is clearly already in the zone. His hair looks immaculate, he's smartly attired – so much so that you'd suspect he'd iron his anorak jacket, if only it were possible. Without showboating or swagger, Peter exudes an air of professionalism, determination and, implicitly because of his business-like demeanour, confidence. If I was a Swindon rider and I caught sight of him in the pits, I'd definitely feel a twinge of anxiety about the evening ahead. Only yards away from the hubbub of the pre-meeting preparations, number 96 – aka the Blunsdon track staff cubbyhole-cum-dining area and chill-out room – there's another delicious fruit-packed cake baked by Swindon Robins sports therapist Karen Pantry. Elsewhere in the pits, Swindon club historian Robert Bamford stands with *Express & Star* speedway reporter Tim Hamblin. Rob is Swindon through-and-through, "It's our biggest meeting in 42 years, you've got to ride for your lives!"
[Tim] "It's your biggest meeting in two years!"
[Rob] "Well, we could get a 4-2 and a 5-1 and then Tai might be nervous at the tapes."
[Tim] "When I spoke to PK and Freddie after last week's meeting, they both said independently of each other, we're going to go there and treat it as a 0-0. If we're at all complacent, we're going to get beat!"

Graham Cooke & Robins physio Karen Pantry

Group photo

Sky in the Legends Lounge

The always helpful Wayne Russell suggests I base my bookstall on the concrete just inside the turnstiles before the slope that leads up to the stadium terraces. Positioned here every fan will have to pass my table. With so much on their minds, let alone the early darkness of an October night, pretty well everyone who does pass is determined to rush off to their favourite spot within the stadium rather than dawdle long enough to consider a book purchase. The 50/50 draw man and his helper take an outgoing approach to solicit interest. Even they struggle. I tell them, "Some of the excuses you get for not buying raffle tickets are worse than the ones I get!" The 50/50 man has heard them all before, "I know – some of them are awful!" Wolverhampton club presenter Ian 'Porky' Jones is one of the earlier arrivals. He's in confident mood and stops at my stall to inform me, "You'll have a new edition by the end of the night – *How Wolves Won the Title*!" Poole's *Speedway Star* salesman (known as Starman) was tasked with enormous responsibility prior to the meeting: "I've had the Elite League trophy at my house for the last four days. Imagine what people would say about me if it had been stolen! It's very heavy! I polished it for two hours earlier today, so that it was looking really nice!" Eastbourne uber-fan Sid Greatley also arrives early, "I said to Lewis Bridger, 'you've got to live, eat and breath this sport! You've got to invest all your money in your equipment and bikes' and I told him to cut out the drinking!" Reading club historian Arnie Gibbons turns up in good time, too. Old Berkshire/Wiltshire rivalries die hard, "I'm just off to see Swindon fail to win the league for the 42nd year in a row!"
[Jeff] "No, no, Arnie – believe!"
[Arnie] "I do believe [pause] that Wolves can win! Have you been relegated to down here?"
[Jeff] "No it's a promotion as everyone can see me before they go elsewhere in the stadium."

One fan lingers by the table, fingers the stock and then exclaims, "Oh, it's a speedway book! I suppose it is a speedway meeting." Speedway reporter Paul Burbidge arrives in full expectation of a Wolverhampton victory. "I think it'll be close but Wolves will just have the edge. For example, Travis McGowan probably won't do that well. Leigh Adams – his partner – will have to pull him along!" Paul believes that the Elite League could learn some valuable lessons from the Speedway Grand Prix series. "I think, long term, the SGP is the way to go! Meetings like this have big crowds and the atmosphere and that – but there's a lot that is wrong with league racing in this country."
[Jeff] "There's lots wrong with the GPs, too."
[Paul] "Gordon Day was saying to me that there's too much speedway in this country. Whether or not they have the bottle to go to two nights a week remains to be seen! Something needs to change!"
[Jeff] "Well, I think, the Speedway Grand Prix could work much more supportively with British speedway, but that hasn't happened."
[Paul] "That cuts both ways!"
[Jeff] "I see Ole Olsen is going to the FIM."
[Paul] "That should improve things."
[Jeff] "What do you do in the speedway close season?"
[Paul] "I'll do lots of articles over the winter. I'm doing lots on the Speedway Grand Prix website. Visitor numbers are up and that could really take off!"

As they funnel through the turnstiles, many fans clutch a card specially produced by the *Swindon Advertiser*. Each card features the *Swindon Advertiser* and Robins logos, along with – in giant letters – a prominently displayed 5-1 in bold type. With a local population of 155,432 and a countywide catchment area, a big crowd at Abbey Stadium is always on the cards, particularly given that this is the only significant sports event that'll be staged in the city tonight. [1]

News travels fast in the cloistered world of speedway. Mobile phones, text messaging and the Internet have accelerated communication to warp-level speed. No doubt we'll all soon start to tweet as well. Often this information is incorrect according to speedway's most prolific author, Robert Bamford: "If you looked on the British Speedway Forum, you'd think that Phil Bartlett was in the [Weymouth] referee's box all night [during the meeting versus Plymouth]. But I spoke to Christina Turnbull and she said he was in there for one minute max. He only went up there to take her the keys so that she could lock herself in 'cause the natives were getting restless!" Paul Oughton, who works in the Swindon Robins commercial department, has close Weymouth connections. "Since Phil Bartlett has been there I haven't been back! Weymouth is my club and I hope that things will get sorted out. If a club is run badly, it should be allowed to go to the wall. Some kind people give money, made generous donations and give sponsorships thinking they're helping the club but, really, they're propping up someone who treated a lot of people badly when he arrived at the club. If they really knew, they wouldn't be so generous! Still, it will sort itself out and I just hope the club survives! I keep out of it completely." A tempestuous meeting on Saturday night at Arlington saw Troy Batchelor and Lewis Bridger cross each other off their respective Christmas card lists. Swindon speedway club statistician and historian Robert Bamford surfs the Internet superhighway as part of his research so is *au fait* with something they call Facebook. "Lewis Bridger said on Facebook to Troy that he's happy to have rounds two and three at Poole and Ipswich later this week!" Another club historian with an extensive number of bookmarked websites (including foreign language ones) on his computer is Reading's Arnie Gibbons. "On the US Speedway Rider Yahoo forum they said that each half of the Newport promotion was in different minds about whether the meeting [against the US Dream team] should go ahead or not!"

These days, due to the unfortunate effects of anxiety and stress, Robert Bamford perches himself behind the Swindon track-shop table on race-nights where he is looked after by good friends and long-time track-shop regulars – Lucy Aubrey and her partner, Lee. Sensibly Rob's got a stool to stand on so that he can see over the packed home-straight terrace crowd. Ten minutes after the scheduled start time there are still lengthy queues of fans keen to gain access to the stadium at all three turnstiles. Rob asks rhetorically, "Who said the crowds wouldn't come? Look at it! [waves

[1] In December the *Sun* reports that though Swindon is famous for its appearance in the Doomsday Book of 1086, its baffling "magic roundabout" and its reputation as "home to model Melinda Messenger, Doctor Who's ex-sidekick Billie Piper and blonde bombshell actress Diana Dors", it's also now been chosen – from a field of 25 other British cities – to be officially twinned with Walt Disney World in Florida! It will be interesting to see what Swindon Speedway makes of this new-found connection in 2010!

his hand proprietarily and expansively at the sea of people in front of him]. Well, I did for one!" Out on the track the riders have made a grand entrance for the finale of the Elite League season. Each of the 14 riders arrives at the start-line on a Harley Davidson, each with chrome shined to within an inch of its life. Bright red fireworks spark and light the sky while, over the public address system, Frankie Goes to Hollywood's *Two Tribes* plays at excessive volume. Shouting above the hubbub, Rob embraces his inner heavy metal fan, "That was almost Polish style!"
[Jeff] "What, clichéd and hackneyed?"
[Rob] "It probably is in your book!"
[Jeff] "Actually, I love this sort of thing!"

Usually a habitué of Premier League and National League meetings, 62-year-old Chris Golding has come to soak up the atmosphere at Blunsdon and also look at the track-shop stock. "The question I'd like to ask is how Howard Jones gets away with publishing such expensive crap? If you know the track in question – for example, Crayford – you have to wonder if he's even been there! There are inaccuracies galore!" Also drawn to the track-shop stall is a gaggle of off-duty riders including Hans Andersen and Ben Barker. They proceed to laugh ecstatically (almost manically) as they hold a Scott Nicholls car sticker between, them as if it was a championship trophy, to pose for the camera phone of Super7even start girls organiser Shelly Ann Willetts. Not aware of their prior conversation, in-joke or exact reason for their mirth at the sight of the Scott Nicholls car sticker, I go to take a photo of this happy group only for Hans Andersen to bluntly assert, "No! No!" Always a fount of knowledge but also a Manchester United supporter, Rob Bamford instructs me, "Do include the fact that Ben Barker is a fan of the Mighty Reds and often goes to Old Trafford!" Sight of my notebook and camera prompts an observant but curious Hans Andersen to come over and ask suspiciously, "What are you writing – a book?" Lost for words after I've confirmed that I am, I dorkily tell Hans, "I admire your riding."
[Hans] "Oh, really. Thank you."
[Jeff] "You have a higher away Elite League average than a home one."
[Hans, disinterestedly] "Do I?"
Rob Bamford is also an admirer of Hans Andersen, "He's a good bloke!"

Tim Hamblin mingles with the crowd, "It'll be 4-2 in the first heat, but not to Swindon!" Freddie Lindgren's first race victory is a worrying sign for the Swindon team and their fans. Though Lindgren comes under considerable pressure from the talismanic Robins captain Leigh Adams – on the first bend, bends one and two of the third lap plus bends three and four of the last lap – the young rider holds on to win. It's symbolic and, possibly, signals a structural change in hierarchy since this has, for many years, been Adams's very own happy hunting ground. Rob Bamford appreciates the spectacle, "What a start that was and what a race! Lindgren is too good nowadays." Though he's well versed in the whys and wherefores of speedway racing, one of the lapsed fans attracted along tonight hasn't quite mastered the intricacies of a speedway programme race-card. "Can you help me fill out my programme – it's my first time doing it? I used to work on the track here a few years ago, but I don't usually get a programme." Swindon seem likely to immediately reply with a 5-1 in heat 2 until the third bend of the last lap when Ty Proctor – riding at Blunsdon for the first time in his career – sneaks under Cory Gathercole to split the Robins partnership and reduce their heat advantage to 4-2. "Oh no, disaster!" is one of the politer phrases uttered around me. Rob Bamford splutters, "Cory Gathercole! We had it in the bag! He made a mess of it on the second lap [points to bend 1] and then he did it again! Balls up!" The ex-track worker takes a more philosophical view of events, "Unfortunately, he had that wobble – I just think he tried too hard!" Loss of superior early race position suddenly infects the whole Robins line-up. As he exits the second bend in heat 3, Ryan Fisher leads Tai Woffinden until an unforced error on the second bend of the third lap rewards the close attentions of the young British rider. Last-lap bunching enables the experienced Adam Skornicki to pass Simon Stead and, thereby, relegates him to last place. Rob is downcast at the Robins heat disadvantage, "We're not getting the run of the track! Tell you what, it's cracking racing! Going for it, but I think it's cup final nerves." Brian Burford believes the issue is one of psychological and physical dominance, "The problem is we don't own the track!"

With the scores level at 9 points apiece after three races, before the fourth heat Rob Bamford bigs up the Zagar/Risager partnership who are about to face Wolverhampton's Peter Karlsson/Ty Proctor pairing. "This could be a key race – we need to get a 5-1!" Though you always think that PK can pass Matej Zagar, the Swindon heat-leader refuses to budge. Unfortunately for the Robins, Morten Risager finishes last and the drawn heat ensures that – after four races – the meeting remains tied and Wolverhampton retain their overall 16-point advantage. Rob Bamford identifies their strategy, "As I kind of expected: Wolverhampton are just stone-walling their way through this meeting but, then, they've earned the right to do that, haven't they?" Wolverhampton track-shop owner Dave Rattenberry savours the atmosphere and likely Wolves win, "I think we've got this! That should wipe the smug grin off Rossiter's face!" Dave is surprised to see Rob Bamford in the stadium let alone positioned in the track-shop, "What are you doing here? Someone told me you were banned!"

Heat 5 provides drama up at the front and at the rear. Lindgren gates, but Simon Stead battles past him on the back straight of lap two. The battle for third place is even more hotly contested between Ryan Fisher and Nicolai Klindt as they exchange positions with some frequency. The natural speedway reporter in Rob Bamford surfaces, "All you can say is they're chucking the kitchen sink at it and Wolverhampton are responding!" Usually the quiet man of speedway history, tonight Rob Bamford has been transformed and his ebullient speedway commentator alter ego is to the fore, "Stead battled past Lindgren while simultaneously Fisher was engaged in a duel for supremacy at the back with Klindt. First he passed Klindt and then was passed himself. The crowd went barmy!" If Rob's engagement levels were high after heat 5, then the sight of Leigh Adams ahead of Peter Karlsson with Travis McGowan in third – to, thereby, establish the bridgehead of a Swindon 2-point lead on the night – registers frantically highly on his delight-o-meter. "You must say an ebullient Rob Bamford said – hyped up by the occasion – ripped off his usual cloak and the quiet man has gone berserk! Can we rise to this remains the question? People will think I'm bloody nuts. I'm enticed by the occasion! Is that the right word? What is the right word? Help me, Jeff – put the right word in. Look at that man on the mobile phone. He looks in real pain. He's obviously a Swindon fan running through the gamut of emotions." With Wolverhampton's aggregate lead slashed to a mere 14 points, Dave Rattenberry's personal small dark psychological cloud prompts him to lash out and pre-emptorily demand, "Where's my commission for the books you sold at the meeting I wasn't at – Stoke – you sold four!"

The emotional rollercoaster ride continues into heat 7 where, with Tai Woffinden up front, a drawn heat looks highly likely until the final back-straight lap where Adam Skornicki sneaks past Cory Gathercole to secure third place for a heat advantage that levels the score on the night. Rob can't quite believe it, "It's getting to the point where I won't comment anymore! It's a question of plucking the right word out of the air! Fortudie; invincibus; Shackleton! Wor Jackie!" I've a sixth sense that Rob's circuits are overloaded and temporarily verge on going on the fritz! Rob glances ahead in the programme, "There's three sudden-death heats and then a match-race!" On the second bend of the third lap of "sudden-death heat" 8, Morten Risager passes Ty Proctor to seize second place behind Travis McGowan. The boisterous Blunsdon crowd greets it with loud acclaim, particularly since it's the first home 5-1 of the evening (plus it reduces the Robins aggregate deficit to 12 points). Simon Stead leads heat 9 until the fourth bend where Peter Karlsson passes him. Holding his imaginary worldwide television audience in rapt attention, Rob takes this latest set-back in his stride, "What a wily old character PK is – everything we've chucked at them, they've responded to!" The race ends as the fourth drawn heat of the night to leave Swindon with only six races left to engineer an unlikely victory. Caught up in the moment Rob sings along with the oral entertainment, "What the world needs now is love sweet love it's the only thing there's just too little of! (Put in brackets that you also sang along to that one!)" Track-shop owner Nick Barber looks on in bemused fashion, "Is Rob Bamford on heat?!"

For the first lap of Heat 10, Leigh Adams races in what appears to be a slightly slow-motion fashion as if he's encountered the resistance of a hidden force-field or, perhaps, that his bike has been held back by a great length of elastic band that's just about to snap back into position. At the start of the second lap, Adams gains release and fires forward accompanied home by his teammate, Travis McGowan, to secure the Robins second 5-1 heat advantage in three races and, thereby, catapult them into an 8-point lead on the night. Rob Bamford ignores the possibility that there may have been some gamesmanship involved and, instead, celebrates ecstatically, "Wuffy at the back!" Rob then grabs a pale green bottle emblazoned with the word "Generate" on the side and drinks a deep draught of the liquid it contains. "This isn't good for my health. Do you think it's got that ingredient in?" "What, caffeine?" "No, you know, what's its name? They were giving it out to the riders – our riders – earlier! It was given out by the Sergeant Major that is our clerk of the course, Michael Hunt – not Mike Hunt – be careful how you say that. They'll be able to say 'as drunk by the victorious Robins – Elite League Champions!' Tell you what, if we do get another 5-1!"

[Jeff] "They could use a tactical ride."

[Rob] "Yeah, that's the trouble. If you do write this up, do show it to me, won't you? I have problems with my health – I shouldn't get ignited like this."
[Jeff] "We have the oxygen tent at the ready."
[Rob] "If I have a heart attack you can put in what you like! When you get to my age, you've seen it all before."
[Jeff] "I'm older than you."

Swaying on his stool, Rob spots the large television screen that flickers above us inside the Legends' Lounge. "Look they've got Hans Andersen in the [Sky] studio. Look at his eyes, he's drunk! He's not with it! He had a half in his hand when I saw him earlier. Nigel Pearson's smiling knowingly!" Hans Andersen sports the headset and microphone mouthpiece favoured by air traffic controllers the world over (when you see them in the movies). Unused to this equipment, Hans is unconsciously biased towards the microphone and so finds himself talking out the side of his mouth. In comparison, Kelvin Tatum suddenly looks smoothly professional – well, at least in body language terms – since we can't actually hear either of them.
[Rob] "Rosco's still smiling!"
[Jeff] "He's been on the 'Generate'!"
[Rob] It's quite tasty actually – a lemony flavour – don't forget 'Generate – it's Great!'"

Talk of greatness prompts Rob's mind to wander to lascivious thoughts of speedway referee Barbara Horley, "She's a Christian teacher, you know? Very attractive, don't you think?" Cory Gathercole is side-by-side with Fredrik Lindgren as they exit the second bend for the first time at the start of heat 11, before he appears to suddenly remember exactly who he is and immediately dramatically drops back into third place. Matej Zagar completes the formality of the win to take the score to 38-28. This ensures that Wolverhampton can now use their tactical ride. At the track-shop, Lee Poole considers the possible permutations of the last four races of the Robins Elite League season, "I'm not saying we can, but, if we can hold the two tacticals and win heat 15, then we can!" Wolverhampton team manager Peter Adams immediately seizes the tactical opportunity to send out Adam Skornicki in black-and-white. He's not the most predictable choice. Adams also brings in Ty Proctor in place of Chris Kerr whose name, tonight, sounds like Chris de Burgh because of the accent of the announcer. Fisher and Risager gate with alacrity and arrive into the first bend ahead. But, when Adam Skornicki cuts back to take the lead, you could hear a pin drop throughout the stadium apart from a frustrated shout of "Put him in the fence!" Rob Bamford looks downcast, "Has that buggered it?"
[Jeff] "Rob, rush your bottle of 'Generate' down to the pits."
[Rob] "They had him out of the gate. They should have sat on him and he'd never have got inside them!"

With Skornicki's race points doubled, the 3-6 heat result narrows the Swindon lead on the night to 7 points. Mathematically, three 5-1s would still guarantee a Robins victory. The first rerun of the vital heat 13 finds Freddie Lindgren sandwiched between Adams and Zagar on the first bend until he loses control, hammers across the apex of the bend to collect Peter Karlsson and smacks him into the air safety barrier to loud cheers from the Swindon crowd. Like every other Swindon fan in the stadium, Rob knows the decision that referee Dave Robinson has to make, "He's got to be excluded!" Nick Barber disagrees, "No – he got a nudge from Adams!" We all look upwards at the Sky replay on the television screen hung on the wall of the Legends' Lounge above us. Nick's scepticism proves well-founded, "Look – he knew Zagar was there and he tried to avoid him but lost control!" The "all four back" decision is greeted with derision, loud boos, shouts of "cheat" and some downcast faces. The modern sports experience dictates that you can see the action live, review it almost immediately on an action replay and also, almost simultaneously, get text messages and phone calls about what has actually been said on-screen. Though we can see Rosco smiling madly we learn that he's apparently just said "I don't know who to talk to without swearing!" With aggregate defeat strongly on the cards, Rob Bamford is magnanimous as the Robins teeter on the brink of their 42nd year of frustration. "I have to say this is a fantastic effort from Swindon! Whatever happens now, they've shown tremendous character. A cliché, I know – but I mean that!" In the re-rerun of the race, Freddie Lindgren wins to guarantee Wolverhampton's victory. A murmuration of Wolverhampton fans overlooking the exit of the second bend go bonkers while the home-straight terrace echoes to boos while loud cries of "cheat!" also ring out. Over the public address system Cliff Richard's *Congratulations* plays and, shortly afterwards, the announcer throws in the verbal towel, "In order to win, we need two 5-0s and that's highly unlikely!"[2]

Without so much as a backward glance, a huge number of Swindon fans start to stream away from the stadium. I half suspect there's been a silent call for all fair-weather fans to immediately muster and congregate in the car park to re-board their mother ship. Lucy Aubrey looks on contemptuously from behind her track-shop table as the hordes rush past her, "Fans who've only seen tonight's meeting can leave now!" The formality of the remainder of the meeting gets quickly wrapped up. There's a win for Tai Woffinden. He's followed home by Simon Stead and Morten Rizz-air. This is then followed with the third 5-1 of the night for the Robins – this massages the score for the history books to an acceptable but not quite good enough 52-41. It's doubtful that Ronnie Russell will conduct any post-meeting analysis of the three teams he split the Swindon squad into prior to tonight's meeting. In retrospect, Ronnie's budgeted team scores have failed to take account of the possible impact of tactical rides. Nonetheless, though Team 1 achieve their original 24-point budget, both Team 2 and Team 3 fall 1 point short on 19 and 9 points, respectively. Whichever way you analyse the score-card, Wolverhampton run out deserved winners of the 2009 Elite League trophy.

12th October Swindon v. Wolverhampton (Elite League Play-off final, second leg) 52-41

[2] Gary Patchett later recalls the events of the night for the *Speedway Star*, "We lost it at Monmore Green, end of story ... we congratulate Wolverhampton as League Champions, but don't go for the rot from Peter Adams that Wolves were the better team over the final three months of the season. They were the better team in the Play-offs, and effectively we fell at the final hurdle."

Afterword

I hope that you enjoyed the journey.

Phew! What a fantastic year I had and what another brilliant experience. I was genuinely overwhelmed with the kindness of strangers and amazed how people went out of their way to help me. There are, of course, exceptions to every rule.

Obviously all mistakes remain my own. If you have any comments, of either persuasion, please get in touch via my website on www.methanolpress.com

Every effort has been made to get in touch with all copyright holders but, again, I would be delighted to hear from you to make the appropriate credits or acknowledgements.

I mentioned earlier that I have been overwhelmed with help and kindness. I hesitate to name everyone as, inevitably, I will make a mistake and miss someone I'm extremely grateful to, so, with sincere apologies to those who I do manage to miss out I would like to thank the following people: Peter Adams, Rachael Adams, Graham Arnold, Robert Bamford, Nick, Johnny, Bev, Molly and Colin Barber, George and Linda Barclay, Dick Barrie, Ian Belcher, Joyce and Malcolm Blythe, Christine Bond, Tim Booler, Mick Bratley, Jim and Steven Brykajlo, Brian Burford, Peter Butcher, John Campbell, Alison Chalmers, Steve Chilton, Ray Collins, Jon Cook, Graham Cooke, Dougie Copland, Mick Corby, ICA Crook, Lucy Cross, Dave Croucher, Jonathan, Keith and Cheryl Chapman, Martin Dadswell, Gordie Day, Alan Dick, Jem Dicken, Steve & Debbie Dixon, Chris Durno, Graham and Denise Drury, Steve and Debbie Dixon, Neil Dyson, George and Joan English, Dave Fairbrother, Jim Fleming, Richard Frost, Emma Gardner, Chris Gay, Arnie Gibbons, Bill Gimbeth, Darcia Gingell, Rob Godfrey, Mike and Anita Golding, David Gordon, Andy Griggs, Tim Hamblin, Graham Hambly, Debbie Hancock, Steve & Jan Harland, Julie Harrowven, Brian Havelock, Steve Hilliard, Liz Hunt, John Hyam, John, Jordan, Karen, Mark and Judy Hazelden, Richard Hollingsworth, Dave Hoggart, Lynn Hunt, Mike Hunter, Tony Jackson, Sue Jackson-Scott, Billy Jenkins, Emma Lemon, Graeme Lemon, Sheila Le-Sage, Kevin Ling, Kevin Long, Gary Lough, John Louis, Michael Max, Tony and Susie MacDonald, Ian and Jean Maclean, Neil Machin, Steve & Nicky Mallett, Julie Martin, Dennis McCleary, Charles McKay, Allan Melville, Steve and Sarah Miles, Chris Morton, Mike Moseley, Jayne Moss, Hazal Naylor, Bill Norris, Peter Oakes, Paul Oughton, Brian Owen, Gordon Pairman, Les Palmer, Dave Pavitt, Nigel Pearson, Rob Peasley, Di Phillips, Mark Poulton, Andy Povey, Colin Pratt, Dave Rattenberry, Dave and Margaret Rice, John Rich, Giles Richards, Gareth Rogers, Laurence Rogers, David Rowe, Wayne Russell, Craig Saul, Mark Sawbridge, Len Silver, Andrew Skeels, Tony Steele, Trevor Swales, Richard Talbot, Bob Tasker, Peter Toogood, Stuart Towner, Ian Thomas, Christina Turnbull, Chris Van Stratten, Alan Walker, Nick Ward, Alf Weedon, The Reverend Michael Whawell, Bryn Williams, Steve Winter, Dave Wright and Malcolm Wright.

To pick out anyone in particular would be invidious. However, I owe so many 'thank yous'. The book wouldn't look as lovely as it does without Vicky Holtham's artistic skills. The look and feel of the covers, website and book layout were all originally conceived by Rachael Adams. There would be many more errors than there are without the help of Vy Shepherd. Graham Russel has shown tremendous pedantry and knowledge to wrangle with my words to convert them into some sort of sense. Robert Bamford also kindly copyedited the Swindon chapters. Michael Payne and Billy Jenkins have continued to offer encouragement, advice and support. My true friend Sue Young has encouraged me often in so many things and really saved me when I needed that most – for which she has my eternal gratitude. Of course, without the love and guidance of my parents – Mary and Alan – none of this book or so many other things would ever have been possible. Finally, you can never have too many teachers and I was lucky enough to have been inspired to write my speedway books by a truly great teacher, poet, musician and wit – Michael Donaghy. He remains greatly missed.

Before I go, we only get one chance to make a first impression – this holds for speedway clubs as much as people. If you've read to here, it's safe to say that you've probably been bitten by the speedway bug (for which, apparently, there is no permanent antidote). We can all no longer go to speedway for the first time. However, we can take new people and relive this experience vicariously once more, albeit second hand. I always like taking newcomers. During 2009, one of these was cardiac nurse Emma "I mend hearts as well as break them!" Gardner. After her trip to a Sky meeting at Arlington, she kindly sent me her impressions. They do capture a certain something about her immediate thoughts – some accurate, others not quite – but they also gesture towards one possible answer to the question I'm still trying to unravel: 'what is speedway?'

OK Jeff this is purely just a few phrases or badly written sentences describing what I thought of Monday night's experience!!
The smell four stroke fuelled with adolescent hormones oozing from the riders, teenage WAGs and me!!
Spray of shale as the riders started and cornered and the piles of dirt along the faded padded advertising boards along the inside of the track.
Bob [Dugard] behaving like a matador as he drove the tractor around the track after every race. Stay pressed trousers, ironed shirt, polished shoes smoking a fag, ignoring the crowd but well aware of the presence he had.
The speedway WAGs with bleach blond hair, gold and hard look. An achievable boyfriend as a result of mixing with the riders in the pits. Teenage hormones combined with four stroke oil. Sweaty, sexy leathers laden with sponsors and baseball caps giving the riders an added NYC homie look. The riders don't maintain eye contact but know that they are being admired by the girls! The pit boys are more approachable – having a laugh – but still totally loyal to their rider.
No evidence of Snap on Halfords tool kits – just Teng tools! A poor man's TT – more like the boy next door's garage rather than Barry Sheene. Living the dream!
The teenage girls delight of mixing and talking to their idol – unlike football – where their longing to be a WAG might be achievable.
Kids getting autographs.
Adults writing in the scores and thinking I used to do that, I could do that, or I want to do that!
80's style memorabilia. Bargains and the selling of autograph books and unposed signed photos of the riders. No airbrushing, no set backdrop – just a natural amateur shot.
A wanna be DJ who likes the idea of being in with the in crowd.
The floodlights and rising moon.
The synchronised heads of the riders – two looking left, two looking right – watching and waiting for the tape release.
Alan [Rolfe] the starter who performs the same ritual of taking three steps after the race has started, exhaling once the bikes make the first corner and lifting his forearms up. I CAN'T DESCRIBE THIS BUT IT'S WORTH WATCHING!!!
The whole night oozed tension, excitement, hormones – and air of gangster like underground roughness, full of rogues with history and a story to tell. But families there too! Everyone mixes.
A more achievable dream for the girls because you can mingle with the stars!
A spectacle of rituals and routines. Like Lewis stopping before the tape with a back wheel slide. People standing in the same spot. Taking your own chairs. Writing in pencil, Alan and his starting routine, the hairy second starter [Terry] always being the first to pull down his side of the tape and the unchanging way he hands the second to last lap and final lap flags to Alan.
Smell of cheap milky coffee and onions.
Competition for [her adorable dachshund] Stan with a cute dog and a neck scarf
The frenzied rush to the car park and the field filled with flashing hazard lights as doors unlocked!! The need to be first out/win fuelled by the night's racing.
The desire to have a go.
The fear of a rider actually crashing.
The deaf tingling ears at the end of the night.
A lovely time."

It just remains to say: if you go to speedway already why not make a point of taking even more friends and/or first timers this year? And, if you haven't been for a while or have never been, now is as good a time as any to start!

Yours in speedway!

Thank you for coming on my latest journey round the tracks.

Brighton, 24 May 2010

INFORMATION

Jazz Musicians
www.billyjenkins.com
The one and only Billy J – the incomparable speedway/bowls loving Bard of Bromley and progenitor of a distinctively British kitchen-sink jazz sound

Stain Glass
www.catrinjones.co.uk/culture.html

ACCOMMODATION

All the following warmly welcome speedway fans and have special rates for us:

Waverley Hotel, Workington
01900 603246
www.waverley-hotel.com

Beeches Guest House, King's Lynn
01553 766577
www.beechesguesthouse.co.uk

Lower Farm
Harpley, King's Lynn
01485 520240

Jurys Inn Glasgow Hotel
0141 314 4800
www.glasgowhotels.juryinns.com

Brent Knoll Lodge Hotel, Highbridge, Somerset
01278 760008
www.brentknolllodge.com

Aston Hotel, Sheffield
0114 261 5609
www.astonhotels.co.uk

Garrison Hotel, Sheffield
0114 249 9555
www.garrisonhotel.co.uk

FOR ALL THE LATEST NEWS AND FIXTURES GO TO:

www.british-speedway.co.uk
Other useful speedway websites:
www.speedwayplus.com
www.speedway-forum.co.uk
www.speedwayupdates.proboards103.com:8080/index.cgi
www.tattingermarsh.co.uk/blog
www.worldspeedway.com
www.subedei.proboards.com/index.cgi
www.keep-turning-left.blogspot.com
www.sideburnmag.blogspot.com
www.all4back.com
www.allspeedway.tv

speedwaystar
BUY IT... OR WE'LL SHOWER YOU IN SHALE!
SPEEDWAY-STAR IS PUBLISHED WEEKLY (£2.60). A ONE YEAR SUBSCRIPTION (52 editions) IN THE UK COSTS £104 (just £2.00 a week). TELEPHONE OUR CREDIT CARD HOTLINE ON (020) 8335 1113 OR WRITE WITH YOUR NAME, ADDRESS, CREDIT CARD NUMBER AND EXPIRY DATE TO: PINEGEN LIMITED, 9 COPPERGATE MEWS BRIGHTON ROAD, SURBITION KT6 5NE

ALSO AVAILABLE FROM METHANOL PRESS

Quantum of Shale

Around the Tracks

"a prose that possesses a kind of petrol-driven Dirty Realism, as though Raymond Carver had decided to turn up at a speedway meeting"

IAN MCMILLAN, *The Times*

328 pages 190 Black & white photographs **£20.00** Paperback

Concrete for Breakfast

More Tales from the Shale

NOMINATED FOR BRITISH SPORTS BOOK OF THE YEAR AWARD 2009

"Jeff Scott's Concrete for Breakfast *is possibly Speedway's War and Peace, or its Ulysses, or, in some of the chapters, its local newspaper gossip page. It's the epic by which all other books on the sport will be judged ... Read this book for a glimpse of a lost tribe, for an examination of collectivism and individuality somehow working together, for endless descriptions of English weather, and for a brave attempt to pinpoint a particular branch of human endeavour that often seems to be far from the centre of things."*

IAN MCMILLAN, *The Times*

302 pages 223 Black & white photographs **£20.00** Paperback

When Eagles Dared

"A remarkable read and something completely different to any other books on the overcrowded market. Jeff has a very personal style that you might either love or hate but I found it riveting and enjoyed almost every word"

PETER OAKES, *Speedway Star*

172 pages 158 Black & white photographs **£10.00** Paperback

Showered in Shale

One Man's Circuitous Journey Throughout the Country in Pursuit of An Obsession – British Speedway

"It's all here, in almost soap opera style proportions ... this is British Speedway stripped bare, this is how it really is and some of it isn't pretty ... many years into the future, historians will gladly hold this book to their bosom for its insight ... what the author has achieved – an it will be interesting to see how many people take this on board – is that he's provided a book that will stand-up as a fly on the wall type narrative of where and what our sport really is in the early millennium ... Showered in Shale *is a quirky book, it's different and off-the-wall"*

BRIAN BURFORD, *Speedway Star*

508 pages 409 Black & white photographs **£20.00** Paperback

Shifting Shale

2006 A Race Odyssey

"Nobody else writing about speedway at the moment can capture the speedway experience in the way that Scott can. As always the beauty of his work is in the description of the minutiae"

JIM HENRY, *Speedway-Researcher*

345 pages 143 Black & white photographs **£10.00** Paperback

Shale Britannia

A Sideways Glance at Speedway

"A marvellously evocative book"

JOHN INVERDALE, *Daily Telegraph*

"Superbly produced, I found it absolutely fascinating"

PETER OAKES, *Speedway Star*

256 pages 345 colour photographs **£10.00** flexiback

All available from **www.methanolpress.com**

methanol press

Lightning Source UK Ltd.
Milton Keynes UK
24 June 2010

156014UK00001B/26/P